Christian Wille, Rachel Reckinger, Sonja Kmec, Markus Hesse (eds.)
Spaces and Identities in Border Regions

Culture and Social Practice

CHRISTIAN WILLE, RACHEL RECKINGER, SONJA KMEC,
MARKUS HESSE (EDS.)

Spaces and Identities in Border Regions
Politics – Media – Subjects

Bibliographic information published by the Deutsche Nationalbibliothek
The Deutsche Nationalbibliothek lists this publication in the Deutsche Nationalbibliografie; detailed bibliographic data are available in the Internet at http://dnb.d-nb.de

© 2016 transcript Verlag, Bielefeld
transcript Verlag | Hermannstraße 26 | D-33602 Bielefeld | live@transcript-verlag.de

All rights reserved. No part of this book may be reprinted or reproduced or utilized in any form or by any electronic, mechanical, or other means, now known or hereafter invented, including photocopying and recording, or in any information storage or retrieval system, without permission in writing from the publisher.

Cover layout: Kordula Röckenhaus, Bielefeld
Cover illustration: misterQM / photocase.de
English translation: Matthias Müller, müller translations (in collaboration with Jigme Balasidis)
Typeset by Mark-Sebastian Schneider, Bielefeld
Printed in Germany
Print-ISBN 978-3-8376-2650-6
PDF-ISBN 978-3-8394-2650-0

Content

1. **Exploring Constructions of Space and Identity in Border Regions**
   (Christian Wille and Rachel Reckinger) | 9

2. **Theoretical and Methodological Approaches
   to Borders, Spaces and Identities** | 15
   2.1 Establishing, Crossing and Expanding Borders
   (Martin Doll and Johanna M. Gelberg) | 15
   2.2 Spaces: Approaches and Perspectives of Investigation
   (Christian Wille and Markus Hesse) | 25
   2.3 Processes of (Self)Identification *(Sonja Kmec and Rachel Reckinger)* | 36
   2.4 Methodology and Situative Interdisciplinarity *(Christian Wille)* | 44
   2.5 References | 63

3. **Space and Identity Constructions
   Through Institutional Practices** | 73
   3.1 Policies and Normalizations | 73
   3.2 On the Construction of Spaces of Im-/Morality. A Power Analysis Perspective
   on the Problematization of Prostitution c. 1900 *(Heike Mauer)* | 81
   3.3 Castles as Instruments of Hegemonial Space Construction and
   Representation. The Example of the County of Vianden *(Bernhard Kreutz)* | 94
   3.4 Biogas – Power – Space. On the Construction of Energy Regions in Border
   Areas *(Fabian Faller)* | 105
   3.5 'Sovereignty' and 'Discipline' in the Media. On the Value of Foucault's
   Governmentality Theory: The Example of an Interdiscursive Analysis of the
   Migration Discourse in Luxembourg *(Elena Kreutzer)* | 121
   3.6 Conclusions | 131
   3.7 References | 133

4. Space and Identity Constructions Through Media-Related Practices | 141
4.1 Representations and Projections | 141
4.2 Multilingual Advertising and Regionalization in Luxembourg *(Julia de Bres)* | 146
4.3 The Artistic and Cultural Stakes for the Works Selected for the *Robert Schuman Art Award*: Exhibition and Publication Spaces – Places of Transformation as well as Artistic and Cultural Interstice? *(Paul di Felice)* | 158
4.4 The Threshold of Exhibition Venues: Access to the World of Culture *(Céline Schall)* | 172
4.5 Literature of the In-between. The Multilingual Stagings of the Publisher *ultimomondo (Till Dembeck)* | 185
4.6 "Mir gesinn eis dono op *facebook*" – (Self-)Stagings of Luxembourg Teenagers in Social Media as Virtual Identity Constructions *(Luc Belling)* | 193
4.7 Petrol Stations as In-Between Spaces I: Practices and Narratives *(Sonja Kmec)* | 204
4.8 Petrol Stations as In-Between Spaces II: Transfiguration *(Agnès Prüm)* | 218
4.9 Conclusions | 229
4.10 References | 231

5. Space and Identity Constructions Through Everyday-Cultural Practices | 241
5.1 Subjectifications and Subjectivations | 241
5.2 Sustainable Everyday Eating Practices from the Perspective of Spatial Identifications *(Rachel Reckinger)* | 252
5.3 Gender Spaces *(Julia Maria Zimmermann and Christel Baltes-Löhr)* | 266
5.4 Identity Constructions and Regionalization: Commemoration of the Dead in the Treveri Region (2nd/3rd century AD) – Family Identities on Tombstones in Arlon *(Andrea Binsfeld)* | 278
5.5 Workers' Housing Estates and their Residents: Constructions of Space and Collective Constitution of the Subject *(Laure Caregari)* | 292
5.6 Periurban Luxembourg. Definition, Positioning and Discursive Construction of Suburban Spaces at the Border between City and Countryside *(Markus Hesse)* | 305
5.7 Remembering the Second World War in Luxembourg and the Border Regions of its Three Neighbours *(Eva Maria Klos and Benno Sönke Schulz)* | 315
5.8 Beyond Luxembourg. Space and Identity Constructions in the Context of Cross-Border Residential Migration *(Christian Wille, Gregor Schnuer, Elisabeth Boesen)* | 326
5.9 Linguistic Identifications in the Luxembourg-German Border Region *(Heinz Sieburg and Britta Weimann)* | 338
5.10 Conclusions | 353
5.11 References | 356

6. **"Luxembourg is the Singapore of the West" – Looking Ahead**
   (Markus Hesse) | 369

7. **Interview Guidelines** | 377

8. **Authors** | 381

1. Exploring Constructions of Space and Identity in Border Regions

Christian Wille and Rachel Reckinger

This volume explores spaces and identities in border regions. The programme thus pointedly phrased is based on a multi-layered research concept that combines methods of spatial and identity studies and integrates various thematic approaches. The point of departure is the notion that spaces and identities are brought about by social practices. Corresponding praxeological approaches that can also be expressed as *doing space* and *doing identity* focus on the performative or processual character, graphically conveyed with concepts such as 'doing geography', '(de)spatialization' or 'identity work' and 'identity politics'. This perspective, also adopted here, not only offers a wealth of starting points for the disciplines participating in this volume, it is moreover the one called for when dealing with investigations *of* and *in* border regions. For it is only constructivist and contingency-oriented approaches that provide adequate access to spatial and identity constructions in border regions which we argue conform only in a very limited way to 'nation-state orders' or to 'binary orders' of the here/there. Rather, in the case of border regions, one has to assume space- and identity-related 'logics of disorder' that manifest themselves in 'transversal' patterns of articulation, which themselves can be qualified as border regions or interstices, leading to practices that aim at the (re)institution of 'orders'. These and other processes of spatial and identity constructions are the subject matter of this volume and are reconstructed via institutional, media-based and everyday-cultural practices in border regions.

This thematic overview already suggests that in this volume the term of border region – and thus the border – will present itself in different forms and contexts. First of all in a political-administrative sense, it is Luxembourg and the adjoining regions in Germany, France and Belgium that provide the framework for the empirical research of the individual contributions in this volume. In addition, the term is used in a categorial sense when (mostly dichotomously defined) categories are applied or questioned. Finally, the term refers to 'spaces of the border' or (categorial) interstices that are produced by means of dynamic negotiations of differences.

Constitutive for the term 'border region' or 'border area'[1] are therefore borders or differences that are not understood as fixed and unquestioned positings, but rather as results of contingent practices. On the analytical level we differentiate between three intertwined 'practices of the border', through which spaces and identities not only materialize but which these also contribute in shaping: (1) the institution of borders as differentiations or regulations by the self or by other agencies with respect to the exterior; (2) the crossing of borders as an affirmative or subversive action with transformative potential and (3) the expansion of borders as an 'in-between' of manifold relations and overlaps (see section 2.1). Differentiating 'practices of the border' in this way helps to obtain an analytical perspective on the processes of negotiations of borders or of differences that are constitutive for constructions of space and identity. The case studies in this volume deal with practical relationalizations and topologies as well as with attributions of significations relating to the physical-material world which in turn inform about identity constructions. This is because distinctions, relations, 'speaking' of a here/there not only indicate (spatial) differentiations, but at the same time reveal information about (self)-positionings and thus identities.

This approach to spatial and identity constructions – on the basis of and along establishments, crossings and expansions of borders – is further differentiated conceptually in this volume, so that we can distinguish between two perspectives of investigation: with regard to spatial constructions we are dealing with institutional and media-based semanticizations and performative techniques of attribution and representation, as well as with everyday geographies as topological structures and symbolic spatializations on the subject level (see section 2.2). Similarly, identity constructions are investigated as identifications *with* and identifications *of*, focussing the attention on processes of attribution through specific institutions and, on the other hand, on everyday-cultural processes of appropriation of these attributions (see section 2.3). These two perspectives of investigation – one looking at the attributed and the other at the appropriated spaces and identities – are not considered separately but rather connected to reveal their empirical intersections and interlinkings in cross-border contexts. For this we draw primarily on Foucault's concept of governmentality – a concept sensitive to the constructedness of social reality, to issues of spatial and identity theory as well as to the interaction of different aspects and levels of the social (see section 2.3).

The three perspectives of investigation outlined above are dealt with in this volume in the framework of three research areas. They comprise (1) a power-critical perspective on spaces and identities that addresses particularly policies and

---

1 | The synonymous use of the terms 'border region' and 'border area' in this volume is due to the different levels of investigation and is linked to the approach of the "social geography of everyday regionalizations" (Werlen 1997) (Personal translation of: "Sozialgeographie alltäglicher Regionalisierungen") (see section 2.2).

normalizations that become effective and are negotiated in construction processes; (2) a media-oriented perspective on spaces and identities that sees media as constructors and projection surfaces and even as spaces (of negotiation) and (3) a subject-centered perspective that investigates the production of space and identity constructions in the course of everyday-cultural practices. The perspectives on spaces and identities adopted within the research areas complement each other and are developed both theoretically as well as empirically in chapters 3, 4 and 5 in a number of case studies.

1.1 About this Publication

The present publication was produced in the framework of a research project at the University of Luxembourg. The university-funded project with the title *IDENT2 – Regionalizations as Identity Constructions in Border Areas*[2] (2011-2014) not only comprised a challenging and complex subject matter, but also relied on the participation of numerous scholars of the research unit IPSE (Identités, Politiques, Sociétés, Espaces), i.e. around 30 colleagues of its eight member institutes.[3] The cross-disciplinary research context was conceived as a follow-up of the previous project *IDENT – Socio-Cultural Identities and Identity Policies in Luxembourg*[4] (2007-2010) (see IPSE 2010; IPSE 2011a; IPSE 2011b) that already centred on identity constructions. The present volume not only brings up to date the results attained there but also develops them substantially further. This is reflected in the expansion of the research question to include spatial construction and the particularities of cross-border investigation contexts; there is also a clear development on the conceptual and structural level, indicated by the complex research concept and the increased collaboration of the participating disciplines.

---

2 | Project management: Assoc. Prof. Dr. Sonja Kmec and Prof. Dr. Markus Hesse; project coordinators: Dr. Rachel Reckinger and Dr. Christian Wille.
3 | They comprise the Institute of Gender, Diversity and Migration, the Institute of Geography and Spatial Planning, the Institute of Philosophy, the Institute for History, the Institute of German Language, Literature and for Intercultural Studies, the Institute for Romance, Media and Art Studies, the Institute for Luxembourgish Language and Literatures, and the Institute of Political Science.
4 | Project management: Prof. Dr. Christian Schulz, project coordinators: Dr. Rachel Reckinger and Dr. Christian Wille.

	Workgroup Politics	Workgroup Media	Workgroup Subject Constitutions
Number of members	6	12	13
Number of participating IPSE institutes	4	6	5

Table 1: Composition of the content-related workgroups in the project IDENT2 – Regionalizations as Identity Constructions in Border Areas

The work for this volume was carried out by the participating scholars in the framework of thematic and accompanying workgroups. The *thematic workgroups* each concerned themselves with one of the three research areas, tailoring them to the project's cross-disciplinary research concept in terms of theoretical and empirical principles. Despite the fact that the case studies are the product of individual research, the results of the collaboration are, as chapters 3, 4 and 5 show, the outcome of regular exchange and close coordination. The content-related project work was flanked by three *accompanying workgroups* that concentrated on theoretical issues, methodological aspects and the collaboration of the participating disciplines. As will become clear in chapter 2, the work accomplished here was critically important for the cross-disciplinary research concept and the collaboration of the participating scholars. The necessary exchange between content-related and accompanying workgroups was guaranteed via the colleagues and the project coordinators who were represented in both types of workgroups.

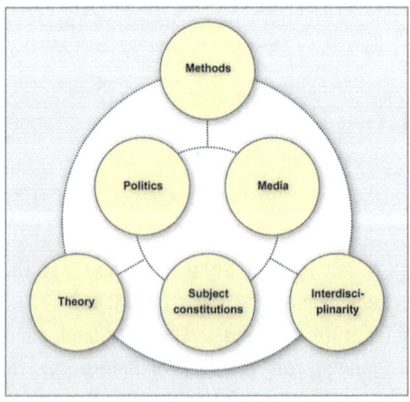

Figure 1: Content-related and accompanying workgroups in the project IDENT2 – Regionalizations as Identity Constructions in Border Areas
(design: Christian Wille, realization: Gilles Caspar and Malte Helfer)

Finally we would like to thank all those without whom the IDENT2 project *Regionalizations as Identity Constructions in Border Areas* would not have been possible and who have been involved in supporting this enterprise and this publication. They include the 3,300 residents of Luxembourg and the adjoining regions who participated in the quantitative and qualitative surveys and all those who have actively supported and accompanied the project, in particular Gilles Caspar, Tilo Felgenhauer, Georg Glasze, Rouven Hehlert, Peggy Jacobs, Fem Alina Kaup, Bertrand Lévy, Guy di Méo, Birgit Neumann, Peter Schmitt-Egner, Verena Schreiber, Benno Werlen, Ruth Zimmerling, Sabine Zinn-Thomas and many more who remain unnamed. We express our gratitude to the University of Luxembourg for the generous financial support it lent to this cross-disciplinary research project. Last but not least we would like to thank the publisher transcript-Verlag for its professional cooperation as well as the translator and editor Matthias Müller who from a multilingual[5] book manuscript marked by different disciplines and academic traditions has produced a German and an English version, the latter with the assistance of his colleague Jigme Balasidis.

REFERENCES

IPSE (2010) (ed.): Doing Identity in Luxemburg. Subjektive Aneignungen – institutionelle Zuschreibungen – sozio-kulturelle Milieus, Bielefeld: transcript.
IPSE (2011a) (ed.): Doing Identity in Luxembourg. Subjective Appropriations – Institutional Attributions – Socio-Cultural Milieus, Bielefeld: transcript.
IPSE (2011b) (ed.): Construire des identités au Luxembourg. Appropriations subjectives – Projections institutionnelles – Milieux socio-culturels, Paris: Berg International.
Werlen, Benno (1997): Sozialgeographie alltäglicher Regionalisierungen. Band 2: Globalisierung, Region und Regionalisierung, Stuttgart: Franz Steiner Verlag.

---

5 | The participating researchers were free to write their contributions in either German, French or English.

2. Theoretical and Methodological Approaches to Borders, Spaces and Identities

Wilhelm Amann, Christel Baltes-Löhr, Brigitte Batyko, Elisabeth Boesen, Till Dembeck, Martin Doll, Fabian Faller, Sylvie Freyermuth, Johanna M. Gelberg, Frank Hofmann, Markus Hesse, Sonja Kmec, Elena Kreutzer, Heike Mauer, Agnès Prüm, Rachel Reckinger, Gregor Schnuer, Gianna Thommes, Lucie Waltzer, Christian Wille

2.1 ESTABLISHING, CROSSING AND EXPANDING BORDERS

Martin Doll and Johanna M. Gelberg

What first comes to mind when faced with the abstract notion of the 'border' is a line that separates at least two areas or spheres from each other, thereby introducing a differentiation. The notion can also imply something zonal, as a number of etymological studies have shown (see e.g. Böckler 2007; Eigmüller 2007; Lask 2002). Here the border not merely appears as a line but is perceived as a threshold, a liminal space, enabling all kinds of interactions. In addition, a border can be concretized on various levels: as a territorial border, marked by turnpikes and custom controls; as a social border that can be expressed via status symbols or consumption patterns; or also as an aesthetical border, which can be staged paratextually or museologically. Depending on the specific concretization, different approaches lend themselves to different scientific disciplines: the border is of key importance not only to geography and social sciences, but also to research in cultural studies and history (see Faber/Naumann 1995; Lamping 2001; Audehm/Velten 2007; Roll/Pohle/Myrczek 2010). Thus the border is *per se* a concept used across boundaries of disciplines. A striking example for this are the border studies which see themselves as an interdisciplinary field and are (increasingly) less concerned with the nature of spatial or social borders, but rather with the social, political, economic and cultural processes which question, shift or institute borders of whatever nature (see Walter-Wastl 2011). Since the 1990s this social-constructivist perspective of bordering that is concerned with social practice has become firmly established in social and cultural studies (see e.g. Albert/Brock 1996; Newman 2001; Houtum/Naerssen 2002).

The interdisciplinary approach to the concept of 'border' also reveals its complex profile. There are not only varying levels of concretization of the border, the respective features of the border and the dynamic processes that occur along it also diverge. The studies presented in this volume generally take a praxeological perspective on these dynamics. The focus is on the 'social practices' performed on the border and in the border region, i.e. "[...] behavioral routines that are dependent on know how and held together by a practical 'understanding'"(Reckwitz 2003: 289)[1], which should be seen as material in the broadest sense and which contribute in shaping border, space and identity.

This section offers an overview of various concepts of the border. The studies in this volume, which have on the geographical level for the most part Luxembourg and the bordering regions as their subject, examine different types of boundaries that however should not be seen as merely duplicating national borders. In addition, the abstracting overview of various concepts of the border explicitly encourages their application to further concretizations of the border, for instance in the realm of media. Drawing on Benjamin Bühler's overview of the history of the ways in which the border has been theorized, we can distinguish the following three structurizing differentiations: the "establishment of the border", the "crossing of the border" and the expansion of the border to an "unmarked area of the in-between"[2] (Bühler 2012: 34).

2.1.1 Establishing the Border

Borders are not a given, natural fact. On the contrary: they are established – and established over and over again. If the creation of a so-called 'European area' conveys the impression that stable borders that have always existed have now been overcome, a brief glance at history already tells us that stringent boundaries are actually only the result of certain historical developments – e.g. the emergence of nation states. Seen from a diachronic perspective, historical maps also provide sufficient evidence of the temporal variability of borders.

Besides revealing the changeability of borders, the historical perspective offers us a second important insight: that the materiality of the border *line* is a fiction. It seems self-evident that it is only on the drawing board that the border can take the form of a perfect line. Until the end of the 18th century borders tended to be conceived "as a margin, a broad strip that acted as a contact space and zone of

---

1 | Personal translation of: "[...] *know how* abhängige und von einem praktischen 'Verstehen' zusammengehaltene Verhaltensroutinen."

2 | Personal translation of: [das] "Einsetzen der Grenze", [das] "Überschreiten der Grenze" [und die Ausdehnung der Grenze zu einem] "unmarkierte[n] Bereich des Dazwischen."

transition, frequently leading to conflicts and shifts of these marginal regions"[3] (Kaufmann/Bröckling/Horn 2002: 12). This zonal character of the border also becomes apparent in the passport system established since the 15th century which enabled the control of travellers along the border margins; however, these controls did not occur at an exact border line, but preferably in the interior (see ibid.: 14). With the formation of modern nation states the notion of the border as an imagined line increasingly took root, while the border itself never completely lost its zonal and marginal character. The establishment of the border (as a line) here first of all occurs as a gesture of domination.

At the same time, the border is also established as an implementation in a bottom-up direction. Borders are confirmed or shifted through social practices. Actions performed along a territorial border result in the practical establishment of a specific space. Hans Medick summarizes:

"Borders shape the structure and dynamics of the societies whose margin they form. The border opens up latitudes for action for the individuals and communities living in their vicinity; but as a space controlled in a special way by sovereign authority, it also produces special patterns of behaviour"[4] (Medick 1995: 223).

Thus (politically effective) latitudes for action open up at the border both on the side of those governed and the side of those governing. Very much in the sense of Michel Foucault's concept of governmentality (see sections 2.3, 3.1 and 5.1) there is at the border an encounter between political government and technologies of the self; the result of this encounter is the constantly repeated establishment of borders.

What marks the establishment of a border is its power of differentiation. Every demarcation is an act of differentiation, which implies the constitution of meaning, just as every definition is based on the principle of bordering. The border differentiates, categorizes and hierarchizes and puts the differentiated units into relation with each other (see Audehm/Velten 2007: 18). The establishment of borders is therefore of paramount importance for forming symbolic and social orders. It is through borders that units are determined as supposedly homogenous units and also put in relation to other units (see Kaufmann/Bröckling/Horn 2002: 16). According to Pierre Bourdieu, a social field can be structured through differentiations; the "fine differences" then manifest themselves as "lines of social

---

3 | Personal translation of: "[...] als Saum konzipiert, als ein breiter Streifen, der als Kontaktraum und Übergangszone fungierte, wobei es dabei häufig zu Streitigkeiten und Verschiebungen dieser Randgebiete kam."

4 | Personal translation of: "Grenzen prägen die Struktur und Dynamik der Gesellschaften, deren Rand sie bilden. Die Grenze eröffnet den in ihrer Nähe lebenden Individuen und Gemeinschaften Handlungsspielräume; sie bedingt aber als ein in besonderer Weise herrschaftlich kontrollierter Raum auch besondere Verhaltensweisen."

distinction without an expansion of their own"[5] (Parr 2008: 29) and enable the subject to be situated in the social field. The act of establishment of borders and of differentiation is of equally elementary significance in the context of identity-constructing subject constitutions (see chapter 5).

Drawing on Jacques Derrida, differentiations and thus the establishment of borders can also be considered semiotically. Meanings and relations created through borders then need not be fixed as clear-cut and permanent, but can be described as ambivalent. In contrast to Bourdieu, (linguistic) differentiations do not signify unchangeable social distinctions[6] for Derrida, but rather open up a performative area in which constant differentiation processes occur and shifts of meaning are made possible. Kathrin Audehm and Hans Rudolf Velten translate these considerations to social and cultural contexts and conclude "that differences should be understood as results of discursive and social processes that possess a performative latitude, and not as hierarchic essences from whose fixed structures borders emerge"[7] (Audehm/Velten 2007: 24). Differentiations or distinctions that produce meaning are therefore *per se* performative acts that enable ambivalences; both aspects conflate in the dynamic process of the establishment of the border.

The establishment of the border basically always defines a situation that is subject to specific organizational principles: the border can, following Erving Goffman, also be understood as a situative "frame" (Goffman 1974: 10f.). The situations thus established – whether as cultural events, socio-cultural patterns of behaviour or historical occurences – follow particular rules. The specific situation is not only defined from within, but it is notably the relationship to the bordered exterior that is also regulated. Goffman emphasizes the major significance of the interplay between the spaces created through the differentiations, the interior and the exterior. Crossing the border as a frame reinforces it by reproducing it at the same time. Goffman's frame analysis therefore implicitly puts the focus on the performative aspect of the establishment of the border and at the same time points to the fundamental interplay between the border and its crossing.

2.1.2 Crossing the Border

Every border implies its own surmounting. As a process, the establishment of the border depends on confirmation and reproduction. The border can only be reproduced following a temporary questioning, its crossing. According to

---

5 | Personal translation of: "[...] feinen Unterschiede" [zeigen sich dann als] "Linien sozialer Distinktion ohne eigene Ausdehnung."

6 | This criticism is shared by recent research drawing on Bourdieu (see e.g. Warde 2005; Warde/Martens/Olsen 1999).

7 | Personal translation of: "[...] dass Differenzen als Ergebnisse diskursiver und sozialer Prozesse zu verstehen sind, die einen performativen Spielraum besitzen, und nicht als hierarchische Essenzen, aus deren feststehenden Strukturen Grenzziehungen emergieren."

Goffman these crossings are however subjected to specific rules determined by the establishment of borders itself. These rules for crossing do not neutralize the border but rather confirm it. This regulated form of crossing is structurally affirmative.

Besides the regulated crossing there is also the unplanned border crossing, the border violation. This non-regulated form of crossing is structurally subversive. Here, instead of an affirmative reproduction of the border, a transformation of the border is enforced. The interplay of border and crossing, whether affirmative or subversive, thus becomes more complex and clearly shows that the establishment and the crossing of the border are mutually dependent.[8]

In their study on figures who pass as well as test the border, Kaufmann *et al.* note that borders "only exist *in actu* as technical mechanisms and social arrangements of exclusion and inclusion as well as opening"[9] (Kaufmann/Bröckling/Horn 2002: 7). Every establishment of a border requires a specific border regime that controls or limits its crossing or decides who is authorized to cross the border or not. Particularly in the light of this situation specific power structures and border regimes become visible in the differentiation between the allowed or sometimes even desired cross-border commuting and the illegitimate violation of borders[10] – always related to particular identitary inclusions and exclusions, particularly along the external borders of the EU: "Borders not only produce nationals and foreigners", the editors write, "but also border violators" (ibid.: 7). In crossing it, the border may be subverted or simply ignored; the power of the border's linear demarcation, the mechanism of exclusion, is questioned in either case. However, questioning the border by crossing it should not be equated with its dissolution. Crossings can in fact stabilize borders. The violation of a border in the sense of an unauthorized crossing can result in its tighter control. Similar mechanisms are at work when so-called white hat hackers access computer data to reveal security loopholes that can then be closed. Kaufmann *et al.* conclude: "Crossing does

---

8 | See also Dieter Lamping's study: "In this sense the border is not only the place of distinction and demarcation, but also the place of passage, approach and mixing. It is at the same time beginning and end, creating its particular dialectics [...]" (Lamping 2001: 13). (Personal translation of: "Insofern ist die Grenze nicht nur der Ort der Unterscheidung und der Abgrenzung, sondern auch der Ort des Übergangs, der Annäherung und der Mischung. Sie ist Anfang und Ende zugleich, und daraus erwächst ihre besondere Dialektik [...].")
9 | Personal translation of: "[...] nur *in actu* [existieren], als technische Vorrichtungen und soziale Arrangements des Aus- und Einschließens wie des Öffnens."
10 | Audehm and Velten thus warn against "[...] equating cross-border commuting in every instance with transgression" (Audehm/Velten 2007: 26). (Personal translation of: [Grenzgängertum] "[...] in jedem Fall mit Transgression gleichzusetzen.")

therefore not only lead to perforation, but also to an ever more perfect securing of the border"[11] (ibid.: 10).

Both Goffman and Kaufmann *et al.* point to the enormous significance of crossing as an essential border dynamics. Whether potentially affirmative or subversive, there is a fundamental consequentiality inherent to the crossing (see Audehm/Velten 2007: 26ff.); the unity of border and crossing thus has the potential for transformation – whatever its specific nature may be.

The elementary interdependency of border and crossing is emphasized by Michel Foucault particularly succinctly: "The limit and transgression depend on each other for whatever density of being they possess: a limit could not exist if it were absolutely uncrossable and, reciprocally, transgression would be pointless if it merely crossed a limit composed of illusions and shadows" (Foucault 1998: 73). The crossing of the border therefore constitutes neither its dissolution nor the questioning of its validity, but rather the fundamental mode for experiencing the border and its transformative potential. Only in crossing it, can the border become tangible and understandable. If Foucault in this context speaks of the space of the transgression and characterizes the crossing also as a "passage", as a "trajectory", then the border itself is spatialized, i.e. can be experienced in its expansion as an 'in-between' (ibid.: 72). In a much-cited passage from the first notes of the 'The Arcades Project' Walter Benjamin describes such "zone[s] of transition" (Benjamin 1999: 856) as thresholds.[12] These expanded border zones are of particular interest in this volume. They offer, as phenomena that are effective in more ways than one, the possibility to reflect in multiple perspectives space, region and identity in the context of the border.

2.1.3 Expanding the Border

Envisaging borders as thresholds, i.e. not as lines, but as areas with an expansion of their own, opens up a broad range of analytical approaches. If we remind ourselves again that it is an essential part of borders to make distinctions, i.e. to separate at least two spheres from each other, the notion of threshold in particular offers the possibility to ask how the two units, which are connected and separated at the same time, relate to each other. This question has been answered in different ways by theorists from various disciplines. This is because thresholds are multidimensional entities that show themselves in a different light depending on the perspective adopted. For instance, one can ask how a threshold divides the

---

11 | Personal translation of: "Überschreitung führt so nicht nur zur Perforation, sondern auch zur immer perfekteren Absicherung von Grenzen."

12 | Even though Benjamin, without explaining himself, insists that "the threshold must be carefully distinguished from the boundary" (Benjamin 1999: 494), we will in the following consider the border *as* threshold. For a concise summarization of Benjamin's polyvalent use of the image of the 'threshold', see Parr (2008).

features of the realms between which it is situated and how it shares them at the same time: that is, whether, first, it forms an additional independent element; whether, secondly, overlaps occur between the spheres or subsets through superimposition; or, thirdly, whether it literally represents an in-between state and, as a fuzzy fringe and through a nuanced cross-fade of different spheres, generally makes it unclear where one sphere ends and the next begins.

If one considers 'threshold' in the first sense, it forms a clearly delineated area of the 'in-between' with a quality of its own. Then it can be understood as a place of passage which necessarily connects two adjoining separate spheres and mediates between them, in the way that one can for instance step on a door sill (see Audehm/Velten 2007: 14).[13] If it is understood spatially, there is an in front and behind, an exterior and an interior. Understood in terms of time, there is a before and an after.

Drawing on Arnold van Gennep's observations on rites of passage (*rites de passage*[14]), Victor Turner has placed thresholds into a processual and praxeological context, and related them to particular structural features: in the rites of passage that accompany incisive changes – e.g. when individuals within a society undergo a change of social status – van Gennep identifies three phases, namely separation, transition and incorporation. The intermediate phase, also designated with the Latin word for threshold, *limen*, is to be understood as a transformational phase – as a phase of antistructure, of ambiguity, of a blurring and a levelling of differences – because, while passing through it, specific socially valid structures liquify, enabling new structures to form (see Turner 1982). The (temporal) change of status is frequently accompanied by a (spatial) passage, whether it be the crossing of a door sill to a temple, a long pilgrim's journey or moving to another domicile, another area (see ibid.: 24f. and 27f.).

Returning here once more to the question of how the threshold relates to the characteristics of the before and after, one should observe that the transformational phase, in terms of structures, does not adopt all structural features of the before but rather has only a few elements in common with the previous structures: liminality thus essentially consists in opening, within this orderless antistructure – this betwixt-and-between as a neither-nor –, the possibility of both adding to the existing, accustomed elements of culture new ones and enabling a "free or 'ludic' recombination in any and every possible pattern, however weird" (Turner 1982: 28). In this kind of no-man's-land of indeterminacy, a society releases its creative potential, not only for its analytical (critical) self-reflection, but also for its own

---

13 | Drawing on Erika Fischer-Lichte, the authors emphasize that in contrast to borders that attempt to prevent their crossing, thresholds – in their function of actually inviting passage – lose the subversive potential of crossing (see Audehm/Velten: 2007: 15).

14 | Benjamin also begins his observations on liminal experiences with van Gennep's *Rites de passage* (see Benjamin 1999: 494).

innovation. Seen in this way, *antistructure* appears as *protostructure* (see ibid.: 32 and 42).

In contrast to this model, which, while allowing for cyclically recurring processes, sees them as unidirectional, other theorists understand thresholds as zones of mutual overlappings. This in turn leads to two conceptual patterns that can be distinguished analytically: namely, as already mentioned above in second and third place, a superimposing and a cross-fading. The former evokes more the image of an intersection, i.e. a multiple affiliation of the involved elements, the latter more the image of their blending and interlacing, connected with indeterminacy.

These two modes are for instance underpinned by the concept of overlaps and fuzzy sets to overcome thinking in terms of binary oppositions, of either-or logics. With the introduction of these terms, Vilém Flusser has questioned the border as a stable demarcation line and conceived it in its expansion as a border region – even though he does not use the term threshold. This clearly de-emphasizes the separating aspect in favour of the "relational and connective dimension of borders"[15] (Guldin 2011: 45): according to Flusser, borders are to be understood as areas in which regions have a particular relationship with each other (see Flusser 2009: 244). In the case of the overlap they intersect and form "grey zones, in which fields superimpose each other"[16] (Flusser 1996: 62), as Flusser explains citing, significantly, the example of Luxembourg:

"The whole of Luxembourg is a question of borders. Granted, there is a specific Luxembourgish language, but in actual fact at the same time French and German are spoken in this border region. There one refers to regions in which cultures are superimposed"[17] (ibid: 93).

In the case of the fuzzy set, on the other hand, "one of the regions penetrates deeply into the centre of the other and vice-versa"[18] (ibid.). Here it is of particular importance not to principally negate differences, but place them in a multidimensional field of complex relationships. For only because the spheres remain distinguishable can they interact, intersect and mesh in the border regions: Flusser accordingly emphasizes that the areas "do not merge with each other, also not superimpose

---

15 | Personal translation of: "[...] Beziehungs- und Verbindungsdimension von Grenzen."

16 | Personal translation of: "[...] graue Zonen, in denen sich Felder überdecken."

17 | Personal translation of: "Ganz Luxemburg ist eine Frage von Grenzen. Es ist wahr, daß es eine bestimmte luxemburgische Sprache gibt, aber in Wirklichkeit wird in diesem Grenzgebiet zur selben Zeit Französisch und Deutsch gesprochen. Man spricht dort von Regionen, in denen Kulturen aufeinanderliegen."

18 | Personal translation of: "[...] dringt eine der Regionen tiefgreifend ins Zentrum der andern ein und umgekehrt."

each other, but rather become fuzzy sets"[19] (ibid.: 246). This thinking in "fuzzy sets" makes it possible to analyse gradual affiliations, also prove that an element can not only be attributed to multiple, incongruent spheres but also that this occurs in varying, not clearly delineated degrees of affiliation ("slightly", "strongly" etc.[20]) (Guldin 2011: 40f.).

More recent observations from planning studies indirectly tie in with this 'fuzzy logic', namely when referring to 'fuzzy boundaries' and 'soft spaces'. This enables a new, more small-scale mode of planning in regional development, which no longer only operates in the framework of existing rigid political administrative boundaries. Instead, also 'soft', functionally conceived planning regions – that at times also diverge among each other – can be taken into account. Regional planning thus becomes an interplay of different, overlapping and interacting levels: in the planning process issues of the existing geography, transport and infrastructure, real estate market, health and education for example are put in relation to each other and evaluated. This can help to reveal overlappings of different types of borders, for instance the fact that specific territorial and sociocultural boundaries are not necessarily congruent or are not stereotypically mapped one on top of the other – as approaches favouring the concept of space as a container tend to do. This interest in new, multiple planning factors has also led to fuzzy professional boundaries of spatial planning, i.e. to an expansion of the disciplines involved in the planning process (see Allmendinger/Haughton 2009: 617f., 620, 625ff.). Here there is an increased emphasis on functional issues and specific social practices and no longer only on a topographically conceived space. This analytical perspective enables in particular in border regions the reconstruction of spatial entities that traverse or cut across national borders and emerge from specific cross-border practices.[21]

Theories of transdifference are connected in a more general way to these modes of incongruence, mixing and indeterminacy. Similar to the approach of 'overlaps' and 'fuzzy sets', the 'trans' of transdifference does not aim to level differences but to use them to develop complementary points of view. The concept of transdifference allows differences to be considered in a novel way in order to investigate elements "of incertitude, indecidability and paradox that are edited out on the basis of binary logics of order"[22] (Lösch 2005: 27). As Britta Kalscheuer has shown, this concept can in turn be connected to spatial configurations: Transdifference makes borders visible not as demarcation lines but rather as

---

19 | Personal translation of: "[...] nicht ineinander verschwimmen, auch nicht einander überdecken, sondern daß diese zu *fuzzy sets* werden."
20 | Personal translation of: "('Ein bisschen', 'stark' usw.)."
21 | A corresponding heuristic framework is provided by the approach "Spaces of the Border" (Wille, 2014).
22 | Personal translation of: [Momente] "der Ungewissheit, der Unentscheidbarkeit und des Widerspruchs" [...] "die auf der Basis binärer Ordnungslogik ausgeblendet werden."

zones "of intercultural dialogue"[23] (ibid.: 43), in which conflicting images of Self and of the Other of the participating cultures are negotiated. In this context, transdifference refers to the transient and always ephemeral destabilization of a clear differentiation between an 'own' and an 'other', between a 'we' and a 'them', inasmuch as any attempt at a clear-cut and stable establishment of a border can be aborted via alternative borderings (see Kalscheuer 2005: 74; Lösch 2005: 36). This also has consequences for the identity attributions caught in the same complex: they are subject to a continuous repositioning (see Kalscheuer 2005: 75).[24] In this way the border becomes a space of interaction, and, as Klaus Lösch puts it, drawing on James Clifford, cultures become the "product of the *interaction* of systems, whose borders are only established in this process of exchange (and not before) and are continuously revised"[25] (Lösch 2005: 33).

Considering the border as a threshold finally leads us back to the question of how it is at all possible to establish borders – or, more precisely: to mark them and make them visible. A review of historical forms of border administration has already shown that territorial borders as a rule require a 'margin', however small, if their effectiveness is to be ensured. Jacques Derrida's deconstruction of Kant's "Analytic of the Beautiful" from the *Critique of Judgement* suggests formulating this even more radically: every 'inner order' enclosed by a border (understood by Derrida/Kant: that which is considered a beautiful object) would then only appear to be independent of the margin marking this border. In effect it could not exist without it, could not be detached from it (see Derrida 1982 [1978]).

It would however require further detailed discussion whether this applies to every kind of border, i.e. whether one always has to presume a form of expansion of the borderline to a threshold. The fact that this question remains unanswered for the time being in no ways diminishes the analytical need to distinguish the above-mentioned three aspects of the border, its establishment, its crossing and its expansion to a threshold. They will be taken up and further elaborated in the contributions of this volume and discussed in the specific empirical studies under the aspect of constructions of space and identity.

---

23 | Personal translation of: [Zonen]"interkulturellen Dialogs."
24 | Kalscheuer here refers to Lossau 2002: 176.
25 | Personal translation of: "[...] Produkt der *Interaktion* von *Systemen*, deren Grenzen freilich erst in diesem Austauschvorgang gezogen und beständig revidiert werden."

2.2 SPACES: APPROACHES AND PERSPECTIVES OF INVESTIGATION

Christian Wille and Markus Hesse

Since the end of the 1980s cultural studies and social sciences have been giving increased attention to the category of 'space'. The concomitant valorization of 'space' under the term 'spatial turn' has gone on to produce a series of differentiations of which the 'topographical turn' plays a role particularly in literary and media studies. The term 'spatial turn' follows up on discussions of post-modernity and was promoted in particular by the geographer Edward W. Soja. In using this term, he called for giving greater consideration to spatial categories and conditions of social development in general, but also understood these as a social contingency of space – not as a spatial constitution of society. Drawing on Henri Lefebvre (1991 [1974]), Soja (1989 and 1996) argues in favour of departing from space as a fact of natural space and instead directing the focus on its processes of social production. Practically around the same time Benno Werlen used the identical approach for developing an action-theoretical conception of geography as a social science that aimed to overcome the notion of geography as a science concerned exclusively with space (see Werlen 2008).

It is precisely this frame of reference in which the present volume investigates 'space' in its processes of social construction in various thematic contexts. What is relevant here is the socially emergent perspective on space broadly received via Lefevbre, in turn building on Simmel (1992 [1903]). Its unabated currency and continuous development commenced in the 1990s, triggered by a series of social and technological changes. These prompted an increasing number of questions in the social sciences and cultural studies that can be narrowed down to two seemingly opposing positions: the apparent disappearance of space and the apparent return of space. This refers first of all to the despatialization thesis which argues that space has lost a great deal of its significance with the development of transport and communication media, space-time convergencies and the borderless society. At the same time, the spatialization thesis proceeds – with the same arguments – on the assumption that there is a growing diversification of spatial contexts (see Kajetzke/Schroer 2010: 195). This already suggests that the apparent disappearance and a corresponding return of space are not consecutive but simultaneously observable processes that are furthermore dependent on interpretation. Also, both need not necessarily be seen as being contradictory, but can be conceived as closely linked dialectic categories. The relationship between despatialization and spatialization, which has to be defined empirically, constitutes one of the subjects in this volume that deals with phenomena in the context of borders and border regions. This is prompted by the consideration that it is particularly in the context of border negotiations that special demands are made on the theoretical category of 'space'; or in other words: here, processes of despatialization and spatialization can be observed particularly well on an empirical level. Bachmann-Medick (2006: 297) supports this observation when she points to "borders and border-crossings" as "salient research areas of the spatial turn."[26] One of the recurring research questions in this volume therefore concerns itself with spatial constructions that emanate from practices of institutions, the media and everyday life and are linked to processes of the establishment, crossing and expansion of borders.

The spatial concepts called on to this purpose represent in each case different analytical approaches to 'space'. This diversity is reflected in the relevant literature also there where the disappearance of space is emphasized and reference is primarily made to geographical spaces and nation states. By contrast, studies that highlight the return of space tend to draw on – besides the physical-material or territorial space – a relational figure of space as expressed, for instance, in social, virtual or transnational spaces (see Schroer 2008: 135). These different types of space (that also circulate within the disciplines) already suggest that is impossible to find a universally valid definition of space and that a number of different spatial types are – and need to be – mustered simultaneously to investigate the productions of space. We will therefore proceed to first clarify some essential approaches to 'space' and subsequently present the research perspectives chosen in this volume.

2.2.1 Approaches to 'Space'

Regarding the subject of 'space', we can differentiate between various concepts and their theoretical preconceptions that each have had their own specific historical development in spatial discourse. To start with, one widely held view of classical geography is based on an understanding that posits space *first* as a material substance, attributing to it an influence on the objects contained therein and assuming an entity with a nature of its own. This understanding of space is rooted in the classical scientific school of thought in the tradition of Isaac Newton, which holds that space is the causally effective container for all natural, material as well as human processes and artefacts. This mechanistic classification of space has also come to be referred to with the metaphor of the container. Building on a series of causal-analytical fallacies, thinking in categories of container space also informed the first conceptions of human geography developed in the early 20th century by Friedrich Ratzel and Alfred Hettner. Soon after, the logical connection made between terrestrial conditions and a specific disposition of society was to become, with fateful consequences, a key feature of the Nazi policy of conquest, which was also justified with the polemical term of *Lebensraum* (living space) drawn from biology and the notion of the alleged '*Volk ohne Raum*' ('people without space'). Even today, such an essentialist, territorialized notion of space

---

26 | Personal translation of: "Grenzen und Grenzüberschreitungen" [als] "[...] herausgehobene[n] Forschungsfelder[n] des *spatial turn*."

continues to be at the root of many concepts of spatial planning, even though the binding powers of the spatial have long become fluid and the circulation of people, commodities, capital, information, policies etc. have rendered spatially-oriented hierarchical patterns of order almost obsolete.

In addition, a relational perspective understands space *secondly* as structure or as an abstraction of dispositional structures of the physical-material objects that constitute it. This understanding of space still has its origins in the abstract conception of geography as a spatial science, which was promoted by Walter Christaller's central-place theory as well as the emerging quantitative methodology of regional sciences and geography (particularly in the USA). While the original assumption of geography as a causal science of the earth's surface remained in place, space now constituted itself as a "form of order of things in juxtaposition across varying distances"[27] (Werlen 2009: 150). Accordingly it is understood as a "constellation of conditions that are marked by a specifically arranged structure and a multiplicity of functional links and relations"[28] (ibid.) that are subject to this structure. While in this sense, space was already considered to be a product of relational systems instead of a quasi natural result of terrestrial conditions, at that time one still attempted to understand and explain the matter in terms of the methodological system of spatial science, in particular through identifying causalities and laws that one sought to clarify analytically chiefly with quantitative empirics and modelling. It was not until the 1990s and 2000s that broader approaches gained currency in the relational research paradigm, for instance those that have emphasized the constitution and organization of stakeholder agency or the role of institutions of various kinds (see e.g. Bathelt/Glückler 2012).

In the course of a further diversification of notions of space in the context of the cultural-theoretical turn, space is *thirdly* emphasized as having significance when considering in particular attributions and ascriptions of meaning in the conflict with the physical-material world. Basically this is about redefining the relationship between space and society. This is done ontologically through a strict separation of physical-material, socio-cultural and mental space, and epistemologically via a reversal of the relationship of space and society. Space is understood in the sense of Werlen's concept of social geography as a manifestation of societal structures (regulative systems, communication, policies) as well as individual experiences, positings and practices that 'produce' space (see below for this central concept in Lefebvre).

---

27 | Personal translation of: "[...] Form der Ordnung des Nebeneinanders der Dinge über unterschiedliche Distanzen hinweg."

28 | Personal translation of: "[...] Konstellation von Gegebenheiten verstanden, die sich durch eine bestimmte Anordnungsstruktur und eine Vielzahl funktionaler Verknüpfungen bzw. Relationen auszeichnen."

"There is an urgent need to systematically take into account the fundamental principles of Modernity, on which postmodern societies are based in many ways, not only in a socio-cultural sense, but – moving on – also in relation to a corresponding geographical view of the world. That means that a space preceding every action can no longer be in the centre of our view of the world, but rather the acting, physical subjects, who from their terrestrial-spatial position [...] realize an appropriation of the world around them"[29] (Werlen 2009: 153).

This aims at leaving behind the traditionally strong position of space in the sense of the above-mentioned container space in favour of the analysis of societal spatial relationships. Space is here also differentiated in a metaphorical sense, when material aspects are largely ignored and structures of order or relationships are subsumed under one umbrella term.

2.2.2 Approaches to Spatial Constructions in this Volume

The totality of the approaches mentioned here enables us to observe social phenomena with their physical-material aspects as a relational network, as well as the meanings embedded or mobilized in the processes that produce such spatial relations. These two specific perspectives on space, one relational-descriptive and the other symbolic-interpretative, are often discussed together in space-sensitive studies and, in the context of the border, are usually considered against the foil of a territorial nation-state order. This foil is then frequently employed to serve as an 'underlay' for the social, forming a mosaic of container spaces, which however need to be regarded in relational and symbolic terms.

The presented approaches and their nexuses, which in many studies are only implied and not explicitly detailed, encourage a blurred use of the category of 'space'. At the same time, however, they offer multiple points of reference across disciplines that have been instrumental in assuring the popularity of the spatial turn and that are also applied fruitfully for this volume. In the context of the border, the concepts of space concerned with relations and significations have proven to be particularly productive. They help in overcoming the notion of the impact and influence of (national) container spaces – from which scientific thought is often unable to detach itself – and examining the dissolution, particularly visible in cross-border contexts, of the seemingly 'national' unity of territorial space and

---

29 | Personal translation of: "Es ist dringend erforderlich, den Grundprinzipien der Moderne, auf denen spätmoderne Gesellschaften in vielerlei Hinsicht aufbauen, nicht nur in sozial-kultureller Beziehung, sondern – weiterführend – auch bezogen auf ein entsprechendes geographisches Weltbild konsequent Rechnung zu tragen. Das heißt, dass nicht mehr ein jedem Handeln vorausgehender Raum im Zentrum des Weltbildes stehen kann, sondern die handelnden, körperlichen Subjekte, die von ihrer erdräumlichen Position aus [...] 'Welt-Bindungen' [...] verwirklichen."

the social space inscribed in it. The various concepts of space therefore help to analytically decode and empirically examine the 'nesting' of spatial types assumed here and the processes of their 'denesting' yet to be investigated. So this volume is not concerned with displacing the diversity of spatial notions in favour of one model but instead with productively exploiting their plurality and the approaches linked to them. Accordingly the case studies attempt to "take into account the single case and in doing so make use of the theoretical diversity of conceiving space"[30] (Kajetzke/Schroer 2010: 203).

This approach to space using multiple perspectives is not new but was and continues to be practised by a number of scholars. One of these is the above-mentioned French social philosopher Henri Lefebvre. He sees space as socially produced and links the process of its production to questions of social theory (see Lefebvre 1991 [1974]); he distinguishes between three spatial formants: (1) the spatial practice (*pratique spatiale*) that produces a materially perceived space (*l'espace perçu*) in the course of everyday action; (2) the representation of space (*représentation de l'espace*) in the course of influential practices that create a space of knowledge, signs and codes (*l'espace conçu*) and (3) the space of representation (*espace de représentation*) of the experiencing subjects who produce a lived space (*l'espace vécu*) in a symbolic sense. While it is not possible to dwell on Lefebvre's work here, we can note that his concern is to conceive physical and social space together in favour of a practice-oriented perspective, to decode the empirical interaction of different spatial concepts, to emphasize the role of the (human) body for space constructions and to adopt a perspective on space that is directed towards contingency or process (see Kajetzke/Schroer 2010: 196).

Michel de Certeau pursues the same idea when he introduces the distinction between place (*lieu*) as the 'objective' physical-material world and space (*espace*) as a materiality 'coated' with meaning (see de Certeau 1984 [1980]). The French historian and philosopher focuses on so-called practices of place (*pratiques de lieu*) which designate the way we deal with and conduct ourselves in places and which ultimately result in the production of space. Practices of place then stand for how individuals appropriate the physical-material world and confer meaning on it. The much-quoted passage that a road only turns into a space by someone walking along it (see de Certeau 1984 [1980]) should however not obscure the fact that places also 'transform' into spaces via narrations and via the ascriptions of meaning connected to them. De Certeau is thus also building a praxeological bridge between physical and social space; but he conceives space explicitly as a social production embedded in time and movement that can be reproduced as a topological structure and connected back to the relational concept of space.

The approach of "media spaces of identity" (Hipfl 2004: 16ff.) follows epistemologically Lefebvre and de Certeau, but for Brigitte Hipfl codes and

---

30 | Personal translation of: "[...] den Einzelfall [zu] berücksichtigen und sich dabei der theoretischen Vielfalt, Raum zu denken, [zu] bedienen."

representations as well as the metaphorical concept of space play a prominent role. The media and cultural studies scholar assumes that "media, identity and space are inseparably connected and constitute each other"[31] (Hipfl 2004: 16). Against this backdrop, she distinguishes (1) the production of geopolitical spaces that are produced via news coverages or the attributions of meaning and differentiations embedded in them. She is thus concerned with 'imaginative geographies' (see Said 1978) which construct identities and can be linked to the notion of 'imagined communities' (see Anderson 1983). In addition, Hipfl understands media themselves as spaces, namely as (2) semiotic spaces which display formations of identity apparent in differentiations, border crossings, inclusions and exclusions produced in them. Finally Hipfl (2004) opens up an analytical approach that centres on the reception of media. The concept of (3) the in-between spaces that are created in the interaction between media and recipients aims to direct the focus to the identity choices (of the semiotic spaces) conveyed by media. At the same time, it seeks to draw attention particularly to their reinterpretation or their contingent appropriations which are not rooted in the media themselves but in the relationship between media and recipients. Even though Hipfl (2004) develops a different trialectics of spatial types to Lefebvre, she succeeds in using the plurality of the notion of space to find an overarching grasp on social productions of space and identities and make them analytically accessible.

These examples of conceiving 'space' in multiple ways and making productive use of this circumstance assume the social dependency and processuality of spaces. In investigating them it is not the spaces 'as such' that are examined but the practices of their production with the involved subjects, bodies, artefacts, world views, meanings and power relations. This "methodological investigative setting"[32] (Bachmann-Medick 2006: 303) – *based on* and *following* social practices and their materializations – can be applied to various forms of spatial constructions, which however frequently overlap empirically. Linguistic-communicative spatial constructions (e.g. imaginative geographies, semiotic spaces, *l'espace conçu*) are more accessible via approaches of discourse theory and semiotics for revealing space-related semantizations and their performative techniques of attribution and representation. Spatial constructions of everyday practices (e.g. *l'espace vécu, les espaces/pratiques de lieu*) can be more easily reassembled via practice-related approaches that address the subjects' everyday geographies as topological structures and symbolic spatializations. Crucial for both forms of spatial production are relations and topologies as well as attributions and interpretations of meaning related to the physical-material world, which in turn permit statements about identity constructions. For while differentiations, relations, 'talking' of an

---

31 | Personal translation of: "[...] Medien, Identität und Raum untrennbar miteinander verknüpft sind und sich gegenseitig konstituieren."

32 | Personal translation of: "Methodische Untersuchungseinstellung."

interior/exterior indicate (space-related) differentiations, these at the same time inform about (self-)positionings and thus about identities.

Based on the above, the level of meaning and the contingency of spaces and/or identities constitute a guiding theme in this volume. We differentiate between three perspectives of investigation which, drawing on different concepts of space, are developed in the following chapters, but also overlap. These are (1) a power-critical perspective on space that addresses in particular policies and normalizations that take effect and are negotiated in spatial construction; (2) a media-oriented perspective on space which sees these as constructors and projection surfaces, with media themselves being identified as spaces and (3) a subject-centered perspective that examines spatial constructions in the course of everyday practices. These perspectives focus partly on different matters, but consistently on the construction processes of spaces while avoiding thinking in preset spatial categories.

The *power-critical perspective on spatial constructions* pervades this volume as a whole, in particular chapter 3. Point of departure here is the assumption that spaces are more or less manifestly shaped by power relationships, more precisely by policies and normalizations. These are revealed by examining differentiations, attributions of meaning, hierarchizations and other techniques of the exercise of power that are inherent in spatial constructions. Here we will also draw on observations by Julia Lossau (2004) and Michel Foucault (1977) among others.

In her studies of the early 2000s, which are more along the lines of linguistic-communicative spatial constructions, Lossau (2004) examines in how far the social is naturalized through practices of location or via symbolic spatializations. Her observations, drawing on Said (1978), are based on a constructivist understanding of space, i.e. that reality is always "created via continuous attributions of meaning; via speaking or writing" and that the representations used for this "are always also embedded in questions about power and domination"[33] (Lossau 2003: 104). 'Doing representation' – as a performative practice of spatial construction – is thus always linked to a "policy of localization"[34] (Lossau 2002). Adopting a power-critical perspective then means enquiring who represents or "localizes" what and how and to what purpose. The analytical work is thus less concerned with the objects used in spatial constructions, but rather with "which way these objects are perceived and thus (re)produced"[35] (Lossau 2003: 110).

Another but similar perspective was developed by Foucault who focuses more on spatial constructions of everyday practice. These primarily refer

---

33 | Personal translation of: "[...] erst [entsteht] durch kontinuierliche Bedeutungszuweisungen; durch Sprechen oder Schreiben [...]" [und dass die dafür verwendeten Repräsentationen] "[...] immer auch in Fragen nach Macht und Herrschaft eingelassen sind."
34 | Personal translation of: "Politik der Verortung."
35 | Personal translation of: "[...] auf welche Art und Weise diese Gegenstände [...] betrachtet und damit (re-)produziert werden."

to architectures as media of control that produce, via their dispositions and materialities, steering effects, i.e. technologies of power with which bodies and cultural practices can be arranged and controlled (see Foucault 1977). Consequently one can inquire about the territorialization strategies of architecture or – as is partly done in chapter 3 – in an even more fundamental way, "which functions spatial productions fulfill in controlling a population and how human action and social participation can be controlled through territorialization and zoning"[36] (Schreiber 2009: 202). In addition, Foucault enables a power-critical perspective where everyday practices are seen as focal points of spatial constructions. It is only in a second step that the analytical attention then directs itself to the spatial figures produced in each case; the primary focus is on the subjectifications and subjectivations[37] which more or less 'guide' the spatial practices. These can be examined on the level of the subject by looking at logics of everyday culture that manifest themselves in social practices and the spatial relationships produced in them (see chapter 5). From the perspective of subjectifications, space-related representations can be examined for symbolic charging and coding – similar to the concept of the "policy of localization"[38] (Lossau 2002) (see chapters 3 and 4). With his concept of governmentality, Foucault provides an effective tool for examining spatial constructions from a power-critical perspective and via a variety of approaches.

The *media-oriented perspective on spatial constructions* in this volume for the most part follows the research conducted in the context of the topographical turn (see Wagner 2010; Weigel 2002). This refers both to the examination of spatially constitutive codings and technologies of representation in cultural media and the semiotic reading of physical-material spaces. Space-creating construction mechanisms play a key role in such 'topographical readings'. They are at the centre of the above-mentioned concept of 'imaginative geographies' developed by literary studies scholar Edward W. Said (see Said 1978). In his work he reconstructs among other things the orientalist discourse of the West and shows how the Other constructed there is instrumentalized for the colonial expansion of the West, or in other words "how imagined geographies were able to turn into powerful instruments for exercising power and also transforming the physical-material

---

36 | Personal translation of: "[...] welche Funktionen Raumproduktionen bei der Steuerung von Bevölkerung erfüllen und wie sich durch Territorialisieren und Zonieren menschliches Handeln und gesellschaftliche Teilhabe lenken lässt."

37 | We differentiate between processes of subjectification (see Althusser 1971) and subjectivation (see Bührmann/Schneider 2008: 176), the former meaning top-down, mostly institutional attributions and the latter bottom-up, generally individual appropriations within the general, neverending practices of identity-building.

38 | Personal translation of: "Politik der Verortung."

2. Theoretical and Methodological Approaches

space"[39] (Döring 2010: 96). Besides the power-critical aspects this is primarily about the performative dimension of the practices of the media discourse, more precisely about symbolic processes of attributions and representations of meaning through which spatial relationships and identities are established. Birgit Neumann's (2009: 118) reading of Said emphasizes this clearly: "Thus the acts of establishing borders have the function of increasingly homogenizing heterogenous spaces and creating spaces that are structured in a binary way and that can be put into the service of the self-affirmative separation of the own and the other."[40]

The social geographers Annegret Harendt and Dana Sprunk (2011) also examine spatializing practices under performative aspects, specifically in the context of media coverages. They have developed, drawing on notions of literary studies, the concepts of 'narrated space' (*erzählter Raum*) and 'narrative space' (*Erzählraum*), attempting to emphasize two dimensions of imaginative geography that are analytically separable but interlock in their effect. In the 'narrated space' they focus on what is said and thus on space-related codings; the 'narrative space' by contrast centres on what is shown and thus the 'stage' and materiality of the staging of space. The latter opens up an additional aspect of media-related productions of space, since it complements the enquiry into the symbolic orders with that into the *mise en scène* of spatial stagings.

In this volume, cultural media are themselves also regarded as spaces. For this we use, among others, the notion of the interstice[41], which is employed both for denoting physical-material arrangements and symbolic-metaphorical ones. While it places less emphasis on the aspect of power asymmetries, it does draw on post-colonial thought, when, in chapter 4, interstices form the counterfoil to binary logics and the dissolution of boundaries becomes constitutive. Interstices then denote zones where borders are crossed and questioned, where a productive-creative negotiation of differences takes place and the own coexists beside the other or the private beside the public.

The *subject-centered perspective on space* in this volume addresses everyday practices and the spatial productions generated in them. As mentioned above, these can be reconstructed via practice- and/or action-theoretical approaches. The point of reference here is the approach of "everyday regionalizations"[42] (Werlen

---

39 | Personal translation of: "[...] wie aus imaginierten Geographien machtvolle Instrumente zur Herrschaftsausübung und zur Umgestaltung auch des physisch-materiellen Raums werden konnten."

40 | Personal translation of: "So haben die Akte der Grenzziehung die Funktion, heterogene Räume zunehmend zu vereinheitlichen und binär strukturierte Räume zu schaffen, die in den Dienst der selbstaffirmativen Separation des Eigenen und Fremden gestellt werden können."

41 | This only partly overlaps with Hipfl's (2004) concept of the in-between mentioned above.

42 | Personal translation of: "[...] alltäglichen Regionalisierungen."

1997a), which focuses "on the human practice with particular consideration for the material means of action, their social interpretation and meaning"[43] (Werlen 2007a: 66). Werlen thus takes the practices of the subjects as a point of departure for examining staged geographies in everyday life. On an analytical level, this involves constellations of objects and/or structures of relationships between artefacts and bodies that are created by subjects in social practices (relationalizations). A further aspect are attributions and signifcations that flow into social practices, condense into representations and in turn take effect on a social level. Both aspects – the observable and relationalizing action as well as the processes of meaning – refer to the physical-material world. Space is then regarded as a conceptional medium that in a relational-descriptive regard expresses "the different relationalizations of bodily subjects with other physical-material circumstances"[44] (Werlen 1997b: 10). In a symbolic-interpretative respect it represents the subjects' attributions and significations produced in the course of relationalizations.

This approach is fundamentally suited for the investigation of spatial constructions in the context of the border since it overcomes the idea of powerful container spaces in favour of a relational and meaning-oriented perspective on space. However, the concept of action that this approach is based on limits the analysis of spatial practices in cross-border contexts. Werlen (2008: 282) sees 'doing space' as an "activity in the sense of an intentional act"[45], focussing on intentions and purposes that subjects attune their actions to. This process is guided "more or less consciously by an intersubjective context of meaning" in the sense of a "socially and culturally prepared orientational grid" that "exists independently from the individual actor"[46] (Werlen 2008: 287). This understanding of everyday practices follows an orientation along the lines of purpose and rules, thereby linking up with classical approaches of explaining agency, which, in the context of the border, only have limited efficacy. This is because they operate *firstly* with rational orientations of action (*homo oeconomicus*), with a normative-collective consensus on (il)legitimate action (*homo sociologicus*) as well as with intersubjectively and stably conceived orders of knowledge (*homo significans*); *secondly* they disregard the observable bodily agency and its materializations (see Reckwitz 2003). However, the analysis of everyday practices in this volume, particularly chapter 5, calls for spatial-theoretical links (via bodies, artefacts and their relationalizations),

---

43 | Personal translation of: "[…] auf die menschliche Praxis unter besonderer Berücksichtigung der räumlichen Bedingungen der materiellen Medien des Handelns, ihrer sozialen Interpretation und Bedeutung."

44 | Personal translation of: "[…] die unterschiedlichen Relationierungen der körperlichen Subjekte mit anderen physisch-materiellen Gegebenheiten […] zum Ausdruck [bringt]."

45 | Personal translation of: "[…] Tätigkeit im Sinne eines intentionalen Aktes."

46 | Personal translation of: "[…] mehr oder weniger bewusst an einem intersubjektiven […] Bedeutungszusammenhang" [im Sinne eines] "gesellschaftlich und kulturell vorbereitete[n] Orientierungsraster[s]", [das] "unabhängig vom einzelnen Handelnden besteht."

and furthermore, in cross-border contexts there is usually less reason to impute rational assessment and expectancy of attaining a desired goal, an intersubjectivity as a 'social lubricant' or a 'proper' execution of (wherever) valid systems of rules and symbols. Rather, in the context of the border, everyday practices are marked by discontinuities, interpretative uncertainties and ambivalences (see Boeckler 2012: 48) that should be identified with a suitable concept of practices – as a focal point of spaces.

Here it is the praxeologically oriented approaches (e.g. Pierre Bourdieu, Anthony Giddens, Theodore Schatzki, Bruno Latour, Andreas Reckwitz) which – with their own specific emphases – develop a perspective on human activities that takes cultural contingency and physical involvement with the physical-material world in equal measure into account. They understand social practices as physical representations and acts of comprehension that are held together by implicit knowledge and interlink with artefacts and natural things (see Moebius 2008: 59 and 61). Furthermore, the knowledge referred to here, i.e. the interpretations and attributions of meaning, has neither a supersubjective existence nor is it 'embedded' in the consciousness of the *homo in praxi*. Rather, it is part of the practical performance within which it is produced and forms the frame for "how concrete things should be interpreted in a practice and be dealt with practically"[47] (Reckwitz 2010: 193). Therefore praxeological approaches are less concerned with the normative attunement of actions, or with the intersubjectivity of cultural codes, but primarily with the physical execution of practices that conceptionally include artefacts and in which attributions and interpretations of meaning are (re)produced in not necessarily predictable ways (see section 5.1). Blending the praxeological perspective on human activity with the concept of "everyday regionalizations"[48] (Werlen 1997a) provides suitable approaches to the subject-centered investigation of spatial constructions in the context of the border (see Wille 2014). This is because contingent interpretations and attributions of meaning become visible as a symbolic-interpretative dimension of spaces through the observation of practices while they occur, just as bodies and artefacts that participate in social practices make the relational-descriptive dimension of spaces empiricially manageable.

In this volume, the perspectives on spatial constructions presented here and the possible approaches for investigating them are adjusted according to the specific subject matters, further developed and empirically connected. We have thus in a way 'materialized' the plurality of the concept of space discussed above, while at the same time linking it to the 'neighbouring' fields of identities and borders in the individual case studies. Point of departure here is always the social element of 'doing' which is translated into institutional, media-related and everyday practices and examined in a power-critical and performative dimension.

---

47 | Personal translation of: "[...] wie konkrete Dinge in einer Praktik zu interpretieren und [...] praktisch zu handhaben sind."
48 | Personal translation of: "[...] alltäglichen Regionalisierungen."

2.3 PROCESSES OF (SELF)IDENTIFICATION

Sonja Kmec and Rachel Reckinger

If the recent publication of two handbooks (Wetherell/Mohanty 2010; Elliott 2011) may serve as indicator, identity studies are in the process of establishing themselves as a field of cross-disciplinary investigation. Early critics of such studies objected to the very notion of 'identity', mainly due to the semantic reference to sameness (being identical to oneself or, in the case of collective identity, to someone else) and its function of domination and exclusion of 'others' as well as the implicit refusal of the contingency and the heterogeneity of an individual's self-conception. However, the concept of identity has since been revised, taking onboard such criticism (Renn/Straub 2002: 12). Most identity theorists nowadays understand identity as an ongoing, always provisional and open-ended yet ambivalent process of self-definition – as the term *Identitätsarbeit* (Keupp et al. 2006) suggests – shaped by social (inter)actions and mediated through discourse and knowledge:

"The person, that is, the concrete individual, whom the I understands itself to be [or to have become] is cast always anew, in a process that is never closed, never free of the intervention and – as the case may be – confirmation by others and finally mediated through public language, is linked to identity, not directly to that which is identical with the I [...]"[49] (Renn/Straub 2002: 11).

The focus is thus on "the gap between the I who has a relation with something and the I who functions as the something in that relation"[50] (ibid.: 10-11). The investigation of this "gap" can only be understood with reference to the theoretical framework of post-structuralism, which will be sketched out below. In a second step we will seek to render the notion of identity operational for empirical studies, before presenting the concrete approaches to identity and space constructions within border regions that will be developed subsequently in the chapters 3, 4 and 5.

---

49 | Personal translation of: "Die Person, aufgefasst als das konkrete Individuum, als das sich das Ich immer wieder neu, nicht abschliessbar und niemals frei von der Intervention und gegebenenfalls von der Bestätigung durch andere, schliesslich im Medium der öffentlichen Sprache 'versteht', ist auf Identität bezogen, nicht unmittelbar auf sich als das mit dem Ich Identische [...]."
50 | Personal translation of: "[...] Abstand zwischen dem Ich, das zu etwas ein Verhältnis unterhält, und dem Ich, das in diesem Verhältnis als das Etwas fungiert."

2.3.1 Post-Structuralist Stances on 'Identity'

To actually close the 'gap' between, on the one hand, what a person is (or has become) and, on the other hand, how this is expressed meaningfully by individuals who are always dependent in their expectations and scopes of potentials on social recognition (Abels 2006; Krappmann 2005; Rosa 2007) is deemed impossible by poststructuralist thinkers, drawing among others on Jacques Derrida and Jacques Lacan. This impossibility is, however, not entirely negative; it opens up creative spaces to partially (re)cast oneself in different relational contexts, within limits of social resources.

In a highly influential lecture given at the John Hopkins University in 1966, Derrida not only reinforces Ferdinand de Saussure's claim that the sign (the relation between signifier and signified) is arbitrary, but suggests that any communication is built on a foundation of sand due to the arbitrariness or "freeplay" of the system (Han 2011: 87). The 'philosophy of presence' or realism, which Derrida considers a metaphysical remnant of Platonism, has also been challenged by the psychoanalyst Jacques Lacan and his students. Lacan opposes the idea of the Platonic psyche or soul to Descartes' *cogito ergo sum*. In his 1949 essay on the Mirror Stage, he argues that a person's identity is never unitary and total, but fragmented. When a child recognizes itself for the first time in a mirror, it is a *mis*recognition, built only on an image, an ideal 'I', an "armor of an alienating identity that will mark his entire mental development with its rigid structure" (cited by Han 2011: 88). Lacan argues for the social nature of the formation of the ego, whose centre remains void.

A decentered formulation of selfhood may also be found in Paul Ricoeur's work *Oneself as Another* (1992 [1990]), which distinguishes within 'identity' two major strands of significances, namely the notion of "selfhood" (corresponding to ipseity, from Latin *ipse*, self) and that of "sameness" (corresponding to identity, from Latin *idem*, same, identical): "identity in the sense of ipse implies no assertion concerning some unchanging core of the personality" (ibid.: 2). Ricoeur's reflection provides a common touchstone for the research unit IPSE (Identités. Politiques, Sociétés, Espaces) at the University of Luxembourg and has allowed for a fruitful interdisciplinary cooperation in the context of a first common project, *IDENT – Socio-Cultural Identities and Identity Policies in Luxembourg*, uniting researchers from the various disciplines represented in IPSE (Reckinger/Schulz/Wille 2011: 7-9). Regarding our common understanding of the concept of identity in this follow-up research project, we continue to subscribe to the view of a "consistent but contingent"[51] (Straub 2004: 287) dynamic structure of 'selfhood'. The reasons for this are that this view puts more emphasis on change and subjectivity (see Reckinger/Wille 2011: 20). It also reflects our skepticism towards classical understandings of identity as 'sameness', which have – according to Reckwitz

---

51 | Personal translation of: "[...] stimmig[e] aber kontingent[e] Struktur."

(2001: 25) – "a universalistic and competence-theoretical orientation and center on the problem of the relationship between the individual and social constraints as well as on the problem of temporal constancy."[52]

Ricoeur's hermeneutics emphasize the embeddedness of personal identity in narrative identity, that is, in signs, symbols and texts (1992 [1990]: 140-148). Life and narrative are seen as intrinsically linked, in a fundamentally ambivalent way, seeing as always provisional identities are the ongoing results of never-ending social interactions, making identifications move in loops, "as a shifting and contextual phenomenon" (Butler 2006 [1990]: 14).

The case studies in our current book draw – inevitably – on a very heterogeneous set of authors and references, but it was important to have a basic common understanding of how we envisage 'identity'. This understanding takes on board Judith Butler's analysis of identity as performative and enacted, rejecting the notion that there is a core or 'real' identity a person could hold on to or strive to achieve (Butler 2008a). Butler also expounds Derrida's neologism *différance*, that is, the constant process of differing (*en différant*), which allows for a more nuanced observation than the static notion of *différence* (Derrida 1982b [1978]: 3): differences, for instance between men and women or between homosexual and heterosexual, are naturalized in order to enforce hegemonies. Gender, Butler writes, "is a kind of imitation for which there is no original." Drawing on Michel Foucault's studies about power relations and "regimes of truth" or truth-generating apparatuses of society, Butler concludes that "identity categories tend to be instruments of regulatory regimes, whether as the normalising categories of oppressive structures or as the rallying points for a liberatory contestation of that very oppression" (Butler 2008b: 121). As a consequence, the notion of social or group identity is also called into question. For instance, if there is no ontological 'woman' the reality of 'us, women' as a category also needs to be reconsidered. In that sense, the canonical distinction between personal and collective identity no longer applies. We do not regard the notion of collective identity as determined by objective group affiliation (as for example Halpern 2009 or Ruano-Borbolan 1998 do), but rather view the collective as an inescapable – though possibly playful or subversive – reference to moral norms, resources and repertoires of knowledge.

On an empirical level, it is thus important to consistently explore the manner in which every single action, which can be regarded as an identity project, can be understood as influenced by this layer referring to 'us' ("*Wir-Schicht*", Elias 1986). In this we follow research traditions which centre primarily, on a theoretical level, on "the balance between individual demands and social expectations"[53] (Abels

---

52 | Personal translation of: "[...] universalistisch und kompetenztheoretisch orientiert und auf das Problem des Verhältnisses zwischen Individuum und sozialen Zwängen sowie das Problem der temporalen Konstanz zentriert."

53 | Personal translation of: "[...] Balance zwischen individuellen Ansprüchen und sozialen Erwartungen."

2006: 254; see Krappmann 2005) and do not limit themselves to the functional (manifold) affiliations (Goffman 1959; Lahire 1998) that have multiplied in late modernity (see Reckinger/Wille 2011: 16-17).

Most of the following case studies address these questions in the here and now, Luxembourg and the border region in the 2010s, but this book also includes historical studies that raise identity issues. Subjects in Gallo-Roman or medieval times also reflected on their (perceived) position, their social standing and their allegiances. 'Reflexivity' may thus not be the most appropriate expression to characterize the specific late modern self-awareness, as Anthony Giddens (1991) proposes. He claims that the anxieties triggered by the disintegration of old communal ties encourage self-awareness. On the one hand, this 'disembedding' increased the felt need to stabilize self-identity; on the other hand it gives people a greater choice over what kind of self they want to be and in what kind of relationships they want to be (Chaffee 2011: 103-104). However, as Reckwitz has pointed out, there is a risk of exaggerating the "permanent changeability of identities" in drafting "the image of a hyper-flexible subject permanently changing its identities [...], which seems disconnected from everyday practices"[54] (Reckwitz 2001: 34-35). Despite this pluralization of possibilities of identity constructions, their scope is limited by the quantity and quality of social interactions as well as economic and everyday-cultural resources – and therefore by structural capitals of social inequality (Bourdieu 1972). This social limitation has a concrete impact on identity constitution through processes of "recognizing oneself, being recognized and acknowledged"[55] (Greverus 1995: 219). "Identity constructions thus are ambivalent: due to eroding dependencies on predefined paths there is, on the one hand, an *obligation to make a choice*, which still holds the possibility of either success or failure, and, on the other hand, there is the *freedom of choice* which still is socio-culturally moulded"[56] (see Reckinger/Wille 2011: 15).

Ulrich Beck, who has further developed the concept of "reflexive modernity" (Beck/Giddens/Lash 1994), argues that the old categories such as nation-state, family and class have become "zombie categories" (Beck/Beck-Gernsheim 2001: 203). They are still around, but have lost the meaning they once had. Beck is more pessimistic than Giddens about human agency, being limited by corporate capitalism, the flexibilization of the job market and the internalization of social norms. Whilst for Beck freedom of choice remains possible (through informed

---

54 | Personal translation of: [Risiko einer] "Dramatisierung der permanenten Veränderbarkeit von Identitäten", [d.h. das] "Bild eines hyperflexiblen, seine Identitäten austauschenden Subjekts [...], das den Boden der Alltagspraktiken zu verlassen scheint."
55 | Personal translation of: "Sich Erkennen, Erkannt- und Anerkanntwerden."
56 | Personal translation of: "Somit beinhalten Identitätskonstruktionen eine doppelte Ambivalenz: wegen erodierender vorgefertigten Pfadabhängigkeiten gibt es einerseits einen *Zwang zur Wahl*, die dennoch Gelingen oder Scheitern birgt, und anderseits die *Freiheit der Wahl*, die dennoch sozio-kulturell überformt ist."

public participation and empowerment), Foucault considers freedom of choice a distinct modern fact that is *intrinsically* part of the technology of power. Nowadays, he argues, sheer physical force is no longer necessary to sway control, as subjects have accepted their social roles and 'identities' via ever more pervasive forms of government and self-government (see below). The degree to which this may have been different in premodern times is open to discussion. But the features of social contingency and thus changeability of identities seem to be universally valid. "The 'working out' of identities on the part of the subjects should be seen as a performance of continuity and on no account as something substantially adherent to their selves" (Reckinger/Schulz/Wille 2011: 293).

2.3.2 Rendering 'Identity' Empirically Operational

Having thus decentered selfhood and unhinged it from an ontological definition, how can we examine identity at all? The notion comprises different psychological and sociological actions, which first need to be disentangled. We will briefly present the terminology proposed by Rogers Brubaker (2001), Martina Avanza and Gilles Laferté (2005) as well as Peter Weichhart (1990) when dealing with identity and examine whether they may be compatible.

Rogers Brubaker (2001) distinguishes between three different phenomena: first, the identification of certain categories of people by social actors or discourses; secondly, self-identification (cognitive self-representation), which he considers to be relational and changeable over time; thirdly a feeling of groupness (akin to Max Weber's *Zusammengehörigkeitsgefühl*), which is derived by the individual from alleged shared category and connectedness.

Martina Avanza and Gilles Laferté (2005: 146-147) reformulate Brubaker's model and propose to focus on the interactions between the following social processes: identification in the sense of categorization (*attribution catégorielle*) or external labelling; discursive production of a social image of a certain collectivity, for instance historical, geographical, artistic or literary representations of 'us' and 'them'; active individual self-identification with a group, shaped by socialization and individual choices.

Drawing on Carl Friedrich Graumann (1983), Peter Weichhart (1990) offers a very similar triad: individuals define physical objects or spatial structures in a certain way (identification of); individuals are being associated with certain groups and opposed to other groups (men/women, northerners/southerners), endowed with positive or fraught with negative character traits (being identified by); individuals identify themselves with an object or a certain place (identification with). The latter is, according to Weichhart, often referred to as spatial identity.

When comparing the typologies established by Brubaker, Avanza and Laferté as well as Weichhart, it appears that they complement each other and may be condensed to two different strands of identity analysis: attribution and appropriation, seeing as the analysis of feelings or attributions of group belongings can be classified into either of those two larger dimensions. Indeed, on the one hand, the distinction Avanza/Laferté (2005) as well as Weichhart (1990) make between the labelling of people and the cognitive characterization of objects may both be considered as attribution, since Brubaker (2001) makes no difference between who or what is being discursively produced. On the other hand, Brubaker's second and third type of identity (self-identification and feeling of group belonging) refer to the individual appropriation of social images. The proposed triads thus overlap and cover in fact only two very distinct notions of identity: identification *by/of* (or: attribution) and identification *with* (or: appropriation) – as proposed in our previous study *Doing Identity in Luxembourg. Subjective Appropriations – Institutional Attributions – Socio-Cultural Milieus* (IPSE 2011a and 2011b):

"To sum up, we have, in order to stress the relational nature of identity patterns, directed our attention to the intricate interplay between the different forms of internal self-understanding and self-relationship and external influences, or, in other words, on the interplay between *bottom up* 'identifications with' and *top down* 'identifications of' (Hark 1999). The circulating identity projects and options – analysed here in the form of representations and negotiations – are intrinsically dialogical and political. There is a negotiation of 'power struggles over the meaning, status and value of life-styles, characteristics, activities and behaviors' (Rosa 2007: 52)" (Reckinger/Schulz/Wille 2011: 21).

2.3.3 On the Concept of Identity in this Volume

As the above discussion has shown, the concept of identity can be subdivided in two major components that reflect its complexity and polyphony: first *attributions* (*identification by*) by normative institutions (of any kind) that possess a certain power to name and define (*identification of*), and second, the *appropriation* (*identification with*) by recipients (of any kind). The mutual interaction of both components ensues in processes of more or less implicit constraints as well as through processes of internalization.

In order to describe this dialectic in more detail, we draw on Foucault's concept of governmentality that seeks to systematically reveal the links between technologies of power (constraints) and technologies of self (internalizations). The contributions in this volume address this context in different ways. While the studies in chapter 3 focus on the analysis of power relationships, chapter 5 is primarily concerned with the aspect of relationships of the self, and especially with forms of subjectivation. Chapter 4 comprises studies that chiefly focus on apparatuses of interstitiality, which in particular reveal the complexity and the processuality of identity constructions.

The concept of governmentality has gained a certain currency in recent social science research. It is a malleable and broadly defined praxeological concept that shows very divergent issues to be linked with each other, thus sharpening our awareness for the constructedness of political, social and (everyday-)cultural evidences. The neologism of *gouvernementalité* coined by Foucault is usually understood to imply a combination of the terms *gouverner* and *mentalité*, i.e. a 'government mentality'. However, we prefer Lars Gertenbach's reading of the term, since

"the term is derived from the French 'gouvernemental' – concerning the government – a translation as 'the way of governing' seems more appropriate. Furthermore, the nominalization of 'gouvernemental' to 'gouvernementalité' makes it possible to use the term as an opposing concept to 'souveraineté' and put it as a third form of power next to sovereignty and discipline"[57] (Gertenbach, 2012: 112; see Sennelart, 2006: 564).

This opposition holds primarily for the historiographic use of the concept and is of particular relevance for the contributions in chapter 3. For its microanalytical use by contrast, as in chapter 5, it is essential that the governmental way of governing "finds its specific expression in influencing the agency of subjects and in the shaping of particular forms of subjectivity"[58] (Gertenbach 2012: 112).

These interlinked aspects of government are emphasized by Foucault's recipients in different degrees, depending on their own line of research, either macropolitically or with focus on everyday-cultural power structures. Foucault himself however always conceived these two aspects together. He was particularly concerned with the "field of relations of forces", in which "the art of government is deployed" (Foucault 2007 [2004]: 312). In the series of lectures *Security, Territory, Population* he emphasizes that it would be productive to see the state as a "way of doing things" instead of as a "transcendent reality" (ibid.: 358). He adds:

"We can see that there is not a sort of break between the level of micro-power and the level of macro-power, and that talking about one does not exclude talking about the other. In actual fact, an analysis in terms of micro-powers comes back without any difficulty to the analysis of problems like those of government and the state" (Foucault 2007 [2004]: 358).

Governmentality, explains Gertenbach, is an "execution of power through and via freedom. It is a form of power that does not operate directly and imperiously, but

---

57 | Personal translation of: "Da sich der Begriff vom französischen 'gouvernemental' – die Regierung betreffend – herleitet, ist er eher als 'Art und Weise des Regierens' zu übersetzen. Darüber hinaus ermöglicht die Substantivierung von 'gouvernemental' zu 'gouvernementalité', den Begriff als Gegenkonzept zu 'souveraineté' zu verwenden und als dritten Typus der Macht neben Souveränität und Disziplin zu setzen."
58 | Personal translation of: "[...] spezifischen Ausdruck [...] im Einwirken auf den Handlungsbereich der Subjekte und in der Formung und Gestaltung bestimmter Formen von Subjektivität."

rather indirectly and mediatingly, not via rigidly fixed norms, but via probabilities"[59] (Gertenbach 2012: 114). In the same way that Bourdieu's concept of habitus does not assume precise *contents* of action, but rather a broad, albeit not arbitrary, *latitude* for action, which is in particular shaped by social-structural and class-specific differences (see Bourdieu 1980), these probabilities can be recognized in the context of governmentality most clearly if analysis "systematically begins at the microphysics of power"[60] (Füller/Marquardt 2009: 97), in order to understand its scope(s) and functioning(s). For power "exists only when it is put into action even if […] it is integrated into a disparate field of possibilities brought to bear upon permanent structures" (Foucault 1983: 219). Thus power structures or relationships are best examined by looking at practices and revealing "the positivity of their interlinkage, their arrangement and their relationships" – not so much by retracing a "historical development or chronology"[61] (Füller/Marquardt 2009: 97).

Thomas Lemke (2008: 261) sums up the concept of governmentality by emphasizing that "forms of political government draw on techniques of 'self governing'."[62] But this one-sided representation lacks the reciprocal movement which is characterized more succinctly with the following quote by Foucault:

"[One] has to take into account the interaction between those two types of techniques – techniques of domination but also techniques of the self. [One] has to take into account the points where the technologies of domination of individuals over one another have recourse to processes by which the individual acts upon himself. And conversely, [one] has to take into account the points where the techniques of the self are integrated into structures of coercion or domination" (Foucault, 1993: 203f.).

What makes governmentality conceptually interesting as a principle of government is that it expressly does not suppress subjectivity but relies on its '(self)-production' or "on the invention and promotion of technologies of the self that can be linked to governmental goals"[63] (Bröckling/Krasmann/Lemke 2000: 29). By implication, this means that Foucault does not advocate the "substitution of the political with the personal", but "a different form of politics and the design of new technologies

---

59 | Personal translation of: "[…] eine Machtausübung über und durch Freiheit. Es ist eine Form der Macht, die nicht direkt und befehlend wirkt, sondern indirekt und vermittelnd, nicht über strikt festgesetzte Normen, sondern über Wahrscheinlichkeiten."
60 | Personal translation of: "[…] konsequent an der Mikrophysik der Macht ansetzen."
61 | Personal translation of: [indem] "die Positivität ihrer Verkettung untereinander, ihre Anordnung und ihre Beziehungen […]" [aufgedeckt werden – jedoch weniger dadurch, dass eine] "historische Entwicklung oder Abfolge nachvollzogen wird."
62 | Personal translation of: "[…] Formen politischer Regierung auf Techniken des 'Sich-Selbst-Regierens' rekurrieren."
63 | Personal translation of: "[…] auf die Erfindung und Förderung von Selbsttechnologien, die an Regierungsziele gekoppelt werden können."

of self", with whose help "political goals can be realized in a considerably more 'effective' way via individual 'self-realizations'"[64] (ibid.: 30) than through explicit-legal limitations of individual freedom.

All in all, this broad understanding of social, cultural and political performativities provides a suitable bracket for conceptually underpinning the chapters in this volume and emphasizing their coherence despite the considerable variety of subject matters addressed in the individual case studies: chapter 5 examines technologies of self; chapter 3 deals with technologies of government; in addition, a further chapter (4) is concerned with apparatuses that are marked by interstices, fuzzy zones and blurrings of these effects. In this way the ongoing constitutive processes of identity construction – attributions (*identification by/of*) and appropriations (*identification with*) – can be presented with a clearer structure in terms of concepts and empirics in their dialectic with spatial constructions in border spaces.

2.4 METHODOLOGY AND SITUATIVE INTERDISCIPLINARITY

Christian Wille

The investigation of constructions of space and identity in this volume focuses on social practices and on specific sub-aspects linked to them (e.g. bodies, artefacts, spatial networks of relationships, logics of power, attributions of signification with their specific differentiations and situatedness). If we take practices as the point of departure of our considerations, this raises the question of how these can be investigated in terms of research practice. In this context, Reckwitz (2008: 195) points out that the presence of the researchers *in situ* is only possible to a limited extent. Even though *current practices* are directly accessible via the present and perceivable materiality of bodies and artefacts, interpretations of meaning through visual and auditive perception remain concealed. These need to be deduced indirectly, "i.e. one has to draw conclusions about the implied schemata from explicit statements, actions, ways of dealing with things etc."[65] (ibid.: 196). Here, the qualitative interview seems to be a suitable method for revealing verbally formulated interpretations of meaning. In the case of *past practices* the issue of direct access to practices becomes more acute: the materiality of the bodies and

---

64 | Personal translation of: [die] "Ersetzung des Politischen durch das Persönliche" [plädiert, sondern für] "eine andere Form von Politik und den Entwurf neuer Selbsttechnologien", [mit Hilfe derer] "politische Ziele [sich] wesentlich 'ökonomischer' mittels individueller 'Selbstverwirklichung' realisieren lassen."

65 | Personal translation of: "[...] das heißt, aus expliziten Äußerungen, Handlungen, Umgangsweisen mit Dingen usw. muss auf die impliziten Schemata rückgeschlossen werden."

artefacts involved in the practices is not open to direct scrutiny, even though it is possible to make observations via media (e.g. film, photography). Here too, interpretations of meaning can only be identified indirectly (e.g. via interviews of contemporary witnesses). Textanalytical processes in particular can be useful here, if for instance written descriptions of practices or ego documents (e.g. letters, diaries) are examined for the subjectifications and subjectivations 'contained in them'.

The above considerations are intended to sensitize us to the fact that the investigation of spatial and identity constructions – which are always only temporary results of practices – almost unavoidably depends on working with data *about* the practices and their sub-aspects. This is also true for the case studies in this volume, although we do not differentiate here between present and past practices, but rather between *three* key methodological approaches that allow us to reconstruct the practices of institutions, media and everyday life together with the constructions of space and identity contained in them.

These *firstly* concern textanalytical processes for examining (non)standard written cultural manifestations (e.g. exhibition catalogues, films, advertisements, virtual environments, gravestones, newspaper articles etc.). They include further approaches from content and discourse analysis as well as semiotics and will be discussed specifically in the corresponding case studies.

Secondly they involve a quantitative survey and a series of qualitative interviews with persons in Luxembourg and its adjoining regions. A special feature of this second methodological approach is the cross-border character of the surveys in Luxembourg, Germany, France and Belgium, and the authors' interdisciplinary *modus operandi* in developing the survey tools and conducting the survey as such. The forms of survey with a more social-scientific approach were used in different ways in the case studies – depending on the epistemic interest – and the collected data were partly combined with each other. This permitted to bring together various aspects of a particular phenomenon and thus expand and complete the perspective on the subject matter under scrutiny.

Besides the techniques of collecting data mentioned above, we will, *thirdly*, take a closer look – as an auto-reflexive method – at the way the contributors to this volume collaborated. Representing different disciplines of the humanities, they met regularly over a period of three years, shared and discussed their insights and thoughts with the aim of looking beyond the limits of their own discipline and, guided by their subject, setting foot on terrain 'alien' to their field (see chapter 1). One of the concerns of this research context was therefore the collaboration between scholars of different disciplines, which in general is subsumed under the term of interdisciplinarity. This term is itself, however, rarely the subject of reflection, and interdisciplinary research is often regarded as a repository for researchers who were "not quite able to gain a foothold"[66] elsewhere (Löffler

---

66 | Personal translation of: "[...] nicht recht Fuß fassen konnten."

2010: 158). This was the reason for a number of authors to take a critical look at 'interdisciplinarity' and develop the concept of 'situative interdisciplinarity' as a common guideline for their collaboration.

In the following we will comment on some research-practical aspects of the quantitative survey and the series of qualitative interviews as well as the corresponding samples, and discuss how we handled the cross-disciplinary collaboration in the making of this volume.

2.4.1 Quantitative Survey

One of the major sources of data for the case studies of this volume is the quantitative representative survey. A total of 3,300 people were interviewed in the sovereign nation state of Luxembourg, in the bordering areas of the federal states of Saarland and Rhineland-Palatinate (Germany), and the regions of Lorraine (France) and Wallonia (Belgium). Considering the issues investigated in this volume, we for the most part interviewed people living in the border region in relative proximity to a national border. The aim was to collect data about various practices and evaluate these under the aspect of the construction of space and identity in the context of the border. The questionnaire used for this and developed by the various disciplines is subdivided in a number of subjects[67] that were operationalized with the help of semi-open and closed-ended questions. Due to Luxembourg's multilingualism and the different languages spoken in the neighbouring regions (see section 5.9) it was necessary to translate the questionnaire (as well as the interview guideline of the qualitative survey) into Luxembourgish, German, French and English. However, a correlation of the survey results was only possible if the meanings of the subjects discussed and key terms matched in the multlingual survey tools. This refers to the socio-cultural spectrum of lexical elements' meaning which, in the translation of survey tools, raises the question whether and in how far the target language possesses an equivalent phrasing that precludes semantic shifts. An equivalence test can be performed via re-translation, but also via discursive procedures where the specific translations are critically discussed with persons sensitive to equivalences. Since a number of authors participating in this volume are bilingual, we applied the discursive procedure for testing the equivalence of the survey tools.

---

67 | These include: socio-demographic information, leisure time and contacts, shopping, household, political life, communication and language, Greater Region and mobility, men and women. The questionnaire is listed in the data collection of the quantitative survey and can be accessed at the library of the University of Luxembourg.

	n	Total Sample in %	Sample of Respondents in Border Area in %
Respondents in Luxembourg	1,021	30.9	.
Respondents in Border Area	2,279	.	100
Saarland	314	9.5	13.8
Lorraine	867	26.3	38
Rhineland-Palatinate	581	17.6	25.5
Wallonia	517	15.7	22.7
Total	3,300	100	.

Table 1: Sample of the quantitative survey (overview) (University of Luxembourg, IDENT2 2012/2013)

The collection of the samples in Luxembourg and the neighbouring regions was entrusted to a Luxembourg survey institute, which was also responsible for carrying out the representative survey. Between December 2012 and February 2013 a total of 1,021 persons aged 16 and above living in Luxembourg and 2,279 persons of the same age segment living in the neighbouring regions were questioned. Almost two fifths of the respondents living in the border area are located in Lorraine, one quarter in Rhineland-Palatinate, slightly more than a fifth in Wallonia and 14 % in the Saarland (see Table 1). The survey was carried out via internet (computer-assisted web interviews) and the subsamples were weighted according to different features: the sample in the Grand Duchy according to the variables of region of residence, age, nationality, gender and (un)employment; persons living in the border area according to region of residence, age and gender. The data were analysed with the procedures of descriptive and inductive statistics.[68]

---

68 | The collected data can be accessed in the library of the University of Luxembourg.

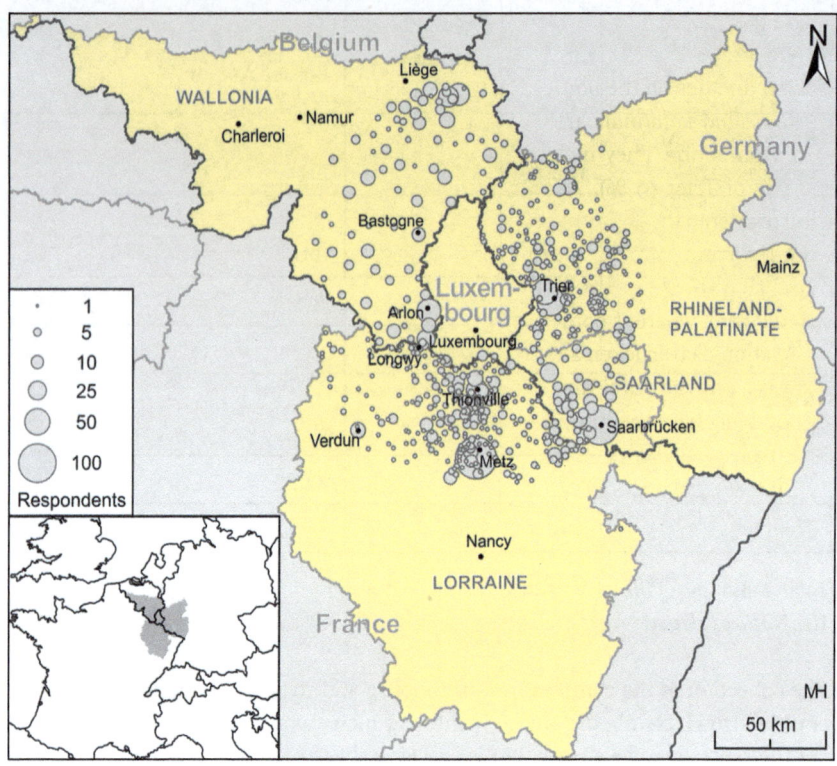

Figure 1: Distribution of the places of residence of the respondents in the quantitative survey in the border area (overview) (University of Luxembourg, IDENT2 2012/2013) (design: Christian Wille, realization: Malte Helfer)

A closer look at the the geographic distribution of the places of residence of persons living in the border area shows that they don't live further away than 50 km from a national border and the majority of them close to a national border (see Fig. 1 and 2). Thus the majority of the survey respondents in *Lorraine* live in northern Lorraine immediately bordering Luxembourg and Belgium; more than two fifths (43 %) live in Thionville (28 %) and in Briey (15 %), both located close to the border. A further 17 % live in eastern Lorraine close to the border to Germany, distributed across Forbach (10 %), located directly on the border, and Boulay (7 %). 37 % of the respondents live further in the hinterland of the Metz agglomeration, of these 13 % in the town of Metz , 6 % in Verdun and 18 % in the Metz region (18 %). Only 2 % live in Nancy and in the Nancy agglomeration. 50 % of the respondents in *Wallonia* have their place of residence in the province of Luxembourg bordering France and Luxembourg. The majority of them live in the border town of Arlon (16 %), followed by Virton (9 %), Neufchâteau (9 %), Bastogne (9 %) and further in the hinterland around Marche-en-Famenne (7 %). 42 % of the respondents in Wallonia live in the province of Liège which borders Germany and Luxembourg.

There they mainly reside in the cities of Verviers (27 %) and Liège (13 %) as well as in Huy (2 %). Further 6 % live in the town of Dinant which is in the province of Namur and lies on the border to France. More than half of the respondents (57 %) in *Rhineland-Palatinate* are distributed across the three communities bordering on Luxembourg. They include Trier-Saarburg (26 %), Bitburg-Prüm (22 %) and the city of Trier (9 %). As many as 22 % of the respondents are domiciled in the rural district of Bernkastel-Wittlich, despite being somewhat further away from the border, followed by the community of Vulkaneifel (12 %). The majority of the survey respondents in the *Saarland* lives in the west and the north of the federal state, where it borders France and Luxembourg. 42 % live in the regional association Saarbrücken and along the river Saar in the district of Saarlouis (30 %) as well as in the rural district of Merzig-Wadern (18 %). Only 7 and 3 % of the respondents have their home in the rural districts of St. Wendel and Neunkirchen which are further away from the border.

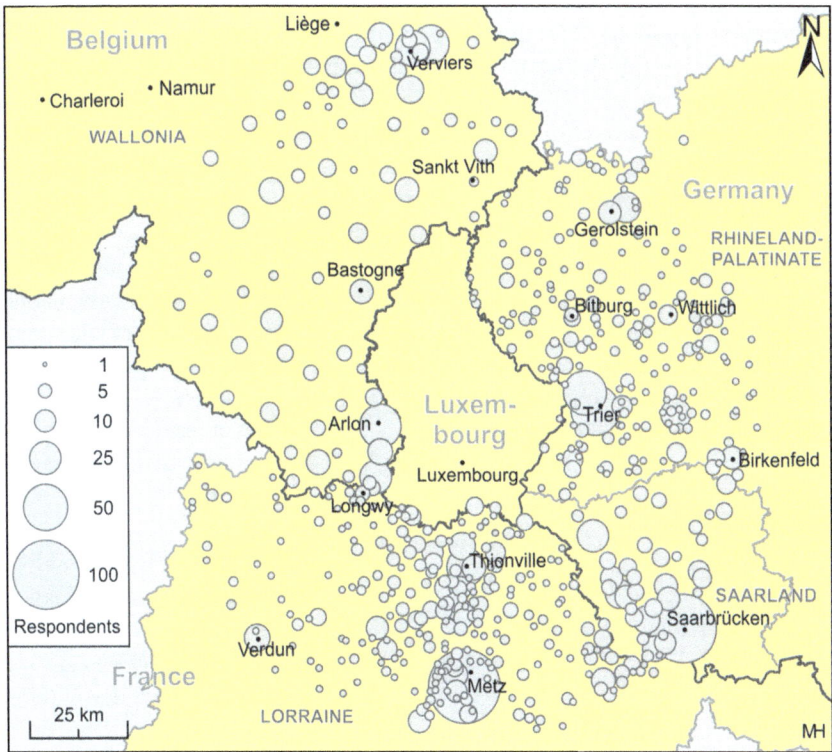

Figure 2: Distribution of the places of residence of the respondents in the quantitative survey in the border area (detailed view) (University of Luxembourg, IDENT2 2012/2013) (design: Christian Wille, realization: Malte Helfer)

2.4.2 Qualitative Interviews

Based on the quantitative representative survey, in spring 2013 in-depth interviews were conducted with residents of Luxembourg and in the neighbouring regions who had agreed to do so in the preceding questionnaire.[69] The aim was to collect, via the wide ranging series of interviews, qualitative data about practices and particularly about the attributions of meaning connected to them for which a standardized procedure is less suited. The qualitative interviews were therefore carried out with a semi-standardized interview guide with fully phrased questions and conversation-generating impulses.[70] In addition, the authors of the present volume, who contributed the individual questions to this guide, were asked to briefly state the epistemic interest and purpose of each question. These were then explained and discussed internally. This made it possible to proceed in a cooperative fashion which would allow the interviewers to also prepare for the interviews by additionally familarizing themselves with the 'thrust' of their colleagues' questions. For this purpose the interviewers recast the detailed interview guide into bullet points, which permitted flexible and largely open interviewing.

It was not the aim of the interview series to establish frequencies, but rather develop a more detailed understanding of processes of the construction of space and identity in the context of the border. We were thus not concerned with acquiring a random sample in order to make subsequent inferences on a population, but rather with studying individual and varied cases, in order to capture information about practices with their specific subaspects. This required a calculated compilation of samples specified according to gender, age, nationality and level of education. Finally, on this basis and minus cases that did not materialize, 47 persons in the area under consideration were interviewed, 24 of them in Luxembourg and 23 in the border area (see Table 2).

---

69 | In their cases studies, some authors in this volume draw additionally on their own and specifically indicated interview series (including expert interviews).
70 | The abridged interview guide is included at the end of this volume.

2. Theoretical and Methodological Approaches

	Luxembourg	Border Area	of these in Rhineland-Palatinate	of these in the Saarland	of these in Lorraine	of these in Wallonia
Gender						
Men	14	12	2	4	3	3
Women	10	11	.	3	4	4
Age groups						
15-24	3	.	.	.	.	.
25-34	4	6	.	2	2	2
35-44	2	7	.	1	2	4
45-54	6	6	1	2	2	1
55-64	4	3	1	1	1	.
65-74	3	.	.	.	.	.
75-84	2	.	.	.	.	.
85-94	.	1	.	1	.	.
Status						
Non-foreigner	12	17	2	6	6	3
Foreigner	12	6	.	1	1	4
Level of education*						
ISCED 1	2	.	.	.	.	.
ISCED 2	5	5	1	3	.	1
ISCED 3	7	5	1	.	2	2
ISCED 4	2	3	.	1	2	.
ISCED 5 and 6	7	9	.	3	3	3
No response	1	1	.	.	.	1
Net sample	24	23	2	7	7	7

Table 2: Sample of the qualitative survey (University of Luxembourg, IDENT2 2012/2013) *According to International Standard Classification of Education (ISCED)

The interviews were conducted by the authors according to language preferences and availability and took place by appointment at the home of the interviewees and frequently in the mornings or evenings. In a conversation usually lasting between one and one and a half hours, various subject areas were discussed following the interview guide, and the interviewees had the opportunity to express themselves freely – but within a certain thematic frame of reference. In this way the interviewees' interpretations and reactions were collected and aspects the researchers had not anticipated were allowed to emerge. Since what concerns us in this volume are the contents of the interviews and not their linguistic form, we employed, for the processing of the digitally recorded interviews, the transcription procedure of the standard language conversion (see Mayring 2002: 91) that consists in minimal emendations of syntactical errors and in streamlining the speech flow. The transcription of the interviews into Luxembourgish, German, French and English was entrusted to transcriptors specifically employed for this purpose. The interview transcripts were then computerized and evaluated via deductive-selective coding as well as inductive-open coding. This means, we first performed a broad coding consisting in assigning responses from the interviews to the subject areas discussed in them. Using the emerging code tree as a basis, the authors of the individual interview questions proceeded to fine-code, with an inductive-open coding, interviewees' answers by argumentative units of signification. The researchers also took responses into account that referred to their colleagues' subject areas in order to be able to record chains of reasoning in the empirical material that cut across thematic fields.

2.4.3 Cross-Disciplinary Collaboration[71]

In academia there are few terms where the discrepancy between frequency of use and theoretical reflection is so extreme as that of interdisciplinarity (see Jungert 2010: 1). It has become a fixture of rhetorics accompanying scientific projects and its inflationary use reinforces the frequently adopted stance that interdisciplinary research supposedly can't be expected to yield any real insights. In order not to risk letting the interdisciplinary or cross-disciplinary collaboration deteriorate to an empty phrase, a number of the contributors to this volume have formed a workgroup to examine the potential and the risks of interdisciplinarity (see chapter 1). Their aim was to systematize the term and the concepts linked with it and develop a common guideline for the work in the framework of the present volume.

When dealing with interdisciplinarity, one first needs to clarify what is to be understood under disciplinarity. In this context Sabine Hark (2005) draws attention to the concept of discipline/disciplinarity which comprises two dimensions, a *discipline generating* one, and a *disciplining* one. Disciplines – as a basis for the organization and structuring of scientific knowledge – should here not be understood statically but rather as dynamic points of intersection of different theoretical-methodological paradigms. Hark defines disciplines as complex bundles of relationships, drawing on Foucault's concept of discursive formation. It is the relationships "between institutions, economic and societal processes, forms of behaviour, systems of norms, techniques, classification systems and manners of characterization"[72] (Hark 2005: 71) that constitute a discipline. Accordingly,

---

71 | This section was written in collaboration with Brigitte Batyko, Heike Mauer, Agnès Prüm and Rachel Reckinger.

72 | Personal translation of: "[...] zwischen Institutionen, ökonomischen und gesellschaftlichen Prozessen, Verhaltensformen, Normsystemen, Techniken, Klassifikationstypen und

the discipline-generating effect manifests itself in the continued updating of this network of relationships. From this social-emergent and relational perspective, discipline can be seen as an ensemble of heterogenous elements such as communities of communication, objects of knowledge and institutions. Hark explains the disciplining dimension (2005: 75ff.) by highlighting disciplines as political institutions. This involves three functions: (1) the *production* of knowledge, which is connected to the production of (in)valid statements, knowable objects, hierarchically ordered subjects (e.g. academic degrees) or practices of knowledge (e.g. plenary lectures); (2) the *regulation* of knowledge which takes effects when determining the recognized subject areas as well as the cognitive structure of the actors and their academic practices; (3) the *reproduction* of knowledge which ensures the continuity in the academic field via the transmission of knowledge and the socialisatory exercising of academic practices. The disciplining dimension is particularly prominent in the reproductive function, when, for example, disciplines organize and classify what is worth knowing and thus regulate what is remembered and what is forgotten.

Taking these considerations into account a discipline can be seen as a space in the academic field which regulates and reproduces itself via specific practices of knowledge and the involved objects, schools of thought, traditions of theory and methodology as well as embedded power relations and self-conceptions. These aspects go generally unquestioned and their interaction is constitutive for individual disciplines. However, they become untenable in research contexts in which different disciplines work together. The fault lines and thus the boundaries of the discipline begin to show up in a praxeological sense where practices of knowledge are no longer self-evidently effective, where formerly constitutive relationships need to be explicitly explained, and previously unquestioned foundations of signification are cast into doubt. Figuratively speaking we are then dealing with a 're-wiring' of complex bundles of relationships or ensembles of heterogenous elements which – as we shall see – can vary in intensity, irritation and innovation.

A glance into the relevant literature shows that besides the term of interdisciplinarity there exist other competing terms which are not used consistently and partly overlap in their meaning. When systematizing terms of interdisciplinarity and related concepts we are thus faced with a problem of demarcation. We will therefore introduce the term of 'cross-disciplinary collaboration'[73], in order to be able to topicalize different forms of collaboration under one umbrella term. For this we have chosen two approaches: in a first step, we will establish which terms are used in research funding for cross-disciplinary collaboration and what significance they have there. In a second step, the relevant concepts are presented synoptically and classified by structural criteria.

Charakterisierungsweisen."
73 | Personal translation of: "Disziplinenübergreifende Zusammenarbeit."

We will thus first examine whether cross-disciplinary collaboration plays a role in funding policies and which terms are used in each case. To this end, calls for proposals of specific funding programmes in the field of humanities and science as well as annual reports (2012) of national and European funding institutions and agencies were analysed (see Table 3).

Level	Institutions/Funding Agencies	Funding Programmes
Regional	University of Luxembourg	Intra-University Project Funding
National	Luxembourg: *Fonds National de la Recherche* (FNR)	FNR: CORE, INTER, ATTRACT, AFR, PEARL
	Germany: *Deutsche Forschungsgemeinschaft* (DFG)	DFG: *Schwerpunktprogramme, Graduiertenkollegs, Sonderforschungsbereiche, DFG Forschungszentren, Forschergruppen, Kolleg-Forschergruppen, Aufbau internationaler Kooperationen*[75]
	France: *Agence nationale de la Recherche* (ANR)	ANR: various thematic calls: *Biologie-Santé, Energie Durable, Environnement et Ressources Biologiques, Ingénierie, Procédés et Sécurité, Partenariats et compétitivité, Programmes transdisciplinaires, Recherches exploratoires et émergentes, Sciences Humaines et Sociales*[76]
	Belgium: *Fonds de la Recherche Scientifique-FNRS* (F.R.S.-FNRS)	F.R.S.-FNRS: *Appels 'Crédits et projets'*, FRESH II – *Recherche collaborative en sciences humaines et sociales.*
European	European Commission	• ERC grants: Proof of Concept, Synergy Grant, Advanced Grant, Starting Grant, Consolidator Grant • Seventh Framework Programme (FP7): specific programmes 'Cooperation' and 'People' (Marie Curie Actions) • Horizon 2020: Programmes 2014-2015

Table 3: Reviewed calls for proposals by selected funding agencies (July 2013)

---

74 | Priority Programmes, Research Training Groups, Collaborative Research Centres, DFG Research Centres, Research Units, Humanities Centres for Advanced Studies, Initiation of International Collaboration.

75 | Biology and Health, Sustainable Energy, Environment and Biological Resources, Engineering, Processes and Security, Partnership and Competitiveness, Transdisciplinary Programmes, Exploratory and Emerging Research, Social Sciences and Humanities.

The analysis of the calls for proposals was conducted in three languages per search query of frequently used terms in connection with cross-disciplinary collaboration.[76] The most frequently found terms were *disziplinär/interdisziplinär*, disciplinary/disciplinarity, interdisciplinary/interdisciplinarity, *interdisciplinaire/ interdisciplinarité* and frontier research, indicating *a priori* that the term 'interdisciplinarity' was widely used. In addition, we noticed that in the calls for proposals there was no further explanation what exactly the funding institutions meant with the searched terms – and thus with cross-disciplinary collaboration. This confirms the impression that the term of interdisciplinarity and related concepts remain blurred and are often mere accompanying rhetorics. All the more important to address this very diverse field and structure it along the relevant terms.

Multi-/Pluridisciplinarity: The term of multidisciplinarity entered academic language in the 1950s and refers to the coexistence of disciplines within one subject area. The disciplines involved here each work on a sub-aspect of the common area of investigation which is within 'their' subject matter. In this form of collaboration, common research questions, mutual references or cross-disciplinary efforts to create a synthesis are largely absent. However, in contrast to purely disciplinary research one can assume that the participating disciplines share pertinent information about their work and that there is potential for broadening the perspective on the common field of investigation (see Jungert 2010: 2). The term of pluridisciplinarity is often used synonymously with multidisciplinarity. However, some authors, for instance Jungert (see ibid.) differentiate between these terms and see pluridisciplinarity as a first step of a truly cross-disciplinary collaboration. This involves the intensification of relations between related disciplines via a loose exchange of findings and problems within a common subject area. However, this in general unstructured collaboration has little effect on the subject matters and on the self-concept of the participating disciplines.

Interdisciplinarity: The term 'interdisciplinarity' is the one most frequently used in the context of cross-disciplinary collaboration. This is also confirmed by the analysis of the calls for proposals by national and European research funding (see Table 3). Interdisciplinarity – albeit without further explanation and with varying emphasis – is firmly anchored in these texts. The Luxembourgish and Belgian funding institutions are more reticent about the interdisciplinary character of research projects and merely indicate that interdisciplinary research is desirable. German and French programmes emphasize the interdisciplinary character of projects more frequently and put a stronger focus on the promotion of interdisciplinarity. European funding programmes also welcome and support the

---

76 | Search terms used in three languages: *disziplinär, multi-, inter-, transdisziplinär, Disziplinarität, Multi-, Inter-, Transdisziplinarität, Pionierforschung*, disciplinary, multi-, inter-, transdisciplinary, cross-disciplinary, disciplinarity, multi-, inter-, transdisciplinarity, frontier research, inter/cross-faculty, disciplinary boundaries, cross-programme, *disciplinaire, multi-, inter-, transdisciplinaire, disciplinarité, multi-, inter-, transdisciplinarité.*

interdisciplinary orientation of research projects. Here the grants of the European Research Council (ERC) play a particular role because they are expressly designed to promote interdisciplinary project work and so-called pioneer research. The European programme Horizon 2020 likewise clearly emphasizes interdisciplinary research as an important aspect worthy of funding – as the *Seventh Framework Programme (FP7)* had already done before. While we see that the concept of interdisciplinarity is indeed supported by public funding policies, there is still the impression that it is as yet not really strategically embedded and that the addressees are assumed to have an understanding of interdisciplinarity which is not further specified. This can however differ significantly and – as we shall see – partly show variously large overlaps with related concepts. For a further discussion of the concept of interdisciplinarity we will focus on its complexity and attempt an internal differentiation. Drawing on Löffler (see 2010: 164ff.) and Heckhausen (quoted in Jungert 2010: 4ff.), we will outline a possible spectrum of interdisciplinari*ties*.

- Heckhausen uses the term 'indiscriminate interdisciplinarity' (*unterschiedslose Interdisziplinarität*) to describe the idea of the *studium generale* in which various disciplinary contents are 'juxtaposed' to offset high levels of specialization and the narrowing of perspectives that accompany them. Mutual references between the disciplines are not intended here, nor is there any cross-disciplinary collaboration in the area of research.
- 'Nice-to-know interdisciplinarity' (*Nice-to-know-Interdisziplinarität*), a term coined by Löffler, applies to a situation where the participating disciplines refer to one common subject but where no points of contact or relationships of exchange develop. Nevertheless, research contexts or events with a nice-to-know factor are useful, for instance as a social event in academia for networking or when, in decision-making processes, it is necessary to consider different perspectives on one subject.
- With the term 'pseudo-interdisciplinarity' (*Pseudo-Interdisziplinarität*), Heckhausen refers to the common assumption that one can already speak of interdisciplinarity when different disciplines work with identical models or methods. This is however in his view not sufficient for bridging differences between the disciplines, for example regarding 'typical' subject domains or levels of theoretical integration.
- 'Auxiliary interdisciplinarity' (*Hilfsinterdisziplinarität*) is used by Heckhausen to describe the use of methods within one's own discipline that are foreign to it. But, according to Heckhausen, it cannot be described as a true collaboration, since it is merely a matter of treating 'typical' questions within one's own disciplines with the help of 'borrowed' methods.
- The grouping of various disciplines around a common complex of problems or subjects is subsumed by Heckhausen under the term of 'composite interdisciplinarity' (*zusammengesetzte Interdisziplinarität*). But there is neither an overlap of subject areas of the participating disciplines nor of the methods

employed. The cohesion of the common research context is in this case only based on the common area of problems and themes.
- 'Supplementary interdisciplinarity' (*Ergänzende Interdisziplinarität*) is situated, according to Heckhausen, on the fringes of disciplines, where there is in part a real attempt to establish a nexus between the different theoretical approaches.
- For a high degree of interaction between disciplines, Heckhausen uses the term of 'unifying interdisciplinarity' (*Vereinigende Interdisziplinarität*). This refers to the convergence and synthetization of different disciplinary theories and sets of conceptual and methodological tools.

This cursory synopsis of interdisciplinarities not only addresses different aspects of the research process, it also reveals different forms of disciplinarity that can be located on a continuum between the affirmation and the subversion of disciplinary boundaries. As we shall see, the conceptual understanding of interdisciplinarity that was relevant in the making of this volume refers to a number of the interdisciplinarities featured above.

Transdisciplinarity: The concept of transdisciplinarity, in turn, denotes a form of working where specific issues are addressed together with actors outside academia and where there is an attempt to overcome the specialization of academic knowledge (see Jungert 2010: 6). So this is *firstly* about crossing the threshold between academia and 'the world outside' in order to find scientific solutions for complex societal problems; and *secondly* about the questioning of the (disciplinary) order of academic knowledge as such (see Després/Lawrence 2004: 399). Transdisciplinarity also implies a critique of disciplinarity as a specific academic practice and aims at regrouping questions, theories and methods without linking them back to individual disciplines (see Maihofer 2005: 199).

Postdisciplinarity: The concept of postdisciplinarity dissociates itself even more clearly from the dichotomy of academic knowledge production on the one hand and the non-academic knowledge production on the other. Postdisciplinarity aims at a research process that does not commit itself to one or more disciplines regarding subject matter and research questions nor proceeds deductively in the development of theories and solutions. Rather, it is concerned – similar to the transdisciplinary approach – with an inductive-reflective process in which the questions to be examined, methods used and theories and solutions developed are generated (see Maihofer 2005: 201).

The forms of cross-disciplinary collaboration presented above show multiple overlaps. Nevertheless they can be distinguished from each other and classified with the help of specific criteria.

For our essay at systematization (see Fig. 3) we have proceeded from the basis of the criterion of disciplinarity as a continuum explained above which grades forms of cross-disciplinary collaboration where discipline-generating and disciplining mechanisms are (in)effective. Forms of cross-disciplinary collaboration where disciplinarity progressively loses its effect are also marked by increasing complexity. This results from the 'rewiring' of bundles of relationships (between objects, methods, concepts etc.) that exist within and outside of academia.

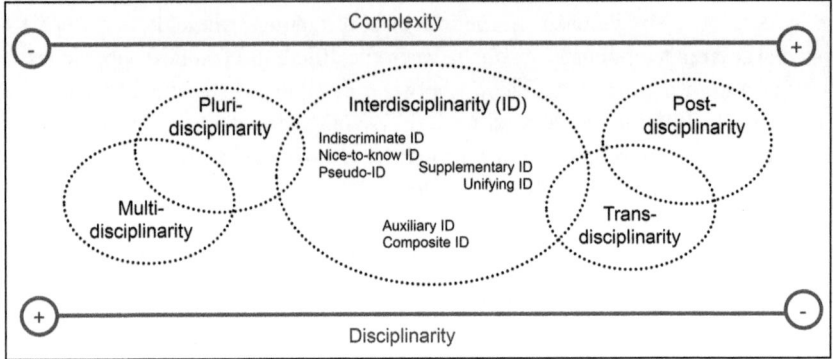

Figure 3: Forms of cross-disciplinary collaboration by the criteria of 'complexity' and 'disciplinarity' (design: Christian Wille)

2.4.4 Situative Interdisciplinarity

From the typology of multi-/pluri-/inter-/trans- and postdisciplinarity presented above – as a series of increased complexity with diminishing disciplinarity – we can derive three basic models of cross-disciplinary collaboration:

(1) Cross-disciplinary collaboration as *addition* should be understood as a collection of different disciplines that work on a common (research) subject and merely share information. In this scientific practice, which would belong to multi- and/or pluridisciplinarity, there is no real exchange and thus no crossing of disciplinary borders.

(2) Cross-disciplinary collaboration as *interaction* can be found where there is an actual exchange between disciplines grouped around a common (research) topic, but without the participating disciplines 'dissolving'. Here we are dealing with different methods of elaboration of or empirical approaches to a common research question – partly the aim behind the concept of interdisciplinarity – which are linked to each other and promise to yield more insights than would be possible to achieve from only one single disciplinary perspective. Even though the individual disciplines remain for the most part 'untouched', this form of collaboration is potentially prone to critical moments that come to bear in 'disorders' of the familiar research practice and require the participating researchers to display certain social faculties (e.g. tolerance for ambiguity, empathy) in order to be able to put up with them and/or exploit them productively (see Wiesmann/Biber-Klemm et al. 2008: 174ff.).

(3) Qualifying cross-disciplinary collaboration as a *synthesis* suggests scientific practices that overcome disciplinary and institutional systems in a problem- and/or solution-oriented way. Similar to the concepts of trans-/postdisciplinarity, here

the (research) topics as well as the necessary conceptual and methodological tools are not predefined, but rather these are developed in a deductive-recursive procedure – mostly also involving non-academics (see ibid.: 172f.). A prerequisite for this kind of collaboration is a high degree of communication and exchange, a strong orientation towards application and the privilege to be able to act without linking up with reproductive-disciplinary communities.

Building on the basic models of addition, interaction and synthesis, the authors of this volume have attempted to pinpoint the academic practice that has already emerged after eight months of project work as a snapshot and develop an ambitious, but realistic vision for further collaboration. Looking back, what has become clear is that the collaboration varied depending on the specific aspect of the research process and that it is difficult to define it in a nutshell: a point frequently emphasized was the wide thematic variety of case studies reflected in this volume, which made an actual exchange between the authors difficult; but at the same time the overarching topical areas structuring the research context (see chapters 3, 4 and 5) as well as the theoretical-conceptual tools (see chapter 2) were highlighted, which virtually call for a productive interaction of all the participating authors. Attention was also given to the methods used, however in equal measure as means of addition and of interaction. This initial assessment already makes clear that the academic practice that was quick to establish itself among our contributors oscillated between disciplinary addition and interaction.

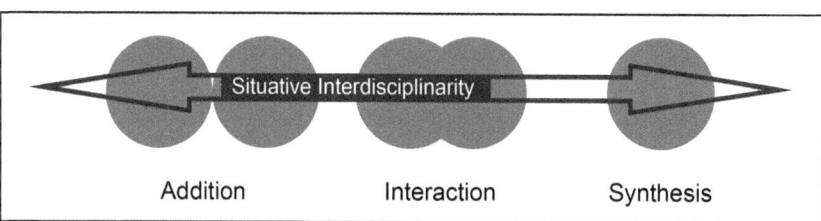

Figure 4: Basic models of cross-disciplinary collaboration (continuum) and position of the concept of situative interdisciplinarity (design: Christian Wille)

In order to reinforce and develop the cross-disciplinary collaboration in the further process of the project, the first experiences were taken on board and, building from these, we developed the concept of *situative interdisciplinarity*. This common guideline refers to the interaction between the disciplines participating in this volume which did not take place in the same degree at every point of the research process. Rather, it was a matter of limited interactions in specific phases of collaboration considered useful. This was governed by the subject matters and phases that structured the research process such as topics, questions, theories, terms and concepts, methods or interpretation. Interaction between the authors – here understood as interdisciplinarity – were thus not meant to take place as an end in itself, but examined for its added value and implemented depending on the situation, during the research process. The following stages were considered particularly suited for this:

1. The development of theoretical-conceptual frameworks within the topic areas (see the introductory sections 3.1, 4.1 and 5.1);
2. The development of common tools of research and analysis (questionnaire, interview guideline);
3. The joint interpretation of empirical data.

A systematic and critical evaluation of the practical implementation of situative interdisciplinarity was only possible after finalizing this book manuscript. Nevertheless, the results of a written survey among 16 authors in an internal colloquium provide first insights into the practice of situative interdisciplinarity and thus into the genesis of this volume. The selected assessments (see Tables 4, 5 and 6) seek to reproduce a broad range of opinions on different aspects of the collaboration and in particular point to the challenges of situative interdisciplinarity.

Positive Assessments	Negative Assessments
"The case study connects my disciplinary perspective with aspects from other disciplines that I got to know in the workgroup meetings."	"No, research topic, sources etc. are (too) different from the other case studies."
"Yes, because I work on a corpus with methods that transcend my discipline. In addition, I'm confronted with theories that are unknown in my discipline."[78]	"The case study is only partly interdisciplinary, since I continually need to coordinate with my colleagues (of other disciplines) and this has an influence on the fundamental perspective on the topic as well as on the analytical approach. On the other hand, the case study is hardly interdisciplinary since I work on the interface of various disciplines anyway."

Table 4: Assessment of the interdisciplinary nature of the authors' own case studies (selected opinions) (University of Luxembourg, IDENT2 2013 – internal survey among the authors)

---

77 | Personal translation of: "Oui, parce que je travaille sur un corpus et surtout avec des méthodes qui dépassent ma discipline; par ailleurs je suis confronté avec des théories inconnues dans ma discipline."

Positive Assessments	Negative Assessments
"I've received constructive criticism in the sense that I carefully observed how colleagues in other disciplines work and argue. This makes me question my own work methods and develop a better understanding for positions foreign to my field."	"I have to admit, I don't master the interdisciplinary background that other colleagues seem to have. I prefer to comment on things which I believe I can have some command over."[79]
"In the workgroup, the exchange between the disciplines was fairly good, marked by mutual respect and interest."	"Some disciplines seemed to be superior to others, since important concepts and terms were adopted from them."
"No rank pulling, the doctoral candidates collaborated on a completely equal footing and often even provided valuable incentives."[80]	"Academic rank influenced the choice of topics."
"I didn't notice any conflicts or showing-off between individual people. It was a good cooperative collaboration."	"Very diverse characters, timid, reticent, others very sure of themselves, result-oriented; others who pondered for a long time on fundamental questions. This mixture is probably more difficult to manage than interdisciplinary collaboration or the different academical positions."[81]

Table 5: Assessment of the collaboration in workgroups (selected opinions) (University of Luxembourg, IDENT2 2013 – internal survey among the authors)

---

78 | Personal translation of: "J'avoue ne pas maîtriser le background interdisciplinaire que semblent partager les autres membres du groupe. Je préfère n'intervenir que sur ce que je crois pouvoir maîtriser."

79 | Personal translation of: "Pas de rank pulling; les doctorants ont participé de manière tout à fait égalitaire et ont même souvent donné des incentives très précieux."

80 | Personal translation of: "Tempéraments très différents, des timides, des réticents, des personnes très convaincues d'elles-mêmes, des gens orientés vers le résultat, d'autres qui restent penchés sur des questions de fond: ce mélange est probablement plus difficile à gérer que le mélange interdisciplinaire et de différents statuts académiques."

Positive Assessments	Negative Assessments
"I got to know many colleagues better and learned something about their work methods."	"Sometimes it was difficult in the work meetings to follow up on the last meeting."
"Read various texts which were extremely productive also for my own field of research; the opportunity to work with interesting people (when they happened to be present)."	"Sometimes I'm lost; the discussions are only helpful in a rather limited way. I have noticed that the idea of interdisicplinarity has its limits."[82]
"For me the project was a great challenge, since I have no experience with interdisciplinary work as it is practiced here. In this sense the project was very helpful even if just to understand how interesting it can be, but also how challenging."[83]	"A considerable expenditure of time one could avoid; the initial theories developed in the groups were later dropped again; intensive research work in no relation to the size of the contribution in the book manuscript; relatively numerous small internal deadlines, here it was sometimes difficult not to lose sight of the bigger picture."

Tabelle 6: Overall assessment of the collaboration (selected opinions) (University of Luxembourg, IDENT2 2013 – internal survey among the authors)

The concept of situative interdisciplinarity should be understood as a temporary and variable intermeshing of the basic models of addition and interaction. It provides a realistic guideline for the cross-disciplinary collaboration in larger cooperative contexts without dissolving disciplines or fundamentally questioning the familiar academic practice of those involved. Rather it is a matter of partially breaking open self-referential research practices as well as a productive combination of 'disciplinary clichés' in favour of intellectual exchange and progress in knowledge.

---

81 | Personal translation of: "Sentiment parfois de n'importe quoi ; de discussions me semblant mener à un résultat bien limité. J'ai ressenti des limites réelles à l'idée d'interdisciplinarité."

82 | Personal translation of: "Pour moi le projet était un grand défi, n'ayant pas l'expérience du travail interdisciplinaire comme il s'est fait ici. En ce sens, cela m'a certainement apporté beaucoup si ce n'est de comprendre à quel point cela peut être intéressant mais aussi demandant."

2.5 REFERENCES

Abels, Heinz (2006): Identität. Über die Entstehung des Gedankens, dass der Mensch ein Individuum ist, den nicht leicht zu verwirklichenden Anspruch auf Individualität und die Tatsache, dass Identität in Zeiten der Individualisierung von der Hand in den Mund lebt, Wiesbaden: Verlag für Sozialwissenschaften.

Albert, Mathias/Brock, Lothar (1996): "Debordering the World of States. New Spaces in International Relations", in: New Political Science 18/1, 69-106.

Allmendinger, Phil/Haughton, Graham (2009): "Soft Spaces, Fuzzy Boundaries, and Metagovernance: The New Spatial Planning in the Thames Gateway", in: Environment and Planning A 41, 617-633.

Althusser, Louis (1971 [1970]): "Ideology and Ideological State Apparatuses" (trans. Ben Brewster), in: L. Althusser (ed.), Lenin and Philosophy and other Essays, New York: Monthly Review Press, 121-176.

Anderson, Benedict (2006): Imagined Communities: Reflections on the Origin and Spread of Nationalism, London/New York: Verso.

Audehm, Kathrin/Velten, Hans Rudolf (2007): "Einleitung", in: Kathrin Audehm/ Hans Rudolf Velten (eds.), Transgression – Hybridisierung – Differenzierung. Zur Performativität von Grenzen in Sprache, Kultur und Gesellschaft (= Scenae, vol. 4), Freiburg i. Br./Berlin/Wien: Rombach, 9-40.

Avanza, Martina/Laferté, Gilles (2005): "Dépasser la 'construction des identités'? Identification, image sociale, appartenance", in: Genèses 61, 134-152.

Bachmann-Medick, Doris (2006): Cultural Turns. Neuorientierungen in den Kulturwissenschaften, Reinbek bei Hamburg: Rowohlt.

Bathelt, Harald/Glückler, Johannes (2012): Wirtschaftsgeographie: ökonomische Beziehungen in räumlicher Perspektive, Stuttgart: UTB.

Beck, Ulrich/Giddens, Anthony/Lash, Scott (1994): Reflexive Modernization: Politics, Tradition and Aesthetics in the Modern Social Order, Stanford: Stanford University Press.

Beck, Ulrich/Beck-Gernsheim, Elisabeth (2001): Individualization: Institutionalized Individualism and its Social and Political Consequences, London/Thousand Oaks: Sage.

Beetham, Gwendolyn/Fernández, Melissa (2010): "Inter/Trans/Post-Disciplinarity: Explorations of Encounters across Disciplines", in: Graduate Journal of Social Science 7, 7-13.

Benjamin, Walter (1999): The Arcades Project, prepared on the basis of the German volume ed. by Rolf Tiedemann (trans. Howard Eiland and Kevin McLaughlin), Cambridge MA: The Belknap Press of Harvard University Press.

Boeckler, Marc (2012): "Borderlands", in: Nadine Marquardt/Verena Schreiber (eds.), Ortsregister. Ein Glossar zu Räumen der Gegenwart, Bielefeld: transcript, 44-49.

Böckler, Stefan (2007): "Grenze und frontier: Zur Begriffs- und Sozialgeschichte zweier Schließungsparadigmen der Moderne", in: Petra Deger/Robert Hettlage (eds.), Der europäische Raum. Die Konstruktion europäischer Grenzen, Wiesbaden: Verlag für Sozialwissenschaften, 25-48.

Bourdieu, Pierre (1972): Esquisse d'une théorie de la pratique. Précédé de trois études d'ethnologie kabyle, Paris: Seuil.

Bourdieu Pierre, (1980): Le sens pratique, Paris, Minuit.

Bröckling, Ulrich/Krasmann, Susanne/Lemke, Thomas (2000): "Gouvernementalität, Neoliberalismus und Selbst-technologien. Eine Einleitung", in: Ulrich Bröckling/Susanne Krasmann/Thomas Lemke (eds.), Gouvernementalität der Gegenwart. Studien zur Ökonomisierung des Sozialen, Frankfurt a. M.: Suhrkamp, 7-40.

Brubaker, Rogers (2001): "Au-delà de l'identité", in: Actes de la recherche en sciences sociales 139, 66-85.

Bühler, Benjamin (2012): "Grenze. Zur Wort- und Theoriegeschichte", in: Trajekte 24, 31-34.

Bührmann, Andrea/Schneider, Werner (2008): Vom Diskurs zum Dispositiv. Eine Einführung in die Dispositivanalyse, Bielefeld: transcript.

Butler, Judith (2006 [1990]): Gender Trouble, London/New York: Routledge.

Butler, Judith (2008a [1990]): "Bodily Inscriptions, Performative Subversions", in: Sara Salih (ed.), The Judith Butler Reader, 7th ed., Oxford: Blackwell, 90-118.

Butler, Judith (2008b [1990]): "Imitation and Gender Insubordination", in: Sara Salih (ed.), The Judith Butler Reader, 7th ed., Oxford: Blackwell, 119-137.

Chaffee, Daniel (2011): "Reflexive Identities", in: Anthony Elliott (ed.), Routledge Handbook of Identity Studies, London/New York: Routledge, 100-111.

de Certeau, Michel (1984 [French original 1980]): The Practice of Everyday Life (trans. Steven Rendall), Berkeley/Los Angeles: University of California Press.

Derrida, Jacques (1982a [French original 1978]): The Truth in Painting (trans. Geoff Bennington and Ian McLeod), Chicago: University of Chicago Press.

Derrida, Jacques (1982b [French original 1978]): "Différance" (trans. Alan Bass), in: Margins of Philosophy, Chicago: University of Chicago Press, 3-27.

Després, Carole/Lawrence, Roderick J. (2004): "Introduction", in: Futures 36, 397-405.

Döring, Jörg (2010): "Spatial Turn", in: Stephan Günzel (ed.), Raum. Ein interdisziplinäres Handbuch, Stuttgart: Metzler, 90-99.

Eigmüller, Monika (2006): "Der duale Charakter der Grenze. Bedingungen einer aktuellen Grenztheorie", in: Monika Eigmüller/Georg Vobruba (eds.), Grenzsoziologie. Die politische Strukturierung des Raums, Wiesbaden: Verlag für Sozialwissenschaften, 55-73.

Elias, Norbert (1986): "Figuration", in: Bernhard Schäfers (ed.), Grundbegriffe der Soziologie, Opladen: Leske + Budrich, 88-91.

Elliott, Anthony (ed.) (2011): Routledge Handbook of Identity Studies, London/New York: Routledge.

Emirbayer, Mustafa (1997): "Manifesto for a Relational Sociology", in: American Journal of Sociology 103/2, 281-317.
Faber, Richard/Naumann, Barbara (eds.) (1995): Literatur der Grenze – Theorie der Grenze, Würzburg: Königshausen & Neumann.
Fischer-Lichte, Erika (2005): "Grenze oder Schwelle? Zum Verhältnis von Kunst und Leben", in: Sprache und Literatur 36, 3-14.
Flusser, Vilém (1996): Zwiegespräche. Interviews 1967-1991, Göttingen: European Photography.
Flusser, Vilém (2009): Kommunikologie weiter denken. Die Bochumer Vorlesungen, Frankfurt a.M.: Fischer.
Foucault, Michel (1977 [French original 1975]): Discipline and Punish: The Birth of the Prison (trans. Alan Sheridan), New York: Pantheon Books.
Foucault, Michel (1982): "The Subject and Power", in: Hubert Dreyfus/Paul Rabinow, Michel Foucault. Beyond Structuralism and Hermeneutics (trans. Robert Hurley et. al), Chicago: The University of Chicago Press, 208-226.
Foucault, Michel (1993): "About the Beginning of the Hermeneutics of the Self" (orig. in English, ed. by Thomas Keenan and Mark Blasius), in: Political Theory, vol. 21/2, 198-227.
Foucault, Michel (1998 [French original 1963]) "A preface to transgression" (trans. Donald F. Bouchard and Sherry Simon, slightly modified), in: James D. Faubion (ed.), Aesthetics, method and epistemology, New York: New Press, 69-87.
Foucault, Michel (2007 [French original 2004]): Security, Territory, Population. Lectures at the Collège de France, 1977-1978 (trans. Graham Burchell), New York: Picador.
Füller, Henning/Marquardt, Nadine, (2009): "Gouvernementalität in der humangeographischen Diskursforschung", in: Georg Glaszke/Annika Mattissek (eds.), Handbuch Diskurs und Raum. Theorien und Methoden für die Humangeographie sowie die sozial- und kulturwissenschaftliche Raumforschung, Bielefeld: transcript, 83-106.
Gertenbach, Lars (2012): "Governmentality Studies. Die Regierung der Gesellschaft im Spannungsfeld von Ökonomie, Staat und Subjekt", in: Stephan Moebius (ed.), Kultur. Von den Cultural Studies bis zu den Visual Studies. Eine Einführung, Bielefeld: transcript, 109-127.
Giddens, Anthony (1991): Modernity and Self-Identity: Self and Society in the Late Modern Age, Cambridge: Polity Press.
Goffman, Erving (1974): Frame Analysis. An Essay on the Organization of Experience, Boston: Northeastern University Press.
Goffman, Erving (1959): The Presentation of Self in Everyday Life, New York: Anchor Books.
Graumann, Carl Friedrich (1983): "On Multiple Identities", in: International Social Science Journal 35, 309-321.
Greverus, Ina-Maria (1995): Die Anderen und Ich, Darmstadt: Wissenschaftliche Buchgesellschaft.

Guldin, Rainer (2011): "Ineinander greifende graue Zonen. Vilém Flussers Bestimmung der Grenze als Ort der Begegnung", in: Christoph Kleinschmidt/ Christine Hewel (eds.), Topographien der Grenze. Verortungen einer kulturellen, politischen und ästhetischen Kategorie, Würzburg: Königshausen & Neumann, 39-48.

Halpern, Catherine (2009): Identité(s). L'individu, le groupe, la société, Paris: Editions Sciences Humaines.

Han, Sam (2011): "The Fragmentation of Identity Theories", in: Anthony Elliott (ed.), Routledge Handbook of Identity Studies, London/New York: Routledge, 83-99.

Harendt, Annegret/Sprunk, Dana (2011): "Erzählter Raum und Erzählraum: (Kultur-)Raumkonstruktion zwischen Diskurs und Performanz", in: Social Geography 6, 15-27.

Hark, Sabine (2005): "Inter/Disziplinarität. Gender Studies Revisited", in: Heike Kahlert/ Barbara Thiessen/Ines Weller (eds.), Quer denken – Strukturen verändern. Gender Studies zwischen Disziplinen, Wiesbaden: Verlag für Sozialwissenschaften, 61-89.

Heckhausen, Heinz (1987): "Interdisziplinäre Forschung zwischen Intra-, Multi- und Chimären-Disziplinarität", in: Jürgen Kocka (ed.), Interdisziplinarität: Praxis – Herausforderung – Ideologie, Berlin: Suhrkamp, 129-145.

Hipfl, Brigitte (2004): "Mediale Identitätsräume. Skizzen zu einem 'spatial turn' in der Medien- und Kommunikationswissenschaft", in: Brigitte Hipfl/Elisabeth Klaus/Uta Scheer (eds.), Identitätsräume. Nation, Körper und Geschlecht in den Medien. Eine Topografie, Bielefeld: transcript, 16-50.

van Houtum, Henk/van Naerssen, Ton (2002): "Bordering, Ordering and Othering", in: Journal of Economic and Social Geography 93/2, 125-136.

IPSE (2010) (ed.): Doing Identity in Luxemburg. Subjektive Aneignungen – institutionelle Zuschreibungen – sozio-kulturelle Milieus, Bielefeld: transcript.

IPSE (2011a) (ed.): Doing Identity in Luxembourg. Subjective Appropriations – Institutional Attributions – Socio-Cultural Milieus, Bielefeld: transcript.

IPSE (2011b) (ed.): Construire des identités au Luxembourg. Appropriations subjectives – Projections institutionnelles – Milieux socio-culturels, Paris: Berg International.

Jungert, Michael (2010): "Was zwischen wem und warum eigentlich? Grundsätzliche Fragen der Interdisziplinarität", in: Michael Jungert/Elsa Romfeld/Thomas Sukopp/Uwe Voigt (eds.), Interdisziplinarität. Theorie, Praxis, Probleme, Darmstadt: Wissenschaftliche Buchgesellschaft, 1-11.

Kajetzke, Laura/Schroer, Markus (2010): "Sozialer Raum: Verräumlichung", in: Stephan Günzel (ed.), Raum. Ein interdisziplinäres Handbuch, Stuttgart: Metzler, 192-203.

Kalscheuer, Britta (2005): "Die raum-zeitliche Ordnung des Transdifferenten", in: Lars Allolio-Näcke/Britta Kalscheuer/Arne Manzeschke (eds.), Differenzen anders denken. Bausteine zu einer Kulturtheorie der Transdifferenz, Frankfurt a.M.: Campus, 68-85.

Kaufmann, Stefan/Bröckling, Ulrich/Horn, Eva (2002): "Einleitung", in: Stefan Kaufmann/Ulrich Bröckling/Eva Horn (eds.), Grenzverletzer. Von Schmugglern, Spionen und anderen subversiven Gestalten, Berlin: Kulturverlag Kadmos, 7-22.

Keupp, Heiner/Ahbe, Thomas/Gmür, Wolfgang/Höfer, Renate/Mitzscherlich, Beate/Kraus, Wolfgang/Straus, Florian (2006): Identitätskonstruktionen. Das Patchwork der Identitäten in der Spätmoderne, Reinbek bei Hamburg: Rowohlt.

Krappmann, Lothar (2005): Soziologische Dimensionen der Identität. Strukturelle Bedingungen für die Teilnahme an Interaktionsprozessen, Stuttgart: Klett-Cotta.

Lahire, Bernhard (1998): L'homme pluriel. Les ressorts de l'action, Paris: Nathan.

Lamping, Dieter (2001): Über Grenzen – eine literarische Topographie, Göttingen: Vandenhoek & Ruprecht.

Lask, Tomke (2002): "Wir waren doch immer Freunde in der Schule". Einführung in die Anthropologie der Grenzräume – Europäisches Grenzverständnis am Beispiel Leidingens, Saarbrücken: Röhrig.

Lefebvre, Henri (1991 [French Original 1974]): The Production of Space (trans. Donald Nicholson-Smith), Oxford: Blackwell.

Lemke, Thomas (2008): "Gouvernementalität", in: Clemens Kammler (ed.), Foucault-Handbuch. Leben – Wirkung – Werk, Stuttgart/Weimar: Verlag J. B. Metzler, 260-263.

Löffler, Winfried (2010): "Vom Schlechten des Guten: Gibt es schlechte Interdisziplinarität?", in: Michael Jungert/Elsa Romfeld/Thomas Sukopp/Uwe Voigt (eds.), Interdisziplinarität. Theorie, Praxis, Probleme, Darmstadt: Wissenschaftliche Buchgesellschaft, 157-172.

Lösch, Klaus (2005): "Begriff und Phänomen der Transdifferenz: Zur Infragestellung binärer Differenzkonstrukte", in: Lars Allolio-Näcke/Britta Kalscheuer/Arne Manzeschke (eds.), Differenzen anders denken. Bausteine zu einer Kulturtheorie der Transdifferenz, Frankfurt a.M.: Campus, 26-49.

Lossau, Julia (2002): Die Politik der Verortung. Eine postkoloniale Reise zu einer "ANDEREN" Geographie der Welt, Bielefeld: transcript.

Lossau, Julia (2003): "Geographische Repräsentationen: Skizze einer anderen Geographie", in: Hans Gebhardt/Paul Reuber/Günther Wolkersdorfer (eds.), Kulturgeographie. Aktuelle Ansätze und Entwicklungen, Heidelberg/Berlin: Spektrum Akademischer Verlag, 101-111.

Maihofer, Andrea (2005): "Inter-, Trans- und Postdisziplinarität. Ein Plädoyer wider die Ernüchterung", in: Heike Kahlert/Barbara Thiessen/Ines Weller (eds.), Quer denken – Strukturen verändern. Gender Studies zwischen Disziplinen, Wiesbaden: Verlag für Sozialwissenschaften, 185-202.

Mayring, Philipp (2002): Einführung in die qualitative Sozialforschung, Weinheim: Beltz.
Medick, Hans (1995): "Grenzziehungen und die Herstellung des politisch-sozialen Raumes. Zur Begriffsgeschichte und politischen Sozialgeschichte der Grenzen und der frühen Neuzeit", in: Richard Faber/Barbara Naumann (eds.), Literatur der Grenze – Theorie der Grenze, Würzburg: Königshausen & Neumann, 211-224.
Moebius, Stephan (2008): "Handlung und Praxis. Konturen einer poststrukturalistischen Praxistheorie", in: Stephan Moebius/Andreas Reckwitz (eds.), Poststrukturalistische Sozialwissenschaften, Frankfurt a.M.: Suhrkamp, 58-74.
Neumann, Birgit (2009): "Imaginative Geographien in kolonialer und postkolonialer Literatur: Raumkonzepte der (Post-)Kolonialismusforschung", in: Wolfgang Hallet/Birgit Neumann (eds.), Raum und Bewegung in der Literatur. Die Literaturwissenschaften und der Spatial Turn, Bielefeld: transcript, 115-138.
Newman, Davis (2001): "Boundaries, Borders, and Barriers: Changing Geographic Perspectives on Territorial Lines", in: Mathias Albert/David Jacobson/Yosef Lapid (eds.), Identities, Borders, Orders. Rethinking International Relations Theory, Minnesota: University of Minnesota, 137-151.
Parr, Rolf (2008): "Liminale und andere Übergänge. Theoretische Modellierungen von Grenzzonen, Normalitätsspektren, Schwellen, Übergängen und Zwischenräumen in Literatur- und Kulturwissenschaft", in: Achim Geisenhanslüke/Georg Mein (eds.), Schriftkultur und Schwellenkunde, Bielefeld: transcript, 11-63.
Reckwitz, Andreas (2001): "Der Identitätsdiskurs zum Bedeutungswandel einer sozialwissenschaftlichen Semantik", in: Werner Rammert/Gunther Knauthe/Klaus Buchenau/Florian Altenhoner (eds.), Kollektive Identitäten und Kulturelle Innovationen: ethnologische, soziologische und historische Studien, Leipzig: Leipziger Universitätsverlag, 21-38.
Reckwitz, Andreas (2003): "Grundelemente einer Theorie sozialer Praktiken: Eine sozialtheoretische Perspektive", in: Zeitschrift für Soziologie 32/4, 282-301.
Reckwitz, Andreas (2008): "Praktiken und Diskurse. Eine sozialtheoretische und methodologische Relation", in: Herbert Kalthoff/Stefan Hirschauer/Gesa Lindemann (eds.), Theoretische Empirie. Zur Relevanz qualitativer Sozialforschung, Frankfurt a.M.: Suhrkamp, 188-209.
Reckwitz, Andreas (2010): "Auf dem Weg zu einer kultursoziologischen Analytik zwischen Praxeologie und Poststrukturalismus", in: Monika Wohlrab-Sahr (ed.), Kultursoziologie. Paradigmen – Methoden – Fragestellungen, Wiesbaden: Verlag für Sozialwissenschaften, 179-205.
Reckinger, Rachel/Schulz, Christian/Wille, Christian (2011a): "Preface", in: IPSE (ed.), Doing Identity in Luxembourg. Subjective Appropriations – Institutional Attributions – Socio-Cultural Milieus, Bielefeld: transcript, 7-9.

Reckinger, Rachel/Schulz, Christian/Wille, Christian (2011b): "Identity Constructions in Luxembourg", in: IPSE (ed.), Doing Identity in Luxembourg. Subjective Appropriations – Institutional Attributions – Socio-Cultural Milieus, Bielefeld: transcript, 291-294.

Reckinger, Rachel/ Wille, Christian (2011b): "Researching Identity Constructions", in: IPSE (ed.), Doing Identity in Luxembourg. Subjective Appropriations – Institutional Attributions – Socio-Cultural Milieus, Bielefeld: transcript, 11-34.

Renn, Joachim/Straub, Jürgen (2002): "Transitorische Identität. Der Prozesscharakter moderner personaler Selbstverhältnisse", in: Joachim Renn/Jürgen Straub (eds.), Transitorische Identität. Der Prozesscharakter des modernen Selbst, Frankfurt a.M.: Campus, 10-31.

Ricoeur, Paul (1992 [French original 1990]): Oneself as Another (trans. Kathleen Blamey), Chicago: University of Chicago Press.

Roll, Christine/Pohle, Frank/Myrczek, Matthias (eds.) (2010): Grenzen und Grenzüberschreitungen. Bilanz und Perspektiven der Frühneuzeitforschung, Köln/Weimar/Wien: Böhlau.

Rosa, Hartmut (2007): "Identität", in: Jürgen Straub/Arne Weidemann (eds.), Handbuch interkulturelle Kommunikation und Kompetenz. Grundbegriffe – Theorien – Anwendungsfelder, Stuttgart: Metzler.

Ruano-Borbolan, Jean-Claude (1998): L'identité. L'individu, le groupe, la société, Auxerre: Sciences Humaines.

Said, Edward W. (1978): Orientalism, New York: Pantheon Books.

Schreiber, Verena (2009): "Raumangebote bei Foucault", in: Georg Glasze/Annika Mattissek (eds.), Handbuch Diskurs und Raum. Theorien und Methoden für die Humangeographie sowie die sozial- und kulturwissenschaftliche Raumforschung, Bielefeld: transcript, 199-212.

Schroer, Markus (2008): "'Bringing Space Back In' – Zur Relevanz des Raums als soziologische Kategorie", in: Jörg Döring/Tristan Thielmann (eds.), Spatial Turn. Das Raumparadigma in den Kultur- und Sozialwissenschaften, Bielefeld: transcript, 125-148.

Sennett, Richard (1996): "Etwas ist faul in der Stadt", in: Die Zeit, 26. Januar, 47-48.

Simmel, Georg (1992 [1903]): "Der Raum und die räumlichen Ordnungen der Gesellschaft", in: Otthein Rammstedt (ed.), Georg Simmel: Soziologie. Untersuchungen über die Formen der Vergesellschaftung (= complete edition, vol. 11), Frankfurt a.M.: Suhrkamp, 687-790.

Soja, Edward W. (1989): Postmodern Geographies: The Reassertion of Space in Critical Social Theory, London: Verso.

Soja, Edward W. (1996): Thirdspace: Journeys to Los Angeles and Other Real-and-Imagined Places, Oxford: Blackwell.

Somers, Margaret R./Gibson, Gloria D. (1994): "Reclaiming the Epistemological 'Other': Narrative and the Social Constitution of Identity", in: Craig Calhoun (ed.), Social Theory and the Politics of Identity, Oxford: Blackwell, 37-99.

Straub, Jürgen (2004): "Identität", in: Friedrich Jaeger/Burkhard Liebsch (eds.), Handbuch der Kulturwissenschaften. Grundlagen und Schlüsselbegriffe, Stuttgart: Metzler, 277-303.

Turner, Victor (1982): "Liminal to Liminoid, in Play, Flow, and Ritual: An Essay in Comparative Symbology", in: Victor Turner, Ritual to Theatre: The Human Seriousness of Play, University of Michigan, Ann Arbor: Performing Arts Journal Publications.

van Gennep, Arnold (1960 [French original 1909]): Rites of Passage (trans. Monika B. Vizedom and Gabrielle L. Caffee), Chicago: University of Chicago Press.

Wagner, Kirsten (2010): "Topographical Turn", in: Stephan Günzel (ed.), Raum. Ein interdisziplinäres Handbuch, Stuttgart: Metzler, 100-109.

Walter-Wastl, Doris (ed.) (2011): The Ashgate Research Companion to Border Studies, Farnham: Ashgate.

Warde, Alan/Martens, Lydia/Olsen, Wendy (1999): "Consumption and the Problem of Variety. Cultural Omnivorousness, Social Distinction and Dining out", in: Sociology 33/1, 105-127.

Warde, Alan (2005): "Consumption and Theories of Practice", in: Journal of Consumer Culture 5/2, 131-153.

Watkin, Christopher (2009): Phenomenology or Deconstruction? The Question of Ontology in Maurice Merleau-Ponty, Paul Ricoeur, Jean-Luc Nancy, Edinburgh: Edinburgh University Press.

Weichhart, Peter (1990): Raumbezogene Identität. Bausteine zu einer Theorie räumlich-sozialer Kognition und Identifikation, Stuttgart: Franz Steiner Verlag.

Weigel, Sigrid (2002): "Zum 'topographical turn'. Kartographie, Topographie und Raumkonzepte in den Kulturwissenschaften", in: KulturPoetik 2/2, 151-165.

Werlen, Benno (1997a): Sozialgeographie alltäglicher Regionalisierungen, vol. 2: Globalisierung, Region und Regionalisierung, Stuttgart: Franz Steiner Verlag.

Werlen, Benno (1997b): "Einleitung", in: Benno Werlen (ed.), Sozialgeographie alltäglicher Regionalisierungen, vol. 3: Ausgangspunkte und Befunde empirischer Forschung, Stuttgart: Franz Steiner Verlag, 9-16.

Werlen, Benno (2008): Sozialgeographie. Eine Einführung, Bern: Haupt.

Werlen, Benno (2009): "Geographie/Sozialgeographie", in: Stephan Günzel (ed.), Raumwissenschaften, Frankfurt a.M.: Suhrkamp, 142-158.

Werlen, Benno (2010): Gesellschaftliche Räumlichkeit 1. Orte der Geographie, Stuttgart: Franz Steiner Verlag.

Wetherell, Margaret/Mohanty, Chandra Talpade (eds.) (2010): The Sage Handbook of Identities, Los Angeles/London/New Delhi/Singapore/Washington DC: Sage.

Wiesmann, Urs/Biber-Klemm, Susette/Grossenbacher-Mansuy, Walter/Hirsch Hadorn, Gertrude/Hoffmann-Riem, Holger/Joye, Dominique/Pohl, Christian/Zemp, Elisabeth (2008): "Transdisziplinäre Forschung weiterentwickeln: Eine Synthese mit 15 Empfehlungen", in: Frédéric Darbellay/Theres Paulsen (eds.), Herausforderung Inter- und Transdisziplinarität. Konzepte, Methoden und innovative Umsetzung in Lehre und Forschung, Lausanne: Presses Polytechniques et Universitaires Romandes, 174-179.

Wille, Christian (2014): "Räume der Grenze. Eine praxistheoretische Perspektive in den kulturwissenschaftlichen Border Studies", in: Friederike Elias/Albrecht Franz/Henning Murmann/Ulrich Weiser (eds.), Praxeologie. Beiträge zur interdisziplinären Reichweite praxistheoretischer Ansätze in den Geistes- und Sozialwissenschaften (=Materiale Textkulturen, vol. 3), Berlin: De Gruyter, 53-72.

3. Space and Identity Constructions Through Institutional Practices

Fabian Faller, Heike Mauer, Bernhard Kreutz, Elena Kreutzer, Wilhelm Amann

3.1 POLICIES AND NORMALIZATIONS

The investigation of processes of social structuration in this volume concentrates on processes of spatial and identity construction. Along with media- and subject-related aspects (see chapters 4 and 5), the research also focuses on normalizations and policies. These refer to 'strategic' practices collective actors use to produce specific spatialities and identities considered to be 'desirable'. This chapter deals with the analysis of such processes of construction and attempts to examine the respective policies and normalizations practised to produce spatial and social categorizations. The aim is to determine the mechanisms and characteristics of spatial and border constructions, to provide some concepts for their analysis and, to a lesser degree, identity constructions that are brought about by social actors. The empirical and theoretical focus is thus on social processes of attribution.

Policies and normalizations as attributions and their appropriations contain various dimensions of power. Power here is understood, in the sense of governmentality studies, as a phenomenon manifesting itself at the levels of self-governing and/or being governed (see Füller/Marquardt 2009). It is seen as a "productive authority for shaping reality"[1] (Gertenbach 2012: 116) and thus enables a constructivist approach to questions of spatial and identity constructions in border areas. Since the questions this chapter seeks to analyse explicitly address power relationships and negotiation processes, this Foucauldian perspective – presented in more detail below – appears to lend itself particularly well to the task. Each of the four case studies presented here is concerned with a specific field of power which in each case varies in intensity and emanates from different actors. The contributions focus in particular on the negotiation processes of those fields of power in which attributions, normalizations and power relationships play

---

[1] | Personal translation of: "[...] produktive Instanz der Gestaltung von Wirklichkeit."

a relevant role. However, the case studies do not in every instance show these aspects as clearly defined areas; instead, there is as a rule a certain degree of overlap and simultaneity. Concepts such as power, governmentality or processes of normalization thus carry varying weight. The common approach of the case studies in this chapter is their focus on border areas where negotiation processes can be observed especially clearly as governmental, i.e. as self-regulating. For instance, traditional forms of government are abandoned and the inhabitants of these border areas engage in a variety of forms of migration which promote the idea of self-regulation. Actors in cross-border contexts are therefore suitable examples for studying governmentality processes because they continually practise them. The term 'actors' here expressly refers not only to elites or normative authorities, but also to persons who make constitutive use of differences depending on the available resources.

The first case study presented here traces the boundaries related to the construction of "spaces of (im)morality" due to the problematization of prostitution in Luxembourg around 1900. At the same time, it analyses the logics of power at work in these construction processes. The following study about castles examines how the hegemonial and social practices emanating from them constituted spaces and their boundaries by means of strategies that continuously changed across the centuries. At the same time, it examines in which ways castles represented the rule of the nobility and what conclusions we may draw from them concerning the nobility's identity constructions. The third case study understands bioenergy regions as constructs of social negotiations. It analyses the emergence of structures and processes that are revealed when the practices of economic actors relate back to policies and normalizations. The final study sheds light on physical, social and semiotic constructions of space. It examines the media discourse on migration in the *Luxemburger Wort*, Luxembourg's most widely circulated daily newspaper, as well as the cross-border expansion of this discourse to the two neighbouring regions of Saarland and Lorraine, or to the entire border region of SaarLorLux, in the period under consideration, i.e. from 1990 to 2010.

The underlying concept of these case studies – the distinction between the logics of power of sovereignty, discipline and governmentality (see below) – serves as a guideline for our collaborative work and should not be understood as static. The social and space-related categorizations inherent in institutional agency are accessed through appropriate analytical approaches and revealed with the aid of expert interviews and text analysis.

3.1.1 Heuristics: A Foucauldian Approach to Power Analysis

One thing has already become clear from this brief overview of the subjects under investigation here: they are extremely diverse. Not only are different periods of history examined (the Middle Ages, recent history and the present), but also different social phenomena (prostitution, castle development, the energy sector, public media). A particular concern of our group of researchers coming from very different disciplines (gender studies, history, geography and literary studies) was to find a common theoretical approach to these heterogeneous fields of study. We concluded that a power analysis approach drawing on the work of Michel Foucault lends itself particularly well to analysing normalizations and policies that enable social actors to create constructions of 'desirable' spaces and identities.[2]

For our interdisciplinary research context and the disparate subjects of investigation, the often criticized ambiguity of Foucault's analysis of power[3] has proved to be exceedingly rewarding. It enables us to refer to a common frame of analysis with a consistent terminology and at the same time to emphasize specific features where necessary.

Regarding the complexity of Foucauldian power analysis, one should bear in mind that Foucault continued to develop it while turning to the study of governmentality and government.[4] This more advanced analysis of power, which Foucault began to use in the mid-1970s, enables an even more subtle differentiation of power phenomena than his previous distinction between discipline, as the only 'productive form of power', and a juridical sovereign power, understood as primarily repressive. With the addition of governmentality, phenomena of power can now be more precisely analysed on the basis of the different types of their functional logic, the techniques and strategies they utilize, and the alliances into which these forms of power enter in historical constellations (see Lemke 2008: 261; Lemke 1997; Gertenbach 2012: 112ff.).

Before connecting this perspective with the subjects investigated in the case studies, we will briefly outline our interpretation of Foucauldian power analysis along its central axes of sovereignty, discipline and governmentality.

At the centre of the logic of power of *sovereignty* is law, which distinguishes what is permitted from what is forbidden and couples forbidden actions to a penalty. Foucault also calls it a "juridical" or "prohibitive" form of power. Sovereignty establishes the sovereign-subject axis, demanding obedience from the latter. Sovereignty exercises a regulatory function by setting basic norms, a function which is negatively determined, however, since order can only arise if what is forbidden is actually prevented. With reference to spatial action patterns,

---

2 | An initial systematization and synthesis of Foucault's analysis of power that this section draws on can be found in Reckinger 2013.

3 | Lemke (1997: 15-23) provides an overview of criticisms of Foucault.

4 | Foucault uses the term governmentality primarily in his lecture series "Security, Territory, Population" (1978-79) (Foucault 2007 [2004]). Previously he only speaks of the problem of "biopower" (Foucault 2003 [1997]: lecture of 17 March 1976). In later lectures, the term of governing increasingly replaces that of governmentality (see Foucault 1997, 2000 [1981], 1982 [1982], 1988 [1984]). In the following, these terms – if not otherwise indicated in the case studies – will be used as synonyms.

sovereignty aims at dominion over a territory or at the assertion of law in a territory (see also in the following Foucault 2007 [2004]: Lectures 1 and 2).

By contrast, *discipline*, as another logic of power, focuses on what is to be done in a binding sense. While the 'juridical' form of power allows for the indeterminate, discipline gives clear instructions for action so that the indeterminate remainder is forbidden (Foucault 2007 [2004]: 46). At the same time, discipline broadens the binarity of what is allowed and forbidden by adding a third element: the delinquent person. Disciplinary techniques accordingly aim at controlling individual physical bodies. The practices used for purposes of control are intended to act both preventively on the total population and correctively on offenders. At the same time, discipline makes a basic distinction between normal and abnormal. The norm – the predefined ideal – forms the basis which makes it possible to stipulate what is normal and abnormal in the first place. To express this primacy of the norm in terminological form, Foucault designates the operation of disciplinary techniques as "normation" (Foucault 2007 [2004]: 57).

The logic of power of *governmentality*, for its part, is closely connected to security mechanisms. While discipline regulates "by definition [...] everything" (Foucault 2007 [2004]: 45) and aims at letting nothing escape its notice, security grants leeway (*laisser faire*). At the same time, governmentality departs from the sovereign/subject axis and relates to the population. Instead of norms, prohibitions and delinquent bodies, the governmental logic of power takes the whole of society as its reference. In this way it enables governing (in contrast to obedience and control). Security mechanisms are not interested in individual (criminal) cases, but rather their effects on society as a whole and their statistical predictability depending on a local, historical context and on social milieus. In the process, the social costs of delinquency and prosecution are also calculated. This makes it possible to enquire into the economically and socially acceptable limitations of undesirable phenomena such as crime, disease, poverty etc. Instead of defining boundaries by what is permitted or forbidden, the bounds of the acceptable are defined by an average. Hence security mechanisms reverse the approach of discipline: instead of stipulating beforehand a norm which defines individuals as normal and abnormal, it first determines the normality of the distribution – the normal distribution. Subsequently, regulatory policies are employed to optimize the reality thus ascertained. That is why Foucault refers to the operation of the apparatuses of security as normalizing.

The concepts of sovereignty, discipline and governmentality can be brought together into an analytical framework as in Table 1, which is of heuristic benefit for the case studies that follow.

	Sovereignty	Discipline	Governmentality
Definition of the problem of power	How can dominion over a territory be exercised?	How can bodies be disciplined and controlled?	How can influence be exerted on social development so as to encourage what is desired and limit what is not?
Instruments and techniques of exercising power	Laws and juridical instruments which lead to isolated instances of obedience	Control mechanisms and disciplining techniques which are to be used on individual subjects and by means of which a distinction is made between what is normal and what is abnormal	Apparatus of security: calculations of probability and risk in relation to the entire population
Form of the exercise of power	Setting norms/ prohibitive	Normative/ controlling	Normalizing/ optimizing
Goal of the exercise of power	Asserting the law in a territory by actually preventing what is forbidden	Bodies/subjects function according to a predefined norm	(Self-)government/ regulation of the population

Table 1: Dimensions, functional logic, techniques and strategies of Foucauldian power analysis, following Füller and Marquardt (2009: 88)

The terms 'governmentality' and 'government' also exhibit additional constitutive facets. "And by 'government' I mean the set of institutions and practices by which people are 'led', from administration to education", Foucault summarizes (1991 [1981]: 176), although – as shown – not primarily power of authority or disciplinary normalizations, but normalizing and regulatory "procedures and techniques [are used] which have a guiding effect on human behaviour"[5] (Gertenbach 2012: 111). Here, an analytical distinction must be made between the political technologies described above (for example, security mechanisms) and technologies of the self. Governmentality can thus be described as a process of transformation and a (re) formation of statehood, in whose wake the power regime of government becomes more significant than that of discipline and sovereignty (see Foucault 2007 [2004]: 108-110). However, it is characteristic of this process

"that state formation or political structures and subjectivation are seen as mutually dependent processes (see Lemke 2008) which act in both directions: from technologies of domination to technologies of the self and vice versa, from technologies of the self to technologies of domination"[6] (Reckinger 2013: 3).

Foucault's approach to technologies of the self constitutes a crucial expansion of power analysis. The analysis of technologies of the self makes it possible to consider, with regard to the constitution and action of subjects, elements of power and domination based essentially on freedom (and expressly not on discipline and control) (see Soiland 2005: 12-18). At the same time, Foucault develops a historical genealogy of modern knowledge of government and its specific rationality in relation to state formation.[7] In addition, governmentality provides an analytical framework for specifying various forms of governing, that is, the variable interplay of sovereignty, discipline and governmentality (see for instance Füller and Marquardt 2009: 87).

Foucault himself emphasizes that the analytical separation of sovereignty, discipline and governmentality does not mean that they are necessarily mutually exclusive:

"The territorial sovereign became an architect of the disciplined space [...] and almost at the same time, the regulator of a milieu, which involved not so much establishing limits and frontiers, or fixing locations, as, above all and essentially, making possible, guaranteeing and ensuring circulations" (Foucault 2007 [2004]: 29).

---

5 | Personal translation of: "[...] Prozeduren und Techniken [zum Einsatz kommen] welche steuernd auf das menschliche Verhalten einwirken."
6 | Personal translation of: "[...] dass Staatsformierung bzw. politische Strukturen und Subjektivierung als sich gegenseitig bedingende Prozesse angesehen werden (vgl. Lemke 2008), die in beide Richtungen wirken: von den Herrschaftstechnologien zu den Selbsttechnologien und, umgekehrt, von den Selbsttechnologien zu den Herrschaftstechnologien."
7 | In the lectures series "History of Governmentality", he elaborates on this from antiquity to early modern times and finally ends with an analysis of neoliberalism (Foucault 2007 [2004], 2008).

3. Constructions of Space and Identity Created by Institutional Practices

Sovereignty, discipline and security refer here to differing logics of the exercise of power over territory and subjects, which can occur simultaneously as political technologies. He explicitly postulates no chronological evolution, which would have a society of sovereignty at its beginning, superseded by a society of discipline and leading to a society of government.

Instead, our analysis proceeds within a 'triangle' described by Foucault: "Sovereignty, discipline and governmental management, which has population as its main target and apparatuses of security as its essential mechanism" (Foucault 2007 [2004]: 107-108).

The following case studies refer to this analytical triangle in order to identify logics of power in the construction of space, limits and identities through policies and normalizations, and to be able to identify them in their relation to one another. This includes an empirical examination of the complexity of the resources and techniques on the part of the holders of power. To this end, the power regimes identified above are "not understood as mutations which supersede one another teleologically, but rather studied specifically in their simultaneous imbrications and modes of interaction"[8] (Reckinger 2013: 9-10). Accordingly, the triangle is not equilateral, but dynamic, depending on the object studied and the empirical shaping of the power relations. This is expressed in Fig. 1 as an asymmetrical triangle.

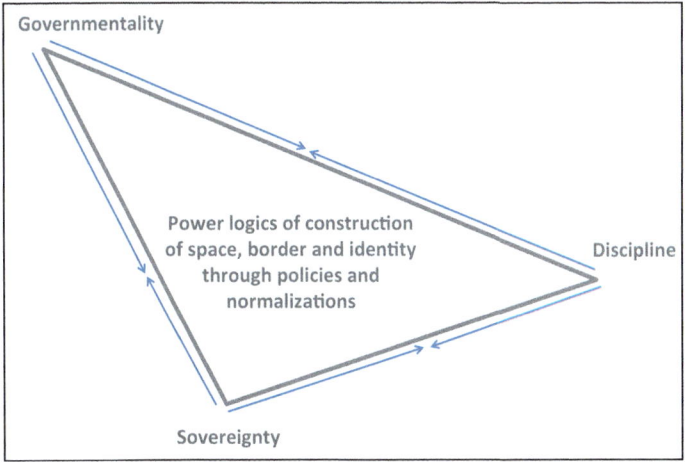

Figure 1: Power logics of construction of space, border and identity through policies and normalizations (own representation)

---

8 | Personal translation of: "[...] nicht als sich jeweils teleologisch ablösende Mutationen begriffen, sondern gerade in ihren zeitgleichen Überlappungen und Interaktionsweisen erforscht [...]."

The three interwoven analytical approaches to policies and normalizations each focus on a partial aspect of power issues and do not yield a coherent picture until they are considered together. Not every case study examines all the dimensions or interrelations of sovereignty, discipline and governmentality; instead, each treats key aspects, which permit conclusions to be drawn concerning the characteristic polymorphous structure of power relations. The concrete research work in this context includes discourses as well as materialities (see Gertenbach 2012: 118) and relates them to legal and institutionalized forms of control, taking account of the "formation of spatial knowledge"[9] (Füller and Marquardt 2009: 91 and 93).

By taking up the problem of prostitution c. 1900, the study on spaces of im/morality refers first to the sovereignty/discipline axis, since "commercial fornication"[10] (Mémorial 1855) was a punishable offence in the Grand Duchy at the time. However, it is shown that use was simultaneously made of governmental logics of power, which contributed to a 'government of the population' and a sexual 'self-government' by means of security mechanisms and self-conduct.

The case study on castles examines these logics of power under the aspect of sovereignty, as instruments of hegemonial spatial construction and representation, using the canton of Vianden as an example, and enquires how the political and social practices emanating from and centred on a castle constituted hegemonial spaces and their boundaries.

In the context of biogas production, the relation of sovereignty and governmentality becomes clear by reference to the structurally affirmative practices of biogas producers. Here the question arises as to how actors deal with policies and normalizations and how this constitutes an energy region. The relations between discipline and governmentality are shown in the biogas producers' subversive work of constitution, in particular the changes in established practices of biogas production.

Finally, the current discussion of migration in the media in Luxembourg is examined by means of a content and discourse analysis. The focus of this case study lies on the sovereignty/discipline axis. The study analyses the relation between sociopolitical debates and their semantic implementations on the part of the journalists and editors of the most widely circulated Luxembourg daily newspaper, the *Luxemburger Wort*, from 1990 to 2010.

---

9 | Personal translation of: "[...] Formierung von räumlichem Wissen."
10 | Personal translation of: "[...] Gewerbsmäßige Unzucht."

3.2 On the Construction of Spaces of Im-/Morality. A Power Analysis Perspective on the Problematization of Prostitution c. 1900

Heike Mauer

The objects under examination in this case study are the 'problematization' of prostitution in Luxembourg in the early twentieth century and the related construction of spaces. Michel Foucault uses the term problematization to refer to the process of questioning the answers provided by politics to the problems posed them (see Foucault 1984: 385). This problematization is permeated with power relationships, which are also examined. Files of legal and police authorities, parliamentary debates and newspaper reports are used as sources. First the historical context and the central issue of the paper are presented.

Around the turn of the century, sexuality and especially prostitution rose to the level of a 'problem' throughout Europe. There were many reasons for this: governments, military and colonial administrations held prostitution responsible for the spread of venereal diseases; the public was concerned about the issue of so-called 'white slavery', i.e. the trafficking of girls. At the same time, the everstronger women's movements were criticizing the double standards of the bourgeoisie, which restricted women's sexuality to marriage, yet allowed men extramarital and premarital sexual contacts through regulated prostitution (see Herzog 2011: 6ff.). In Luxembourg, too, the government targeted prostitution as a propagator of venereal diseases. For instance, the health report of 1907 spoke of "a significant increase in venereal diseases in recent years" and the medical inspector demanded "regulation of prostitution to prevent venereal diseases. [...] We must not forget the quality of the people by focusing on quantity"[11] (Collège Médical 1908: 16). Consequently, a government commission was appointed to combat prostitution. The trafficking of girls was also publicly scandalized in the newspapers (see, for instance, *Luxemburger Wort* 1904b). The bourgeois women's movement in Luxembourg only indirectly addressed prostitution by criticizing proletarian living conditions from a moral perspective (see Goetzinger 1997: 67). By contrast, the *Katholische Frauenbund* (Catholic Women's Association) began in 1911 to gather signatures for a petition against the so-called hostess bars (*Animierkneipen*) considered to be the "most dangerous strongholds of venereal disease", because "that is where alcoholism and prostitution join hands"[12] (*Das Volkswohl* 1911).

---

[11] | Personal translation of: "[...] in den letzten Jahren eine bedeutende Zunahme der venerischen Erkrankungen", [...] "durch Reglementierung der Prostitution der Zunahme der venerischen Erkrankungen vorzubeugen [...]."

[12] | Personal translation of: "[...] gefährlichsten Horte der Geschlechtskrankheiten" [...] "Alkoholismus und Prostitution reichen sich hier die Hand."

In a word, around 1900 prostitution was also 'discovered' in Luxembourg as a social problem which seemed to be getting increasingly out of control. This started a debate involving parliament, police, legal authorities and the political public concerning the existing prostitution policies and their practical implementation. The background for the problematization of prostitution was the rapidly advancing industrialization of the country, especially in the so-called Minette Basin (ore basin) and the concomitant increase in (labour) migration (see Scuto 2012: 67ff.). Hence in 1911 the above-mentioned government commission pronounced:

"[W]hen commerce and industry attracted to the newly emerging centres thousands of men living in forced or voluntary celibacy and furnished them with ample, relatively well-paid work, prostitution appeared at the head of those elements which exploit the weaknesses and passions of the workers"[13] (Archives Nationales de Luxembourg (ANLux) J 64/39: 243).

We shall first examine which spaces of im-/morality are in general constructed, which social, political and territorial boundaries are drawn for this purpose and which dimensions these construction processes encompass. Subsequently we shall inquire into the power relationships created, negotiated and transformed by the construction of spaces of im-/morality. Our particular interest here will be the relationship between the various power logics of sovereignty, discipline and governmentality distinguished by Foucault which – as the hypothesis argues – at the same time permeate the construction of im-/moral spaces.

3.2.1 Im-/Moral Spaces as the Result of Demarcatory Policies

One dimension of the construction of im-/moral spaces in Luxembourg is the drawing of boundaries between national and foreign. The nation of Luxembourg, the territory of the Grand Duchy, is here imagined to be a space of moral integrity threatened by debauched foreigners crossing the borders:

"The domestic landlords of Esch are justifiably complaining about unscrupulous competition on the part of foreigners who are routinely [...] allowed to keep a public house. [...] Professional trollops come from neighbouring countries, rent a room in the vicinity of such bars and engage in prostitution"[14] (*Luxemburger Wort* 1904a).

---

13 | Personal translation of: "[L]orsque le commerce et l'industrie attirèrent dans les centres naissants des milliers d'hommes vivant dans un célibat forcé ou volontaire, et leur fournirent un travail abondant et relativement bien rémunéré, la prostitution apparut à la tête des éléments qui exploitent les faiblesses et les passions des travailleurs."
14 | Personal translation of: "Die einheimischen Wirte von Esch beklagen sich mit Recht über eine schmutzige Konkurrenz seitens Ausländer, welche ohne weiteres [...] das Halten einer Schankstelle gestattet wird. [...] Gewerbsmäßige Racoleusen kommen aus den

3. Constructions of Space and Identity Created by Institutional Practices

And in 1907 a member of parliament asked:

"Why do we not more often make use of the legal lever of deportation? [...] If we would make more use of our right of deportation, then many vendible harlots would have to leave the public houses and cross the border, taking much that is sordid with them"[15] (Chambre des Députés 1907: 265).

One reason that this identification of morality with the nation and of immorality with the intrusion of foreigners could function was the exceptional position of prostitution legislation in Luxembourg. Unlike Belgium, France and the German Empire, the regulation of prostitution in Luxembourg at the beginning of the twentieth century was not implemented by the vice units responsible at the local level. Luxembourg had neither established controlled brothels nor a requirement for prostitutes to register with the police. Prostitution was thereby factually prohibited, yet on the other hand prostitutes did not have to fear demeaning forcible medical inspections by the police – as long as they were able to conceal their activities from the police. The authorities were certain that foreign prostitutes – from Metz, for instance, and other cities of the German Empire – were coming specifically to Luxembourg for that reason. A report made by the Hollerich police in 1908 states "[A]fter a time [...] it turned out that the same were largely under police inspection which they had eluded due to venereal disease"[16] (ANLux J 64/39: 392f.). And the *Verein für Volks- und Schulhygiene* (Society for Public and School Hygiene) lamented:

"When it is known that in Germany prostitutes are continuously inspected by the police and forced to undergo treatment if they are found to be diseased, it is easily understandable that all professional prostitutes find their way to our free country and our hostess bars [...]"[17] (Pier/Meyers 1910b: 25).

Nachbarländern herüber, mieten sich in der Nähe solcher Wirtschaften ihr Zimmer und treiben die Prostitution gewerbsmäßig."

15 | Personal translation of: "Warum gebrauchen wir nicht öfters die gesetzliche Handhabe der Ausweisung. [...] Würden wir mehr von unserem Ausweisungsrecht Gebrauch machen, dann müsste manche feile Dirne aus den Wirtshäusern über die Grenze gehen und manches Elend würde mit ihr aus den Wirtshäusern wegziehen."

16 | Personal translation of: "[N]ach einiger Zeit [...] stellt es sich heraus, dass dieselben grösstenteils unter Sittenkontrolle standen, welcher sie sich wegen Geschlechtserkrankung entzogen haben."

17 | Personal translation of: "Wenn man weiss, dass in Deutschland eine Sittenkontrolle besteht, welche die Prostituierten einer dauernden sitten- und sanitätspolizeilichen Kontrolle und im Erkrankungsfalle einer Zwangsbehandlung unterwirft, so ist es leicht begreiflich, dass alle gewerbsmässigen Prostituierten den Weg in unser freies Land und in unsere Animierkneipen finden [...]."

There were similar fears regarding living together out of wedlock (concubinage), which was associated with prostitution. In contrast to neighbouring countries, concubinage was not prohibited, and the canton of Esch became, according to the authorities, a destination for foreigners living in concubinage (ANLux J 64/39: 372).

This already indicates a further dimension: the regionalization of immorality. It was primarily the heavily industrialized south, marked by a 'proletarian culture' (see Chapter 5.5), as well as the area around the train station in the capital city and the neighbouring parishes of Hollerich and Bonneweg, that were declared to be immoral spaces. Bars and cafés employing women as waitresses and/or maidservants were the main places where prostitution was secretly practised; there were hardly any streetwalkers. With regard to waitresses, the police commissioner of the city of Luxembourg stated as early as 1891 that they were "more often than not foreigners" and "a large number of them had a poor reputation for morality or had already been convicted of prostitution or [...] venereal disease"[18] (Archives de la Ville de Luxembourg (AVL) LU 11 - IV/2 447 1891). During a parliamentary debate on a new law governing public houses about the turn of the year 1907-08, the Public Prosecutor's Office told the Minister of State that the "evil of the cabaret is the most hideous wound eating at the body of society"[19] and that restaurants and public houses with waitresses were clandestine brothels (ANLux J 64/39: 412). The new law passed in late 1908 limited the number of such establishments and also provided stricter requirements for foreign landlords, who now had to prove residence in the Grand Duchy for at least five years in order to be able to open a public house (see Mémorial 1908).[20] A nationwide regulation of waitress service was not adopted, though. The local level remained in charge of overseeing and setting up brothels, for safeguarding morals, safety and public peace (see Mémorial 1843). And the inconsistent municipal ordinances (which only existed in the Minette basin and the capital city) regulating women serving tables in the public houses, hotels and restaurants also remained in effect, even though they were held to be inefficient. Thus the problem of prostitution in hostess bars remained largely unresolved for the general public.

However, inns and public houses were ambivalent spaces, not considered exclusively immoral. The *Verein für Volks- und Schulhygiene* for instance emphasized

---

18 | Personal translation of: "[...] ces femmes en majeure partie étrangère"; "Un grand nombre de ces filles jouissaient d'une mauvaise réputation morale ou ont déjà subi des condamnations du chef de prostitution ou pour [...] maladie vénérienne."

19 | Personal translation of: "Le mal du cabaret est la plaie la plus hideuse qui ronge le corps social."

20 | Fayot (1979: 29) holds industrialization responsible for the large number of public houses and rampant alcoholism. This is supported by the spatial concentration of public houses: in 1897, 64 % of the total of 2,856 public houses were located in the canton of Esch. This would equal 56 residents per public house.

a desire to protect "honest landlords against [...] unfair, damnable competition [...] in the fight against the unhealthy excesses of the catering trade"[21] (Pier/Meyers 1910a: 21). Even the popular *Obermosel-Zeitung* in Grevenmacher made a passionate plea for the pub as the people's 'reception room' in 1906:

"At the public house, workers discuss their common interests, the tradesman and the farmer hear of new experiences and goals, the merchant learns what the public would like. [...] The public house is a democratic institution *par excellence*. All classes of the population meet there [...]. The public house thus promotes relations amongst the various classes which are becoming more necessary to the existence of a commendable society"[22] (ANLux J 64/14).

As regards the construction of im-/moral spaces, it is significant that both public and private spheres represent gendered conceptions. Along with regionalization and the dichotomy between the familiar and the foreign, the gendering of public and private forms another dimension in the process of constructing im-/moral spaces. This also aids in understanding the ambivalent position of the public house as a space that is at once social, democratic and morally two-faced.

Nevertheless, the relationship between public and private is complicated, as is the gendering of this relationship. This distinction was crucial to the bourgeois societies of the nineteenth century (see Hausen 1992), which excluded women from public life on pseudoscientific grounds, associating them with private, intimate and family matters (see Krause 2003: 25). The constitution of a public sphere in which men as citizens consort with one another politically and economically but to which women have no legal access is thus itself an expression of gender relations. Gendered power relations are thereby naturalized, normalized and made invisible. Although the separation between a familial private sphere with feminine connotations and public (gainful) activity with masculine connotations became a reality in nineteenth-century bourgeois families at best, the gendered dichotomy of public/private represents nevertheless an important perceptual structure of the social. It produces an interpretation of women's actions – in contrast to their actual public presence – that is different (e.g., unseemly, apolitical etc.) than similar actions of men (see Lang 1995: 83). When it comes to prostitution policies, the state does not restrict itself to setting a framework, as in other areas of

---

21 | Personal translation of: "Beim Kampfe gegen ungesunde Auswüchse des Wirtegewerbes [...]" [die] "[...] ehrlichen Wirte" [schützen zu wollen] "gegen eine unlautere, verdammenswerte Konkurrenz."

22 | Personal translation of: "Im Wirtshause besprechen die Arbeiter ihre gemeinsamen Interessen, hört der Handwerker und der Bauer von neuen Erfahrungen und Zielen, erfährt der Kaufmann manche Wünsche des Publikums. [...] Das Wirtshaus ist eine demokratische Einrichtung *par excellence*. In ihm berühren sich alle Stände der Bevölkerung [...]. Das Wirtshaus vermittelt also Beziehungen der einzelnen Stände untereinander, die zum guten Bestehen der Gesellschaft [...] notwendiger werden."

policy, but intervenes directly in the boundaries between public and private. This particularly affects the ability of prostitutes to safeguard their privacy in the face of state policies that directly control their bodies and pathologize their personalities (see Kontos 2009: 234). Historically, such policies were strongly guided by the norm of bourgeois gender relationships and endeavoured to include the proletariat in such gender arrangements (see ibid.: 240).

In Luxembourg, as well, the problematization of prostitution targeted primarily suspicious women – such as waitresses. The clients were almost entirely ignored by officials and the general public. In 1910, the *Verein für Volks- und Schulhygiene* wrote in regard of the spread of venereal diseases through prostitution:

"From 1898 to 1908 inclusive, 110 female persons in this country were sequestrated by the police due to venereal disease [...]. In the two years 1909 and 1910 [...] 61 + 21 = 82 venereally diseased [...]. We cannot know how large is the number of male persons who were infected by these sources of contagion, how many illnesses, how much misery this brought to how many families"[23] (Pier/Meyers 1910b: 25).

Although men were regarded as a part of the activity of prostitution, it was as a matter of course assumed here that men were infected by the "sources of contagion", that is to say, played a passive role and were certainly not actively involved in passing on diseases to prostitutes. Whether the "misery" refers only to the man's illness, or also to its potential to be passed on to wives and family members, remains implicit.

In 1908, the Hollerich police made an issue of the role of clients with regard to prosecution:

"It is also immensely difficult to find witnesses in order to initiate proceedings against the landlords for running a house of ill repute without permission, because the very same usually turn out to be persons from the upper classes and married, and they all maintain the greatest reserve in their testimonies, even to the point of denying everything to the investigating officers and even the courts, in order to avoid a conjugal scandal"[24] (ANLux J 64/39: 390).

---

23 | Personal translation of: "In den Jahren 1898 bis 1908 einschliesslich wurden hierlands 110 weibliche Personen wegen Geschlechtskrankheiten polizeilich sequestriert [...]. In den beiden Jahren 1909 und 1910 [...] 61 + 21 = 82 Geschlechtskranke [...]. Wie gross die Zahl der männlichen Personen ist, die durch diese Ansteckungsherde infiziert wurden, wieviel Krankheiten, wieviel Elend dadurch in viele Familien gebracht wurde, entzieht sich unserer Kenntnis."

24 | Personal translation of: "Auch ist das Feststellen von Zeugen, um das Verfahren wegen Haltens einer Unzuchtstätte ohne Ermächtigung gegen den Wirt einleiten zu können, eine ungemein schwierige Sache, indem dieselbe sich gewöhnlich aus Personen besserer Stände, und Verheiratheten herausstellen, und sie in ihren Aussagen die grösste

While it is still possible to discern the police's regret in these lines that clandestine prostitution usually remained unpunished due to male reticence to testify, the statements of the public prosecutor in Luxembourg City have an altogether more understanding tone:

"The testimony of persons who are only occasionally involved in such affairs, in a momentary neglect of duty, is detrimental to their reputation and brings unrest and discord into families in such a way that one might ask if the means be not worse than the evil"[25] (ANLux J 64/39: 197).

Prostitution appears to disrupt the bourgeois model of the gendered separation between public and private in that prostitution and sexuality are publicly established and embedded in a market-based economy (see Schulte 1979: 17). Hence, focusing on the prostitutes on the one hand and not pursuing the clients on the other upends the gendering of public and private space. As long as it was primarily men who were pursuing their political and economic interests in the public house, it remained intact as a public space in which the bourgeois order of the sexes was upheld. The presence of waitresses and prostitutes, by contrast, transformed it into an immoral space. Here the immorality is primarily imputed to the prostitutes whereas the behaviour of the clients is tolerated – also by certain authorities – with reference to the protection of their privacy.

3.2.2 Power Logics of Spatial Construction

Now that we have so far identified three dimensions of the construction of spaces of im-/morality, we shall turn to the power relationships inherent in them. Prostitution in the Grand Duchy is connected to sovereignty through the distinction between what is permitted and what is forbidden, it constitutes a statutory offence. From the point of view of disciplinary logic, the prostitute is a delinquent subject. From the perspective of governmental logic, prostitution presents a safety risk, since it spreads venereal diseases through the population.

My further discussion will primarily concern the relationship of the various power logics to one another, since it can be assumed that prostitution policies do not follow a single logic. This manifests itself in the above-mentioned demand of the *Collège Médical* that prostitution be regulated in order to prevent venereal

---

Zurückhaltung bewahren, ja geradezu, um einen Ehescandal zu vermeiden, alles sowohl vor dem untersuchenden Beamten, wie auch vor Gericht in Abrede stellen."

25 | Personal translation of: "Les témoignages de personnes mêlées à des affaires de ce genre par occasion et dans un moment d'oubli de leurs devoirs, ternissent des réputations et portent le trouble et la discorde dans les familles, de sorte que l'on peut se demander si le remède n'est pas pire que le mal."

diseases and improve the 'quality'[26] of the population. A regulatory system which forces prostitutes to be controlled by the police and by doctors corresponds to a 'disciplinary regime' (Kontos 2009: 260). However, this is not an end in itself, since the intention is to protect the population from venereal diseases. To this extent, regulating prostitution is a biopolitical goal (see Foucault 2003 [1997]: 239ff.) which follows the governmental power logic of the security dispositif.

In the first part of this paper, the process of distinguishing between the familiar and the foreign, or between the national and the foreign, was highlighted as a dimension of the construction of im-/moral spaces. It is therefore not surprising that administrative measures – especially deportation – taken by the immigration police play a major part. The Aliens Police Act 1913 defined the practice or promotion of prostitution as a "danger to public safety and order" (Mémorial 1913), so that the expulsion of suspicious foreigners – mostly women – became an integral part of prostitution policy. The practice of deportation can first be characterized as a connection between a sovereign and a disciplinary logic of power: the sovereign state uses police as a means to restore the integrity of the territory. However, a governmental logic also comes to bear in the practice of expulsion in the form of a security dispositif in that the authorities work with a logic of suspicion when exercising it. This logic is intended to minimize risks by identifying dangerous – that is, potentially delinquent – subjects. Hence we read in a police report in Esch/Alzette, for instance, that

"A. is cohabiting with the foreigner S. in B., a local tavern. A. spends nearly the whole day with the guests in the tavern of her lessor. Her pimp [S.] works very little and [therefore] the two cohabitors can have no other source of income than what A. earns through professional prostitution"[27] (ANLux: Police des Étrangers No. 84003 1913).

Based on this suspicion, the authorities revoked A.'s residence permit for the Grand Duchy. This paved the way for deportation without requiring definitive evidence. In 1913, the police in Hollerich wrote:

"The same is under strong suspicion of engaging in professional prostitution and can be seen wandering about for this purpose almost every evening in the streets near the local train station, as well as in the notorious Italian taverns. However, it has not yet been

---

26 | At that time, ideas of the 'degeneration' of society included notions that sexual misconduct not only compromised individuals, but also resulted in effects on the population (for example, on the genetic make-up, criminality etc.) (see Foucault 2003: 252f.).

27 | Personal translation of: "A. in der hiesigen Schenke B. mit dem Ausländer S. in wilder Ehe lebt. A. treibt sich fast den ganzen Tag in der Schenke ihres Wohnungsgebers mit Gästen umher. Ihr Zuhälter arbeitet sehr wenig und [somit] können die beiden Konkubinaten keine andere Erwerbsquelle haben, als dem [sic] Verdienst der A. durch die gewerbsmässige Prostitution."

possible to convict the same of prostitution"[28] (ANLux: Police des Étrangers No. 85665 1913).

The construction of the risk, of the dangerous milieu, or of the prostitutes as a threatening subject, is directly related to the space constructions outlined above. The 'proof' of prostitution, or of the construction of the prostitute as a delinquent subject in need of deportation, is essentially based on their association with spaces connoted as immoral, such as public houses and especially the hostess bars. Spending time in an area 'of ill repute' creates an identity as a prostitute in the eyes of the police and must accordingly be understood as a subjectification process (see Chapter 5.1). At the same time, these power logics are highly gendered: female prostitutes are the ones being identified with these immoral spaces, while the clients' identity remains undetermined, since they – as already quoted – only participate occasionally, in a "momentary negligence of duty."

The initiatives of the moral social purity and abstinence movements, which were closely allied with the elites in state and society and demanded tougher control mechanisms for law enforcement, remained at first firmly committed to sovereign-disciplinary power logics. At the same time, they urgently called for a moral self-guidance of individuals. Both aspects must be understood in their gendered dimensions. The abstinence movement[29], the *Verein für Volks- und Schulhygiene* (Society for People's and School Hygiene), as well as the above-mentioned campaign of the *Catholic Women's Association* demanded from the government primarily measures against the waitresses – some flanked by provisions for the (male or female) operators of public houses. No demands were made for punishment of the clients nor for tougher controls on the male patrons of public houses. At the same time, considerations regarding moral self-conduct were focused on bourgeois gender norms, on the feminine connotation of the private sphere of the family and intimacy, and thus particularly on women: "A woman [...] knows how to make hearth and home a place of happiness and peace, whither a man likes to return from the office, workshop or factory, and where he will enjoy spending his time"[30] (*Das Volkswohl* 1903: 91). So if a woman constitutes

---

28 | Personal translation of: "Dieselbe steht dringend unter dem Verdachte die erwerbsmässige Prostitution auszuüben, und kann man selbe fast allabendlich zu diesem Zwecke sich in den Strassen an hiesigem Bahnhof, sowie in den berüchtigten Italienerkneipen herumtreiben sehen. Selbe konnte jedoch bis dato der erwerbsmässigen Prostitution nicht überführt werden."

29 | The *Verein gegen den Mißbrauch der geistigen Getränke* (Society Against the Abuse of Alcoholic Liquors) published the journal *Das Volkswohl* (The People's Welfare) and was especially active against the hostess bars.

30 | Personal translation of: "Die Frau [...] versteht es, aus dem heimatlichen Herd den Ort des Glückes und des Friedens zu machen, wohin der Mann aus dem Büreau, aus der Werkstatt, aus der Fabrik gerne heimkehrt, wo er gerne verweilt."

herself as a housewifely subject and comprehends the related reproductive practices (cooking, washing, cleaning) as the tasks she is to fulfil, she would be able to fashion her home as a "place of happiness" for her husband. In this perspective, not only is the conjugal household imagined to be a place of morality, but rather the woman should at the same time be able through her self-conduct to keep her husband from entering immoral spaces which could corrupt him with alcohol and prostitution, such as the hostess bars. The *Verein für Volks- und Schulhygiene* also defined the "founding of housekeeping and cookery schools, so that a young woman may know how to make a man's home attractive for him"[31] (Pier/Meyers 1910b: 26) as a preventive component in its battle against the hostess bars. Although an examination of living conditions amongst the Luxembourg working class by the *Verein für die Interessen der Frau* (Association for the Interests of Women) referred to the house as the "quintessential domain"[32] of a woman, the association nonetheless emphasized that poverty could prevent successful self-government. The result of the "housing misery", it said, was that

"[...] even the most capable woman [can] create no 'home' here despite the best of intentions. The man will prefer to spend his evenings at the public house rather than in such rooms, children will prefer to play on the street – and the feeling of home and the sense of family are destroyed"[33] (*Verein für die Interessen der Frau* 1907: 4).

Due to living in confined spaces and taking on male boarders, the morals of the children are at the same time "extremely endangered at the tenderest age"[34] (ibid.). Thus it can also be established that governmental self-conduct and subjectivation techniques (see Chapter 5.1) are closely related to the dimension of the gendered separation of public and private. Since women were directly encouraged to practise self-conduct but men only indirectly, we can speak of a gendered intensification of this power logic. This in turn raises the question of whether men at that time were considered as being at all capable of self-conduct since, as shown above, they were supposed to need the self-conduct of women and the creation of a home to keep them from going to immoral places. At the same time, it is remarkable that men were not generally made the target of disciplinary or legal action.

Finally, a case study shows that women accused of prostitution also bring their moral self-conduct into play towards the authorities in order to avoid being

---

31 | Personal translation of: "[...] Gründung von Haushaltungsschulen und Kochschulen, damit die junge Frau es verstehe, dem Manne sein Heim anziehend zu gestalten."

32 | Personal translation of: "[...] ureigenste Domäne."

33 | Personal translation of: "Wohnungselend" [...] "[...] auch die tüchtigste Frau trotz besten Willens hier kein 'Heim' schaffen [kann]. Der Mann wird seine Abende lieber im Wirtshaus zubringen als in solchen Räumen, die Kinder werden lieber auf der Strasse spielen – und Heimgefühl und Familiensinn werden vernichtet."

34 | Personal translation of: "[...] im zartesten Alter schon schwer gefährdet."

subjected to the legal-disciplinary action of deportation. They often point out that they have not violated the law of the land during their stay in Luxembourg. For instance, Else G. argues in a petition to the Public Prosecutor's Office in February 1915[35] that she had

"[...] lived for nearly six years in Luxembourg without having done anything wrong. [...] I have come to love the Luxembourg countryside very much during my many years there. [...] I neither worked in a café, nor did I cohabit with anyone. I came to live in the Poststrasse because I was running an Épicerie [grocer's shop] there and [...] I only remained nearby because I did not like to foray too far with my many belongings"[36] (ANLux: Police des Étrangers No. 30305 1915).

Else G. refers directly to a spatializing official practice of localizing prostitution in bars and cafés, as well as certain urban problem areas. In attempting to prove her moral self-conduct by mentioning her conformity to the law and her business activity, she hoped to be able to avoid being associated with these immoral spaces and thus being deported, despite the proximity of her place of residence to the aforementioned cafés. The authorities did not agree with her argumentation, however, and expelled Else G. in the spring of 1915 – quite in accord with the governmental logic of suspicion.

3.2.3 Conclusion

This paper shows, based on the example of the problematization of prostitution in Luxembourg c. 1900, that the construction of im-/moral spaces comprises several dimensions: a distinction between the national and the foreign, a regionalization and a gendering of public and private.

These dimensions of space construction take effect in processes of drawing boundaries and are at the same time permeated by power relationships. Although it is easy to identify certain asymmetries of power with regard to those involved in the problematization of prostitution and the actors affected by it, we were here

---

35 | While Luxembourg was occupied by German troops, the Luxembourg authorities were still in charge of civil administration (see Trausch 2002). This did not result in any noteworthy changes to prostitution policies – in contrast to occupied Belgium, for instance (see Majerus 2003).

36 | Personal translation of: "[...] fast 6 Jahre in Luxembourg gelebt, ohne mir auch noch das Geringste zu Schulden kommen zu lassen. [...] Das Luxembourger Land ist mir durch meinen langjährigen Aufenthalt dort [...] sehr lieb geworden [...]. Ich war weder in einem Café beschäftigt, noch habe ich in wilder Ehe mit jemand gelebt, dass ich in der Poststrasse wohnte, kam daher, dass ich eine Episerie [Lebensmittelgeschäft] dort führte und [...] blieb ich nur deshalb in der Nähe wohnen, weil ich mit meinen vielen Sachen nicht gern weit geplündert bin."

less concerned with the question of who possesses power and who lacks it. Rather, the question relevant to this investigation was, in the Foucauldian sense (Foucault 1983 [1982]: 216): how is power exercised? Using the power analysis outlined at the beginning of this chapter we could show that the various power logics of sovereignty, discipline and governmentality are intermeshed with one another in the spatial constructions related to the problematization of prostitution: the deportation of foreign prostitutes was an administrative practice which can first be understood as the interplay of sovereign and disciplinary power logic to secure and control the territory. At the same time, it is essentially based on a security dispositif, the logic of suspicion. The extent to which this intermeshing is a direct result of difficulties in the criminal prosecution of prostitution, which in turn refers to the explosive power of prostitution with regard to the gendering of public and private spaces, will have to be left for other studies to examine. In addition, it becomes clear that the spatial constructions, as well as the function and mode of operation of the power logics, have to be understood as gendered. Hence primarily women are deported on suspicion of prostitution. This is shown both by the absolute figures as well as the fact that prostitution accounted for more than fifty percent of the reasons for the expulsion of women throughout the period under review, while this proportion among men is inconsequential.[37] The dimensions of the drawing of boundaries between the national and the foreign, as well as the regionalization described above, lead to the formation of gendered identities, so that 'the foreign waitress' becomes the prototypical prostitute. Finally, the governmental techniques of self-conduct concentrate on female self-conduct, which is then indirectly supposed to keep men from entering immoral spaces. This power logic refers to the importance of the gendered separation of public and private in maintaining the bourgeois order in general, and in constructing spaces of im-/morality in particular.

Sources

Luxembourg National Archives

ANLux J 64/14 Revision du régime des cabarets, 1900-1912 (dossier).
ANLux J 64/39 Prostitution: rapports; reglements; propositions..., 1907-1917 (dossier).
ANLux J 71/1-J71/27 Police des étrangers – expulsions et renvois, interdiction (1881-1918).
ANLux Police des Étrangers No. 30305 (Else G.), 1915.
ANLux Police des Étrangers No. 84003 (Louise A.), 1913.
ANLux Police des Étrangers No. 85665 (Angèle T.), 1913.

---

37 | These data are based on my own statistical evaluations of the deportation orders (ANLux J 71/1-J71/27 (1881-1918)).

Luxembourg City Archives

AVL LU 11 - IV/2 447 Police amusements, cabarets et spectacles, 1891.

Luxembourg National Library

Chambre des députés (1907): Compte-Rendu des Séances de la Chambre des Députés du Grand-Duché de Luxembourg. 1907-1908, Luxembourg: Chambre des députés.

Collège Médical (1908): "Situation Sanitaire du Grand-Duché de Luxembourg pendant l'année 1907", in: Annexe au Mémorial A n° 61 de 1908.

Das Volkswohl. Organ des Luxembourger Vereins gegen den Alkoholismus (1903): "Der Alkohol und die Frau", edition of June 1903, 88-92.

Das Volkswohl. Organ des Luxembourger Vereins gegen den Alkoholismus (1911): "Die Animierkneipen in Luxembourg", edition of January-July 1911, 23f.

Luxemburger Wort (1904a): "Mehr als Schmutzkonkurrenz", edition of 12.3.1904, 2.

Luxemburger Wort (1904b): "Verschiedene Nachrichten", edition of 26.3.1904, 2.

Mémorial A Nr. 17 (1843): "Gesetz über die Einrichtung der Gemeinden und Distrikte vom 24. Februar 1843".

Mémorial A Nr. 17 (1855): Arrêté royal grand-ducal du 14 mai 1855 et règlement du 5 juin suivant, concernant les maisons de débauche et les personnes qui se livrent à la prostitution.

Mémorial A Nr. 49 (1913): "Gesetz vom 18. Juli 1913, über die Fremdenpolizei".

Mémorial A Nr. 76 (1908): "Gesetz vom 26. Dezember 1908, über die Schankwirtschaften".

Pier, J.P./Meyers, Michel (1910a): "Animierkneipen", in: Verhandlungen des Vereins für Volks- und Schulhygiene während des Vereinsjahres 1910, 20-21.

Pier, J.P./Meyers, Michel (1910b): "Die Animierkneipen", in: Verhandlungen des Vereins für Volks- und Schulhygiene während des Vereinsjahres 1910, 22-30.

Verein für die Interessen der Frau/Verein für Volks- und Schulhygiene (1907): Einiges über Wohnungsverhältnisse der ärmeren Arbeiterbevölkerung in Luxembourg. Luxembourg: M. Huss.

3.3 CASTLES AS INSTRUMENTS OF HEGEMONIAL SPACE CONSTRUCTION AND REPRESENTATION. THE EXAMPLE OF THE COUNTY OF VIANDEN

Bernhard Kreutz

Over the past twenty years, medieval research has rediscovered the castle as a subject of study. It has broken away from the older, often purely architectural or military-historical perspective (see for example, Piper 1912; Ebhardt 1939-1958) and begun to pose new questions related to cultural history and even sociology. This was initiated primarily by Joachim Zeune's study that carried the programmatic title *Burgen. Symbole der Macht. Ein neues Bild der mittelalterlichen Burg (Castles. Symbols of Power. A New View of the Medieval Castle)* (1995).

Recent research describes the medieval and early modern castle as a 'multifunctional structure'. It served as both fortification and residential complex, fulfilling military functions and at the same time acting as the home of a lord and his family, soldiers and servants. In its function as a military base, the castle served to control transport routes and borders. It was a weapons arsenal and a prison, as well as an administrative and judicial centre. Finally, a castle was a place to collect and store the levies demanded by the lord, such as grain, wine, wool and, not least, money. However, castles also had a significant representative function. This applied to their interior design as a stage for courtly culture, as it did to their exterior appearance as a symbol of power visible from afar, dominating the surroundings also in a visual sense (see Zeune 1995: 34ff. and 171ff.; Burger 2010: 72ff.; Hope 2010: 197ff.; Ehlert 2010: 144ff.). The castle thus played a part in medieval aristocratic rule similar to that described by Michel Foucault for the metropolis as a centre of the territorial state in the seventeenth and eighteenth centuries (see Foucault 2007 [2004]: 12ff.).

Against this background and from the viewpoint of the Foucauldian concept of sovereignty (see ibid.: 11ff.), we shall now examine the functions exercised by castles in the system of rule in medieval and early modern times, exemplified by the County of Vianden in the Grand-Duchy of Luxembourg. How did these functions reflect in the architecture of a castle? What social practices, emanating from and centred on the castle, were used to constitute a sovereign space? How did castles mark the boundaries of this space? And finally, how did castles represent feudal rule and how did they contribute to conceptions of aristocratic identity? The Vianden records in the *Luxembourg National Archives* (ANLux) and the *Koninklijk Huisarchief* (Royal Archives) in The Hague (KHA) were evaluated under these aspects along with sources already published.

Apart from the eponymous seat of the Counts of Vianden in today's Grand Duchy of Luxembourg, a total of fifteen additional castles can be found in the Eifel-Ardennes region, which the House of Vianden put to various uses in their reign until their demise in the French Revolution. These castles or their ruins are located in modern Luxembourg (not only in Vianden, but also in Brandenburg, Fels/Larochette, Klerf/Clervaux and Schengen), in Belgium (St. Vith, Bütgenbach, Salm and Sterpenich) and in Germany (Dasburg, Neuerburg, Hamm, Dudeldorf, Schönecken, Neuenstein and Schleiden) (see Fig. 2).

3.3.1 Functions and Architecture: The Example of Vianden Castle

We will take a closer look at Vianden Castle to exemplify the functions of the castle in the counts' system of rule. This also includes examining the effects which the different functions had on the architectural design of the castle during the various building phases (see Zimmer 1996: 262ff. and 2010: 96ff. on the history of the castle's construction).

As early as the mid-fourth century AD, the Romans built a watchtower, surrounded by a square wall, on the Vianden spur above the river Our. The building served to keep watch on the Our Valley and control a river crossing (see Hunold 2011: 359). Around the year 1000 the first medieval stone fortification was erected on this site. It had a curtain wall with an oval layout, containing a hall (*aula*) and a square-shaped chapel. The owners and builders were the lords of Hamm on the Prüm in the western Eifel. They held office as stewards[38] of Prüm Abbey in the eleventh century, responsible for the abbey's secular affairs. As laymen, it was the stewards' task to implement those disciplinary mechanisms among the abbey's subjects which the monks themselves, as clerics, were not permitted to carry out (see Foucault 2007 [2004]: 6ff.). This included administering justice, collecting debts and providing military protection (see Huyghebaert 1984: 34ff.). Apart from controlling the crossing on the Our, the fortification in Vianden was now also used to govern and control the surrounding territory.

---

38 | The historical German term used here is that of *Vogt*. "The terms 'Vogt' and 'Vogtei' originate from the Latin *advocatus, advocatia*. They refer to a wide range of institutions. What the various connotations have in common is the fact that individual persons acted on behalf of a third party or at least on formal authorization, exercising power, organizing administration, collecting taxes, presiding over a court of law or taking over legal representation in a trial [...] The *Vogt* was a layman who represented a cleric, a church, a cloister or a monastery in secular affairs, particularly in court, and administered church property." Personal translation of: "Den Begriffen 'Vogt' und 'Vogtei' liegen lat. advocatus, advocatia zugrunde. Sie bezeichnen eine breite Palette von Institutionen. Gemeinsam ist den unterschiedl. Begriffsinhalten die Tatsache, daß Personen im Auftrag – oder zumindest formal beauftragt – Herrschaft ausübten, Verwaltung organisierten, Abgaben einzogen, Gericht hielten oder bei Prozessen die rechtl. Vertretung übernahmen. [...] Der V. war ein Laie, der einen Geistl., eine Kirche, ein Kl. oder ein Stift in weltl. Angelegenheiten vertrat, v.a. vor Gericht, und das Kirchengut verwaltete." (see H.-J. Schmidt 2003, LexMa, vol. VIII: col. 1811-1814)

Towards the end of the eleventh century, the lords of Hamm moved their residence to their new castle above the Our. From then on, they called themselves Counts of Vianden after their new residence (see Beyer 1860: 447, No. 390). This incisive change was also reflected in the architectural design of the castle. A square keep, serving as a residential tower, was built in the northern part of the structure. The castle remained the counts' residence for around three hundred years (see Margue 2012: 1562ff.). Like the main city of a territory, the castle now also added aesthetic and symbolic purposes to its political and economic functions (see Foucault 2007 [2004]: 14). In the course of the following roughly 150 years the complex was expanded into a monumental, prestigious seat.

The first step was taken around 1170, when the square chapel was replaced by a two-storey, decagonal central structure. Around 1200, Vianden Castle reached its greatest extent. A large, prestigious *palas*[39] was added to the northeast side, to be used for receptions and celebrations. A majestic gallery with large, cloverleaf windows was constructed connecting the new *palas* and the chapel. In the mid-thirteenth century, finally, all the buildings were furnished with high roofs and stepped gables in the Gothic style. The castle retained this late medieval state of construction essentially until its demolishment in the 1820s (see Milmeister 2003: 261ff.) and was restored to this former state in the twentieth century.

The County of Vianden was inherited by the Counts of Nassau in 1417. They did not reside at Vianden, however, but in the Netherlands. Having lost its function as a residence, the castle continued to serve an important function in territorial rule. It became the seat of a district magistrate who performed governmental functions for the absentee counts. The halls in the *palas* were now used as grain store, weapons arsenal and powder magazine (KHA, C2, No. 72).

Starting with the Roman hill fort intended to keep watch over the Our crossing, from the turn of the millennium on, the medieval castle in Vianden constantly acquired new functions and was redesigned accordingly. While the first *aula* was still used by the stewards of Prüm for judicial purposes, once these had taken up permanent residence in Vianden, the castle was redesigned successively, until the mid-thirteenth century, into an ostentatious building of the ruling nobility. After losing its residential function in 1417 the castle remained frozen, as it were, in its late medieval state of construction. From then on, the building was used as an administrative castle with only minor additions being made to it (see Zimmer 1996: 401f.).

---

39 | A *palas* (Lat. *palatium*) is "a residential hall of a medieval German palace or castle. The *palas* houses the ceremonial rooms in one, or more often two storeys above a partly deepened basement, initially in royal and episcopal palaces, and since the 10th century also in castles." Personal translation of: "Wohn- und Saalbau einer ma. Pfalz oder Burg in Dtl. Der P. beherbergt die Repräsentationsräume in einem oder zumindest zwei Geschossen über einem teilw. eingetieften Untergeschoß, zunächst in kgl. und bfl. Pfalzen, seit dem 10. Jh. auch in Burgen" (see G. Binding 2003, LexMa, vol. VI: col. 1631f.).

3. Constructions of Space and Identity Created by Institutional Practices

Figure 1: Vianden Castle after restoration. The chapel can be seen beneath the ridge turret, next to it the gallery with its four cloverleaf windows, at left in the background the palas with the stepped gables (photo: Jengel)

3.3.2 Spatial Construction and Boundaries

As an administrative castle, Vianden Castle continued to be the centre of rule in the county even after 1417 (see Meyer 2010: 18ff.; Burger 2010: 72ff.; Mersiowsky 2010: 126f.). Apart from Vianden, the rule of the counts was built upon three other administrative castles. Since the late Middle Ages, the county also comprised the fiefdom of Dasburg on the northern border, today a part of the German West Eifel, as well as the fiefdoms of St. Vith and Bütgenbach, now in Belgium. In each of these four territories the eponymous castle was the seat of a district magistrate and the centre of the system of rule.

The earliest evidence of Dasburg being owned by the Counts of Vianden dates from 1222. The castle, the appurtenant village and the surrounding country to the north with 34 villages formed the dominion of Dasburg (see Milmeister 2003: 67ff.). A castellan is first mentioned as governor of the count in Dasburg in 1399 (ANLux, LV, No. 192). In 1380, Count Simon of Sponheim-Vianden was able to secure the castles and dominions of St. Vith and Bütgenbach in the Ardennes for the County of Vianden for good (see Mötsch 1993). A governor at St. Vith Castle is documented for the first time in 1388 (ANLux, LV, No. 114). From 1403 onwards this governor was also in charge of Bütgenbach (see Milmeister 1993: 95). Except for Dasburg, which was a fiefdom of the Abbot of Prüm, the Vianden dominions were under the suzerainty of Luxembourg. This applied to the County of Vianden proper from 1269, and to St. Vith and Bütgenbach from 1380 (see Margue 2012: 1566f.; Mötsch 1993: 268f.). However, there is no evidence that the suzerainty of Prüm and Luxembourg, and the implications resulting from it under feudal law, had any direct effects on the everyday life and the relations between the count's office-holders and subjects inside the Vianden territories.

The administrative castles of Vianden, Dasburg, St. Vith and Bütgenbach were the backbone of the territorial sovereignty of Vianden until the county's dissolution in 1795. They formed a chain running from south to north along the Our. Several villages were assigned to and governed by each of the four administrative castles. The collection of the manorial rents, both monetary and in kind, was the hegemonic practice which most strongly affected the everyday life of the population.

The counts' territorial dominions were divided up into sub-districts (feudal estates) with several villages assigned to each, along with agricultural properties and common rights to forestry, grazing and hunting. The administrators of the feudal estates, the stewards, were responsible for collecting the tributes from the peasants in the villages of their district. The stewards were directly subject to their superior, the district magistrate, whose seat was the respective administrative castle. There were seven estates in the County of Vianden proper: Lahr, Nussbaum, Geckler, Mettendorf, Karlshausen, Geichlingen and Krauthausen, with a total of 38 villages (KHA C2, No. 66). The fiefdom of Dasburg included the estates of Eschfeld, Daleiden and Leidenborn, with a total of 34 villages (see Vannérus 1928: 94f.). The seven estates of Weiswampach, Neundorf, Recht, Amel, Büllingen, Bütgenbach und Pronsfeld, with a joint total of 64 villages, were governed from the administrative castles of St. Vith und Bütgenbach (see Vannérus 1928: 97ff.).

A list of properties and revenues compiled in 1615 by Philip William, Prince of Orange, provides an insight into the organization of the manorial system in Vianden (KHA C2, No. 66). Owing to the armed conflicts between the House of Orange-Nassau and the Spanish Habsburgs in the Netherlands, which had been affecting the County of Vianden since 1567 (see Milmeister 2003: 177ff.), it seems that severe irregularities in the payment of the tributes had occurred in the previous decades. Philip William, Count of Vianden, made use of the brief period of peace during his reign from 1604 to 1618 to restore and consolidate the economic base of his rule. He had the Vianden tax collector Gilles Bouvet compile a list of tributes setting down in detail the procedure centred in the administrative Castle of Vianden (KHA C2, No. 66, f. 2r-4r).

First Bouvet summoned all seven of the county's stewards to the castle, where they were asked to provide information under oath concerning the number and size of the taxable farms, as well as the amount of all monetary fees and rents in kind in their districts. This information would then be compared with the older records available in the castle. The stewards, however, stated that they were unable to do so. Even the subjects could no longer provide precise information, since the goods had in the meantime often been divided up and the payment obligations for them were also divided up amongst several persons. The tax collector responded by giving the stewards a few days' time to obtain exact information. If they were unsuccessful, he would summon the subjects individually to the castle for questioning or go to the villages himself to appraise the situation. After the deadline passed, the stewards again claimed they were unable to obtain accurate information on the amounts of the rents. Thereupon the tax collector carried out his threat and summoned all the farmers in the County of Vianden to the castle starting on 1 June 1615. After being cautioned and sworn in, each of them provided information on the size of their property and the consequent monetary fees and rents in kind. Contentious cases were clarified by mutual agreement among the farmers, stewards and the tax collector, or postponed to be decided at a later time.

The role of the stewards in these proceedings becomes apparent from their delaying tactics. They obviously did not see themselves primarily as overseers of the tax collector's interests and thus of the count's regime. Instead, they acted in the interest of the subjects, whose tax obligations they at first attempted to conceal – in their own interest, as well, since they themselves were obligated to pay taxes on the farms they owned. The farmers, probably on the advice of the stewards, accepted having to appear at Vianden Castle and disclose the size of their properties. This seemed better than having to undergo a visit by the tax collector. However, tax collector Gilles Bouvet also expressed his satisfaction. Even though the subjects may have withheld some due payments, the questioning put the taxation of the subjects on a new and – since it involved a consensus with those obligated to pay – legally firm basis. Weighing the costs against the benefits, the tax collector can be said to have achieved selective obedience from the subjects (see Foucault 2007 [2004]: 64ff.). The result of the survey of 1615 was a detailed inventory listing, in French, all 218 taxable farms in the County of Vianden, along with their owners and the individual amounts of the annual rents, divided up according to the seven estates and the appurtenant 38 individual villages.

Apart from the four administrative castles, the counts made use of additional castles, those of their relatives and branch lines in Hamm, Klerf, Salm, Schönecken and Neuerburg (see Fig. 2). The ancestors of the House of Vianden, who had been the stewards of Prüm Abbey, came from Hamm Castle in the Eifel. In the mid-thirteenth century, an independent branch of the family of the Counts of Vianden established itself in Hamm (see Milmeister 2003: 39ff.; Klein 1997: 426ff.). Another branch was founded by Count Gerhard, a brother of Frederic I of Vianden in the twelfth century. Its seat was Klerf (Clervaux) Castle on the eponymous river in the Ösling (see du Fays 1985: 39f.). In 1163, the House of Vianden acquired through marriage the castle and the County of Salm in the Ardennes, today Vielsalm in Belgium. In 1248, the Salm-Vianden branch had to recognize the suzerainty of Luxembourg (see Du Fays 1985: 26ff., 40, 83f.; Margue 2012: 1562 and 1568). The Schönecken branch of the family broke away from the House of Vianden in the course of an inheritance dispute in 1264 (see Du Fays 1985: 168ff.). One final branch line had its seat in Neuerburg in the western Eifel. Around 1230, the castle and fiefdom of Neuerburg separated from the county of Vianden and became the seat of a branch line (see ibid.: 93ff.; Margue 2012: 1567). The castles of the branch lines, to which the Counts of Vianden still had sovereign rights in some cases, formed a ring around the central area with the four administrative castles. No longer belonging to these, they marked the boundaries of the sovereign territory of Vianden proper.

A third group of castles were the vassal castles and *Offenhäuser*. These were castles over which the House of Vianden had suzerainty, in which it had proportional ownership or had a so-called *Öffnungsrecht*, meaning that the counts were able to use these castles as a military stronghold on the basis of a contractual agreement, that is, the castles were 'open' to them. At the same time, the lord of the castle was not allowed to make his castle available to any enemy of the House of Vianden (see Rödel 2010: 66f.). This third group included Brandenburg (see Wampach 1949: 313, No. 226), the castles of Fels (see Friedhoff 2013: 130f.), Dudeldorf (see Vannérus 1919: 275), Schengen (ANLux, LV, No. 335, 430, 457, 469), Sterpenich (see Vannérus 1919: 235), Schleiden (KHA C2, No. 22) and Neuenstein (ANLux, LV, No. 348). The seven vassal castles and *Offenhäuser* formed a second, wider ring around the sovereign territory of the Counts of Vianden.

In the Middle Ages, and to some extent into modern times, as well, it is not possible to identify a clearly defined territory, with linear borders and coherent laws, for the County of Vianden. The exercise of power in medieval times operated via a range of specific legal relationships that individuals entertained with their ruler. These could consist of obligations under the manorial system to provide labour and pay taxes, obligations of noble vassals under the feudal system to provide military services and aid, or obligations to open and hand over castles. The feudal rights of princes often overlapped and interfered with one another. It was non uncommon for various landlords to be represented in one village, and noble vassals frequently had several competing overlords. Hence the House of Vianden in Dasburg were vassals to the Abbots of Prüm, while their family seat of Vianden had been under the suzerainty of Luxembourg since 1269. So although the Counts of Vianden were able to use the castles of other noble lords for their own purposes, they had to open their family seat to the Counts of Luxembourg upon request (see Estgen 2009: 30ff., No. B. 26). Nonetheless, the example of the Vianden castles shows how the counts' policies by degrees produced a sovereign space. The practices of sovereignty thus here had the object to gradually create a territory (see Foucault 2007 [2004]: 11f.). The first part of this paper already showed that castles also had functions other than that of consolidating claims to a territory.

The building of Vianden Castle by the lords of Hamm c. 1000 already marked a local claim to power at the crossing over the Our. The sovereign's hold over the tax-paying villagers was greatest in the vicinity of Vianden Castle and the three additional administrative castles in Dasburg, St. Vith and Bütgenbach. It was institutionalized by the district magistrates and stewards, and stabilized through daily enforcement. The creation of written registers of tributes, as in 1615, as well as their maintenance and enforcement, made for an effective practice of sovereignty in the construction of a space. This hegemonial space was constituted by the taxable farms, the villages in which they were located and their districts. Several villages formed a feudal estate and the estates taken together in turn established an administrative district assigned to an administrative castle. The castles of the branch lines of the House of Vianden were grouped outside this immediate vicinity. They marked no clear, linear border, but probably staked out a zone within which the Counts of Vianden held a dominant position. The outer ring of vassal castles and *Offenhäuser* formed an advanced line to the south and east made up of castles which could not readily be used against the House of Vianden. They constituted a sort of secure area which Vianden could at least militarily neutralize in the event of conflict. The three different groups of castles served to varying degrees to secure the rule of the House of Vianden. The farther from the centre on the Our, the weaker the counts' power and their ability to assert it.

Figure 2: The castles of the County of Vianden (yellow: administrative castles, green: branch lines, blue: vassal castles and Offenhäuser*) (design: Bernhard Kreutz, realization: Malte Helfer)*

3.3.3 Representation and Aristocratic Identities

The first identity-establishing function of a castle for a noble family was providing a name. Many noble families named themselves after their family seat. This name was transferred to the dynasty, from there to the principality and later to the successor states. Some of these castle names are still found in the names of present-day states, such as Luxembourg, Limburg, Mecklenburg or Brandenburg. Vianden Castle also took on an identity-establishing function of this nature. After the lords of Hamm, who came from the eponymous castle on the Prüm, had settled in the new castle, they named themselves after their new seat. At the same time as the castle was being converted to a residential edifice in the late eleventh century, the sources mention a certain Gerhard of Vianden (*Gerardus de Vienna*) in 1096 (Beyer 1860: 447, No. 390).

The expansion of Vianden Castle in the twelfth and thirteenth centuries, with the aligned two-storey chapel, gallery and majestic *palas*, was modelled on Salian and Hohenstaufen imperial architecture. A typical example of this imperial type of construction is the Imperial Palace (*Kaiserpfalz*) of Goslar. Here we also find a two-storey chapel with a polygonal layout, an open gallery and a *palas* set in a line (see Knapp 2008: 55ff.). There is no evidence to suggest that the Goslar palace was the direct model for Vianden Castle. However, the similarities would have been obvious to contemporaries. The Counts of Vianden used this architectural reference to position themselves as partisans of the Hohenstaufen faction and as imperial princes of the highest rank (see Margue 2012: 1572f.).

The expansion of the castle also created the stage for the courtly culture which was an integral part of aristocratic identity in the Middle Ages. The biography of Yolanda of Vianden, written in the late thirteenth century (see Moulin 2009) provides us with a vivid picture of the kind of feasts that were held at Vianden Castle. This young daughter of Henry I, Count of Vianden and his wife Margaret refused an arranged marriage befitting her station, renounced courtly life and, against her parents' will, entered the Dominican monastery of Marienthal in 1248. In order to emphasize all that Yolanda was willing to forego, her biographer, Hermann von Veldenz, describes the courtly feasts at Vianden Castle in scintillating colours, such as the marriage of Yolanda's brother Frederic to Mathilde of Salm in 1247 (see Moulin 2009: 267ff., v. 5277-5324). Yolanda's refusal to take part in this feast and join the others in exuberant dancing marked her breach with her former aristocratic world in favour of a life of monastic poverty and humility. The author of the Yolanda epic compares the majestic Castle of Vianden to the humble monastery of Marienthal as examples of these two medieval ways of life (see Margue 2001: 106ff.).

The Vianden castles retained their function as symbolic centres of sovereignty in Foucault's sense until the county's dissolution. They were not only political and economic centres, but also the scene of the symbolic legal acts, which had a key legitimating significance for the aristocratic rule of the *Ancien Régime* (see Foucault 2007 [2004]: 11f.). This becomes clear in 1683, when John, Prince of Isenghien[40], whom Louis XIV had been able to install temporarily as Count of Vianden in his fight against William III of Orange (see Milmeister 2003: 210ff.). A detailed report of the handover of the County of Vianden to the Prince of Isenghien on 9 August 1683 has come down to us (see Bassing 1913: 1ff.). On this day, the envoys of Louis XIV, the mayor, the judges and jurymen of the City of Vianden, as well as representatives of all the estates and all the other office-holders in the county gathered at Vianden Castle. There he forbid them in future to accept instructions from William III, Count of Orange and commanded them to obey their new lord, John, Prince of Isenghien, exclusively from then on. Then he handed over the County of Vianden with the fiefdoms of Dasburg and St. Vith to the nobleman Gabriel Lefebvre of Bierbais, who was representing the absent Prince of Isenghien. The French king's envoy handed him the keys to the castle, to the *Vorstadt* (part of a city outside the city walls) and to the city itself, lit a fresh fire in one of the castle's fireplaces and symbolically gave Lefebvre, in front of the city gates, a handfull of earth representing the entire county. Then, in Vianden City Hall, he discharged all the judges, jurymen and mayors of the town and the seven stewards from their duties, only to reinstate them immediately in the name of the Prince of Isenghien. Finally, the gathering made its way to the parish church of Vianden, where Gabriel Lefebvre took an oath by proxy for the prince, vowing to rule the county in a manner agreeable to God and to safeguard the rights of the subjects. Three days later, the fiefdoms of St. Vith and Bütgenbach were handed over in a similar ceremony (KHA C2, No. 123).

Vianden Castle was used *pars pro toto* to represent the entire county at the handover. The count's office-holders were gathered at the castle and sworn to their new lord. Here a fire was lit in a fireplace for the new landlord, here he or his envoy accepted the keys to the city. John, Prince of Isenghien, however, was only able to keep his position as Count of Vianden for barely fourteen years. The Treaty of Ryswick in 1697 obliged Louis XIV to yield the occupied territories in the Low Countries. William III of Orange, now also King of England, repossessed the County of Vianden along with the fiefdoms of Dasburg, St. Vith and Bütgenbach in February of 1698 (see Milmeister 2003: 219f.).

3.3.4 Conclusion

Although Michel Foucault developed his concept of sovereignty with regard to the absolutist territorial state of the seventeenth and eighteenth centuries (Foucault 2007 [2004]: 11ff.), his ideas on techniques of domination, securing the territory, selective obedience achieved by judicial means, and power symbolism can, however, be profitably applied to the history of castles in the Middle Ages.

---

40 | Izegem in Flanders.

Using their castles as a base, the Counts of Vianden were able, in the course of the centuries, to create a hegemonial space by means of practices of sovereignty. The core area was formed along a south-north axis by the seat of Vianden and the three other administrative castles of Dasburg, St. Vith and Bütgenbach. Collection and control of the manorial rents ensured that the sovereign's hold over the residents of this region was strongest. This control was institutionally strengthened by the district magistrates and stewards. The core territory was surrounded by outlying castles of the Vianden branch lines of Schönecken, Hamm, Neuerburg, Klerf and Salm. The outermost ring was composed of the vassal castles and *Offenhäuser* of Schleiden, Neuenstein, Dudeldorf, Brandenburg, Fels, Schengen and Sterpenich. They marked an area of the counts' influence which put limitations on the ability of neighbouring, competing rulers to act against the interests of Vianden.

The residents were subject to disciplinary control in the form of hearings held at the castle on certain days, the compulsory labour the subjects had to perform there, and the summonses to determine the amounts of rents and taxes. However, the counts often achieved only selective obedience by these means. This shows up, for instance, in the double role played by the stewards who, although they were the counts' administrators, in practice also acted in the interest of the subjects and, not least, of themselves.

Finally, the castles of Vianden, and especially the family seat, were an integral part and the source of aristocratic identity models. From Vianden Castle, the name passed over to the dynasty and to the county. The houses of Nassau and Orange also added it to their many titles after 1417. The architecture of the castle embodied an imperial political programme and identified the House of Vianden as a supporter of the imperial House of Hohenstaufen. Life at Vianden Castle was described in contemporary literature as the epitome of courtly culture and as the antithesis of the monastic ideal. In the castle, aristocratic rule manifested and legitimized itself through symbolic legal acts up into modern times.

Owing to the sources, this analysis focuses primarily on the actions of the protagonists and the perspective of the aristocratic rulers and their functionaries. The compilation of the tax lists in 1615 shows, however, that the subjects even in pre-democratic systems of government were by no means mere recipients of orders. Sovereignty in the *Ancien Régime* was often a process negotiated between the rulers and the ruled, who not infrequently met as equals.

Sources

Archives Nationales du Luxembourg (ANLux), fonds LV: comté de Vianden, No. 114, 192, 335, 348, 430, 457, 469.

Bassing, Theodor (1913): Quelques documents relatifs à la prise de possession de la ville, du château, de la terre et du comté de Viandan, ainsi que des seigneuries en dépendantes, de St. Vith, Dasbourg et Butgenbach, par la Maison d'Isenghien, Luxembourg: Fr. Burg-Bourger.

Beyer, Heinrich (1974 [1860]): Urkundenbuch zur Geschichte der mittelrheinischen Territorien, Band 1: Von den ältesten Zeiten bis 1169, Aalen: Scientia-Verlag.

Estgen, Aloyse/Pauly, Michel/Pettiau, Hérold/Schroeder, Jean (2009): Die Urkunden Graf Johanns des Blinden (1310-1346), part 2: Die Urkunden aus den Archives générales du Royaume, Brüssel (= Urkunden- und Quellenbuch zur Geschichte der altluxemburgischen Territorien bis zur burgundischen Zeit, vol. 11; Publications du Cludem 22) Luxemburg: Cludem.

Koninklijk Huisarchief Den Haag (KHA), C2: Graafschap Vianden, No. 22, 66, 72, 123.

Milmeister, Jean (1993): "Inventaire de documents concernant la ville et le comté de Vianden", in: Ous der Veiner Geschicht 11, 91-101.

Moulin, Claudine (2009): Bruder Hermann von Veldenz: Leben der Gräfin Yolanda von Vianden. Textgetreue Edition des Codex Mariendalensis, (= Beiträge zur luxemburgischen Sprach und Volkskunde, vol. 36), Luxemburg: Imprimérie Centrale S.A.

Vannérus, Jules (1919): "Le premier livre de fiefs du comté de Vianden", in: Publications de la Section Historique de l'Institut Grand-Ducal de Luxembourg 59, 219-338.

Vannérus, Jules (1928): "Les biens et revenus domaniaux du comté de Vianden au XVIIe siècle", in: Publications de la Section Historique de l'Institut Grand-Ducal de Luxembourg 62, 33-158.

Wampach, Camille (1940): Urkunden- und Quellenbuch zur Geschichte der altluxemburgischen Territorien bis zur burgundischen Zeit, vol. 4 (Covering the last period of Count Henry V the Blondell's rule until his death on 24 December 1281), Luxemburg: Editions Saint-Paul.

3.4 Biogas – Power – Space. On the Construction of Energy Regions in Border Areas

Fabian Faller

The use of renewable energy sources has generally come to be recognized as a promising way to tackle some of the greatest social challenges of our time, such as climate change, issues of resource efficiency or aspects of social justice. Decentralized power generation systems are the most effective and most efficient approach to the use of renewable energy. These can be adapted flexibly to regional needs and to the respective context, and enhance regional economies. In addition, plants for generating renewable energy are less complicated and less expensive in terms of investments, planning and maintenance than large infrastructures, such as coal-fired power stations. They also require less professionalism, thereby enabling actor groups from local and regional civil society to become active in the energy sector. These aspects are directly tied to the question of the spatial effects of such processes: Which regions gain or lose? Who profits where and how from using 'green' energy?

This case study deals with a dimension of the energy debate which lies behind such questions: the processes of regionalization linked to each 'who' and 'where'. It discusses power generation from biomass, in particular biogas generation in small and medium-size plants, as is often practised in agricultural enterprises. The investigation is based on seventeen interviews with plant operators in the Grand Duchy of Luxembourg and western Rhineland-Palatinate.

Regionalization here is understood, following Benno Werlen (1999; 2007; 2010a; 2010b) and Anssi Paasi (2004 und 2011), as processes of constitution of societies and their geographies.[41] These processes include various practices of (re)productions and transformations of the 'situation' (occurrences, behaviour patterns, historical events)[42], the drawing of new borders and new cross-border relationships and thus processes of continuous, performative *borderings* (see chapter 2.1). The situation in the energy sector results from those social practices directly related to the generation and use of power. The case study therefore focuses on practices of the energy transition and how these (re)produce something 'social', whatever form it may take. This brings questions of power into view: which normalizations and territorial policies are embedded in the regionalization processes of the energy transition and how do they take effect? This question, that is how the dimensions of sovereignty and discipline relate to governmentality, is answered from a power-analytical perspective on regionalizations (see chapter 3.1).

The aim of the following analysis is to understand the creation of so-called 'energy regions' as a construct of social negotiation. Juridical forms of power and normalizations of various actors are examined, as well as how these affect the practices of the operators of biogas plants; how sovereignty and discipline are reflected in the practices of the biogas industry, how they are governmentally embodied, how energy regions are affirmatively (re)produced. In addition, energy regions will be considered as individual perceptions and bases for action, which are articulated by economic and political actors and take effect in everyday practices. In this way, normalizing patterns of the energy transition can be revealed and examined in the sense of security dispositifs (Foucault 1977) and how they constitute and reproduce themselves as a phenomenon of 'circulation' within the biogas industry.

---

41 | These geographies are the result of, and precondition for, individual as well as collective actions and interpretations, negotiation processes and practices.
42 | On the concept of 'situation', see chapter 2.1, which refers to Goffman (1974).

3.4.1 Spatial Policies and Normalizations of the Energy Transition in the Border Area of Luxembourg and Rhineland-Palatinate

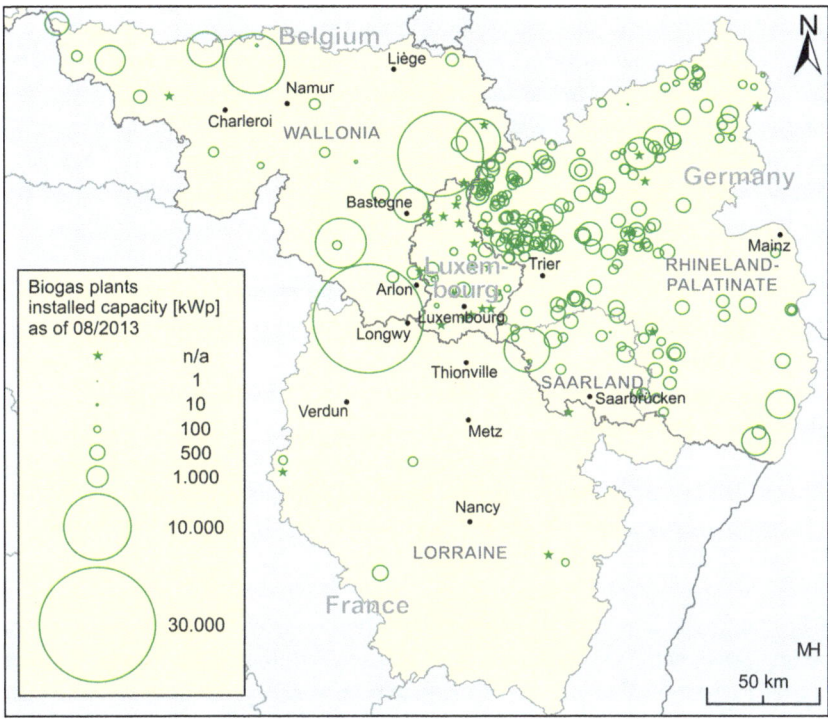

Figure 1: Locations of biogas plants in the Greater Region (design: Fabian Faller, realization: Malte Helfer)

The territorial point of departure for the case study's research context is the so-called Greater Region.[43] In September 2013, there were 266 biogas plants in this area with a generating capacity of roughly 420 MW_{el}.[44,45] Plants in Wallonia and Lorraine generate

---

[43] | The Greater Region has been in existence since 1998 and its objective is the collaboration of institutional actors in Saarland, Rhineland-Palatinate, Luxembourg, Lorraine and Wallonia (see http://www.granderegion.net, accessed 19.09.2013; Wille 2012: 106ff.).

[44] | As of 19.09.2013, data: Länderarbeitskreis Energiebilanzen RLP (2013); Statistisches Landesamt Rhineland-Pfalz (2013); Institut national de la statistique et des études économiques du Grand-Duché du Luxembourg (STATEC) (2013); Institut wallon de l'évaluation, de la prospective et de la statistique (IWEPS) (2013); Institut national de la statistique et des études économiques (INSEE) (2013).

[45] | By way of comparison, the nuclear power plant in Cattenom (the third largest in France): 5,448 MW; the pumped storage hydro power station in Vianden (the third largest in the EU): 1,096 MW; the Wörrstadt wind farm (the largest in Rhineland-Palatinate): 55.5 MW.

about one-third of the power, roughly 20 % comes from Rhineland-Palatinate, 6 % from Luxembourg and 1 % from Saarland, although these figures do not by any means correspond to the number of installed plants. More than two-thirds of the plants are located in Rhineland-Palatinate, slightly more than 10 % each in Luxembourg and Wallonia, 6 % in Saarland and 2 % in Lorraine. This discrepancy between generating capacity and installed plants is primarily explained by the fact that a large proportion of the plants in Rhineland-Palatinate and Luxembourg only generate up to 500 kW$_{el}$. A look at the locations of the plants furthermore shows a concentration in western Rhineland-Palatinate and in Luxembourg, whereas the plants in Lorraine, as well as Wallonia, are widely spread (see Fig. 1). The goal of the following analysis is to explain which processes have led to this concentration in Luxembourg and western Rhineland-Palatinate. Special attention will be paid to the operator side of various territorial policies and normalizations in relation to governmentality.

Setting Standards and Normalization through State Policies in Reference to Biogas

"It cannot be too strongly emphasized that controlling energy is a condition for the exercise of power. [...] Each segment of the energy sector is intensely interrelated with politics"[46] (Brücher 2009: 33).

The energy sector is strongly marked by political control. As a consequence of the liberalization of the European energy market since 1996, both the European Union as well as the individual member states have been working constantly on controlling it politically. Currently there are ten different regulations, guidelines and laws governing the biogas segment in the EU and in Luxembourg, and in Germany as many as 31. Added to these are other state frameworks, such as zoning or tax laws, obligations of use or investment grants. The national states and the EU are obviously 'sovereigns of energy', which also constantly comes up in the interviews:

"This whole biogas affair is political. If it no longer suits the government, then they just change the general framework so it becomes uninteresting or gets either funded or penalized somewhere"[47] (male, German, Rhineland-Palatinate).

Here we clearly see the juridical exercise of power and normalization of (supra) state actors, who enact laws to build up a regulative structure which follows the

---

46 | Personal translation of: "Dass Macht die Kontrolle der Energie voraussetzt, kann nicht oft genug wiederholt werden. [...] Jeder Bereich der Energiewirtschaft steht in intensiver Wechselbeziehung mit der Politik."

47 | Personal translation of: "Die ganze Biogasgeschichte ist ein Politikum. Wenn das der Politik nicht mehr passt, dann werden die Rahmenbedingungen so verändert, dass es uninteressant wird oder dass es irgendwo entweder gefördert wird oder dass es bestraft wird."

binary coding of allowed/prohibited and places sanctions on unauthorized practices. Establishing norms in such ways are practices with which actors purposely set up, distinguish, and categorize energy regions, organize them into hierarchies and put them into relation with one another. However, it cannot be assumed that these norms are followed *per se*, or that the biogas producers necessarily embrace the normalized energy region in the sense of technologies of the self. It is worth examining how the normalizations show up in practices or feed back into one another and thus initiate everyday regionalizations. Since the policies mentioned refer primarily to nation states, they are of little use when it comes to explaining local processes in border areas. We will therefore first proceed to compare these more or less obvious ways of exercising power through normalization with governmental processes, which constitute energy regions in a local, cross-border context.

On the Relationship between Sovereignty and Governmentality in the Context of Biogas Production

The relationship between sovereignty and governmentality in the context of biogas production is especially reflected in the structurally affirmative practices of the biogas producers: how do they deal with 'the law' and how does this enable an energy region to constitute itself? This process of negotiation between juridical power and self-conduct is examined by asking the following questions:

- Which laws and regulations are mentioned/perceived by the biogas producers as crucial?
- How is that which is allowed and not allowed perceived and how are decisions/actions taken accordingly?
- Which laws and regulations are presented as impossible to circumvent?

Initial insights into the relationship between sovereignty and governmentality can be gained from the interviewees' statements on the significance of setting standards. In Rhineland-Palatinate, they particularly emphasize the importance of the law for giving priority to renewable sources of energy (Renewable Energies Act, in German: *Erneuerbare-Energien-Gesetz* or EEG). Some of the interviewees mentioned that the EEG encouraged them to decide in favour of the plant:

"The plans were already almost finished. Then when the new EEG came along in 2004 we decided straight off to get into the biogas business because that just seemed to us to make good business sense"[48] (male, German, Rhineland-Palatinate).

---

48 | Personal translation of: "Die Pläne waren schon soweit geschaffen. Als dann 2004 das neue EEG kam haben wir uns direkt entschieden doch in die Biogasbranche einzusteigen, weil es sich da für uns einfach wirtschaftlich dargestellt hat."

"We liked the idea of the twenty-year fixed feed-in tariff. And the plant did not make for too much work, and that's what led to our decision"[49] (male, German, Rhineland-Palatinate).

For others, the EEG, in conjunction with its auxiliary regulations, was or is in fact a necessary condition for a cost-efficient operation of a biogas plant.

"Without this funding through the EEG, biogas would not be profitable, you might say. This applies to all renewables, you know, it's exactly the same for photovoltaics and wind"[50] (male, German, Rhineland-Palatinate).

"Without the manure bonus I'd have to say it would be pretty tight. We'd lose around about 60,000 €. And the whole cost calculations, including the cowshed, it's based in the end on the payout we're getting at present. My income is fixed, you know"[51] (male, German, Rhineland-Palatinate).

The EEG created incentives to build plants that changed the socio-material situation in the territory under study. Plants are built, networks between operators form, there is 'space' for exchanging experiences and discussion (see below). Besides discussing market incentive programmes, the interviewees often broached the issue of approval procedures. These are seen by the operators as being restrictive and obligatory, which puts the power logic of sovereignty above that of self-regulation:

"It's harder to get a permit for a petrol station here than if you want to build Cattenom [nuclear power plant nearby in France]"[52] (male, Luxembourger, Luxembourg).

"The approval procedures are simply impossible. You submit something and then you're kept waiting. Then you ring them up and some time later you get a paper saying: 'You still have to submit this, you have to explain that and the like.' [...] By the time you get all this together weeks have passed. Then you send it in, and again nothing happens. [...] And the

---

49 | Personal translation of: "Das hat uns gut gefallen mit dieser festen Einspeisevergütung über 20 Jahre hinweg. Und der Arbeitsaufwand, den die Anlage macht, ist auch übersichtlich gewesen und dadurch kam der Entschluss."
50 | Personal translation of: "Ohne diese Förderung durch das EEG wäre ja Biogas nicht wirtschaftlich, sagen wir mal so. Das gilt ja nun für alle Erneuerbaren, das gilt für Photovoltaik und für Wind ja genauso."
51 | Personal translation of: "Ohne Güllebonus muss ich sagen, das wäre schon sehr eng. Wir verlieren dann gleich mal so um die 60.000 €. Und die ganze Betriebskalkulation auch mit dem Kuhstall, alles basiert letztendlich auf den Auszahlungspreisen wie wir sie momentan haben. Meine Einnahme ist ja fest."
52 | Personal translation of: "Wenn du für eine Gastankstelle hier eine Genehmigung willst, das ist schlimmer, als wenn du Cattenom [Kernkraftwerk im nahegelegenen Frankreich] errichten willst."

3. Constructions of Space and Identity Created by Institutional Practices

requirements are so high and there are more and more of them, more are constantly being added. [...] If at some point I don't just say to the contractor: 'C'm on, let's get started!', I don't get anything done. Again and again, people come by who stand there and say 'You have to do something for me, as well! And then you have to do this here and what are you doing?' But if you submit an application... you hear nothing. That's the biggest problem, it's bigger than not being able to pay back the investment. It's really awful"[53] (male, Luxembourger, Luxembourg).

"But what's been going on lately with all these requirements for water pollution control, requirements for the materials used, requirements related to TÜV [Technical Control Board] issues. We'd already started construction when the first biogas plant blew up and that got it all going: completely different requirements for fire prevention, structural conditions, then the Liability Insurance Association, explosion protection. Every week something went wrong somewhere in the country and every time new things came up. A lot of it makes sense, I must say, but some of it is totally exaggerated. Every construction material needs some sort of permit from this Berlin testing authority for materials, but they don't approve everything, and if not, you get no permit"[54] (male, German, Rhineland-Palatinate).

Thus the topic here is actually the relationship between sovereignty and governmentality: the distinction between what is allowed or not, the practices derived from this distinction and the regionalization processes resulting from

---

53 | Personal translation of: "Die Genehmigungsverfahren sind halt unmöglich. Dann reicht man das ein und dann kommt nichts. Dann ruft man an und irgendwann kommt dann ein Papier, da steht drauf: 'Das musst du noch nachreichen, das musst du erklären und so.' [...] Bis das wieder zusammengestellt ist: wieder so viel Wochen weg. Dann geht das rein, dann wieder nichts. [...] Und die Auflagen sind so hoch, es wird immer mehr, es kommt immer hinzu. [...] Wenn ich nicht einfach irgendwann sage zu dem Bauunternehmer: 'So, jetzt legen wir los!', dann mache ich nichts. Da kommen immer wieder Leute, die stehen auf und sagen: 'Bei mir musst du auch noch! Und dann musst du noch hier und was machst du da?' Aber wenn man dann einen Antrag einreicht... Stille. Das ist das größte Problem, das ist größer, als dass ich das *Invest* nicht zurückbezahlen kann. Das ist wirklich ganz schlimm."

54 | Personal translation of: "Aber was sich in der Zeit entwickelt hat, mittlerweile an Auflagen für Gewässerschutz, an Auflagen für die eingesetzten Materialien, an Auflagen, was den TÜV [Technischer Überwachungsverein] anbelangt. Wir waren am Bauen und dann ging die erste Biogasanlage mal hoch und schon ging das los: ganz andere Anforderungen an Brandschutz, an bauliche Gegebenheiten, dann Berufsgenossenschaft, Explosionsschutz. Jede Woche ging ja irgendwas irgendwo in der Republik schief und jedes Mal kamen dann neue Dinger. Vieles ist sinnvoll, muss man einfach sagen, aber manches ist dann auch vollkommen überzogen. Da muss jedes Baumaterial irgendwie 'ne Zulassung von dieser Berliner Prüfstelle für Materialien haben, die es nicht gibt für alles, sonst kriegt man keine Genehmigungen."

it. On the one hand, this relationship is based in the governmental regulatory framework, and on the other is also reflected in non-governmental normalizations or political expressions of intent.

"We produce milk here. We are going to carry on producing milk. And I'm glad that I've found an alternative in biogas. As things now stand, what is politically intended, we will further expand this second mainstay"[55] (male, German, Rhineland-Palatinate).

Here it becomes clear that the interviewee feels that his individual business policy is the normal state of affairs, but which at the same time depends on governmental policy; sovereignty and self-conduct are juxtaposed as a matter of course. This can also be seen in the context of projects, when an individual plant is embedded in a larger joint project and thus assigned to a larger strategic concept. This constitutes a specific situation and introduces limitations which, however, the operator himself does not see as problematic:

"We don't have to at the moment, nor can we change a lot with this project. Now we first have to wait until it's finished to see how it goes, but then we can take action again"[56] (male, German, Rhineland-Palatinate).

Comparable patterns of argumentation can also be found in various interviews with regard to other aspects. For instance, the argument of regional production is used in almost all discussions of raw materials transport, in order to depict a normal state of affairs which is followed and justified by practical logic:

"- It's a regional issue if only because it's to do with acreage. I can't make a biogas plant that would farm land within a radius of 100 kilometres. That won't work simply because it would be too expensive and that's not what it's all about.
- But then there's that still if you somehow don't find anything here?
- I mean then you just have to look for an alternative, I can't let the biogas plant run idle. That won't work. Because, well, the problem as I see it is that if I don't keep feeding enough, then I fall down on performance first and then again there's also, say, after two or three weeks, I finally get enough substrate, then I'll need another four weeks before I get it back

---

55 | Personal translation of: "Wir machen hier Milch. Wir werden auch weiterhin Milch erzeugen. Und ich bin froh, dass ich über den Weg Biogas eine Alternative gefunden habe. So wie jetzt der Stand der Dinge ist, wie es politisch gewollt ist, werden wir dieses zweite Standbein weiter ausbauen."

56 | Personal translation of: "Wir müssen jetzt momentan nicht, wir können auch durch das Projekt nichts Großes ändern. Jetzt müssen wir erstmals den Ablauf abwarten, bis es abgeschlossen ist, aber dann können wir noch mal tätig werden."

3. Constructions of Space and Identity Created by Institutional Practices

up there. That's not worth it. That one time I got substrate from farther away, that was an emergency, that was really an emergency"[57] (male, Luxembourger, Luxembourg).

What is already intimated here is the significance of social norms for the practices of the plant operators ("what it's all about" as a common construct). The following interview segment shows how social norms and neighbours' expectations cause plant operators to choose a different location from the one originally preferred:

"We didn't have any citizens' action group here that protested, either. We had enough acreage to build the plant right on the farm. But I didn't want that for several reasons. Everything we need for the plant would then have to be taken through the village and up to the plant. All the manure up the same way. That would be a huge strain on the village high street. Up there you practically don't need to worry at all about the smell, either, due to the wind direction alone. So that was clear to everyone here in the village right from the outset and that's why it wasn't a problem"[58] (male, German, Rhineland-Palatinate).

The last aspect of the relationship between sovereignty and governmentality we will look at here deals with the affirmative acceptance of normalization. Various laws, regulations or standards are all referred to as inescapable, and the energy region is thus reproduced. This relationship is often reflected in the interviews, especially with regard to the manure bonus and the official requirement to own a gas flare in Germany:

---

57 | Personal translation of: "- Allein von der Flächenabhängigkeit ist es ja eine regionale Sache. Ich kann keine Biogasanlage machen, die 100 Kilometer im Umkreis Flächen bewirtschaftet. Das geht nicht, weil es einfach zu teuer wird und das ist auch nicht Sinn der Sache. - Aber das gibt es dann trotzdem, wenn Sie hier irgendwie nichts finden? - Ich meine dann muss man eben Alternativen suchen, ich kann nicht die Biogasanlage leerlaufen lassen. Das geht nicht. Weil, ich sehe leider das Problem, wenn ich die nicht genug füttere, dann falle ich erst mit der Leistung runter und dann brauche ich auch nochmal, nehmen wir mal an ich bekomme dann nach zwei bis drei Wochen, bekomme ich dann mal genug Substrat, dann brauche ich auch nochmal vier Wochen, bevor ich sie wieder da hab'. Das bringt nichts. Das eine Mal Substrat von weiter weg, das war ein Notfall, das war wirklich ein Notfall."

58 | Personal translation of: "Wir hatten hier auch keine Bürgerinitiative, die protestiert hat. Wir hätten Fläche genug gehabt um die Anlage direkt am Hof zu realisieren. Nur aus mehreren Gründen wollte ich das nicht haben. Alles, was wir für die Anlage brauchen, muss dann hier durch das Dorf durch und zu der Anlage geschleppt werden. Die gesamte Gülle denselben Weg hoch. Das wäre für die Dorfstraße eine enorme Verkehrsbelastung geworden. Auch eventuelle Geruchsbelästigungen sind da oben zu fast 100 % ausgeschlossen, schon allein von der Windrichtung her. So, das war auch jedem hier im Dorf ganz klar von Anfang an und deswegen war das gar kein Problem."

"About this 30 % manure with the substrate. Well, we'd also already spoken to an environmental consultant: - 'What happens if at some point a technical problem crops up and I can't put anything into it that day?' - 'That just can't be allowed to happen,' he said. [I can't say:] 'Put twice as much in the next day and then it's all OK.' No, it has to be more than 30 % every day. These laws are there and they have to be observed"[59] (male, German, Rhineland-Palatinate).

"Now we have to put in a gas flare, we just bought one. I personally don't think that's the most sensible thing, because we don't need one, but the law says we have to have it starting on 1st January 2014"[60] (male, German, Rhineland-Palatinate).

"And we were under pressure. We had to have the motor running by 31st December because we weren't allowed to use any more heating oil after 1st January 2007 or we'd have lost our status"[61] (male, German, Rhineland-Palatinate).

It becomes apparent that the normalizations discussed at the beginning circulate effectively in practice and encourage selective obedience. They are observed "because that's just how it is", or because otherwise sanctions are expected. The fact that the normalization seems to be accepted as a matter of course in the technologies of the self can be interpreted as optimized control of a territory. This applies both to political and social parameters. Deciding to invest in a biogas plant and choosing a location thus reflect various negotiation processes on the part of the actors. The interview segments last quoted, however, also point to another aspect: the issue of discipline and its relationship to governmentality.

On the Relationship between Discipline and Governmentality in the Context of Biogas Production

The aims of discipline are control and surveillance, actions taken to moralize and improve; it concentrates, focuses and encloses. It strives to regulate every detail

---

59 | Personal translation of: "Mit diesen 30 % Gülle beim Substrat. Also da hatten wir auch schon mit dem Umweltgutachter gesprochen: 'Wie sieht das denn aus, wenn da irgendmal ein technisches Problem ist und ich kann dann heute nichts da reintun?' - 'Das darf einfach nicht sein', sagte er. [Ich kann nicht sagen:] 'Tust du halt am nächsten Tag das Doppelte rein und dann ist das auch okay'. Ne. Nein, das muss jeden Tag über 30 %. Diese Gesetze bestehen und die müssen dann eingehalten werden."

60 | Personal translation of: "Wir müssen jetzt, das haben wir jetzt gekauft, eine Gasfackel nachbauen. Das halte ich zwar nicht unbedingt für die sinnvollste Sache, weil wir sie nicht brauchen, wir müssen sie vom Gesetzgeber her ab 1.1.2014 haben."

61 | Personal translation of: "Und wir hatten ja den Druck. Zum 31.12. mussten wir den Motor am Laufen haben, weil nach dem 1.1.2007 durften wir kein Heizöl mehr einsetzen, da hätten wir den Status verloren."

(see Foucault 2007 [2004]: 67 ff.). Governmentality (technologies of the self or apparatuses of security), by contrast, is oriented towards averages or normal distributions of social rule, towards normalization or *laisser faire*, in order to promote the desirable and limit the undesirable (the phenomenon of circulation, see ibid.). How do these apparently contrasting dimensions come together?

The relationship between discipline and governmentality in the context of biogas production is reflected particularly in the subversive constitutions the biogas producers accomplish: instead of (re)producing the energy region affirmatively, we are here dealing with transformations of the situation, of negotiations between discipline and *governmentality*. Their analysis aims at finding answers to the following questions:

- How do biogas producers perceive control, how do they judge it?
- What courses of action are seen as 'normal'?
- What sort of 'circumventions' take place?

As shown in chapter 2.1, transitions can also be understood as ambiguities, blurring or levelling differences. The resulting no-man's land of uncertainty enables the actors to become creative, for example, by developing alternative technologies of the self in relation to discipline or individual interpretations of legal frameworks. Such in-between areas are necessary to mediate between the adjoining categories of 'discipline' and 'governmentality'.

The interviewees mention various dimensions of control:

"And the surveillance, even far worse than in agriculture!"[62] (male, German, Rhineland-Palatinate).

"I recently said to my wife: 'We're going to have go get another file cabinet, one simply isn't enough for everything.' Nothing can be done without paperwork any more. And I say, paperwork is only good for keeping you under control, that's what I always say, right?"[63] (male, German, Rhineland-Palatinate).

Control is seen as restrictive, thus fulfilling its goal of normalization. But by the same token, it stimulates responses and technologies of the self of governance that are just as specific and play a part in commercial relationships. Without exception, the interviewees all reported that contractual certainty is necessary

---

62 | Personal translation of: "Und die Überwachung, noch viel schlimmer wie in der Landwirtschaft!"

63 | Personal translation of: "Ich habe letztens zu meiner Frau gesagt: 'Wir müssen unbedingt noch mal einen zweiten Aktenschrank kaufen, in den einen passt einfach nicht mehr alles rein.' Ohne Papierkram läuft nichts mehr. Und ich sage, der Papierkram ist ja nur dafür gut, dass man kontrolliert werden kann, sage ich dann immer, nicht?"

when collaborating with large companies, although this is often an unaccustomed experience for the farmers:

"We also noticed, whenever we [had dealings] with the companies, the ones coming down from up there [...] With us, it was still the case that we didn't need to write everything down: no sooner said than done. A promise is a promise. That's not the case with them, though. Not generally. 'Where does it say that? Where is that written down? If it's not set down in writing, we don't need to do anything'"[64] (male, German, Rhineland-Palatinate).

This quote reflects forms of control in the self-guidance and external control of the operators. Companies use contracts to establish certainty and include or exclude one's own actions; they serve companies which are not locally based ("from up there") as instruments of mediation between discipline and governmentality. In addition, they enable an effective circulation of practices and thus the spread of technologies and knowledge (socio-technical regionalization). The distinction to "those up there" helps establish identity. The "we" emphasized in the quote can in this case be evaluated as an important criterion for the density of biogas plants in the territory: the social networks in Luxembourg or in Rhineland-Palatinate are developed to such a degree that a common identity is represented linguistically – as the following arguments will show. A professional, regionally based identity can therefore help develop and stabilize the industry *in situ*. In such a situation, however, contracts are unsuitable instruments of control:

"Written contracts among farmers is always difficult. I mean, if it doesn't work on the basis of trust, then you might as well forget it altogether. We already had contracts here, we had supply contracts, but we never insisted that we fulfil them. No point in that. So if someone here in the village tries to enforce contracts, that's a problem, it won't work"[65] (male, Luxembourger, Luxembourg).

Rather, instruments of discipline and *laisser faire* encounter each other in such a way that specific practices and forms of control and security become necessary for joint economic activity.

---

64 | Personal translation of: "Wir haben auch festgestellt, wenn wir mit den Firmen, die da von oben runterkommen... Bei uns war es immer noch so, wir brauchten nicht alles aufzuschreiben: Gesagt, getan. Ein Mann, ein Wort. Bei denen stimmt das alles nicht. Generell nicht. 'Wo steht das? Wo steht das geschrieben? Wenn das nirgends steht, brauchen wir nichts zu machen'."

65 | Personal translation of: "Schriftliche Verträge unter Landwirten ist immer schwierig. Ich meine, wenn das nicht auf Vertrauensbasis geht, dann kann man das sowieso vergessen. Wir hatten hier schon Verträge, wir hatten Lieferverträge gehabt, da haben wir auch nie darauf bestanden, dass wir die erfüllen können. Das bringt auch nichts. Also wenn man hier im Dorf versucht, Verträge durchzusetzen, dann hat man ein Problem, das geht nicht."

"The farmers, the others, have to know you're not dependent on them. If you make yourself dependent, in a way you make it easy for them to put the squeeze on you. So if you always go to the limit, there are people already starting to look round in May, like 'Where can you still sell some maize?!' And when the others get wind of it, then in the autumn maize is already up by 100 € per hectare"[66] (male, German, Rhineland-Palatinate).

Knowledge of a situation enables the actors to respond accordingly to the control mechanism in their own practices. This process of negotiation of one's own situation contains an element of transformation, which aims at the perceived individual options for action. Personal experiences and options for action become relevant to the relationship of discipline and governmentality. We can observe something similar in the following segment referring to financing the plant. Here it becomes clear that the image the operator entertains of himself does not agree with the attribution of the refinancing institute, and that, as a result, the house bank refuses to finance the plant and thus another institution takes over this role:

"The house bank desperately wanted, that is, desperately wanted to. Only then they were tripped up by their refinancing office. They had reservations: 'Plants of this size only with farmers ... mmh ... are you sure, farmer XY? Can you really run it, are you sure of what you are doing there?' I had this good man from the refinancing office on the telephone for two hours and had to listen to him ask me, a farmer, whether I knew what I had to do there on my field. At some point then I said to him: 'OK, people. You know what you do in your bank, we know what we do on our field. We'll just drop it, then.' There's no point, it just doesn't make any sense"[67] (male, German, Rhineland-Palatinate).

The social *bordering* taking place here indicates a withdrawal from the familiar environment and at the same time a circumvention through which the plant operator constitutes his apparatuses of security. The presumed control

---

66 | Personal translation of: "Die Bauern, die anderen, müssen wissen, du bist nicht von denen abhängig. Wenn man sich abhängig macht, und schon ist man in einer gewissen Weise erpressbar. Also, wenn Sie immer auf Rille fahren, es gibt welche, die fangen dann irgendwann an im Mai schon zu gucken: 'Wo ist noch Mais zu verkaufen?!' Und wenn die anderen das mitbekommen, dann ist der Mais im Herbst schon von vorneherein 100 € im Hektar teurer."
67 | Personal translation of: "Die Hausbank wollte unbedingt, also wollte unbedingt. Nur die sind dann wieder über ihren Rückfinanzierer gestolpert. Die hatten Bedenken: 'Anlagen in dieser Größe nur bei Landwirten ... Mmh ... bist du sicher, Landwirt XY? Kannst du die auch wirklich betreiben, bist du dir sicher, was du da machst?' Ich hatte diesen guten Mann von dem Rückfinanzierer zwei Stunden am Telefon und musste mir tatsächlich als Landwirt sagen lassen, ob ich weiß, was ich da betreiben muss auf meinem Acker. Irgendwann habe ich zu dem gesagt: 'Ist gut, Leute. Ihr wisst, was Ihr in Eurer Bank macht, wir wissen, was wir auf unserem Acker machen. Wir lassen es dann sein.' Es hat keinen Sinn, es macht keinen Sinn so was."

mechanisms of the financial sector are contrasted with bodies of knowledge and self-image, producing a 'normal' image of one's own profession. In this way, the role of the refinancing office transforms itself for the operator from an authority into a marginal figure – in the end the financing was ensured by another bank. At the same time, this case is also an example of the differing interpretations of banks' security demands. Ultimately, the farmer managed to secure the desired financing. Experiences such as these and their propagation in social networks help create a more relaxed attitude towards control mechanisms. This behaviour can also be observed with regard to statutory provisions. A regulative framework is clearly identified while its legitimacy is questioned. In other cases, its non-observance is taken entirely for granted and even expressly emphasized. Possible consequences are neither mentioned, nor presumably feared:

"And then we also manipulated, don't worry, you can leave that in [in the interview report] with the acreage because they otherwise don't get approved. But then again that was still sort of illegal: the approval was for 180 kW. But then starting that year, starting in November 2005, we officially went up to 180, but as far as capacity was concerned, we could go up to 250 kW"[68] (male, German, Rhineland-Palatinate).

"We have, I'd say, the approval is on hand for 400 kW. These 400 kW are also realized in the construction. The idea behind it, though, is that because we have two times 400 kW in block-type thermal power stations, we also have the approval from RWE [power company] up to two times 400. When we're finished with the construction phase, we'll subsequently submit a BImSch [approval in accordance with the Federal Control of Pollution Act] and can then run the 800 kW without any illegal operations"[69] (male, German, Rhineland-Palatinate).

This non-observance is also reflected in the interviews with regard to social aspects. The interviewee still sees himself as a farmer and not primarily as an energy producer (for example, he holds a high-level function with the farmers' association), yet the biogas plant is an instrument to safeguard him against social changes. In the process, the way he deals with his own product also changes:

---

68 | Personal translation of: "Und dann haben wir auch manipuliert, das können Sie auch ruhig drin lassen [im Interviewprotokoll], mit der Fläche, weil sie kriegen ja sonst keine Genehmigung. Aber das war dann auch noch halb illegal: die Genehmigung war für 180 kW. Aber wir sind dann ab dem Jahr, ab November 2005 sind wir halt eben offiziell mit 180, aber von der Leistung her konnten wir bis 250 kW hochgehen."

69 | Personal translation of: "Wir haben das, ich sag mal, die Genehmigung liegt mit 400 kW vor. Diese 400 kW werden bautechnisch auch umgesetzt. Der Hintergedanke ist aber der: Weil wir zweimal 400 kW an Blockheizkraftwerken haben, die Genehmigung von RWE [Energieversorgungskonzern] auch auf die zwei Mal 400 haben. Wenn wir fertig mit der Bauphase sind, werden wir eine BImSch [Genehmigung nach Bundesimmissionsschutzgesetzt] nachreichen und können dann halt eben auch ohne illegalen Betrieb die 800 kW fahren."

"If people here are not willing to pay at least a reasonably decent price for our products, if they're not willing to pay us enough so that we can make a proper living from it, or at least an acceptable living, then the stuff goes into the biogas plant"[70] (male, German, Rhineland-Palatinate).

This justification, which almost comes across as a threat, also shows how social standards can be circumvented through technologies (of the self), how supposed conflict potentials – depending on the angle of vision – can be exacerbated or attenuated, and one's own practices optimized. The following quote illustrates in particular the positive aspects of these possibilities for self-guidance, although the interviewee provides no proof for the thesis of improvement.

"Back then we already had the idea to ferment the [slurry]. When the [substrates] are properly fermented you can normally drive right up past the walls of the houses, so there's really no problem [with neighbours bothered by the smell]"[71] (male, German, Rhineland-Palatinate).

To summarize, we can say that the relationship between discipline and governmentality operates at various levels and usually manifests itself in subtle and implicit perceptions (instruments of control and discipline; technologies of the self of (1) governance, of (2) negotiating one's own situation and ensuring and representing one's own ability to act, of (3) the constitution of the apparatuses of security, of (4) non-compliance with norms and of (5) self-guidance). The transformative potential resides in the everyday nature of the technologies of the self (governmentality) in dealing with the situation, while tensions are clearly revealed in regard of the instruments of disciplinary action.

3.4.2 Conclusion

The use of biomass to generate power is tied to various spatial policies and normalizations. Actors try to assert their goals and control other actors. This case study examined interviews with biogas producers in Luxembourg and western Rhineland-Palatinate to discover how they develop their practices in the tangled web of politics, civil society, business and the environment, how they deal with their situation and create technologies of the self to achieve their goals and in this

---

70 | Personal translation of: "Wenn die Menschen hier nicht bereit sind, zumindest einen einigermaßen anständigen Preis für unsere Waren zu zahlen, wenn die nicht bereit sind, uns dann auch das dafür zu bezahlen, dass wir gut davon leben können, oder vernünftig davon leben können, dann geht es bei uns in die Biogasanlage."

71 | Personal translation of: "Damals war das schon die Idee, dass die [Gülle] vergärt wird. Wenn die [Substrate] richtig vergoren sind, da kannst du die normalerweise an die Häuserwand fahren, also da hast du kein Problem [mit Geruchsbelästigung der Anrainer]."

way constitute the 'local' energy sector. It becomes clear that tensions, conflicts and trade-offs are important aspects of these regionalizations. At the same time, they reflect the relationship between governmentality and sovereignty which, as shown, helps stabilize energy regions and (re)produce the situation. In contrast to this, the relationship between governmentality and discipline seems to run harmoniously, which encourages the circumvention of the situation.

The continuous *bordering* on which the triangular relationship between governmentality, discipline and sovereignty is based seems to play a decisive part in the concentration of the plants in the area under study. The differentiation of social groups, of what is allowed and what is not, of the possible and the impossible or of supporting and prohibiting factors, runs like a logic through the technologies of the self of the biogas plant producers in dealing with the situation. The continuous change of affirmative and subversive crossing of boundaries clearly shows that the complex practices of setting and crossing boundaries are mutually dependent, creating situation-dependent regionalizations. Although national laws naturally play a part in this, other aspects are at least equally important, such as:

- Social networks and the related exchange of knowledge and experience;
- The self-conception of plant operators and the related patterns of interpretation;
- The respective perceptions and evaluations of various practices in the biogas sector and related courses of action.

The first and third aspects seem to be particularly specific and of greater importance in the border area, since different situations come together here. These produce multiple networks and practices that in turn can again reproduce or transform the situations. Thus setting and crossing boundaries are as much a part of the everyday practice of biogas producers in the border region as continuous, performative *bordering*. This clearly shows that regionalizations are crucially dependent on the actors involved and their relationships in social as well as spatial contexts.

3.5 'Sovereignty' and 'Discipline' in the Media. On the Value of Foucault's Governmentality Theory: The Example of an Interdiscursive Analysis of the Migration Discourse in Luxembourg

Elena Kreutzer

"Mass media are technologies of government. They elevate certain subject areas to the status of systematic knowledge and intermesh regulating practices with practices of self-conduct. They are technologies of government in a twofold sense: they are subject and object of governmental rationalities. They are thus at the same time governmentalized and governmentalizing practices"[72] (Wedl 2008: 1).

Following Juliette Wedl's thesis quoted above, the central question of this case study is how Foucault's governmentality concept can be harnessed for media theory and practice. The goal of this paper is therefore to determine in particular the practical value of Foucault's comprehensive concept of governmentality for media and media analyses, something which has been little discussed hitherto. Its value for media analyses will be shown by focusing on the two poles of governmentality theory, 'sovereignty' and 'discipline'.

Using an interdiscursive analysis of the migration discourse in Luxembourg media during the period from 1990 to 2010, the initially theoretical statements on the value of Foucault's governmentality concept will be given practical application. Interdiscourse analysis sees itself as "a further development and modification of discourse analysis as developed by Michel Foucault and is an applied discourse analysis that concerns itself with the link to practice and empiricism"[73] (Amann/Bourg et al. 2010: 165). Hence the present case study forms a point of intersection between two largely separate receptions of Foucault in sociological research: the political and sociological governmentality debate and the discursive analysis of media texts (see Wedl 2008: 1).

This contribution will first consider the relevance that 'migration in Luxembourg' has for politics, media and research as a subject of investigation. This will be followed by a discussion of the theoretical and practical value of Foucault's governmentality theory within the scope of an interdiscursive analysis

---

[72] | Personal translation of: "Massenmedien sind Regierungstechnologien. Sie erheben bestimmte Gegenstandsbereiche in den Status systematischen Wissens und verschränken regulierende Praktiken mit Praktiken der Selbstführung. Regierungstechnologien sind sie in doppelter Weise: Sie sind Subjekt und Objekt gouvernementaler Rationalitäten. Sie sind somit zugleich gouvernementalisierte und gouvernementalisierende Praktiken."
[73] | Personal translation of: "Eine Weiterentwicklung und Modifikation der von Michel Foucault entwickelten Diskursanalyse und ist als eine angewandte Diskursanalyse um den Bezug zur Praxis und Empirie bemüht."

of Luxembourg media's discourse on migration. The case study concludes with the results of the empirical survey and their evaluation in the context of Foucault's governmentality theory.

3.5.1 The Importance of 'Migration in Luxembourg' to Politics, the Media and Research

Migration is a topic that is generating controversial public discussion in Europe. As a consequence migration movements, and the appurtenant questions of integration, are regularly part of the political and media agenda in many European countries.

In Luxembourg, too, traditionally portrayed as a country of immigrants (see Scuto 2008; Kmec/Lentz 2012), the topic of migration is currently a part of political and public reality. One significant reason for this is that 61.2 % of Luxembourg's population have a migrant background (see STATEC 2013). Since sociopolitical topics and debates are usually seen as worth reporting, depending on their topicality and news value in the sense of an informative function of media (see Jarren/Meier 2002: 101), they receive ample coverage in Luxembourg's media. Nonetheless, the representation of migrants in Luxembourg's media has thus far been only marginally studied.

While the public image of migrants in the media of the Federal Republic of Germany has been under study since the 1970s (see Delgado 1972) and in the USA since the 1930s (see Inglis 1938), academic papers on the situation in Luxembourg (see Bailey 2012; Skrijelj 2012; Cirikovic 2013), are few and far between, unpublished and limited to a single immigrant group (for example, Muslims or refugees). Instead, studies of migration in Luxembourg have so far concentrated on historical migration (see Scuto 2008; STATEC 2008: 573ff.; STATEC 2013: 159ff.), some of which make cross-border comparisons of migration in Luxembourg and the SaarLorLux region (see Leiner 1994; Trinkaus 2014). The subject of the present case study is the trilingual (German, French, Luxembourgish[74]) daily newspaper with the highest circulation in Luxembourg: the *Luxemburger Wort*, which has been appearing since 1848.[75]

---

74 | The articles written in Luxembourgish are largely announcements of events, as well as local and private ads, which were left out of the research for pragmatic reasons. Accordingly, the sample only takes account of German and French articles.

75 | Luxembourg's media landscape consists of the two dailies with the highest circulation, the *Luxemburger Wort* and the *Tageblatt*, their French-language counterparts, *La Voix du Luxembourg* (up to the end of September 2011) and *Le Quotidien*, as well as the liberal daily, the *Lëtzebuerger Journal* and the Communist *Zeitung vum Lëtzebuerger Vollek*. The weekly press comprises the three weeklies *Woxx*, *Le Jeudi* and *d'Lëtzebuerger Land*, the family and television magazines *Télécran* and *Revue*, the publications published in Portuguese *Contacto* and *Correio*, as well as the satirical newspaper *Den neie Feierkrop*.

The study limits its observations moreover to the period from 1990 to 2010[76] and does not concentrate – as earlier research literature – on specific nationalities or generations. Instead, the paper is based on a typologization of migration according to status groups[77]: 'foreigners' (*étrangers*), 'refugees' (*réfugiés*), 'asylum seekers' (*demandeurs d'asile*) and 'migrants/immigrants' (*migrants/immigrés*), 'ethnic German emigrants" and finally, the *sans papiers*.[78] The question now is: how can this media topic be understood in terms of Foucault's governmentality theory?

3.5.2 On the Benefit of Foucault's Theory of Governmentality for an Interdiscursive Media Analysis

Foucault did not himself publish any work on media studies nor did he explicitly envision the governmentality concept to be used for media texts. Although one can find repeated references to his terms and methodical approaches in sociology and media studies (see Parr/Thiele 2007: 85), there seem to be only very few media-related concepts directly inspired by Foucault's governmentality theory and these are only to a very limited degree application-oriented (see Stauff 2005; Schneider 2006; Wedl 2008). Applying Foucault's concept of governmentality to the subject of media by means of analysing interdiscourses offers therefore an approach that has hitherto received little attention.

Drawing on Foucault, every order of knowledge has its own specific choices or options of representation. These options determine their subjects, that is, their

---

[76] | Because Luxembourg's laws concerning foreigners were revised in the early 1990s and the topic of 'migration' thus took a place on the political agenda, it must be assumed that the mass media were interested (see Willems/Milmeister 2008: 75). In addition, not all relevant issues of the *Luxemburger Wort*, in the sense of a complete count, could be considered for practical reasons in the research. Instead, the systematic 'constructed week' sampling method was chosen, in which each nth element is selected according to a stipulated interval, starting from a specific point in time. For the analysis, we selected the first Monday in January of the first year, the second year, and so forth, the Tuesday of the next week and then one weekday further on for each following week throughout the period under study.

[77] | Depending on specifications of laws regarding foreigners concerning the length or purpose of their stay, which usually precedes a public discussion of national migration policy, a distinction is made between various legal status groups. The designations of the status groups are thus related on the one hand to legal categorizations, on the other to designations emerging from public discussions of migration policies.

[78] | The phenomenon of the *sans-papiers*, which arose around 1980, goes back to French immigrant society and France's colonial past (see Schwenken 2003: 129). In its German counterpart – criminalized immigrants – the term does not occur in the discourse of Luxembourg media and is therefore not quoted in German.

possibility, composition, interrelation and visibility (see Wedl 2008: 5). In these orders of knowledge, the sayable becomes visible, just as the unsayable is excluded. A discourse in Foucault's sense therefore is also marked by its limitations, that is, by prohibitions, exclusions of the sayable or the visible. At the same time, there are always connections to other discourses. Collective symbols are seen as connecting links between the discourses. These include interdiscursive elements which at a specific point in time occur in several discourses. They serve as a source of evidence and interpretability.

In interdiscourse analysis these recurring interdiscursive elements are analysed in terms of collective symbols and metaphors. Based on Foucault, Jürgen Link defines discourses as follows:

"Contrary to natural languages, discourses are much more strongly variable historically and culturally and stipulate [cross-linguistically] specific spaces of sayability and knowledge, as well as their boundaries. They are institutionalized, regulated manners of speaking as spaces of possible statements which are coupled to actions"[79] (Link 2006: 410).

Foucault's discourses should be seen as special discourses, since they transfer special knowledge to narrowly limited spaces of sayability and knowability. However, these special discourses have to be transformed and framed, by means of integrational mechanisms, into re-integrated, interdiscursive processes so as to be generally understandable (see Parr 2009: 100). In other words:

"While the discourses analysed by Foucault were largely concerned with the formations of positive knowledge and institutionalized studies (jurisprudence, medicine, the humanities, etc.), interdiscourse analysis is concerned with discursive complexes which are specifically not limited by specialization, but have overarching effects and can therefore be called 'interdiscursive'"[80] (Amann/Bourg et al. 2010: 165).

Link's concept of interdiscourse thus starts from a systematic and 'free' definition of the term discourse, contrary to Foucault's conception of discourse, yet also includes power analysis, a component of Foucault's concept (see Link 2006: 410).

---

79 | Personal translation of: "Diskurse sind im Unterschied zu natürlichen Sprachen historisch-kulturell sehr viel stärker variabel und legen [sprachübergreifend] jeweils spezifische Sagbarkeits- und Wissensräume sowie deren Grenzen fest. Es sind institutionalisierte geregelte Redeweisen als Räume möglicher Aussagen, die an Handlungen gekoppelt sind."
80 | Personal translation of: "Während es bei den von Foucault analysierten Diskursen weitgehend um Formationen positiven Wissens und institutionalisierte Wissenschaften (Recht, Medizin, Humanwissenschaften etc.) ging, interessiert sich die Interdiskursanalyse für Diskurskomplexe, die gerade nicht durch Spezialisierung begrenzt sind, sondern übergreifend wirken und deshalb als 'interdiskursiv' bezeichnet werden können."

3. Constructions of Space and Identity Created by Institutional Practices

Power analysis also forms the foundation of Foucault's governmentality concept with its polarized and simultaneously overlapping power-analytic approaches of 'governmentality', 'discipline' and 'sovereignty'. Originally, Foucault's governmentality theory, with its power dimensions of 'sovereignty', 'discipline' and 'governmentality', was aimed at technologies of control of the population. These technologies arise from the question, first posed in the sixteenth century, of how to 'properly' govern the subjects of a state (see Wedl 2008). Foucault examines governmental technologies of control that concern power over a territory (sovereignty), mechanisms of control and disciplining of bodies (discipline) and socially desirable development (governmentality) (see sections 2.2, 2.3 and 3.1). The aspects of 'sovereignty' and 'discipline' lend themselves well to revealing (media) power, control and disciplining mechanisms and can be employed in the present media analysis, which uses no other methods of data collection (e.g. survey) nor external data (intra-extra-media comparison) (see Maurer/Reinemann 2006: 38).

The 'governmentality' pole is secondary in this case study for reasons of research methodology: this is not a reception study. There is no (qualitative) empirical material from which to derive governmental self-relations, which indeed take place on a large scale in the interaction between media and recipients. However, this concept would become relevant in terms of theory, empirics and methodology if the reception of media were taken into account.

With reference to the media, the power logic of 'sovereignty', originally concerned with the possibilities of exercising power over a territory, can therefore be defined as follows: first, in the sense of a Fourth Estate as an influence of the media on political or economic actors, as when investigative journalists uncover scandals and test the legitimacy of the political or economic exercise of power (see Kunczik/Zipfel 2005: 73). Second, media can influence recipients through their manner of reporting. The media's power therefore unfolds its effect in the moment of reception and is enhanced by specific journalistic control mechanisms.

The exercise of mass-media power discussed above can also be examined via the analytical approach of 'discipline'. It is likewise evident in journalistic control mechanisms particularly concerning attributions to specific status groups used in the *Luxemburger Wort*. Attributions are one of the components of the identity concept employed in the present volume (see section 2.3).

We can use media analysis for examining the way the issue of migration is covered in the media – as shown in the following – with the aim of identifying possible journalistic control mechanisms, but not for diagnosing explicit media effects.

3.5.3 Discursive Analytical Findings

An analysis of the frequency with which the issue was topicalized (agenda setting) showed that 2001 marked a high point in migration coverage in the *Luxemburger Wort* (see Fig. 1).

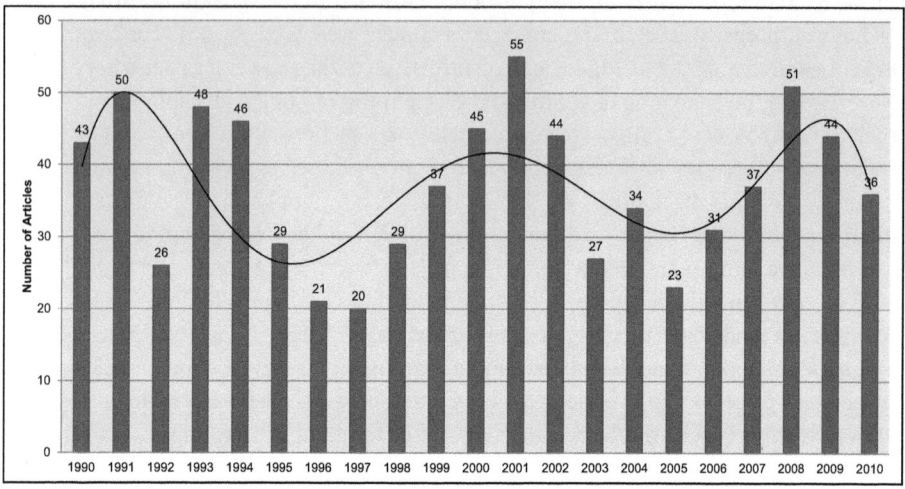

Figure 1: Distribution of articles in the Luxemburger Wort *from 1990 to 2010*

Since the complex issue of migration can be structured in various ways, it seemed practical to assign topics to either a primary or a secondary category. The former places articles into the context of national, regional, cross-border or global migration policy, while the latter subsumes immigration issues (for example, family reunification, asylum procedures, labour migration, measures taken to secure borders) on the one hand, and on the other matters concerning migrants already living in the EU, such as integration, discrimination, racism, (dual) citizenship or participation (see Schwenken 2003: 123).[81]

For the peak year of 2001, this yields the following distribution of topics: of the 55 articles, 52 % cover Luxembourg's migration policy and 20 % European migration policy. The focus of the national migration discourse for 2001 is on the regularization problems of the *sans-papiers*, the 'illegals'. The fact that there is a stronger focus on the attribution of 'illegals' could be put down to the law on asylum procedure adopted in Luxembourg in 1996, which was intended to limit the right of recently immigrated migrants to reside and work, and thus, according to Willems/Milmeister (2008: 76), led to a rise in illegal immigration. On the

---

81 | Although, depending on the article, multiple entries are possible, a classification only according to the various migrations policies is also conceivable, however, without addressing further topics which require secondary categorization.

3. Constructions of Space and Identity Created by Institutional Practices 127

other hand, illegal immigration was on the European Commission's agenda in 2001 and thus also on Luxembourg's, which may also explain this national focus.

Drawing on Benjamin Bühler (2012: 34), who distinguishes three temporal aspects of the border – the "institution of the border", the "crossing of the border" and the "extension of the border" – (see section 2.1), we can note that for the topic of 'illegal immigration', which in 2001 received particularly wide coverage in the *Luxemburger Wort*, the main focus was on the crossing of the border. The *sans papiers* are considered illegitimate border trespassers due to the fact that they have traversed the outer borders of the EU in the sense of a forbidden border crossing. At times, this leads to a tighter regulation of the border, as for instance by the border security measures explicitly prioritized by the EU in 2001.

While most other studies of migration coverage in print media rate the percentage of migrants as subjects participating in society to be less than 10 % (see Kreutzer 2009: 336), the *Luxemburger Wort* focuses comparatively frequently on the participation of migrants, as shown by its percentage of 13 % for the period under review. These are largely accounts by those directly affected. This shows that in the articles migrants are not only talked 'about', but also 'to'; migrants are given a chance to tell their own individual stories. That migrants are not presented primarily as objects of the coverage, but as subjects, may be due to the fact that the *Luxemburger Wort* considers itself to be a newspaper committed to Christian-humanist principles (see Hellinghausen 1998: 233).

Elements of discourse that can be the object of interdiscourse analysis need to be identified via contextual relationships. Interdiscursive elements, such as collective symbols, are considered to be "complex, iconically motivated, paradigmatically expanded signs"[82] (Parr 2008: 204), which unite two sides, an image (*pictura*) and what is actually meant, the meaning concealed behind it (*subscriptio*). For the present analysis of interdiscursive or collective symbols, it is necessary to make an inventory by first ascertaining the *pictura* elements and then assigning the appurtenant *subscriptio* elements.

Of the German-language articles, 33 % of the articles exhibit interdiscursive elements while 67 % have none. These interdiscursive elements constitute for the most part collective symbols, especially flood metaphors. Collective symbols form the "overall sphere of symbolism, imagery, use of metaphors, descriptive stereotypes and clichés"[83] (Keller 2011: 33). Additional collective symbols found in the sample are '(in-)flow', 'facilitator', 'siege', 'boat' and 'dyke'.

The German collective symbols can be found in in-house reports (14 %) and press agency reports from the *Deutsche Presseagentur* (dpa) (11 %). This means that not only Luxembourgish, but also German sociopolitical symbol-generating

---

82 | Personal translation of: "[...] komplexe, ikonisch motivierte, paradigmatisch expandierte Zeichen."

83 | Personal translation of: "[...] Gesamtbereich der Symbolik, Bildlichkeit, Metaphorik, der anschaulichen Stereotypen und Klischees."

conditions are relevant to the interpretation of results. Collective symbols are also found in the French-language sample of the *Luxemburger Wort* (30 %), again largely flood metaphors, albeit distinctly fewer than in the German-language sample.

What is remarkable is that the German boat metaphors found in the *Luxemburger Wort* only appear in the dpa reports and only in reference to Germany, resulting in a corresponding ascription of the *subscriptio* element. This yielded the general ascription of *pictura* and *subscriptio* elements on the media migration discourse in the *Luxemburger Wort* shown in Table 1.

Pictura ('image')		Subscriptio ('meaning')	
p1	Flood/*flux*[84]	s1	Sum of the status groups
p2	(in-)Flow or wave/*vague*	s2	Sum of the status groups
p3	Facilitators/people smugglers	s3	Criminal gangs which enable illegal immigration
p4	Siege	s4	Successful (illegal) (mass) immigration to Luxembourg
p5	Boat	s5	Germany (since the *pictura* element is only found in dpa reports and with an explicit reference to Germany)
p6	Dyke	s6	National border of Luxembourg

Table 1: Description of the pictura *and* subscriptio *elements (own compilation)*

Needless to say, these collective symbols do not occur simultaneously in the articles.

In the following in-house article by a local editor of the *Luxemburger Wort* two *pictura* and *subscriptio* elements occur:

"If the flood of foreign players to Luxembourg is not stopped, then in a few years it could well be that practically no Luxembourgish player will be found any more on a referee sheet. No fewer than 102 foreigners lined up on the first day of play last Wednesday for the various

---

84 | French 'flux' has a similar meaning to that of German 'Flut' for the present analysis of migration discourse in the media. First, however, 'flux' has a more neutral connotation, for instance, as in traffic flow. Only in the second sense does 'flux' capture the same ideological idea as the German term 'Flut'. This embodies the idea of a flood caused by a rainstorm as well as a metaphorical flood, powerful tides that are threatening and uncontrollable.

national division clubs. So only 63 of the total of 165 players sent in were Luxembourg nationals. On the first day, a mere two Luxembourgers played for the promoted team from Schifflange. The two players Duarte and Del Bon were merely substitutes. This means that Schifflange started the match with eleven foreigners. Three Luxembourgish players were used by Hobscheid and Mertzig. At least there were four home-grown players on the field for F91 Düdelingen, Wiltz and Rümelingen. So the clubs are investing more and more money in foreign players instead of promoting domestic junior talent"[85] (*Luxemburger Wort* 1999).

While the first *pictura* element 'flood' corresponds to the *subscriptio* element 'sum of the foreign athletes', the second image element 'home-grown' stands for Luxembourgish footballers. "[B]y way of the metaphorical use of words from a specific range of origin, [the group of topics related to migration] is cognitively pre-structured and interpreted for the recipient"[86] (Niehr/Böke 2010: 331). Thus the interdiscursive element 'flood' can be ascribed to the 'water' type of metaphor, which can be subsumed under the target field of 'labour migration'. A connection is made between maritime elements and the discussion of immigration in general and the development of the foreign population in particular. Applied to civil society discourse, this expresses the idea that migrants are a heavy burden on the labour market and – in the case of the article quoted – enter into a competitive situation with domestic footballers.

As a rule, foreign athletes are considered to be 'desirable' migrants, as many German studies on media-migration research have established (see Bonfadelli 2007: 99). The text example "Akzente in der Nationaldivision" (Accents in the National Division) shows that this is the case for Luxembourg if the number of foreign athletes remains within limits. The fact that the Portuguese and French

---

85 | Personal translation of: "Wenn die Flut der ausländischen Spieler nach Luxembourg nicht gestoppt wird, dann kann es gut sein, dass in einigen Jahren fast kein Luxembourgischer Spieler mehr auf einem Schiedsrichterbogen zu finden ist. Nicht weniger als 102 Ausländer wurden am vergangenen Mittwoch am ersten Spieltag bei den verschiedenen Nationaldivisionsvereinen aufgestellt. Von den insgesamt 165 eingesetzten Spielern waren also nur 63 Fußballer im Besitz der Luxembourgischen Nationalität. Am ersten Spieltag kamen gerade mal zwei Luxembourgische Spieler beim Aufsteiger aus Schifflingen zum Einsatz. Die beiden Akteure Duarte und Del Bon wurden sogar nur eingewechselt, dies bedeutet, dass Schifflingen die Begegnung mit elf Ausländern begonnen hat. Bei Hobscheid und Mertzig kamen drei Luxembourgische Spieler zum Einsatz. Beim F91 Düdelingen, Wiltz und Rümelingen standen immerhin vier Eigengewächse auf dem Spielfeld. Die Vereine investieren also immer mehr Geld in ausländische Spieler, anstatt die eigene Jugend zu fördern."
86 | Personal translation of: "[...] über den metaphorischen Gebrauch von Wörtern aus einem bestimmten Herkunftsbereich [wird der Themenkomplex Migration] für den Adressaten kognitiv vorstrukturiert und interpretiert."

names of the two footballers Duarte and Del Bon indicate that they are of foreign origin is not mentioned.

So what do these findings from interdiscourse analysis mean with a view to Foucault's governmentality theory? Power effects as understood by Foucault can be revealed in (media) discourses with the help of interdiscourse analysis, since collective symbols are used to draw on the everyday knowledge of recipients from all social strata. Mass media therefore contribute to the construction of the sayable through cross-strata interdiscursive elements. They constitute a key locus of truth production, yet they not only organize knowledge, but also generate it by presenting and ordering social reality through visual or textual statements. They "thus treat problems which at the same time are constructed by being treated as problems in the media"[87] (Wedl 2008: 6). By drawing on governmentality theory, Wedl describes this generation of knowledge as an interconnection of technologies of self-conduct and external conduct: since mass media are not isolated from political, economic and statal conditions, nor from the discourses, and are thus to a certain extent 'externally guided', they are embedded in sociopolitical circumstances of dominance. At the same time, they are not subject to any direct constraint and are therefore in a certain sense free, they therefore 'govern' themselves. As a critical public, they exercise a controlling function over other social institutions, such as the economy, the state and politics, in the sense of the 'sovereignty' approach of governmentality theory (see ibid.).

3.5.4 Conclusion

Seeing media as technologies of government means asking "how the media contribute to problematization, knowledge production, control of subject areas"[88] (Stauff 2005: 92). This section's aim is to discuss in theory and practice how, by way of journalistic control mechanisms of the interdiscourses used in the migration discourse in the *Luxemburger Wort*, media emerge as technologies of government in the sense of the governmentality concept. As the example of the collective symbol of 'flood' showed, certain discursive elements 'wander' out of a specific everyday discourse as metaphors and *through* a large number of discourses (for example, through the political and media discourses), whereby they become fundamental ideological concepts of civil society (see Keller 2011: 33). This civil society discourse is also a discourse in Foucault's sense, since it makes ritualized forms of speech, ways of acting and effects of power visible. In the sense of Foucault's governmentality concept and his analytical approach of 'sovereignty', these effects of media power develop at the moment of reception

---

87 | Personal translation of: "[...] bearbeiten demnach Problemfelder, die gleichzeitig durch die mediale Problematisierung erst konstruiert werden."

88 | Personal translation of: "[...] wie Medien zur Problematisierung, zur Wissensproduktion, zur Steuerung von Gegenstandsbereichen beitragen."

of such interdiscourses. The power-oriented measures of control and discipline identified with the analytical approach of 'discipline' are revealed in the present case study in the attributions conveyed on the 'migrant' by the media. An analysis of the agenda setting showed that the 'illegals' constituted a temporarily prevalent attribution in the migration discourse of the *Luxemburger Wort*. In addition, the *Luxemburger Wort* surprisingly often ascribes a status of 'subject' to the migrants by increasingly focusing on the fate of individuals and letting them tell their own personal stories. Although it was possible to show by way of example that media can indeed be considered "as processors of order, as technologies of government, at the same time as a power factor, a regulatory force"[89] (Schneider 2006: 86), it would require an analysis of Luxembourg's entire range of public opinion and media outlets on migration coverage as well as additional longitudinal, cross-sectional and reception studies of other (media) discourses in order to prove or disprove conclusively the assertion made at the beginning of this paper that media are technologies of government in the sense of the governmentality concept.

Sources

Luxemburger Wort (1999): "Akzente in der Nationaldivision. Nur zwei luxemburgische Spieler bei Schifflingen aufgeboten", Issue 191 of 20 August 1999, 21.
Federal Refugees Act as amended in the notice of 10 August 2007 (Federal Law Gazette I, 1902), which was last changed through Article 1 of the Act of 6 September 2013 (Federal Law Gazette I, 3554), http://www.gesetze-im-internet.de/bundesrecht/bvfg/gesamt.pdf, accessed 14.01.2014.

3.6 Conclusions

The case studies presented in this chapter combine extremely heterogeneous subjects of research under the perspective of Foucault's discussion of a specific power logic which achieves its impact and its extensive validity primarily through a variable combination of the various power logics of sovereignty, discipline and governmentality. We can see the interrelationship of these power logics as a tendentially historical sequence of technologies of power proceeding from the 'extrinsic' pole (sovereignty) to the 'intrinsic' pole (governmentality). On the other hand, the three logics still constantly intertwine with one another.

Hence it was argued that the varied architectural history of Vianden Castle in the Middle Ages was closely tied to the establishment of a system of domination which was able to assert its sovereignty to a great degree in the form of symbolic representations. As the case study on spaces of im-/morality showed, the problem

---

89 | Personal translation of: "[...] als Prozessoren von Ordnung, als Regierungstechnik, zugleich als ein Machfaktor, eine Ordnungsmacht."

of prostitution became acute in Luxembourg c. 1900 as a disciplinary-legal problem. At the same time, the authorities also operated with governmental security mechanisms, and techniques of self-regulatory, governmental conduct developed which had distinct gender-specific traits. The entirely different topic of biogas generation in the Greater Region places the actors between the poles of sovereignty and governmentality, between a system of public-law standards and the practices of individual operators. Finally, the analysis of a part of the recent migration discourse in Luxembourg's media focused in particular on the aspect of how interests of sovereignty are asserted by using specific journalistic sets of symbols, with the media also producing both disciplinary and governmental effects insofar as the underlying assumptions of normality are hardly ever questioned – also and especially by the journalists.

The four case studies concentrate on historically and topically very different social practices, which nonetheless have in common the construction of a political space. They perceive themselves as facets aimed at the national territory of Luxembourg as well as the entire border region. The studies also propose considering political spaces, such as 'Luxembourg' or the 'Greater Region', not in their static limitations and as definitive places, but focussing more closely on the many and varied practices of territorial policies subsumed under them. It was clearly shown that historically there are no territorial constants. Not only did the borders of the sovereign territories change in the course of time, but the sovereign areas of power themselves were continuously being redefined, by means of multifaceted practices of the exercise of power, in which the building of castles played a key role. In the nineteenth and twentieth centuries, the borders of the national states solidified, as the problematization of prostitution shows. Undesirable conduct was associated with the 'foreign' and the 'sick', which were to be kept away from the *'Volkskörper'*, or 'body of the people' – quite physically through expulsions of non-Luxembourgers whose lifestyle was deemed morally and/or politically suspicious. The police, judiciary and parliament equated the borders of the national state to those of the bourgeois order and consolidated them. A hundred years on, national borders, while seemingly weakened within the Schengen Area, continue to play an important part both discursively as well as in practice. Thus the analysis of recent articles on migration in the press shows that the collective symbol of the 'body of the people' may have been abandoned, but other metaphors – such as that of the 'flood' – continue to establish the distinction between external and internal as naturally given and implicitly carry a warning against 'inundation'. Here, the media reflect parliamentary debates and legislation while influencing them at the same time. At the legislative level, national borders are still a potent force within the territory of the EU, as the analysis of biogas production in the border region between Germany and Luxembourg shows. While some producers creatively circumnavigate these borders, others have internalized the guidelines. Borders are moreover not only recognized and designated between states, but also between farmers who produce energy and those who do not, between corporations and individual biogas producers, as well as between national states and the overarching framework of the EU.

This perspective, together with the specific instruments of Foucault's concept of power, provides us with propositions that can be taken up by subsequent studies. The hypothesis of the successive shift of technologies of power from sovereignty to governmentality will most certainly prove a rewarding starting point for clarifying, in terms of power politics, the problem of transition of a limited national space into cross-border spaces. In contrast to constructions of national identity, such transnational spatial constructions and models for everyday life in cross-border contexts presuppose flexible, complex governmental governance which demands from all actors a high degree of self-regulating forms of conduct.

3.7 References

Amann, Wilhelm/Bourg, Viviane/Dell, Paul/Lentz, Fabienne/Di Felice, Paul/Reddeker, Sebastian (2011): "Images and Identities", in: IPSE – Identités, Politiques, Sociétés, Espaces (ed.), Doing Identity in Luxembourg. Subjective Appropriations – Institutional Attributions – Socio-cultural Milieus, Bielefeld: transcript, 165-226.

Bailey, Brian (2012): La répresentation des réfugiés dans la presse luxembourgeoise, unpublished bachelor thesis, Luxemburg.

Binding, Günther: 2003. "Palas" in: Lexikon des Mittelalters, vol. VI, Munich, col. 1631-1632.

Bonfadelli, Heinz (2007): "Die Darstellung ethnischer Minderheiten in den Massenmedien", in: Heinz Bonfadelli/Heinz Moser (eds.), Medien und Migration. Europa als multikultureller Raum?, Wiesbaden: Verlag für Sozialwissenschaften, 95-118.

Brücher, Wolfgang (2009): Energiegeographie, Berlin/Stuttgart: Gebrüder Borntraeger Verlagsbuchhandlung.

Burger, Daniel (2010): "Burgen als Orte der Justiz und Verwaltung – Zum Funktionstypus der spätmittelalterlichen und frühneuzeitlichen Amtsburg", in: G. Ulrich Großmann/Hans Ottomeyer (eds.), Die Burg, Dresden: Sandstein Verlag, 72-85.

Cirikovic, Damir (2013): Darstellung der Migranten aus dem ehemaligen Jugoslawien in der luxemburgischen Berichterstattung (1990-2000). Die Rolle der Presse als Integrationsmedium, unpublished bachelor thesis, Luxembourg.

Delgado, Manuel (1972): Die 'Gastarbeiter' in der Presse. Eine inhaltsanalytische Studie, Opladen: Leske + Budrich Verlag.

Ebhardt, Bodo (1939-1958): Der Wehrbau Europas im Mittelalter. Versuch einer Gesamtdarstellung der europäischen Burgen, 2 vols., Berlin: Deutsche Verlagsgesellschaft.

Ehlert, Trude (2010): "Die Burgküche des Hoch- und Spätmittelalters im Spiegel literarischer Quellen", in: G. Ulrich Großmann/Hans Ottomeyer (eds.), Die Burg, Dresden: Sandstein Verlag, 144-157.

Fayot, Ben (1979): Sozialismus in Luxemburg, vol. 1, Luxembourg: C.R.E.S.

du Fays, Dominique (1985): La maison de Vianden. Des origines à 1337, unpublished master thesis, Liège: Université de Liège.

Foucault, Michel (1980 [French original 1977]): "The Confession of the Flesh. Interview". in: Colin Gordon (ed.), Power/Knowledge: Selected Interviews and Other Writings, 1972-1977 (trans. Colin Gordon, Leo Marshall, John Mepham, Kate Soper), New York: Pantheon Books, 194-228.

Foucault, Michel (1983 [French original 1982]): "The Subject and Power", in: Hubert Dreyfus/Paul Rabinow (eds.), Michel Foucault: Beyond Structuralism and Hermeneutics (trans. Robert Hurley *et. al*), 2nd edition, Chicago: The University of Chicago Press, 208-226.

Foucault, Michel (1984): "Polemics, Politics, and Problematizations: An interview with Michel Foucault", in: Paul Rabinow (ed.), The Foucault Reader (trans. Lydia Davis), New York: Pantheon Books, 381-390.

Foucault, Michel (1988 [French original 1984]): "The political technology of individuals", in: Luther H. Martin/Huck Gutman/Patrick H. Hutton (eds.), Technologies of the Self: A Seminar with Michel Foucault, Amherst, MA: University of Massachusetts Press, 145-162.

Foucault, Michel (1991) [French original 1981]): Remarks on Marx: Conversations with Duccio Trombadori (trans. R. James Goldstein and James Cascaito), New York: Semiotext(e).

Foucault, Michel (1997): "What is Critique?" in: Sylvère Lotringer (ed.), The Politics of Truth (trans. Lysa Hochroth and Catherine Porter), Los Angeles: Semiotext(e).

Foucault, Michel (1998): "Polemics, Politics and Problematizations", in: Paul Rabinow (ed.), Essential Works of Foucault, vol. 1 "Ethics", New York: The New Press.

Foucault, Michel (2000 [French original 1981]): "'Omens et singulatim': Towards a Critique of Political Reason", in: Essential Works of Michel Foucault 1954-1984, vol. 3 New York: The New Press, 298-325.

Foucault, Michel (2003 [French original: 1997]): Society Must Be Defended. Lectures at the Collège de France, 1975-1976 (trans. David Macey), New York: St Martin's Press.

Foucault, Michel (2007 [French original 2004]): Security, Territory, Population. Lectures at the Collège de France, 1977-1978 (trans. Graham Burchell), New York: Picador.

Foucault, Michel (2008[French original 2004]): The Birth of Biopolitics. Lectures at the Collège de France, 1978-1979 (trans. Graham Burchell), New York: Picador.

Friedhoff, Jens (2013): "Die Ganerbschaft zu Fels (Larochette). Ein Fallbeispiel gemeinschaftlichen Burgenbesitzes im Luxemburgischen", in: Olaf Wagener (ed.), Burgen und Befestigungen in der Eifel. Von der Antike bis ins 20. Jahrhundert, Petersberg: Michael Imhof Verlag, 124-137.

Füller, Henning/Marquardt, Nadine (2009): "Gouvernementalität in der humangeographischen Diskursforschung", in: Georg Glasze/Annika Mattissek (eds.), Handbuch Diskurs und Raum, Bielefeld: transcript, 83-106.

Gertenbach, Lars (2012): "Governmentality Studies. Die Regierung der Gesellschaft im Spannungsfeld von Ökonomie, Staat und Subjekt", in: Stephan Moebius (ed.), Kultur. Von den Cultural Studies bis zu den Visual Studies, Bielefeld: transcript, 108-127.

Goetzinger, Germaine (1997): "Der 'Verein für die Interessen der Frau' oder Bürgerliche Frauenbewegung in Luxemburg", in: Germaine Goetzinger/Antoinette Lorang/Renée Wagener (eds.), "Wenn nun wir Frauen auch das Wort ergreifen...", Frauen in Luxemburg 1880-1950, Luxembourg: Ministère de la culture, 63-79.

Goffman, Erving (1974): Frame Analysis. An Essay on the Organization of Experience, Boston: Northeastern University Press.

Großmann, G. Ulrich/Ottomeyer, Hans (eds.) (2010): Die Burg. Wissenschaftlicher Begleitband zu den Ausstellungen "Burg und Herrschaft" und "Mythos Burg". Publikation der Beiträge des Symposiums "Die Burg" auf der Wartburg, 19.-22. März 2009, Dresden: Sandstein Verlag.

Hausen, Karin (1992): "Öffentlichkeit und Privatheit. Gesellschaftspolitische Konstruktionen und die Geschichte der Geschlechterbeziehungen", in: Karin Hausen/Heide Wunder (eds.), Frauengeschichte – Geschlechtergeschichte, Frankfurt a.M.: Campus, 81-88.

Hellinghausen, Georges (1998): 150 Jahre *Luxemburger Wort*. Selbstverständnis und Identität einer Zeitung 1973-1998, Luxembourg: Editions Saint-Paul.

Herzog, Dagmar (2011): Sexuality in Europe. A Twentieth-Century History, Cambridge: Cambridge University Press.

Hilgert, Romain (2004): Zeitungen in Luxemburg 1704 bis 2004, Luxembourg: Service information et presse du gouvernement luxembourgeois.

Hoppe, Stephan (2010): "Hofstube und Tafelstube – Funktionale Raumdifferenzierungen auf mitteleuropäischen Adelssitzen seit dem Hochmittelalter", in: G. Ulrich Großmann/Hans Ottomeyer (eds.), Die Burg, Dresden: Sandstein Verlag, 196-207.

Hunold, Angelika (2011): Die Befestigung auf dem Katzenberg bei Mayen und die spätrömischen Höhenbefestigungen in Nordgallien (= Monographien des Römisch-Germanischen Zentralmuseums, vol. 88; Vulkanpark-Forschungen, vol. 8), Mainz/Regensburg: Schnell und Steiner.

Huyghebaert, Nicolas (1984): "Pourquoi l'église a-t-elle besoin d'avoués?", in: Publications de la Section historique de l'Institut grand-ducal de Luxembourg 98

(Avouerie en Lotharingie. Actes des 2ᵉ Journées Lotharingiennes 22-23 octobre 1982), 33-42.
Inglis, Ruth (1938): "An Objective Approach to the Relation between Fiction and Society", in: American Sociological Review 3, 526-533.
Keller, Reiner (2011): Diskursforschung. Eine Einführung für SozialwissenschaftlerInnen, 4th ed., Wiesbaden: Verlag für Sozialwissenschaften.
Klein, René (1997): "Genealogie und Ursprung der ersten Herren von Hamm in der Eifel (1239-1357)", in: Hémecht 49, 423-430.
Knapp, Ulrich (2008): Stätten deutscher Kaiser und Könige im Mittelalter, Darmstadt: WBG.
Kmec, Sonja/Lentz, Fabienne (2012): "Immigration", in: Sonja Kmec/Pit Péporté (eds.), Lieux de mémoire au Luxembourg/Erinnerungsorte in Luxemburg, vol. 2: Jeux d'échelles/Perspektivenwechsel, Luxembourg: Editions Saint-Paul, 109-114.
Kontos, Silvia (2009): Öffnung der Sperrbezirke. Zum Wandel von Theorien und Politik der Prostitution, Sulzbach: Ulrike Helmer.
Krause, Ellen (2003): Einführung in die politikwissenschaftliche Geschlechterforschung, Opladen: Leske + Budrich Verlag.
Kreutzer, Elena (2009): "Die Einwanderer in der Wahrnehmung der regionalen Presse des Saarlandes 1990-2005", in: Clemens Zimmermann/Rainer Hudemann/Michael Kuderna (eds.), Medienlandschaft Saar. Von 1945 bis in die Gegenwart, vol. 3: Mediale Inhalte, Programme und Region (1955-2005), München: Oldenburg Wissenschaftsverlag, 325-344.
Kunczik, Michael/Zipfel, Astrid (2005): Publizistik. Ein Studienhandbuch, 2nd ed., Köln: UTB.
Lang, Sabine (1995): "Öffentlichkeit und Geschlechterverhältnis. Überlegungen zu einer Politologie der öffentlichen Sphäre", in: Eva Kreisky/Birgit Sauer (eds.), Feministische Standpunkte in der Politikwissenschaft, Frankfurt a.M.: Campus, 83-121.
Leiner, Stefan (1994): Migration und Urbanisierung. Binnenwanderungsbewegungen; räumlicher und sozialer Wandel in den Industriestädten des Saar-Lor-Lux-Raumes 1856-1910, Saarbrücken: Fischer Verlag.
Lemke, Thomas (2011): Eine Kritik der politischen Vernunft: Foucaults Analyse der modernen Gouvernementalität, 2nd ed., Hamburg: Argument.
Lemke, Thomas (2008): "Gouvernementalität", in: Clemens Kammler/Rolf Parr/Ulrich Johannes Schneider (eds.), Foucault Handbuch, Stuttgart: Metzler, 260-263.
Link, Jürgen (2006): "Diskursanalyse unter besonderer Berücksichtigung von Interdiskurs und Kollektivsymbolik", in: Reiner Keller/Andreas Hirseland/Werner Schneider/Willy Viehöver (eds.), Handbuch Sozialwissenschaftliche Diskursanalyse, vol. 1: Theorien und Methoden, 2nd ed., Wiesbaden: Verlag für Sozialwissenschaften, 407-430.

Margue, Michel (2001): ""Wy ritterlîche sy dâ streit!" Kloster und Burg. Der historische Rahmen zur und in der Yolanda-Dichtung", in: Guy Berg (ed.), "Man mohte schrîven wal ein bûch." Ergebnisse des Yolanda-Kolloquiums 26.-27. November 1999. Luxemburg, Vianden und Ansemburg (= Beiträge zur luxemburgischen Sprach- und Volkskunde, vol. 31), Luxemburg: Imprimérie Centrale S. A., 105-125.

Margue, Michel (2012): "Vianden", in: Werner Paravicini (ed.), Höfe und Residenzen im spätmittelalterlichen Reich. Grafen und Herren (= Residenzenforschung, vol. 15, IV), Ostfildern: Jan Thorbeke Verlag, 1560-1574.

Majerus, Benoît (2003): "La prostitution à Bruxelles pendant la Grande Guerre: contrôle et pratique", in: Crime, Histoire & Sociétés 7/1, 5-42.

Maurer, Marcus/Reinemann, Carsten (2006): Medieninhalte. Eine Einführung, Wiesbaden: Verlag für Sozialwissenschaften.

Mersiowsky, Mark (2010): "Burg und Herrschaft – Ein Blick in die spätmittelalterliche Praxis", in: G. Ulrich Großmann/Hans Ottomeyer (eds.), Die Burg, Dresden: Sandstein Verlag, 126-133.

Meyer, Werner (2010): "Burg und Herrschaft – Beherrschter Raum und Herrschaftsanspruch", in: G. Ulrich Großmann/Hans Ottomeyer (eds.), Die Burg, Dresden: Sandstein Verlag, 16-25.

Milmeister, Jean (2003): Geschichte der Grafen von Vianden. 1090-1795, Vianden: Edition des Amis de l'Histoire de Vianden.

Mötsch, Johannes (1993): "Der Erwerb der Herrschaften St. Vith und Bütgenbach durch die Grafen von Sponheim", in: Jahrbuch für westdeutsche Landesgeschichte 19, 255-270.

Niehr, Thomas/Böke, Karin (2010): "Diskursanalyse unter linguistischer Perspektive – am Beispiel des Migrationsdiskurses", in: Reiner Keller/Andreas Hirseland/Werner Schneider/Willy Viehöver, Handbuch Sozialwissenschaftliche Diskursanalyse, vol. 2: Forschungspraxis, Wiesbaden: VS Verlag für Sozialwissenschaften, 359-385.

Paasi, Anssi (2004): "Place and Region: Looking Through the Prism of Scale", in: Progress in Human Geography 28/4, 536-546.

Paasi, Anssi (2011): "Geography, Space and the Re-Emergence of Topological Thinking", in: Dialogues in Human Geography 1/3, 299-303.

Parr, Rolf/Thiele, Matthias (2007): "Foucault in den Medienwissenschaften", in: Clemens Kammler/Rolf Parr (eds.), Foucault in den Kulturwissenschaften. Eine Bestandsaufnahme, Heidelberg: Synchron Wissenschaftsverlag der Autoren, 83-112.

Parr, Rolf (2009): "Diskursanalyse", in: Jost Schneider (ed.), Methodengeschichte der Germanistik, Berlin: de Gruyter, 90-107.

Reckinger, Rachel (2013): Der Gouvernementalitätsbegriff. Eine Perspektive zur Untersuchung von Raum- und Identitätskonstruktionen, IDENT2-Working Papers 4, 1-16.

Rödel, Volker (2010): "Burg und Recht – Ein Bereich vielfältiger Gestaltungs- und Wirkungsmöglichkeiten", in: G. Ulrich Großmann/Hans Ottomeyer (eds.), Die Burg, Dresden: Sandstein Verlag, 64-71.

Schmidt, Hans-Joachim: 2003. "Vogt, Vogtei" in: Lexikon des Mittelalters, vol. VIII, Munich, col. 1811-1814.

Schneider, Irmela (2006): "Zur Archäologie der Mediennutzung. Zum Zusammenhang von Wissen, Macht und Medien", in: Barbara Becker/Josef Wehner (eds.): Kulturindustrie reviewed. Ansätze zur kritischen Reflexion der Mediengesellschaft, Bielefeld: transcript, 83-100.

Schulte, Regina (1979): Sperrbezirke: Tugendhaftigkeit und Prostitution in der bürgerlichen Welt, Frankfurt a.M.: Syndikat.

Schwenken, Helen (2003): "'Papiere für alle'. Selbstorganisationen und Protestmobilisierung in der EU im Bereich der illegalen Migration", in: Ansgar Klein/Ruud Koopmans/Hans-Jörg Trenz/Ludger Klein/Christian Lahusen/ Dieter Rucht (eds.), Bürgerschaft, Öffentlichkeit und Demokratie in Europa, Opladen: Leske + Budrich Verlag, 117-140.

Scuto, Denis (2008): "Historiographie de l'immigration au Luxembourg", in: Hémecht 60/3-4, Actes des Deuxièmes Assises de l'historiographie luxembourgeoise, 391-413.

Scuto, Denis (2012): La nationalité luxembourgeoise (XIXe-XXIe siècles), Bruxelles: Édition de l'Université de Bruxelles.

Skrijelj, Arnela (2012): Der Islam in den luxemburgischen Printmedien 2000-2011, unpublished master thesis, Luxembourg.

Soiland, Tove (2005): "Kritische Anmerkungen zum Machtbegriff in der Gender-Theorie auf dem Hintergrund von Michel Foucaults Gouvernementalitätsanalyse", in: Widersprüche 25, 7-25.

STATEC (Statistics Portal Grand-Duchy of Luxembourg), Bibliographie zur wirtschaftlichen und sozialen Entwicklung in Luxemburg ab Beginn des 20. Jahrhunderts, http://www.statistiques.public.lu/fr/publications/series/bibliographie/bibliocomplete-2008.pdf, accessed 14.01.2014.

STATEC (Statistics Portal Grand-Duchy of Luxembourg), Bibliographie zur wirtschaftlichen und sozialen Entwicklung in Luxemburg, http://www.statistiques.public.lu/fr/publications/series/bibliographie/bibliocomplete-2013.pdf, accessed 14.01.2014.

STATEC (Statistics Portal Grand-Duchy of Luxembourg), Migration background of the population of Luxembourg, http://www.statistiques.public.lu/en/news/population/population/2013/04/20130409/index.html, accessed 02.01.2014.

Stauff, Markus (2005): Das neue Fernsehen: Machtanalyse, Gouvernementalität und Digitale Medien, Münster: Lit Verlag.

Trausch, Gilbert (2002): "Les deux occupations allemandes (1914-1918 et 1940-1944) en comparaison. Mémoire collective et précédent", in: Musée d'histoire de la ville de Luxembourg (ed.), "...et wor alles net esou einfach." Questions sur le Luxembourg et la Deuxième Guerre mondiale, Luxemburg, 346-361.

Trinkaus, Fabian (2014): Arbeiterexistenzen und Arbeiterbewegung in der Eisen- und Stahlindustrie. Die Hüttenstädte Neunkirchen/Saar und Düdelingen/Luxemburg im historischen Vergleich (1880-1935/40), Saarbrücken: Eigenverlag der Kommission für Saarländische Landesgeschichte und Volksforschung e. V.
Wedl, Juliette (2008): Medien in der Triade von Wissen, Macht und Subjektivierung. Der Nutzen Foucaults Gouvernementalitätstheorie für eine diskursanalytische Medienanalyse. 6./7. März, Vortrag auf der Tagung "Theorien und Methoden der sprach- und diskursbezogenen Produktforschung", unpublished manuscript, Trier, http://www.strategiespielen.de/wordpress/wp-content/j_wedl_medien_als_regierungstechnologien.pdf, accessed 02.01.2014.
Werlen, Benno (1999): Sozialgeographie alltäglicher Regionalisierungen, vol. 1: Zur Ontologie von Gesellschaft und Raum, 2nd ed. Stuttgart: Franz Steiner Verlag.
Werlen, Benno (2007): Sozialgeographie alltäglicher Regionalisierungen, vol. 2: Globalisierung, Region und Regionalisierung, 2nd ed., Stuttgart: Franz Steiner Verlag.
Werlen, Benno (2010a): Gesellschaftliche Räumlichkeit, vol. 1: Orte der Geographie, Stuttgart: Franz Steiner Verlag.
Werlen, Benno (2010b): Gesellschaftliche Räumlichkeit, vol. 2: Konstruktion geographischer Wirklichkeiten, Stuttgart: Franz Steiner Verlag.
Wille, Christian (2012): Grenzgänger und Räume der Grenze. Raumkonstruktionen in der Großregion SaarLorLux (= Luxemburg-Studien/Etudes luxembourgeoises, vol. 1), Frankfurt a.M.: Peter Lang.
Willems, Helmut/Milmeister, Paul (2008): "Migration und Integration", in: Wolfgang Lorig/Mario Hirsch (eds.), Das politische System Luxemburgs. Eine Einführung, Wiesbaden: Verlag für Sozialwissenschaften, 62-92.
Zeune, Joachim (1995): Burgen. Symbole der Macht. Ein neues Bild der mittelalterlichen Burg, Regensburg: Pustet.
Zimmer, John (1996): Befort, Bourscheid, Fels, Luxemburg und Vianden (= Die Burgen des Luxemburger Landes, vol. 1), Luxembourg: Editions Saint-Paul.
Zimmer, John (2010): Brandenburg, Dudelange, Koerich, Larochette, Septfontaines, Stolzembourg, Vianden (= Die Burgen des Luxemburger Landes, vol. 3), Luxembourg: Editions Saint-Paul.

4. Space and Identity Constructions Through Media-Related Practises

Luc Belling, Julia de Bres, Claudio Cicotti, Till Dembeck, Paul di Felice, Jeanne Glesener, Sonja Kmec, Anne-Marie Millim, Hérold Pettiau, Agnès Prüm, Céline Schall, Mónika Varga

4.1 Representations and Projections

The study of the relationship between media and identity received a new impetus in the 1990s through the work of radical constructivists such as Jean Baudrillard (1984 [1981]) and Siegfried J. Schmidt (1994). Drawing on the latter (among others), the BOAG (Bochumer Arbeitsgruppe für Sozialen Konstruktivismus und Wirklichkeitsprüfung) introduced the neologism "media identity" (*Medienidentität*). The authors advance that

"[globally ubiquitous] electronic mass media [...] have been feeding us for almost 50 years with the kind of 'implicit knowledge' we presume others have and we presume others presume we have. We know from mass media how to behave in certain contexts and situations and what we are allowed to say in them. The realities of local contexts are being infiltrated by acute media realities to such an extent that common knowledge has rather become secondary reality"[1] (BOAG 1997: 7).

Although media do not influence personal identity in a linear, causal or complete way (ibid.: 19), and the question concerning exactly how media shape personal

---

[1] | Personal translation of: "Geht es um die globale Allgegenwart elektronischer Massenmedien. Sind sie es doch, die uns seit nahezu 50 Jahren flächendeckend mit genau dem "impliziten Wissen" versorgen, das wir anderen unterstellen können und auch unterstellen können, daß diese anderen es uns unterstellen. Aus den Massenmedien wissen wir, wie wir uns in bestimmten Kontexten und Situationen verhalten sollen und was in ihnen sagbar ist. Die Wirklichkeiten lokaler Kontexte werden durch die akuten Medienwirklichkeiten infiltriert. Dies in einem Ausmaß, das kommunales Wissen eher zur Sekundärwirklichkeit werden läßt."

and collective identity constructions (and vice-versa) remains open to debate, there appears to be a general consensus among media theorists that media and identity are intrinsically linked. Thus, Hepp *et al.* (2003: 18, cited by Kneidinger 2013: 44) advance that current identities are – whether the concerned are aware of this or not – "media identities", since many of the pattern, structures, discourses and themes that shape and affect our identity have been internalized solely via media. Bernadette Kneidinger (ibid.) adds that it is only through media that Benedict Anderson's "imagined communities" take shape, as media determine how geopolitical spaces are being represented, transporting certain ideas about a land and its people. Frequently, a territory, 'its' people and 'its' culture are constructed as a homogeneous, self-contained entity. Nonetheless, media are not simply providers of collective images and stereotypes users identify with or distance themselves from. They only have an influence on perceptions of reality and modes of behavior, if actively appropriated by individual users. Some media even offer a "platform for active self-presentation" (ibid.: 45), such as Web 2.0, but also traditional letters to the editors of a newspaper or to the producers of a TV show that are being (partially) reproduced and disseminated via those channels.

Media: Definitions of what may count as a 'media' vary widely. Following Herbert Marshall McLuhan's line of reasoning, anything that may be used as an extension of the human body and modifies the human sensory perception may be considered a media, including language, script, print, numbers, money, light, roads, any means of transportation, weapons etc. (McLuhan 1964, see Mein 2011: 14, Tore 2011: 19-20). On the other extreme, some definitions limit media to technology based aids or means of communication. The former seem too broad, the latter too restrictive for our purpose, which hinges on the relational character of media. Media are not viewed as machines that 'transmit' readymade identities, but as social arrangements whose particularity it is to link social actors to social situations and social actors among themselves. Thus, media may be seen as 'contact zones' where relations among different participants are being negotiated (see Clifford 1997: 188-219). Similarly, Jean Davallon defines media as a "place of interaction" (*lieu d'interaction*) as well as as a "place of production and reflection of social discourse" (*lieu de production et de réflexion de discours social*) producing meaning and contributing to the organization of the social space it builds on (Davallon 1992: 103). Moreover, media are at the same time products and producers of language and social ties and thus always linked to issues of power (ibid.). The "implicit knowledge" media feed us with (see above) is unstable and establishes the real solely through recitations, as Michel de Certeau (1984: 186) put it:

"Social life multiplies the gestures and modes of behavior (im)printed by narrative models; it ceaselessly reproduces and accumulates 'copies' of stories. Our society has become a recited society, in three senses: it is defined by stories (*récits*, the fables constituted by our advertising and informational media), by citations of stories, and by the interminable recitation of stories."

4. Constructions of Space and Identity Created by Media-related Practises

The statistical survey as well as the qualitative or expert interviews some case studies examine show the reception of media images and their integration into everyday speech and thought. As the interviewees were aware of the fact that their utterances (transcribed and thereby rendered anonymous) would be read by others and discussed in the present book, one could even argue that their statements may be considered as media themselves. At any rate, they help us to understand how media function.

Looking at media produced or consumed in Luxembourg and the border areas, we examine a variety of questions: how dominant a role did state borders play in the twentieth century? Have they disappeared following the Schengen agreements or have they been replaced by other types of borders? What other material and immaterial borders emerge when examining multilingual advertisements, the cross-border *Robert Schuman Art Award* launched by the Quattropole[2], museums as means of mediation between visitors and the content they display, paratexts generated by a multilingual publishing houses, *facebook* walls of teenagers and films featuring petrol stations – a symbol of different types of border zones? What spatial identities do they project and reflect?

Spaces: Media analysis led to the identification of a variety of spaces that were often immaterial rather than material: two or more spheres coexist or collide, producing a certain tension and amalgamation. Depending on the case studies, these spaces are linguistic (advertisements). They concern the interaction of art with commerce (art awards), everday spaces and the world of arts, culture or science (museums) or the subtle interplay of literary and non-literary concerns (paratexts). Content analysis allows us to question binary constructions, such as public and private (*facebook*) or reality and fiction (films).

In order to understand how these spaces intersect in the media, different metaphors may be used. They allow us to examine how these binaries are being constructed and deconstructed in social and cultural spaces in which identities are subject to constant (re)negotiations.

Co-spatiality: Spaces can be connected in different ways, categorized by Jacques Lévy and Michel Lussault (2003: 523-524) as three types of "interspatiality": "interface", "spatial scaling" (*emboîtement*) and "co-spatiality". The first one, interface, concerns actions that establish, shift or question a border dividing adjacent spaces, for instance a religious, political or linguistic delimitation (ibid.: 522). The second one, spatial inclusion, posits a multiscalar approach, combining different levels of analysis, such as the local, the regional, the national, the continental or the global (ibid.: 306). Finally, co-spatiality infers that one space can mean different things to different people. Drawing on the findings of the Chicago School in the 1920s, which examined the various cities within a city, co-spatiality acknowledges the

---

2 | Quattropole is a cross-border city network linking Metz, Luxembourg, Trier and Saarbrücken. URL: http://www.quattropole.org/en/home

subjective perception of individual actors and the coexistence of multifarious spatial arrangements. Lévy and Lussault link the concept of co-spatiality to the image of Deleuze and Guattari's "thousand plateaus" (*millefeuille*) and the microfissures that allow for communication between them (ibid.: 213-214). These passages or "commutators" (ibid.: 186) may be physical places such as harbours, train stations or airports, allowing types of different spaces to interact and people with different social backgrounds to mix and mingle. The absence of passages does not call into question co-spatiality, which may also consist of a number of hierarchically structured, impermeable spaces.

When looking at the representation of (material as well as immaterial) spaces in various media, the notion of co-spatiality appears to be the most useful one, as the spaces we shall examine are neither territorially adjacent, divided by a clear border, nor included in one another, but may rather be conceived of as superposed layers of existence with passages in-between. We would like to focus on these in-between spaces that allow for transformations and creative appropriations, while remaining alert to the refusal or impossibility to cross them.

Hybridity and Third Space: The study of in-betweenness has gained momentum since the 1990s under the impetus of postcolonial studies, where 'hybridity' has become one of the most widely employed and most disputed terms. Drawing on Marie-Louise Pratt's "contact zone" and notion of "co-presence" (2007: 390-396) and Homi Bhabha's "third space" (1994: 37-39), 'hybridity' commonly refers to the creation of new 'transcultural' forms. Based on Mikhail Bakhtin's description of the disruptive co-existence of diverse and sometimes contradictory voices and discourses within one speech utterance or language, 'hybridity' stands for a change of paradigm: "[Language] is transformed from the absolute dogma it had been within the narrow framework of a sealed-off and impermeable monoglossia into a working hypothesis for comprehending and expressing reality" (Bakhtin 1981: 1039-1040). In the wake of postcolonial studies, this paradigmatic shift from "sealed-off and impermeable" mono-entities to intersecting and cross-fertilizing diversities has also been applied to cultures. Over the past twenty years, "third space" has become "a talisman of the current academic endeavours to reconceptionalize difference by means of spatial thinking", despite the inherent logic of any spatial language, which "does not only allow for difference but also for the fixation of difference by locating identities" (Lossau 2009: 63). The positive normative connotation of hybrid forms and "third spaces" originate from a critical position, aiming at undermining and subverting the hegemonic power of dominating cultures and discourses. However, empirical transnational studies do not always bear out this celebratory subtext (Mitchell 2002: 81-82). This scepticism may hark back to a more traditional reading of in-betweenness as problematic.

The Transformatory Power of Interstitiality: Writing in the 1920s, Frederick Thrasher characterised "interstitial" urban areas – at the threshold of two concentric circles, according to the then dominant explanatory model – by "deterioration, shifting population and cultural isolation" (cited by Cordasco/Galatioto 1971: 56). Half a century later, "interstitial communities" were still considered to be "plagued" by shifting population (ibid.). Following the observation that ethnic self-affirmation was neither limited to the "slums" nor to a transitory phase, scholars subsequently revised the findings of the Chicago School. Working on Paris, Albert Piette (1990) examined different types of "interstitial" neighbourhoods. His focus was on the interactions that took place in the "contact zone": either there was much contact but no sustainable interaction, no contact whatsoever or there were intensive exchanges. Nonetheless, the legacy of the Chicago School is still palpable, as the 'interstice' is defined as a meeting ground of various populations, as if it were surrounded by culturally homogenous neighbourhoods. This seems highly problematic when the focus is on social realities, but it may be applied much more adequately to the realm of imagination.

In our case studies, imagined spaces are indeed constructed as binaries (distinct languages or cultures, art/commerce, non-place/place etc.), whose very constructedness is revealed by investigating their meeting grounds. This 'contact zone' or 'interstice' – or rather the processes that constitute this unstable space, i.e. 'interstitiality' – is our object of analysis. The standard definition of the term 'interstice' refers to an intervening space, deriving its etymology "from Latin *interstitium*, from *intersistere* 'stand between', from *inter-*'between' + *sistere* 'to stand'" (Oxford Dictionaries). In biology 'interstitial space' refers to fluid compartments, surrounding individual cells. Interstitial fluid "provides a path through which nutrients, gases, and wastes can travel between the capillaries and the cells" (Concise Dictionary of Biology 2012: 107). Without taking the organic metaphor too far, we would like to stress the dynamic and liquid aspect of 'interstitiality', which denotes a passage between two (or more) clearly defined regimes.

The notion of 'passage' is a particularly popular spatial metaphor in literature and literary studies (Parr 2008). It is also used to describe the process of 'mediation' (Caillet/Lehalle 1995; Davallon 2004: 42, 46, 48). Moreover, 'passage' implies the idea of transformation of one's perception, that is the "transfiguration of the common place" (Danto 1974): when (tres)passing one implicitly challenges the strict dualism and separation of the distinct (linguistic, literary or symbolic) regimes. Even if one refuses to cross the threshold, one cannot negate its existence and the challenge it constitutes. Embracing the threshold, that is, constantly oscillating between different spaces and refusing to decide for one or the other, is the most radical way of experiencing the co-presence of both and the transformatory power of this middle ground. As Deleuze and Guattari (1987: 25) claim:

"The middle is by no means an average; on the contrary, it is where things pick up speed. *Between things* does not designate a localizable relation going from one thing to the other and back again, but a perpendicular direction, a transversal movement that sweeps one and the other away, a stream without beginning or end that undermines its banks and picks up speed in the middle."

By investigating the representation of this in-between space or interstice in various media, our case studies will show whether the "river banks", that is, the strict delimitation of binary regimes, are being undermined, or whether they are being reinforced, or both.

More concretely, we will examine firstly whether multilingualism and references to the cross-border context in advertising in Luxembourg contribute to the construction of transnational spaces, or whether they merely reinforce national spaces. We will then turn to the cross-border *Robert Schuman Art Award* and the interstitial space opened by the exhibitions and their representations in the official catalogues. The third subchapter will deal with museums and analyse to what degree their thresholds allow for a passage between public space and the space of high culture. Focusing on the self-representation of the multilingual publishing house *ultimo*mondo, the following case study will examine how literature can escape its attribution to clearly delimitated, territorially bounded linguistic spaces and thus embed itself as it were in a linguistic in-between space. The self presentation techniques of teenagers in cyberspace constitute another angle of approach of spatial identities in a subchapter investigating how *facebook* online profiles supplement identity projections and how they influence offline friendships. Finally, we will turn to petrol stations as interstitial places, both by their physical location and by their symbolic ambivalence (between numb routine and creative appropriation) and explore how this oscillation is practiced and narrated, both by interview partners and in films.

4.2 Multilingual Advertising and Regionalization in Luxembourg

Julia de Bres

This contribution analyses the connections between multilingual advertising and regionalization in Luxembourg, from a sociolinguistic perspective. Advertising is a fertile area for examining identity construction. Advertisers seek to appeal to consumers through a variety of techniques, one of which is orienting to features of their assumed identities, including linguistic identities. While consumers may resist these identity constructions, their constant reiteration is still likely to have some impact on appropriated identities. Advertisers also play a role in reinforcing and/or reconstructing spatial boundaries, through both linguistic and extralinguistic means. Interstitiality in this context can be approached from two angles. First, linguistic interstitiality could be represented by the use of more than one language variety in advertisements, through code-switching between varieties within an advertising text. Such interstitial linguistic practices disrupt the norm of monolingualism in written texts and are relatively frequent in advertising, a genre that often displays creative and transgressive forms of language use. Second, spatial interstitiality could be represented by the depiction of border-crossing practices in advertisements, for example depictions of the lived reality of cross-border workers or references to a transnational region. Moreover, use of languages associated with particular geographical spaces can itself be seen as a form of spatial representation, which may tend more towards the national (reflecting a state's dominant language use) or the transational (reflecting a more hybrid, i.e. interstitial, language use). Both these linguistic and spatial forms of interstitiality stand in opposition to other more dominant constructions of language and space, which would keep languages firmly separate and the borders between national spaces clearly defined. Using data from a large corpus of print advertisements in the free daily newspaper *L'essentiel*, as well as additional advertisements from the public space in Luxembourg, this contribution addresses two themes related to interstitiality. The first is how multilingual practices in the advertisements indirectly reference national and/or transnational spaces. The second considers advertisements that directly address the cross-border context. Overall, the contribution argues that multilingual practices and references to borders in the advertisements, while superficially interstitial, do little to create transnational identities, and rather tend to reinforce existing national state borders.

The research was undertaken within the theoretical framework of sociolinguistic research on multilingualism in advertising. Such research often focuses on advertisements produced in contexts where there is a clear default or majority language, including Japan (Haarman 1989), Germany (Piller 2001) and Ireland (Kelly-Holmes 2005). Researchers highlight the (stereotypical) associations of language varieties that advertisers draw upon in an attempt to transfer these connotations onto the products advertised (Cook 2001, Myers 1999). We find, for example, French as the language of romance, Italian as the language of food, German as the language of technical expertise, and English as the language of business (Haarman 1989, Piller 2001, Kelly-Holmes 2005). In such cases, researchers speak of the "linguistic fetish", "fake multilingualism" (Kelly-Holmes 2005) or "mock language" (Piller 2003), given that the multilingualism of the advertisements fulfills symbolic (and commercial) purposes rather than reflecting the linguistic realities of its target audience, many of whom may not understand the languages used at all. The situation is quite different in societies with a substantial tradition of multilingualism, where a range of languages are used for everyday communicative purposes and society members have a diverse linguistic repertoire. Luxembourg, with its official trilingualism in Luxembourgish, German and French, and ever-more complex forms of multilingualism as a result of recent patterns of migration and globalization, is one such setting par excellence. Here, while advertisers may still draw upon the symbolic associations of languages in designing their advertisements, the languages used may also reflect actual multilingual practices (and identities) in the community. For researchers, the languages of advertising in such settings can provide insights into language relationships in a multilingual context.

This case study involves analysing multilingualism in advertising in line with current approaches in sociolinguistics. At the same time, drawing on the common themes of this chapter, analysis of the advertisements takes into account not only multilingual aspects, but also the advertisements' relationship to the construction of interstitial spaces in particular. The research questions addressed are:

- How does multilingualism in advertising contribute to the construction of national and/or transnational spaces?
- How do references to the cross-border context in advertising contribute to the construction of national and/or transnational spaces?
- How does multilingualism interact with border references in advertising in constructing national and/or transnational spaces?

The data is a selection of advertisements from 2009-2011 in the free French language daily newspaper *L'essentiel*. German was traditionally the main (although not exclusive) language of the print media in Luxembourg. This has recently changed, with a range of publications available in other languages, including Portuguese, French and English, to cater for the increasingly diverse population of the country. The newspaper that is the subject of this research, *L'essentiel*, is read by a comparatively young, ethnically diverse, French-speaking and less wealthy audience (Lamour and Langers 2012). Its introduction to the Luxembourg context both represents a response to the growing French language readership and forms part of a general rise in free daily newspapers across Europe (ibid.: 2012).

The choice of *L'essentiel* as a source for analysing multilingualism and border construction is related to its close connections to the economic and demographic developments currently underway in Luxembourg, which have resulted in a high prominence of migrants and cross-border workers. Distributed in Luxembourg in areas of transit (e.g. train stations, city centres, pedestrian zones, bus stops, service stations, as well as entries to numerous companies)[3], the paper aims to reach both residents of Luxembourg and cross-border workers who commute to Luxembourg for work. In 2012, *L'essentiel* had 192,000 daily readers, exceeding those of the most read conventional daily newspaper, the *Luxemburger Wort* (172,100 readers). The readers of *L'essentiel* included 124,800 residents of Luxembourg, their nationalities mirroring the diversity of the resident population (46,900 Luxembourgish, 34,800 Portuguese, and 43,100 of other nationalities). The remaining readers consisted of 67,200 cross-border workers (49,500 French and 17,700 Belgian).[4]

---

3 | Personal correspondence with *L'essentiel*, 18 October 2012.

4 | Data from personal correspondence with *L'essentiel*, 4 October 2012. These figures are taken from a 2012 national survey of media consumption by Luxembourg residents,

4. Constructions of Space and Identity Created by Media-related Practises   149

Cross-border workers thus made up just over a third of the *L'essentiel* readership (35 %), and the proportion of French cross-border workers in particular (25.8 %) exceeded that of residents of Luxembourgish nationality (24.4 %). The integral relationship of *L'essentiel* to the diverse population of Luxembourg and the economic developments currently underway is well described by Lamour and Langers (2012: 18), who observe that "the viability of [free daily newspapers] rests on the presence of a dense and mobile population that can be captured during its daily movement in spaces of transit" and that they "capture a very eclectic readership made up of nationals and foreigners attracted by the grand-ducal urban economy."[5] In these ways, *L'essentiel* is a useful source of data on multilingualism in Luxembourg in a context of intense cross-border migration.

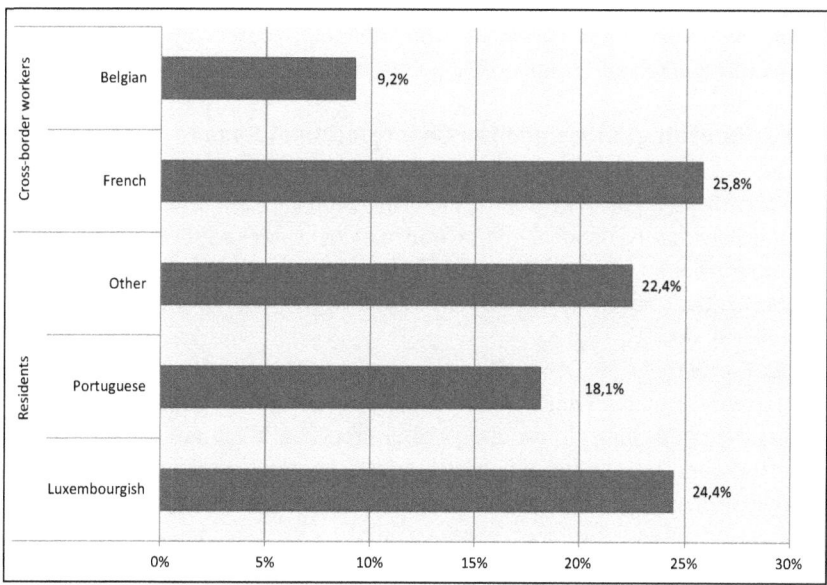

Figure 1: L'essentiel *readership in 2012 (source: L'essentiel)*

The period chosen for analysis was 2009-2011 (the three years leading up to the time the research was undertaken). Given the large number of advertisements

---

in addition to a supplementary survey focusing exclusively on cross-border workers. In response to my question as to whether German cross-border workers also read *L'essentiel*, *L'essentiel* noted that their number was not considered significant enough to include them in the survey. This was attributed to the language of the newspaper being French.

5 | Personal translation of: "La viabilité de [la presse quotidienne gratuite] repose sur la présence d'une population dense et mobile pouvant être captée lors du déplacement quotidien dans les espaces de transit"; "Elle capte un lectorat très éclectique fait de nationaux et d'étrangers attirés par l'économie urbaine grand-ducale" (Lamour/Langers 2012: 18).

in each issue, rather than collecting all advertisements across the period, it was decided to undertake a detailed analysis of advertisements from the available issues in three particular months: January 2009, June 2010 and December 2011 (the beginning, middle and end of the chosen period). The total number of issues analysed was 55 (out of an actual 63 issues produced across the three months[6]) and the number of advertisements in the final data set was 1,038. All of the advertisements in each issue were photographed, coded for date, page, company, sector and languages used, and analysed quantitatively to identify patterns across the period. Advertisements identified as especially salient in terms of multilingualism and/or the cross-border setting were then analysed qualitatively for aspects of language use, following established approaches to analysis of the discourse of advertising (e.g. Cook 2001). This contribution focuses on the qualitative analysis. Advertisements from other data sources are also included in the results that follow, to support the points made.

4.2.1 Multilingualism and the Construction of Space

The first theme to be discussed is the relationship between multilingualism and the construction of national and/or transnational spaces in the advertisements. Two main points are considered in this section: use of languages in relation to the national origin of the advertiser, and degree of multilingualism in the advertisements.

In the periods analysed, the advertisements placed came from a mixture of Luxembourgish, French and Belgian organizations. The French and Belgian organizations almost always used French as the main language of the advertisement, and the Luxembourgish organizations mostly used French or (very rarely) German, the traditional written languages of Luxembourg, as the main language of the advertisement. This general pattern reflects the dominant written language use associated with each nation-state (France, Luxembourg) or, in the case of Belgium, the French-speaking region of the nation-state.

One aspect that departs from this trend for reproducing written language use associated with particular national spaces is the use of Luxembourgish in the advertisements. Horner and Weber (2008) argue that the rise in salience of Luxembourgish in Luxembourg is particularly apparent in its increased use as a written language. This has been facilitated by ongoing processes of standardization. While previously regarded by many as a spoken dialect of German, Luxembourgish was progressively standardized over the nineteenth

---

6 | Access was only available to those issues that had been collected at the time by a contact, and some issues were missing. This involves four missing issues for January 2009 (16 out of 21 issues were available), one missing issue for June 2010 (20 out of 21 issues were available) and two missing issues for December 2011 (19 out of 21 issues were available).

and twentieth centuries so that a standard written variety now exists, with an official orthography, dictionaries and grammar.[7] This written standard is taught to migrants (e.g. in evening classes) but only minimally at school and is not widely known. Luxembourgish is, however, increasingly used in written domains, particularly the new media (see e.g. de Bres/Franziskus 2014), with wide orthographic variation. Present in 11.5 % of advertisements in the data, Luxembourgish was not a major language of advertising in *L'essentiel* but its presence is significant given its more recent use as a written language. When used, Luxembourgish appeared most often in minimal forms (e.g. slogans in advertisements otherwise in French), but was sometimes used more extensively (e.g. some stretches of text in French, others in Luxembourgish) and occasionally made up the entire text of the advertisement. What is especially interesting for the purpose of this contribution is who was using Luxembourgish. The most frequent users of Luxembourgish were Luxembourgish organizations. Examples include the bank Spuerkeess, using the slogan *Äert Liewen. Är Bank.* – Your life. Your bank. – and the insurance company Foyer, using *Äert Vertrauen a sécheren Hänn* – Your confidence in safe hands. Luxembourgish organizations were the only ones to produce advertisements written entirely in Luxembourgish. These included, for example, the Luxembourgish Ministry of Transport, the cultural broadcaster Radio 100,7, promoters of the film about Luxembourg *Mir wëllen net bleiwen*, and political parties advertising national elections. In these cases, the strategy appears to be to appeal to Luxembourgish national identity in order to foreground authenticity in advertising products with a national or local character (see also Reddeker 2011). Luxembourgish was also used by some foreign-owned companies in the data, however. In some cases, this appeared to represent a change during the course of the period analysed. The multinational Pearle opticians and the Belgian supermarket Delhaize, for instance, had French slogans in January 2009, but Luxembourgish slogans in June 2010 (*Är Aen a gudden Hänn* – Your eyes in good hands, and *Einfach méi fir äert Geld* – Simply more for your money, respectively). A more extensive example was an advertisement by Brico Plan-It, a hardware store in Belgium. This advertisement included a slogan in Luxembourgish (*Alles fir d'Haus* – Everything for the house) and the top half of the ad was entirely in (non-standard) Luxembourgish, so that readers needed to be able to understand Luxembourgish to understand the message about the offer (in large font *Du muss déch awer entscheeden, well den 23. Juni -20 % op 1 Artikel vun Ärer Wiel* – You need to decide though, because 23 June -20 % on

---

[7] | Current orthography is based on the rules of the *Luxemburger Wörterbuch* (1975), with a slight reform in 1999 (Mémorial 1999). In 2009 the Ministry of Culture formed a working group to modify and simplify the current rule system. A comprehensive official dictionary that will be based on the new rules – the *Lëtzebuerger Online Dictionnaire* (LOD 2007ff.) – is still in production (see Gilles forthcoming).

a product of your choice).⁸ Still, the majority of the text, including the technical details of the offer, remained in French. This advertisement is a good example of a polyphonic advertisement (Backhaus 2007), in that readers needed to be able to understand both French and Luxembourgish in order to get the full information, the advertisement thereby assuming a multilingual audience.

What can we make of the use of Luxembourgish by foreign companies? One possibility is using this language to appear local. This recalls the example of minority language use provided by Kelly-Holmes (2005) in which the foreign supermarket Tesco adopted Irish-English bilingual signage in Ireland, imitating the local supermarket Superquinn, "perhaps to make it look more Irish, or perhaps to show goodwill and an openness to the local culture" (Kelly-Holmes 2005: 134). Advertisers might also use Luxembourgish to target a specifically Luxembourgish audience. For example, a retail association across the border in France ran an advertisement in June 2010 wishing readers a good Luxembourgish national day and inviting them to come to Thionville where shops would remain open on the public holiday.⁹ Luxembourgish was used to say *Hierzlech Wëllkomm zu Diendenuewen* – a warm welcome to Thionville –, even using the Luxembourgish version of the town's name, *Didden(h)uewen*, albeit in markedly non-standard spelling.¹⁰ Residents with Luxembourgish nationality are a significant part of the *L'essentiel* readership and are perceived as being relatively wealthy, meaning they are especially targeted by retailers in France, Belgium and Germany. Use of Luxembourgish forms part of this attraction strategy. Advertisers from across the border in this data did not, however, take the further step of producing advertisements fully in Luxembourgish. Use of Luxembourgish is a powerful means of constructing space through language in the advertisements discussed above. In the case of Luxembourgish organizations, it is a tool that can be used to emphasize a national or local identity, setting oneself apart from non-Luxembourgish organizations, and implicitly reinforcing national boundaries. For foreign companies, use of Luxembourgish performs a different function, moving to deconstruct ideas of Luxembourgish as only being relevant for national actors and instead appropriating it for use by actors deriving from a broader regional space.

If use of Luxembourgish is one way in which advertisers of different national origins could be distinguished in the data, the degree of multilingualism they employed in their advertisements was another. Most cases of multilingualism in the advertisements involved an advertisement mainly in one language with a

---

8 | The text is unusual in its use of *awer* (however), which seems out of place in this context, the absence of a verb in the second half of the sentence and the inconsistent use of *du* (informal 'you') followed by Ärer (polite 'you' or plural form).

9 | The Brico Plan-It example above is a comparable example originating from Belgium.

10 | *Hierzlech* is also non-standard, possibly representing the Luxembourg city pronunciation of *häerzlech*.

small element such as a slogan in another language. There were very few highly multilingual advertisements, in the sense that one could not really say which was the main language of the advertisement. This is in accordance with a widespread norm of monolingualism in written texts (see Sebba *et al.* 2012). When these advertisements did appear, however, the level of multilingualism could be quite striking. For example a 2010 Luxembourg Airport advertisement promoting a running event included the text:

junior-kulturlaf/yuppi-mini-kulturlaf/team-run/walking
sport et musique – une combination unique

Here elements of (sometimes non-standard) French, Luxembourgish and English can all be detected. Similarly, a 2010 advertisement for an equestrian event included the following text:

CSI Luxembourg
Reiser Päerdsdeeg 2010
Jeudi:
Youngsters Tour
Vendredi:
International Qualifyings
Polo Night
Samedi:
Toyota Lexis Masters
STar Chef Cooking
Dimanche:
Grand Prix de Roeser
Prix P&T Luxembourg
Aire De Jeux Pour Enfants/Shopping Village
Et Specialités Culinaires

Again French, Luxembourgish and English blend together, with it being difficult to determine one main language for the advertisement.

Other instances of multilingualism in the data were more subtle, with some advertisements showing the influence of other languages in the use of non-standard forms in a particular language. Examples involving English in advertisements include non-standard grammatical structures or morphology, such as use of the 'Germanic hyphen' to connect compound nouns, formation of compound nouns as a single word, or excessive use of capital letters, revealing the influence of German or Luxembourgish in English and French. One bilingual example showing several of these features is a travel advertisement from 2009, which advertises *Events & Sightseeing, Parcs d'attractions, Day Spa, Minitrips, Citytrips, Comédies musicales, Foires et expositions* (events and sightseeing, fun parks, day spas, mini trips, city trips, musicals, fairs and exhibitions), ostensibly in a combination of French and English but also showing Germanic influences in the use of capital letters and compound nouns.

It can be questioned why there are so few highly multilingual advertisements in the data. This could reflect the application of the monolingual norm for written texts, which may apply even to highly multilingual Luxembourg. Nevertheless, all of the above instances of multilingualism came from the advertisements of Luxembourgish organizations, and in the data as a whole we can again see a distinction between organizations of different national origins in relation to their apparent degree of comfort with multilingual practices. A good example of this is advertisements by supermarkets of different national origins in the data. The Luxembourgish supermarket Cactus mainly produced advertisements in French, often with small elements in Luxembourgish (e.g. *pickeg Präisser–* spiky prices, *2009*). A more subtle feature of its advertisements was to not translate words on pictures of foreign-origin products when referring to them in the body of the advertisement. An example from 2009 was an advertisement that included pictures of products with the words *Blattspinat* and *Schinkenwurst* (spinach and ham sausage) on the packaging. Although the rest of the advertisement was in French, captions for these products reproduced the terms in German as on the packages, rather than using the French translations *épinards* and *saucisson au jambon*. This was also the case for a Cactus advertisement in 2010, where a caption reproduced the English term *tealight* from the packaging in the associated picture, rather than using the French term *bougie chauffe-plat*. In contrast, advertisements of the French supermarket Auchan were always fully in French, with careful translation of any products with non-French names into French in the captions. Delhaize was also most likely to translate product names into French, although in 2010 it included a Flemish caption (*harengs-matjes*). This language use reproduces perceived national trends of language use (multilingual in Luxembourg, monolingual in France, bilingual in Belgium).

In general, it seems that Luxembourgish organizations in the data did advertise in (sometimes subtly) more multilingual ways than organizations from the neighbouring nations, despite the fact that these latter organizations were also advertising in Luxembourg. While generally advertisers from all national origins stuck to one main language in the advertisements (showing the force of the monolingual norm), Luxembourgish advertisers occasionally showed a much higher degree of multilingual practices, perhaps reflecting the multilingualism of the national space.

4.2.2 Borders and the Construction of Space

If the multilingual practices discussed in the previous section indirectly contribute to the construction of largely national spaces, the data also includes more direct references to national and transnational spaces. This section focuses

4. Constructions of Space and Identity Created by Media-related Practises

on how the advertisements relate to the cross-border context. It was commonplace to see advertisements by companies located across the border and/or promoting events across the border. These advertisements implicitly lend a regional and supranational context to the newspaper advertisements. Here, however, the focus is on cases where the cross-border context was explicitly referenced in the advertisements, thereby contributing to the construction of national and/or transnational spaces.

There were very minimal explicit references to the 'Greater Region' in the data. In 2009 one Luxembourgish language school offering classes in English, French, German and Luxembourgish had *Grande Région* as part of its name (*inlingua Grande Région*), and in 2010 the Commune de Sanem advertised a garden show that it referred to as *une manifestation unique dans sont [sic] genre dans la grande région* – a unique manifestation of its kind in the Greater Region. The term did not appear in any other advertisements.

Several advertisements referred to the cross-border context by targeting cross-border workers in particular. In 2009, the Luxembourg gym Fitness Zone advertised a *Pack Frontaliers* – cross-border workers' package. In 2010, the LCGB union advertised itself as being *le syndicat luxembourgeois pour frontaliers* – the Luxembourg union for cross-border workers – and the French bank Banque Populaire Lorraine-Champagne claimed that it accompanied clients beyond "our borders" – *vous accompagne au-delà de nos frontières* – and that it was *la banque des frontaliers* – the bank of the cross-border workers. Many such advertisements had a tendency to reinforce the border rather than diminish its importance. For example, the Luxembourg bank BGL placed an advertisement in 2010 showing cross-border workers being interviewed on the point of arriving at the Luxembourg railway station, which is highly symbolic of the border, and a LUXGSM advertisement in 2010 constructed an intricate metaphor of cross-border workers having two pairs of glasses, one spectacles for the week and the other sunglasses for the weekend, asking them: *frontaliers, vous en avez marre de choisir?* – cross-border workers, are you sick of choosing? – and suggesting that they buy a phone that they could use both in Luxembourg and their country of residence. Such advertisements emphasize the border as a disruption, rather than constructing a borderless region.

An instance of more implicit reference to borders in the advertisements is the approach advertisers took to indicating their geographical location. Across the data set, some advertisements simply mentioned the place name (e.g. *Messancy*), while others noted the country (e.g. *Messancy (Belgique)*). In 2009, an advertisement for the concert venue Rockhal specified that its location, Esch-sur-Alzette, was in Luxembourg, before noting how far it was in kilometres from Nancy (France), Metz (France) and Saarbrücken (Germany). In 2010, there were two interesting instances of marked *lack of* reference to national locations in advertisements. Firstly, the retailer McArthur Glen Luxembourg uses the term Luxembourg in its product name, whereas it is actually situated in Belgium (just across the border, in Messancy). Whereas one could also interpret the name as referring to the 'province de Luxembourg' region of Belgium in which it is located, the use of this name within the Grand Duchy is more likely to be interpreted in national terms. This interpretation is supported by the text on the company's website, which gives directions to the shopping centre from Belgium, Luxembourg and France, but offers GPS coordinates rather than specifying the country: *Le centre McArthurGlen Luxembourg est situé à l'intersection de grands axes de communication entre le Grand-Duché de Luxembourg, la France et la Belgique. Coordonnées GPS: Longitude: 05 degrés 48'30" Latitude: 49 degrés 36'29".*[11] Secondly, the 'Chocolaterie du Luxembourg', on further research, is actually located just across the border in France. Both marked references to locations and strongly unmarked references to locations suggest that national differences are perceived by advertisers as being important. Why go to such lengths to obscure them if they are not? I would claim that the borders are again reinforced rather than deconstructed in these advertisements.

So far, this contribution has considered two themes separately in relation to the advertising data, multilingualism and the construction of space on the one hand, and border references and the construction of space on the other. In fact, these two themes can coincide within an advertisement. As an example, in September 2012 the telecommunications company Tango launched a billboard campaign in the forecourt of the Luxembourg city railway station. The campaign involved four posters attached to a metal frame, and was aimed at cross-border workers – presumably those who were likely to pass it on their way out of the train station en route to work. In the main poster it was stated that cross-border workers, like the three pictured, should *[choisir] Tango FreeBorders pour appeler, surfer et envoyer des SMS depuis [leur] pays d'origine* – choose Tango FreeBorders to call, surf and send SMSes from their country of origin. Underneath the main image, the text referred to the product as *la solution que tous les frontaliers attendaient* – the solution that all cross-border workers were waiting for. Each of the other three posters showed one cross-border worker each, introduced as *Marc le frontalier, Lisa die Grenzgängerin* and *Amélie la frontalière* – Marc the cross-border worker, Lisa the cross-border worker and Amélie the cross-border worker. It was stated under the image of each person that they had chosen Tango FreeBorders to call all their friends wherever they were. The message of this advertising campaign seems at first glance to involve surpassing borders, the product name *FreeBorders* and the content of the advertising text suggesting that the border presents no barrier to making use of the product in either Luxembourg or France, Belgium or Germany. The linguistic and visual features of the advertisement suggest otherwise, however. First, language choice is telling. While the main poster was entirely in French, the language choice for the other posters followed that of the featured cross-border worker's country

---

11 | Personal translation: "The centre McArthurGlen Luxembourg is situated at the intersection of large axes of communication between the Grand Duchy of Luxembourg, France and Belgium. GPS coordinates: Longitude: 05 degrees 48'30" Latitude: 49 degrees 36'29"."

of origin: we find French for Marc, German for Lisa, and French for Amélie. This reproduces the standard national (or in the case of Belgium regional) language use of each country, and reflects the widespread "one nation, one language" ideology (Woolard 1998), which posits that each nation state (or in the case of Belgium, region) has only one legitimate language associated with it. This language use was reinforced by the use of national flags in two circles to each side of the cross-border worker's head (placing him/her in the no man's land inbetween), with the text reinforcing a divide between nation states through the verbal opposition *il vit en France* (in the circle to the left) and *il travaille au Luxembourg* (in the circle to the right) – he lives in France, he works in Luxembourg. The overall effect of the advertising campaign, despite attempting to focus on the 'borderless' practices of cross-border workers, is to reproduce these borders, through both linguistic and non-linguistic means.

4.2.3 Conclusion

This contribution has drawn from a large corpus of newspaper advertisements, as well as a further advertising campaign outside the newspaper context, to examine the connections between multilingual advertising and regionalization in Luxembourg. The focus has been on identifying interstitial practices in both linguistic and spatial terms in the data. Interstitial linguistic practices are not absent in the data. We can for instance highlight the (rare) use of Luxembourgish by foreign companies and the adoption of multilingual practices to at least some degree by advertisers of all national origins. These advertisements depart from the monolingual norm applying to written texts, and suggest a possibility for more fluid linguistic and spatial relationships. Nevertheless, the general pattern is for language use to closely reflect dominant language use within the nation-state of the advertiser, markedly multilingual practices remain restricted to advertisers originating from multilingual Luxembourg, and even use of Luxembourgish by foreign advertisers can be seen as a reference to the national space of Luxembourg, rather than as creating a common regional space. This linguistic reinforcement of the national is also apparent in more direct references to the cross-border context within the advertisements, which tend to reinforce spatial borders even while focusing on those people who cross them. The overall conclusion is that both multilingual practices and references to borders in the data, while superficially interstitial, do little to construct a transnational region, but rather tend to reinforce existing national state borders. When it comes to the advertising data considered here, identity constructions involving truly interstitial linguistic and spatial practices seem rather thin on the ground.

4.3 THE ARTISTIC AND CULTURAL STAKES FOR THE WORKS SELECTED FOR THE ROBERT SCHUMAN ART AWARD: EXHIBITION AND PUBLICATION SPACES – PLACES OF TRANSFORMATION AS WELL AS ARTISTIC AND CULTURAL INTERSTICE?

Paul di Felice

"In an art exhibition complex relations come into play between what is shown and what is said; between the visitors and what they are able to read or understand. What also comes into play here are what the social notions of an exhibition (of contemporary art), a mediating text or a visit should be"[12] (Glicenstein 2013: 166).

Created in 1991 as an art biennale for promoting cultural and artistic exchange and reinforcing common 'identities' between the four cities of Luxembourg, Metz, Saarbrücken and Trier, the award[13] is named after Robert Schuman, one of the founding fathers of the European Community. This event, which takes place every two years in one of the four cities, has been organized since 1995 in such a way that the city hosting the award determines the curators (one for each city) who in turn select the artists, each represented with five works. These works are presented in an exhibition, accompanied by a bilingual (German-French) catalogue and assessed by eight jurors.

The complicated but well-structured organization remains very organic and dynamic through the constantly changing artistic and cultural players (artists and curators, jury and representatives of the cultural establishment).

The artistic and cultural stakes for the organizing city are considerable, because it is the one that determines the exhibition locations and coordinates the choice of curators. It has to consider issues of the works' mediation and reception, place the works in the context of its own local cultural policy and at the same time help them to find recognition in the world of contemporary art beyond its borders. But how does the exhibition's disposition and the concept of the catalogue relate to the dynamics resulting from the opposition between local or regional artistic and cultural discourses on the one hand and international contemporary art on the other?

---

12 | Personal translation of: "Dans des expositions se jouent des relations complexes entre ce qui est montré et ce qui est dit ; entre les différents auteurs de ce qui est dit et le contexte où ils le disent ; entre les visiteurs et ce qu'il leur est possible de lire ou de comprendre. Ici se jouent aussi des représentations sociales de ce que doit être une exposition (d'art contemporain), un texte de médiation, une visite."

13 | The *Robert Schuman Art Award* includes a prize money of 10,000 € for one or more of the selected artists. Besides this sum of money, being awarded also lends greater public visibility and recognition to the artist and his or her work.

If one considers the catalogue, as the only official and permanent reference to the exhibition, to be an additional space for presenting the exhibition, one may ask how this space can encourage the transition of the nascent work from the studio to the exhibition. Do the exhibition and the catalogue allow the works to be related to each other in a space of opposition and exchange?

This chapter will also deal with the question of artistic recognition connected to topics that are inherent to the event of the *Robert Schuman Art Award*, i.e. the opposition between regionalism and internationalism, as well as the contrast between local and international contemporary art.

Furthermore, I will look into the question of artistic and cultural representation by referring to specific works presented at the exhibition and their accompanying texts. I will examine the mediation and the reception of the works by verifying in how far the catalogue has the potential to be an additional exhibition space, even becoming an interstitial space where the transfiguration of 'local/regional' artistic work can take place, aiming at international recognition via cultural and artistic identity constructions and deconstructions.

In terms of methodology, I will proceed by analysing, using examples from the catalogue of the organizing city, four topics that show the prize as a "place of interaction" and as a "place of production and reflection of the social discourse"[14] (Davallon 1992: 103). More precisely, I will show how the prize expresses an interstitiality and a productive tension between two types of discourse and practice, between international orientation of contemporary art on the one hand and regional embeddedness on the other. The selected works frequently play with or dissociate themselves from this local rootedness by making use of the cross-border character of the respective region, precisely in order to endeavour to establish an international artistic and cultural discourse. This oscillation between the local and the global takes place in various ways. I have distinguished four different themes that emerge in the following editions of the prize:

- Luxembourg 1995: Can one speak of a European orientation and of an inscription of cross-border regional art into international contemporary art?
- Metz 2001: Art as a dissolution of borders?
- Saarbrücken 2005: Political discourses, socially engaged, aesthetical works?
- Trier 2007: The catalogue as a space of aesthetic exchange and a facilitator for the appropriation of new artistic tendencies?

---

14 | Personal translation of: "Lieu d'interaction", "Lieu de production et de réflexion du discours social."

The 1995 edition which took place in the framework of the event *Luxembourg – European Capital of Culture* relaunched the prize – after the fiasco of 1993 – giving it a European orientation and inscribing regional cross-border art into international contemporary art. Metz 2001, where the concept of art as a dissolution of borders was a key theme, constituted a further important step.

Saarbrücken 2005 attempted to go beyond the regional framework by turning to political, ethical and aesthetical discourses without any apparent link to the location of the exhibition. This was however not a linear development: the 2007 Trier edition which took place, again, in the framework of *Luxembourg and Greater Region – European Capital of Culture* returned to art as a link between the region and the world of contemporary art. What was more apparent here than in other editions, however, was that the radical treatment in the regional and global artistic productions chosen by the artists in 2007 was not always fully appreciated by the not very experienced regional audience. The communication projected by the exhibition and the catalogue nevertheless reveals the concern of the prize's major players to encourage the public's acceptance of contemporary art. We shall see in how far the catalogue has contributed to a better understanding of new international artistic trends in a regional context.

4.3.1 Luxembourg 1995: Can one speak of a European orientation and of an inscription of cross-border regional art into international contemporary art?

After an initial attempt in 1991 (a sort of test run) and after the fiasco of 1993 the *Robert Schuman Art Award* was relaunched in 1995 in Luxembourg.

In the framework of the cultural year *Luxembourg – European Capital of Culture*, the award gave itself a new structure compared to 1991 in order to ensure a higher degree of artistic quality: four renowned curators were invited to propose four artists from one city.

Luxembourg's decision to entrust the project coordination to the Swiss Urs Raussmüller, 1982/83 founding member of the *Hallen für Neue Kunst* in Schaffhausen[15], was a decisive step. Responsible for redesigning the *Casino Luxembourg – Forum d'art contemporain* to an exhibition space during the cultural year, Rausmüller was also assigned by the city of Luxembourg to select the Luxembourg candidates for the *Robert Schuman Art Award*. He had made himself a name with his activities as director of the *Hallen für Neue Kunst* in the field of museography of contemporary art. With the so-called *White Cubes*, the *Casino Luxembourg* established an exhibition concept which respected the classical architecture of the building, creating a neutral atmosphere particularly effective

---

15 | With an exhibition area of over 5,000 m² this museum, housing a large collection of concept art, *arte povera*, *minimal art* and *land art*, served for a longtime as a model for other museums of contemporary art.

for exhibiting contemporary art. As the curator for the *Robert Schuman Art Award*, he was also responsible for the museography of the exhibition space, the Halle Victor Hugo. As the mayor Lydie Würth-Polfer emphasized in her preface to the catalogue: "With the Halle Victor Hugo, Urs Rausmüller succeeded in creating an exhibition architecture that is very sobre and very appropriate"[16] (catalogue 1995: 4).

For Rausmüller, the *Robert Schuman Art Award*, one of many art events in the programme of the cultural year, became a challenge to create an artistic approach that was original and convincing. It aimed for a process that embraced the logics of contemporary art rather than for one qualitatively superior single oeuvre.

His particular concern was therefore contrasting the works and the artists in a space and he favoured the reception through documentation and diffusion:

"There is only a point in bestowing an art award if the purpose is not to honour an individual but rather to engage with many. The award provides the pretext to launch a work and orientation process which involves much more than the participating artists, and that is where its primary importance lies"[17] (ibid.: 7).

As the politically responsible office-holder, Lydie Würth-Polfer also mentions the importance of the event with regard to the cross-border mingling of ideas and concerns. In her view, the art award shows the quality of contemporary art production that reaches beyond the Greater Region:

"For a long time already the cultural commonalities of the inhabitants of the border region around the cities of Luxembourg, Metz, Saarbrücken and Trier have been inspiring those responsible for cultural politics to constantly new projects. The European spirit is expressed – more than in any other event – in the *Robert Schuman Art Award*, which after being redesigned gives an overview of the best contemporary works of art in our cross-border and cross-regional space"[18] (ibid.: 5).

---

16 | Personal translation of: "[...] réunit seize créateurs retenus dans une présentation architecturale très sobre et très adaptée."

17 | Personal translation of: "Die Verleihung eines Kunstpreises hat nur dann einen Sinn, wenn das Ziel nicht in der Auszeichnung eines einzelnen, sondern in der Beschäftigung mit vielen gesehen wird. Der Preis liefert den Vorwand, einen Arbeits- und Orientierungsprozess auszulösen, in den weit mehr als die betroffenen Künstler einbezogen sind, und darin liegt seine primäre Bedeutung."

18 | Personal translation of: "Im Robert-Schuman-Preis, der nach seiner Neugestaltung einen Überblick über die besten zeitgenössischen Kunstwerke in unserem grenz-und regionenübergreifenden Raum gibt, findet – mehr als in jeder anderen Veranstaltung – der europäische Geist seinen Ausdruck."

This European and international dimension was also underscored by the choice of the nominated artists. It was above all the curator for Saarbrücken, Jo Enzweiler, who, while deploring the poor level of the 1993 submissions, raised the political and artistic stakes of the prize by justifiying his choice of artists as follows:

"In order to reach this desired level from the very beginning, I have pledged to consider in my selection artists who already possess an expressive, rich and visually convincing œuvre"[19] (ibid.: 18).

It was he who nominated the artist Wolfgang Nestler who would go on to become the prize-winner of Luxembourg 1995. All four coordinators favoured putting the emphasis on the strong personality and expressive freedom of the nominated artists. Rausmüller reminds us in the catalogue:

"The learnable mastery in handling materials and forms on the surface or in space or the visually successful realization of a specific topic are therefore in themselves insufficient criteria for assessing artistic quality. The only thing that counts in art is boundless individuality – the artist's subjective stance which, in its condensation in the work of art (regardless of the form it takes), attains universality in the course of time"[20] (ibid.: 6).

The French version of the catalogue renders the German "uneingeschränkte Individualität" as "personnalité unique et libre de s'exprimer", reflecting a shift

---

19 | Personal translation of: "Damit von Anfang an dieses angestrebte Niveau auch erreicht werden kann, habe ich mich darauf festgelegt, bei meinem Vorschlag Künstler zu berücksichtigen, die über ein anschauliches, umfangreiches und öffentlich wirksames Œuvre verfügen."
French version of the catalogue text: "Afin de parvenir à ce niveau, je me suis engagé à choisir, en soumettant ma proposition, des artistes dont l'œuvre est expressive, riche et visuellement convaincante."
20 | Personal translation of: "Das erlernbare Geschick im Umgang mit Materialien und Formen auf der Fläche oder im Raum oder die visuell geglückte Umsetzung einer bestimmten Thematik sind darum als solche keine ausreichende Vorgabe für eine Bewertung künstlerischer Qualität. Was in der Kunst zählt ist einzig uneingeschränkte Individualität – die subjektive Haltung des Künstlers, die in der Verdichtung im Kunstwerk (welche Erscheinungsform es auch immer annimmt) im Verlauf der Zeit Allgemeingültigkeit erlangt."
French version of the catalogue text: "La maîtrise acquise des matériaux et des formes, à plat ou dans l'espace, ou la transposition réussie d'un sujet donné ne suffisent pas, en soi, à évaluer la qualité artistique. Ce qui importe dans l'art, c'est la personnalité unique et libre de s'exprimer, le comportement subjectif de l'artiste qui, en se concentrant sur son œuvre (quelle que soit son apparence) parvient, avec le temps, à la reconnaissance universelle."

in content and emphasizing the significance of the artist's "singular personality" and his or her "freedom of expression."

Sculptor Wolfgang Nestler, who before had participated (in 1977 and 1987) in the major art exhibition *Documenta* in Kassel that takes place every 5 years, presented an oeuvre that confirmed this longtime involvement with a new visual concept inspired by minimal art. His international recognition – art critics compare him to the great American artist Richard Serra, known in Luxembourg for his sculpture *Exchange*, which was erected on the Kirchberg in 1996 – makes him the ideal representative of this European and international development of an art that has emancipated itself from regionalism: "Wolfgang Nestler was, parallel to the American Richard Serra, the decisive protagonist of the new paradigm – for here there is a paradigm, not a rapidly exhausted stylistic variation"[21] (Schneckenburger 2013).

Luxembourg 1995 thus aimed more at an oeuvre that would endure over time, at the visual and formal qualities of the artistic approach and its international recognition, in other words at the total output of an artistic personality, rather than at the aesthetic qualities of an individual work.

The event taking place in the framework of this cultural year therefore highlighted the visual qualitites of the region's artists by giving the award to an artist whose work had already attained the status of European and international art. Instead of serving as a stepping stone to an international career for a young artist, the award here used an artist's reputation in order to reinforce its own recognition and standing, by nominating a personality that had already attained international artistic recognition.

4.3.2 Metz 2001: Art as a dissolution of borders?

The particular feature of the 2001 edition in Metz was the challenge of organizing an event that comprised three exhibitions at three renowned venues in the city.[22] "The work of art invites us", wrote Jean-Marie Rausch, mayor of Metz, in his preface, "to once more discover new paths and traverse the rifts of history. In this European space, everyone can grow and bring a part of himself or herself to the table"[23] (catalogue 2001: 7).

---

21 | Personal translation of: "Wolfgang Nestler war, parallel zu dem Amerikaner Richard Serra, der maßgebliche europäische Protagonist des neuen Paradigmas – denn es handelte sich um ein Paradigma, nicht um eine rasch erschöpfte Stilvariante."
22 | The exhibition venues in Metz were the Musée de la Cour d'Or, the Arsenal and the Ecole des Beaux-Arts.
23 | Personal translation of: "Das Kunstwerk lädt uns ein, noch einmal neue Wege zu entdecken und über die Gräben der Geschichte zu gehen. In diesem europäischen Raum kann jeder wachsen und ein Teil von sich selbst aufbringen."

The coordinators also emphasized the event's originality and participatory format. The variety of exhibition venues and the fragmentation of the art works – presented in such diverse forms as video, installation, photography, text and painting – lent a pronounced dynamism to Metz 2001.

With its novel orientation, the *Robert Schuman Art Award* now had the aim to remodel the disposition of the exhibition as well as the communication with the public by creating spaces that were more suited for the presentation of processes than of finished works. The elimination of all sorts of borders was also supposed to show in the style of presentation. The exhibition was to be regarded as a dynamic and permeable dispositif, as Reesa Greenberg described it:

"A model which posits the exhibition less as entity and more as event, less as finite and fixed and more as temporally fluid phenomenon, less as an insular construct and more as a relational structure in its internalized and externalized connections, less as address and more as conversation" (Greenberg 1995, 118-115).

In this Metz edition, the emphasis was on the fluidity and flexibility of the artists who via their creative work evoked openings, transitions and spaces of exchange that supersede ideological and geographical boundaries. Laure Faber and Bettina Heldenstein, the coordinators for the city of Luxembourg, emphasized:

"Artistic work does not stop at borders. Artists do not even need to ignore or delete borders, since these technically do not exist for them. They are only fictional lines that delineate a sphere of activity within which a number of people exercise power. The artists' sphere of activities however is the whole world as they experience and perceive it. It is at the same time matter and subject"[24] (catalogue 2001: 13).

Her choice of artists, particularly with Su Mei Tse (laureate), a young artist who comes from a multicultural background (born in Luxembourg, English mother, Chinese father) and Yvan Klein, who presented his series in Japan, contributes to this idea of opening which contemporary art can convey by breaking through the imposed boundaries. In the text of their presentation, the two Luxembourg coordinators formulated this very clearly:

"Neither their background, nor their training nor their interests are limited to Europe. In our view, the choice of these artists, whose works testify to an open-mindedness and a real

---

24 | Personal translation of: "Künstlerische Arbeit macht nicht an Grenzen halt. Künstler brauchen Grenzen noch nicht einmal zu ignorieren oder zu tilgen, da diese für sie, genau genommen, nicht existieren. Es sind nur fiktive Linien, die ein Wirkungsfeld begrenzen, innerhalb dessen einige Menschen Macht ausüben. Das Wirkungsfeld der Künstler ist jedoch die ganze Welt so wie sie sie erleben und wahrnehmen. Sie ist gleichzeitig Materie und Subjekt."

4. Constructions of Space and Identity Created by Media-related Practises

involvement in the present, seems justified for an award on a regional level which at the same time claims international recognition"[25] (ibid.: 13).

This edition seems to be expressly directed at a distant world, an artistic journey that aims to take the spectator far beyond the regional borders and the topics connected to the city network of the *Quattropole*. As if the coordinators had invited the artists to "wander about in the Afterworld, far removed from geographical borders and ideological limitations they would have been subjected to in order to reduce them to a cultural product that would be treated as a commodity"[26], as Bernard Copeaux, coordinator of Metz, put it in the catalogue. (ibid.: 23).

The dyptichs of the series *Nippon Inside/out* of Luxembourg artist Yvan Klein illustrate this transition into another culture where static interiors contrast with dynamic exteriors in an opposition of tradition and modernity. The association of aleatoric images, frequently determined by the formal components of photography, provoke in the beholder a cultural shift of involvement.

Figure 1: Cover of the catalogue Robert Schuman Art Award 2005

---

25 | Personal translation of: "Weder ihre Herkunft, noch ihre Ausbildung oder ihre Interessen beschränken sich auf Europa. Die Auswahl dieser Künstler, deren Arbeiten Zeugnisse einer offenen Sichtweise sowie eines wirklichen Engagements in der Gegenwart sind, erscheint uns gerechtfertigt für einen Preis auf regionaler Ebene, der gleichzeitig international Geltung beansprucht."

26 | Personal translation of: "[...] im Jenseits zu irren, weit entfernt von geografischen Grenzen und ideologischen Einschränkungen, die ihnen aufgezwungen wären, um sie zu einem kulturellen Produkt, das wie Ware behandelt würde, zu reduzieren."

In the installation *Si lo desea, cante!* by Dieter Kunz, an artist nominated by Saarbrücken, there is also no evidence of a regional topic. Far away from home, at the bus station and the metro station *Bellas Artes* in the centre of Caracas, Venezuela, he set up a two-part installation (video and audio) which retraces the surroundings in shifted reality and time, while the cityscapes of the Trier artist Rut Blees, steeped in mysterious and magical light, seem to transport us into the photographic non-places between reality and fiction.

In focusing on the dissolution of borders, the award of Metz 2001 not only presents works of art that pinpoint the cultural transfer from one region to another, but it also created a platform of reflection and of political, social and artistic discourse. In their contrast, the works of art, frequently inspired by personal, local, regional and national themes, took on a global dimension.

4.3.3 Saarbrücken 2005: Political discourses, involved, aesthetic works?

"Visual art is suited like no other to be an ambassador of lively exchange", wrote Charlotte Britz, mayor of Saarbrücken, in the preface of the catalogue of the *Robert Schuman Art Award*[27] (catalogue 2005: 6). Further on in the catalogue, in his presentation of the Luxembourg nominees, the art historian and critic and coordinator for the city of Luxembourg, René Kockelkorn, regrets that "precisely the political, the ideological plays no role whatsoever in the annals of the so-called *Schuman Art Award*, barring the usual babble at the opening of the respective exhibitions"[28], and he explains his choice of artists, "in order to change this", by proposing works "which fathom human existence on various levels of society"[29] (ibid.: 10).

The Luxembourg contribution is, appropriately, an installation by Jerry Frantz titled *Schandmaul* ('malicious tongue'), consisting of a video production and a 17th century iron mask, a loan from the Medieval Crime Museum in Rothenburg ob der Tauber.

In the Saarbrücken projection we see a film which records without sound the facial expressions of people reacting to questions posed by a female journalist. The people interviewed in Luxembourg were asked provocative questions such as: "Would you murder your wife if you were certain you could get away with it?" or "Do you think Hitler did good things?" The installation shows the people filmed with a video camera and their different facial expressions in slow motion.

---

27 | Personal translation of: "Die Bildende Kunst ist wie keine andere dazu geeignet, Botschaften eines lebendigen Austausches zu sein."

28 | Personal translation of: "[...] dass gerade das Politische, das Ideologische, in den Annalen des so genannten Schuman-Kunstpreises, außer in den üblichen Sonntagsreden zur Eröffnung der jeweiligen Ausstellungen, keine Rolle spielt."

29 | Personal translation of: [...] "dies zu ändern", [indem er Werke vorschlägt,] "[die] auf verschiedenen Ebenen die Gesellschaft und die menschliche Existenz aus[loten]."

In this installation which relates the iron scold's bridle – in the shape of a pig's head – to the mute facial expressions shown in close-up, the artist invites us to reflect on the freedom of opinion and self-censorship in a liberal democracy. The relevance of the work with its references to history and politics, the geographical transfer from one city to another, the aesthetic and artistic prejudice are treated here, as always with Frantz, with a certain irony, while the viewer is still accorded a good measure of interpretational freedom.

The award winner Margit Schäfer, nominated by the city of Saarbrücken, takes her inspiration more from her family than from society at large, but with her series *Zehn Leben* ('Ten Lives') and *Vermächtnis* ('Legacy') she questions, through photo album pictures, the representation of the woman as seen by the petty-bourgois male. In these series, the artist plays with the synchronization of self-identification and identification by others by staging herself as her own mother on an old family photograph taken by her father.

These works by Frantz and Schäfer *in situ* testify to a political involvement that was announced by certain exhibition curators, even though in this edition not only social issues but also purely visual and aesthetic aspects played a role.

Figure 2: Video-stills excerpts from the catalogue Robert Schuman Art Award 2005 (Jerry Frantz)

4.3.4 Trier 2007: The catalogue as a space of aesthetic exchange and a facilitator for the appropriation of new artistic tendencies?

Looking at the catalogue of 2007, one immediately sees that the graphic design has not changed between 2005 and 2007. There is a shift from orange to the complimentary colour blue, but format and typography have remained unaltered. As already in 2005, the catalogue came with a DVD to reproduce the works presented as videographic works to their best advantage.

Even though in terms of form changes are not significant, they are all the more so in terms of content. The catalogue's introductory text is indeed something special since it is an excerpt from a text by the art theorist Bazon Brock on aesthetics: *Der Barbar als Kulturheld* (2007) ('The Barbarian as a Cultural Hero'). Why is the text which figures as an introduction to the catalogue so important? The fame of the author most certainly plays a part here. But what makes it significant is above all the topic of his contribution, with its thesis that "the demand for beauty is revolutionary, because it forces one to equally appreciate the ugly"[30] (catalogue 2007: 8).

In the text, Bazon Brock develops his theory of the conception and reception of the contemporary artwork by emphasizing – drawing on Duchamp's art of the *ready-made,* which he relates to the self-declared forgery in art – the difficulties, even the uselessness of judging:

"The transition from normative to non-normative aesthetics, from that of the beautiful 'to that of the no longer beautiful arts', therefore implies judging forgery no longer as a criminal act but rather as a creative performance. It is only as a declared forgery that the work can become a work of art"[31] (ibid.: 13).

Did the organizers have the need to justify the new artistic tendencies by relying on a theorist of renown? In substantiating their choice, the Luxembourg coordinators Kevin Muhlen and Anne Kayser point to the diversity of contemporary art production in Luxembourg under which they subsume different techniques such as installation, video art, photography and painting. The disposition of the installation and the diversity of tools of expression is emphasized, as well as the *mise en abyme* of contemporary art production. A number of art works from Trier 2007 illustrate this choice of topic very well. Selected by the Metz coordinator Jean-

---

30 | Personal translation of: "Die Forderung nach Schönheit ist revolutionär, weil sie das Hässliche gleichermaßen zu würdigen zwingt."
31 | Personal translation of: "Der Übergang von der normativen zur nicht-normativen Ästhetik, von der der schönen 'zu der der nicht mehr schönen Künste', bedeutet dem zufolge, Fälschung nicht mehr als kriminellen Akt sondern als schöpferische Leistung zu bewerten. Das Werk kann nur noch als deklarierte Fälschung zum Kunstwerk werden."

Jacques Dumont under the title *Travelling*, Samuel François highlights the concept of the artist as a nomad who acts superregionally via exhibitions, exchanges and residencies.

The artist's geographical location reveals much about his inspirations. Living in Lorraine, in the small community of Hettange-Grande (some 30 kilometers from Metz, but also from the borders to Luxembourg, Belgium and Germany), he realized his first artistic projects in the open countryside and in the urban environment. These were temporary actions that take on various forms in the catalogue. The dispositif of the presentation is constitutive for this ephemeral and de-sacralized art, giving it, via the international exhibition and the catalogue, the legitimacy to exist in the world of art. This reveals the full meaning of Bazon Brock's introduction which ties in with the ideas of the American philosopher Arthur Danto and his concept of the transfiguration of the banal object into art. In the face of an object that transforms into art we are confronted with the intentionality of the artist and the "incarnation of his significance"[32] (Thériault 2010: 60).

In a certain sense the exhibition as well as the catalogue become this interstice where the object transforms into art, the idea into matter, and where reflection finds its space of aesthetic exchange.

Figure 3: Cover of the catalogue Robert Schuman Art Award 2007

Trier 2007, organized in the framework of the year called *Luxembourg and Greater Region – European Capital of Culture 2007*, also presented itself as an event that contributed to the superregional and national dialogue and aimed at changing the

---

32 | Personal translation of: "L'incarnation de sa signification."

attitudes of the public and the image of the region (see Sonntag 2013). As Monika Sonntag noted in her study on cross-border cooperation, the aim of the cultural year was to cross borders and boundaries and attempt the unexpected.

"The aim to promote cross-border mobility of the public and its openess towards new forms of art shows itself to be basically a social problem. In the face of this problem, the cultural-political challenge seems to be primarily to overcome social borders of cultural education"[33] (Sonntag 2012: 95f.).

The *Robert Schuman Art Award* of 2007 was able to contribute via the exhibition and the catalogue to overcoming cultural borders by making contemporary art accessible to a larger public.

4.3.5 Conclusion

The works assembled in the various exhibitions and catalogues of the *Robert Schuman Art Award*, presented via different schemes and accompanied by texts and discourses, testify in equal measure to a specific culture through the participation of regional art schools as well as to a common culture that is reflected in a particular timeliness of the works. However, this sometimes only becomes clear to the untrained public with a certain time delay. If the (Greater) region hardly ever appeared as a topic in the art works, it was because one wanted to prevent artistic regionalism by favouring more general topics, and because the award feels committed to a high-level European culture. In terms of presentation everything is done to blur the actually existing differences and discrepancies between the four cities that have no common production budget.

The emphasis is, particularly in the catalogues, on contemporary art, which asks more questions than it gives answers. In this way it is possible to bring works into contact with the international art world, while at the same time creating a new platform for the exchange between artists and regional public.

Can one therefore say that the award in its function as an interstice really contributed to the development of contemporary art in the region? Does it, after eleven editions, enjoy the international recognition in the world of art that it has striven to achieve?

In the years 2007 and 2008 the award winners exhibition *The Best of* took place in the framework of *Luxembourg and the Greater Region – European Capital of Culture 2007* at the same time as the regular award event, first in Trier and subsequently in

---

[33] | Personal translation of: "Das Ziel, die grenzüberschreitende Mobilität des Publikums und dessen Offenheit gegenüber neuen Kunstformen zu fördern, stellt sich im Kern als soziale Problematik heraus. Die kulturpolitische Herausforderung scheint angesichts dieser Problematik in erster Linie darin zu bestehen, soziale Grenzen der kulturellen Bildung zu überwinden."

Luxembourg, at various major exhibition venues. As a sign of an opening to the east, Dumitru Gorzo, an artist from Sibiu in Romania, was also part of the selection of the *Robert Schuman Art Award* 2007, as a guest *hors concours*.

If one looks at the list of young artists that participated in the award, one can note that the event has contributed to the artistic development of some participants. Personalities such as Su-Mei Tse who in Venice in 2003 was awarded the Golden Lion for the Luxembourg pavilion (two years after her participation in the *Robert Schuman Art Award*), or Martine Feipel, who together with Jean Bechameil represented Luxembourg at the 54th Biennale in Venice, received their first visibility and recognition via the award's exhibition and catalogue.

But there were also critical remarks by artists and curators who participated in the award. For the Luxembourg artist Marco Godinho, who was invited as curator (2009 for Metz) and as artist (2011 for Luxembourg), the award – which he described as an interesting and important initiative – permits "to deconstruct local representations, to highlight the notions of territory, interstice and multiculturality, but should be developed more consistently regarding its artistic concept and its mediation"[34], so that the participating artists and above all the young laureate can profit from the award for his or her professional development.[35] Nevertheless the award creates a scheme which allows to contrast the works and reflect them in their reference to multiculturality and contemporary art.

Finally, this ephemeral space which establishes a transition between local production and international art production and a connection between artist and spectator, can only be realized if it is appropriated and recognized by the public.

These four examples of the 1995, 2001, 2005 and 2007 editions of the *Robert Schuman Art Award* have shown how both the exhibition venue as well as the space of the catalogue have contributed in shaping the way of dealing with local, regional and national culture with regard to the globalization of art. By creating a 'space of passage', the award partly succeeds in turning the different artistic stances into complex and hybrid options, which, taking into account the different identities and spaces, can complement instead of confront each other. Even if this space only appears occasionally, it will legitimize the interplay of the cultures of production and reception in art and contribute to building new transcultural bridges.

---

34 | Personal translation of: "[...] die lokalen Vorstellungen zu dekonstruieren, die Vorstellungen von Territorium, von Zwischenraum und Multikulturalität zu thematisieren, doch sollte er hinsichtlich des künstlerischen Konzepts und der Vermittlung konsequenter weiterentwickelt werden."

35 | Marco Godinho, Interview at the book fair of Walferdange, November 2013.

Sources

Catalogue Prix d'art/Kunstpreis Robert Schuman, Luxemburg (1995): Musées de la Ville de Luxembourg.
Catalogue Prix d'art/Kunstpreis Robert Schuman, Metz (2001): Ville de Metz, Musée de la Cour d'Or.
Catalogue Prix d'art/Kunstpreis Robert Schuman, Saarbrücken (2005): Landeshauptstadt Saarbrücken.
Catalogue Prix d'art/Kunstpreis Robert Schuman, Trier (2007): Stadtmuseum Simeonstift Trier.

4.4 THE THRESHOLD OF EXHIBITION VENUES: ACCESS TO THE WORLD OF CULTURE

Céline Schall

A museum exhibition is not a medium like others: By nature it is spatial and involves the visitor as an active participator (see Davallon 1999). For a visit to a museum it is therefore necessary to leave one's home, go to the museum and enter it. In addition, a visit to a museum requires an intellectual effort – which aims at comprehending the meaning of the exhibition – and a symbolic effort: it presumes the entrance into a heavily valorized place of culture, a place of experience and knowledge, which is not yet accessible to all members of society (see Donnat 2008). Visiting a museum exhibition thus implies a physical, intellectual and symbolic passage from the space of everyday life to that of the museum, to the world of art, science, history, in brief, to 'culture'. It is worth noting that one third of Luxembourg's residents have declared that they have never set foot in a museum (see University of Luxembourg, IDENT2 2012/2013 – quantitative survey).

It is this threshold of museums and exhibition venues that constitute the subject of this case study, understood as the more or less expanded space which both separates and connects the everyday space and the exhibition space of cultural objects and knowledge. Using a variety of examples, my concern will be to understand the symbolic function of the threshold and to examine under which circumstances it facilitates the passage between the two spaces and creates a positive 'visitor attitude' in those who cross it.

After establishing how the notion of the threshold is employed in different contexts, I will present a communication-oriented method for analysing museum thresholds, followed by a typology of the latter. The study will conclude with a discussion of the results and perspectives of this analysis.

4.4.1 The Museum Threshold: Interstice, Paratext, Border Area

A Spatial, Symbolic and Contractual Fact

First of all, the notion of threshold indicates a spatial fact: it is a space of the 'in-between', an 'interstice', whose function it is primarily to enable the passage from one place to another (see Starwiarski 2010). But whereas the interstice often suggests a space that is situated between functionally clearly defined constructions or spaces and is fallow (see Dumont 2006), of temporary or uncertain status, without a specific attribution, often associated with the notion of non-place (see Guillaud 2009), the threshold, on the other hand, is more a space that occupies a potentially strategic role of reception and of passage. Thus the theshold is *a priori* a specific interstice that results from one or more sophisticated strategies. The seminar *Zones du seuil* has in fact shown that a building's threshold is something increasingly neglected by architects, while it has the important function of receiving or rejecting, depending on who identifies themselves (see Coll. 2012). Contemplating the threshold thus also means contemplating its crossing: the threshold manifests itself in the crossing, it is a barrier *and* a crossing, a closing *and* an opening (see Starwiarski 2010).

In addition, the threshold contains symbolic values: it acquires a phantasmagoric quality which is connected to the notion of passage, rite and metamorphosis (see Bonnin 2000), which at the same time brings it close to the notion of *liminalité*. This concept has its origin in the analysis of rites of passage developed by Arnold van Gennep (1909) and signifies the "moment in which an individual has lost a first status and not yet acquired a second one; it finds itself in an intermediate situation and hovers between two states"[36] (Calvez 2000: 83).

Finally, the notion of threshold points to that of the paratext, used particularly in literature (see section 4.5), which is more than a border or a boundary, namely "a 'vestibule' that offers everyone the possibility to enter or turn back"[37] (Genette 1987: 7). The role of the paratext is then to make a text accessible, to facilitate its consumption, its reception. This enunciative context thus contributes in establishing a communicative contract between reader and work and allows for a more "relevant reading"[38] of the text (ibid.: 8) by indicating how it should be read (it provides keys to reading) and who is speaking.

---

36 | Personal translation of: "Le moment où un individu a perdu un premier statut et n'a pas encore accédé à un second statut ; il est dans une situation intermédiaire et flotte entre deux états."

37 | Personal translation of: "Un 'vestibule' qui offre la possibilité à tout un chacun d'entrer ou de rebrousser chemin."

38 | Personal translation of: "Une lecture plus pertinente."

The Functions of the Museum Threshold

In one of the few well-known studies on museum thresholds, Monique Renault focuses on the passage between the urban space and the museum space and defines the latter's threshold as that "which crystallizes the tensions between the two worlds"[39] (Renault 2000: 15). The museum threshold – understood as the space that separates and connects the everyday space and the exhibition space – is in fact first of all a physical space, an 'in-between space' between two different spaces: the public everyday space, potentially the space of living, passage, taking a walk, commerce, work, unrest, action etc. and the museum, the space of culture, knowledge, but also of esthetical pleasure, silence, calm etc.[40]

Etymologically the word 'museum' points to the holy grove of the Muses, protectors of the arts (see Gob/Drouguet 2006) and thus to a 'separated' space, such as the forest. The separation of objects from the everyday world is moreover the actual condition of existence of the museum object – in the sense of the *objet muséal* (see Davallon 1999): this separation is indeed the "first phase of the operation of musealization by which the real items are dislocated from their original environment and acquire the status of museum objects or museal realities"[41] (Desvallées/Mairesse 2011: 661). The 'closed' space of the museum also ensures the functioning of the exhibition as a text (see Davallon 1999 for a more in-depth discussion): the objects are decontextualised and relocated, re-expressed within a tour which is the carrier of meaning.

However, the museum has pledged to be "in the service to society" according to the definition of the International Council of Museums (Mairesse/Desvallées 2011: 14). It therefore has to increasingly open up to society and take on a genuine social role (see Fourès/Grisot/Lochot 2011). But precisely this shift has always been a problem for the museum: the fact remains that there is still a cultured class, a 'separate' medium, a 'special' place, whose doors are sometimes difficult to pass. These doors can at times not only be daunting (and exclude particular social groups), but also in a way 'invisible' and in turn exclude certain social groups for whom they are not part of the universe of the intelligible, thinkable and doable (see Bourdieu/Darbel 1991 [1966]).

The museum threshold also has different practical functions: it has to generate the desire to enter the museum, has to enable visitors to inform themselves about the visit, opening times or entry fees (and thus potentially also to turn back or

---

39 | Personal translation of: "[...] ce qui cristallise les tensions entre ces deux mondes."

40 | Nevertheless, the exterior is never entirely without reflection, observation or art, and the museum area is never free of influences from the outside world. It would therefore be more correct to say that the threshold of the museum offers a passage or a transition between two spaces which are *a priori* different but can approach each other.

41 | Personal translation of: "La première étape de l'opération de muséalisation par laquelle les vraies choses sont séparées de leur milieu d'origine et acquièrent le statut d'objets de musée ou de muséalies."

4. Constructions of Space and Identity Created by Media-related Practises

to stay in order to rest or meet up with somebody), to pay possible entry fees or acquire documents that help them to orientate themselves in the exhibition both in terms of space and content. Often there is a cloak room where one can make oneself comfortable for the visit (or sometimes change or rest). In most museums, entrance and exit adjoin, and there is a museum shop where one can buy something as a souvenir of one's visit. The threshold is thus the space that prepares for the visit or the departure and enables the exchange between the two spaces.

As a border space the threshold has to enable the visitors to extract themselves from their everyday lives in order to enter a different time and a different world. It therefore marks the difference between these spaces, and a visit to a museum can resemble a journey into another time-space: the threshold is

"[...] mental preparation, forgetting the self, the previously experienced, it is the conditioning for the challenging and solitary tension of these spaces without voice, invitation to an aesthetic encounter, to a dialogue of the eyes, senses and the intellect"[42] (Renault 2000: 16).

The museum therefore has to ensure that the visitors are deprived of their accustomed spatial-temporal orientation in order to prepare them for the aesthetic and cognitive experience, and in doing so it becomes the access to another world. As in a journey "the visitor is 'decoupled' from everyday life and immersed, for the duration of his visit, in a new universe"[43] (Davallon 1999: 174f.). For the visitor this not only involves a passage from one space to another, but from one 'attitude' to another: the passerby, the stroller, tourist, consumer is called upon to become an interested and attentive visitor and aesthetic. But according to Renault (2000), and also in my view, this change necessitates a space and a time that permit the visitor to adopt an attitude that is adequate to the visit.

Furthermore, crossing the museum threshold presumes, like the paratext of books, an implicit contract between visitor and museum. Once the threshold is crossed a certain behaviour is expected of the visitor: the exhibition is usually visited in silence, with a certain slowness and attention, without touching the exhibits etc. The visit to the museum is thus a social regulation of 'good taste' and 'good' behaviour (see Jacobi/Meunier 2000). And it is the museum threshold that imposes upon the visitor a certain deceleration, a certain time of observation, of exchange with the museum personnel or with the group he or she has arrived with (family, friends), a preparation for an encounter with the world of culture. It

---

42 | Personal translation of: "Préparation mentale, oubli de soi, de son vécu précédent, il est conditionnement à la tension exigeante et solitaire de ces lieux sans voix, invitation à une rencontre esthétique, à un dialogue des yeux, des sens et de l'intelligence."
43 | Personal translation of: "Le visiteur est 'déprogrammé' du quotidien et plongé, pour le temps de sa visite, dans un univers nouveau."

is the preparation for the encounter which allows the adoption of a specific visitor's attitude appropriate to the exhibition to be visited (the visitor may be prompted to be more or less attentive, more or less quiet, more or less nostalgic or open towards the new, depending on the exhibition).

And vice-versa this contract also involves obligations for the museum, right from the threshold: it has to suggest a special relationship to the objects and items of knowledge (see Renault 2000) and this contract has to be honoured with the visit – e.g. an exhibition focusing on aesthetics or emotionality or knowledge transfer has to be advertised as such from the point of its threshold.

Finally, Renault (2000) shows that historically, when comparing the neoclassical art museum with contemporary buildings, museum architecture increasingly tends to 'deactivate' the rupture created by the threshold. The visit to the museum in this way turns into a transit event that links two urban moments, bringing it into the vicinity of places of transit, such as railway stations or subway stations. She thus favours a museum that is discrete from the public space, the condition "necessary in order to bring forth the meaning of the works"[44] (ibid.: 20). As we shall see, this position is debatable. In any event, the role of the threshold seems important: if it is (too) open, it banalizes; if it is (too) closed, it sacralizes, with the risk that passage is prevented. So a great deal comes into play at the level of the threshold: it is not a neutral place.

Thresholds of Exhibition Venues: A Communicative and Semiotic Study

In order to examine the question how thresholds of exhibition venues function, how they behave in terms of the communicative contract and the attitude of the visitor, and what their current development is, I have conducted a communicative analysis of the thresholds of 77 museums and exhibition venues in the Grand Duchy of Luxembourg. The subject of the study is therefore a heterogenous sample of exhibitions in terms of scale (small, medium-sized, large museum), form (amateur project, professional), geographical location (city, rural) or type (art, history, ethnology, industry etc.).

Thanks to this relatively large corpus, I was able to pursue both a quantitative and a qualitative approach. I have photographed the thresholds of the 77 exhibition venues following a fixed protocol that segmented the museum space according to the principle of spatial and semantic scaling *(emboîtement)*, "i.e. according to a regressive process from the general to the particular"[45] (Gharsallah 2008: 48f.). The photographs are produced by first beginning with general views, followed by views of the individual exhibition elements, from the largest to the smallest. These

---

44 | Personal translation of: "[...] nécessaire pour faire surgir le sens des œuvres."

45 | Personal translation of: "[...] c'est-à-dire selon un procédé régressif allant du général au particulier."

are arranged in such a way that the space can be reconstructed on the basis of the pictures.

I have described each threshold on the basis of these photographs: the context of each exhibition venue – type of city, neighbourhood etc.; the architectural elements of the threshold – infront of the entrance and behind it – and of the external environment up to the door and from the door to the exhibition; but also how the threshold is expressed via the existing communicative elements – the name of the museum, reception boards, contents, languages etc.; the moment when one sees the museum's displays – around the museum, from the foyer, behind the foyer etc.; similarly the functions of the places of reception – information, sale, repose etc.

This quantitative approach makes it possible to evaluate the significance of specific tendencies of threshold design and formulate a typology of these thresholds. The qualitative approach to certain 'representative' thresholds is in principle based on a semiotic analysis that aims to highlight the conditions of the possibilities (and the constraints) of certain effects of meaning (see Davallon 1999; Gharsallah 2008). In other words: the semiotic analysis helps us to understand how the threshold acts as a signifier by searching in the expographical dispositif what it expresses independently from the intentions of those who designed it (the *intentio auctoris* according to Umberto Eco 1991 [1990]). The analysis thus returns to searching in the expographical dispositif for what Eco calls the intention of the work or the *intentio operis* (see ibid.). The thresholds are therefore analysed as they appear to the visitor, at the same time formulating hypotheses as to the effects of their meaning. These hypotheses concern the threshold's symbolic effect, the communicative contract established by each type of threshold, and the way the threshold could take effect on the visitor's attitude. We should note here that the threshold of a museum is first and foremost the result of architectural constraints (all the more because in Luxembourg the majority of the buildings housing museums were originally not designed for this purpose), but it can also be structured, designed, reinforced or blurred through a series of strategic measures (through the placing of objects, texts, images etc).

4.4.2 The Threshold: A Typological Approach

For defining the threshold we use in principle three criteria: 1) the rupture between the (external) environment and the contents of the exhibition (between the external context in which the museum and the exhibition is situated and between the building and the exhibition); 2) the 'moment' when one glimpses the displays or works for the first time (before entering the museum or behind the reception hall) and 3) the elements preparing for entering the exhibition (the number and kind of elements preparing – or not – this entering). Even though the following typology reduces the particularities of each threshold, it is nevertheless suited to formulate a general reflection on the significant elements of the threshold.

Exhibitions 'without Place'

First of all there are museums 'without place' and therefore also without a threshold (8 % of the sample). These are very small museums which are located without any separation in the public space: e.g. the *Musée Sybodo de la médecine* ('Sybodo museum of medicine'), which is located in a wing of the hospital of Kirchberg, in the middle of a patients' waiting area, or the *Musée des instruments de musique* ('museum of musical instruments') which is housed in a corridor and a stairwell of the *Conservatoire de Luxembourg*. These museums consist of ensembles of showcases displaying exhibits and texts (labels and boards). They resemble the exhibitions staged in (media) libraries, but have the feature of not distinguishing themselves from their environment, i.e. there is no rupture between the exhibition area and the surrounding space: the *Musée de la physique* ('museum of physics'), for instance, is in the corridor of a secondary school next to the physics rooms. The *Musée du relais postal et des écritoires et salle de classe d'autrefois* ('museum of the postal relay station, writing material and classrooms of olden times') in Asselborn is situated on the first floor of an old post office, with a restaurant on the ground floor that already offers a glimpse of a number of exhibits.

Here the museum is inextricably connected with the everyday public space. These exhibitions offer no entrance or exit and therefore also no circuit that needs to be followed. It is difficult to determine where they begin and where they end. Only the show cases make it possible to separate the displays from reality, but the ensemble of the show cases is not sacralized or 'discrete'. The banality of everyday space has the tendency to incorporate the exhibits located in the middle of a space meant for other purposes, thus becoming the object of a passing glimpse, but rarely of a purposeful tour. Symbolically, the lacking separation between external public space and exhibition does not permit the visitor to see it as a coherent text, to follow a meaningful tour or to move around in another time-space. Since the museum merges entirely with its direct surroundings the rupture between the two worlds is blurred and one is not stimulated to decentre oneself in order to approach the exhibits. Such exhibitions thus have much in common with non-places or interstices: places of passage and not of observation that deprive the exhibits of their aura. Only experts (of museums or of the exhibition's theme) can in my view recognize an exhibition venue, a 'mini museum', in these show cases and will be able to adopt a 'visitor' attitude by taking the time to explore the exhibition and acquire knowledge. But in the geat majority of cases visitors will be no more than passers-by (or patients, or students etc.) while waiting to move on to another activity relating to the place in question (seeing the doctor, attending class, having a meal etc.).

Exhibitions where the Threshold has no Function

53 % of the sample (41 exhibitions) are in closed buildings specifically intended for housing exhibitions, but once visitors have come through the entrance they have direct access to the works and exhibits. These museums therefore have no

threshold in the actual sense, or, more precisely, their threshold is limited to the entrance door. It is above all the small and medium-sized museums that display this type of threshold. This sudden immersion into the world of the exhibition can be explained with a lack of space or with lacking awareness for the symbolic role of the threshold.

One can distinguish two sub-types of this kind of threshold. The first type is represented in 34 % of the exhibitions. They are marked by a 'hard' entrance and a clear break with their surroundings: the *Musée de l'abeille* ('bee museum') evokes nature even though it is located in the centre of Diekirch, or the *Musée de la Poste* conjures up the postal past of Luxembourg city in the very urban business district around the station of Luxembourg city. The second exhibition type, represented with 19 %, displays an abrupt entrance, but is, at the same time, intimately connected with its direct surroundings: the *Musée A Schiewech* in Binsfeld presents collections relating to the rural world in a rural environment. With this exhibition subtype the threshold seems to begin already well before the door: the geographical space surrounding the museum would then already be a preparation for the contents of this museum. This is also true of the exhibition of the *Massenoire* ('black mass'), which is located in the district of Esch-Belval (an old industrial site), the *Site industriel du Fonds-de-Gras* ('industrial site of the Fonds-de-Gras') or *Musée de la mine Cockerill* ('museum of the Cockerill mine'). The exhibitions' industrial environment has an effect on how these are interpreted and prepares the visitor for what is presented in the exhibition. With exhibitions of this kind the threshold therefore begins long before their doors.

In both cases, these 'immersive' exhibitions require the visitor to already have a certain degree of knowledge of the world they are about to enter and risk putting off laypersons or the non-initiated. They establish a special communicative contract with the visitor that might give the impression as if the mere contact with the exhibits could suffice to understand them: not entirely withdrawn from 'reality', the exhibits are placed on the same level as the everyday exterior and thereby lose their aura for visitors who do not have the knowledge to identify by themselves which of the exhibits are the important ones. This is particularly evident in the rural museums: it is as if the familiarity one experiences when seeing these old objects (which are familiar to us from our grandparents) would suffice to also understand them. One therefore passes from an everyday external space into a 'familiar' space as if one were to enter someone's living room. In addition, these exhibitions without threshold do not oblige the visitor to slow down or adopt a visitor's attitude. Depending on the status the visitor has had outside the museum, it is possible that he or she might retain it inside. For instance, the tourist exploring rural Luxembourg and entering one of these museums without threshold is most likely to remain a 'tourist' rather than change into a 'visitor'. The visitor entering a 'familiar' space might also feel uninhibited by the constraints that are usually imposed by a museum (silence and the prohibition to touch objects).

Exhibitions whose Threshold Prepare for an Encounter

Finally, slightly over a third (39 % or 30 cases) have a threshold which consists of a room intended for reception, equally segregated from the everyday external space and from the exhibition. Access to the exhibit is therefore progressive. But these thresholds do not all have the same configuration: we can distingush three sub-types.

1) *Classical thresholds*: 14 % (or 8 cases) of the exhibitions have a reception hall that is separated both from outside and from the collection, which however also serves another function, e.g. for tourist information (*Musée de l'Europe* ('museum of Europe') in Schengen, *Musée et maison du vin* ('museum and house of wine') in Ehnen) or for the sale of objects (*Musée national des mines de fer* ('national museum of iron mines') in Rumelange). To a certain degree this structured space allows visitors to slow down and take a moment's time to extricate themselves from the external reality before approaching the museum's works or exhibits. This space thus separates the exhibit from reality and enables it to acquire a special status and a special aura. Whoever enters there can also take their time to adopt a visitor's attitude appropriate to the visit and the understanding of the exhibition. But this is connected to a choice: visitors can also choose to turn to other activities offered by the space – they can browse or inform themselves about the region, thus retaining their status as consumers, tourists or strollers inside the museum. I therefore argue that for a museum really wishing to prepare for an encounter, it is not sufficient to provide a threshold that is merely physically separated from the interior of the exhibition: it has to multiply the symbols that prepare the passer-by for becoming a visitor.

2) *Visible thresholds*: Certain exhibitions (16 %) have a threshold that is structured, both outside and within the museum, into a number of sections preparing for the encounter with the world of culture. This means, what happens here is not so much a *moment* of reception rather than a *process* of reception. This is for instance the case with the *Musée Forteresse, histoire, identités* ('museum fortress, history, identities') or *Villa Vauban – Musée d'art de Luxembourg* ('Luxembourg art museum') for whose visit it is necessary to first cross a park and subsequently traverse a very calm and sober lobby. Everything along the way leading to the exhibitions is an invitation to calmness and contemplation of the works. And in the lobby, the only place in the *Villa Vauban* where one can see the external world, there are comfortable easy-chairs facing the park that invite reflection. Other examples: the new exhibitions *The Bitter Years* in the *Pomhouse* in Dudelange and *The Family of Man* in the *Château de Clervaux* offer a multiplication of the architectural thresholds and a very present paratext. In *The Family of Man*, the visitor is required to follow the signboards from the city centre and then use a path up to a castle. Standing infront of the castle's entrance one sees a large sign with the inscription 'The largest photo exhibition of all times'[46], followed by a text

---

46 | Personal translation of: "La plus grande exposition photographique de tous les temps."

which outlines how the exhibition was created. Directly after entering the castle two large banderoles indicate the exhibition's title and identify it as part of the Unesco cultural heritage. In the castle yard a board invites the visitor to climb some steps. Inside the castle one notices a large inscription on the wall *"The Family of Man* Unesco Memory of the World" and "A photographic cultural heritage created by Edward Steichen for the MoMA in New York in 1955"[47]. An arrow indicates that the visitor should take an elevator. On arriving on the respective floor visitors are 'received' by two photographs of the exhibition (a face and the head of a statue, looking at him or her), as well as by the same large board as on the previous floor, but with the following information: "503 images, 273 photographers, 68 countries."[48] The visitor walks through the corridor and reaches the lobby. In the back, one finds the information regarding entrance fees and the multimedia visit. In addition, a text elaborates on the history of the exhibition – an exhibition that has travelled around the world and will in the future be 'legendary'. One also learns that the exhibited prints are originals and that the visitor is thereby asked to show the appropriate respect and consideration. Finally the visitor can turn around, open a door and enter the exhibition. The multiplication of the threshold elements is very marked here: it prepares the visitor for an encounter, announcing itself as 'extraordinary' and unique, with an equally unique cultural heritage – with the seal of Unesco serving as a guarantee for quality. Furthermore, various interpretations of the exhibition are suggested long before one actually sees the works: the significance of the photographs as objects of cultural heritage, of the subject matter represented in the photographs, of the exhibition etc. By contrast, inside the exhibition mediation is reduced to a bare minimum: the visitor has additional information in a portable media dispositif, but the exhibition offers no written texts besides those used in the original exhibition in the *Museum of Modern Art* (MoMA) in 1955. Thus this very elaborated threshold already provides the crucial information in order to roughly understand the project and the exhibition and fulfills the function of paratextual information – it is a medialization in the proper sense.[49] One can also see very well that it is not only the architecture that 'makes' a threshold: here it is all the elements of the museum's paratext that clothe the threshold and multiply its sections and effects.

The *Musée national de la résistance* ('national museum of resistance') in Esch-sur-Alzette also has a clearly visible threshold. It requires the visitor to cross a large open square, climb a dozen steps, approach a very impressive neoclassical building with high columns, pass a monument that carries the inscription "Died for their

---

47 | Personal translation of: "Un patrimoine photographique créé par Edward Steichen pour le *MoMA* de New York 1955."

48 | Personal translation of: "503 images, 273 photographes, 68 pays."

49 | The medialization is here understood as "the production and materialization of social relationships that enable the exchange" (personal translation of: "La production et la matérialisation de relations sociales qui rendent possible l'échange" (Davallon 2007: 10)).

fatherland" and push open a heavy door. Then the visitor enters a dark room, the 'sacred hall' with large paintings, in front a column with an urn containing soil from various concentration camps. Here the threshold clearly invites the visitors to remember and to collect themselves and suggests the adoption of a humble attitude. This is not only a promise relating to the exhibited works but a truly psychological preparation of the visitor for the exhibition.

In this case, we see that the threshold can also extend beyond the doors of the museum. This is also the case with the *Musée national d'histoire naturelle* ('natural history museum') in which the tour begins at a room of *concernation*[50]: a room which is right at the beginning of the tour, directly behind the foyer, and which is intended to make the visitors look forward to their encounter with the scientific contents they are about to 'enter'. One can observe very well here that the exhibition's threshold can not only be in the museum's foyer but also a little further back, at the beginning of the exhibition. Similarly, the *Musée d'histoire de la ville de Luxembourg* ('museum of the history of the city of Luxembourg') and the *Musée national d'histoire et d'art* ('national museum of history and art') both have a glass elevator directly behind the reception which takes the visitor to the permanent exhibition. The elevators extend the threshold of these exhibitions by providing a physical journey and a symbolic ascent in time. They decontextualize the visitors, pull them out of their daily routine and recontextualize them in another time-space (a sombre room, surrounded by rocks, evoking a time long past). In the *Musée Tudor* in Rosport, the journey by elevator is even more symbolic since the visitor arrives in a very sombre, almost black room which evokes the time before the invention of the electric generator by Henri Tudor. Light appears on the tour at the moment when Tudor invents the generator.

Here the passage between the exterior and the interior of the museum takes place via a threshold which fulfills symbolic and paratextual functions. Due to the architecture, but also and primarily through the use of scripto-visual, scenographic or iconic signs the threshold appears as something continually accompanying the visitor. It enables the exhibits to take on a specific value: as a constant of a (more or less) long tour, the threshold directs the visitor's attention to the exhibits and emphasizes their exceptional aspects. The threshold also enables a transformation of the passer-by into a visitor and conveys him or her into a mental state attuned to the following exhibition even before becoming aware of the exhibits. The visitors are accompanied in their transformation and are occasionally even prompted to become more than a visitor: an 'attentive observer' in the *Villa Vauban* or the *Musée Dräi Eechelen*; a 'witness' in the *The Family of Man, The Bitter Years* or the *Musée national de la résistance*; a 'scientific apprentice' who asks questions in the *Musée national d'histoire naturelle* or the *Musée Tudor*; a 'temporal explorer' in the

---

50 | This term was coined by the museologist André Giordan. It refers to a space that 'concerns' (*concerner*) the visitor, that is intended to arouse his or her interest in the subject matter (see Giordan 2013).

Musée d'histoire de la ville de Luxembourg and the *Musée national d'histoire et d'art*. Here we clearly see how via the museum's threshold identitary micro-adjustments are made.

3) *'Transparent' thresholds*: Finally, the most modern museums also have thresholds that accompany the visitors, but without the latter clearly perceiving them as such: these museums (5 % of the corpus, i.e. four cases) do not display the features of overt accompaniment as described above. Instead, they offer a progressive threshold which facilitates the access to the works by playing with transparency and letting the exhibition communicate with the surroundings. Examples of this type are for instance the Mudam, the *Casino – Forum d'art contemporain* in whose foyer and pavilion, the 'aquarium', artist encounters and all kinds of forums take place (visible from the street), the *Musée d'histoire de la ville de Luxembourg* with its large glass wall decorated with colours, logos and symbols of the current temporary exhibitions, or the *Musée d'histoire(s) de Diekirch* ('museum of the history [and stories] of Diekirch') where a part of the permanent exhibition is visible from outside and particularly from the threshold of the church opposite. But at the *Musée d'histoire(s) de Diekirch* and the *Casino* the building is not entered via these transparent spaces, which diminishes the effect of transparency.[51]

The Mudam is the most representative of this type of museums that establish a connection between interior and exterior.[52] It indeed offers an architecture (a work by Ieoh Ming Pei) which is completely geared towards establishing connections between the urban and the artistic space. The use of glass, of passages, of glass roofs permits a visual exchange between interior and exterior: from outside, works can be discovered which are located outside the building, in the moat that runs around the Mudam, and also works that are inside the museum. The northern facade contains small wall openings that point to the square by which the visitor enters the building, but the southern facade, completely of glass, faces the districts of Clausen and Pfaffenthal. Through the large glass facades facing the city the latter becomes an integrated element of the museum.

These thresholds establish a dialogue between surroundings, city, museum, art and cultural heritage which here is primarily performed by the architecture and not so much through scripto-visual or iconic elements. Access to culture is here perhaps an easier one, less impressive than in those museums that show themselves as an accompanist of the visitor: the path leads 'quite naturally' to the museum. For Monique Renault (2000), these thresholds are 'hidden thresholds'[53] which deactivate the rupture with the urban space. In her view, museums with hidden thresholds are increasingly becoming a backdrop for a stroll, such as a round of afternoon window shopping, and intentionally mislead the visitors by

---

51 | One could say these museums have, in a certain sense, a 'hybrid' threshold.
52 | It is also one of the only six museums of the corpus expressly designed and built for this function.
53 | Personal translation of: "Seuils occultés."

suggesting that they have access to art after paying the entrance fee, that it is sufficient to stroll around and buy a souvenir in order to impregnate oneself with the aura of cultural heritage. I, by contrast, am of the opinion that the transformation from passer-by to visitor happens progressively (since he/she sees the works from outside, prepares for his/her encounter with them and crosses a threshold devoted to the reception). The passage is effected in a subtle way, like an 'unconscious' transition in the visitor who is thus 'guided' to the work, while in actual fact the visitor is engaged in veritable preparatory work. Far from being demagogic, this type of threshold proves on the contrary to be very efficient in transforming passers-by into visitors. It finally leads to the encounter with the work inside the museum, there where mediations can multiply, depending on the kind of public, be it expert or not.

4.4.3 Conclusion

The threshold of the museum can be both passage and barrier, outside as well as inside. It can hide or show, receive or exclude, encourage or forbid, hide itself or show itself. It can extend spatially into the exterior and interior area of the museum. It can be a key to understanding the exhibition, and above all it promises to establish a specific connection the world of culture. This space consisting of multiple dimensions, neglected by museology and certain museums, is nevertheless an important place where a crucial part of the museum's mediation can take place.

Naturally, my typology would have to be further refined and one would need to examine what concrete effects the various types of threshold have on the visitors by observing how the latter appropriate them. One could also develop other dimensions, in particular linguistic and symbolic boundaries that are added to the threshold.[54] But at its present point my study indicates that, in terms of quantity, the thresholds show themselves to be more of a boundary than a passage, and more of an interstice (an 'in-between' that is implemented without a particular strategy) than a paratext (which connects two spaces and determines how the second one is to be read) or a border space (which permits performing identitary micro-adjustments in the visitor and preparing him/her in the best possible way for a visit to the exhibition).

---

54 | In most museums the scripto-visual register is used to identify the museum but also to impose boundaries: opening times (sometimes limited), entrance fees, all kinds of prohibitions (don't touch, smoking and taking pictures prohibited etc.) – and it rarely happens that a text invites the visitor to enter the museum. In addition, the language used for informing the visitor is in the majority of cases French – only eight places offer all the information in French, German and English – so that the choice of the receiving language can constitute a significant symbolic boundary for the visitor.

According to my analysis, only those among the various identified types of thresholds fulfill a truly mediating function and a symbolic role that allow a progressive approach to the work. Only they create a framework where a visitor's attitude can be adopted and where this process of identitary micro-adjustments, with its fluid boundaries, can be accompanied. Even if these elaborated thresholds are often found in those museums that are best equipped in terms of funds and location, the problem can certainly not be reduced to these (albeit important) elements: it is above all the strategic aspect of the museum's mediation that has to be reconsidered – for which the threshold is no doubt only an indication.

4.5 LITERATURE OF THE IN-BETWEEN. THE MULTILINGUAL STAGINGS OF THE PUBLISHER *ULTIMO*MONDO

Till Dembeck

This case studies looks into the linguistic and spatial situatedness of literary communication. It follows a line of research that has grown in recent years and which attempts to focus on literature beyond the limitations set by monolingualism – that is, beyond the segmentary differentiation according to territorially localizable languages. Point of departure of these studies is the observation that monolingualism is a norm that came about relatively late in history and was maintained only with massive cultural-political pressure. This norm – research also refers to it as the 'monolingual paradigm' (Yildiz 2012: 6) – consists in the notion that individual speakers 'by nature' have a (standardized) mother tongue and can produce literature appropriately only in this language (see Martyn 2014). In as far as it is subject to this paradigm, literature adjusts to national language segmentation on the one hand and to the mechanisms of transformation between the national monolingualisms on the other (see Gramling 2014). A great number of institutions are involved in this process, not the least and in particular the publishers which, besides the authors, have the most interest in the marketability of literary works (see Lennon 2010).

It is, however, by no means the case that the monolingual paradigm has at any time really had an all-pervasive effect. There are many examples of literature beyond monolingualism, not only but particularly so in a multilingual state such as Luxembourg. This literature uses as it were the interstices that necessarily remain from attempts to delineate and limit languages and linguistic areas. It draws on the fact that, historically and systematically, languages are and always have been hybrid, that is, they emanate from processes of creolization – and are therefore always open for new amalgamations. And it makes use of differences between languages to fuel its creative energy. The emerging new literary forms exploit a linguistic interstice when they generate structures that cannot be clearly attributed to one language and occupy a place beyond the limits of all single languages.

In the following, I will discuss literature of interstitiality by taking a closer look at the way the Luxembourg publisher *ultimo*mondo and its associate and leading author Guy Rewenig stage themselves in the public sphere. More precisely it is about an example of what Gérard Genette in his study on paratext has described as a publisher's "epitext" (Genette 1997 [1987]: 9). Here I turn to the border region of literary works themselves: Genette's study subsumes all those elements of a text or book under the term of paratext that constitute the threshold between text and non-text and serve the purpose of guiding reception. It is the paratext that makes a text identifiable in the first place, because it limits the text 'locationally' from various sides (e.g. as title, preface, footnote) and referentially, i.e. by identifying it as an entity (this too is a key function of the title). At the same time it is the privileged place where the "author and his allies"[55] (Genette 1997 [1987]: 2), in particular the publisher, can ensure, in their view, an appropriate reception. It is therefore a border region both in the sense that it marks the border between text and non-text, and in the sense that it regulates the recipients' access to the book. Epitext comprises that which is not directly attached to the text or the book, but circulates independently. Epitexts, in particular when they are produced by the publisher (programme leaflets, announcements, advertisements of any kind), are a primary medium for conveying literature into the (linguistic) spaces of the public sphere – and even more than that: they take a part in shaping this space or at least attempt to do so.

In the case of the publisher *ultimo*mondo this happens under the premise that the space of reception is precisely not a monolingual one. In that sense the central question of this case study is not so much how epitextual conveyance of literary texts functions in multilingual spaces of communication, but rather how it itself attempts to relate language and space to each other. The epitextually conveyed language policy of the publisher *ultimo*mondo is thus not only examined as a key factor of the publisher's identity construction but also considered as an attempt to influence the spatial localization of literature.

4.5.1 A Publisher's Book as a Family Album and Bible

On 25 October 2010, a book was presented in Luxembourg's *Centre national de Littérature* which already by its cover distinguished itself from the vast majority of books that currently appear on the European market (see Fig. 1). The title is in four languages: *Bicherbuch. Livre des livres. Bücherbuch. Book of Books* (n. a. 2010); the name of the publisher, *ultimo*mondo, comes from a fifth language; and on the back of the cover there is at least one word from a sixth language (*aficionados*). Obviously a book such as this does not conform to the mechanisms of a market

---

55 | Personal translation of: "Autor und seine Verbündeten."

primarily geared towards monolingualism and translation. It is therefore only logical that none of the books were released for sale. All of the one thousand copies were given away and in addition most of the pages are each identified as a gift by a sponsor.

The *Bicherbuch* belongs to a not so voluminous genre that could be referred to as a 'publisher's book'. This genre comprises books in which publishers showcase themselves and their history, i.e. in particular the books they have published and the authors linked to them. A similiar book was published by the German publisher *Suhrkamp* in 2010 for its 60th anniversary (Fellinger 2010). A year later, a book was published about the then 32-year old publisher MÄRZ-*Verlag* (Bandel/Kalender/Schröder 2011). And in Luxembourg the 'predecessor', as it were, of *ultimo*mondo, the PHI-*Verlag*, celebrated its 20th year of existence with a publisher's book that was also a catalogue for an exhibition dedicated to the publisher in the *Centre national de littérature* (Delvaux/Janus/Marson 2001).

Figure 1: Bicherbuch, front cover

What is interesting about this genre? One could be tempted to disqualify publisher's books – as instruments of self-advertisement and self-display – as a suitable subject of philological labour. One would then have to say that literature may pragmatically depend on publishers and markets, but its essence can only be understood independently of these conditions. This is the prevalent attitude and it is partly also justified. Indeed, as a reader of what would then be referred to as 'autonomous' literature one feels called on to judge texts only by 'literary' criteria, even by criteria that the specific texts provide *themselves*. However, one must also assume that their institutional frame in no way remains external to literary texts, but rather, as a 'parergon', never leaves their core untouched (see Derrida 1987 [1978]). Here the publishing house, as the author's 'ally', plays a key role, being already an institution of the public the text seeks to influence. It represents author and text, but at the same time has an agenda of its own. The interplay of text, paratext and publisher's epitext reveals all those strategies and tensions that constitute the cultural-political field in which literature operates. Publisher's books illustrate this interplay – albeit abridged and strategically staged – and thereby provide the opportunity to examine literature as a part of culture politics. What is additionally interesting in the case of the *Bicherbuch* is that the publisher – or at least Guy Rewenig as its leading author and associate – advocates, in certain respects, a 'pure' understanding of literature and culture and, in doing so, is intentionally engaging in cultural policy, a point I will return to later.

But back to the *Bicherbuch* itself and to its outer appearance, which is important since we are here dealing with the publishing aspect of books. It is, like all of the publisher's titles, a high-quality book production, a hardcover of over 250 pages with elaborately designed text and illustrations. A remarkable contrast is that many photographs in the book expressly do not have a professional finish but are – clearly an intended effect – recognizable as snapshots. The personal and private touch is also evident in the volume's dedication to Roger Manderscheid who had died shortly before publication ("Fir de Rosch" ('For Roger') (n. a. 2010: 5) with a personal message by Frank Wilhelm to Guy Rewenig) and the references to the home towns of the authors presented in the main section of the book. Even the already mentioned references to sponsors and the thanks to a series of organizations and persons in the imprint, in Guy Rewenig's introduction dealing with the publisher's history as well as the extensively illustrated section *Partnership* seem to testify more to personal obligations than to business ones. The publisher thus presents itself – "amitié oblige" ('friendship obliges') (n. a. 2010: 16) – as part of a network of Luxembourg institutions and public figures in which even the institutions are personalized: all have known each other for a long time and are looking back together.

However, despite the informal atmosphere, this is more than 'only' about personal remembrance. This is indicated by the names of both the book and of the publisher: the French and English version of the term *Bicherbuch* suggests a biblical format, and the very publishing house announces itself, almost somewhat apocalyptically, as a witness of a 'last world'. Both terms should be understood in a strictly ironic sense (considering we are here dealing with a publisher who describes the Catholic Church as a "folkloristic club"[56]) – they symbolize, in Friedrich Schlegel's words, a manner of speaking where "everything should be playful and serious"[57] (Schlegel 1991: 13).

---

56 | Personal translation of: "[...] folkloristische[n] Verein."

57 | Personal translation of: "[...] alles Scherz und alles Ernst."

4.5.2 Texts from the Last World

Regarding the name of the publishing house, we find statements by Rewenig who for instance remarked "the last world is the world of books and literature which for me is the ultimate refuge. So the world of free imagination, of dreams and yearnings, if you will"[58] (Rewenig 2010: 19). This fits well with the fact that the publisher was indeed established as a kind of refuge, namely when Francis van Maele left the PHI-*Verlag* – until then the regular publisher of Rewenig and Roger Manderscheid, the second prominent *ultimo*mondo author and associate – and the publishing house was taken over by *editpress* with whose ideological and political connotation the authors were unable to identify (see n. a. 2010: 9). Apparently, van Maele had successfully mediated between these authors and a market that in the 1970s and 1980s had yet to be tapped into. In this sense, Manderscheid lauded his erstwhile publisher in the celebratory volume of the PHI-*Verlag*: van Maele had like no other conveyed 'local' literature to a 'local' audience (see Manderscheid 2001: 72) – and this seemingly without ever having come under suspicion of being commercially biased.

This already describes the claim which the new publisher makes: it vows to explicitly reject commercial thinking – the imprint of the *Bicherbuch* says the publisher is "toujours dans une situation précaire" ('always in a precarious situation') (n. a. 2010: 2). One sees oneself "inscrit dans la mouvance de gauche" ('inscribed in the Left movement') (n. a. 2010: 15) and refuses, with much clangor, to join the association of the *Lëtzebuerger Bicherediteuren* ('Luxembourg book publishers'). Since 2010, because of a dispute with the ministry of culture, the publishing house has claimed for itself the 'honorary title' of "Editeur discriminé par l'Etat luxembourgeois" ('publisher discriminated by the state of Luxembourg') (Dimmer/Rewenig/Scheuren/Thiltges 2010: 17). From a recent statement by Rewenig in which he rigorously contrasts the "radical open-mindedness of the creative artists" with the "unctuous, electorally useful fabrications" of Luxembourg's cultural-political "representatives"[59] (Rewenig 2012a: 12), one can deduce that the publisher and author Rewenig – but actually also the publisher *ultimo*mondo – is concerned with creating a space within which alternative accesses to the 'world' can be tested beyond economic and political stratagems. This creates ideally "[h]eiße Texte" ('hot texts') (n. a. 2010: 210), as the first part of the title for the launch event of the "Tour de lüx" (n. a. 2010: 209) was called with which the publisher celebrated its 10th anniversary. Whether the choice of the

---

58 | Personal translation of: "[...] die letzte Welt [...] die Welt der Bücher und der Literatur, die für mich der ultime Zufluchtsort ist. Also die Welt der freien Imagination, der Träume und Sehnsüchte, wenn man möchte."

59 | Personal translation of: "[...] radikale Weltoffenheit [der] Kulturschaffende[n]" [gegen die] "salbungsvollen, elektoral nützlichen Zwecklügen [der kulturpolitischen] Repräsentanten."

term used by the GDR censure jargon for 'dangerous' texts was a conscious one or not is not really important. Because it is clear by now that the publisher of the last world stages a form of subversive outsiderism.

This staging takes up a pragmatic challenge that in principle all Luxembourg publishers face, and even raises it. Because the field of activities of Luxembourg publishers is anyhow fundamentally different from that of publishers in most of the other European countries. On the one hand, they serve a multilingual readership and on the other, they have to almost completely refrain from publishing translated literature, since this business is firmly in the hands of German and French publishers.[60] This implies to a large degree a limitation to the Luxembourg market and to literature 'from here' – and this is what needs to be kept in mind when assessing *ultimo*mondo's publishing policy. Because the gesture of the 'Nestbeschmutzer' ('one who dirties his own nest') which Rewenig cultivates as an author is also of significance for the publisher – and for the the reading of the *Bicherbuch*. In the celebratory volume for the PHI-*Verlag*, Rewenig defines, in a glossary on the "Innenleben des Editörs" ('inner life of the editor'), the "Großherzogtum" ('Grand Duchy') as a "kleinkulturtum" ('petty culture-ty') (Rewenig 2001b: 84). As a satirist, there is little that Rewenig does not find fault with regarding his "home country" ("the only sports field where immobility is an athletic discipline")[61], or the language policy for Luxembourgish – for instance when he denounces the "Aktioun Lëtzebuergesch" ('Action Luxembourgish') as "a quasi-racist variety of heritagism"[62] (Rewenig 1983: 35). Rewenig has made out a currently prevailing "identity stammering" in Luxembourg which serves no other purpose than that of self-isolation. Against this he sets the stipulation: "Identity is something that no national institution should be allowed to have a claim on, it belongs exclusively to the individual and it is only for the individual to be in charge of it"[63] (Rewenig 2012a: 12).

So what could it be that Rewenig seeks to achieve with his publisher? If one considers that his name is after all associated with the first modern novel in Luxembourgish, *Hannert dem Atlantik ('Beyond the Atlantic')* (1985), and that *ultimo*mondo initially announced it would exclusively publish works by Luxembourgish authors (see n. a. 2001), it is quite obviously not a matter of turning one's back to everything Luxembourgish. But that is not only because whoever dirties their nest also needs their nest. Rather it shows that the kind of

---

60 | This of course does not regard translations into Luxembourgish, which are however rare. Recently the publisher *Capybara Books* has ventured into this field – it remains to be seen how successful this project will be.

61 | Personal translation of: "[...] einziger Sportplatz, wo die Unbeweglichkeit eine athletische Disziplin ist."

62 | Personal translation of: "[...] eine quasi-rassistische Spielart der Heimattümelei."

63 | Personal translation of: "Über Identität hat keine nationale Instanz zu verfügen, sie ist das Ureigene, über das allein jedes Individuum entscheidet."

4. Constructions of Space and Identity Created by Media-related Practises

literature that Rewenig and the publisher is passionate about can be produced, if not exclusively, but particularly in a place like Luxembourg, which in turn also has to do with language, also with the Luxembourgish one. Regarding his book *Ein unwiderstehliches Land* ('*An irresistible country*'), Rewenig writes: "My concern here is the cosmopolitanism of provinciality"[64] (Rewenig 1986). In a space that is patently restricted in multiple ways – what is at stake is literature 'from here', non-commercial texts *and* texts that cannot be politically co-opted – the publisher *ultimomondo* seeks to create urbanity against the odds. The staged blending of the formats 'family album' and 'bible' that we see in the *Bicherbuch* shows this very clearly.

How does this work in detail? Here is a sample: "Leef Landsleit! Mir mussen hei am Pays alleguer Lëtschtebeudjesch reden. Dat ist jo awer parfaitement klar. Wie sech weigert, eis Nationalsprache quotidiennement ze parléieren, deen ass weiter nichts wéi e Landesverräter" ('Dear countrymen! We have to speak Luxembourgish everywhere in this country. That's totally clear. Anyone who refuses to speak our national language in daily life is nothing more than a traitor to their country') (Rewenig 2012b: 12). These sentences from a satirical comment by Rewenig on the subject of 'national language' indicate a strategy which brings us back to the point of departure of this case study, the extreme multilingualism of the cover of the *Bicherbuch*. Rewenig here attempts to play out the identity-political language purism of Luxembourgish *ad absurdum* by, as it were, overstraining the existing possibilities of incorporating French and German words into Luxembourgish. One does not *have* to say "quotidiennement" instead of "alldeeglech", but it also can't be entirely excluded. This possibility is what seems to be Rewenig's concern – or, conversely, the impossibility to keep language pure as a fixed entity. For Rewenig – and this could also be the reason for working with formats such as dictionary and glossary – what is concentrated in Luxembourgish is the possibility (actually present in all languages) to use the 'impurity' of language to be not only aesthetically innovative but also cosmopolitan – in any case more cosmopolitan than a merely patriotic and local literature would be, but also more so than the national literatures of the 'large' neighbouring countries.

One could describe the stipulation with which the publishing house *ultimomondo* presents itself and 'its' literature as an alternative, equally ironic and subversive cosmopolitanism. While the national literatures of for instance Germany and France have at least since the end of the 18th century tended to expect the standardization of competencies in the mother-tongue on the part of the recipients and producers, indeed even have regarded it as the precondition for producing any kind of literature of artistic quality, compensating the resulting encapsulation by institutionalizing translation; so while the German and French literary public has been staging a cosmopolitanism of monolingualism as it were, the self-presentation of *ultimomondo* precisely reverses this strategy. The

---

64 | Personal translation of: "Es geht mir [...] um die Weltläufigkeit in der Provinzialität."

publishing programme's multilingualism forms a sharp contrast to the marked limitation of the area of distribution. And the 'scandals' that in particular Rewenig has recently provoked stage in a self-mocking way 'storms in a tea cup', which also point to the fact that there is nothing unusual in producing literature that subverts the establishment of linguistic and cultural borders.

4.5.3 Publishing Policy in the Times of Babel

The enterprise of *ultimo*mondo is however not merely subversive but also constructive in the sense that it implies an alternative option for the spatial structuring of language and literature. This becomes clear when we revisit the *Urtext* of all western theories of multilingualism, the Old Testament story of Babel. We can safely draw on this parallel passage, considering the biblical format the publishing house has given its anniversary book.

At the beginning of the story of Babel is the wish of men to preserve the unity of their language – they want to "make a name for themselves" and avoid being "scattered" over the face of the earth (Genesis 11; see also Dembeck 2014). They erect the tower visible from afar as a beacon to ensure togetherness. Here the unity of language guarantees the very existence of a centre – and only in being too far removed from the centre lies the danger of being scattered. The notion of language unity that the business model of almost all European publishers relies on is a totally different one – as I have pointed out at the beginning: the monolingual paradigm presumes that individual languages are bound to a more or less clearly defined territory, but also each represent close systematic orders in themselves.

If *ultimo*mondo subverts these linguistic barriers, on the one hand, and on the other, finds it important to operate from a precisely determined place; if, in pronounced self-sufficiency, it nevertheless seeks to be more cosmopolitan than all great powers, then it basically attempts to establish, tongue-in-cheek, a new Babel that aspires to being the point of departure of a movement for overcoming rigid language differences. This enterprise is tongue-in-cheek because it acts on the assumption that it can only claim universality under conditions of (self-)limitation. The *Bicherbuch* is a manifest of cultural-political claim that is voiced in a both muted and ironic manner. But what is laid claim to is precisely not the domain of single or national languages, but rather a space beyond the boundaries formed by the systematic and territorial basis of languages. Beyond these boundaries and on the basis of a limited locality the publisher seeks to create a literature of the in-between. And it is in creating this in-betweeness, this interstitiality, that it attempts to find its identity.

4.6 "Mir gesinn eis dono op *Facebook*" – (Self-)Stagings of Luxembourg Teenagers in Social Media as Virtual Identity Constructions

Luc Belling

The topic of this case study are identity constructions by Luxembourg teenagers in the social network *facebook*. I will examine how teenagers stage themselves on this virtual platform. Nowadays, digital media exert a strong influence on young people, with parents playing a less crucial role than friends (see Boyd 2006). As a result, certain peer dynamics evolve on virtual platforms such as *facebook* where we can observe self-stagings and identity constructions.

The contribution examines such identity-generating self-stagings in the context of digital social networks. This means transferring theoretical concepts of identity construction that relate to non-virtual identities and face-to-face situations into a digitalized space with self-generated online identities. The term of online identity can be compared to Döring's definition of virtual identities (2000: 65): "We refer to virtual identities when we examine how people present themselves when communicating computer-based with each other."[65] One should however be careful not to generalize computer-based communication, since the users in social networks, in contrast to web forums and chats, do not conceal themselves behind pseudonyms but rather represent a virtual image under their proper name – after all, the idea is to be recognized and acknowledged. These virtual identities exist only within digital social networks (in this case *facebook*), described by Boyd/Ellison (2007: 211) as follows:

"We define social network sites as web-based services that allow individuals to (i) construct a public or semi-public profile within a bounded system, (ii) articulate a list of other users with whom they share a connection, and (iii) view and traverse their list of connections and those made by others within the system."[66]

The definition also refers to interstitial characteristics of social networks such as creating a personal profile in a 'semi-public' environment, whereas the interactional orientation of social networks is disregarded in the context of this contribution. Creating a profile basically constitutes only the access to a social network, with no particular focus on the communicative possibilities of these platforms.

---

65 | Personal translation of: "Wir sprechen von virtuellen Identitäten, wenn es darum geht, wie Menschen sich selbst präsentieren, wenn sie computervermittelt [...] miteinander kommunizieren."
66 | Smith (1976) has made similar observations. He distinguishes between object *versus* acting self.

This case study's two aspects of examination imply the following research questions:

- Which techniques of self-representation are used in online profiles of teenagers?
- Which role does the wall play as a contact zone in self-staging?

One theoretical approach dealing with identities in the context of social media is symbolic interactionism. Already Mead (1934) pointed to the crucial step in the forming of an individual's identity that consists of self-reflection (view of one's identity from an exterior perspective) and the perception of reactions of society (in this case the self-constructed network contacts in *facebook* that form a kind of community). In social networks, this objectivation is particularly evident during the creation of online profiles. Here, considerations concerning the manner one wants to present oneself to one's own community (see Döring 2003: 334) become apparent.

For capturing the dimension of self-reflection/reflexivity, we draw on a contrasting staging method described by Anthony Giddens (1984) in his model of presence/absence. He developed the conceptual pair of front and back regions, with the front region expressing a display or performance and the back region a concealment (see Werlen 1997: 174). Frontal aspects of presentation cannot be authentic because they represent a facade; only what is concealed behind it, the back presentation, should be considered real/authentic (see Giddens 1984: 124). These two staging techniques will be examined in the context of virtual identities in order to show the relationship between frontal and back stagings and the communicative content conveyed.

Goffman's self-representation in everyday life (impression management) partly draws on symbolic interactionism which states that communicative actions are crucial for identity formation (see Goffman 1959: 3). Complementing the analysis of interaction-based, communicative actions with that of other forms of making contact is indispensable for this contribution. In the virtual social networks, communicative actions can be detected on the walls with both profile owners as well as their 'contacts' (i.e. the members of their network) leaving messages and also being able to comment on these visibly for everyone.

Given this communally constructed self-image on *facebook*, the study seeks to shed light on two specific perspectives of analysis, since virtual identities feed on self-generated profile pages as well as on interactional walls. These two self-staging techniques are examined in the context of virtual space which constitutes an interstice of private and public environment. According to Boyd (2006) these are "places where youth gather to hang out amongst friends and make public [...] spaces their own." Although the virtual identities are visible by many other users, they represent for teenagers a private space where they can interact with friends without supervision such as by parents or teachers.

4. Constructions of Space and Identity Created by Media-related Practises

The first research topic examines the hybrid construction of personal profile pages as an interplay of front and back staging techniques. The second research topic highlights the wall as a contact zone that enables situations of private communication in a public space.

The data for the case study was gathered from examining online identities of six Luxembourg teenagers from one school class. The project was presented in an 11th grade and three male and three female participants[67] were determined by random selection among the volunteers. All wall messages posted by these six participants from July to December 2012 were gathered and analysed. Besides monitoring the wall activities, I recorded the information on the profile page and noted any changes made to the profiles during these six months.[68] In order to influence the data as little as possible, the results were not presented to the school class until the project's conclusion in January 2013.

After evaluating and analysing the walls, semi-structured interviews were conducted that related to the teenagers' communication practices. By linking the quantitative evaluations of the online profiles with qualitative evaluations of the interviews, the case study also provides, besides the statistical evaluation, insight into the teenagers' user motives.

4.6.1 Practices of (Self-)Staging in Online Profiles

For examining self-staging techniques in online profiles I draw on a modified concept by Zhao *et al.* (2008) for identity construction on *facebook* which is subdivided into four categories: visual (profile photo), enumerative (interests, hobbies, favorite books etc.), narrative (self generated texts by the users about themselves) and self-labelling (information about gender, relational status, home town, education etc.) The model reflects a continuum of public presentation that is arranged between implicit and explicit. The practice of self-labelling is for instance a very explicit method of self-staging,

"[...] since individuals choose labels to describe themselves, thereby straightforwardly and unambiguously placing themselves in categories, [...] enumeration of hobbies and interests, on the other hand, is a less explicit form of identity construction, since there is a less straightforward connection between statements about one's hobbies and interests

---

67 | In general, however, the analysis revealed no significant differences between the sexes, which is why the further discussion will not include differentiation by gender.
68 | Changes in profile information are displayed on the wall and could therefore be considered in the analysis. In the case of the participants the changes related exclusively to the publication of a new profile photo. Only the group memberships and the quantity of Likes increased continuously during the period under review. The information in Table 2 refer to the last day of monitoring (31.12.2013). The remaining information did not vary during the six months.

[...], and the type of identity one constructs for oneself through such a claim" (Bolander/Locher 2010: 166).

The visual practice of uploading profile photos represents the most implicit form of self-staging, since contents are only shown, but not described or explained (see Zhao et al. 2008: 1816).

Table 1 lists the information published by teenagers in their online profiles.

Form of public staging	Staging practices	Melanie	Sam	Sophie	Raoul	Manon	Marc
Implicit	Visual	23	18	8	11	7	13
	Enumerative	504	257	33	150	86	394
Explicit	Narrative	No	Yes	No	No	No	No
	Self-labelling	5	8	5	8	7	7
	Network contacts	1,506	1,352	1,107	481	738	683

Table 1: Staging practices of the reviewed teenagers on their profile pages (quantitative count) (own study) [69]

The first research question discusses the self-representation practices of teenagers on their profile pages. The self-reflection/reflexivity described by Mead (1934) and the inherent exclusion of certain information is an important process in the staging of virtual identity. The investigation analyses the interstitial character of the profile pages on which the users convey authenticity through the reproduction of selected private information (back), but at the same time consciously stage themselves (front) in order to stand out among the mass of network contacts.

Visual self-staging: The category of visual presentation techniques constitutes, through the regular updating of profile photos, a continuous working on identity. In this immaterial 2.0 work (Coté/Pybus 2011) the profile pages appear not as static elements but as consciously employed tools to attract the attention of network contacts. Profile photos constitute an implicit method of presenting oneself on platforms such as *facebook* without using textual explanations.

---

69 | The test subjects' names were changed for reasons of privacy. Only the gender of the user is expressed with the chosen name.

4. Constructions of Space and Identity Created by Media-related Practises 197

The analysis of the photos revealed that the test subjects were indeed visible on each of the 80 uploaded pictures, but often not alone. On 34 pictures (42 %) the teenagers appeared together with another person or group. Manon's comment was: "Mostly I upload pictures together with my boyfriend. I want everyone to see we're a couple."[70] Besides partly very private representations of relationships, group pictures with friends are a particularly favorite motif. The teenagers also confirm that they post pictures with their friends to demonstrate their closeness with these persons.

In general, regular updates of profile photos are an important presentation method of virtual reality, with the pictures partly conveying a very private and authentic impression of the teenagers, apparently without too much concern about their reception within the network's extensive realm.

Enumerating self-staging: So-called enumerating profile information (books, films, music, places visited, *facebook* groups etc.) are extensively used by the teenagers (see Table 1). They inform about selected interests and preferences which again point to a dynamic staging of identity. Regular information about places visited or films watched allow a continuously updated glimpse into the teenagers' non-virtual life. The enumerating self-staging presents the audience with information that deviates from the usual standardized profile information. This is also confirmed by Melanie who, with 504 enumerations of interests, conveyed the most information:

"I click on everything that interests me in some way or that I like. Since meanwhile all kinds of things can be found on *facebook*, it's easy to quickly *like* something. I don't really worry that the other contacts can see this information. After all, they're unimportant things that don't reveal much about me."[71]

The carefree way in which Melanie provides her information confirms that implicit presentation methods (pictures and enumeration) tend to be back stagings that do not seek public display. These more spontaneous techniques of self-presentation form a contrast to the narrative staging.

Narrative Self-staging: "Oh no, that's too much work writing about myself. And I don't really know what to write."[72] This comment by Raoul is representative for all test subjects (except Sam). The effort in terms of time seems to play a role in the

---

70 | Personal translation of: "Meeschtens lueden ech Fotoen héich op deenen ech mat mengem Fränd sinn. Ech wëll, datt jidderee gesäit, datt mir eng Koppel sinn."
71 | Personal translation of: "Alles, wat mech interesséiert oder mir gefält, klicken ech un. Mëttlerweil fënnt een alles op *facebook* an et kann een et séier un ouni Problemer *liken*. Ech denken am Fong net driwwer no, datt déi aner Leit déi Saache kënne gesinn. Et si jo nëmmen onwichteg Saachen, déi näischt mat mir ze dinn hunn."
72 | Personal translation of: "Oh nee, dat ass mir zevill Aarbecht, fir eppes iwwert mech ze schreiwen. Ech wéisst och guer net, wat ech do schreiwe sollt."

creation of a profile. Raoul also adds that without the categories pre-set by *facebook* it is difficult to present oneself. Sam is the only test subject who uses this narrative self-staging method, even though paradoxically his text underscores the difficulty of the self-image: "You want to know something about me? Ask the others. They always know everything better anyway." Asked about it, Sam was unable to explain why he had chosen precisely this phrasing in his profile.

Due to a lack of profile information, an analysis of this self-staging method could not be carried out, maybe – a possible interpretation of Sam's example – because the self-representation here is so explicit that it has a paralyzing effect. But in how far the test subjects are aware of an audience cannot be determined. The fourth category is perhaps the most classic category within online profiles, but it also shows the greatest differences between the test subjects' self-stagings.

Self-labelling self-staging: The explicit profile information comprises the name (obligatory), date of birth, relationship status, family members, language skills, gender, hometown and education (school). Already with the obligatory labelling with a name, we can observe various techniques of self-staging since three teenagers give their official name, the three others a slight variation of their offical name or a nickname, by which they are, however, known in their peer group and thus recognizable. Raoul, whose profile gives his real name, comments: "That's not at all relevant for me. I want other people to be able to find me. How are they supposed to do that if I give a false user name?"[73] Raoul's comment corresponds to the basic idea of *facebook*: to serve as a platform on which people can find other people they know. By contrast, three teenagers used an artificial name which is not really a classic pseudonym but rather a typographical-phonetic play with their own name. Manon for instance uses letter reiterations in her name ("Maaaannnooonnn"); Melanie only uses her first name which she however divides with a space into a first and second name ("Mel Anie") and Sam chooses besides his correctly given first name an imaginary second name ("Miseler") which points to his home region (Moselle region). This creates a certain charaterization of the person, but at the same time makes finding it via *facebook*'s search function difficult. Asked about this Sam said: "I don't want everybody to know my name. That's too private for me. My friends know my pseudonym and know how to find me on *facebook*."[74] Stating one's name can therefore very well be regarded as part of one's private sphere which – in this for the test subjects public space – is protected with an artificial name (front facade). Indirectly Sam indicates that the potential for networking with other network contacts is not that important to him. These results confirm Boyd and Ellison's (2007: 211) statement about the change in the notion of networking:

---

73 | Personal translation of: "Dat ass jo guer net relevant fir mech. Ech wëll, datt déi aner Leit mech op *facebook* fanne kënnen. Wéi solle se dat da maachen, wann ech e falsche *Username* hunn?"

74 | Personal translation of: "Ech wëll net, datt jidderee weess, wéi ech heeschen. Dat ass mir ze privat. Meng Frënn kenne mäi *facebook*-Numm, mat deem se mech fanne kënnen."

4. Constructions of Space and Identity Created by Media-related Practises

"On many of the large SNSs [social network sites], participants are not necessarily 'networking' or looking to meet new people; instead, they are primarily communicating with people who are already a part of their extended social network."

Besides the name, the listing of family members is an interesting feature of self-representation with the teenagers. With the exception of Sophie's profile, all other profiles named referred to friends as family and pointed via a link to their *facebook* profile. Here the test subjects agree in the interviews, as Manon explains: "That's perfectly normal at school. It's become a trend. My best friends are like family to me."[75] On the one hand, the use of this profile category shows the strong attachment of the teenagers among each other (already indicated by the profile pictures), but on the other, it can also be seen as evidence that naming the actual family members might be too private or that these do not have a *facebook* profile.[76]

The analysis shows a clear combination of implicit back and explicit front stagings. Authentic (back) information is made public with the implicit presentation techniques of contents which the teenagers do not perceive as primary identity markers. By contrast, in the case of the self-labelling profile category the teenagers partly erected a front facade because they regard the communication contents as too private to share with a larger audience. This process of self-reflection therefore occurs in explicit profile categories in which the public display of non-virtual realities is avoided.

4.6.2 Identity Constructions on *facebook* Walls

The data listed in Table 2 was gathered and evaluated to answer the second research question relating to wall activities.

For the quantitative counts, one can already observe significant differences in the number of published posts as well as in the type of these posts (textual status messages *versus* photos). These figures suggest different self-staging techniques on the wall. In addition, besides the active self-stagings, we can also notice discrepancies between the reception of posts through one's own network and the resulting interaction.

The posts were gathered with the help of an egocentric network analysis that exclusively examines the communication on the test subjects' wall – without

---

[75] | Personal translation of: "Dat ass ganz normal bei eis. Et ass en Trend ginn. Meng bescht Frënn si wéi eng Famill fir mech."
[76] | Also regarding other information from the self-labelling profile category were frontal stagings employed for privacy reasons. None of the test subjects gave their actual date of birth and also for 'hometown' Hawaii or Los Angeles was given, but never a place in Luxembourg. Similarly, for 'education' no profile listed the actual school but, in turn, schools on different continents.

looking at their activitites on other walls – in order to record the teenagers' communication processes.

	Melanie	Sam	Sophie	Raoul	Manon	Marc
Posted messages	263	74	56	85	26	194
of these status updates	102	38	24	50	7	57
of these photos	77	27	14	29	17	44
Messages from other users	640	35	267	154	229	123
Comments on messages	2,808	256	583	845	495	2,675
Number of *Likes* received	5,048	562	1,221	1,051	688	1,308

Table 2: Counted wall activities of interviewed teenagers (own study) [77]

On the walls the teenagers communicate daily with their network and draw attention to themselves with updates. The investigation will show whether Bolander/Locher's (2010: 167) hypothesis is confirmed that "implicit means of identity construction is clearly different to the explicit form evident in the self-labelling on the profile pages." This would mean that on walls private information that was protected in the profiles with non-authentic, frontal displays is made accessible to the same audience and discussed quasi publicly.

Functionality of Wall Posts

Table 2 shows the number of published information that varies between 263 (Melanie) and 26 (Manon) wall posts. This wide range suggests that the wall is used in different ways. Melanie comments on her high frequency of messages: "I know I publish a lot. I don't do it consciously. I just have a lot to say, or a photo that

---

[77] | The sum of the status messages and photos does not equal the total sum of published entries. In addition, also other forms such as videos, best results in online games etc. were published. This information was, however, not considered in the analysis.

I want to show others."⁷⁸ Melanie describes her continuous staging as a means of staying in contact with her network friends and regularly sharing information from her life with them. Manon, by contrast, sees writing short messages more of a problem: "I almost never write statuses. If I want to share something I do it with pictures."⁷⁹ She points to the use of pictures as staging measures that show her mostly together with friends. Overall, the analysis shows that the status messages comprise 40 % and the photographs 30 %.

The contents of textual posts chiefly deal with personal topics such as friendships, relationships or school. Bolander/Locher's hypothesis is confirmed here, because the teenagers do indeed discuss private and authentic topics on the walls and therefore act out a back staging infront of an audience. The combination of explicit frontal staging of the profile pages corresponds to an explicit back representation on the walls.

Asked about this, Raoul emphasizes that he fails to see a connection between the two elements: "The profile can be viewed by anyone. But what happens on the wall is for my real friends."⁸⁰ Even though virtual reality feeds from these two categories and both are visible for the members of the network, we can observe that the teenagers are conscious of a separation that subdivides the hybrid profile into a public and a private component.

The network analysis of the walls shows that the teenagers on average made contact with 41 different people on their wall.⁸¹ Even though this figure seems relatively high, it constitutes in terms of contacts in the test subjects' networks (481 to 1,506) only a small percentage of possible interlocutors. What can result from this conversational situation, perceived as familiar and involving mostly the same contacts, is the communicative effect that one forgets the invisible third party – in the shape of the audience reading passively along – and conducts private, mostly dyadic conversations in a quasi-public space.

The wall seems to be a private representation platform for teenagers with a direct correlation between the walls, the profile pages and the non-virtual life. The interlocutors on the walls overlap with the teenagers' profile information regarding their family members. When asked in the interview, it was furthermore confirmed that the contacts on the wall were the closest friends, mostly from school, whom they

---

78 | Personal translation of: "Ech weess, datt ech vill *online* setzen. Ech maachen dat net express. Ech hunn einfach ëmmer eppes ze soen oder eng Foto, déi ech deenen anere weise wëll."
79 | Personal translation of: "Ech schreiwe bal ni Statussen. Wann ech eppes matdeele wëll, da maachen ech dat mat Fotoen."
80 | Personal translation of: "D'Profil gesäit jo jiddereen. Wat awer op der Pinnwand geschriwwe gëtt, dat ass just fir meng Kollegen."
81 | Melanie had the most contacts (59) and Manon the fewest (27). The study disregarded birthday messages. On birthdays, many contacts post a message out of politeness, even though they maintain no online contact with that person.

also meet almost on a daily basis. The wall connections are used by the teenagers as a supplement to the offline world, whereby maintaining relations has an important function in connection with virtual identitites. Bolander/Locher (2010: 165) state that "individuals in *facebook* tend to have 'anchored relationships' (see Zhao et al.), which means their *facebook* relationships are grounded in offline life".

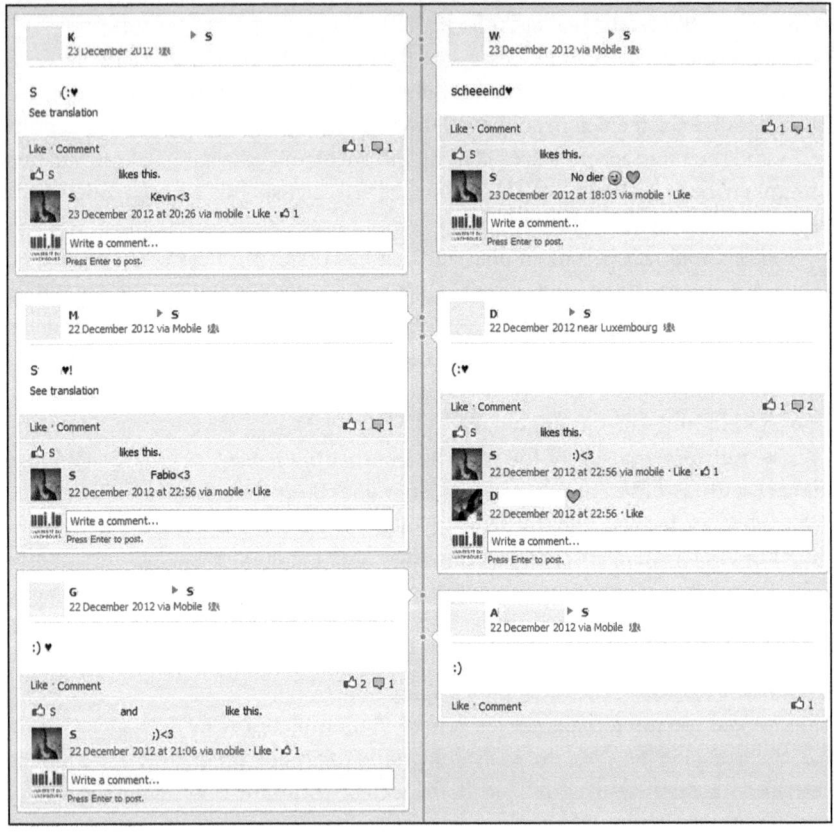

Figure 1: Maintaining relationships through wall posts: Sophie's facebook wall

In my view, this form of short messages (by the profile owner but primarily by the other network contacts) on walls develops a certain "mutual impingement" (see Goffman 1959: 100). Thus messages need not necessarily contain a specific content, but rather act as routine greeting rituals that leave a visitor's trace which in turn leads to a repayment of the visit on other walls. Boyd (2006) also points to the interrelationship of mutual wall messages: "For those seeking attention, writing comments and being visible on popular people's pages is very important and this can be a motivation to comment on others' profiles" (Boyd 2006). This is confirmed by Melanie's comment: "It's exciting when you log into *facebook*. You never know whether someone has posted something on your page. It's always nice when you have other people thinking of you."[82] This also explains the wall activitities like the one in Fig. 1 which depicts an anonymized screenshot of Sophie's wall (recognizable by the S).

A first glance at Fig. 1 underscores the secondary importance of the message content and reinforces the hypothesis that the wall comments, which are chiefly comprised of emoticons, are used for relationship maintenance. What is remarkable in sustaining and developing the virtual identity is not only the attention that is accorded to the teenagers with these comments; also the role that the profile owners themselves fulfill is of crucial importance.

Common Identity Constructions in the Contact Zone (Wall)

One single comment on the wall is not sufficient for relationship maintenance. The profile owner is indirectly called on by the fleeting traces left by the visitor to react to the comment (even if only with an emoticon) as this could otherwise be construed as a lack of respect (see Goffman 2008: 5).

In theatrical performances there is a relationship between actors and audience, described by Goffman as a "performance team" (1959: 71). Communication in social networks, however, has the effect that every user equally fulfills both the role of the actor and that of the spectator and at any moment can leave the passive role of the observer and actively join in the conversation. In this context, Davis and Harre (1990: 46) introduce the notion of acts of positioning, as "the discursive process whereby selves are located in conversations as observably and subjectively coherent participants in jointly produced story lines".

Accordingly Sophie reacted to all comments, both with a comment of her own and by using the *Like* function (as a rapid response option). For maintaining and managing one's virtual identity this phatic function can be of great importance as a response signal. Gerlitz (2011: 103) points to the significance of the *Like* button which "enables to not only materialize but also measure and record positive affects."[83]

All in all, more than 85 % (n= 7,662) of all wall postings (both textual messages and pictures) were commented on in the corpus, and almost 95 % (n= 9,878) of all comments were marked with at least one *Like*. So it is not suprising to hear Melanie state in the interview: "I try to answer every message on my wall. It's exciting when several conversations start up on different walls."[84] The teenagers considered this time-intensive identity editing work to take up between two to three hours a day, with some stating that it could take even longer depending on how many wall conversations they are having at the same time.

---

82 | Personal translation of: "Et ass spannend, wann ee sech bei *facebook* aloggt. Du weess ni, ob een dir op deng Säit geschriwwen huet. Et ass ëmmer schéin ze gesinn, wann anerer un dech geduecht hunn."

83 | Personal translation of: "[...] ermöglicht, positive Affekte mit einem Klick sowohl zu materialisieren als auch zu messen und erfassen."

84 | Personal translation of: "Ech probéieren, op all Message op der Pinnwand ze äntweren. Et ass spannend, wa verschidde Gespréicher op méi Pinnwänn entstinn."

4.6.3 Conclusion

This case study attempted to shed some light on the construction of virtual identities in teenagers, focussing on the hybrid self-staging practices of teenagers as well as the interstitial space of online profiles.

For the profile page, it was possible to show with front and back self-staging techniques that the test subjects are aware of the presence of a public audience and accordingly protect private topics with a facade. We were also able to observe different weightings within the profile categories, with the implicit rubrics being answered most truthfully. A conspicuous profile feature probably typical for teenagers is the inclusion of friends. This was evident both in the profile photos as well as in the labelling of friends as 'family'. This reference to prominent contacts in the network can also be found in the walls of the virtual identity projections. Teenagers seem to attach much more importance to the virtual relationship maintenance with their best friends than self-staging via their online profile.

With the help of an egocentric network analysis it was possible to shed light on this hybrid status of a space in a basically public arena but perceived as private among friends. Despite large personal networks, the number of communication partners is relatively small, which produces a familiar and perhaps also less reflected self-representation in the form of partly very private conversations among the teenagers. This is also evident in the reversal of front and back staging methods, since authentic information is displayed on the wall without a protective facade. In conclusion, the active relationship maintenance of offline contacts turns out to be an important function of virtual identities which every day demands and stimulates a great number of conversations.

4.7 PETROL STATIONS AS IN-BETWEEN SPACES I: PRACTICES AND NARRATIVES

Sonja Kmec

In *Blumme vun der Tankstell* (2011) ("Flowers from the Petrol Station"), the Luxembourgish singer-songwriter Serge Tonnar gives voice to the ambivalent feelings many people have about petrol stations, which have "often become a code, a mundane place and at the same time a modern myth" (Polster 1996: 11).[85] In the song, Sunday marital quarrels are repeatedly appeased by flowers bought at a petrol station, until one day the speaker's wife does not forgive him and stabs him in the chest. The lyrics encode a diffuse, but pervasive feeling that buying

---

85 | The present study has been developed together with Agnès Prüm, whose contribution in this volume centers on the encoding of (petrol-station) experiences into films and other media.

flowers at a petrol station may be considered a *faux pas*. As shall be argued below, this reflects a more general approach towards petrol stations, which fulfil concrete material needs, while generating a sense of unease, possibly linked to the "impersonal" atmosphere and mechanical customer clearance. "[Gasoline stations] tell us that we live in a world of increased place-product-packaging [...], of enhanced corporate dominance [...], of accelerated change" (Jakle/Sculle 1994: 233). At the same time, the standard layout generates a feeling of familiarity: "It is a place of strong behavior expectation" (ibid.: 229).

In their interstitial functioning between impersonality and familiarity, petrol stations fit Marc Augé's description of "real non-places of supermodernity" (Augé 1995: 96). Augé does not specifically categorize filling stations among the non-places of (super)modernity – except as part of the motorway system (ibid.: 97), but they share the characteristics of other sites of anonymous mass transit, such as train stations, airports and supermarkets, which create "neither singular identity nor relations; only solitude, and similitude" (ibid.: 103). "Non-places" are not defined ontologically, as things in themselves, but in contrast to the "relational" character of "places" (Augé 2012: 0:16-1:58). Augé himself acknowledges that "non-places" may well open up new spaces for (inter-)action, thereby destabilising the seemingly clear-cut distinction between "place" and "non-place".

Although, at first sight, "non-places" preclude any kind of identification, there are many ways this space is being appropriated – both in everyday practices and in creative appropriations. The latter may appear in the qualitative interviews[86], which do not simply relate past experiences and recurring routines, but cast them in a language that is steeped in (popular) culture. They refer to images such as exploding petrol stations, a relatively common occurrence in films across all genres.[87] This intersection of locally embedded practices and global frames of reference are a first aspect of the interstitial character of petrol stations. Moreover, they may be seen as interstitial spaces, defined as zones of contact and transformation of different forms of spatiality, on the following accounts:

Firstly, in their hybrid state – increasingly mechanized, though relying on organic matter (fossil fuel) – petrol stations constitute a type of contact zone, whose transformative power insidiously reconfigures the 'human' and blurs the distinction between man and machine, as illustrated in the Luxembourgish documentary *Plein d'essence* (Mersch 2007, see Kmec/Prüm 2014).

Secondly, driving a car and stopping for petrol is emblematic for the shift from adolescence to adulthood. This symbolic significance is underlined by Hayley G.

---

86 | University of Luxembourg, IDENT2 2012/2013 – qualitative survey.

87 | The synopsis of 818 films listed on the *Internet Movie Database* (http://www.imdb.com – accessed 22.10.2012) mention a "gas station" scene, 103 thereof may be classified as violent scenes. This includes 59 explosions of the site, mostly in the genres of drama, thrillers, action, crime and horror films, but also in science fiction films and even in romantic comedies (see section 5.8).

Hoover, whose user-generated video entitled *Gas Stations* (2009) starts with a 'declaration of (consumer) independence': "I am a big kid now and that means two very exciting things. One: I can order things off the TV. And two: I get to pay my own gas."

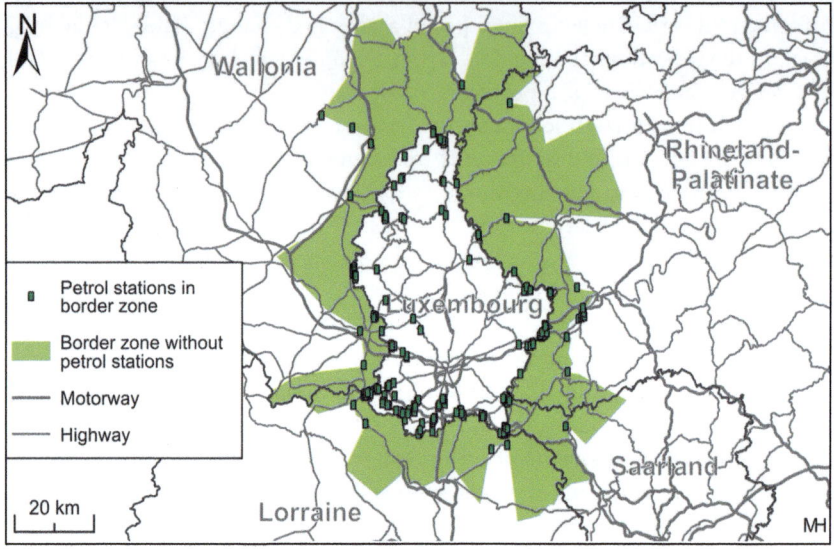

Figure 1: Petrol stations as border markers (source: Ullrich 2009, realization: Malte Helfer)

Thirdly, on a political level, petrol stations have become markers of state borders and tax regimes. Within the Schengen area, border posts have been abolished or turned into art centres to encourage cross-border exchanges.[88] However, these internal borders have not disappeared altogether. Within the EU, nation states use different instruments such as fiscal regimes, nationality laws, language policies or immigration restrictions, to establish and demarcate their zones of influence. The implementation of these mechanisms generates regional practices, which may disrupt official discourses and demarcations. It is in particular at the borders that state hegemony is renegotiated through the everyday practices and the choices of

---

88 | In 2007, when Luxembourg and the Greater Region were "European Capital of Culture", the project *hArt an der Grenze* was initiated in 2007 by the *Saarländisches Künstlerhaus* (http://www.kuenstlerhaus-saar.de/index.php/hart-an-der-grenze.html – accessed 06.01.2014). In a similar vein, the project *Borderline*, managed by Claudia Passeri and Michèle Walerich, transformed former borders at Esch/Grenz, Mondorf-Mondorff and Differdange-Hussigny into art exhibition and meeting places. The work of Guillaume Paris is still to be seen at the French custom office of Hussigny, whereas the former customs office at Mondorf continues to be used by the local tourist office.

individuals. In our case study, petrol stations have emerged as the specifically local physical markers of the overlapping of fiscal regimes in and around Luxembourg. Interestingly, their concentration at the outer limits of Luxembourg's zone of fiscal influence redraws the lines the Schengen treaties aimed to 'erase'. In the digital atlas of the Greater Region SaarLorLux, a map by Daniel Ullrich (2009) shows that the last petrol stations in Luxembourg (often located on or near the country's national borders) and the first petrol station in the neighbouring country define a new border zone spanning 10 to 25 km.

The reason for this phenomenon may be traced back to low excise duty and value-added tax rates in Luxembourg.[89] As a result, "petrol tourism" has a strong impact not only on Luxembourg's fiscal revenues but also on its image. The fiscal regime may be rigid, but people play the system by buying petrol, stocking up on cigarettes and alcohol, to be distributed or sold 'back home'. This transgression is not merely tolerated by the authorities; it is the very cause of existence of border petrol stations.

Finally, the perception of petrol stations wavers between that of a functional, impersonal "non-place" and that of a relational "place". Filling up the car may be an entirely mechanical gesture, pertaining to what Georges Perec (1989) calls the "infra-ordinary". It appears completely unreflected, while at the same time the petrol station triggers a sense of disturbance, as the unknown appears familiar (for instance through recognizable brands) and the familiar becomes strange and threatening.

The present study focuses on this last aspect of interstitiality or co-spatiality. It eschews all ambition of representativity, but explores the intersubjective and intertextual construction of meaning using the hermeneutical approaches of literary and cultural studies (Thompson *et al.* 1994). First, an analysis of everyday petrol station routines[90] will examine whether the empirical, statistical material reveals similar fissures and inconsistencies as the narratives do. In a second step, these narratives are explored further, showing three different ways the 'threshold' of the petrol station is experienced, narrated and transfigured – simultaneously "decoded" and "encoded [...] into and out of discursive form" (Richardson 2005) – in interviews and in various media.

---

89 | European Commission, Taxation and Customs Union, Excise duties on alcohol, tobacco and energy, http://ec.europa.eu/taxation_customs/taxation/excise_duties/index_en.htm (accessed 24.12.2014); VAT live, 2013 European Union EU VAT rates, http://www.vatlive.com/vat-rates/european-vat-rates/2013-eu-vat-rates-2/ (accessed 24.12.2013). A similar phenomenon may be observed at other state borders in Europe and worldwide.
90 | University of Luxembourg, IDENT2 2012/2013 – quantitative survey.

4.7.1 Stopping at the Petrol Station: A Mere Routine?

According to our survey, the vast majority of people living in the borderlands use a car in their daily life (94 %) and to reach their holiday destination (86 %). One objective of the survey was to find out about people's practices and preferences when filling up their car: which petrol station do they choose and why? Do they frequent petrol stations for other reasons than … buying petrol?

Pecuniary Incentives
Pecuniary advantages are frequently mentioned in the qualitative interviews as determining the choice of petrol station, as are the factors of proximity and convenience: 42 % explain their choice with reference to proximity, 24 % link it to the station's loyalty programme (*carte de fidélité*), 15 % to the friendliness of staff and 8 % to the shop attached to the petrol station, often a franchise of a local supermarket. The remaining 40 % declare that they do not make a conscious choice. One could argue that the former merely assume that they are acting of their own free will, when their choice may in fact be dictated by routine (proximity), public policy (excise duties and VAT) and marketing devices (*cartes de fidélité*). Despite their name, which suggests a form of personal connection, the latter do not generate a sense of community, but rather of loyalty to a corporation: clients are cast as "vassals" who remain unknown to one another as they pledge "fealty" (*fidélité*) to their "lord". The card may establish a bond, but it does not involve any personal interactions – as opposed to relating to the friendliness of the staff.

Locations
In their everyday life, most people prefer to use petrol stations located in villages or towns (62 %), whereas only 6 % choose to stop along the motorway. By far the highest percentage of any group using motorways to fill up on petrol are cross-border commuters (14 %). By contrast, Luxembourg residents are least likely to use motorways in their daily routine: only 3 % claim to do so. This relative reluctance to use motorway petrol stations contrasts markedly with people's behaviour when on vacation. In that case, one third (33 %) stops at service stations along the motorway, while only 27 % (in contrast to the 62 % mentioned above) opt for petrol stations in a village or town. The contrast is even more significant if one looks at Luxembourg residents, almost half of whom (45 %) actually prefer motorway stations when on vacation.

Age and Gender
There is no general gender bias, but age does seem to play a significant role in the choice of petrol station: 59 % of all young people (16-24 years old) prefer the motorway on their holidays, 9 % in their everyday life. Generally, the older one is, the more one is disposed to stop in a town or village for petrol. Young people are

also more likely to use petrol stations as a meeting place. This is also the only age group in which there is a marked gender difference: 21 % of men aged 16 to 34 state that they sometimes meet people at a petrol station, compared to an average of only 11 %. However, a significantly larger proportion of our sample, in particular young men again, state that they will eat or drink at a petrol station (logically often on their own).

According to one 23 year-old interview partner, petrol stations are a popular meeting point after nightclubbing:

"There is a petrol station in Leudelange, which I often go to … after clubbing in order to eat … a pizza or something of the kind, to be among friends. […] I think it is awesome, it's …, they put a pizza in the oven for us – you can buy a pizza for 2.50 or 3 € – and we eat together at about 4 or 5 am, at a time where we are still in harmony. After that, everybody goes home"[91] (male, 23, Luxembourgish, Luxembourg).

Whether situated in a small town like Leudelange or alongside the motorway (the same interviewee mentions the Aire de Berchem and the Aire de Capellen as meeting points), what attracts this young man and his friends are the all-night-long opening hours and the cheap food that is being served. However, not everyone finds "harmony" at petrol stations. A cross tabulation shows that people who visit nightclubs and cinemas frequently are more likely to meet at petrol stations, than those who spend their free time in sport halls and outdoors. For a majority of people the petrol station is not a *lieu de rencontre* but a *lieu de passage*. The main aim is to buy petrol, which 62 % do regularly, that is, more than once a month. Three other products people buy there regularly are bread/food (19 %), cigarettes (18 %) and newspapers/magazines (12 %), whereas only 8 % claim that they buy alcohol at petrol stations. Age matters again: cigarettes and alcohol are purchased mostly by the youngest age groups (with a bias towards cigarettes by young women, and alcohol by young men), newspapers/magazines most frequently by men aged 24 to 35 and food is bought most frequently by the 35 to 44 age group.

The Petrol Station: Beloved Enemy

Contrary to our expectations, people who shop in organic grocery stores are more – not less – likely to buy their bread or other food in petrol stations too. The choice appears to be less ideologically motivated than linked to the amount of money one

---

91 | Personal translation of: "Il y a une station de service à Leudelange, je la fréquente souvent après … de sortir de discothèque pour aller manger … une pizza ou quelque chose comme ça, être entre amis. […] je trouve ça génial, c'est … , ils nous mettent la pizza ou four – on peut acheter une pizza à 2.50 € ou 3 € – et on mange tous ensemble vers quatre, cinq heures du matin, donc, où on est encore en harmonie. Après, tout le monde part à la maison."

is disposed to spend on food.[92] Similarly, a statistical cross tabulation has shown that people who buy food in delicatessen have fewer qualms about buying it at petrol stations than people who frequent discount stores. Luxembourgers are most likely to buy food and least likely to buy cigarettes at the petrol station. This may be linked to the minimarket one finds attached to Luxembourgish petrol stations and its function as emergency solution (*dépannage*) to buy food after closing hours, whereas cigarettes can also be bought in bars till 1 am. According to a market research commissioned by Shell, shops with late opening hours attract a young urban clientele, mostly singles, who are either working long hours, are generally disorganized in their shopping or just need a quick fix (Paragon Communications 1992, cited by Polster 1996: 145). The consumer behaviour of this 'top-up society' is not limited to the singles and yuppies of big cities, but seems to apply more generally to young or middle-aged people living close to such convenience stores. As (1) strict regulations regarding shop opening hours do not apply to petrol stations in Luxembourg, (2) Luxembourg borders are replete with petrol stations and (3) no one in Luxembourg and the border areas we surveyed lives more than 30 km from the border, it is not surprising that about half of our interview partners consider petrol stations useful stopgap solutions ("*Abhilfe*", "*Noutstopp*") or even emergency exits ("*sortie de secours*"). The minimarkets are considered – mostly free of value judgment – to replace the traditional little shop ("*Tante Emma Laden*" or "épicerie"). Very few interviewees refuse categorically to buy anything there except petrol, considering those shops taboo ("*tabu*" or "*Unleben*"). Some are sceptical about meat, fresh fruits and vegetables or flowers, but express themselves very ambivalently. Asked whether he would buy food at the petrol station, one interviewee replies:

"Not at all! It's a real no-go for me! Most of the time, I go to my shop, where I [usually] go, there I know where I will find things. At petrol stations, I am never really sure, whether the goods meet the quality standards I really expect. [...] I would never buy a sandwich or something like that there. Well, I will buy a ... sausage as a snack, but nothing else!"[93] (male, 62, German, Rheinland-Pfalz).

The strict opposition between "my shop" (which is well known and can be trusted) and petrol stations (in the plural), where the food quality is uncertain, is overcome by the search for instant gratification. This spur-of-the-moment decision obliterates the dichotomy between 'place' and 'non-place' and creates an

---

92 | See section 5.2.
93 | Personal translation of: "Gar nicht! Das kommt gar nicht in Frage für mich! Meistens gehe ich zu meinem Laden, wo ich hingehe, da weiß ich, wo ich was finde. Bei den Tankstellen bin ich mir nicht sicher, ob das wirklich die Qualität hat, die ich auch wirklich bevorzuge. [...] Ich würde auch nie irgendwie mal ein Brötchen oder so was kaufen. Gut, für den kleinen Hunger mal zwischendurch so eine ... Wurst, aber alles andere nicht".

interstitial situation, where the adamant 'never' becomes 'maybe'. According to a 2006 market research commissioned by Aral, this behaviour is linked to the interstitial character of petrol stations:

"Each fuelling procedure is a mixture of pure routine and immersion into a very specific microcosm. [...] The subject perceives themselves as in an *in-between world*: for a brief moment, the visit to the petrol station has torn them out of their normal everyday routine. In this 'no man's land', the obligations and the rules of everyday life are less palpable, the subjects are more open towards the unknown and new products, and they will follow impulsive feelings and wishes more spontaneously. [...]. This alien/unfamiliar *in-between world* also generates fears and perhaps even a diffuse sense of threat and insecurity"[94] (Rheingold Institut 2006, author's italics).

While the market researchers recommend installing good lightning and using well-known brand logos to convey a feeling of orientation, order and safety, this study looks more closely at how customers behave on the threshold between the mechanical, mindless routine practiced at an anonymous 'non-place', on the one hand, and the creative appropriation of that same space, be it through (inter)action or imagination, on the other.

4.7.2 The Petrol Station as Threshold Between "Non-Place" and "Place"

The idea of transformation is key to the notion of "threshold" as conceptualized by the ethnographer Arnold Van Gennep (1909, cited by Turner 1982: 24). His highly influential study of rites de passage in traditional European societies distinguished between three phases: separation, transition and incorporation. Victor Turner further developed this model and examined whether it could be applied to (post)industrial societies. He found that "liminal" phenomena still exist "in the activities of churches, sects, and movements, in the initiation rites of clubs, fraternities, masonic orders", but that "liminoid" phenomena linked to leisure activities are more common. These are generally individualized, although they may have a "mass" effect (Turner 1982: 54-55). Contrary to rites of passage in traditional societies or structures, which invert but rarely subvert the *status quo*,

---

94 | Personal translation of: „Jeder Tankvorgang ist eine Mischung aus reiner Routine und dem Abtauchen in einen ganz eigenen Mikrokosmos. [...] Die Probanden fühlen sich wie in einer *Zwischenwelt*: Der Tankstellenbesuch hat sie für kurze Zeit aus ihrem normalen Alltagsgeschehen gerissen. In diesem Niemandsland sind Zwänge und Regeln des Alltags weniger spürbar, die Probanden sind offener gegenüber Neuem, neuen Produkten und eher bereit, spontanen Gefühlen und Wünschen nachzugehen. Und auch mal Dinge auszuprobieren, die sie sich im Alltag nicht trauen würden. Diese fremde *Zwischenwelt* löst allerdings auch Ängste und teilweise sogar ein diffuses Bedrohungsgefühl aus."

liminoid experiences "are often subversive, satirizing, lampooning, burlesquing, or subtly putting down the central values" (ibid.: 41). As the spatial metaphor of the interstitial space suggests, one may a) enter the "liminoid" and undergo a transformation; (b) recognize a potential threshold, but refuse to release control; or, (c) remain undecided or suspended in the interstice.

Entering the "Liminoid"

A rather straightforward way to cross the border between 'non-place' and 'place' is to initiate social interactions:

"My wife got to know the cashiers, it's for the atmosphere, it's more like a family atmosphere, less like a factory. Because the large stations, it's really ... [...] if you calculate the ratio [of petrol pumps per inhabitant] in Schengen[95], there must be something like 800 inhabitants [...]. Taking into consideration the number of stations in Schengen, this is impressive!"[96] (male, 58, French, Lorraine).

In this interview extract a clear dichotomy is established between the anonymity of mass consumption ("factory") and face-to-face interactions ("family"): one way to disrupt the 'industrial' routine is becoming acquainted with the staff.

A more radical transformation of the unreflected "infra-ordinary" (Perec 1989) setting of the petrol station may be observed in the following extract, recounting how a group of young women used it to stage a hen night.

"They came there with a supermarket trolley and they were already a little drunk [laughter]. [...] I think they wanted to wash the cars, but it wasn't very clever, because [loud laughter], just next to them, there was the petrol sta... – er – the automatic carwash station [...] they must have stayed two, three hours before they left for – I don't know – Clausen [pubs and clubs district of Luxembourg city], well, and confront the bride with further dares. They made – er – a lot of noise. Me, I passed by twice with my dog and you could hear them in the entire village [laughter] laughing like crazy. That was really funny"[97] (female, 30, Portuguese-Luxembourgish, Luxembourg).

---

95 | Schengen is a village in Luxembourg, bordering Germany and France, where the Schengen agreements were signed in 1985 and 1990.

96 | Personal translation of: "Mon épouse a fait connaissance avec les vendeuses, c'est pour l'ambiance, c'est plus familial, moins usine. Parce que les grosses stations, c'est quand même... [...] Et si on fait un peu un ratio sur Schengen où vous devez avoir, si je me souviens bien, quelque chose comme 800 habitants [...], et voir le nombre de stations qu'il y a, c'est impressionnant, il faut le dire!"

97 | Personal translation of: "Elles étaient venues avec un caddie et elles étaient déjà un petit peu ivres [laughter]. [...] Je crois qu'elles voulaient laver les voitures, mais c'était pas malin, parce que [loud laughter] juste à côté, elles avaient la station essence, euh, de lavage automatique [...]. Elles ont dû rester deux, trois heures avant de partir, je sais

A hen night or bachelorette party is part of most western weddings and constitutes the 'separation' or 'first phase' of this classic rite of passage. It involves the future bride being challenged by her girlfriends to 'misbehave' one last time before entering the safe harbour of marriage. The custom is far less formalized in Luxembourg than in Britain or the US (Kalmijn 2004; Montemurro 2006) and does not always involve disguises and dares. In this case, it includes a taunt apparently modelled on another US custom, the so-called bikini carwash, a fundraising event where sparsely clad young women offer to wash cars against a fee. No matter what the actual intention and behaviour of the women at the Luxembourg petrol station were, the amused account provided by our interview partner refers to their state of inebriation, "crazy" laughter and loud noise, that is, to transgressions and transformations of expected social behaviour. It may thus point at the "antistructure" said to characterise the "liminoid" (Turner 1982: 32-33). Although the stereotypical bikini carwash does not question, but rather reinforce, gender roles and the sexualized objectification of women, this chauvinist message tends to be subverted when it is used in an oblique or 'queer' way – as in the petrol station scene of the film *Zoolander* analysed by Agnès Prüm in her contribution to this volume.

Indeed, a parodic-travestying intervention (Bakhtin 1981b: Kindle Locations 1028-1029) may be seen as social critique: at a large motorway petrol station on the Luxembourgish-German border, a young man – observed and filmed by one of the authors (Aire de Wasserbillig 2012) – seizes a traffic cone and uses it as a speaker cone. He announces to the laughter of his friends and other clients: "Attention ladies and gentlemen! Three packs of cigarettes for the price of five!"[98] His ironical message derides the Luxembourg fiscal regime and the symbolic border posts petrol stations have become. The common laughter creates an (ephemeral) bond between strangers and disturbs the routine, just as the removal of the traffic cone disrupts the imposed order.

Implicit criticism of a certain consumer behaviour frequently emerges from the interstice between jest and seriousness, even when no concrete action is being related, only a hypothetical "what if" story. In that case, the threshold is crossed but in mind, producing even more radical associations with the petrol station.

"What If...?"

Asked what they would never do in a petrol station, two interview partners answer jokingly: "to smoke while filling up the car" (male, 42, Belgian, Wallonia) and "to play with the lighter" (female, 19, Portuguese, Luxembourg). The imagined threat

---

pas, à Clausen, voilà, et faire d'autres défis pour la future mariée. Elles avaient fait un euh, beaucoup de bruit. Moi, j'étais passé avec le chien deux fois et on les entendait dans tout le village [laughter] rigoler comme des folles. Ça, c'était drôle."

98 | Personal translation of: "Aufgepasst meine Damen und Herren! Drei Pack Zigaretten zum Preis von fünf!"

is such a cliché[99] that it leads to smile. Other interviewees, however, underline how dangerous the practice of filling up jerrycans with petrol is. As one of our interview partners phrased it: "Except for people who transform their cars into bombs, I cannot think of anything serious [laughter]"[100] (male, 57, German, Saarland).

Thus, in some interviews, there are hints at the potential danger of the place, but most people appeared perplexed when asked for their spontaneous associations with petrol stations. One man summed it up succinctly: "Not much happens at the petrol station. You drive up, fill up your car, pay, and drive off, eh"[101] (male, 52, Luxembourgish, Wallonia). This kind of reaction confirms our working hypothesis of a strong discrepancy between the absence of reflection about petrol stations as a place of everyday life and their significance in films and popular culture, where they are portrayed as uncanny, disquieting places, where bad things are expected to happen.

This underlying threat is linked less to the anonymous customer clearance than to actual interactions with station attendants. In her video blog, *Gas Stations* (2009), Hayley recounts how she had to step into the station shop due to a failure of the credit card reader and came across a man who "happen[ed] to resemble the creepy uncles from a second grade sexual harassment videos." Displaying the on-screen message "Stay Safe", she animates sock puppets and mimes a voice talking to children: "Although I recognize your face, you cannot touch my private space." The petrol station thus appears to generate (sexual) anxieties, linked to its perception as 'place' of human interactions (even if they are but imagined) rather than anonymous 'non-place'.

In a similar vein, one of our interview partners reports a "rather negative" anecdote, "even though nothing happened to anyone." He took exception to a station attendant in Austria who insisted on filling up his car:

"This is dreadful, because I really don't like it. [...] I don't want anybody else to fill up my car, I want to do this myself. Most people fill it to the brim, but I want to fill up my car the way I always do, and I don't want another person to do this. [...] I would let anybody drive my car – that is different. I'm not the type of person that cherishes their car, but somehow I don't like this service generally, or if a service is forced on me. I'm that type of person, I also prefer buffets. That's my disposition. And that [attendant] would not be stopped and immediately started to faff about. I really wanted to say ..., and I got very angry at myself because I didn't intervene. I really wanted to tell him: 'Here, take 5 or even 10 € as a tip, but just leave me alone' [laughs]. I did tell him: 'Please, leave it be', but he just did it and

---

99 | As in the petrol station scene in *Zoolander*, analysed by Agnès Prüm.
100 | Personal translation of: "Abgesehen von den Leuten die ihre Autos in eine Bombe verwandeln, fällt mir da nichts Ernstes auf [laughter]."
101 | Personal translation of: "Op der Tankstell erlieft een net vill. Et fiert ee bäi, et tankt een, et geet ee bezuelen, an et fiert ee rëm, he."

afterwards I was so very angry at myself, I should have struck his fingers and told him: 'Just go, I'll do this myself'" [102] (male, 29, German, Saarland).

Both the blogger and the interviewee reject human interactions on the grounds that they fear a violation of their private space and want to remain in control of the situation. They see the threshold, but perceive an abyss that would destabilize their personality, and thus cling to the anonymity and the safety of interactions with machines.

A third type of reaction when faced with the interstitial space of petrol stations is to perceive both the 'non-place' and the 'place', but to remain unable to move on.

Undecidability

The state of suspension implied in the notion of undecidability may be detected in the ambivalent attitude of a female interviewee, who affirms that she dislikes petrol stations due to the smell of diesel, but

"Once I'm there, it no longer bothers me, and actually, I rather like [petrol stations], it's tidy, sometimes you can get rather nice chocolates, beautiful flower arrangements, and in general, the girls are nice ... In fact, I do not like going there, I keep telling myself: 'Oh shit, I have to go and get fuel', but once I'm there, it does not bother me. It's fast, and rather comfortable, well thought-through, well laid out" [103] (female, 33, French, Lorraine).

---

102 | Personal translation of: "Ich finde das ganz schlimm weil ich so was gar nicht mag. [...] Ich will nicht, dass einer für mich tankt, ich will selber tanken. Die meisten lassen dann bis zum Rand volllaufen und ich will aber so tanken wie ich das immer mache und nicht dass ein anderer das macht. [...] Ich würde jeden fahren lassen, das ist was anderes. Ich habe zum Auto jetzt nicht die Bezüge dass man das hegen und pflegen muss, sondern irgendwie ich mag generell nicht diesen Service. Wenn mir Service aufgedrängt wird. Ich bin selbst der Typ, ich mag auch am liebsten Buffet. Das ist so meine Einstellung dazu. Und der ließ sich gar nicht aufhalten und hat direkt angefangen da rumzumachen. Ich hätte am liebsten gesagt ..., und da habe ich mich dann über mich selber geärgert, dass ich nicht reagiert habe. Ich hätte am liebsten gesagt: 'Hier bekommen Sie 5 € Trinkgeld oder sogar 10, wenn Sie mich einfach in Ruhe lassen' [lacht]. Ich hab auch gesagt: 'Bitte lassen Sie das', aber er hat das dann gemacht und nachher hab ich mich echt über mich selber geärgert, ich hätte dem auf die Finger hauen sollen und sagen sollen: 'Los weg da, ich mach das selber'".
103 | Personal translation of: "Une fois que j'y suis, ça ne me dérange pas, j'aime assez bien finalement, c'est bien rangé, des fois on trouve des chocolats qui sont pas mal, des bouquets de fleurs qui sont jolis, en général les filles sont sympas... En fait, je n'aime pas y aller, je me dis: 'Oh merde, il faut que j'aille maintenant faire le plein', mais une fois que j'y suis, ça ne me dérange pas. Ça va vite, et je trouve que c'est quand-même assez agréable, je trouve que c'est bien pensé, bien aménagé."

In fact, despite some reluctance, and once she is set on following her routine, she seems to approve of some aspects of its 'non-place' character (the organisation, the service, the speed, etc.). Outside of that routine, on the way to her holidays, she positively appreciates stops at petrol stations:

"Moreover, if we are not talking about petrol stations in Luxembourg, when you drive down to the south, the only ray of hope [sunbeam] of the journey [small ironic laughter] is to stop at petrol stations. During a long journey, I love it! But the stations are different from the ones you find here. There, you can see people, lorry drivers from different countries, you see people who take a sort of shower in the toilets, well, I think it's very lively. On the motorway, [petrol stations] are very lively, in fact, whereas here, it's not the same, it's fast [and impersonal]. You fill up and you leave, whereas a big station on the motor way is rather nice [...]. I've always liked that, ever since I was little. [...] And then, you see people, and there are people who make you laugh, some of them are fighting, and it's a very, very lively environment! And then, you get a coffee, a chocolate or something, and I like that" [104] (ibid.).

The difference between an orderly, well equipped, time-efficient 'non-place' and an enjoyable 'place' – described three times as "very lively" – lies not so much in the dissimilarity of petrol stations in Luxembourg and abroad, but may be ascribed to alterations of her state of mind. Daily routines only allow for 'non-places', whereas her holiday mood allows for 'places' to emerge and other people to be noticed.

The state of suspension and undecidability that might be experienced at the threshold between overlapping social spaces, or between 'place' and 'non-place' may be illustrated by the following extract from an interview with the Beatles-drummer Ringo Starr:

"We stopped at – errr – a motorway café – t'eat some grease [chuckles]. Now Paul had the keys, and George was sitting behind the wheel [mimics steering motion] as we came out. And there – an argument went on for at least an hour and a half. 'I've got the keys!' -'Well, I'm sitting behind the wheel!' [mimics steering motion]. And it was like we had to sit

---

[104] | Personal translation of: "Et je dirais, si on ne parle pas des stations-service à Luxembourg, quand on descend dans le sud en voiture, le seul rayon de soleil du trajet [small ironical laughter], c'est de m'arrêter aux stations-service. Pendant un long voyage, j'adore! Mais ce ne sont pas les mêmes stations qu'ici. Là, on voit des gens, des routiers qui viennent de tous pays, on voit des gens qui prennent une sorte de douche dans les WC, enfin je trouve que c'est très vivant. Sur l'autoroute, elles sont très vivantes, en fait. Alors que celles-ci, c'est pas la même chose, c'est vite fait. On fait son plein et on part. Alors qu'une grosse station sur l'autoroute, c'est quand même sympa [...]. J'ai toujours aimé ça, depuis toute petite [...] Et puis, on voit des gens, il y a des gens qui font rigoler, il y en a qui s'engueulent, c'est très, très vivant comme environnement! Et puis on prend un café, un chocolat ou quoi, moi je trouve ça sympa."

there and go through this 'cause one of them – none of them was gonna give up! You know, 'I've got the keys' - 'I've got the wheel!' [mimics steering motion]" (George Harrison 2011: 26:45-27:23).

For the viewer of this interview, diverse social and cultural spaces collide and intermingle in his account: childhood games and rivalries; the freedom, self-determination and rites of passage associated with driving cars, and by extension, petrol stations; youth culture; constructions and perceptions of the sixties culture and counter-culture; the band's global marketability, and the transformation of four young men into money-generating businesses that endure beyond their own natural life span (George and John are already dead); their profound (transforming) effect on popular culture, the music industry and entire generations etc.; all these situate *The Beatles* – the b®and – at the intersection between the relational and the non-relational, the human and the mechanical, the local and the global, the 'place' and the 'non-place'.

4.7.3 Conclusion

The petrol station, at first sight a symbol for supermodernity, routine and anonymity, serves to highlight the co-existence, intersection and mutual transformation of many different types of spaces. Firstly, an analysis of social practices linked to petrol stations showed that certain consumer patterns and leisure habits rely on the late opening hours of the stations' shop or eatery. The petrol station becomes – for some people, under some circumstances – a congenial meeting place or was part of a diffuse feeling of adventure when on vacation. In the end, the perception of petrol stations wavers between that of a functional, impersonal 'non-place' and that of an individualized 'place', depending on whether the mechanisms of (capitalist) supermodernity are activated fully, partially or not at all. It is important to note that this 'activation' depends on the subject's choice, which is itself contingent, momentary and dependent on the situation: they may choose to merely be led by the injunctions of consumer logics, or they may break the routine and initiate, rekindle or live out human relationships. The system itself is neither abolished nor affected by this choice: it is merely allowed to operate or to remain dormant.

The shift from 'non-place' to 'place' was then investigated in more detail, drawing on the reactions and anecdotes our interview partners imparted. Petrol stations act as threshold between 'non-place' and 'place', between absent-minded gestures and stimulus to the imagination ("what if ..."), between boredom and exuberance. A chore may become a creative, even subversive, act. Sometimes the narrative also lingers in the interstitial space or passage between the different frames of mind. This undecidability shows how meaning is reconfigured through mimesis, parody or travesty. This links in with Ricoeur's hermeneutics, according to which "the manner of existing [...] is from start to finish a being-interpreted" (Watkin 2009: 77).

This intermingling of diverse social and cultural spaces (co-spatiality), the unpredictable quality of thresholds, their openness and ever-latent potential for reconfiguration are markers of interstitiality, which may be experienced in non-places such as petrol stations. In and through (popular) culture, however, the petrol station itself undergoes one further transformation, or *transfiguration*: the *site* becomes a *sign*, complex and multi-layered, as blatant as its 'original' was discrete; evasive, ambiguous, and yet eminently recognisable. This aspect will be developed in "Petrol Stations as In-Between Spaces II: Transfiguration."

Sources

Aire de Wasserbillig (2012) (Luxembourg, Director: Agnès Prüm), Unpublished iPhone Video Filmed on 20.10. 2012.
Blumme vun der Tankstell (2011) (Luxembourg, Serge Tonnar & Legotrip, Klasseklon, Maskénada).
Gas Stations (2009) (USA, Director: Hayley G. Hoover), YouTube Video posted on 06.02.2009, http://www.youtube.com/watch?v=t_1a8nWbMHY, accessed 15.12.2013.
George Harrison: Living in the Material World (2011) (UK, Director: Martin Scorsese), DVD, posted on YouTube: http://www.youtube.com/watch?v=fEL4_qadPp4, accessed 15.12.2013.
Plein d'essence (2007) (Luxembourg, Director: Geneviève Mersch).
Zoolander (2001) (USA, Director: Ben Stiller).

4.8 Petrol Stations as In-Between Spaces II: Transfiguration

Agnès Prüm

"Nothing special"[105] (male, 62, Luxembourger, Luxembourg). This expression, used by one of our interview partners about the things he would do or buy at a petrol station, aptly voices the quasi-consensus among our interviewees about the role and significance of petrol stations in everyday life. Petrol stations may sometimes, as Sonja Kmec has shown, become the scene of extraordinary events and experiences, and thus momentarily acquire the qualities of a 'place'. These transformations are inadvertent and contingent, however, and petrol stations remain, in most situations, relegated to the realm of the "infra-ordinary" (Perec

---

105 | Personal translation of: "Näischt spezielles."

1989).[106] In movies and popular culture in general, however, this tendency is reversed: the frequency with which they are associated with the out-of-the-ordinary seems out of all proportion, especially in relation to lived experience (Kmec/Prüm 2014). This contrast between 'real' petrol stations and their fictional counterparts is both puzzling and significant, because it reveals the transformation lived experience (Lefebvre 1986: 48-49) undergoes in the process of continual participatory encoding and decoding. This section proposes the concept of *transfiguration* as a tool to investigate the back and forth movement between lived experience and code. Firstly, transfiguration may be observed in the transformation of a material *site* into a mediated *sign* or 'code' everyone is able to access. In a second step, we will show how this process relies on a distancing from and dislocation of 'the real' in (pop)-cultural artefacts. Finally, we will explore the fundamentally participatory character of transfiguration and the performative appropriation of space it allows.

4.8.1 From Site to Sign

Fears and anxieties associated with the uncertain status of the petrol station are not merely *transposed* into literary or filmic narratives about disturbing disappearances[107], explosions (e.g. *Zoolander* 2001) or the undead.[108] While transposition presupposes a one-way process, in which an object or idea is encoded into popular culture once, and then decoded, in a presumably uniform manner, by various audiences, our qualitative interviews show that the process is more dynamic and relies on active participation.

The register in which our interview partners relate incidents or experiences they deem worth remembering or mentioning is a first indicator of this phenomenon. In most instances, the petrol station is both perceived and constructed as "infra-ordinary" and hardly elicits any reactions, but when it is associated with a particular memory or commentary, the register in which the incident is conveyed acquires a relational quality: it translates the interviewee's anger (buffet-man), appreciation (the tidiness of petrol stations), wonder (number of pumps at Schengen) and, most frequently, self-deprecation or humour (bombs on wheels) (see section 4.7).

---

106 | The present study has been developed together with Sonja Kmec. It builds on her discussion of petrol stations as interstitial spaces and focuses on the encoding of lived experience into film and other media. The same body of empirical data has been used in this analysis.
107 | This preoccupation is not new: *Es geschah am hellichten Tag* (1958) was based on Friedrich Dürrenmatt's screenplay. Unsatisfied with the result, the author published *Das Versprechen. Requiem auf den Kriminalroman* the same year – released in 2001 as *The Pledge*. Tim Krabbé's psychological thriller *Het Gouden Ei* (1984) was brought to the screen in 1988 as *Spuurloos* and its remake *The Vanishing* in 1993.
108 | E.g. *Zombie 3* (1988).

Our interview partners do not merely refer to cultural representations of petrol stations, they expect their conversation partner to grasp both the trope and the emotion it engendered for them in order to understand – and perhaps share – the ideas they (now) associate with petrol stations. In other words, the shift in register, which interpellates their audience and invites them to participate, becomes the instrument by which they activate the code and reconfigure 'the petrol station': they draw on pre-existing interpretive frameworks while charging the trope with dynamic meaning(s) of their own. Interestingly, the relational dimension observed in the shift from 'place' to 'non-place' can be observed in the reconfiguration of the petrol station trope.

Drawing on the 'petrol-station-flowers' trope and Hayley G. Hoover's internet rant *Gas Stations* (2009) discussed by Sonja Kmec in this volume, this section explores the relational and participatory dimensions of the transfiguration of material site into mediated sign.

The meaning of the 'petrol station' trope is not fixed nor necessarily negatively charged, but in combination with certain situations and/or other tropes, such as 'flowers from the petrol station', it generates a stronger sense of unease, though it does remain ambivalent: two of our interview partners find flowers from the petrol station utterly "unromantic", and they are often either associated with unacceptable disrespect, if the flowers are meant for one's love interest[109], or with humorous disregard, when the recipient is one's mother-in-law. The quandary one of our respondents evidently faces, for instance, as he tries to reconcile the conflicting social imperatives associated with dating (personal register) and practicality (impersonal register), is telling:

"It is of course perhaps nicer if you [go] to a real florist's, if, I say, if you have a date with a girl whom you really like; it is perhaps better to go to a florist's and spend 10 € more, to get something personal. I can see that er – er, but if you pay a visit to your mother-in-law on a Sunday morning, and you are pressed for time, would there really be a problem? You may have to remove the price – oh – oh, my God"[110] (male, 31, Luxembourgish, Luxembourg).

Sonja Kmec links the 'general sense of unease' associated with flowers from the petrol station to the latter's 'impersonal' and 'non-space' character (see section

---

109 | They top the list of worst gifts for Valentine's Day (Winter 2013) and are perceived as tools for breaking up relationships (sheldonprice/nealdoran 2008).

110 | Personal translation of: "Et ass äh, ähem, et ass natierlech villäicht méi schéin, wanns de an e richtege Blummebuttek, wann, ech soe mol, wanns de dann e Rendezvous mat engem Meedchen hues, dat de wierklech gär hues, ass et villäicht besser, an de Blummebuttek ze goen, eng Kéier 10 € méi auszeginn, eppes Perséinleches ze maachen. Dat gesinn ech schonn, mä äh, wanns de sonndes moies d'Schwéiermamm besiche gees an du bass am Stress, wat sprécht dogéint ne. Muss villäicht de Präis erofhuelen, oh, oh, mäi Gott."

4.7). One may further argue that this impersonal character has been encoded into different compound tropes, where, in combination with other tropes, the petrol station acts as a qualifier and determines hierarchical relationships between social actors and situations. It is clear that for our interview partner, the date, with its need to impress and succeed, trumps the mother-in-law, both in practice and 'in code'. The difficulty he is struggling with is thus two-fold: on the one hand, both recipients, 'the love interest' and 'the mother-in-law', may well be real persons, but they are also cultural codes, whose activation in this context reveals the various layers of meaning that intersect with the speaker's perception and construction of petrol stations. On the other hand, our interview partner's hesitation may also be caused by the fact that none of the tropes he draws on are stable, and that he is caught at the intersection between a variety of possible meanings, "none of them original", which "blend and clash" in a "tissue of quotations drawn from innumerable centres of culture" (Barthes 1967 [1968]).

As this example shows, the real world petrol-stations our interview partner visits have become inextricably entwined with their cultural representations, as have the social dilemmas he faces. The conflation of the 'petrol-station flowers' and 'mother-in-law' tropes, for instance, pervades discursive practices and fiction/popular culture. In an episode from the ITV series *Midsomer Murders* (2008), the inversion of the love interest/mother-in-law hierarchy is signalled by two different bouquets the same woman receives. She is offered flowers from "all-night garage" by her husband, Chief Inspector Tom Barnaby, in order to make up for being late (a running gag throughout the series). His ill-fated flowers are instantly relegated to the rubbish bin, and are later markedly contrasted to the very impressive bouquet she receives from their daughter's soon to be official fiancé. Significantly, in this particular situation, wooing one's (future) mother-in-law is about as important as wooing one's fiancée: indeed, because the flowers+garage subtext combination disrupts accepted constructions of the 'mother-in-law' trope, the audience realizes, long before it has been announced, that a wedding, or a similar event, may be in the works. This example shows the hermeneutic versatility of these codes. Indeed, transfiguration is only possible because cultural codes remain fluid and open to reinterpretation, yet shared and easily accessible in socio-cultural contexts that may be as distinct and diverse as interview situations, personal conversations or media reception.

In popular culture, the site of the petrol station is not only transfigured into a sign conveying disregard for one's loved ones, but taps into deep-rooted anxieties. Hayley G. Hoover's self-generated video *Gas Stations* (2009) is *performed* in the rant mode, suggesting that she is letting off steam about something that 'really happened'. However, she both exploits and parodies the genre of the internet rant by blending modes of expression such as first person narratives and testimonies, puppet theatre performances (sock puppets), informational sexual harassment videos, self-parody and parodic re-enactments, in such a way that boundaries between these discursive practices are blurred. For instance, when the card reader instructs her: "Please see attendant", she fumes: "*No! No*, I cannot *see* an attendant right now: it is early in the morning, the flu is going around school and if I get another whiff of that corn-dog, I am going to *puke*."[111] Despite these grievances, Hayley eventually surrenders: "I see the attendant [demonstrative pause] because I am a good citizen." Though her annoyance at having to interact with a gas station attendant may well be 'real' and may also provoke 'real' responses, it is important to note that the episode as recounted is not: Hayley admits at the end of her rant that a significant part of the incident at the gas station is merely "imagined".

The 'gas station' thus becomes the site where the different discursive practices and their corresponding social spaces blend, clash and generate new meaning(s): adulthood and good citizenship, for instance, are equated with, and reconfigured as, responsible consumer behaviour. Drawing on associations with its 'non-place' character – the dehumanized cyborg space and other signifying chains such as the "creepy uncles" (see section 4.7), the stereotypical "attendant", who expects Hayley to "pay with plastic" as a typical representative of her generation etc. – Hayley/Hoover simultaneously decodes and encodes the petrol station. The fluidity of the reconfiguring encoding/decoding process is marked by the absence or the shifting of boundaries between the fictional and the so-called 'real', and the 'real' is perceived and constructed through the medium of fiction.

Hoover's rant presents attributes that Limor Shifman considers "fundamental to popular culture":

"The first is the postmodern representation system of simulacra and pastiche (Jameson, 1991) [...]. The second is the constant reworking of texts by internet users, reflecting a so-called 'participatory culture'. Conceptualized as a set of intertwined cultural practices, participatory culture is manifested in new forms of expression, problem solving, circulation and affiliation (Jenkins et al. 2007). Fundamental to this complex web is the practice of reconfiguring content and publicly displaying it in parodies, mashups, remixes and other derivative formats" (Shifman 2011: 188).

In her examination of participatory practices, Shifman distinguishes between "viral videos", clips "that spread[s] to the masses via digital word-of-mouth mechanisms *without significant change*" (ibid.: 190) and "memetic videos [...] that generate extensive user engagement by way of creative derivatives" (ibid.: 188). Though according to the criteria defined in this study, *Gas Stations* may not be classified fully memetic (we did not find any derivatives of this video), its parody of the rant genre and creative appropriations evident in various enactments (the gas station attendant, sock puppets etc.) clearly aligns it with participatory culture of the 'new media', Web 2.0 and internet memes.

---

111 | The italics in this excerpt mark the passages where the speaker's intonation denotes outrage.

Hoover's rant transfigures the 'gas station', transforming an infra-ordinary situation into a critical and participatory proclamation.[112] Significantly, though its meaning has been reconfigured, the actual 'gas station' itself remains constant and unchanged.

4.8.2 Dislocating the Real

The distancing that occurs between the initial encounter with a random customer at the petrol station, his construction as a potential threat, and the 'creepy uncle' simulacrum (Baudrillard 1981) he transforms into in *Gas Stations* is critical to the process of transfiguration. According to Arthur C. Danto, "'That it is not really happening' remains even now an important contribution to our enjoyment of art which manages to distance the real and to disarm it" (Danto 1974: 146). On the one hand, this suggests that, beyond the "enjoyment" it procures, one of the primary aims of Hayley's rant might be to defuse the "real" anxieties she associates with petrol stations. On the other hand, the threat that is both there and not there, and its displacement from Hoover's 'reality' to Hayley's 'rant' may serve to further illuminate the process of transfiguration. Danto's analysis of transfiguration hinges on the semantic ambiguity of the concept of 'appearance', which can signify both 'real physical presence' (1) and its contrary, the 'appearance of physical presence' (2): depending on the interpretive frameworks in place, an object such as Cimabue's crucifix[113] may be read as "*about* the crucifixion rather than the crucifixion itself, and represented rather than present again" (ibid.: 146).

"Doubtless a different attitude towards the artist will be taken depending upon whether we attribute to him the power to make a charged reality present again, rather than the power to represent reality. In any case, the shift from the first to the second sense of appearance would exemplify just the transfiguration of life into art which Nietzsche describes in his geneology [sic] of attic tragedy. There, the boundaries of the sacred precinct are transformed into the walls of a theater, as, in the case of Cimebue, the altar where the sacred event eternally occurs is changed into an elaborate frame housing a work of art, as the church itself undergoes alteration into a kind of inadvertent museum. And all of this without the object itself being changed at all" (ibid.: 146).

---

112 | On 15.12.2013, *Gas Stations* was viewed 36,451 times since its upload on 06.02.2009, obtained 952 likes, 30 dislikes and generated 265 comments.
113 | Danto refers to a painted crucifix (c. 1280) that is generally attributed to the thirteenth century artist Cimabue (Cenni di Peppi). Though badly damaged by the flood of 1966, it is located at the Santa Croce Church and Museum in Florence (West 1996 and Santa Croce Church and Museum, Florence, http://www.museumsinflorence.com/musei/museum_of_opera_s_croce.html).

Danto's conception of the "transfiguration of life into art", which is triggered by the "shift from the first to the second sense of appearance", or from "present again" to "represented" (ibid.: 146), relies on two main features: first, the (transfigured) object, in this case the cross of Cimabue, remains unchanged and, secondly, transfiguration has a profoundly transformative effect, as both the architectural and the ideological constructs erected around it have evolved and continue to evolve in time. To put it plainly, what has changed is not the object itself, but the way we look at it and the meanings we ascribe to it. The cross acts as an interstice, a bridge between the different meanings and worldviews it elicits.

In the context of this study, then, the process of transfiguration implies that our object, petrol stations as actual places or types of places, do not undergo any material alterations, but that the meanings, emotions and cultural significance ascribed to them adjust to match the frames of mind in which they are both experienced and represented. This may shed further light on why the same person can experience petrol stations as both a "time efficient 'non-place' and an 'enjoyable place'" (see section 4.7). It may also provide us with a more dynamic model to describe the oscillation between site and sign petrol stations undergo through discursive practices and cultural encoding. Indeed, petrol stations provide a prime example of the 'transfiguration of life into art', as the 'freak gasoline fight accident' in Ben Stiller's 2001 movie *Zoolander* will demonstrate.

On one level, within the universe of the movie, we witness a creative appropriation of a petrol station by Derek Zoolander, a parody of a male supermodel, and his friends. Before their arrival, the petrol station is very much a 'non-place', dehumanized and anonymous, but as they drive up to the pump, dressed in individualized colours reminiscent of *Power Rangers* combat suits (Mighty Morphin Power Rangers 1993-1995) and perform a pastiche blending dance, martial arts routines and bikini carwash moves that quickly mutates into a water fight, the fictional petrol station is transformed into a 'place'. Like the hen night observed by our interview partner (see section 4.7), this scene is witnessed by two male onlookers. Unlike our interviewee, however, they are not amused by what they see, and their disapproving demeanours signal that the gender-bending appropriation of the sexually charged bikini carwash practice by four young men severely disrupts their heteronormative expectations. Of course there is no direct causal link between the interview situation in our case study and the scene in the movie, which actually predates our research. Their juxtaposition, however, does reveal a dialogic relationship (Bakhtin 1981a) between everyday practices and cultural artefacts. Significantly, as this example shows, movies do not merely transfer existing social or cultural practices into fiction: they actively transform or exaggerate them, they offer commentary or critiques, and they invite laughter or outrage, and so forth.

As the viewer navigates in and out of fictional, 'real' and simulated space, the water fight degenerates into a gasoline fight, and … one of the characters lights a cigarette. The viewer is able to predict the subsequent explosion from a form of culturally generated 'foresight' that blends experience of practice (the combination of petrol and flames may lead to fire and explosions) and of sign/simulation (they will hopefully not have experienced the explosion of a 'real' petrol station). More significantly, however, the simulated filmic explosion blows up more than the petrol station: the various chains of signification that are active in this extract are revealed to be hollow and decentred, not rooted in the 'real'.

As this brief account suggests (see Kmec/Prüm 2014 for an in-depth analysis), the 'freak gasoline fight accident' both highlights and relies on the fact that petrol stations can be experienced as both sites and signs, and the film itself acts as a form of gateway, or interstice, between the various interpretive layers individual viewers may or may not activate. To expand on Danto's metaphor, 'transfiguration of life into art', or (popular) culture, may be defined as the shift from presence to simulation, or from site to sign. Combined with the idea of interstitial spaces as sites of potential participatory practices and culture, this shift becomes an oscillation, a back and forth movement between material petrol stations and their creative appropriations. In other words, transfiguration denotes the process by which lived experience, including its spaces and objects, is continuously and simultaneously encoded, decoded, and reconfigured at the threshold of interaction between various actors of (participatory) culture. Indeed, like Hayley's rant, *Zoolander* exhibits memetic qualities: combining parody and mimesis, it has sparked numerous re-enactments[114], disseminated as user-generated videos, and the jeep ride to the petrol station, set to Wham!'s *Wake Me Up Before You Go Go* (1984), has spawned its own meme, the 'Zoolander Dance' or 'Jeep Party', and a plethora of compilations, remixes and parodies, casting British football stars, the Obamas, Hillary Clinton or Michael Jackson in the roles of Zoolander and his friends (Zoolander Dance/Jeep Party 2005).

4.8.3 Performing (in) Space

As interstitial spaces, and because of their 'standard' 'non-place' status, petrol stations thus provide a perfect location to observe the ways in which participatory practices emerge from the collision between various social spaces. The widespread internet practice of pastiche, imitation and parody raises one last additional question, however. None of the processes described above happen *outside* human consciousness and/or interaction, and the human body itself can become the interstice, the instance of transfiguration. The unpublished iPhone video caught on camera at a large petrol station at the border between Luxembourg and Germany (Aire de Wasserbillig 2012), will serve to illustrate this claim.

We argued above that the young man's impromptu traffic cone performance expresses a humorous critique of the effects of the Luxembourgish fiscal regime

---

114 | For example, Matt Hemphill-Zoolander Gasoline Fight Parody, http://www.youtube.com/watch?v=qKoj6jSu4AY.

on the (im)permeability of the country's borders (see section 4.7). One may also argue, however, that in this clip, or through this clip, different spaces, such as national, fiscal and legal spaces, social networks and internet culture etc. are brought into contact with one another, and that the bridge between these different types of spaces are the young man, his cone and the setting he has chosen for his performance. He is the medium between interpretive frameworks and platforms, and his performance reconfigures the Aire de Wasserbillig. Like the cross of Cimabue, both the petrol station and the young man himself remain materially unchanged by this performance, though they do, for a moment, channel what could be described as multiple (other) voices.

This episode may be expounded by reference to the discipline that coined the concept of transfiguration: theology. Dorothy Lee's analysis of the process of Jesus' transfiguration or metamorphosis into incandescent light (Lee 2004: 2), one of the central miracles celebrated by the Eastern Orthodox Church, may help us decode the mundane scene observed at the Aire de Wasserbillig. In seemingly oblique ways, this episode is reminiscent of the Transfiguration scene in the Bible, which Lee describes as follows:

"The transfiguration tells the story of Jesus' ascent of the mountain somewhere at the mid-point of his ministry, in the company of his disciples. There his physical appearance is changed, metamorphosing into incandescent light, a light that blazes from his face and clothing. Two of the greatest (long-dead) prophets of Israel's past appear beside him, conversing with him. The disciples, meanwhile, are overawed at the spectacle and respond with incomprehension and bewilderment, Peter proposing to erect three tents to house Jesus and his celestial guests. At this point a cloud intervenes, overshadowing the heavenly figures, and a voice speaks from the cloud, declaring Jesus to be the beloved Son. Then the miraculous signs recede and Jesus is left alone to descend the mountain with his bemused disciples" (Lee 2004: 2).

Lee's account of the biblical transfiguration identifies a set of characteristics, which once divested of their religious import and specific narrative aspects, can be abstracted and applied to our analysis of petrol stations as combinations of site and sign: first, a particular setting is chosen (mountain/petrol station); secondly, the medium's body undergoes a visible, though temporary, transformation (incandescent light/cone); thirdly, routines of third party onlookers are disrupted (the disciples/the customers); fourthly, a dialogue is established between different actors that are co-present only because the medium has invoked them (the long-dead prophets and the clouds, the different social, fiscal, social and cultural spaces); and finally, after the event, neither place nor medium are changed: the "miraculous signs recede", Jesus leaves the mountain, and the young man drops his cone, leaves the petrol station and the bemused onlookers revert back to their routines.

If Jesus in the transfiguration scene is "the meeting-place between human beings and God, between the temporal and the eternal, between past, present and future, between everyday human life [...] and the mystery of God" (ibid.: 2), the young man and his performance become, for the onlookers, and for a fleeting moment, the visual carrier of critique and the trigger of oscillation between 'space' and 'non-space'. As the young man's declaration disrupts the customers' routines, the petrol station as a site is transfigured into sign, its signification temporarily changed and expanded way beyond the physical space that it occupies materially, even beyond the territorial, political and fiscal co-spatiality his intervention critiques. Indeed, his performance also draws on the 'VLC Player in Real Life' series of image macros, in which orange and white traffic cones are reconfigured into megaphones or converted into embodiments of the VLC Player icon.[115] Significantly, both performer and observer may or may not be aware of the fact that the computer software VLC Media Player uses an orange and white traffic cone as an icon, and that the association between traffic cones and the VLC Media Player is a common internet joke.

By appropriating the Aire de Wasserbillig in this particular way, the nameless young man simultaneously perpetuates and activates internet culture – thus transforming, without changing his being, for a brief moment, into the incarnation of a new media, a new culture, and perhaps 'his generation'. As he becomes the gateway between the various spaces and interpretive frameworks his performance activates, the latter is also revealed as fundamentally participatory:

"However, in contrast to textual memes, memetic videos and their derivatives focus much more on the performative self. Uploaders become both the medium of the meme and its message: their faces and bodies are integral parts of these clips" (Shifman 2011: 200).

4.8.4 Conclusion

This study has examined the intertwining of practical, textual and ideological dimensions and developed the concept of 'transfiguration' as fundamentally participatory and relational, and going beyond a unilateral 'transposition' of lived reality into fiction or vice-versa. Indeed, as we have shown, social spaces and interpretative frameworks are co-present; far from invalidating each other, they actually reinforce each other. Fuelled by anxieties of sexual harassment and human interaction, Hayley G. Hoover's user-generated video exorcises her fears through a creative reconfiguration of the petrol station. The second example, a highly intertextual Hollywood production, *Zoolander*, features a comic/tragic explosion of a petrol station that has spawned a series of internet memes and other

---

115 | The "Protestor assists in the installation of VLC Media Player" image macro, for instance, was disseminated on different social networks platforms such as http://imgur.com/gallery/oWzuoOG and http://9gag.com/gag/aozgAYX.

derivative practices. Finally, a spontaneous creative appropriation of a Luxembourg petrol station, lampooning fiscal regimes, fortuitously caught on film, reveals the complexity of the relationship between co-spatiality and transfiguration.

In the end, petrol stations continue to exist as components of daily routines relegated to the margins of everyday life. Unlike many of their filmic counterparts, they remain mostly ordinary, and our interview partners were generally surprised to be asked questions about a place with which they associate "nothing special". As objects of analysis, however, they have provided an invaluable medium that has allowed us to shed light on the hidden intricacies of the 'common place' and its transfiguration into (popular) culture.

Sources

Aire de Wasserbillig (2012) (Luxembourg, Director: Agnès Prüm), unpublished iPhone Video Filmed on 20.10.2012.
Blumme vun der Tankstell (2011) (Luxembourg, Serge Tonnar & Legotrip, Klasseklon, Maskénada).
Es geschah am hellichten Tag (1958) (Germany, Director: Ladislao Vajda).
Gas Stations (2009) (USA, Director: Hayley G. Hoover), YouTube Video posted on 6 February, http://www.youtube.com/watch?v=t_1a8nWbMHY, accessed 15.12.2013.
George Harrison: Living in the Material World (2011) (UK, Director: Martin Scorsese), DVD, posted on YouTube: http://www.youtube.com/watch?v=fEL4_qadPp4, accessed 15.12.2013.
Midsomer Murders (2008) (UK, Director: Richard Holthouse). Season 10, Episode 59: "Death in a Chocolate Box", TV Series, ITV, aired on 11.05.2008.
Plein d'essence (2007) (Luxembourg, Director: Geneviève Mersch).
Mighty Morphin Power Rangers (1993-1995) (USA/Japan, TV series).
sheldonprice/nealdoran (2008): "Man Dismayed As Petrol Station Flowers Fail To End Relationship", in: NewsBiscuit: The news written by you, 14.02.2008, http://www.newsbiscuit.com/2008/02/14/man-dismayed-as-petrol-station-flowers-fail-to-end-relationship-301/, accessed 15.12.2013.
Spoorloos (1988) (Netherlands/France, Director: George Sluizer).
The Pledge (2001) (USA, Director: Sean Penn).
The Vanishing (1993) (USA, Director: George Sluizer).
Wake Me Up Before You Go-Go (1984) (USA/Canada, George Michael & Wham!, Make it Big, CBS Records / Epics Records).
Winter, Kathy (2013): "What NOT to get a girl on Valentine's Day: Petrol station flowers, all-you-can-eat buffet vouchers and tickets to see his favourite football team top the gift list of shame", in: Mail Online, 11.02.2013, http://www.dailymail.co.uk/femail/article-2277007/What-NOT-girl-Valentines-Day-Petrol-station-flowers-eat-buffet-vouchers-tickets-favourite-football-team-gift-list-shame.html#ixzz2nZQ1qvEZ, accessed 15.12.2013.

Zombie 3 (1988) (Italy, Director: Lucio Fulci/Claudio Fragasso/Bruno Mattei).
Zoolander (2001) (USA, Director: Ben Stiller).
Zoolander Dance/Jeep Party (2005-), http://knowyourmeme.com/memes/zoolander-dancejeep-party, accessed 15.12.2013.

4.9 Conclusions

The present chapter attempts to shed light on the connection between space and identity with regard to media. Here, media are defined spatially, as zones of contact, i.e. as areas in which boundaries and differentiations are negotiated. The notion of space in this chapter is specified accordingly. On the assumption that spatial structures are both precondition and result of social practices, the focus is directed to *interstices*, understood as areas that cannot readily be attributed to delineated and clearly defined spaces.

The common feature of the case studies in this chapter is that they establish connections between spatial structures on different levels. This procedure stems from considering media of representation with their possibility of a (projective) re-description of reality. A particularly important point here is in how far boundaries on different levels tend to subvert or confirm each other (or both at the same time!).

Thus the case study on museum thresholds relates two structural levels to each other: the cultural space constituted by the exhibition and the space of everyday life. Thresholds – for instance the entrance area of a museum or even the showcase in a publicly accessible hall – here present themselves as an area of transition and mediation between these two spaces. Their effect can differ strongly depending on the type of threshold. The boundary between cultural space and everyday space can be rendered almost wholly invisible, or, conversely, fleshed out in detail as a *rite de passage* turned into architecture. The case study on the self-representation of Luxembourg teenagers on *facebook* makes a connection between the levels of presentation in the social network, on the one hand, and the real-world self-positioning, on the other. Here one can see that the boundary between private and public space that the teenagers presume as given and attempt to maintain in their social network has more or less already been subverted by the conditions of the medium. At the same time it becomes evident that the teenagers' 'real' self-image does not remain unaffected by the network's structural presettings, e.g. the categorization of other users as 'family' – for instance when good friends are first rubricated as family and then also regarded as such. The case study on language choice in Luxembourg advertisements, by contrast, points to a relatively clear confirmation of boundaries through mediated representation. It shows that the on the whole sporadic mixture of languages in newspaper and poster advertisements in Luxembourg – i.e. the temporary suspension of boundaries between languages 'on paper' – has in the adverts basically the function of reinforcing the existence of national and linguistic borders on the sociocultural (and political) level. In this case we therefore only find an apparent subversion of borders in mediated representation.

When looking at national and linguistic borders and boundaries, a further distinction comes into focus which plays a more or less crucial role in the other three case studies, that between particularity and universality. The case study on the *Robert Schuman Art Award* of the *Quattropole* Saarbrücken-Metz-Trier-Luxembourg shows that the cultural-political staging, the selection of the award-winning artists and their works as well as the exhibition concept all attempt to link the award's local situatedness to an international or universal claim. As a result, local references become somewhat detached on all levels. This should, however, not go too far if the art region the award is intended to represent or even create is to be internationally recognizable. The case study on the self-staging of the Luxembourg publisher *ultimomondo* also reconstructs a similar strategy of cultural-political assertiveness. In an even more radical way the publishing house attempts to claim for itself – no matter how ironically broken – a general pioneering role on the foundation of a multilingualism that is taken for granted in Luxembourg. In any event, what both case studies deal with is confirming the boundaries on one level (marking the local origin of artistic or literary works) in order to suspend it on another (an international, even universalistic claim).

The case studies on petrol stations as an interstice distinguish themselves from the other studies in the sense that they are the only ones in this chapter that are based on an empirical survey as well as on the reading of treatment of motives in terms of popular culture. Here the quantitative and qualitative survey (University of Luxembourg, IDENT2 2012/2013) also provides evidence that petrol stations are in more ways than one perceived as a kind of interstice. Under the assumption that the empirical approach opens up a popular semantics of the petrol station, the authors attempt in a second step to also reconstruct their treatment in films of different formats. In these case studies, levels are therefore crossed also methodologically: the focus here is on the interactions between spatial constructions in popular semantics and filmic treatment producing the methodological connection of empirical and hermeneutic procedures. At the same time, there is also in this case a tension between a more local semantics – for the petrol station is at least in external perception representative of Luxembourg – and a cross-border appropriation on the level of popular cultural.

On the whole, we can see that media of representation, understood as zones of contact, can indeed enable 'passages' to be opened up between different descripitive levels (see section 4.1): different figurations of border are placed in parallel to and at the same time contrasted with each other. The levels mediated with each other have a spatial structure in the sense that they make it possible to set boundaries, cross borders and initiate movements in various directions – whether conceived in a concrete or in an abstract sense. The notion of level is, after all, already an exclusively spatial concept. Perhaps media will thus prove to be those very interstitialities the case studies seek to examine.

4.10 References

n. a. (2001): "Les Editions Phi, c'est fini?", in: Gewan 56, Frühjahr, 11.
n. a. (2010): Bicherbuch. Livre des livres. Bücherbuch. Book of Books, Sandweiler: *ultimo*mondo.
Augé, Marc (1995 [French original 1992]): Non-places: Introduction to an Anthropology of Supermodernity (trans. John Howe), London & New York: Verso.
Augé, Marc (2012): Architecture and Non-Places, Seminar, Estonian Institute of Humanities, Tallinn University, 12 October 2012, http://vimeo.com/51662299, accessed 07.12.2013.
Backhaus, Peter (2007): Linguistic Landscapes. A Comparative Study of Urban Multilingualism in Tokyo, Clevedon: Multilingual Matters.
Bakhtin, Mikhail (1981a): "The Dialogic Imagination", in: Michael Holquist (ed.), Four Essays by M. Bakhtin, Kindle Edition, Austin: University of Texas Press.
Bakhtin, Mikhail (1981b [Russian original 1940]): "From the Prehistory of Novelistic Discourse", in: Michael Holquist (ed.), Four Essays by M. Bakhtin (trans. Caryl Emerson and Michael Holquist), Austin: University of Texas Press, Kindle Locations 794-1305.
Bandel, Jan-Frederik/Kalender, Barbara/Schröder, Jörg (2011): Immer radikal – niemals konsequent. Der MÄRZ Verlag – erweitertes Verlegertum, postmoderne Literatur und Business Art, Hamburg: Philo Fine Arts.
Barthes, Roland (1967 [French original 1968]): "The Death of the Author" (trans. Richard Howard), in: David Lodge/Nigel Wood (eds.), Modern Criticism and Theory: A Reader, Harlow, Essex: Longman, 146-151.
Baudrillard, Jean (1984 [French original 1981]): Simulacra and simulation (trans. Sheila Glaser), Ann Arbor: University of Michigan Press.
Bhabha, Homi K. (1994): The Location of Culture, London/New York: Routledge.
Bochumer Arbeitsgruppe für Sozialen Konstruktivismus und Wirklichkeitsprüfung (BOAG) (1997): Medien, Identität: Medienidentität, in: Bochumer Bericht 4, http://www.boag-online.de/papers-bb04.html, accessed 20.02.2014.
Bolander, Brook/Locher, Miriam (2010): "Constructing Identity on *Facebook*: Report on a Pilot Study", in: Karen Junot/Didier Maillat (eds.), Performing the Self SPELL (= Swiss Papers in English Language and Literature, vol. 24), Tübingen: Narr, 165-187.
Bonnin, Philippe (2000): "Dispositifs et rituels du seuil", in: Communications 70, 65-92.
Bourdieu, Pierre/Darbel, Alain (1991 [French original 1966]): The Love of Art: European Art Museums and their Public (trans. Caroline Beattie and Nick Merriman), Redwood City, CA: Stanford University Press.
Boyd, Danah (2006): "Identity Production in a Networked Culture: Why Youth Heart MySpace, http://www.danah.org/papers/AAAS2006.html, accessed 06.03.2014.

Boyd, Danah/Ellison, Nicole B. (2007): "Social Network Sites: Definition, History, and Scholarship", in: Journal of Computer-Mediated Communication 13/1, 210-230, http://jcmc.indiana.edu/vol13/issue1/boyd.ellison.html, accessed 07.09.2013.

Brock, Bazon (2002): Der Barbar als Kulturheld III, Gesammelte Schriften 1991-2002, Ästhetik des Unterlassens, Kritik der Wahrheit – wie man wird, der man nicht ist, Köln: DuMont.

Caillet, Elisabeth/Lehalle, Etienne (1995): À l'approche du musée, la médiation culturelle, Lyon: Presses universitaires de Lyon.

Calvez, Marcel (2000): "La liminalité comme analyse socioculturelle du handicap", in: Prévenir 39/2, 83-89.

Clifford, James (1997): Routes: Travel and Translation in the Late Twentieth Century, Cambridge (Mass.)/London: Harvard University Press.

Coll. (2012): L'architecture au niveau du seuil, Magazine Siedle 2, SSS Siedle.

Conter, Claude D. (2012): "Von Neubrasilien nach Sibirien. Gegenwartsromane aus Luxemburg: Guy Helminger und Guy Rewenig", in: Ralf Bogner/Manfred Leber (eds.), Die Literaturen der Großregion Saar-Lor-Lux-Elsass in Geschichte und Gegenwart, Saarbrücken: Universitätsverlag des Saarlandes, 213-233.

Cook, Guy (2001): The Discourse of Advertising, 2nd ed., London/New York: Routledge.

Cordasco, Francesco/Galatioto, Rocco G. (1971): "Ethnic Displacement in the Interstitial Community: the East Harlem (New York City) Experience", in: The Journal of Negro Education 40/1, 56-65.

Coté, Mark/Pybus, Jennifer (2011): "Social Networks: Erziehung zur Immateriellen Arbeit 2.0", in: Oliver Leistert/Theo Röhle (eds.), Generation *Facebook*: Über das Leben im Social Net, Bielefeld: transcript, 51-74.

Danto, Arthur C. (1974): "The Transfiguration of the Commonplace", in: The Journal of Aesthetics and Art Criticism 33/2, 139-148.

Danto, Arthur C. (1981): The Transfiguration of the Commonplace. A Philosophy of Art, Cambridge MA: Harvard University Press.

Davallon, Jean (1992): "Le musée est-il vraiment un media?", in: Publics et Musées 2, 99-123.

Davallon, Jean (1999): L'exposition à l'œuvre: stratégies de communication et médiation symbolique, Paris: L'Harmattan.

Davallon, Jean (2004): "La médiation: la communication en procès?", in: MEI – Médiation et Information 19, 39-59.

Davallon, Jean (2007): Le don du patrimoine: une approche communicationnelle de la patrimonialisation, Paris: Hermès-Lavoisier.

Davies, Bronwyn/Harré, Rom (1990): "Positioning: The Social Construction of Self", in: Journal for the Theory of Social Behavior 20, 43-63.

de Bres, Julia/Franziskus, Anne (2014): "Multilingual Practices of University Students and Changing Forms of Multilingualism in Luxembourg", in: International Journal of Multilingualism 11/1, 62-75.

de Certeau, Michel (1984 [French original 1980]): The Practice of Everyday Life (trans. Steven Rendall), Berkeley: University of California Press.

Deleuze, Gilles/Guattari, Felix (1987 [French original 1980]): A Thousand Plateaus. Capitalism and Schizophrenia (trans. Brian Massumi), Minneapolis: University of Minnesota Press.

Delvaux, Jean/Janus, Jean-Philippe/Marson, Pierre (eds.) (2001): 20 ans d'éditions Phi, un défi: exposition et catalogue, Mersch: Centre national de littérature.

Dembeck, Till (2007): Texte rahmen. Grenzregionen literarischer Werke im 18. Jahrhundert (Gottsched, Wieland, Moritz, Jean Paul), Berlin/New York: de Gruyter.

Dembeck, Till (2014): "Für eine Philologie der Mehrsprachigkeit. Zur Einleitung", in: Till Dembeck/Georg Mein (eds.), Philologie und Mehrsprachigkeit, Heidelberg: Winter, 9-37.

Derrida, Jacques (1987 [French original 1978]): The Truth in Painting (trans. Geoffrey Bennington and Ian McLeod), Chicago & London: Chicago University Press.

Desvallées, André/Mairesse, François (2011): Dictionnaire encyclopédique de muséologie, Paris: Armand Colin.

Dimmer, Michel/Rewenig, Guy/Scheuren, Micheline/Thiltges, Paul (2010): "Discrimination Prend Effet, Madame Modert", in: Tageblatt, edition 162 of 15.07.2010, 17.

Donnat, Olivier (2008): "Démocratisation de la culture: fin... et suite?", in: Jean-Pierre Saez (ed.), Culture et société: un lien à reconstruire, Toulouse: Éditions de l'Attribut, 55-71.

Döring, Nicola (2000): "Identität + Internet = Virtuelle Identität?", in: forum medienethik 2/2000, 65-76, http://www.mediacultureonline.de/fileadmin/bibliothek/doering_identitaet/doering_identitaet, accessed 04.11.2013.

Döring, Nicola (2003): Sozialpsychologie des Internet. Die Bedeutung des Internet für Kommunikationsprozesse, Identitäten, soziale Beziehungen und Gruppen, Göttingen: Hogrefe.

Dumont, Marc (2006): Penser la ville incertaine: périmètres et interstices, http://www.espacestemps.net/generate-pdf/?idPost=22689, accessed 19.12.2013.

Eco, Umberto (1991 [Italian original 1990]): The Limits of Interpretation, Bloomington: Indiana University Press.

Fellinger, Raimund (ed.) (2010): Suhrkamp, Suhrkamp. Autoren über Autoren – 60 Jahre Suhrkamp Verlag, Frankfurt a.M.: Suhrkamp.

Fourès, Angèle/Grisot, Delphine/Lochot, Serge (2011): Le rôle social du musée: agir ensemble et créer des solidarités, Paris: OCIM.

Genette, Gérard (1987): Seuils, Paris: Seuil.

Genette, Gérard (1997 [French original 1987]): Paratexts. Thresholds of Interpretation (trans. Jane E. Lewin), Cambridge MA: Cambridge University Press.

Gerlitz, Carolin (2011): "Die *Like* Economy: Digitaler Raum, Daten und Wertschöpfung", in: Oliver Leistert/Theo Röhle (eds.), Generation *Facebook*: Über das Leben im Social Net, Bielefeld: transcript, 101-122.

Gharsallah, Soumaya (2008): Le rôle de l'espace dans le musée et dans l'exposition. Analyse du processus communicationnel et signifiant, thèse de Doctorat, sous la direction de Jean Davallon et Catherine Saouter, Université d'Avignon/ Université du Québec.

Giddens, Anthony (1984): The Constitution of Society. Outline of the Theory of Structuration, Cambridge: Polity.

Gilles, Peter (forthcoming): "From Status to Corpus: Codification and Implementation of Spelling Norms in Luxembourgish", in: Wini Davies/Evelyn Ziegler (eds.), Macro and Micro Language Planning, Palgrave Macmillan.

Giordan, André, Musées et expositions, http://www.andregiordan.com/museologie/Museologie.htm, accessed 01.12.2013.

Glicenstein, Jérôme (2013): L'art contemporain entre les lignes, Paris: PUF.

Gob, André/Drouguet, Noémie (2006): La Muséologie. Histoire, Développement, Enjeux actuels, Paris: Armand Colin.

Goffman, Erving (1959): The Presentation of Self in Everyday Life, New York: Doubleday Anchor Books.

Goffman, Erving (2008): Interaction Ritual: Essays in Face-to-face Behavior, New Jersey: Transaction Publishers.

Greenberg, Reesa (1995): "The Exhibition as Discursive Event", in: Lucy R. Lippard (ed.), Longing and Belonging: From the Faraway Nearby, Santa Fe: SITE, 120-125.

Guillaud, Clara (2009): "Interstices urbains et pratiques culturelles", in: Implications philosophiques, dossier 2009, http://www.implications-philosophiques.org/Habitat/Guillaud3.html, accessed 01.12.2013.

Haarmann, Harald (1989): Symbolic Values of Foreign Language Use: From the Japanese Case to a General Sociolinguistic Perspective, Berlin: Mouton de Gruyter.

Hepp, Andreas/Thomas, Tanja/Winter, Carsten (2003): "Medienidentitäten: Eine Einführung zu den Diskussionen", in: Carsten Winter/Tanja Thomas/Andreas Hepp (eds.), Medienidentitäten. Identität im Kontext von Globalisierung und Medienkultur. Köln: Harlem, 7-26.

Horner, Kristine/Weber, Jean-Jacques (2008): "The Language Situation in Luxembourg", in: Robert Kaplan/Richard Baldauf/Nkonko Kamwangamalu (eds.), Current Issues in Language Planning 9/1, Clevedon: Multilingual Matters, 69-128.

Jacobi, Daniel/Meunier, Anik (2000): "La médiation, projet culturel ou régulation sociale du "bon" goût ?", in: Recherches en communication 13, 37-60.

Jakle, John A./Sculle, Keith A. (1994): The Gas Station in America (Creating the North American Landscape), Baltimore/Maryland: The Johns Hopkins University Press.

Jameson, Fredric (1991): Postmodernism, or the Cultural Logic of Late Capitalism, London: Verso.

Jenkins, Henry/Clinton, Katie/Purushotma, Ravi/Robinson, Alice J./Weigel, Margaret (2007): Confronting the Challenges of Participatory Culture: Media Education for the 21st Century, Chicago: The MacArthur Foundation.

Kalmijn, Matthijs (2004): "Marriage Rituals as Reinforcers of Role Transitions: An Analysis of Weddings in the Netherlands", in: Journal of Marriage and Family 66/3, 582-594.

Kelly-Holmes, Helen (2005): Advertising as Multilingual Communication, Houndmills/Basingstoke/Hampshire/New York: Palgrave Macmillan.

Kmec, Sonja/Prüm, Agnès (2014): "De l'insoutenable banalité des lieux-cyborgs. Les stations-essence dans l'imaginaire de l'extrême contemporain", in: Sylvie Freyermuth/Jean-François Bonnot/Timo Obergöker (eds.), Ville infectée, ville déshumanisée, Bruxelles: Peter Lang.

Kneidinger, Bernadette (2013): Geopolitische Identitätskonstruktionen in der Netzwerkgesellschaft, Wiesbaden: Springer Fachmedien.

Lamour, Christian/Langers, Jean (2012): La Presse Quotidienne Gratuite au Luxembourg. Vers un renouveau générationnel et populaire de la presse? (= Les Cahiers du CEPS/INSTEAD, cahier n° 1/2012), Luxembourg: CEPS/INSTEAD.

Lee, Dorothy (2004): Transfiguration: New Century Theology, London/New York: Continuum.

Lefebvre, Henri (1986): La Production de l'Espace, Paris: Anthropos.

Lennon, Brian (2010): In Babel's Shadow: Multilingual Literatures, Monolingual States, Minneapolis/London: Minnesota University Press.

Lévy, Jacques/Lussault, Michel (ed.) (2003), Dictionnaire de la géographie, Paris: Belin.

Lëtzebuerger Online Dictionnaire – LOD, http://www.lod.lu/lod, accessed 04.12.2011.

Lossau, Julia (2009): "Pitfalls of (Third) Space. Rethinking the Ambivalent Logic of Spatial Semantics", in: Karin Ikas/Gerhard Wagner (eds.), Communicating in the Third Space, London/New York: Routledge, 62-78.

Mairesse, François/Desvallées, André (2011): "Vers une nouvelle définition du musée", in: François Mairesse/André Desvallées (eds.), Vers une redéfinition du musée?, Paris: L'Harmattan, 13-20.

Manderscheid, Roger (2001): "francis", in: Jean Delvaux/Jean-Philippe Janus/Pierre Marson (ed.), 20 ans d'éditions Phi, un défi: exposition et catalogue, Mersch: Centre national de Littérature, 70-72.

Martyn, David (2014): "Es gab keine Mehrsprachigkeit, bevor es nicht Einsprachigkeit gab. Ansätze zu einer Archäologie der Sprachigkeit (Herder, Luther, Tawada)", in: Till Dembeck/Georg Mein (eds.), Philologie und Mehrsprachigkeit, Heidelberg: Winter, 38-51.

McLuhan, Herbert Marshall (1964): Understanding Media: The Extensions of Man, New York: Routledge.

Mead, George Herbert (1934): Mind, Self, and Society with an Introduction of Charles W. Morris, Chicago: University of Chicago Press.

Mein, Georg (2011): "Medien des Wissens – Anstelle einer Einführung", in: Georg Mein/Heinz Sieburg (eds.), Medien des Wissens. Interdiziplinäre Aspekte von Medialität, Bielefeld: transcript, 7-21.

Mémorial (1999): "Règlement grand-ducal du 30 juillet 1999 portant réforme du système officiel d'orthographe luxembourgeoise", in: Mémorial A. Journal Officiel du Grand-Duché de Luxembourg/Mémorial A. Amtsblatt des Grossherzogtums Luxemburg 112, 2040-2048.

Meunier, Dominique (2007): "La mediation comme 'lieu de relationnalité'. Essai d'opérationnalisation d'un concept", in: Questions de communication 11, http://questionsdecommunication.revues.org/7363, accessed 20.02.2014.

Mitchell, Katheryne (2002): "Cultural Geographies of Transnationality", in: Kay Anderson/Mona Domosh/Steve Pile/Nigel Thrift (eds.), Handbook of Cultural Geography, London: Sage, 74-87.

Montemurro, Beth (2006): Something Old, Something Bold: Bridal Showers and Bachelorette Parties, New Brunswick: Rutgers University Press.

Myers, Greg (1994): Words in Ads, London: Edward Arnold/New York: Routledge.

Oxford Dictionaries, Interstice, http://oxforddictionaries.com/definition/english/interstice?q=interstice, accessed 20.02.2014.

Parr, Rolf (2008): "Liminale und andere Übergänge. Theoretische Modellierungen von Grenzzonen, Normalitätsspektren, Schwellen, Übergängen und Zwischenräumen in Literatur- und Kulturwissenschaft", in: Achim Geisenhanslüke/Georg Mein (eds.), Schriftkultur und Schwellenkunde, Bielefeld: transcript, 11-63.

Paragon Communications (ed.) (1992): The Top-up Society. A Report on a Newly Defined Retailing Sector, London: Shell UK Ltd.

Perec, Georges (1989): L'infra-ordinaire, Paris: Éditions du Seuil.

Piette, Albert (1990): "L'école de Chicago et la ville cosmopolite d'aujourd'hui: lecture et relectures critiques", in: Albert Bastenier/Felice Dassetto (eds.), Immigrations et nouveaux pluralismes, Bruxelles: De Boeck, 67-83.

Piller, Ingrid (2001): "Identity Constructions in Multilingual Advertising", in: Language in Society 30, 153-186.

Piller, Ingrid (2003): "Advertising as a Site of Language Contact", in: Annual Review of Applied Linguistics 23, 170-183.

Polster, Bernd (1996): Super oder normal. Tankstellen – Geschichte eines modernen Mythos, Köln: DuMont.

Pratt, Mary Louise (2007 [1992]): Imperial Eyes: Travel Writing and Transculturation, Kindle edition, London: Taylor & Francis eLibrary.

Reddeker, Sebastian (2011): Werbung und Identität im multikulturellen Raum. Der Werbediskurs in Luxemburg. Ein kommunikationswissenschaftlicher Beitrag, Bielefeld: transcript.

Renault, Monique (2000): "Seuil du musée, deuil de la ville?", in: ICOM 70, 15-20.

Rewenig, Guy (1983): "Der Schriftsteller Guy Rewenig. Lernen durch Lachen", in: Forum 65/66, 33-36.
Rewenig, Guy (1986): "Satiren sind das Sommerkleid der Verzweiflung. Gespräch mit Guy Rewenig über sein neues Buch", in: De Bicherwuerm 9, n. p.
Rewenig, Guy (2001a): Dein Herz aus Eis macht mich ganz heiß. Fußnoten, Echternach: Phi.
Rewenig, Guy (2001b): "Was macht den Verleger verlegen? 16 Stichworte zum Innenleben des Editörs. Für Francis van Maele", in: Jean Delvaux/Jean-Philippe Janus/Pierre Marson (eds.), 20 ans d'éditions Phi, un défi: exposition et catalogue, Mersch: Centre national de littérature, 82-85.
Rewenig, Guy (2010): "Über Melancholie und Heimat – und was die 'ultima fiesta' mit X-Mas zu tun hat. Ein Gespräch mit *ultimo*mondo-Mitbegründer Guy Rewenig", in: Lëtzebuerger Journal 177, 14.09.2010, 19.
Rewenig, Guy (2012a): "Es luxemburgert", in: D'Lëtzebuerger Land, edition of 20.07.2012, 12.
Rewenig, Guy (2012b): "Lëtschtebuedjesch ", in: D'Lëtzebuerger Land, edition of 16.11.2012, 12.
Rewenig, Guy (2013): "Wir Gewalttäter", in: D'Lëtzebuerger Land, edition of 11.01.2013, 9.
Rheingold Institut, Frauen fühlen sich an Tankstellen unwohl – Aral-Mobilitätsstudie, http://www.rheingold-salon.de/veroeffentlichungen/artikel/Frauen_fuehlen_sich_an_Tankstellen_unwohl_-_Aral-Mobilitaetsstudie.html, accessed 17.12.2013.
Richardson, John, E. (2005): "Decoding", in: Key Concepts in Journalism Studies, London: Sage UK, http://proxy.bnl.lu/login?qurl=http %3A %2F %2Fwww.credoreference.com/entry/sageukjour/decoding, accessed 06.12.2013.
Schlegel, Friedrich (1991): Philosophical Fragments (trans. Peter Firchow), foreword by Rodolphe Gasché, Minneapolis, London: University of Minnesota Press.
Schmidt, Siegfried J. (1994), Kognitive Autonomie und soziale Orientierung, Frankfurt a.M.: Suhrkamp.
Schneckenburger, Manfred (2013): "Wolfgang Nestler – Kontemplation mit dem Körpergefühl", in: Künstlerlexikon Saar, http://www.kuenstlerlexikonsaar.de/personen-a-z/artikel/-/nestler-wolfgang, accessed 13.01.2014.
Sebba, Mark/Mahootian, Shahrzad/Jonsson, Carla (2012): Language Mixing and Code-Switching in Writing: Approaches to Mixed-Language Written Discourse, New York/London: Routledge.
Shifman, Limor (2011): "An Anatomy of a YouTube Meme", in: New Media and Society 14/2, 187-203.
Smith, Adam (1976): The Theory of Moral Sentiments, Oxford: Claredon Press.
Sonntag, Monika (2012): "Grenzüberschreitende Kooperation im Kulturbereich. Interkulturalität in Luxemburg und der Großregion", in: Thomas Ernst/Dieter Heimböckel (eds.), Verortungen der Interkulturalität. Die Europäischen Kul-

turhauptstädte Luxemburg und die Großregion (2007), das Ruhrgebiet (2010) und Istanbul (2010), Bielefeld: transcript, 95-111.

Sonntag, Monika (2013): Grenzen überwinden durch Kultur. Identitätskonstruktionen von Kulturakteuren in europäischen Grenzräumen (= Luxemburg-Studien/Études luxembourgeoises, vol. 3), Frankfurt a.M.: Peter Lang.

Thériault, Mélissa (2010): Arthur Danto ou l'art en boîte, Paris: L'Harmattan.

Thompson, Craig J./Locander, William B./Pollio Howard R. (1994): "The Spoken and the Unspoken. A Hermeneutical Approach to Understanding Cultural Viewpoints that Underlie Consumers' Expressed Meanings", in: Journal of Consumer Research 21, 432-451.

Thrasher, Frederick (1927): The Gang, Chicago: University of Chicago Press.

Tore, Gian Maria (2011): "'Médias' et 'médiations': pour penser et analyser la communication", in: Marion Colas-Blaise/Gian Maria Tore (eds.), Médias et médiations culturelles au Luxembourg, Luxembourg: Editions Binsfeld, 15-26.

Turner, Victor (1982): From Ritual to Theatre: The Human Seriousness of Play, New York: Performing Arts Journal Publications.

Ullrich, Daniel, GR-Atlas: Tanktourismus, http://gr-atlas.uni.lu/index.php/de/articles/tr1191/ta1196, accessed 17.12.2013.

van Gennep, Arnold (1909): Les Rites de passage, étude systématique des rites de la porte et du seuil, de l'hospitalité, de l'adoption, de la grossesse et de l'accouchement, de la naissance, de l'enfance, de la puberté, de l'initiation, de l'ordination, du couronnement, des fiançailles et du mariage, des funérailles, des saisons, etc., Paris: É. Nourry.

van Gennep, Arnold (1960 [French original 1909]): The Rites of Passage (trans. Monika B. Vizedom and Gabrielle L. Caffee), Chicago: The University of Chicago Press.

Watkin, Christopher (2009): Phenomenology or Deconstruction? The Question of Ontology in Maurice Merleau-Ponty, Paul Ricoeur and Jean-Luc Nancy, Edinburgh: Edinburgh University Press.

West, Shearer (1996): "Cimabue (Cenni Di Peppi) (C. 1240-?1302)", in: The Bloomsbury Guide to Art, London: Bloomsbury Publishing Ltd, http://proxy.bnl.lu/login?qurl=http %3A %2F %2Fsearch.credoreference.com.proxy.bnl.lu %2Fcontent %2Fentry %2Fbga %2Fcimabue_cenni_di_peppi_c_1240_1302 %2F0, accessed 17.12.2013.

Werlen, Benno (1997): Sozialgeographie alltäglicher Regionalisierungen, vol. 2: Globalisierung, Region und Regionalisierung, Stuttgart: Steiner.

Woolard, Kathryn A. (1998): "Language Ideology as a Field of Inquiry", in: Bambi B. Schieffelin/Kathryn Woolard/Paul Kroskrity (eds.), Language Ideologies: Practice and Theory, Oxford: Oxford University Press, 3-47.

Yildiz, Yasemin (2012): Beyond the Mother Tongue: The Postmonolingual Condition, New York: Fordham University Press.

Zhao, Shanyang/Grasmuck, Sherri/Martin, Jason (2008): "Identity Construction on *Facebook*: Digital empowerment in anchored relationships", in: Computers in Human Behavior 24/5, 1816-1836.

5. Space and Identity Constructions Through Everyday-Cultural Practices

Christel Baltes-Löhr, Andrea Binsfeld, Elisabeth Boesen, Laure Caregari, Norbert Franz, Markus Hesse, Eva Klos, Rachel Reckinger, Gregor Schnuer, Benno Sönke Schulz, Heinz Sieburg, Gianna Thommes, Britta Weimann, Christian Wille, Julia Maria Zimmermann

5.1 SUBJECTIFICATIONS AND SUBJECTIVATIONS

The present chapter ties up with chapter 3 and completes the theoretical-conceptual perspective adopted there. While the latter primarily analyses technologies of domination, normalizations and attributions of meaning, we will here address the question of how such technologies and positings of subjects are lived and/or how they influence the individuals' self-conceptions. Both chapters are based on Foucault's approach of governmentality (see Foucault 2007) in order to shed light – each with a different focus – on the interplay of technologies of domination (see chapter 3) and subjectivation (see this chapter) and their inherent constructions of space and identity. For examining this interplay we distinguish, in the case studies presented here, between the aspect of subjectification, i.e. the addressing or 'interpellation' as subject (see Althusser 1971) and that of subjectivation, the understanding of self (see Bührmann/Schneider 2008); or in other words, between the processes of attribution and appropriation as well as their intermeshing in the course of everyday practices (see Reckinger/Schulz/Wille 2011). The following considerations focus on the subjectivations that can be observed empirically in the case studies.

At present, the concept of the subject is experiencing a certain revival in cultural studies. However, today's approaches have detached themselves significantly from the earlier abstract, philosophical discussion of the concept. The subject analysis in culture studies deals with the empirical subject and its different (historical) 'modes of subjectivation'. It is therefore based on a reversal of the classical relationship between the philosophical concept of subject and the empirical subject characteristic for the 18th and 19th centuries.

In the following, we will first show how the classical understanding of the subject has been questioned since the late 19th century and the distinction between transcendental and empirical subject dissolved. Subsequently we will present the theoretical foundation of subject analysis as encountered in the case studies and discuss the link between governmentality and subjectification/subjectivation. We will conclude by describing the operationalization of the developed conceptual framework in terms of research practice.

5.1.1 Development of the Concept of the Subject: A Synopsis

During the 18th century epistemology developed a specific understanding of the subject. This development can be traced back to René Descartes' dualism and leads to Immanuel Kant's transcendental philosophy (see Benedikter 2011: 767). Kant's subject is, in contrast to the object, an actively perceiving entity and exists *a priori* – it is not a result of sensory perceptions, but it is a "transcendental unity of self-consciousness" (see Kant 1999: 247). With this he describes a subject that is a given as a basis for sensory perceptions (see ibid.: 246f.) and can overcome subjective influences on itself through 'understanding' (*Verstand*). The subject here is centred, i.e. it perceives actively and the understanding of these perceptions is universally and objectively possible, since the mind and pure reason are given *a priori*.

In the 19th and in the early 20th century a series of concepts of the subject emerged that questioned the abstract, transcendental subject as a basis of the self. One can here point to Marx and Engels who maintain the subject-object dichotomy and transfer it onto the relationship of worker-product. Their concept of the subject describes the 'self' as the product of social agency (Marx/Engels 1970: 51). The works of Sigmund Freud and Friedrich Nietzsche were ground-breaking for the development of the later, postmodern notion of the decentralization of the subject. The question of how self-awareness originates plays an important role in Sigmund Freud's psychoanalysis. The instinctual 'id' and the value-oriented 'super-ego' are in conflict; this leads to the creation of the 'ego' or the self. There is therefore no transcendental subject in Kant's sense, but rather a balancing act that manifests itself in our consciousness as a clash of norms, urges and reflection. The influence of Freud's concept of the subject is very much in evidence in post-structuralist thinkers such as Jacques Lacan, Roland Barthes, Julia Kristeva and Judith Butler.

Of particular importance for the more recent discussion of the concept of the subject in cultural studies is Friedrich Nietzsche, for whom the notion of a transcendental subject, and the concept of freedom linked to it, is an illusion:

"Knowing, in an absolute and thus also relative sense, is likewise *a mere fiction*! So this also does away with the necessity to posit a something that 'knows', a subject for knowing, some pure 'intelligence', an 'absolute spirit': - this mythology that even Kant has not entirely relinquished [...] has now had its day"[1] (Nietzsche 2009 [1885]: 38 [14]).

Nietzsche understands the 'self' as plural, as unequal to itself, not centred and calls for 'self-overcoming' as a form of freedom. His philosophy and its notion of the subject are considered a prelude to postmodern theory and an escape from modernity (see Habermas 1990: 86). At the same time, in early sociology (Emile Durkheim, Max Weber, Georg Simmel) the notion of the subject is understood in the sense of 'personality' or 'identity'. Until the second half of the 20th century, however, the conception of the individual in social sciences is based largely on the idea of an *a priori* given, self-aware 'self' that has a specific relationship to society to be explored.[2]

It is finally the late- and postmodern thinkers who once more radically question the subject as something given. Andreas Reckwitz (see 2008: 124) describes two concretizations of this perspective which are gaining increasing acceptance: 1) Michel Foucault's concept of the subject and the analysis of modes of subjectivation in cultural studies influenced by him and 2) the concept of a specifically postmodern 'self'. Foucault sees Kant's concept of the subject as a historical-contextual construction and rejects, like Nietzsche, the idea of a transcendental 'self'. In his view the subject is not a precondition that, under the influence of social structures, enables actions, but rather is itself a result of actions which in turn are situated in a historical-cultural context. The second concretization consists in the formulation of new postmodern forms of the subject and is proposed by scholars such as Mike Featherstone (1995) or Zygmunt Bauman (2000) who deal with the dissolution of solid social structures in postmodernity hitherto considered natural. The classical differentiation between an abstract (transcendental) and an empirical (positivistically/deterministically prescribed) subject is now no longer a key element of subject analysis. What grounds these studies is the notion of the subject as one that is, on the one hand, socially constituted and, on the other, constitutes the social.

---

1 | Personal translation of: "Das Erkennen, das absolute und folglich auch das relative, ist ebenfalls *nur eine Fiktion*! Damit fällt denn auch die Nöthigung weg, ein Etwas das 'erkennt', ein Subjekt für das Erkennen anzusetzen, irgend eine reine 'Intelligenz', einen 'absoluten Geist': – diese noch von Kant nicht gänzlich aufgegebene Mythologie [...] hat nunmehr ihre Zeit gehabt."
2 | Here society is more than the sum of its individuals, in this sense becoming the actual subject of investigation – functionalism and structuralism do not deal with the relations between individuals but with those between the individual and society.

5.1.2 Theoretical Principles of Subject Analysis in Cultural Studies

The current subject analysis in cultural studies deals with the empirical subject, i.e. it is not concerned with the philosophical problem of determining a general concept of the subject. Nevertheless, the underlying theoretical understanding is widely shared: the subject is not an autonomous *a priori* given factor constituting the basis of knowledge and agency, but rather the result of certain modes of subjectivation and subjectification that need to be examined. The interest in cultural studies is therefore not directed towards the subject but the historically and culturally specific types of subject, more precisely, the processes of their formation. But more recent research has directed its attention expressly to the modes of subjectivation. The concern here is not an analysis of the relationship between the individual and society, where individualization is regarded as a liberation of the individual from social constraints, but rather "how this individual, in its physical or mental features, which supposedly ensure its autonomy, is made up of highly specific schemata" (Reckwitz 2008a: 15).[3]

Subject analysis in cultural studies therefore maintains a critical distance towards its subject: features are understood as only seemingly given and pre-cultural, and the object of enquiry are the "barely conscious or transparent processes of stabilization and destabilization" of these features – "of the societal subject categorizations in which the individual inserts herself in a more or less unproblematic fashion"[4] (Reckwitz 2008a: 16f.).[5] The interest in cultural modes of subjectivation and subjectification was stimulated by fundamental theoretical developments of poststructuralism; an important impulse came from the hypothesis of a postmodern transformation of the self, which forms the basis both of the revision of the bourgeois concept of the subject and the contemporary processes of subjectivation and subjectification processes.

In this chapter, subject analysis is primarily understood to mean an enquiry into social practices about the constitutions of subjects articulated in them, with subject constitution being understood as the dynamic relationship of subject formations and subject positionings or attributions (*subjectifications*) and forms of self-understanding and self-relationship or appropriations (*subjectivations*). In this process, implicit precepts are internalized, reproduced, shifted or also overcome in various ways. Subject constitutions are therefore contingent formations – as are the identities resulting from them, not devoid of contradictions and always

---

3 | Personal translation of: "[...] wie sich dieses 'Individuum' in [...] körperlichen oder psychischen Eigenschaften, die ihm vermeintlich Autonomie sichern, aus hochspezifischen Schemata zusammensetzt."
4 | Personal translation of: "[...] kaum bewussten oder transparenten kulturellen Prozessen der Stabilisierung und Destabilisierung"[dieser Eigenschaften] – "de[r]n gesellschaftlichen Subjektordnungen, in die der Einzelne mehr oder weniger unproblematisch einrückt."
5 | Partly inspired by the American Culture and Personality School.

temporary. Subject constitution is a ubiquitous, continuous process that permeates social practice.

The 'subject' focused on here should not be equated to an individual. Rather, these are historically changeable subject forms that allow the individual to be addressed as a subject, *to be subjectivated*, and to perceive him/herself as a subject, to *subjectivate him/herself*. Subjectifications comprise attributed cultural typings, catalogues of requirements or patterns of what should be attained. Subjectivations by contrast stand for self-designs of the individual that are guided by subjectifications, which also includes the possibility that the individual might fail in meeting the challenge of becoming a subject in his or her attempt to fulfill the subjectifications. The theoretical approach that focuses on this empirically open and partly conflictual tension between subjectification and subjectivation is described by Reckwitz as follows:

"The most important feature of the poststructuralist perspective on the subject consists in the fact that the subject categorizations are not analysed as results of homogenous and clear-cut codes but as cultural entities in which a contradiction-free and stable subjectivity is continuously defeated and subverted: for instance by different discourse categories overlapping each other in unpredictable ways, by attributions of signifiers to signified identities turning out to be ambivalent or subject cultures emerging as spaces of permanent conflicts of definition"[6] (Reckwitz 2008b: 80).

Drawing on Foucault's notion of governmentality, the case studies in this chapter shed light on processes of subject constitution by focusing on certain practices and discourses of spatial and identity construction in border regions. They thus examine contexts where particularly ambiguous, contradictory and fragile subject constitutions may be presumed. In the following, we will argue how the conceptual tools used here are linked to Foucault's concept of governmentality and subject analysis that plays a crucial role in this volume.

5.1.3 Governmental Approach to Subject Constitutions

The governmentality approach has shown itself to be a particularly useful tool for subsuming the examination of subject constitutions emerging from processes

---

6 | Personal translation of: "Das wichtigste Merkmal der poststrukturalistischen Perspektive auf das Subjekt besteht [...] darin, dass sie [...] Subjektordnungen nicht als Resultate homogener und eindeutiger Codes analysiert, sondern als kulturelle Gebilde, in denen eine widerspruchsfreie und stabile Subjektivität immer wieder scheitert und torpediert wird: etwa dadurch, dass sich unterschiedliche Diskursordnungen unberechenbar überlagern, dass Zuordnungen von Signifikanten zu Identitätssignifikaten sich als mehrdeutig erweisen oder Subjektkulturen sich als Räume permanenter Definitionskonflikte herausstellen."

of subjectification and subjectivation under one single analytical bracket, thus providing a common basis for the different research interests of the authors of this chapter. This is an integrative concept which focuses on the interaction between technologies of domination and of self by "generally addressing the mutual constitution of forms of power, practices of knowledge and forms of subjectivation"[7] (Bührmann/Schneider 2008: 70). Put differently: governmentality points to "the different forms of agency and fields of practice that in manifold ways aim at the guidance, or the conduct of individuals and collectives"[8] (Lemke 2008: 260). This can refer to the conduct of *others* (e.g. on the macrosocial level of a national administration or on the microsocial level of self-help literature) as well as the conduct of the *self* (on the microsocial level of ethical self-disciplining).

The approach gives particular attention to the *interconnection of technologies of domination and of self*, the latter of which are the focus of the present chapter, as already indicated above. Governmentality "not only integrates numerous inter-, sub-, and transnational actors, but also points in particular to the numerous intersections of power relations where concrete actions, particular dispositions and subjectivities are created in the first place[9] (Gertenbach 2012: 112). On the microanalytical level favoured in this chapter, the governmental form of government "finds its specific expression in the influence on the subjects' sphere of agency and in the shaping and forming of certain kinds of subjectivity"[10] which are analysed in the case studies with regard to constructions of space and identity in everyday-cultural practices.

Recent publications on the concept of governmentality frequently emphasize its function as a hinge between power, knowledge and subjectivity. This refers to the fact that the interplay of power and knowledge in each case produces or 'suggests' different forms of subjectivity (see ibid.: 114). Knowledge is understood by Foucault extremely heterogenously as an umbrella term for scientific findings, legitimate 'high culture', various official 'canons'; but it also includes everyday-cultural evidences, non-discursive inventories of experience etc. This knowledge is not only never neutral, but it also regulates what appears as 'true' in the various social fields or periods. Within this scope, individuals have a certain latitude for

---

7 | Personal translation of: [indem es] "allgemein die wechselseitige Konstituierung von Machtformen, Wissenspraktiken und Subjektivierungsformen adressiert."

8 | Personal translation of: "[...] auf unterschiedliche Handlungsformen und Praxisfelder, die in vielfältiger Weise auf die Lenkung und Leitung von Individuen und Kollektiven zielen."

9 | Personal translation of: "[...] integriert nicht nur zahlreiche zwischen-, sub- und transstaatliche Akteure, sondern verweist v.a. auf vielfältige Kreuzungspunkte von Machtverhältnissen, in denen überhaupt erst konkrete Handlungsweisen, bestimmte Dispositionen und Subjektivitäten erzeugt werden."

10 | Personal translation of: [ihren] "spezifischen Ausdruck [...] im Einwirken auf den Handlungsbereich der Subjekte und in der Formung und Gestaltung bestimmter Formen von Subjektivität."

agency with extremely numerous – but not arbitrary – choices (see Baltes-Löhr/ Prüm/Reckinger/Wille 2011).

The following case studies focus on the governmental positioning of self-relationships in connection with spatial aspects of identity construction. In this field of research one can find a considerable number of terms that are partly used synonymously: in the context of subjectification, we come across processes of subject formation, subject positioning, governmental practices, disciplining practices etc., while in the context of subjectivation we encounter self-practices, technologies of self, self-government, self-conduct etc. (see Bührmann/Schneider 2008). These different terms each point to aspects of the following basic context: "Technologies of government aim at certain practices of self-care, conduct individuals to self-responsible and rational behaviour"[11] (Gertenbach 2012: 117). This kind of conduct in which "individuals – without being forced to – adapt, frequently unresistingly and via internalized norms or values, to the fabric of power relationships"[12] (Füller/Marquardt 2009: 89) shows the inherent ambivalence of the term 'conduct': "To 'conduct' is at the same time to 'lead' others (according to mechanisms of coercion that are, to varying degrees, strict) and a way of behaving within a more or less open field of possibilities" (Foucault 2000 [1982]: 341). This 'conduct' of subjects based on internalized knowledge and the examination of its adaptation in specific contextual-normative frameworks constitute the common subject matter of the eight case studies. These plural, relational, reflexive and ambivalent identifications and self-disciplinings concern everyday life choices and positionings – in short 'identity work' (see Keupp et al. 2006) – that are made on the basis of unequally distributed resources. Despite this inequality, "choices follow discursive structures that are oriented towards a specific risk scenario and make certain choices more or less likely"[13] (Füller/Marquardt 2009: 90). These probabilities are not the same for everybody, but their principle obtains to everybody. Paying particular attention to processes of agency, we therefore understand the *relational* subject in the case studies of this chapter neither as

"something transcendental with features that it possesses a priori, i.e. prior to any experience, nor can it be rendered, in its mental structure, independently from the cultural context into an object of empirical research. [...] The subject does not simply emancipate

---

11 | Personal translation of: "Regierungstechnologien zielen [...] auf bestimmte Praktiken der Selbstsorge hin, leiten Individuen zu selbstverantwortlichem und rationalem Verhalten an."

12 | Personal translation of: [in der sich] "Individuen – ohne dazu 'gezwungen' zu werden – durch verinnerlichte Normen oder Wertvorstellungen häufig widerstandslos in das Gefüge der Kräfteverhältnisse einpassen."

13 | Personal translation of: "[...] Entscheidungen diskursiven Strukturen, die an einem spezifischen Risikoszenario ausgerichtet sind und bestimmte Entscheidungen wahrscheinlicher oder unwahrscheinlicher machen."

itself from all cultural forms, but is a correlate of changing modes of subjectivation. [...] Instead of presupposing the reflexive subject, it then emerges as a product of highly specific cultural modes of subjectivation"[14] (Reckwitz 2008a: 13 and 16).

Precisely here is the starting point for our empirical analysis: from the perspective of different microanalytical modes of subjectivation we at the same time focus on the aspects of subjectification linked to them. In the sense of governmentality, we mix aspects of subjectification, i.e. the way how individuals are addressed, with aspects of subjectivation, i.e. the way individuals see themselves with regard to the discourses *implicitly* addressed to them and the, in each case different, individually produced internalizations. In summary we can say:

"The relationship between the two analytical dimensions of subjectification/subjectivation is thus one that needs to be examined empirically according to the identity precepts found in each case and their – however seamlessly or refractedly – ascertainable appropriations as empirically reconstructable identity patterns"[15] (Bührmann/Schneider 2008: 71f.).

5.1.4 Operationalization of the Theoretical-Conceptual Framework

Regarding the operationalization of the research approach, we have modelled our work, among others, on the praxeological heuristics as suggested by Reckwitz (2008a: 135ff.) and on the corresponding analytical categories. This heuristics seems particularly suited for research in the context of the border, since it is attuned to the investigation of 'processual realities', so that it is possible to observe contingent processes and examine space and identity constructions both as preconditions as well as results of practices of *Doing Space* or *Doing Identity*. The concept of practices occupies a crucial place within this analytical framework. It allows the examination of subject constitutions that 'cut across national borders', when we can assume in particular for border regions that "meanings, identities and practices do not occur either in one or the other culture", but that the world is "a cultural melange in the sense of a mutual cultural penetration of global

---

14 | Personal translation of: "[...] eine Transzendentalie mit Eigenschaften, die ihm *a priori*, d.h. vor aller Erfahrung, zukommen, noch lässt es sich in seiner mentalen Struktur unabhängig vom kulturellen Kontext zum Objekt empirischer Forschung machen. [...] Das Subjekt emanzipiert sich nicht kurzerhand aus sämtlichen kulturellen Formen, sondern ist ein Korrelat wechselnder Subjektivierungsweisen. [...] Statt das reflexive Subjekt vorauszusetzen, wird es dann als Produkt hochspezifischer kultureller Subjektivierungsweisen sichtbar."

15 | Personal translation of: "Das Verhältnis zwischen den beiden analytischen Dimensionen von Subjektivation/Subjektivierung ist somit ein empirisch zu klärendes gemäß den jeweils vorfindbaren Identitätsvorgaben und deren – wie nahtlos oder gebrochen auch immer – nachweisbaren Aneignungen als empirisch rekonstruierbare Identitätsmuster."

and local references of meaning that are mobilized and reproduced in everyday practices"[16] (Reuter 2008: 270).

The following studies build from this concept of practices to do justice to the creative-eventful potential of subject constitutions, but also to the increased complexity and contingency of cultural forms that can be presumed to be particularly marked in border regions. The concept of practices ties in with the understanding of the subject developed above, since "praxeological subjects are not subjects of cognition but empirical projects that are described within the respective practice"[17] (Berger 2013: 315). This view implies that subjects only exist within the performance of practices, which is why an investigation into subject constitutions or identities can only be dealt with as an investigation into the social practices with the corresponding sub-aspects of subjectivation and subjectification.

The concept of practices contrasts with the concept of action in so far as social agency in the 'classical sense' is understood as a social phenomenon that is generated and guided by a mental centre of action residing in the actors themselves. This internal centre represents a place of non-visible motives, values, norms etc. that guide the externally visible action. This dualism of the guiding internal apparatus and the externally perceivable physical agency is overcome with the concept of practices (see Schmidt 2012: 56). Here it is assumed that

"[...] 'actions' do not occur as discrete, punctual and individual exemplars but that they are embedded, under normal social conditions, in a more comprehensive, socially divided practice held together by an implicit, methodological and interpretative knowledge as a typified, routinized and socially 'understandable' bundle of activities. The social should here not be sought in the 'intersubjectivity' and not in the 'guidedness by norms', but rather in the collectivity of behaviours that are held together by a specific 'practical competence': practices thus form an emergent level of the social which however is not present in the 'environment' of its physical-mental carriers"[18] (Reckwitz 2003: 289).

---

16 | Personal translation of: "[...] Bedeutungen, Identitäten und Praktiken [...] nicht entweder in der einen oder der anderen Kultur [liegen]", [sondern die Welt] "vielmehr einer Kulturmelange im Sinne einer wechselseitigen kulturellen Durchdringung globaler und lokaler Sinnbezüge [gleicht], die in den alltäglichen Praktiken mobilisiert und reproduziert werden."
17 | Personal translation of: [insofern] "es sich bei den praxeologischen Subjekten nicht um Erkenntnissubjekte [handelt], sondern [um] empirische Projekte, die innerhalb der jeweiligen Praktik beschrieben werden."
18 | Personal translation of: "[...] 'Handlungen' nicht als diskrete, punktuelle und individuelle Exemplare vorkommen, sondern [dass] sie im sozialen Normalfall eingebettet sind in eine umfassendere, sozial geteilte und durch ein implizites, methodisches und interpretatives Wissen zusammengehaltene Praktik als ein typisiertes, routinisiertes und sozial 'verstehbares' Bündel von Aktivitäten. Das Soziale ist hier nicht in der 'Intersubjektivität' und nicht in der 'Normgeleitetheit' [...] zu suchen, sondern in der

In the following, we will lay out in more detail individual facets of this concept under analytical-empirical aspects, as used in the following case studies.

Collectivity and Enactment: The concept of practices emphasizes the collective character of human activities, with symbolic categories and cultural codes not regarded as 'being outside of practice', but as inherent in social practices and produced by these. It is only through social practices that interpretative patterns or symbolic power relations develop their existence and effect (see Moebius 2008: 60). Robert Schmidt (2012: 57) emphasizes in this context that the concept of practices by no means ignores "concepts and capabilities such as intentionality, consciousness and reflexivity" but "reformulates these praxeologically"[19]. This means that the analytical focus should be directed to the observable doing and the capabilities and structures of meaning that become manifest in it. These features of the concept of practices allow the case studies to approach questions of spatial and identity construction largely unencumbered by presuppositions. In the reconstruction of (cross-border) linguistic spaces, for example, interviewees are asked about their language choice in order to establish the actual linguistic practices in the border region independently of pre-defined linguistic spaces. Another study examines the interviewees' empirically observable dietary practices and values in order to determine which concepts of sustainability are actually practiced. Also practices of remembering and the interpretations of meaning connected to them are examined in their direct enactment – initially regardless of national or regional normalizations.

Routinization and Unpredictability: The concept of practices also emphasizes the routinized as well as the creative and unpredictable character of human action. This allows both the repetitivity of practices as well as their situative and contextual adaptability to become the subject of analysis (see Reckwitz 2009: 174). In terms of research practice, this makes it possible to focus on the "combinational logic – in detail decipherable, impure – of various cultural elements in the practices, discourses, subjectivations and systems of practice and artefacts"[20] (Reckwitz 2010: 195). The reproductive-routinized character of practices, as emphasized particularly by Bourdieu, and their creative-processual character, as highlighted notably by Derrida or Butler, are two sides of one coin (see Reckwitz 2009: 174). This perspective centers on the contingency of social logics and with that on cultural change – a particularly crucial aspect when examining border regions.

Kollektivität von Verhaltensweisen, die durch ein spezifisches 'praktisches Können' zusammengehalten werden: Praktiken bilden somit eine emergente Ebene des Sozialen, die sich jedoch nicht in der 'Umwelt' ihrer körperlich-mentalen Träger befindet."

19 | Personal translation of: "[...] Konzepte und Vermögen wie Intentionalität, Bewusstheit und Reflexivität" keinesfalls ausblende, sondern diese "praxeologisch reformuliert."

20 | Personal translation of: [die] "im Detail dechiffrierbare[n], unreine[n] Kombinationslogik diverser kultureller Elemente in den Praktiken, Diskursen, Subjektivierungen und Praxis-/Artefaktesystemen."

This is reflected in the case studies when they, for example, show how practices of remembering develop contrary to established discourses, how routinization and reflexivity mix in the context of dietary practices or which strategies are employed in order to deal with linguistic impredictability.

Materiality and Spaces: Practices are, in addition, not only observable through physical performance, which also includes language and other symbolic forms, but they also manifest themselves as well *in* and *with* artefacts. The material dimension of bodies and artefacts can, for instance, comprise technologies, architectures or spatial structurizations and at the same time be understood as part of a discourse. Discourses are then not understood as speaking about certain issues, but rather as elements that produce cultural representations and form objects by speaking about them. Thus discourses themselves are, in turn, practices: "Practices of representation" (*Praktiken der Repräsentation,* Reckwitz 2006: 43) or 'discursive practices' (*pratiques discursives,* Foucault 2002 [1969]) which – like all practices – have a material anchoring (e.g. grave stones, newspaper articles, paintings) and, as "social places that produce orders of knowledge"[21] (Reckwitz 2010: 191), bring forth discourses with their inherent subjectifications or subjectivations. Artefacts are to be understood as "quasi-objects" (Latour 1993) and thus as elements of practices that are examined as to how their use and treatment influence practices, and how they enable or limit practices (see Reckwitz 2010: 193). This focus on modes of appropriation or use of artefacts enables a tie-in with considerations of spatial theory: "The fact that all social practices can be regarded as spatializing and organize space and its artefacts in a certain way, creates a further wide-ranging field of subject analysis"[22] (Reckwitz 2008b: 91). This refers to constellations of artefacts and/or space-generating interpretations of meaning that are here subsumed under the term of spatial construction. The space to be thus examined "is not a container, but a processual, relational space of practices and relationships between embodied participants, artefacts, places and environments"[23] (Schmidt 2012: 240). The following case studies take up this way of considering materiality and space; they discuss for instance the significance of spatial categories in dietary practices, the representations of (cross-border) spaces, workers' estates as a spatial nexus of social practices or the distribution of linguistic practices. They examine how the artefacts involved in the respective spatial constructions influence the practices of representation, for instance in connection with family identities or practices of remembering.

---

21 | Personal translation of: "Gesellschaftliche Produktionsorte von Wissensordnungen."
22 | Personal translation of: "Dadurch, dass sämtliche soziale Praktiken [...] sich als *spatializing* betrachten lassen und den Raum und dessen Artefakte auf bestimmte Weise organisieren, ist [...] ein weiteres umfangreiches Feld der Subjektanalyse gewonnen."
23 | Personal translation of: "Raum ist kein Behälter, sondern ein prozessualer, relationaler Raum der Praktiken und Beziehungen zwischen verkörperten Teilnehmerinnen, Artfakten, Orten und Umgebungen."

Practical Knowledge: Another area of analysis of subject constitutions connected to the hitherto discussed aspects is practical knowledge. This is the term for various kinds of knowledge that form a basis of meaning for social practices; practical knowledge flows into practices while at the same time being produced by them (see Reckwitz 2004: 320). Knowledge is therefore not understood as a given capability for action, rather it can only be reconstructed in its processuality, i.e. in connection with practices. Knowledge of this kind is "structured via differentiations which also provide the context for how specific things should be interpreted in a practice and dealt with practically"[24] (Reckwitz 2010: 193). These differentiations thus give orientation for what is 'correct' or 'discrediting' (see ibid.: 194). They represent codes that are often constructed in a binary fashion, but can also be more complex and comprise entire systems of differentiations. For the examination of subject constitutions, it is necessary to reveal the codes inherent in practical knowledge that determine what the subject 'is' and should be. This also includes pursuing the question in how far different codes that shape culturally desirable or also rejected subject models overlap in subject constitutions or compete with each other.

These processes that shed light on the dynamics of identity constructions direct the attention to the interplay of processes of subjectification and subjectivation, which in each case articulates itself empirically in different ways. This will be illustrated in the following case studies using examples of practices of language choice, diet, remembering and commemorating as well as gender-specific spatial representations.

5.2 Sustainable Everyday Eating Practices from the Perspective of Spatial Identifications

Rachel Reckinger

Food plays an important role in everyday-cultural practices due to the fact that it constitutes a daily necessity, that it is recurrent and that it is subject to choice – even though that importance is reflected unevenly by individuals. Furthermore, it is assumed that as much as 50 % of environmental effects are due to the consumption patterns of individual households (see EEA 2012); a major part of this is food (see EEA 2005), particularly because of its means of production (agricultural manufacturing processes), its distribution (global transport routes and commercial outlets), as well as the demand and the preferences for specific foods on the part of the consumers (orientation of product processing, choice and marketing). This case study deals with

---

24 | Personal translation of: [ist über] "Unterscheidungen strukturiert, die auch den Rahmen dafür bieten, wie konkrete Dinge in einer Praktik zu interpretieren und wie sie praktisch zu handhaben sind."

the everyday appropriations of more or less 'responsible' eating habits – analysed as an ensemble of plural ways of how people live different understandings of sustainability. This perspective makes recourse to the question of subject constitution by focusing on the diversity of everyday practices and the *governmental self-relations*. Here the *subject* – with its various self-technologies of alimentary reflexivity, which is unevenly developed and follows different priorities and constraints – is seen in a dynamic connection with its *discursive practices*, its more or less *implicit knowledge* as well as the *spatial materiality* of food itself (for the terms see section 5.1). The latter refers to the awareness and the practical attributions of meaning of the geographical origin as a relational context of food production. Implicit knowledge refers to classification systems for the ideal of "a 'good' diet/way of eating for our society" as well as to the selection criteria for food relevant in everyday contexts. Finally, relevant discursive practices comprise reasonings for and opinions on the significance of certain criteria in the choice of food, while the interplay between ideal and reality sheds light on different understandings of sustainability.

Sustainable everyday eating practices[25] are understood as a pragmatic set of decisions that will differ considerably depending on the "daily life that people lead"[26] (Kudera/Voß 2000), which in turn will have its very particular requirements determined by milieu-specific resources, gender relations, life stages and age (see Brunner 2007), as well as by divergent subjective values, priorities and general outlook on life (see Herde 2005). All of these are particularly significant in long-term observations (see Jaksche 2005). The approaches developed by Herde and Brunner have shown themselves to be especially helpful when discussing the three analytical pillars of sustainability – the ecological, the social and the economic – on the level of specific consumer practices, as they combine features of the consumed food with individual everyday-cultural practices.

The term of sustainability was not expressly mentioned in our surveys for methodological reasons: on the one hand, we wanted to avoid effects of social desirability in order to arrive at an understanding of emic food-related priorities and criteria of everyday action as well as of the spatial context relating to the chosen form of diet with its potential to shaping people's identity. On the other hand, the goal was to establish, without prejudging the outcome, whether 'responsible' food consumption is more personally, socially, ecologically, economically or geopolitically motivated. To achieve this, we first identified quantitative indicators for documenting possible food-related patterns of sustainability. This survey (University of Luxemburg, IDENT2 2012/2013 – quantitative survey) was

---

25 | Sustainable eating practices in general are for instance defined as *"appropriate to one's needs* and *adequate to everyday life, socially differentiated* and *wholesome, low-risk* and *environmentally sound"* (personal translation of: *"bedarfsgerecht* und *alltagsadäquat, sozialdifferenziert* und *gesundheitsfördernd, risikoarm* und *umweltverträglich"*) (Eberle et al. 2006: 1, italics in the original; see Sedlacko/Reisch/Scholl 2013; SDC 2009).
26 | Personal translation of: "Alltägliche Lebensführung."

supplemented in a second step with qualitative interviews (ibid. – qualitative survey) that aim to provide insights into the meanings and values behind these indicators. This in-depth approach was designed to ultimately reveal the everyday-cultural priorities, criteria, legitimations and consumption strategies in the field of food and eating practices – in short: the performative ways of subjectivation – in a perspective of spatial identifications.

5.2.1 Features of Sustainable Food Consumption

The quantitative indicators for lived patterns of sustainability that were developed are either connected to the individual dietary practices and assessments or directly to the characteristics of the consumed foods.

Knowledge about the Geographical Origin of a Selection of Foods Used on a Daily Basis

The product categories considered in the survey comprise beverages as well as meat and vegetable foods *used on a daily basis*[27] and available on the retail market, originating from international, regional, industrial or non-industrial production contexts, both from biological or conventional manufacturing, i.e. demanding a conscious decision on the part of the customer when there is a choice of several comparable products. We investigated the importance generally attributed to the 'geographical origin' of these foods – without introducing categories such as familiar *produits du terroir*, local producers, farmers' markets etc. which in media and advertising are connoted as convivial and vigorous symbols of authenticity and tempting delicacies (see Reckinger 2012b). What interested us more was the question whether we can assume that consumers reflect on the production contexts of commonly consumed foods and whether the knowledge about their origin also sharpens people's awareness of the conditions of food production as agriculturally and economically highly transformed consumer products with global implications – in short, the ecological, economical and social production costs of food. What understanding do consumers have of the entaglement of different major vested interests in the field of food production on which they could indeed bring their influence to bear via their consumer choices?

The interviewees' high rates of affirmation show that the geographical origin of food is important to them. However, the origin is systematically rated higher in Luxembourg than in the border area, apart from fruit juices, possibly because Rhineland-Palatinate is a fruit and fruit juice producing region, which already points to a cognitive shift in response behaviour from the general question of 'geographical origin' to the specific understanding of 'regional products', which is also evident in the interview material (see below).

---

27 | This draws on the website http://www.foodmap.lu, accessed 20.05.2012, which was created by the luxembourgish *Office national du Tourisme* and the *Ministère des Classes Moyennes et du Tourisme* and lists all regional producers subsuming them in product families.

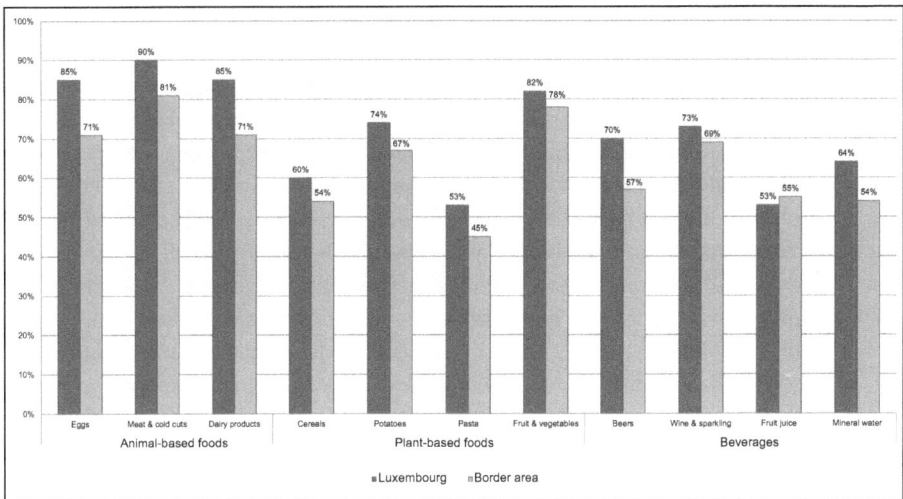

Figure 1: Is the geographical origin of the following foods important to you? Affirmation in percent (University of Luxembourg, IDENT2 2012/2013 – quantitative survey)

Statistically, the origin is considered most important for all animal products as well as for one vegetable category.[28] The former are subject to regulations and controls to meet specific standards of hygiene; trust, which consumers seem to associate with social and geographical 'proximity', plays an important role here. Fruit and vegetables, by contrast, is the food category which is constructed as the emblematic element of a 'healthy' lifestyle; its direct connection to agriculture, i.e. localization, seems to be self-explanatory. But this connection is also present for cereals, potatoes and wine[29] whose origin is, however, considered by the respondents as significantly less important. A product's strong symbolic charge therefore comes with a high degree of valuation of the knowledge about its origin.

Subjective Importance of Foodstuff Attributes

Following the *criteria of possible sustainability inherent to the foods themselves* emphasized by Herder (2005) und Brunner (2003), we also investigated the *subjective importance* that the respondents assign to these attributes.

---

28 | Meat and cold cuts: 83 % within the border area average; fruit and vegetables: 79 %; eggs: 76 %; dairy products: 75 %.

29 | This statement refers to the average of the population. As soon as more specific interest groups with typical preferences are considered (e.g. men and wine, see Reckinger 2012a), this balance shifts. The general principle, however, that the appreciation of a foodstuff increases proportionally to that of the knowledge of its origin and production context remains unchanged (see Reckinger 2011; 2007a; 2007b).

There is for instance a strong consensus that *seasonality* of fruit and vegetables is important (agreement in survey area: 79 %). The sections of the population that attach particular importance to this tend to be elderly people as well as women. In Lorraine the consensus on this question is significantly above average (87 %), while in Rhineland-Palatinate and Saarland it is below average (70 % respectively).

Fair trade as an indicator of a sensitivity for social justice and cultural diversity is seen as significantly less important, with more value being attached to it in Luxembourg than in the border area. The product group attracting the highest degree of affirmation is that of coffee and tea: in Luxembourg 61 % and in the border area 50 % of the respondents state that the fair trade attribute is important with coffee and tea, among them in particular older people and men. Conversely, 40 % of the respondents in the border area and 29 % in Luxembourg consider 'fair trade' in none of these products important. Also in the interviews, fair trade foods were seldom mentioned spontaneously; one person did not even know what it meant: "What do you mean? Products for the poor?!"[30] (female, 66, French, Luxembourg).

Finally, we compared per region the subjective importance of the sustainability indicators *from organic farming* and *from regional production* as well as the pragmatic-egocentric attribute *good value*. Here we see a marked difference between Luxembourg and the border area: while in the first sample, 'regional origin' is, almost exclusively, mentioned most frequently as being most important (apart from coffee and tea: 'good value'), in the border area, it was the item 'good value' that ranked first without exception. 'Regionality', however, features nine times[31] in second place in this sample, while 'from organic farming' is given four times as the second most important criterion.

In both samples, products from organic farming feature not higher than in second place (in total eight times), but mostly in third place (16 times), which suggests that dietary decisions oscillate primarily between the attributes 'regional origin' and 'price-quality ratio'. The interview material (see below) confirms this trend.

5.2.2 Interpretations of 'Responsible' Eating Practices

We were able to access everyday-cultural legitimations for a 'responsible' diet via an open-ended question in the qualitative interviews: "What do you consider to be a 'good' diet or a 'good' way of eating for our society? What does that mean for you?" In the following, this *ideal* is contrasted with the criteria and priorities relevant to daily dealings with food (*practice*): "What do you consider important when choosing the food you buy?" As we will see below, the results clearly show that the spatial context relating to the foods in question provides a meaningful

---

30 | Personal translation of: "Les produits pour les pauvres, c'est ça?!"

31 | In the border area, 'regionality' came in second place for the following foods: meat and cold cuts, dairy products, potatoes, pasta, beer, wine, coffee and tea, juice, mineral water.

identification; this point is discussed at the end of this section separately via the interview question "Do you consider the area from which your food comes to be important?".

Comparison of Dietary Ideal and Practice

In the analysis, the transcribed responses per interview question were coded according to argumentative units (see section 2.4) in order to bring out more or less transversal strands of argumentation in the material.[32] The topical complexes presented here deal in particular with self-referentiality (51 % of all arguments for the ideal and 36 % for the practice), as well as with the origin of foods (50 % for the practice and 28 % for the ideal).

When describing an ideal of 'good' diet/way of eating for society, interviewees relate to a self-defined norm that as a subjectification (identity options) is connected to possible modes of subjectivation (identity designs). Differences between individuals notwithstanding, the prominent self-referential statements show that a 'good' diet/way of eating "for society", as formulated in the interview question, was understood for the most part as 'good' diet/way of eating "for me". By contrast, self-referential considerations are somewhat less significant in those assessment and selection practices that focus on the origin of foods. Rejections comprise passive 'not giving it much thought' (which applies more to the ideal and suggests low relevance for everyday life) or active, explicit distrust (which occurs more frequently for the practice and points to a higher identitary significance). The influence of children in the household is in both questions the same (3 %); it can be rated positively as well as negatively. For instance:

"The kids have meanwhile all left home, so I don't need to buy stuff for the kids that's really not good for me"[33] (female, 48, German, Saarland).

Or the opposite:

"Recently, precisely because my kids asked for it, I prepare much more vegetables than I used to. Everything: uncooked, cooked and stewed vegetables"[34] (male, 42, Belgian, Wallonia).

---

32 | In the analysis of all qualitative statements, the percentages represent the proportional ratio of the individual arguments in the discourses between each other, and the large amount of low percentages show the broad range of issues that were relevant to the interviewees, since they were broached spontaneously.

33 | Personal translation of: "Die Kinder sind alle aus dem Haus mittlerweile, deshalb muss ich keine Sachen mehr für die Kinder kaufen, die für mich gar nicht gut sind."

34 | Personal translation of : "Ces derniers temps, parce qu'il y avait une demande de la part de mes enfants, je cuisine beaucoup plus de légumes qu'avant. De toutes sortes: des crudités, des légumes cuits."

In the following, the two patterns mentioned most frequently, i.e. self-referentiality and origin of foods, are discussed individually.

	Ideal of a 'good' diet for society	*Practice* of criteria in food choice
Ratios of degressive argumentational strands in the interview responses	Self-referentiality (51 %), among which:	Self-referentiality (36 %), among which
	Health-oriented nutritional value (14 %)	Low or moderate price (11 %)
	Balanced and varied (12 %)	Has to taste good (7 %)
	Has to taste good (7 %)	Fresh products (5 %)
	Home-prepared and -cooked (7 %)	Without chemical additives (3 %)
	Without chemical additives (6 %)	Health-oriented nutritional value (3 %)
	Less meat (3 %)	Home-prepared and -cooked (2 %)
	Fresh products (1 %)	Pleasure in the freedom of choice (2 %)
	Eating according to one's own culture (1 %)	Balanced and varied (1 %)
		Long shelf life (1 %)
		Personal testing of quality (1 %)

Figure 2: Argumentational strand "self-referentiality" in the responses to the comparative questions about the ideal of a 'good' diet for society and the practice of criteria in food choice (University of Luxembourg, IDENT2 2012/2013 – qualitative survey)

In the *self-referential* arguments which were developed in the answers to both questions, when discussed in terms of the ideal, health-oriented nutritional value as well as self-disciplining balance and variety were put forward as a priority – in line with what political campaigns have been calling for (see Reckinger et al. 2011). On the practical level, by contrast, nutritional value plays a very minor role and the aspiration to balance and variety, *a priori* appropriate and hedonistically realizable, is even less important. Instead, they are supplanted by the desire for a low or moderate price, i.e. a self-referential argument *par excellence* that ignores all processes in the food sector prior to the individual act of buying and merely aims at an individual cost-profit calculation, something that becomes evident in the often recurring expression "value-for-money ratio" (each time interpreted according to individual standards). In addition, the hedonistic-subjective expectation of good quality – empirically understood as tasty food – occupies a relatively high position in the otherwise rather normative catalogue of discussed food-related ideals. This is also given a certain amount of priority in the practical perspective and is linked to the three arguments of pleasure in the freedom of choice, the expectancy of a long shelf-life and the possibility to personally test the quality of the foodstuffs. In particular fruit and vegetables are handled for this purpose – but when other people are observed doing this in a shop it is considered unhygienic and inappropriate.

	Ideal of a 'good' diet for society	*Practice* of criteria in food choice
Ratios of degressive argumentational strands in the interview responses	Origin of foods (28 %), among which:	Origin of foods (50 %), among which:
	Regional products (11 %)	Regional products (15 %)
	Organic products (3 %)	Fair to the producer (8 %)
	Seasonal products (3 %)	Pollution through transport (5 %)
	Good products from one's own garden (2 %)	Mistrust towards organic farming (4 %)
	Better taste when origin is known (2 %)	Organic products (4 %)
	Mistrust towards organic farming (2 %)	Good products from one's own garden (3 %)
	Pollution through transport (2 %)	General sensitivity to origin (2 %)
	Problems with regional products (1 %)	Seasonal products (2 %)
	General sensitivity to origin (1 %)	Problems with regional products (2 %)
	Fair to the producer (1 %)	Better taste of regional products (2 %)
	Better taste of organic products (1 %)	Better taste of organic products (2 %)
		Better taste when origin is known (1 %)

Figure 3: Argumentational strand "origin of foods" in the responses to the comparative questions about the ideal *of a 'good' diet for society and the* practice *of criteria in food choice (University of Luxembourg, IDENT2 2012/2013 – qualitative survey)*

For the two comparative questions, the arguments concerning *the origin of foods* mention regional products most frequently (11 % for 'ideal' and 15 % for 'practice'). In the assessment and selection practices, further aspects come into play that relate to regionality: this involves "supporting" regional producers economically (whereby this frequently used verb suggests occasional acts of solidarity or clearing one's conscience rather than a continuous shopping practice) or taking personal responsibility in looking out for seasonality of the products. The fact that the latter attribute was, however, only rarely mentioned spontaneously does not contradict the quantitative data that showed a very strong consensus on this point, but confirms implicitly that seasonal food consumption takes place rather unreflectedly. Other statements include wanting to avoid long transport routes, but also preferring regional products because they represent a more trustworthy, local alternative to organic foodstuffs that are sometimes regarded with suspicion; "good products from one's own garden" receive an emotionally particularly positive rating. The recurring, relativating expression "but maybe I'm just imagining things" suggests partly an assumption without justification, i.e. implicit knowledge, which operates far more strongly via general confidence-building and representations than via cognitive channels. Distrust and approval of organic farming are more or less equally strong. The former refers either to deliberate misleading of customers, e.g.: "There are already surveys that say that much more organic food is being sold than produced" (male, 57, German, Saarland) or to pragmatic doubts about feasibility.

"It's practically impossible to produce organic food [...] The other day, I saw choppers spraying vines with chemicals. The wine grower who's got his vines right next to that vineyard, come on, he's not going to tell me he's producing organic wine, because even when there's only light wind he's going to get his share of that stuff!"[35] (male, 58, French, Lorraine).

For interviewees who, by contrast, attach importance to organically farmed food, it is primarily increased confidence that makes a difference, legitimized with stricter production and quality controls (in particular for eggs, meat as well as fruit and vegetables) – besides a subjectively claimed "better taste". Considerations about the geographical origin of organic foodstuffs, on the other hand, are rare, so that presumably little thought is given to environmental issues – for instance that a locally produced, conventional meat dish can have a smaller carbon footprint than an imported organically farmed vegetarian one (see Carlsson-Kanyama 1998). In that sense, the empirical material shows that the approval – or conversely – the

---

35 | Personal translation of: "C'est pratiquement impossible de faire du bio. [...] Je voyais l'autre matin encore des hélicoptères en train de balancer des produits sur les vignes. Celui qui est à côté avec ses vignes, il ne va pas me dire qu'il fait du vin bio, parce qu'avec un peu de vent, il en profite aussi!"

rejection of organic farming is far more often a self-referential profession of faith than a conscious decision for sustainable action.

Even though almost all of these arguments refer to the foodstuffs themselves, the analysis suggests an additional self-referential dimension also in the other topics discussed in the interviews. Thus long transport routes are not so much criticized because of high CO_2 output but rather for the long duration of transport that requires chemical treatment of otherwise perishable products, which is rejected by various interviewees. The same type of reasoning applies to the subjectively-hedonistically experienced "better taste" of food categories with a recognizable origin or from organic farming or regional contexts.

In short, the two main strands of arguments in the ideal and the practice of food-related choices refer to the *self* as well as to the *origin of foods*; in the case of the dietary ideal, the argumentation is primarily self-referential, while in the case of the practice, it is the origin of the foodstuffs that is foregrounded – but what ultimately shows through in both cases is a consistent and pronounced self-referentiality. Within this self-referentiality, comments about the food-related ideal primarily involve attributes for individual health promotion (with the sensitivity to a balanced combination of nutritional values often offset against flavour), while statements about the dietary practice emphasize cost-related criteria on the level of the individual household, followed by hedonistically oriented assessments.

Identifications with the Spatial Materiality of Foods

The tendency that arguments referring to the food sector are less relevant in the constitution of the subject analysed here than directly self-referential ones can be also be observed with the question about the *subjective importance of the geographical origin* of foods.

73 % of the directly elicited statements about origin emphasize its importance and thus the centrality of spatial constructions. But there are also cases of rejection (both verbalized indifference as well as mistrust – together 11 %) and self-referentiality (9 %). The self-referential arguments involve in particular the purely hedonistically motivated taste of foods, followed by requirements for freshness, for a low level of chemical treatment as well for the attribute "good value for money". In the end, taste is the decisive factor for eating decisions, even though it is often described in an unspecific and unsystematic fashion:

"I have to admit that there's a sauce from Australia that I like very much. I know it's a sauce that may have travelled some 15,000 km, but I just like this sauce, so I'm going to buy it [...] But if it's about buying leek, OK, I'd prefer to get my leek from the farmer around the corner rather than one that maybe comes from Italy. In that case, I might actually pay attention [to the origin]"[36] (male, 44, Belgian, Wallonia).

"When I drive down this road here [...] and there's someone selling fresh-picked strawberries, of course I'll buy them. Because their quality is usually better than what I get in a shop, where they have them coming from Spain or wherever. They may be fifty cent cheaper, but then they already go bad after just one day in the fridge. But in general I don't really pay attention to these things"[37] (female, 48, German, Saarland).

These interview passages also show that purchasing decisions are very differentiated depending on the foodstuff and individual hedonistic preference, but far more unreflected – and at the same inconsistent and unsure – regarding their production context.

But the argument chiefly advanced for the subjective importance of origin shows that the majority of interviewees equate "origin" with "regionality" (62 %), if one considers all the motifs of statements on regionality combined (regional products: 23 %; intention of buying regional products: 15 %; better taste of regional products: 13 %; problems with regional products: 8 %; fair towards the producer: 3 %). Despite this striking numerical and discursive prominence of regional products, their approval is far more moderate in terms of *content*. On the one hand, this becomes evident in the *potentialities* that are mentioned in this context; be it a simple *intention* which as a concern is not crucial enough to be followed up consistently (the expression "we try..." appears frequently here) or be it that an intention cannot be carried out due to specific *problems*: not all food categories can be produced locally; regionally produced foodstuffs are not always easily recognizable; even though it would be desirable to support local producers, these are said to be hardly able to work economically due to "European" guidelines and regulations. Some examples:

"We do try, mind you. [...] It' always better to buy seasonal vegetables, and not strawberries in winter, for instance. Of course. But if there was a super bargain ... I don't know, melons in winter – I don't think that would happen very often – then I can't guarantee you that we wouldn't buy them anyway, just because we know that this melon has travelled 1,000 km

---

36 | Eigene Übersetzung von: "Je ne vous cache pas, j'aime bien une sauce qui vient d'Australie. Je sais que c'est une sauce qui a fait peut-être 15,000 km, mais j'aime bien cette sauce-là, donc j'achèterai cette sauce. [...] Mais pour acheter des poireaux, OK, je préfèrerais acheter le poireau qui vient de la ferme d'à côté que celui qui vient peut-être d'Italie. Donc là, je vais peut-être regarder."

37 | "Wenn ich [...] hier die Straße herunterfahre und da steht einer mit frisch vom Feld geernteten Erdbeeren, kaufe ich die, ganz klar. Weil die meistens von der Qualität her besser sind wie wenn ich in den Laden gehe, und da habe ich welche, die aus Spanien kommen, oder sonst wo her. Die sind dann zwar fünfzig Cent billiger, dann habe ich sie aber auch einen Tag im Kühlschrank und sie sind schon hinüber. Aber generell gucke ich nicht danach."

5. Space and Identity Constructions through Everyday-Cultural Practices 263

by plane and produced a lot of carbon dioxide pollution. I think, at least for me personally, that this ecological mentality is not all that ingrained yet. But at least we're aware that one should buy seasonal and local products, if possible. [...] Maybe with vegetables, the origin is often printed on the package, but with other pre-packed things, like cornflakes, you don't know whether they're from the USA or whether they were produced in the Netherlands or at the factory round the corner"[38] (male, 44, Belgian, Wallonia).

"One should really promote [regional products]. Maybe one could play the Greater Region system in some way or other? I mean, subsidizing local products that are consumed locally. [...] A little north of Metz there's a village, it's called Gorze, and until three months ago, the only raw milk cheese of the region was produced there – the *Tomme de Gorze* – which was sold in 15 or more shops in Metz on the market and in some supermarkets. The other day, I asked for *Tomme de Gorze* and at the counter they said: 'No, it doesn't exist anymore.' [...] The producer decided to quit because he had to meet the European standards. [...] He couldn't afford to [...] continue producing his cheese. So now there's no longer any *Tomme de Gorze* that was produced some 15 or 20 km from here"[39] (female, 44, French, Lorraine).

On the other hand, meat and dairy products in particular (especially the Luxembourg brand *Luxlait*) as well as fruit and vegetables (often associated with seasonality) are mentioned in connection with regionality. The reasons for these

---

38 | Personal translation of: "On essaie quand-même [...]. C'est toujours mieux d'acheter des légumes de saison et de ne pas prendre des fraises en hiver, par exemple. Evidemment. Maintenant, s'il y a une super-promo sur... je ne sais pas moi, un melon en hiver – je ne pense pas que ça arrive très souvent –, je ne vous garantis pas qu'on ne le fera pas, parce qu'on a dans l'idée que le melon a peut-être fait 1,000 km en avion et que ça pollue beaucoup en CO^2. Je pense, en tout cas pour ma part, qu'on n'a pas encore cette mentalité écologiste très, très ancrée. Mais en tout cas, on a conscience qu'il faut acheter des produits de saison et des produits locaux si possible. [...] Peut-être pour les légumes, il est souvent marqué la provenance, mais pour d'autres produits préemballés, vous achetez des cornflakes, vous ne savez pas s'ils viennent des Etats-Unis ou s'ils ont été produits en Hollande ou dans l'usine d'à côté."

39 | Personal translation of: "Mais il faudrait réellement promouvoir... [...] On pourrait peut-être faire un truc d'ailleurs de la Grande Région, hein ? C'est-à-dire, voilà, on met une espèce de subvention aux produits locaux consommés localement. [...] Il y a un village un peu au-dessus de Metz qui s'appelle Gorze qui fabriquait jusqu'il y a trois mois le seul fromage au lait cru artisanal du coin qui s'appelait la tomme de Gorze, qui était vendu dans une quinzaine, peut-être plus, de points de vente à Metz, au marché, dans quelques supermarchés etc. [...] Là [...], j'ai demandé la tomme de Gorze et mon fromager, il m'a dit: 'Non, ça n'existe plus.' [...] Le monsieur a décidé d'arrêter parce qu'il devait se mettre aux normes européennes [...]. Il n'a pas eu les moyens [...] pour continuer à produire son fromage. Voilà, donc, il n'y a plus de tomme de Gorze qui était donc à 15, 20 kilomètres d'ici."

preferences are given hesitatingly and it is particularly with the generalizing judgements that the national context is instrumental in building trust:

"With ham [...] we prefer to buy products from Luxembourg rather that any from Belgium or France or Italy, because I think these [local] products are just as good, and you also know ... OK, you don't know everything, but at least I'm pretty confident that these are handled in a decent and clean way. Something you can't be sure about with products from elsewhere"[40] (male, 64, Luxembourger, Luxembourg).

"Five or six years ago there was a reportage [*Envoyé Spécial*] about Spanish vegetables, I'll never eat Spanish vegetables again in my life! [...] And I'll be on the alert, because [...] when you hear how they go about it, [...] with those masses of pesticides and chemicals they put on them, to make the vegetables grow all inflated, no! And the stuff has no taste whatsoever, no taste whatsoever! [...] Now I try buying French, if it's not too exaggerated"[41] (female, 49, French, Lorraine).

A number of interviews reveal the influence of informative and critical TV programmes whose information is not absorbed in a very nuanced fashion and which form the basis for generalized judgements that have a long-term impact on practices. In these cases, scepticism often concerns chemical contamination in conventional agriculture, but also labels and certificates in the organic and fair trade sector (which reduces willingness to pay a higher price for such foodstuffs). What is invariably mentioned is the individual sensory check via the taste (in the two last quoted examples "just as good" or "no taste whatsoever") or the opposite, i.e. that an individual sensory check is not possible (for instance that one cannot detect any difference in taste between organic foods and others from conventional farming). Interestingly, this mistrust refers to organic farming *versus* conventional agriculture, understood as binary opposites, but almost never to regional products whose identification as 'local' seems to leave them 'untouched' by these production contexts. In cases of doubt, they are not confronted with self-referential and generalized mistrust; instead, specific problems are addressed in

---

40 | Personal translation of: "Wann et ëm Hame geet [...], dann huele mer éischter eis Lëtzebuerger Produkter, wéi aus der Belsch oder aus Frankräich, oder aus Italien, well ech fannen déi Produkter si genau sou gutt, an et weess een och, bon et weess een net alles, mee ech menge mol zumindest ze wëssen, dass dat anstänneg a propper behandelt gëtt. Wat een anerwäerts net ëmmer sou genau weess."

41 | Personal translation of: "Il y a cinq, six ans, ils ont fait un reportage [à *Envoyé Spécial*] sur les légumes espagnols, de ma vie, je ne mangerai plus jamais un légume espagnol! [...] Et je fais attention, parce que justement [...], quand on nous explique comment c'est fait, [...] avec le nombre d'insecticides, de produits qu'ils mettent pour les faire gonfler et tout, non! Et en plus ils n'ont aucun goût, ils n'ont aucun goût ! [...] Et maintenant j'essaie, quand c'est pas trop exagéré, j'essaie d'acheter français."

a more reflected and empathetic way. Only when regional products are discussed for their subjectively perceived "better taste", are they expressed in unequivocally positive and emotionally charged terms, e.g.: "The local products, and they are also the best!" (female, 51, Polish, Luxembourg) or:

"-For which reason do you prefer produce from the producer, as you say? -The taste! -So it's the taste and not the place of origin? -Oh yes! And the quality of the meat. You notice the difference between a piece of lamb that you can buy at the *Carrefour* [supermarket] [...] and one which I buy 500m down the road from the local farmer. No comparison, absolutely no comparison!"[42] (male, 58, French, Lorraine).

5.2.3 Conclusion

This case study has focused on constitutions of the subject in daily dealings with an individually interpreted 'responsible' diet, with particular attention to the specific self-relations behind the discursive practices, the (implicit) knowledge mobilized in the process and the attributions of meaning of the consumed foodstuffs' geographical origin. These appear in particular as hedonistic-individual subjectivations which only in the context of ideal *versus* practice, elicited on a contrastive basis, show a correlation with subjectifications for the promotion of health – but noticeably few overlaps with those regarding more broadly conceived sustainability concerns. This means in effect that a 'responsible' diet is interpreted on the level of individual identity as 'appropriate for the maintenance of one's own health' at the most, and rarely as a collective identification with ethically and politically motivated action. Also with arguments that refer explicitly to the food system in general and the geographical origin in particular, it is in the end the inherent self-referentiality that is decisive for shaping everyday practices. The geographical origin of foodstuffs, particularly in the form of regionally produced products (whatever size that region may have), has in the subjectivations shown itself to be a category that generates the most identity and trust, compared to the forms of organic farming and conventional agriculture, which are perceived as being unrelated to the former and as oppositional to each other. However, this prioritization is, again, subject to the price-quality ratio, individually regarded as crucially relevant.

In order to pinpoint plural yet daily practiced understandings of sustainability, food consumption was presented as an interface of social, cultural and institutional contexts, by focusing in particular on the interviewees' practices and sets of argument, which are additionally influenced by more general, partly competing

---

42 | Personal translation of: "-Et pour quelle raison préférez-vous les produits du producteur, comme vous dites? -Le goût! -Donc c'est surtout le goût et pas la provenance? -Ah oui! Et la qualité de la viande. Vous voyez la différence entre un bout de mouton que vous allez prendre chez *Carrefour* [...] et puis celui que je prends 500 m au dessus dans la ferme. Ça n'a rien à voir, rien à voir!"

social discourses on 'good' nutrition, health, ecology etc. The attention to the "daily life that people lead"[43] (Kudera/Voß 2000) highlights the potential for action as well as for inhibition within a combination of various constraints that take effect through the interplay of different areas of everyday life. The analytical sensitivity for the interviewees' specific, practicable prioritizations aims at an understanding that considers those aspects of the polysemic concept of sustainability that are relevant to daily eating practices and reveals food-related modes of governmental reflexivity in border regions.

5.3 Gender Spaces

Julia Maria Zimmermann and Christel Baltes-Löhr

Gender-specific attribution and appropriation of spaces is traditionally seen as constituted along binary lines: the man is assigned the exterior space, the public sphere of work and economy, but also the geographical space, and foreign realms. The woman's domain, by contrast, is the interior space, the private sphere at home or else the virtual space of relationships (see Wucherpfennig 2010). Both sexes appropriate the spaces attributed to them. In processes such as these, both the subject and the spatialized materiality is transformed. This creates genderized 'regions' in the subjects' living environment as well as spatialized subjects of a gender discourse.

Within a pluridimensional concept of identity in which identity markers are seen as intersectional, we define 'gender' as a social construction that manifests itself in its dimensions as a physical, psychological, social and sexual disposition and is considered to be modifiable as well as plural (see Baltes-Löhr 2014). The actors are actively and discursively involved in the construction process and find themselves in an interdependent relationship of attribution and appropriation.[44] In much the same way that we have defined gender, we posit an understanding of 'space' that defines space as a materiality (physical space), as a social space, as an abstract, virtual or experienced space (see also section 2.2). Space, too, is considered to be modifiable and plural.

In this case study, we will examine the attributions actors use to create spaces through discursive-performative acts, the spaces appropriated thus and the effects that attribution and appropriation processes in turn have on subjects.

While the boundary between the genderized spaces is also permeable to some degree (see Baltes-Löhr 2000: 515), it nevertheless has an unmistakeable reality. Thus the interviews conducted in the context of the present case study (University of Luxembourg, IDENT2 2012/2013 – qualitative survey) show significant gender-

---

43 | Personal translation of: "alltägliche Lebensführung."

44 | When in the following we speak of 'women' and 'men', it should be understood that we are referring to representatives of subject forms and not to pre-social 'natural' entities.

specific connotations with regard to attribution and appropriation of spaces, as well as in the relation between interior and exterior space. Even so, the empirical results also indicate a heterosocial interstice, a 'border region' which is attributed to both women and men. With the help of the gathered quantitative data (University of Luxembourg, IDENT2 2012/2013 – quantitative survey) we will therefore examine whether gender-specific attributions and connotations can be deduced from public spaces. The selected spaces, eating and drinking places, places of physical exercise and open-air places are marked by complex and partly ambivalent materializations of a spatialized gender discourse. The study clearly shows that public spaces are for the most part attributed heterosocially, i.e. cannot be construed as being either specifically female or male regarding the presence of one gender. There is nevertheless a subliminal genderization at work indicating that certain spaces tend to be perceived as 'predominantly male' and others as 'predominantly female', and that gender-specific norms of behaviour and perception are connected to them. In a further step we will, proceeding from the evaluation of qualitative interviews, analyse the construction of genderized interior and exterior spaces in terms of their attribution of responsibility and competence (interior space) as well as the threat they constitute (exterior space). What becomes clear here is that the domestic interior space is connoted as mostly female and defined by women. What also becomes clear is that there is a tendency for the exterior space to exclude women under certain conditions, e.g. depending on the time of day, or on the way women move around in the exterior space, i.e. excluding them by turning it into a potentially dangerous space that can offer them no safety whatsoever. In this instance, diagnosing public spaces as heterosocial stands, to a certain degree, on shaky ground in terms of quality. As a result, the conclusion of this paper reaches contradictory findings suggesting that the binary division of space for the sexes has in part become muddled and disrupted. This disruption can, however, be interpreted politically as a gender-neutral liminal space by a situative deconstruction of the subject form of 'gender'.

5.3.1 Genderized Spaces

Using standardized questionnaires, we established which spaces respondents think are frequented predominantly by men and which predominantly by women or by both gender groups in equal measure. The specified spaces constitute exclusively public spaces that according to Wucherpfennig (2010) belong to the category of the male-connoted exterior space, while women tend to be associated with the interior space involving the raising of children, reproduction of sociability and maintaining one's personal network. In the following, we will examine in how far these materializations of a bi-spatial gender discourse apply.

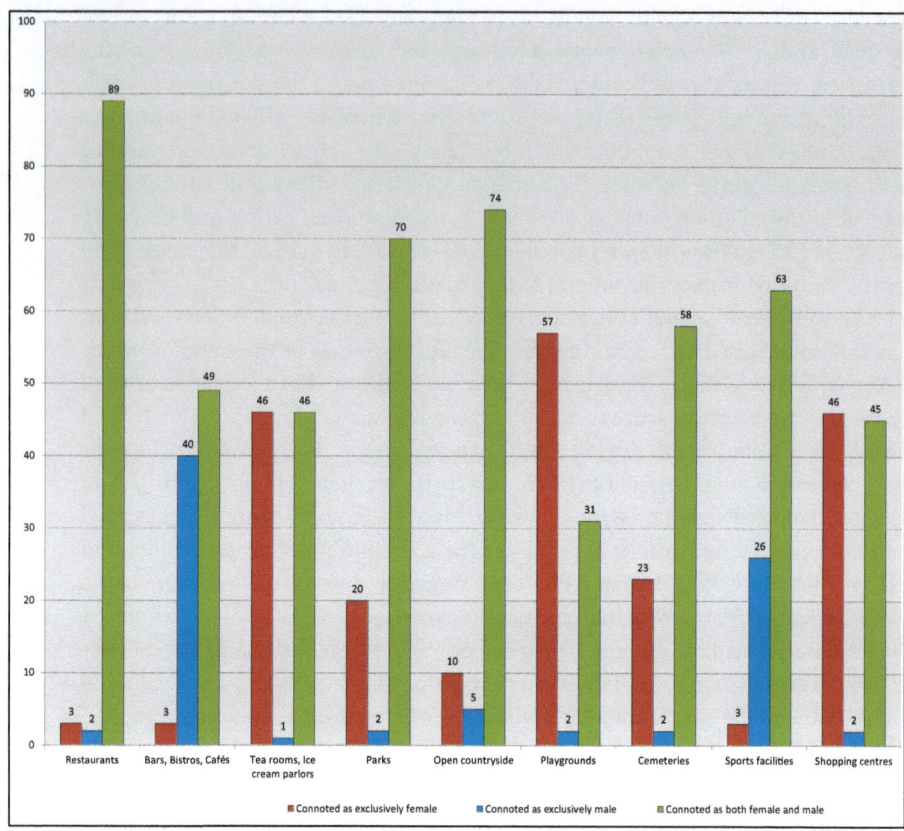

Figure 1: Gender-specific attributions of public spaces in percent (University of Luxembourg, IDENT2 2012/2013 – quantitative survey)

Places of Public 'Reproduction'[45]:
Places of Personal Network Maintenance

Restaurants, bars/bistros/cafés as well as tea-rooms/ice cream parlours[46] are establishments that provide restoration. But since these are in the public space and are only devoted to the consumption of food – the actual reproductive work, the preparation of the dishes, is as a rule invisible in these spaces – their original significance, and with it their respective genderized connotation, has broadened.

---

45 | The term refers to the private reproduction of the individualized domestic management attributed in modern times to the female sphere.

46 | The original German word here is *Konditorei*, a pastry shop where one can buy cake and pastry to take away or enjoy on the premises with coffee or tea. There is no direct equivalent in English, but 'tea room' is close enough, particularly in its function as a social place for predominantly female customers.

As Fig. 1 shows, restaurants are generally regarded as heterosocial places, while cafés, bars and bistros as well as tea rooms and ice cream parlors are connoted almost equally frequently as typically male or female spaces and as heterosocial spaces. These results can be explained with the fact that the mentioned spaces as a rule are not frequented by hungry individuals but specifically by groups and thus also serve personal networking purposes. Here we can distinguish three different gendered forms of personal networking: the afternoon coffee klatsch with cake is considered a traditional space of female homosociality (see Setzwein 2006: 46f.) and its publicly accessible equivalent are tea rooms and ice cream parlors. The network maintained here is of a private nature. The traditional space of specifically male homosociality is the bar, which is, however, frequented in the evenings. Bistros and cafés can also become places of male networking, but usually have a work-related connotation and are typically frequented during business hours. Thus the time of day also determines whether spaces are connoted as male, as female, or as in the following case, heterosocially. Because even though the evening visit to the restaurant is also used for maintaining one's professional network, it is generally more about cultivating private, mixed-gender contacts. According to the now outdated code of etiquette, in the evening women leave the interior space only in male company (see Schrott 2005). This applies particularly to the visit to the restaurant which thereby becomes both a 'male', because public, but also a 'female', because private, space (of social relations).

Nature: Domesticated and Wild Spaces

The questionnaires enquired about four open-air spaces: open countryside, parks, childrens' playgrounds and cemeteries. These are spaces that treat nature in different ways. Open countryside is a space where at the moment no discernible cultivation is taking place, which is therefore apparently little touched by human civilization. Parks by contrast are an example of domesticated, organized nature without being assigned a specific function. Childrens' playgrounds and cemeteries, on the other hand, show a clear functionalization: the systematic reshaping of nature here serves the aim of creating a specific social space. The childrens' playground is a space devoted to care work, and the cemetery too symbolically serves the purpose of maintaining family relationships which are renewed or confirmed by tending the graves of deceased loved ones. According to Würzbach (2004: 54), both spaces are connoted as female, while the park, depending on its use, can be connoted as both male and female. The open countryside symbolizes 'foreign lands', to be conquered by male pioneers and unfit to be entered by women (see ibid.). From this, one can conclude that in the gender-specific topography women occupy the more *cultivated* spaces and merely interact with domesticated, *socialized* nature.[47]

---

[47] | Another example for this is horticulture, in particular the flower garden by the house. But Würzbach (2004: 54) defines the house implicitly as a 'natural' space, in contrast to the civilized and civilizing public space.

Our results permit us to partly question the suggested categorizations. For the interviewees, the open countryside is more of a gender-neutral place, as are parks. Childrens' playgrounds are seen, unsurprisingly, as chiefly female, but also heterosocial spaces. Cemeteries are regarded as a heterosocial space with a tendency towards female connotation (see Fig. 1).

Corporalities: Working on Oneself

The body of the subject is both a constituent part of the space, a medium of appropriation of space as well as something appropriated and reshaped by spaces (see Wastl-Walter 2010: 68ff.; Strüver 2010). With regard to gender, working on one's bodily self is inextricably connected with the (im)possibility of appropriation of space. While the exercise of the male body is aimed at strength, stamina, speed – in short, at all those characteristics of the body which allow it to appropriate as large a space as possible – precisely the opposite is the case with the female body: it is supposed to be 'beautiful', attractive to the eye of the male beholder, not necessarily strong. The female body is the adornment of the interior space, not the instrument of the exterior space. The physical component of gender-specific subjectification is suggested in the questionnaire when dealing with sports facilities and shopping centres: sports facilities as spaces for exercising the body with the aim to optimize it in is functionality can be interpreted as male-connoted spaces, shopping centres with their clothes and shoe shops, perfume and jewellery departments, by contrast, as places of aestheticization of the body and thus as female-connoted spaces. Kerstin Dorhöfer (2000) furthermore suggests interpreting shopping centres as semi-public spaces of transition that have offered women since the 19th century access to spaces outside the private sphere, without doing anything to bringing about a change to their exclusion from the political-industrial city. They therefore find themselves beyond the interior space without however creating a liminal space in the sense of opening up gender-specific spheres. According to our findings these statements need to be differentiated (see Fig. 1): sport facilities are regarded by the interviewees as heterosocial spaces, even though with a strong male connotation. Shopping centres by contrast are seen in equal parts as female and heterosocial spaces: similar to bars/bistros/cafés and tearooms/ice cream parlors, contradictory discourses seem to overlap here.

The evaluation of the quantitative data shows that the discursive classification of public spaces along traditional gender patterns is paradoxically something that seems to exist and not exist at the same time. On the one hand, most of the respondents make no gender-specific distinction in the attribution of public spaces. Nevertheless we can find, besides the heterosocial intepretation by the majority, partly significant gender-specific attributions. What we also see is that spaces are significantly less frequently classified as male than as female (see Fig. 1). The public space, thus the conclusion of the evaluation, is no longer male, as in the traditional spatial order of the sexes. It is primarily heterosocial, with a tendency towards feminization. However, even though the evidence provided by the data is unambiguous, this conclusion should be treated with caution. Social geographers have suggested that in the course of the 20th century there has been a change in the function of public spaces and that in particular the downtown area has acquired an increasing significance as a privatized space of consumption, while the power centres of the state and the economy have been withdrawing from the city centres to segregated areas (see Friedrich 2010: 64). Even though this change of urban function did not necessarily have any consequences for gender-specific subject construction, women could thus become the typical users of urban space. However, female connotations have by no means displaced the male connotations of public space, but in the majority of cases have merely joined the existing ones. One can assume that the respondents based their answers on their own experiences and simply perceived women more vividly even while the sexes were possibly present in equal measure. The higher visibility of women would then not necessarily be due to a female appropriation of the space but to an irritating and therefore conspicuous deviation from the familiar norm. Finally, the quantitative evaluation of a space does not reveal anything about its qualitative interpretation. In order to decide whether and how spaces are constituted in a genderized way, it is therefore necessary to also include the results from the qualitative interviews.

5.3.2 My Home is my Castle – Female Responsibilities and Competences in Interior Spaces

The attribution of responsibilities of the domestic interior space – particularly the care activities – is defined by the respondents predominantly as female-connoted. The responsibility and competence of women is hardly ever questioned, but also not specifically brought up. In the qualitative interviews, the actual distribution of roles among the heterosexual couples frequently tends to be mentioned *en passant*. In this way groceries done by the woman turns into a 'professional' activity: "Hmm, my wife sometimes drives all the way to Trier to do the professional groceries", whereas her real job as a teacher is ironized as a trip into the exterior space: "My wife played the teacher for a few years at the school here"[48] (male, 77, German Luxembourger, Luxembourg).

The following example reveals a strategy of changing the grammatical subject in the course of the conversation, something that can be observed repeatedly in the interviews. Actual responsibilities in the interior or exterior space are concealed by using a "we", suggesting a commonality instead of the actual distribution of tasks. It is more coincidentally, in another context, that the separation of roles is 'confessed':

---

48 | Personal translation of: "Hmm, meine Frau fährt schon mal extra nach Trier, um den Berufseinkauf zu machen [...]", "Meine Frau hat hier ein paar Jahre lang Lehrerin gespielt an der Schule."

[about good food] *"We could still cook, nowadays that's no longer the case."* [italics by the authors]
[later, about his multicultural attitude] "I eat everything though, I don't care where. I can do Japanese, Chinese, Russian, I don't mind, I eat everything.
-But you cook in the Saarland style?
-No, not me, my wife"[49] (male, 49, German, Saarland).

Among the female interviewees, responsibility for the interior space is mentioned particularly when there are children living in the household. When this responsibility is no longer there it can be experienced as a relief. Cases where the man takes over the care activity are rare. The following citation therefore 'deviates' somewhat from the norm:

"No, I'm the one that does the groceries. The house, the garden, the admin, the kitchen, the groceries, I do all that"[50] (male, 42, Belgian, Wallonia).

The interior space is not limited to the home proper but also comprises those places necessary for maintaining the care activity. Thus, even though supermarkets are public spaces, they tend to be female-connoted. In the area covered by the survey, both men and women tend to move around mainly by car. Non-mobility can even turn out to be a privilege for men:

"And he [the son-in-law] also doesn't provide for himself, his wife's got to get the groceries and lug them home all on her own [...] a car is unnecessary [he says]. Even though they have two small kids"[51] (male, 49 German, Rhineland-Palatinate).

In the majority of cases men are attributed the competence for vehicles and technical things in general:

---

49 | Personal translation of: *"Wir konnten immer noch kochen, heutzutage ist das net mehr so. [...] Obwohl, ich esse alles, das ist mir egal wo. Ich kann Japan, China, Russland, das ist mir egal, ich esse alles. -Aber kochen tun Sie saarländisch? -Nee, ich net, meine Frau."*
50 | Personal translation of: *"Non, les courses, c'est moi qui m'en occupe. La maison, le jardin, l'administration, la cuisine et les courses, c'est moi qui fais ça."*
51 | Personal translation of: *"Und er [der Schwiegersohn] versorgt sich auch nicht selber, seine Frau muss alles beischleppen [...] ein Auto ist überflüssig [sagt er]. Obwohl sie zwei kleine Kinder haben."*

"And when I'm running short [referring to the petrol in the tank], I say: 'Hey, dear, I'm almost in the red.' And mostly he's got a full jerrycan anyway. [...] I hate getting petrol. I'm also too stupid to get the fuel tank lock opened"[52] (female, 44, German, Saarland).[53]

Here the subjectivation is linked to a drastic diminishment of one's own technical competence and legitimizes the separation of spheres in the form of spaces of competence. In the case of the family's groceries, however, it is the women that are attributed competence, while men are assigned an accompanying role: "The women say: 'I'm the boss', yeah, I always trot along and am allowed to push the trolly"[54] (male, 49, German, Saarland). What becomes clear here is that the interviewee does not feel as an equal partner, but an outsider who is "allowed" to do certain things, because the women, who are the ones who are actually in charge and competent, give him the permission.

That men experience the female-connoted sphere of care and relationship as something outside their realm of competence and potentially menacing is suggested in another context in the facetious answer to the question where men feel anxious: "At the shrink in a relationship counselling!"[55] [laughs] (male, 57, German, Saarland). The public space is rarely mentioned by the interviewees in a specifically gender-connoted way. This is consistent with the finding expressed above that it is frequently perceived as a gender-neutral space. The following excerpt from an interview suggests, however, that public spaces, even if they are mostly frequented by women, remain male spaces of competence:

"I've been twice to the theatre here in Trier with a good [female] friend of mine. The *Traviata*, that's one of my favorite operas. The first time I was there with this friend of mine, and she didn't know the first thing about opera, a young lady, I have to admit, I wanted to acquaint her a little bit with things cultural, and she really loved it!"[56] (male, 62, German, Rhineland-Palatinate).

---

52 | Personal translation of: "Wird es bei mir knapp [gemeint ist das Benzin im Tank], sag ich: 'Ei Schatz, ich bin fast im roten Bereich.' Und meistens hat er dann sowieso einen befüllten Kanister. [...] Ich bin so ein Tankmuffel. Ich bin auch zu dämlich, um mein Tankschloss aufzukriegen."
53 | We could, however, detect no principal gender difference regarding the interviewees' refueling habits (see section 4.7).
54 | Personal translation of: "Die Frauen sagen: 'Ich bin der Chef', ja, ich geh immer mit und darf den Wagen schieben."
55 | Personal translation of: "Beim Psychotherapeuten in einer Paarberatung!"
56 | Personal translation of: "Ich war mit einer guten Bekannten zweimal hier in Trier im Theater. Die *Traviata*, das ist eine meiner Lieblingsopern. [...]. Das erste Mal habe ich die Bekannte dabeigehabt und die hat noch nie was mit Oper zu tun gehabt, eine junge Dame, muss ich sagen, ich wollte sie mal ein bisschen in die Kultur einweisen, und sie war so was von begeistert!"

The exterior space is here presented as a cultural space, of culture in the singular *notabene* and exclusively understood as 'high culture', as a hegemonial interpretation of the actually multi-layered term. The "acquaintance with things cultural" or subjectification occurs via an already subjectivated subject which in this case presents itself, not quite coincidentally, as male towards a female object: in the interviewee's narrative the term for his friend changes from the sexually more neutral "acquaintance" (*"die Bekannte"* in German) to "(young) lady" (*"junge Dame"*) – a term that can be read in an ironically detached but also pejorative way. Interpreted this way, a 'lady' is a female person that requires guidance by a 'gentleman' at all times. The use of the anachronistic terms gentleman/lady thus reproduces a gender relationship that is defined on different levels as dichotomous and asymmetrical.

5.3.3 Living in Dangerous Spaces – Women at Risk

We have established that the presence of women in the public space on its own says nothing about the qualitative reading of this space. The above citation suggests that despite female presence it is primarily men who in actual fact appropriate the public space, while, even though women also occupy it, a true spatial subjectification in the sense of an attribution of competence occurs chiefly in the personal interior space. It was also indicated that a possible feminization of the public space depends on the time of day: the visit to the tea room or the children's playground suggests a daytime use, while come evening, the public space once more becomes male territory (this also includes male accompaniment of women). We will now examine in how far the public space can even become a space of perceived threat or fear for women.

In principle, threat can be experienced both in exterior and in interior spaces. In actual fact, women are more frequently victims of violence in the interior space at the hands of family members, partners or acquaintances (see European Commission 2010: 55; Ruhne 2011: 30f.). Nevertheless, it is almost exclusively the exterior space that is considered potentially dangerous and is constructed as such (see Becker: 62ff.). This also becomes evident in the interviews.[57]

Often the interviewees experience the nocturnal public space as a space of threat:

"I'd say there certainly are [places where women feel threatened]. Dark corners, generally speaking. Not here, not in Saarburg, but in Trier, Luxembourg, specially around the station, it's so labyrinthine there. I wouldn't want to wander about there alone after dark"[58] (male, 49, German, Rhineland-Palatinate).

---

[57] | Only few interviewees commented on domestic violence in connection with gender-specific spaces of threat.

[58] | Personal translation of: "[Orte, an denen sich Frauen bedroht fühlen] gibt es schon. So allgemein, dunkle Ecken. Bei uns nicht, Saarburg nicht, aber Trier, Luxemburg, gerade

5. Space and Identity Constructions through Everyday-Cultural Practices

So this interviewee considers "dark corners" not only threatening for women but also for himself. Not infrequently the first impulse is to not specifically differentiate the threat in terms of gender, which leads to a logical break in the narrative when the interviewee involves himself directly in the narration and creates a certain ambiguity about whether he is reliving the threat in the sense of a self-identification as a women, or whether he regards the threat all the more serious for women because he is also experiencing it himself as a man. In a few cases, the existence of a threat is denied altogether, but eventually, after further inquiry, admitted, which in some extreme statements even turns into a kind definition of the female condition:

"For a woman it's, well, it's... it's normal. Well, I mean, normal, no, it's not normal, but women, true. We, we don't have, how shall I say, the same rights. Yes, but we're more at risk than men" [59] (female, 66, French, Luxembourg).

Threat as female normality may be inexpressible, but it remains, according to the testimony of this interviewee, a reality. Another statement is notable in that it presents women not as potential victims of crime but rather as a "problem".

"For a woman, that's quite typical, really. Everywhere you have corners where it's dark and someone could be lying in wait for you. [...] The same with paths in the woods or in residential areas that peter out into the woods, if you walk through the park at night, that's where women are the problem on account of getting assaulted one way or another"[60] (male, 29, German, Saarland).

Without saying it in so many words, the interviewee is suggesting that women who at night go to less frequented public places basically have to reckon with the possibility of becoming victims of sexual assault. This kind of culture of 'victim blaming', which partly blames the violence committed against women on their behaviour, or at least sees it as a contributing factor, can also be found in other statements – also from women:

---

am Bahnhof, da ist es so verwinkelt, da würde ich nicht unbedingt gerne alleine im Dunkeln hingehen."

59 | Personal translation of: "Pour une femme, c'est, voilà, c'est, c'est normal, c'est. Enfin, c'est normal non, c'est pas normal, mais les femmes, c'est vrai. Nous, nous n'avons pas les mêmes, comment dirais-je, pas les droits. Si, mais, nous sommes plus en danger que les hommes."

60 | Personal translation of: "Also als Frau eher so ganz typisch, da gibt es überall Ecken, wo es dunkel ist und einem einer auflauern könnte [...] Also auch Wege im Wald oder Wohngegenden, die in den Wald übergehen, wenn man da jetzt nachts im Park lang läuft, da sind Frauen eher das Problem wegen Übergriffen in irgendeiner Form."

"OK, of course, sometimes you have to mind how you dress. If you don't want to get molested you shouldn't wear a miniskirt. You shouldn't provoke people, that's simple common sense"[61] (female, 28, French, Saarland).

A male interviewee links the same 'improper' dress to a specific public space and a specific time as well as to an 'inappropriate' way of occupying the space:

"After all, I don't need to go to the station at ten o'clock at night and then strut about in a miniskirt… at that time the incentive to get yourself raped is of course higher than when you go there at ten in the morning"[62] (male, 29, German, Saarland).

In contrast to the previous citation, the danger is potentially not that of being molested, but rather of being raped. Furthermore the danger is not named as such but phrased as an 'incentive' for the perpetrator, which delegitimizes the victim's perspective which the use of the first person singular might have suggested. As with the above reference to "dark corners", here too it is suggested that at night the public space is no space for women. That this means discursively limiting women's freedom of movement is only rarely mentioned:

"That's a question you can ask yourself in any instance of aggression, but with sexual violence against girls there is unfortunately often the tendency to put some of the blame on the victim, and that as a direct reaction, mind you […]"[63] (male, 42, Belgian, Wallonia).

A threat for men is sometimes denied outright or even ridiculed by interviewees of both sexes: "Maybe in the hospital, when the doctors come at them with their syringes, but otherwise…"[64] (female, 34 Jahre, Belgian, Luxembourg). Or: "Listen, I'm six foot tall, I weigh 110 kilos, I've learnt to defend myself, I'm really not scared to go anywhere!" [ironic laugh][65] (male, 42, Belgian, Wallonia).

---

61 | Personal translation of: "Gut, klar, manchmal muss man aufpassen, was man anzieht. Wenn man nicht belästigt werden will, muss man nicht unbedingt einen zu kurzen Rock anziehen. Man muss die Leute nicht provozieren, das ist menschliche Vernunft."

62 | Personal translation of: "Ich muss ja nicht mehr um zehn Uhr nachts zum Bahnhof gehen und dann mit Miniröckchen durch die Gegend stolzieren … dass natürlich dann der Anreiz, vergewaltigt zu werden, höher ist, als wenn man morgens um zehn Uhr da hingeht."

63 | Personal translation of: "C'est une question qu'on peut se poser dans le cas de n'importe quelle agression, mais dans le domaine des agressions sexuelles sur les filles, on a malheureusement souvent tendance à un peu culpabiliser la victime, et ça comme conséquence immédiate […]."

64 | Personal translation of: "Krankenhaus vielleicht, wenn die Ärzte mit der Spritze auf sie zukommen. Aber ansonsten…"

65 | Personal translation of: "Ecoutez, je mesure un mètre nonante-deux, je fais cent dix kilos, j'ai appris à me défendre, je n'ai pas vraiment peur d'aller nulle part! [ironic laugh]."

When narratives feature men becoming victims of violence it is qualitatively different from that against women; it comes from 'outside' and so acquires the savour of the inevitable or even of war.[66] According to the statements of some of the interviewees, the violence that women fall victim to is considered as basically preventable by women dressing appropriately, moving around in company or simply avoiding certain places at certain times of the day. If they still enter the space of threat they should behave in an adequate – i.e. invisible – way, or, if possible, become 'masculine':

"I remember when we were students, I had a friend who was really very masculine. And she was very very wary. She said: 'when I go home alone, when I'm obliged to go home alone, I dress up as a guy.' She put on a hooded jumper, she was very tall, she sort of did the swagger... And that worked great! I think that's really a good technique! [amused laugh]"[67] (female, 33, French, Lorraine).

5.3.4 Conclusion: Degendered Transitions

The evaluations of the quantitative and qualitative surveys have shown that men and women perceive neutral spaces as well as spaces with specific gender attributions differently. In the first case, we are dealing with an appropriation of spaces (subjectivation), while in the second case it is subjectification processes (attributions) that take effect. In both cases spaces are genderized and have a genderizing effect on the actors. When spaces are brought up as a subject matter, this takes place in a gender-specific framework of activity. What is remarkable here is that it is mostly female spaces of activity that are brought up (groceries, domestic work and child care), while male spaces of activity are only rarely mentioned, primarily referring to things technical. Thus it is still women that seem to be the ones in charge of the household, particularly when children need to be taken care of. The role of men is limited to that of an assistant, what Baltes-Löhr (2006: 189) refers to as threshold activities.

However, taking into account which spaces are not invoked in a genderized way – these include the realms of work, business, leisure time not explicitly examined in this study – and bearing in mind the attributions of spaces made by the interviewees, which in their clear majority have revealed no gender-specific connotations, then we can say that women are definitely present in the public

---

66 | The narrative about crime featuring proletarian male migrants in so-called social hot spots is common in the entire survey area and deserves separate attention. We do, however, wish to emphasize that it is defined intersectionally and also specifically gendered.

67 | Personal translation of: "Je me souviens, quand on était étudiantes, j'avais une amie qui était très masculine, en fait. Et elle, elle était très méfiante. Elle disait: 'Quand je rentre seule, quand je suis obligée de rentrer seule chez moi, je me fais passer pour un mec.' Elle mettait un sweat avec une capuche, elle était assez grande, elle faisait une démarche un peu..., et ça marchait bien! Je crois que c'est une bonne technique, en fait [amused laugh]!"

space. But not in all areas are they represented equally strongly, and they are certainly not as strongly represented as men are. The quality of the appropriation of space also differs greatly. In particular, we should not overlook the mechanisms of displacement of women from the public space that have manifested themselves in the discourse around spaces of threat. Here it is suggested that women who dwell in certain 'spaces of threat' have to reckon with being the target of violence. There is no discursive perception of a comparable threat for men. A – precarious – safety of some sorts is created when women make themselves 'invisible' in these spaces. The latent or overt culture of 'victim blaming' leads to women in effect being denied the right to safety, because 'they only have themselves to blame'. But in this way women are also denied an equal appropriation of public space.[68]

Despite the paradoxical and precarious visibility of women in the public space, it is not an exclusively male one, but rather a heterosocial space. 'Gender' can here at least partially lose some of its significance as a structural and subject category. The individuals are no longer addressed as gender-specific subjects and no longer subjectivate themselves exclusively as a genderized subject: here 'gender' is situatively deconstructed. This is, however, only successful if the public space is also understood as a political space of the deconstruction of identity. This is not an entirely novel idea (see Degele 2010). In many respects it is already being put into practice. For instance the explicit appropriation by homosexual, trans- and intersex persons – e.g. on Christopher Street Day or IDAHOTI (*International Day against Homo-, Trans- and Interphobia*). But so far this is as yet more of a programme than everyday reality. We can nevertheless establish that the boundaries between the male and the female subject position in the public space are becoming increasingly blurred, creating a deconstructivist and complex borderland of encounters (see Baltes-Löhr 2003: 96f.).

5.4 Identity Constructions and Regionalization: Commemoration of the Dead in the Treveri Region (2nd/3rd century AD) – Family Identities on Tombstones in Arlon

Andrea Binsfeld

Family and kinship are the fundamental social orders of Graeco-Roman societies. Families can fulfil diverse functions within these societies: they can be life partnerships and economic entities, they transmit values and traditions and integrate future generations into society. Families are not rigid structures but

---

68 | For Ruhne (2011: 208f.), the insecurity with which women move around in the public space – and which has been instilled into them – is a symptom of the exclusion of women from the public space and of the persistence of a gender-specific separation of spheres.

rather subject to change. By adapting to the general economic, social, political and cultural conditions, families equip subjects with a specific family identity (Bührmann/Schneider 2008: 68, footnote 27). Representations of families thus provide an ideal field of research for examining the question of subjectification and subjectivation as well as the visualization of identities. The representations of families on tombstones in the Roman provinces show in an exemplary way which models these recur to (subjectification), which pictorial formulas are used, how they are modified and which self-conception of the subjects they express (subjectivation).

This case study will primarily examine identity constructions using the example of family representations on Roman tombstones of the *civitas Treverorum*, i.e. the region that encompasses what is today Luxembourg and the neighbouring areas in Belgium (Arlon), France and Germany (Trier). The analysis of a few selected examples aims at identifying the processes of self-definition, the subjectivation techniques and the identity constructions embedded in them. The centre of focus here are practices of remembering and the material form given to them in tombs. These artefacts are part of a visual discourse that generates identities and spaces. This contribution in this way connects two important fields of research: the construction of social and cultural identities taking the example of tombstones as well as research on the Roman family. The focus of the analysis will be on the Arlon tombstones of the 2nd and 3rd century AD that are compared with representations of various regions, in particular Metz and Trier. The paper builds on the work of Hannelore Rose and Henner von Hesberg who are also conducting research on family representations on Gallo-Roman tombstones. Rose (2007: 207ff.) however examined in particular the Metz tombstones, while von Hesberg (2008: 257ff.) analysed general family representations and role models on tombstones in the northwest provinces. The areas of family representations and the construction of social and cultural identities are dealt with in number of other studies this case study draws on. Yasmine Freigang's (1997) research on the tombstones of the Gallo-Roman civilization in the Moselle region has been of fundamental significance for the aspect of self-representation in Gallo-Roman society. In subsequent years, a series of colloquia were also devoted to this particular subject (see Fasold 1998; Heinzelmann 2001; Walde 2007). The romanizing and transformation processes of the Treveri region and the northern border provinces have furthermore been subject of independent research projects (see Haffner/von Schnurbein 2000; Scholz 2012).

For the research on the Roman family, the *Roman Family Conferences*, originally organized by Beryl Rawson, were of great importance. The *Companion to Families in the Greek and Roman World*, published in 2011 by Rawson, covering a broad range of topics, methods, disciplines and sources and also treating aspects of the remembrance culture of household and family, constitutes a comprehensive repository of hitherto conducted family research.

Generally, one can detect a tendency towards studies on the regional level: after the examination of house and family had concentrated in particular on the family in Italy and Rome (see for instance Huskinson 2011: 521f.; Dasen/Späth 2010), it is now the provinces that are receiving more attention. An example for this is the volume published by Michele George with the programmatic title *The Roman Family in the Empire. Rome, Italy and Beyond* (2005a). In this context, the tombstones in particular are very much focus of attention, because especially family images offered the local elites "an effective image through which they could display their social ascendancy and lay claim to a public profile, albeit one conditioned by practical and cultural limitations" (George 2005b: 37f.).

Behind the questions of subject constitutions through subjectifications and subjectivations there is the fundamental question of Romanization and acculturation, since Romanization research devotes itself to the problem to what extent Roman precepts were received by the population of the conquered territories. Notions about the cultural transfer between Romans and the local population in the provinces have changed greatly since the Romanization concept was developed in the 19th century, a process particularly associated with Theodor Mommsen and Francis Haverfield (see Rothe 2005: 1ff.). Initially the focus was on the aspect of subjectification. Romanization was understood as a one-way adoption of Roman culture. More recent research has been focussing on the process of subjectivation, that is on diversity and heterogeneity; points of interest are now the local, variety and plurality (see Deppmeyer 2005: 57ff.; Hingley 2010: 54ff.; Hodos 2010: 9; Scholz 2012: 1ff.; Schörner 2005: Vff.).

5.4.1 Representations of the Roman Family

Examples from the urban Roman context and northern Italy, such as the tomb relief of the family of the Servilii from the 1st century BC (see Fig. 1) in the Vatican Museum in Rome (Kockel 1993: 14f.), show on which models, i.e. on which "patterns of the desirable" (Reckwitz 2008: 140) the cases I will be dealing with here could build on.

Figure 1: Tomb relief of the Servilii, Rome; Museo Gregoriano Profano inv. 10,491 (Kockel 1993: plate 51b)

The inscription indicates that this is a family of released slaves, generally referred to as freedmen or freedwomen.[69] The family members are strictly frontally aligned. The inscription and the attribute, i.e. the *bulla* the boy is wearing around his neck, serve to highlight in particular the son of the family: the inscription refers to the boy twice explicitly as son, the *bulla* identifies him furthermore as the first free-born of the family (see ibid.: 53). Each family member is assigned a function: Hilarus is explicitly addressed as father (*pater*), Sempronia Eune as spouse (*uxor*). As slaves the Servilii had neither the right to marry nor start a family. It is therefore particularly important to them to record and visualize through inscription the civil rights they have acquired with their release. In their self-representation the freedpersons appropriate pictorial forms typical for a family of Roman citizens: the *toga*, the representation as matron and the free-born offspring (see Huskinson 2011: 526f.). The men indicate their status by wearing the *toga*, while women wear the *tunica* and as outer garment the *palla*, which in some cases covered the head. In the *pudicitia* gesture, the women reaches into the *palla* and pulls it slightly in front of her face, suggesting the virtue and modesty of a Roman matron. The grave relief also reflects the particular pride of the freedpersons of their free-born son. The visual representation thus serves not so much private but public purposes. Even though this type of representation of the family is particularly frequently chosen by freedpersons, it is not limited to this group (see George 2005b: 37ff.; Zanker 1975). In addition, the number of depicted family members can be extended by further individuals, as an example from Ravenna from the 1st century AD shows: besides the couple with their child, we also see the women's sister together with her husband as well as two freedpersons (see Pflug 1989: Cat. No. 8).[70] In this case, the tombstone visualizes the complex structures of the Roman family. The term *familia* is thus not limited to blood relations but also comprises slaves and freedpersons who could be granted the right to be laid to rest in the family tomb. Affiliation to a family is connected with rights and duties, such as burial. In this sense the Ravenna tomb also represents a public document, since it visualizes this affiliation. Here too, the documentary character is underscored by the rigid frontality. Another form of family representations can be found on sarcophagi, in particular childrens' sarcophagi that

---

69 | Corpus Inscriptionum Latinarum (CIL) VI 26410: P(ublius) Servilius Q(uinti) f(ilius) Globulus f(ilius), Q(uintus) Servilius Q(uinti) l(ibertus) Hilarus pater, Sempronia C(ai) l(iberta) Eune uxor (personal translation: "Publius Servilius Globulus, son of Quintus, the son, Quintus Servilius Hilarus, freedman of Quintus, the father, Sempronia Eune, freedwoman of Gaius, the spouse").

70 | CIL XI 28: P(ublius) Arrius P(ubli) f(ilius) Montanus, Mocazia Helpis uxor, P(ublius) Arrius Pollux; Q(uintus) Decimius Dacus, opt(io) de (triere) Pinnata, Moca(z)ia Iucunda u(xor), P(ublius) Arrius P(ubli) l(ibertus) Primigenius, P(ublius) Arrius P(ubli) l(ibertus) Castor (personal translation: "Publius Arrius Montanus, son of Publius, Mocazia Helpis, the spouse, Publius Arrius Pollux, Quintus Decimius Dacus, Optio of the trireme Pinnata, Mocazia Iucunda, the spouse, Publius Arrius Primigenius, freedman of Publius, Publius Arrius Castor, freedman of Publius").

illustrate the child's life history. Even though at first sight 'private' aspects seem to predominate here, such as the parents' mourning over their deceased child, the selection of visual themes transmits values and defines norms and areas of function. The mother's purview is birth and child care (together with the wet nurse); particular importance is placed on the representation of the child's education. Cases where the active involvement of the father in the education is depicted are the exception, such as helping the son with putting on the *toga*, symbolizing the transition from child to young man. While these representations certainly offer the possibility to express emotions, such family cycles can also be embedded in the representation of the *pater familias*' achievements and public work for society and thus be a part of the public presentation (see Huskinson 2011: 528ff. and 534ff.). It is however doubtful in how far these portraits represent the actual composition of the family, in particular because on the majority of tombs only one child is depicted, mostly a son. This suggests that the purpose of these family representations was not a truthful reproduction of a nuclear family or an extended family, but rather primarily the representation of rights, values and social status (for issues of demographic research, see Krause 2003: 23ff.; Huskinson 2011: 533; Huebner 2011: 73ff.). The importance of the family as an identity-generating institution appears particularly clearly by the grave reliefs of freedpersons. By having themselves represented as citizens, sons, parents and spouses, they furnish themselves with a specific family identity.

5.4.2 The Arlon Tombstones

Whether and how these identity models were in turn adopted by the population of the northwest provinces of the Roman empire and shaped self-conceptions there is something I will examine by taking a closer look at the tombstones of the Roman *vicus* Arlon. The *vicus* of Arlon was created after the conquest of Gaul in the course of the development of the road network under Emperor Augustus or under the governorship of Agrippa. Arlon was located at the intersection of the roads Reims-Trier and Metz-Tongeren. As with the Roman freedpersons, we also have to ask ourselves here in what way the population of the province of Gaul absorbed influences of Roman civic life. A number of selected examples representative of the most important subject models will serve to illustrate which aspects predominated in the representation of the Arlon families. These examples all date from the 2nd and 3rd century AD, i.e. from the time of consolidation of Roman rule in Gaul.[71]

Professional Success and Wealth
In the first example, the so-called *Pilier aux jeunes époux* (see Musée archéologique 2009: No. 57), a couple is depicted (see Fig. 2a and b).

---

[71] | It is not possible to provide here a comprehensive catalogue-style overview of family representations on tombstones. For this, readers are referred to the publications by Mariën (1945), Lefèbvre (1978) and the current museum catalogue (Musée archéologique 2009).

5. Space and Identity Constructions through Everyday-Cultural Practices

The woman is wearing a local variety of the cloak: a "cloak-like shawl"[72] (Freigang 1997: 302) that is put around the shoulders and over the arm so that the shawl hangs down in front in a point. The man is also wearing an 'indigenous' form of the *tunica* and the *paenula*, i.e. a cloak with a V-collar and hood.[73] They are turned to each other, the woman is holding a cloth, the *mappa*, in her hand, and a small bottle, a *balsamarium* which is closed with a cork, while the man is holding a scroll. On the right side, there is a dancer with *krotaloi* (castanets), nude but for a cloak that is sliding off her shoulders. Such depictions from the Dionysian realm reflect the aspirations of the tomb owners for an eternal life in happiness after death – a motif very common in funerary art from the 4th century BC onwards until the late imperial era (see Andrikopoulou-Strack 1986: 115ff.). On the left side, one also sees a nude woman putting a wrap around her body below her breast. She has deposited her clothes next to her. Very similar to these depictions are for instance bronze statuettes showing goddesses with breastwraps, like the Venus from Hinzerath-Belginum in the Hunsrück[74] or the statuette from the museum Burg Linn which originates from a 3rd century grave from Krefeld Gellep.[75]

On the front side of the tomb of the *Pilier du drapier* (Musée archéologique 2009: No. 109; Mariën 1945: 30ff., No. A1; Freigang 1997: Trev 80; Lefèbvre 1978: 71ff., No. 47), three persons are depicted: a woman between two men (see Fig. 3).

The woman is wearing a full-length *tunica* with tassles, over it a shawl; in the left hand she is holding a *mappa*, in the right a round glas bottle with a long neck whose shape coincides exactly with the sphere-shaped *balsamaria* such as they also occur frequently as burial objects (see Goethert-Polaschek 1980: 8). The *balsamarium* suggests wealth and luxury, while the the *mappa* characterizes the woman as a matron. The two men wear knee-long tunics lined with tassles and a *paenula*. The man on the left is holding a *codex* made of wax tablets in his hand, as well as a stylus, the man on the right a purse (*marsupium*), items pointing to a successful activity in commerce and trade. Since the heads of the three individuals represented are badly damaged, we lack clues for drawing conclusions about the relationship between them (a father and a couple?). What is also lacking here are body language and explanatory gestures. Possibly one has to imagine the scene as in an example from Metz: on the tomb stele for Marcus Maturicius Maternus and Marcianus, a woman is also flanked by two men. According to the inscription the wife Mariana had had the monument erected for the two male deceased, perhaps

---

72 | Personal translation of: "Mantelartiges Umschlagtuch."
73 | The Latin terminology draws on Freigang 1997. For the problems regarding terminology see Rothe 2009: 34ff.).
74 | Present location: Rheinisches Landesmuseum Trier, see Massow 1940.
75 | My thanks go to Franziska Dövener of the *Centre National de Recherche Archéologique de Luxembourg* for pointing this piece out to me. Present location: Museum Burg Linn, Krefeld, see Pirling 1986: 73 and Illustr. 48.

father and son.[76] She is turned to the younger man on her left, while the man on her right is characterized as an older man by his beard style and wrinkles (see Rose 2007: 216).[77] The sides of the Arlon tomb show scenes from the life of a cloth merchant: the right side features a coach ride and a scene of transport, the left two scenes involving a cloth probe and a payment.

Figure 2a: Tomb depicting a young couple (Le pilier aux jeunes époux), IAL GR/S 028 (© Institut Archéologique du Luxembourg, Musée Archéologique d'Arlon); Figure 2b: Left side of the tomb pillar depicting a Venus (© Institut Archéologique du Luxembourg, Musée Archéologique d'Arlon)

A comparison of the two examples with the Roman models reveals distinct differences. The subjects cannot primarily be said to represent Roman citizens – instead of *toga* and *palla* they are wearing local dress. As in the case of the Roman examples, the realms of man and woman are clearly separated and precisely defined by the attributes: wealth and beauty are attributes of the woman, men by contrast are assigned to the world of business, the public-legal sphere and the area of education. This is conspicuously visible in an example from Trier, the so-called 'parental couple pillar' (see Fig. 4): the left side shows the woman engaged with her morning toilet, assisted by four female servants who are most probably slaves. The right side shows the master hunting and conducting his business. The slaves' number, their activity and their well-groomed appearance also serves the purpose of visualizing their master's and mistress' wealth.

---

76 | Année Epigraphique (AE) 1976, 479: M(arco) Maturi[c]io M[ate]rno/et Marcia [no(?)---]/Mariana Mari[---]/defunctis.
77 | Metz, La Cour d'Or, inv. 75.38.60; found in Metz, Ilot-St. Jacques.

5. Space and Identity Constructions through Everyday-Cultural Practices   285

Figure 3: Tomb depicting two men and a woman (Le pilier du drapier, previously: Le Marchand de draps), IAL GR/S 047 (© Institut Archéologique du Luxembourg, Musée Archéologique d'Arlon)

Figure 4: Parental couple pillar from Neumagen, Rheinisches Landesmuseum Trier Nm 184a (© Rheinisches Landesmuseum Trier, photo: Th. Zühmer)

But the role of the woman is here also geared towards representation of status: in these two examples from Arlon, her duties as a mother were obviously not deemed worthy of specific illustration, in contrast to the Roman models. However, Roman pictorial formulas such as the *balsamaria*, the representation of Venus and motifs from the Dyonisian sphere are used to visualize the socially appreciated values and norms. The way how subjects deal with the Roman precepts becomes clear above all in the clothing, which is interpreted sometimes as a Romanized variant of a Gallic costume (see Freigang 1997: 304ff.) and sometimes as a genuinely indigenous garb that 'modernized' under the influence of Romanization (see Rothe 2009: 54ff.). In their adaption of themes, such as education, the Arlon memorials can refer to Roman models. But in contrast to the latter, the focus here is on economic aspects of self-representation: in its self-conception the family presents itself primarily as a unit of economic provision.

Family Bond

But familial attachment as well as the importance of marriage and children can also be found in Arlon. They inform the self-conception of the subjects as, for instance, in the case of the monument of Attianus (see Musée archéologique 2009: No. 52; Mariën 1945: 78ff., No. D3; Lefèbvre 1978: 46ff., Nr. 22; Freigang 1997: Trev 82). Here the inscription helps us to identify the depicted persons (see Fig. 5).

It indicates that Matrausus had the monument erected for his wife and son. The inscription says: *Secundius Attianus et Censorinia Matrausus (or M. Trausus) co(n)i(ugi) (et) fili(o) def(unctis)*[78] (AE 1986: 497). The closeness between mother and son is underlined twofold: mother and son are holding right hands. In addition, the mother is resting her left hand on her son's shoulder. A man, characterized as an older man by his beard, is standing on the right, slightly turned to the group. The son is holding a scroll in his left hand, the father the *codex*, which here has a handle, and the stylus. The sides show a philosopher and a muse – a representation modelled on urban Roman sarcophagi to visualize the deceased's claim to education. There too, the deceased are portrayed in the circle of philosophers and muses.

The main side of the *Pilier au satyr* shows two couples (see Musée archéologique 2009: No. 48; Mariën 1945: 104ff., No. E2; Lefèbvre 1978: 38f., No. 17; Freigang 1997: Trev 81) (see Fig. 6); the men are wearing a knee-length *tunica* and above it a *paenula*, the women a long *tunica* and a shawl. The left couple is turned to each other and extending their right hands to each other, the man is holding a scroll in his left hand, which can be interpreted as a sign for a claim to education, as a testament scroll, a marriage contract, a document of citizenship or as a professional

---

78 | Personal translation: "Secundius Attianus and Censorinia. Matrausus [or: Marcus Trausus] for the deceased spouse and the deceased son."

attribute (for the interpretations, see Freigang 1997: 313), the woman is holding a *mappa*. The second couple is also turned to each other but without joining hands. The woman is holding a *balsamarium* in her hand; the man's left hand is damaged; possibly he also held a scroll in his hand. Above the two couples a length of cloth has been draped on which the shanks of two cupids are resting. The cupids have been interpreted as an indication of the emotional tie of the couples (see Rose 2007: 217). The sides portray a dancing naked bacchante and a satyr.

*Figure 5: Tomb of Attianus, IAL GR/S 022a
(© Institut Archéologique du Luxembourg,
Musée Archéologique d'Arlon)*

Figure 6: Tomb representing two couples (Le pilier au satyr, previously: Les mariés et leurs témoins), IAL GR/S017 (© Institut Archéologique du Luxembourg, Musée Archéologique d'Arlon)

The scene is interpreted as the portrayal of a wedding with witnesses (see Musée archéologique 2009: 101) or, somewhat less boldly, as two couples with however only one pair joining hands. It is also conceivable that two generations of married couples could be united in one scene here (see Rose 2007: 216f.). For this tomb too, there is an equivalent in Metz, which is unfortunately very badly damaged, but it shows a very similar arrangement of figures.[79]

A representation equally unusual for both Gallo-Roman and Roman monuments can be found on the *Pilier de la femme à l'anneau* (see Musée archéologique 2009: No. 53; Mariën 1945: 41ff., No. A.4; Lefèbvre 1978: 48ff., No. 23; Freigang 1997: Trev 83; see Fig. 7): it shows a couple, the woman is turned to the man; she is holding a ring between thumb and forefinger. She is wearing a girdled *tunica* and a cloak, the *palla*, which she has pulled over the back of her head. In the other hand she is holding a small box. This is not the kind of local costume that we have seen in the other examples from Arlon discussed here, but the typical costume of a Roman matron.

---

79 | Metz, La Cour d'Or, inv. 95.10.1; found in Metz, St. Nicolas.

Figure 7: Tomb of the woman with the ring (Le pilier de la femme à l'anneau, previously: La dame à l'anneau), IAL GR/S 023 (© Institut Archéologique du Luxembourg, Musée Archéologique d'Arlon)

The woman with the ring is not the only example for the adoption of Roman costume in the provinces. It is, however, notable that in Arlon only women are portrayed – if at all – in Roman dress, while the men choose exclusively local garb (for further examples, see Rothe 2009). The ring, which is here unmistakably presented to the partner, could point to an engagement or a marital relationship and not only to a symbol for the wealth of the deceased, since the ring is handed over to the woman at the engagement (see Iuvenal 6,27; Digesta 24,1,36; Plinius, Naturalis Historia 33,12). The woman has put the cloak over the back of her head, exactly as in representations of weddings. The man, bearded, is wearing a *tunica* and a *paenula*, in the left hand he is holding a wax tablet and a stylus. The sides are also interesting: the right one shows a young man in a *tunica* and a *paenula*; he is holding a scroll in his hand. The left side is less well preserved; here a young woman was portrayed – maybe the children of the couple?

5.4.3 Conclusion

The representation of the nuclear family or a slightly expanded family circle on the Arlon tombstones serves to visualize the self-image exhibited to the outside world. However, the limitation to the nuclear family reflects not so much the true (archeologically documented) everyday culture, but is used as a visual motif for 'family' and for wealth. We have to assume that only wealthy families were able to afford to have a tomb erected and have their sons run a household of their own, instead of living with their familiy in their father's house (see Huebner 2011: 73ff.). The family presents itself via the tombstones as a nucleus of economic success. Nevertheless, particularly in the case of the Arlon tombstones, there is no lack of emotional gestures, references to an affective attention between married couples, parents and children. This relatedness has not only been understood as an expression of a local style, but also of emotional attachment, additionally underscored by cupids, as in the case of the four-figure stele, as well as erotic motifs (nude dancers, portrayal of Venus) (see Rose 2007: 216f.). In this sense, the portrayal of Venus with the breast wrap as a lateral relief of the stele of the young couple (see Fig. 2) is possibly not only to be interpreted as a positive expectation of the beyond or a general symbol of beauty, but also as an indication for the relation between the partners of the couple. Also the affection for the children is visualized through body posture and gestures, as we have seen in the example of the mother joining hands with her son and putting her other hand around his shoulder (see Fig. 5). Our comparative examples from Rome and northern Italy also portray children in the circle of the family, but these portrayals have more representational purposes and more or less ignore the aspect of emotional attachment between parents and children. In the Gallic province, by contrast, privacy acquires a public value (see Rose 2007): children symbolize the future and the hope of their parents. This is, again, particularly evident on the reliefs of the freedpersons which repeatedly emphasize the civic status of their children by wearing the *bulla* and by referring to the sons as *filius*, as the example of the Servilii clearly shows. That also in the case of the tombstones of *Gallia Belgica* the hope of the parents rests in the children is illustrated by a stele in Metz[80]: mother and son are holding hands – the attachment between son and father is shown in the fact that the son is portrayed as a miniature of his father; he is wearing a *tunica* and *paenula* and has, like his father, grasped the wax tablets at the handle. The wax tablets repeatedly appear on tombstones in scenes of monetary transactions, as an indication of successful professional activity.[81]

---

80 | Metz, Musées de Metz, inv. 75.38.58; found in Metz, Ilot-St.-Jacques; see Freigang 1997: 432f., Med 199, tab. 41. AE 1976, 478: [---]iolae Silvici filiae Sacuri[us ---]/[---]s uxori et Sacer fil(ius) vivi posuerunt.

81 | Metz, Musées de Metz, inv. 75.38.58; found in Metz, Ilot-St.-Jacques.

As in Rome, men and women were assigned to different spheres. It is, however, notable that men never let themselves be portrayed in the *toga*, but rather in a local costume, which does not necessarily mean that they did not possess Roman civic rights. This is disproven by the Metz stones (whose inscriptions have frequently survived) which indicate that the portrayed did indeed possess civic rights. From this we can conclude that there was no obligation to wear the *toga*, that on the contrary the portrayed consciously and self-assuredly presented themselves in local dress. In this the tombs of Arlon and Metz differ from those of Trier: the percentage of individuals letting themselves be portrayed in Roman dress is in Trier, the main city of the *civitas Treverorum*, significantly higher than in Arlon, the second urban centre of the Treveri region (see Rothe 2009: 114, Illustr. 12) and in Metz (see Freigang 1997: 301ff.). The difference between the two main cities of the neighbouring *civitates*, Metz and Trier, is indeed remarkable. Also for Metz, one would expect a higher percentage of *togati*, but here too local dress predominates.

It has already become clear here that, on the one hand, Roman values and Roman pictorial formulas are adopted, but that these show regional variation. Even if the Arlon monuments primarily show a local form of dress and not the *toga* as an emblem of the *romanitas*, one nevertheless cannot interpret the choice of the local dress as an act of dissociation. What predominates in the Arlon monuments is the civil sphere of craft, commerce and trade and not the public-political realm represented by the *toga*.

Besides the representation of family wealth and professional success, wedding and marriage as well as a close attachment between family members are themes that inform the self-conception of the families of the Arlon tombs. These elements determine the social identity of these families. They use pictorial motifs that are clearly taken from the Roman visual repertoire: family, marriage, muses, philosophers, Venus, Dionysian pictorial themes, and, partly, female dress. Also attributes such as glass *balsamaria* are typical Roman burial objects. The motifs are Roman, Roman social values are adopted – but not exclusively. In Arlon, a very unique manner was found in the way these motifs were used and varied, finally developing a visual language which is an expression of a distinct local cultural identity. The creative way of dealing with the Roman models shows that these merely constitute choices and not obligatory norms. What we have here then is not a unilateral transfer of culture, which would correspond to the notion of subjectification or the old notion of Romanization, but instead a differentiated way of treating pictorial motifs. In their manner of expression, the Arlon monuments are much closer to the tombs of Metz than to those of Trier, where Roman motives still predominate. What emerges here are cultural spaces – through regionally shaped and visually represented subjectivation processes – that need not necessarily overlap with the territorial borders of the *civitas Treverorum*.

5.5 WORKERS' HOUSING ESTATES AND THEIR RESIDENTS: CONSTRUCTIONS OF SPACE AND COLLECTIVE CONSTITUTION OF THE SUBJECT

Laure Caregari

Scholarly and popular publications on the subject as well as common usage in Luxembourg employ the term *Kolonie*[82] as a synonym for workers' housing estates. In France and Belgium they are known under the term *cité ouvrière*, in Germany they are referred to as *Arbeitersiedlung*.[83]

Workers' housing estates owe their existence to the mining and smelting of iron ore in the southwest of Luxembourg, the Minette, which during the industrial take-off since the 1880s increasingly attracted international, national and local enterprises. After the First World War, these merged or were incorporated – if it was German capital – into other companies (see Quasten 1970; Trausch 2000). The most important representatives of company housing in Luxembourg included the following industrial enterprises: ARBED (*Aciéries Réunies de Burbach-Eich-Dudelange*), GBAG (*Gelsenkirchener Bergwerks A.G.*), HADIR (*Hauts Fourneaux et Aciéries de Differdange-St. Ingbert-Rumelange*).

The enterprises' aim in establishing workers' housing estates was to settle a controllable 'workers' force' in close proximity to the plants and in this way minimize the contact with 'company-damaging' practices and discourses. At the same time, this system provided workers and their families with convenient accomodation. The deliberately planned short walking distance to the workplace connects with the paternalistic control by the company and shapes the residents' production of space and their social practices.

A special feature of the Grand Duchy is that an estate was not designed as a segregated spatial entity but annexed to the already existing residential structure (see Hudemann/Wittenbrock 1991) or else was supplemented by urban roads built later – an exception being the village Lasauvage that was wedged between steep hills (see Fleischhauer 2013: 10). Geographically, these residential structures can be found in Luxembourg in places where heavy industry established itself.

The present case study deals with the question of how the current estate residents we interviewed – all of them former workers in Luxembourg's steel industry – narratively represent the everyday subjectivation (see section 5.1) they experienced during the time of their employment. Can one deduce from these

---

82 | This paper deals only with workers' housing estates. A further aspect, which however transcends the scope of this study, is the spatial separation from the civil servants' estates. Also in terms of design and size of the houses for civil servants and those for workers, the enterprises established a distinct hierarchization.

83 | Prominent examples are the *Cité de Butte* in Villerupt, the *Bois du Luc* in the Borinage and the *Margarethenhöhen* in Essen.

communal experiences and memories a collective constitution of the subject and identify this as a particular form of blue-collar culture[84]? What effects does this constitution of the subject through everyday behaviour have on the construction of space? Furthermore this paper wishes to fulfil a desideratum that was formulated during the 4^e *Assises de l'historiographie luxembourgeoise* (see Caregari *et al.* 2012) and which consists in not only examining the estates from an economic-historical and architectural perspective (see in particular Lorang 1994), but also in taking a closer look at the 'inner life' of the residents and their individual experiences and perceptions. Historical contextualizations and architectural typologizations here only serve to contribute to a better understanding of the subjective perception and use of space.[85]

The study's empirical basis consists of the qualitative guided interviews which were conducted with nine contemporary witnesses: men between the age of 57 and 75, in the period from May to October 2013; the conversations lasted on average one hour. The evaluation of the integrally transcribed interviews followed the heuristic categories according to Reckwitz (2008: 75ff.): subjectivation/subjectification, practices, (cultural) codes, practical knowledge, discourses, artefacts/materiality.

The sample of interviewees comprises current or previous Luxembourg residents of different workers' estates[86] of the Luxembourg Minette. The microsociological perspective gives us insights into everyday culture. The subject is not considered as the product of a particular environment but is examined under the premise that "the knowledge that [subjects] appropriate in the course of their

---

84 | "But blue-collar culture is, as we know, more than merely a culture of need and deprivation, even though it is frequently that too. My understanding of blue-collar culture continues to constitute 'those manifestations of the proletarian way of life and the workers' movement that express values and are as such are transmittable'" (Tenfelde 1991: 21f.). (Personal translation of: "Aber Arbeiterkultur ist bekanntlich mehr als Not- und Mangelkultur, wenn auch immer wieder auch das. Ich verstehe nach wie vor unter Arbeiterkultur 'diejenigen Manifestationen der proletarischen Lebensweise und der Arbeiterbewegung, die Werthaltungen ausdrücken und als solche tradierfähig sind'".) In line with this quote, life in a workers' estate should not merely be identified with a "culture of need and deprivation" but also include the examination of values.

85 | A bibliography on the subject of company-owned housing in the Greater Region can be found in Caregari/Lorang 2013.

86 | The following selection was made in order to take the diversity of this form of housing into account: *Cité Raty* (Lasauvage), *rue de l'industrie* (Oberkorn), *rue Dr. Welter* (Esch-sur-Alzette), *Saarbrécker Kasäre*, partly demolished (Esch-sur-Alzette), *Kazebierg*, demolished (Esch-sur-Alzette), *op Barbourg* (Esch-sur-Alzette), *Cité Emile Mayrisch* (Schifflange), *Kantine* HADIR, converted (Rumelange), *Brill* (Dudelange).

socialization [can] in practice be confirmed but also confused or contradicted"[87] (Buschmann 2013: 141).

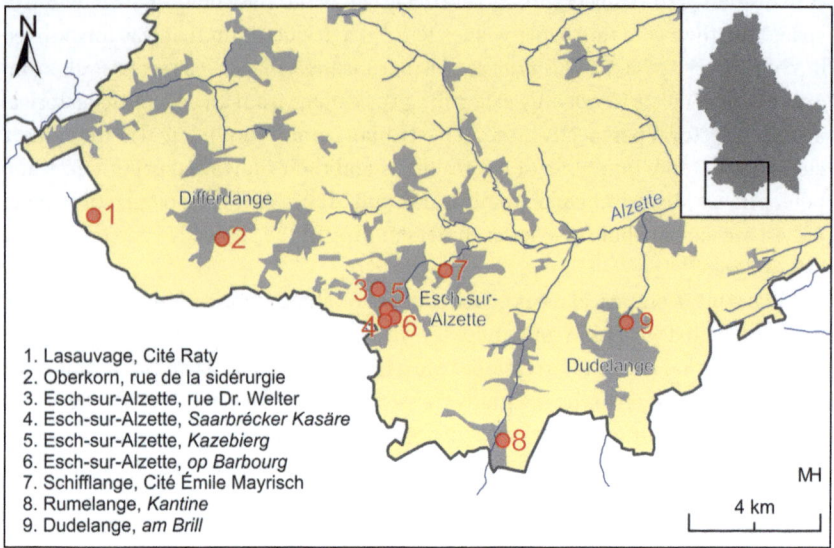

Figure 1: The Minette region with its settlement structures (as per 2013) (design: Laure Caregari, realization: Malte Helfer)

5.5.1 Hierarchy and Homogeneity

This section deals with the social control exerted by the company over the estate while also exploring the latitude of individual agency. The relationship between control and individual latitude, i.e. between subjectification (the perspective of attribution) and subjectivation (the perspective of appropriation) should not be regarded as dichotomous. It is their overlaps, points of encounter and interweavings that determine the constitutions of the subject. The social practices of the estate residents are inherent to the formation of the subject. This human behaviour reinforces and legitimizes the social space of the estate.

Social control continued to be exerted after the Second World War, only that it changed from an explicit to an implicit form. The residents were not autonomous with regard to the furnishing and possible alterations of the estate house; each of the interviewed contemporary witnesses mentioned various authorities that needed to be reported to in case of damage, refurbishing plans or moving house. It was the company that exercised the power of decision over when and to what

---

87 | Personal translation of: [Dass] "das Wissen, das [Subjekte] sich während ihrer Sozialisation aneignen, in der Praxis also einerseits bestätigt, andererseits aber auch irritiert oder konterkariert werden [kann]."

degree changes could be carried out – changing the wallpaper, the colour and quality of paint work, new floorings etc.:

"I still remember their names, the people who came to us. That was Brosius and Deden. Two of them. Must have been Germans. Must have been people from the early times of the German estate. They always came round when there was something that needed to be done. And then the ARBED replaced it. I can also remember that they laid new floors after the Second World War."[88]

The 'inspector' who came by to check remained the exception in the estate after the Second World War. From this period on, an explicit and direct disciplining of the estate residents by the company seemed less necessary. By that time, the practice of turning to an administrator or clerk had already been internalized by the estate residents – even though they were resigned about the procedure's inordinate length and unavoidability.

"When we had something that was broken, for instance when a window was broken, then we went up to the workshop. Then we said in the joinery: 'Our window is broken.' [...] But usually it was a department at the plant. That was the *Service Logement*, let's call it that. Then they came. It took a while, though. What was his name again? [...] No matter what needed to be repaired in the houses, whether the roof was damaged. Then you went to the overseer or to the office [...] of the mine. That was the *Chef-Bureau*. Then he made a call to the mine: 'This and that in that house.' And then it took a while until they had the time to do it. Then two men came round. Then, for instance, the roof was repaired. That's just the way it was."[89]

---

88 | Personal translation of: "Ech weess elo nach, wéi déi zwee geheescht hunn, déi bei eis komm sinn. Dat war de Brosius an den Deden. Zwee. Dat mussen nach Däitscher gewiescht sinn. Dat mussen der nach vum Ursprung vun den däitschen Kolonien gewiescht sinn. Brosius an Deden. Déi sinn ëmmer an d'Haiser kucke komm, wann eppes ze maachen ass. An dann huet d'ARBED dat frësch gemeet. Ech kann mech och erënneren, si huet nom Zweete Weltkrich nei Biedem gemeet."

89 | Personal translation of: "Wa mer eppes futti haten, zum Beispill wann eng Fënster futti war, da si mer eropgaang bei d'Atelieren. Dann hu mer gesot bei der Schräinerei: 'Eis Fënster ass gebrach.' [...] Mä gewéinlech war et och ee Service vun der Schmelz. Dat war de Service Logement, loosse mer dat esou nennen. Déi sinn da komm. Dat huet da gedauert. Wéi huet dee scho méi geheescht? [...] Egal, wat et war an den Haiser, ob den Daach futti war. Dann hutt dee beim Steiger oder am Bureau [...] vun der Minière... Do war ee Chef-Bureau. Dann huet deen op d'Schmelz telefonéiert: 'Dat an dat ass an deem Haus.' An dann huet dat gedauert, bis datt se dann Zäit haten. An da sinn se komm zu zwee Monn. Dann ass dat, zum Beispill um Daach, gefléckt ginn. Dat war eben esou."

All interviewees connected life on the estate with a certain degree of special awareness or even dissociation: subjectivation techniques formulate a clear idea of exceptional situations (e.g. insecurity) which became an everyday experience, as the following speculation about the assignation of a name shows:

"-We always called the [estate] the barracks, or in my time it was the Revolver Ally.
-Revolver Ally? Why Revolver Ally?
-Someone said it at some point, and it stuck.
-Was there a reason for it?
-No, I don't think so. Maybe at some point two guys got into a knife fight over who of the two should kick out the parson."[90]

This quote in connection with the expression "kick out the parson" makes clear in how far space can be considered a result of various kinds of practices. It is the combination of practical knowledge – in this case the implicitly shared knowledge of the tendency towards anticlericalism – and the awareness of its cultural significance that, for the subjects, charges the social space of the estate with meaning.

Figure 2: The Saarbrécker Kasäre aka Revolver Ally in the 1930s (Photo: Photothèque of the city of Luxembourg)

This knowledge constitutes itself around the daily routine, which is in turn closely interwoven with disciplining techniques of equal treatment. All estate residents are subjected in their daily lives to the principle of homogeneity established by the

---

90 | Personal translation of: "Mär hunn et [d'Kolonie] ëmmer Kasäre genannt oder zu menger Zäit war et d'Revolvergaass. -D'Revolvergaass? Firwat dann d'Revolvergaass? -Dat hat op eng Kéier ee lancéiert, an do war et dat. -Gëtt et dofir e Grond? -Nee, ech mengen net. Villäicht sinn de mol zwee Stéck mam Messer unenee gaang, wee vun hinne soll de Paschtouer erausgeheien."

company – the same houses in interior and exterior design, the same possibility to grow vegetables and keep animals etc. This practical knowledge also creates an awareness for the non-observation or the circumventing of the rules established by the company:

"My mum had done the laundry. There was no power in the laundry room, so my dad rigged up something primitive. It almost killed my mum. And then they came from the mine and they set up something solid."[91]

Asked about the practice of allocating houses within the estate, one interviewee answered:

"We did that ourselves. Later you went to the ARBED, to L. I think he was called. Like I said, that was 50 years ago. Then they went to him and said: 'Mine [the house] is too big, and he's got lots of children. I'll swap with him.' -'Sure, that's fine. You can move tomorrow.' The rent, that was always... Every house paid the same amount."[92]

Figure 3: Match of the Red Boys against a British team. In the background, the estate in Oberkorn in 1910 and the ropeway for transporting iron ore (Photo: Collection Erny Hilgert)

---

91 | Personal translation of: "Meng Mamm, déi hat d'Wäsch gemaach. An der Wäschkichen, do war kee Stroum, do hat mäi Papp eppes Primitives gezwafft. Meng Mamm ass bal do leie bliwwen. An do sinn déi vun der Mine komm, an déi hunn eppes gemaach, wat Kapp a Fouss hat."

92 | Personal translation of: "Jo, mer hunn dat vun sech aus gemeet. Herno bass de op d'ARBED gaangen, bei den L., mengen ech huet dee geheescht. Wéi gesot, dat si 50 Joer hier. Da sinn se bei dee gaangen, dann hunn se gesot: 'Meng ass ze grouss, an heen huet vill Kanner kritt. Ech tauschen mat him.' -'Jo, et ass gutt, hei. Muar kanns de plënneren.' Den Hauszëns, dee war jo ëmmer... All Haus huet datselwecht bezuelt."

This practice was exclusively tied to the system of estate allocation. The fact that there was a specific point of contact on the part of the land-owning company, combined with the "behavioural routines dependent on know-how and held together by practical 'understanding'"[93] (Buschmann 2013: 289), makes it possible to identify the estate as a socially homogenous space.

We see, nevertheless, that social disciplining can be further expanded. Concerned about the 'work force' and thus about its own profits, the company not only intervenes in the sphere of daily life and food production, but also attempts to extend its educational influence to leisure-time and after-work culture. This can, however, only succeed if the company is the only authority with "ownership" in the place and has a monopoly on the organization of daily life. The following example illustrates the expansion of the estate as a complex of practices:

"No, there was no private house here. We didn't have that, because everything here was MMR [S.A. *Minière et Métallurgie de Rodange*]. This side up to the hill... This side is France. But all that was MMR. Even the baker, who was on this side. The *Economat*[94] that was there. The pub that was there. All that was MMR. They paid their rent, as was the custom. Then this pub which is on this side... Because during the week, they closed at eight pm. Then everybody got chucked out. They had to go to work in the morning, so you couldn't sit there till eleven or twelve. Or that one got drunk. Out at eight. Only Saturdays were they allowed to stay longer because they didn't work on Sundays. That was the law here. That's the way it was."[95]

---

93 | Personal translation of: "Als *know-how* abhängigen und vom praktischen 'Verstehen' zusammengehaltene Verhaltensroutinen."

94 | "With the shop [*Economat*], a similar logic was at work to that of the houses: considering the insufficient number of retail stores in the industrial zone, its task was to provide the essential basic products to the workers and their families and above all prevent too strong a pricing pressure that could have affected the salaries" (Commaille 2004: 371). (Personal translation of: "Der Kaufladen [*Economat*] unterlag einer ähnlichen Logik wie die Wohnungen: Angesichts der unzureichenden Zahl von Einzelhandelsläden in den Industriezonen war seine Aufgabe, den Arbeitern und Familien die unentbehrlichen Grundprodukte zur Verfügung zu stellen und vor allem einen zu starken Preisdruck zu verhindern, der sich auf die Löhne hätte auswirken können.")

95 | Personal translation of: "Nee, et war iwwerhaapt kee Privathaus hei. Dat ass et net hei ginn, well alles, wat hei war, war MMR. Déi Säit den Hiwwel... Déi Säit ass jo Frankräich. Mä dat ass alles MMR. Souguer de Bäcker, wou déi Säit war. Den Economat, wou do war. D'Wiertschaft, wou do war. Dat war alles MMR. Déi hunn hire Loyer bezuelt, sou wéi et eben hei war. Well déi Wiertschaft, wou déi Säit ass... Well an der Woch ass déi um aacht Auer owes zou gemaach ginn. Dann ass all Mënsch erausgeflunn. Si hu misse mueres schaffe goen, da war et net, fir bis eelef, zwielef Auer do hänken ze bleiwen. Oder datt ee voll war. Um aacht Auer eraus. Just samschdes konnten se méi laang, well se sonndes net geschafft hunn. Dat war gesetzlech hei. Jo, dat war esou."

5. Space and Identity Constructions through Everyday-Cultural Practices

If we take the construction of a complex of practices a step further in its logic, then we are faced with cultural codes. Insights into this interface between practice and constitution of the subject are often narrated using comparisons or episodes and are linked to a specific terminology:

"But I was at the school once. And the doctor said ... He checked the teeth, and the girl, the assistant sat there and then she read: 'Ah, you're from the *Féckerei*, my boy?' Yes, and then he explained to the secretary: 'The German mines, they were closely connected to the *Fugger* system, you know.' And it seems they also called these houses *Fugger* houses. *Fugger*, that was someone in Germany who gave houses to his people. And they could also buy them from him. And these estates were called *Fuggerei*. It's also possible that the seven houses here were called *Fuggerei* because they were built by people from Aachen. And *Fuggerei* changed to *Féckerei* [...]. And that's the origin of the name. *Kazebierg* or *Féckerei*."[96]

We can safely say that the practice is marked by a stable 'system' of constants. These are appropriated and applied in the complex of practices of the 'estate' in assigning names and in the daily routines. In the interviews they form a dispositif of institutional subjectifications, pragmatic considerations and discourses, decodable by the respective estate residents.

The constitution of the subject as a relationship of both analytical categories is expressed through the knowledge of subjectification systems, while it also generates elements of subjectivation. One accepts the choices of lifestyle and housing provided by the company, at the same time pointing to the lack of alternatives regarding other ways of life. As accompanying semantics for the description of the social space, the statements often end on a resigned note: "That's just how it was", "That was the law", "We were glad to be here", "What more can you expect from life?"[97] The estate's residents' appropriation of space results from bridging the gap between the individual living conditions and fitting into a collectivist living environment through everyday practices.

---

96 | Personal translation of: "[...] Mä ech war eng Kéier an der Schoul. An do huet och den Dokter gesot... Do huet en Zänn kontrolléiert an d'Meedchen, d'Assistentin souz do, an do huet e gelies: 'Ah, kënns du vun der Féckerei, mäi Jong?' Jo, an do huet heen der Sekretärin erkläert: 'Déi däitsch Schmelzen, déi waren jo ganz mat deem Fugger-System do verbonnen.' An wéi et schéngt, hunn se déi heiten Haiser och Fugger-Haiser genannt. De Fugger war jo een, deen an Däitschland senge Leit Heiser ginn huet. An si konnten och bei him kofen. An déi Citéen hu Fuggerei geheescht. Elo kann et och sinn, dass déi siwen Haiser hei Fuggerei geheescht hunn, well et vun der Aachener gebaut ginn ass. An aus der Fuggerei ass dann eng Féckerei ginn. [...] An dat ass, wéi den Numm hierkënnt. Kazebierg oder Féckerei."

97 | Personal translation of: "Dat war eben esou", "Dat war Gesetz", "Mär ware frou, datt mer hei souzen", "Wat wëlls de méi hunn?"

5.5.2 Architecture and Technical Installations

This section deals with the ensemble of material objects and its effects on spatial constructions and specific constitutions of the subject. This thematic category comprises the living conditions and the perception of the estate house as such, while also dealing with the technical installations of the company. The aim is to establish the boundaries between the estate and the materiality of the work place, for the technical installations of the heavy industry are closely connected to the estate's environment due to their proximity to the workers' private living quarters.

All interviewees were able to deliver a detailed description of the distribution of rooms and the layout of their estate house. As different as the various 'estate systems' may have been, the estates themselves were uniform in their simplicity. The following narrative is representative of all comments on this subject:

"The houses had four entrances. Two on the side of the road, where the *Kazebierg* began and two on the other side. There was no road, there was only a path [...] There were separate entrances [...] They were not big houses. When you opened the door you had a kitchen. You opened the door and you were immediately in the kitchen. And then you're on your left, then you were in the living room. [...] And then upstairs, two bedrooms. They were all like that. I mean the parents' bedroom and the childrens' bedroom. And considering that there were a lot of children... [...] The toilets were outside, until shortly before the Second World War. Those were little houses for two families. Here was ours. And when this was built, a stable was added, and there was also a toilet in that. [...] You could keep an animal in there."[98]

The descriptions are all value-neutral and there are no discernible differences regarding the specific architectural type of the estates. The exterior architecture, be it the austere barrack type, the symmetrical cottage or the playful garden city concept (see Caregari/Lorang 2013: 52f.), is not reflected in the interior design and thus did not have any disciplining effects on the estate residents.[99] But the

---

[98] | Personal translation of: "Déi Haiser haten véier Entréeën. Zwou op der Säit vun der Strooss, wou de Kazebierg eropgaang ass, an zou déi aner Säit. Do war keng Strooss, do war nëmme Wee. [...] Et ware getrennten Entréeën. [...] Et waren keng grouss Haiser. Der hat eng, wann Der d'Dier opgemeet hutt, Kichen. Der huet d'Dier opgemeet, da war Der direkt an der Kichen. An da sidd Der lénks, da war d'Stuff. [...] An dann uewenop zwee Schlofzëmmer. Dat war alles esou. Dat heescht d'Eltereschlofzëmmer an d'Kannerschlofzëmmer. A vu dass vill Kanner do waren... [...] D'Toiletten, déi ware bis kuerz virum Zweete Weltkrich dobaussen. [...] Dat waren esou Haisercher fir zwou Familljen. Hei war fir eis. A wéi dat dote gebaut ginn ass, do ass e Stall bäikomm, an do war och eng Toilette dran. [...] Do konnt een en Déier halen."

[99] | This is also noted by the contemporary witness Marcel Kieffer: "I certainly didn't know much less than my adult contemporaries about the architectural style and about the historical dimension of our estate (Kieffer 2006: 308)." (Personal translation of: "Vom

materiality of the interior layout of the estate house plays a role insofar as it puts all residents on an equal level. This in turn stimulates the sense of identification.

Figure 4: The Cité Émile Mayrisch in Schifflange in the 1950s (Photo: private)

In addition, all interviewed estate residents, whether asked to do so or not, listed the family names of other estate residents. The enumeration did not go beyond the boundaries of the estate. This shows that the subjectivation is not only determined by the socio-professional identity of the workers employed in the heavy industry, but also by intensive neighbourly relations, which means that this 'doing identity' is interwoven with 'doing space'.

For the estate residents, materiality is not limited to their living structures. The specific aspect of walking proximity obliged the residents to permanently deal with the materiality of the companies' technical installations. The interlinkage of private living environment and economic production site had the effect that no boundary was established between both forms of materiality:

"I must tell you something about the tips. It was not nice of the ARBED how they dealt with these tips. Because what they did with these tips, when there was a crisis… then they created a reserve tip. And this tip, it was so big that the iron ore stones almost flew right into the houses. It almost reached up to here. They totally destroyed the soil. Everyone had a garden there. That's the way it was in the estates. Everyone. But then they just filled it up, garden and everything that was in it. And then, when things were going better, it was stripped again, the tip. Then it was needed again in the smeltery, the iron ore, I mean. Then you could clean up your garden again. Remove all the stones. That wasn't very nice of…"[100]

Architekturstil wie auch von der historischen Dimension unserer Kolonie wusste ich sicher nicht viel weniger als meine erwachsenen Zeitgenossen.")

100 | Personal translation of: "Vun den Typpe muss ech Der och eppes zielen. Dat war net fein vun der ARBED, wéi se mat deenen Typpen ëmgaangen ass. Si huet eis nämlech déi Typpen, deemno wann elo eng Crisis war… dann ass erëm ee Reservetyp ugeluet ginn. An deen Typ, dee war sou grouss, dass d'Minettssteng bal bis an d'Haiser geflu sinn. En ass

Figure 5: The estate Kazebierg beside the technical installations of the Usine Terre Rouge in the late 1920s (Photo: private)

The interviews also reveal the emotional perception which contributes to a permeability between domestic and work environment. The immediate proximity imposed by the company was considered immutable and could become part of subjectivation:

"What I found far more interesting than football were all the installations. All the installations of the mine... the loading site of the Collarts[101]... where you could watch from the street where the train went to and when it was tipped and so on. And on the other side, the division of the ARBED... from the Pierre Kersch Street there was a footbridge across the mine division of the ARBED to the *Ledigenheim*[102]. And I stood quite often on this bridge. I spent a lot of hours there, just watching the trains. That was fascinating. The empty ones that left, that had different locomotives. The full ones arriving, and so on. The full ones that were then taken out of a station, that were then driven to the crusher. And were later parked in the empty station. And later the whole manoeuvre began all over again. That was fascinating. I think I was definitely shaped by this..."[103]

---

da ganz heihinner komm. D'Äerd hunn se all futti gemeet. Jiddwereen hat e Guart do. Dat war jo an de Kolonien. Jiddereen. Mä deen hunn se dann zougetippt, de Guart an alles wat matdrann stoung. An dann wann et erëm gutt gaang ass, ass deen erem opgebaggert ginn, deen Typ. Dann ass et ërem gebraucht ginn an der Schmelz, d'Minett. Da konnts de deng Gäret erëm an d'Rei setzen. D'Steng eraus huelen. Dat war net ganz fein vun der..."

101 | Charles and Jules Collart operated the smeltery in Steinfort and owned mines in Esch-sur-Alzette and other places (see Pagliarini/Clemens 2009).

102 | The *Ledigenheim* in the Hoehl in Esch-sur-Alzette was built for workers who were unmarried or separated from their families.

103 | Personal translation of: "Dat, wat fir mech méi interessant war wéi de Fussball, dat waren déi ganz Installatiounen. Déi ganz Installatioune vun der Mine... De Collarten hire Quai. Wou ee vun der Strooss aus konnt kucken, wou den Zuch gefuer komm ass, an wann

These material objects, today for the most part demolished or lying waste, evoke memories of everyday contexts. They are named, incorporated and convey "cultural capital" to the estate residents.[104] With their – positive as well as negative – comments, they identify themselves as belonging to a particular group which was constrained or fascinated by the materiality. Tips, loading sites for iron ore and mine locomotives create microhistorical identity symbols. They possess, on a smaller scale, an aura[105] similar to that of the furnace silhouette on Belval[106] for instance – the beacon landmark of an entire region.

The materiality is closely connected to the existential basis of the estate. While the technical installations were the precondition for the estate being erected in the first place, they also constituted a threat to the living environment: "Then the houses were pulled down. Because they built the agglomeration with the crusher plant in the 50s."[107] The estate was dominated by a materiality subjected to purpose, which in the case of modernization measures, production increase or non-profitability could diminish or eliminate the human living environment.[108] The specific circumstances of ownership – all estate land and technical installations belonged to the company – allowed the expansion of technical installations into the estate's complex of practices. The result was that the constitution of the subject prevented the construction of an everyday boundary.

---

e gekippt ginn ass. An esou virun. An op der anerer Säit, de Betrib vun der ARBED... Vun der Pierre Kersch-Strooss ass eng Passerelle fortgaang iwwert de Grouwebetrib vun der ARBED an d'Ledigenheim. An ech stoung zimlech oft op déier Bréck. Ech hunn zimlech vill Stonnen do verbruet, fir just den Zich nozekucken. Dat war faszinéierend. Eideler, déi fortgefuer sinn, déi ënnerschiddlech Lokomotiven haten. Déi voll, déi komm sinn, an sou virun. Déi voll, déi ewech geholl gi sinn aus enger Guare, déi op de Brecher gefouert gi sinn. An herno an déi eidel Guare gestallt gi sinn. An herno ass de ganze Manöver rëm vu vir ugaang. Dat war faszinéierend. Ech mengen, ech sinn definitiv geimpft ginn..."

104 | "Cultural capital can be acquired [...] in the absence of any deliberate inculcation, and therefore quite unconsciously. It always remains marked by its earliest conditions of acquisition which, through the more or less visible marks they leave [...] help to determine its distinctive value. It cannot be accumulated beyond the appropriating capacities of an individual agent; it declines and dies with its bearer" (Bourdieu 1986: 241-258).

105 | Contrary to the theory of materialism in Walter Benjamin's 1936 essay, *The Work of Art in the Age of Mechanical Reproduction* (Benjamin 1968 [1955]): despite its serial reproduction, the artefact does not lose its aura, but instead enhances it through its historical testimony.

106 | Central production site of Luxembourg's steel industry (see Knebeler/Scuto 2010).

107 | Personal translation of: "Do sinn d'Haiser afgerappt ginn. Well se déi Agglomeréierung mat der Brecheranlag an de fofzeger Joren gebaut hunn."

108 | The looming deceleration of industrial production and the beginning tertiarization of society induced the enterprises to shed their estates at the end of the 1960s for cost reasons.

5.5.3 Conclusion

Statements about the constitution of the subject in Luxembourg's workers' housing estates are always connected with examinations of isolated but homogenous spatial entities. The estate has to be seen as the alternative to regulations or interventions by the state in company policy. The common denominator is, similar to France, the attitude towards the workers, "consisting in an unswerving [paternalism] which however allows for significant variants."[109]

The spatial perception of the estate residents in the interviews is consistently shaped, on the one hand, by the model of sovereignty of unequal relations (see section 5.1) – the company determining what is permitted and what is not – and by the practice of concentration of one socio-professional category, on the other. This mixture of hierarchy regarding the company and equality between those dominated is also confirmed in the statements. The intensive preoccupation with the other estate residents is based on the principle of equality. This is expressed in the fact that even after sometimes several decades, all the families of the estate are recalled by name. The disciplining hierarchy is exercised everywhere via the design and size of the houses – but not via the architecture itself – and through the control over everyday practices with the help of the possibilities provided by the company for performing them.

Analogous practices exhibited by estate residents can be regarded as overarching constants, since they are connected via implicit knowledge and cultural codes more so than other 'urban residents'. If something needed to get repaired, or a house swapped, one knew which authority to turn to. A further indication for a specific and demarcational spatial awareness is the terminology used for the estate.

Another observation common to all samples is that none of the interviewees failed to mention the perceived proximity to the technical installations. Even more so than the estate, these are charged with emotions that create a sense of identity and, if perceived favourably, are converted into cultural capital. The boundary between work and domestic environment becomes obsolete through the emotional perception that the housing estate and mining, i.e. the smeltery and steel mill, belong together.

The analysis permits us to identify the subculture of a comprehensive blue-collar culture that produces a specific complex of practices, subjectivated by a paternalistic principle of governmentality. This subculture generates the place of the estate as an expression of collective disciplining through equality and materiality.

---

109 | Personal translation of: [Welche in einem] "unerschütterlichen [Paternalismus] besteht, der aber oft beträchtliche Varianten zulässt."

5.6 Periurban Luxembourg. Definition, Positioning and Discursive Construction of Suburban Spaces at the Border between City and Countryside

Markus Hesse

"[...] The in-between city represents places that are 'not quite traditional city and not quite traditional suburban' (Young and Keil, 2010). They are forgotten geographies, where many people live and where [...] the dialectical treatment of urban *versus* suburban neglects the many shades of urban places that require our planning and policy attention" (Kirby/Modarres 2010: 67).

The expansion of urban settlements beyond the borders of the (nucleus) city into previously non-urban spaces is a central feature of spatial development of the pre- and postwar period in the overwhelming majority of western industrialized nations, in Europe as much as in North America and Australia (see Harris/Larkham 1999). Point of departure of this process are the migrations from city to hinterland of households or enterprises, particularly industry, later also of commerce as well as recreational facilities. Ever since the onset of industrialization, more or less continuous population and employment growth has been over lengthy periods the normal mode of urban development. This has produced polycentric urban regions that display very diverse structures (see Kloosterman/Musterd 2001; Parr 2004).

Scientific analysis in geography and spatial research has traditionally assigned the term of suburbanization to the expansion of the city beyond its borders (see Pratt 1994; Harris 2006); in francophone countries, this is also referred to as *périurbanisation* (see Paluch 1997; Piorr *et al.* 2011). This term also includes spaces that are further removed from the centre, spaces whose development is defined in English-speaking countries with the term of counterurbanization (see Champion 1989; Mitchell 2004). Counterurbanization refers to the growth of non-metropolitan locations, with the perspective here being expanded to the category of the rural space – those sparsely populated spaces, in earlier times marked by agriculture and forestry, which today still comprise substantial areas of Europe's large countries.

The expansion of the cities and the concomitant urbanization of society had two important consequences: on the one hand, it created transitory spaces in the in-between area between city and countryside, with, compared to the city, low density of development, a higher percentage of free spaces and fewer places of employment and recreational facilities – but with clearly more intensive land uses than in rural regions. These fringe spaces were, in the beginning, based in a high degree on the division of labor between city and hinterland, partly also peripheral rural spaces. Today this hinterland has in many cases emancipated itself from the core city, has become more urban, a part of the polycentric urban region. On the other hand, the emergence of transitory spaces has created a situation where it has become (almost) impossible to make meaningful and clear distinctions between city, countryside and in-between spaces, particularly in the agglomerations. The various spatial types are parts of a continuum that are increasingly merging into each other, particularly in the fringe areas of the large metropolitan areas. Until now, however, there has been a lack of appropriate conceptualizations for describing these spatial types (see Harris 2010), and over a long period of time they did not feature very prominently as a subject of spatial analyses and spatial planning. In the course of a tendency towards urbanization of modern society perceived as 'planetary', the boundary between city and countryside is even regarded by some observers as entirely obsolete (see Schmid/Brenner 2011). This dictum is explained with the worldwide growing urban population; since 2007, it is assumed that – for the first time in history – there are more people living in cities than in the countryside. This thesis of a universal tendency towards urbanization of society follows the assumption that space is produced socially, but that spatial differences between city and countryside no longer have any real social relevance.

The emergence of hybrid spatial categories or the tendency towards dissolution of clear differentiations between city and countryside are signals of more complex conditions and progressions of spatial development. These include, besides urbanization and the growth of urban spaces, significant social and spatial-temporal differentiations of, for instance, mobility, migration and internationalization. The same applies to the incorporation of regions into larger functional systems, e.g. through cultural and economic globalization. This development has also contributed to territory, city and region no longer being perceived as territorially constituted and clearly defined but rather as relational: as an object of a complex system of relations that is read by very diverse actors along 'variable geometries' (i.e. flexible spatial understandings) and is situated on different levels of scale (local, regional, global) (see Raco 2006).

5.6.1 Spatial Categories and Attributions: The Constitution of Space in City, Countryside and the 'In-between'

"Scholars researching suburbia in the framework of different disciplines still have no easy overview of what the different areas of their subject have in common" (Vaughan et al. 2009: 485).

When social change can no longer be grasped with the traditional inventory of scientific terms, epistemologies and methods, it causes a productive irritation. This basically also applies to spatial development. With regard to this subject, one can draw three possible conclusions in reaction to this situation: the first is to search for a fundamentally new paradigm – in this case, the conceptualization of the 'postmodern' city as a rupture with the 'old' city's logic of development; a second option would be to retain what has been passed down, what has proven its worth also under such marginal conditions that suppose transformation and change – this would here correspond to assuming the universally valid return or renaissance of the city. The third possibility would be to adopt a different conceptual perspective. This is the logic also followed by the present paper. It implies that the research subject is no longer assumed as given, but is understood as a case of individual, subjective constructions.

Such a perspective views space as a result of social agency, as socially constituted and socially constructed (see sections 2.2 and 5.1). This perspective is also well justified with regard to the subject discussed here: the question of what can be called 'urban', 'suburban' or 'rural' is no longer determined via classical parameters of spatial science (such as population potential and density, spatial location, commuter relations to the nearest centre). Instead, 'city' and 'countryside' are actively created, produced. The accompanying attributions detach themselves from scientific categorizations and positings – which themselves of course also constitute constructions – and are increasingly performed by the subjects themselves. Attribution of meaning ensues both in the professional discourse, i.e. through scientists, politicians and planners as well as through the population itself. Here various factors come into play: space-related identities and identifications, demarcations, policies and ideological framing as well as subjectivations and subjectifications, i.e. individual perceptions and positings, but also the concomitant practices.

This is confirmed when we consider the contradictory perceptions and evaluations of what constitutes urban and rural spaces (and lifestyles) or what differentiates them. Spaces that were previously perceived as rural are no longer necessarily peripheral but also appear as highly industrialized, are subject to social integration and social modernization (see Woods 2007); at the same time, some cities ruralize, in particular those that have lost considerable numbers of inhabitants due to deindustrialization or transformation. Interim usages, urban gardening and agricultural subsistence on fallow soil are playing a more prominent role and at least in part are shaping a new perception of the city. This blending of the traditional images of city and countryside corresponds to a coincidence of competing ideal images of both spatial categories: the image of the renaissance of the city in which many people live, work, spend their free time, again is found alongside new urban poverty and exclusion. And in contrast to the reality of many successful agro-industrial and logistic production spaces that have established themselves in rural-peripheral regions, for some time now there has been a remarkable orientation of the urban mainstream society towards the rural. This is also reflected in the high demand for lifestyle magazines that offer country life, country culture and countryside nostalgia as a communicative staging.

The perception of sub- and periurban spaces is also very contradictory: the city fringe has always been both *privatopia* and *dystopia* – i.e. private space of retreat and yearning on the one hand, which offered the perspective to maximize the respective advantages of city and countryside and avoid their disadvantages. And on the other hand, the suburban space was a projection area of a sweeping critique of urban growth (see Nicolaides 2006; Vicenzotti 2011), chiefly from the ranks of architects and urban planners, but also from the core cities themselves. This critique was aimed at the urbanization of free space, the fiscal depletion of the core cities through the haemorrhage of tax-paying households as well as the creation of commuter migrations. But it was voiced primarily from the perspective of the core city and to a lesser degree from the angle of the peripheral regions themselves (see Hesse 2010).[110] The narrative of the dissolution of the city was for a long time very impactful if not hegemonial.

The constructivist perspective on space is guided by an awareness for the particular significance of boundaries. Boundaries are constitutive for spaces and thus also for the traditional understanding of the suburban or periurban. It is administrative boundaries and those drawn by settlement structures that create the fact of the margin in the first place: in purely statistical terms, it is frequently only the crossing of the municipal boundary that transforms the migration from the centre to the periphery into a matter of suburbanization. Furthermore, suburban spaces are found on both sides, inside and outside, of the boundary of the core city. Here, the most distinctive demarcation of boundaries ensued discursively, referring to the heated controversies within the respective policy departments about *suburbia* (see above) that formed a marked contrast to its residents' high appreciation for this spatial category. The core city was assessed positively, while the areas beyond the city limits were given a negative evaluation.

Finally, connections also emerge to 'identity' in a spatial context. Here we differentiate between the attributed identity of a region or a space and the identification of individuals with particular spaces or places (see Paasi 2002 and 2003; Weichhart 1999). Regarding the question of space-related identity, we subscribe to the view of Paasi (2003: 477):

"Regional identity has been recognized as a key element in the making of regions as social/political spaces, but it is difficult to elucidate what this identity consists of and how it affects collective action/politics [...]. The crucial question is how political passions are regionalized, and here institutions constitutive of region-building (economy, governance, language, media, literature) and inherent power relations are significant."

Against this background, the aim of this paper is to explore the constitution and the construction of segmented space at a remove from the big centres. The focus will be on the perspective of the inhabitants of these areas. What interests us is how the inhabitants of the periphery associate their locations and in which way, if any, space-related identity is shaped. It continues to remain unclear how the

---

110 | And it has remained unclear who precisely was the addressee of this critique: the subjects that chose this location type; economic actors who found particularly favourable conditions of exploitation here; or the planning and regulative policies that have created the necessary incentives for the respective social practices.

inhabitants of suburbia, the in-between city, the suburban space actually call the place where they live, which images they associate with it, and in how far this space is perceived as 'home'. In that respect, processes of demarcation of boundaries and identity-building are equally relevant. This particular way of looking at space also makes it possible to question conventional positings and hegemonial discourses and to open and pluralize the perspective. We have chosen the Grand Duchy of Luxembourg and the Greater Region, i.e. including the neighbouring regions Wallonia, Lorraine, Rhineland-Palatinate and Saarland as an example for examining this complex of questions (see University of Luxembourg, IDENT2 2012/2013 – quantitative and qualitative survey). It is an attempt to understand the constitution of sub- and periurban spaces as a product of a specific subjectivation. Building on this, we will discuss a number of implications for further research.

5.6.2 The Suburban and Periurban Regional Scenario in Luxembourg and in the Border Region

Compared to other European countries, the Grand Duchy of Luxembourg, one of the smallest member states of the European Union, has seen an above-average favourable demographic development and an extremely successful economic transformation. This developmental path is moreover characterized by two particular features compared to urban development in other contexts: it took place in a very short period of time and in a relatively small territory, which at the end of 2012/beginning of 2013 comprised around 537,000 inhabitants and around 380,000 resident employees on an area of 2,586 km^2 (see STATEC 2013: 9). Recent spatial development of Luxembourg has been very disparate: a few densely populated areas contrast with a generally more segmented region. The country's north is traditionally regarded as rural. The great majority of the country's 106 municipalities have a population of less than 10,000. In the past, the highest development pressure, measured in absolute figures, was sustained by the metropolitan area, while many smaller municipalities show the highest relative gains in growth.

The country's housing and real estate markets are extremely tense (see Becker/Hesse 2010); even compared to the substantially higher level of income, rents and real estate prices are generally double to those in comparable locations in Germany, Belgium or France. After a first wave of suburbanization in the 1970s and 1980s, these problems created an increased cross-border residential mobility out of Luxembourg. It has been directed primarily to the periurban rural area near the border of Rhineland-Palatinate, Wallonia and Lorraine (see section 5.8). Near the national border, the settlement area dynamics are currently much more pronounced than in the centres. This is not only true for the transformation of erstwhile villages and smaller towns to residential locations of the urban commuter population, but, particularly in Luxembourg, also for the office locations interspersed in the more rural parts of the country, which constitute largely unintegrated workplace concentrations. The spatial imbalances that come with massive daily commuter traffic and continuing problems in the provision of housing are currently considered *the* major problem for regional planning.

If the combination of relatively small territory size, large-scale interlacement and very dynamic growth of economy and population in the past two decades in itself already creates very specific constraints for spatial development, then this applies even more to the ongoing internationalization of the country. This is already evident in the country-wide very high percentage of non-Luxembourg nationals of 44 %, reflecting the various waves of immigration in the country's recent past. But in the small municipalities it encounters a very specific regional scenario: in municipalities of not more than approx. 8,000 inhabitants, such as Walferdange in the northern periphery of the capital, or Mersch in the country's centre, the proportion of foreigners is as high as 30 % or more representing around 90 to 100 or more different nationalities (see the websites of the communes of Mersch and Walferdange). Especially for small municipalities, this is extraordinarily high and poses a particular challenge. This diversity is less marked in the municipalities near the border which instead have a more balanced mixture of nationals from the respective bordering countries.

5.6.3 Empirical Glimpses into Sub- and Periurban Constellations

"It's suburban. You got a forest and, I mean, in Luxembourg nothing is really urban unless you live right in the middle of *Grand-rue*." (male, 48, British Luxembourger, Luxembourg).

This section will provide a few selected empirical glimpses into the constitution of sub- and periurban space in Luxembourg and in the border region. In two rounds of empirical research, we examined the interpretations and attributions of meaning with respect to people's place of residence. First we formulated, as part of the quantitative survey, a short set of questions relating to grading the place of residence according to the degree of urbanization. We asked the interviewees how they rated their residential location: as urban, rural or sub-/periurban. In addition, we conducted semi-standardized interviews with 23 selected respondents who had participated in the quantitative survey and had given their ratings and were willing to discuss the reasons for their choice.

Perceptions of the 'In-Between'

Fig. 1 and 2 show a compilation of the results arrived at in the standardized survey. On the one hand, they refer to the entire area covered by the survey as well as to those areas of the respective countries' territory that constitute a part of the Greater Region, and on the other, to the different regions of Luxembourg. We see here a relatively high degree of correspondence with the classifications suggested by these particular areas on the basis of the features of their space and settlement structure or which have been put forward by the respective spatial planning authorities or the European Spatial Planning Observation Network (ESPON): "The Greater Region shows a clear functional, demographic, and morphological polycentricity that is the basis for the overall functioning of the region" (ESPON/UL 2010). With the exception of Lorraine, most parts of the entire area covered by the survey are rated as having a predominantly rural or sub-/periurban structure; in the Saarland and the Rhineland-Palatinate, part of the survey area ratings of suburban and rural are more or less evenly distributed (see Fig. 1). Among the different areas within Luxembourg, the contrasts are even stronger. Here the area of the capital stands out as urban with 61 % of the ratings. What is remarkable here is the low percentage of ratings given to this category for the rest of the centre. As expected, the south is rated both as sub-/periurban as well as rural; and for Luxembourg's northern and eastern regions the category 'rural' is – also unsurprisingly – the predomiant one (see Fig. 2).

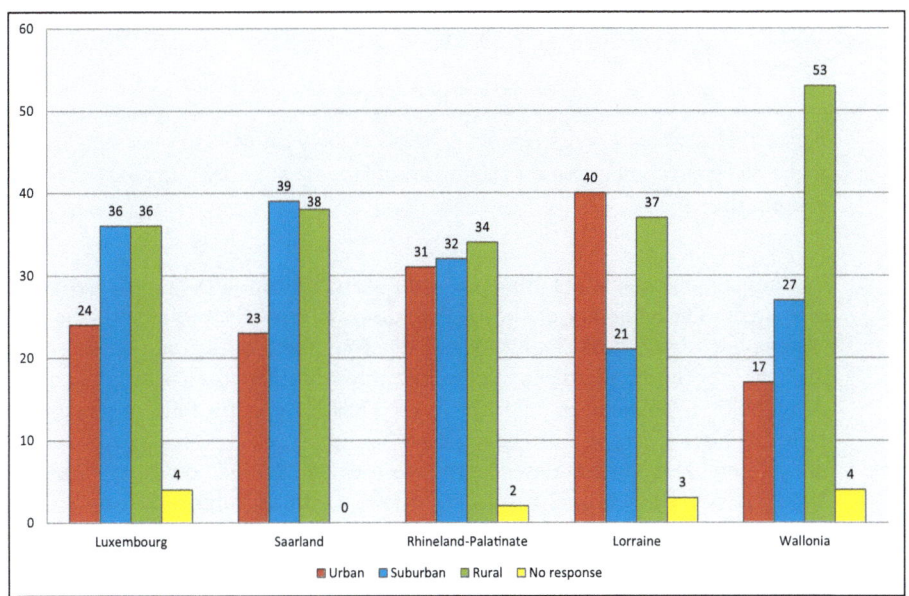

Figure 1: How would you describe your lifestyle in this location? Entire survey area in percent (University of Luxembourg, IDENT2 2012/2013 – quantitative survey)

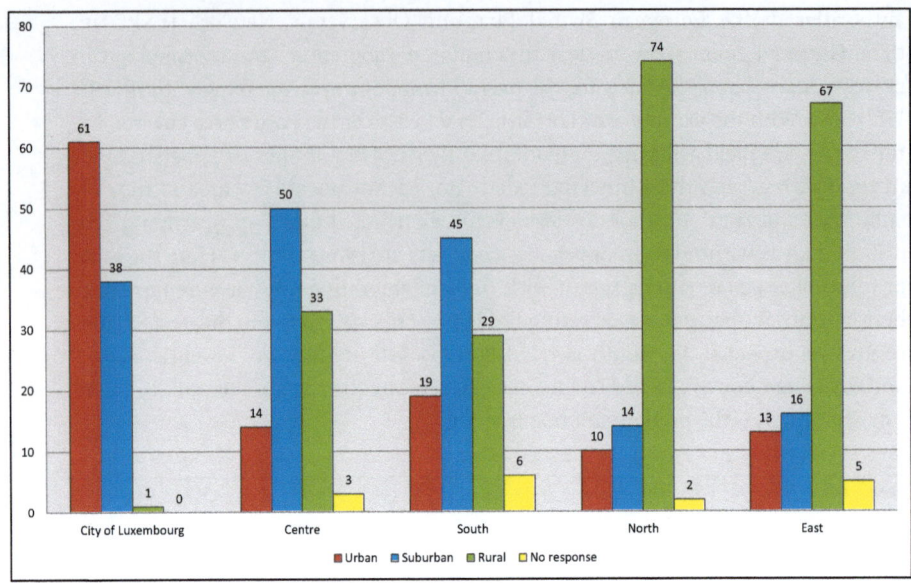

Figure 2: How would you describe your lifestyle in this location? Luxembourg residential population in percent (University of Luxembourg, IDENT2 2012/2013 – quantitative survey)

By comparison, responses from the semi-standardized survey are clearly less consistent. The selection of the in this case 23 respondents followed the self-assessment of the participants who had given their rating of their place of residence for the standardized survey and were willing to discuss the reasons for their choice in detailed personal interviews. These covered the following question: Does the place where you live have a clear boundary? Where does it begin, where does it end? How do you describe the place where you live to acquaintances or strangers? Why do you qualify your home town as urban, suburban, rural? Would you say that you identify with the place where you live? If so, why? If not, why not?

At first, a majority of the interviewees reacted to these questions with puzzlement. Apart from a few exceptions (see below) people are not accustomed to using the classical terminologies of space-related planning and research in their everyday lives. Only a minority of interviewees came up with precise terms on their own accord: instead, the interviewees offered detailed narratives with which they situated themselves in or also identified themselves with their place of residence.

"Where does it begin? At the border, where you can immediately..., but... OK, the whole of Athus also belongs to it, I mean, it's... nowadays it all connects what now..."[111] (female, 31, Luxembourgish, Wallonia).

---

111 | Eigene Übersetzung von: "Wou fänkt en un? Vun der Grenz, wou een direkt zwar... Okay, ganz Athus gehéiert dozou, ech mengen, et ass jo... alles hänkt zesummen, wat elo..."

The transcripts of the conversations document numerous queries on the part of the interviewees attempting to understand the research interest of the survey. This response can have two different reasons: on the one hand, this clearly confirms the marked discrepancy between the use of corresponding terminologies by experts and by residents (this problem was already broadly discussed during the coordination of the interview guideline). Interviewers were obliged to provide explicit assistance and explanations for the interviewees to be able to position themselves. On the other hand, this probably also has to do with the fact that in particular in the urbanized parts of the survey area – i.e. beyond the rural areas –, clear boundaries between city and countryside are more the exception than the rule. This is reflected in the vagueness of attributions made by the residents of those areas.

Next, the evaluation of the empirical findings will focus on the following two question items: How is the place of residence referred to? Are there indications for a space-related identification and how is it reflected? Interviewees living in an urban centre or in a village (centre) gave an unambiguous answer to the question about the place of residence. In the other cases, the terminology is inconsistent and varied, due to the already mentioned problem of demarcating clear boundaries. On Luxembourg territory and in the German-speaking border region, the terms "Stadtrand" and "Vorstadt" or "Vorort" (lux. *Viruert*) are used; an English speaking interviewee was the only one to use the term 'suburban'. The francophone interviewees characterize their place of residence in this case as *"entre les deux"*, i.e. in the in-between between city and countryside, which offers certain advantages (*"un peu des deux côtés – on a des avantages"*). It is only French speaking people that use the term *zone périurbaine*. "Vorstadt" refers as a rule to the nearest centre. In rural Germany, territorial reforms have created the effect that for the inhabitants of smaller neighbourhoods it is not the administrative seat of the municipality that is the chief place of reference but the place of residence.

Here one needs to take into account the particular features of the urban system in Luxembourg whose 106 municipalities consist in large part of small municipalities with less than 10,000 inhabitants. Often evaluations oscillate between the formal municipal charter and the actual significance of the municipality; frequently independent small municipalities are attributed more importance for reasons of political symbolism than they *de facto* have. Occasionally, the label of the rural is also used for settlement nuclei that have, according to the same interviewee's information, around 3,500 inhabitants, therefore, by the standards of the region, exhibiting more of an urban character, i.e. being attributed specifically urban features.

Evaluations of the 'In-between'

This scale connected with good accessibility by car (only public transport is rated as unsastisfactory) has in general a positive effect on the evaluation of the places of residence: "But I'm, like, two kilometres from the city. So it's not countryside, either? No, it's just perfect!" (female, 53, Finnish, Luxembourg). Interviewees give positive ratings throughout to the location of their place of residence and the corresponding local and regional surroundings. This is partly due to the already mentioned scale of the spatial structure, in particular to the fact that the survey area by and large, barring a few exceptions (areas in Rhineland-Palatinate relatively remote from the border), does not consist of peripheral rural areas, and that also many of the locations classified as rural lie in the catchment area of the urban centres and are easily accessible. In this way, the widely scattered in-between spaces permit a high degree of benefit maximization in the interface of settings that lean more to the urban and more to the rural, which belongs to the classic motivations for choosing a place of residence in sub- and periurban areas (see Mitchell 2004; McCarthy 2008).

"I would like to move, but the problem is that I don't want to move away from here. I don't really like my house, but the place is practical, the neighbourhood. We're not cramped, everyone has their garden, that's why I don't know. If I move, I would need to find something here"[112] (female, 33, French, Lorraine).

The interviewees' direct ratings of the quality of their location are positive throughout ("I have here everything I need"; "very nice, small place, very calm, pleasant"[113]; "only advantages.") The empirical material yields only limited indications for space-related appropriations. Corresponding points of reference are in this case clearly linked to social contexts: the determining factors here are family, neighbours, leisure activities:

"And you feel a sense of belonging to that... place, commune?" -"Yes, in the fact that the kids went to school there and that through that I know a lot of the parents. I know a lot of the activities so I get invited to a lot of things where there will be a lot of people from Strassen. My kids used to play for the football team and things. So, yes, you get to know the people. But no, I would never say I am a 'Strassener'. I am more of a… I'm very European in the way I position myself. I have an English passport but, you know, I speak languages. I don't attach myself to a… place" (male, 48, British Luxembourger, Luxembourg).

The ratings and assessments referring to space-related appropriation processes are made in the very specific context of Luxembourg which is marked by a basic contradiction between more segmented spatial configurations and constellations, on the one hand, and an apparently great diversity of social practices, attitudes and assessments, on the other. This situation reflects the critically examined role that the category 'space' plays for subjectivation processes in the context of constructivist approaches to research.

---

112 | Eigene Übersetzung von: "Moi j'aimerais bien déménager, mais le problème, c'est que je ne veux pas partir d'ici. Ma maison ne me plaît pas forcément, mais c'est l'endroit qui est pratique; le voisinage, on n'est pas trop collés les uns sur les autres, on a chacun un jardin, donc je ne sais pas. Si je déménage, il faudrait que je trouve ici, en fait."
113 | Eigene Übersetzung von: "Très sympathique petite localité, très calme, plaisible."

5.6.4 Conclusion

It was the aim of this case study to examine how the category of sub- and periurban space in Luxembourg and in the border region is specifically constituted by its inhabitants. The subjective assessments that emerge in the spatial classifications of place of residence correspond at first glance to the 'objective' features with which these locations are characterized in the professional discourse. At second glance, however, these categorizations are relatively scattered, very segmented and greatly dependent on the local context. As far as statements are made about residential satisfaction, these are all positive, consistent with the research on choice of residential location and motivations (see Beckmann et al. 2006). Close ties are confirmed with respect to the social context. But these are not necessarily explainable in the spatial context. So the question whether there is something like a space-related identity or identification on the basis of this evaluation has to remain unanswered. We should here point out the special importance of infrastructures: it is only thanks to the high degree of motorization and the good spatial development that the dispersed life in the sub- and periurban space has become feasible and attractive.

This picture seems to confirm the afore-mentioned tendency towards dissolution of sharp contours of 'urban' and 'rural' spaces also for the area examined here. This yields at least two points for further discussion: first, one would need to clarify what the concomitant hybridization of spatial contexts actually signifies. Secondly, we have to ask ourselves how meaningful are spatial categorizations at all, in particular when we are dealing with such complex questions as 'identity': "Geographical spaces are now overlapped by many and varied social and cultural ideas, requiring a reconceptualisation of space as a socially produced set of manifolds [...], better recognised as territories of becoming able to produce new potentials rather than as fixed territories of identity" (Cloke 2011: 568).

5.7 Remembering the Second World War in Luxembourg and the Border Regions of its Three Neighbours

Eva Maria Klos and Benno Sönke Schulz

In 2006, the cultural studies scholar Aleida Assmann stated with regard to the Second World War and the Germans: "We live in the shadow of a past that in manifold ways continues to make itself felt in the present and haunt later generations with emotional dissonance and moral dilemmas"[114] (Assmann 2006: 159). The Nazi period is still present in German and European everyday life – be it

---

[114] | Personal translation of: "Wir leben im Schatten einer Vergangenheit, die in vielfältiger Form in die Gegenwart weiter hineinwirkt und die Nachgeborenen mit emotionaler Dissonanz und moralischem Dilemma heimsucht."

in the form of memorial days, representations in schoolbooks or in the popularity of 'histotainment' in TV programmes and on the internet. The media, school lessons, as well as family conversations play important parts in the ways in which people form specific historical knowledge (see Welzer *et al.* 2002: 9, referencing Wineburg 2001: 181), but they position themselves very differently in regard to memories as conveyed by the media or the family.

This diversity of stances is particularly accentuated in border regions: different countries exist side by side in terms of specific memory cultures, while at the same time being in direct relation to and exchange with one another; in border regions, the individual is consequently more intimately confronted with the view of the 'other' and the view on the 'others' in day-to-day life. Our case study takes this lived experience as its point of departure in order to examine the following two questions[115]: What are the identitary attributions that people from Luxembourg and the surrounding border regions of France, Belgium and Germany respectively come and came into contact with through verbalized accounts of the Second World War? And what is the stance adopted towards these accounts?[116] The case study aims to shed light on identity constructions in the border regions articulated in this (tension) field.

Empirically, this study is based on newspaper articles from the years 1950 to 2013[117] that deal with the invasion of neutral Luxembourg by Nazi forces on 10 May 1940. Articles of the *Luxemburger Wort*, the Luxembourg regional edition of the French paper *Le Républicain Lorrain* and the Belgian paper *La Meuse* as well as the German paper *Trierischer Volksfreund* constitute the sources[118] used to initially reconstruct the coverage of 10 May 1940 since 1950. Secondly, identitary attributions as related by print media are considered from a historical perspective,

---

115 | We would like to thank Professor Norbert Franz for his extensive conceptional preparation of the study and critical comments.
116 | Drawing on Reckinger 2013: 12.
117 | We can make no claim to comprehensiveness regarding the selection of the articles, but we have tried to ensure a balanced differentiation in terms of region and period. The newspapers were checked for reports on 10 May 1940 around the time of the anniversaries (until 1960 annually, after that in five-year periods). One should note the Catholic and conservative leaning of the newspapers chosen for Luxembourg (*Luxemburger Wort*) as well as the temporal limitation for *Le Républicain Lorrain*, which only began publishing a regional edition for Luxembourg in 1961. That newspaper articles have a relevance for the everyday life of the residents in the border regions is confirmed by the representative survey conducted for this volume, according to which 92 % of the respondents in Luxembourg state that they read a daily newspaper once in a while (University of Luxembourg, IDENT2 2012/2013 – quantitative survey).
118 | Our thanks go to Danielle Werner (*Bibliothèque nationale de Luxembourg*) for making it possible for us to obtain comprehensive access to this material.

as the newspaper articles are here treated as a reflection of publicly relevant topics and are seen as conveying collectively shared values and moods and, hence as implying subjectifications. 10 May 1940 was chosen as a specific date, as it presented coverage of a direct violation of a border – a point in time when the survey areas' situation was charged with tension, due to which communally held values are observed as having emerged particularly strongly.

This methodological approach is complemented on a third level by the evaluation of the representative survey (University of Luxembourg, IDENT2 2012/2013 – quantitative survey) that focuses on current memory practices. One should, however, note here that the preset response options presented by the survey have the consequence of preliminary structuring the process of remembering, as it only enquires about partial and specific aspects. With the help of the survey, we aim to establish which people regard the Second World War as playing an important role in the construction of their memories and which of the queried contents they remember. Subsequently, we will discuss possible individual stances taken towards the established attributions (subjectivations) which are empirically noticeable in the respondents' behaviour as related to the questions posed.

5.7.1 The Invasion on 10 May 1940 and the Occupation as Represented in the Print Media from 1950 until Today

"There was no cloud in the sky on 10 May 1940. For us it was a day for dying, for Hitler, however, the chosen hour for victory"[119] (*Luxemburger Wort* 1950: 1). These are the words chosen in 1950 by the *Luxemburger Wort* to commemorate the day of the invasion when German military pushed across the border of the neutral Grand Duchy of Luxembourg, an invasion that constituted a clear breach of international law. The article failed to mention the neighbouring states of Belgium and France as well as the Netherlands, which were further targets of this military operation (*Fall Gelb* – 'Case Yellow'). Nevertheless, this quote can be regarded as typical of the journalistic tone adopted in regard to coverage about the Second World War published in the papers of the surveyed border regions outside Germany during the 1950s, because it contrasts the emotional state of the local population with that of the Nazi regime. "My homeland was violated by a ruthless intruder"[120], wrote a Luxembourg author in the Belgian paper *La Meuse* (1952: 2). Here, the contrast between the big and brutal German aggressor and the small and peace-loving Grand Duchy emerges as a continuously recurring theme. Not only the prose of the corresponding articles about 10 May 1940, but also their outer appearance and their placement within the newspaper divulge cohesive similarities in the 1950s. They mostly take the form of relatively short articles, often adopting a very

---

119 | Personal translation of: "Kein Wölkchen trübte den Himmel am 10. Mai 1940. Für uns war es ein Tag zum Sterben, für Hitler aber die auserwählte Stunde zum Siegen."
120 | Personal translation of: "Ma patrie a été violentée par un intrus sans scrupule."

emotional style, and placed on the newspapers' front or second page. A further feature of the articles' content organization in this period is the emphasis on the unbending will of Luxembourg's population during German occupation and their commitment to a free and independent state of Luxembourg. Frequently, 10 May is also used as an opportunity to comment on the geopolitical situation in the Cold War period. The *Luxemburger Wort* in particular draws a parallel between the 10 May and the perceived threat of the Soviet Union on several different occasions. The impact of the 1950s newspaper articles can thus be seen as a chiefly emotional one, an effect that will surely have reinforced the transmission and fixation in the memory of the readers.[121]

By the early 1960s, the formerly rather short pieces published on the occasion of anniversaries were increasingly replaced by longer documentaries. Series of articles such as "History of the War 1939-1945 – Today 20 years ago"[122] (*La Meuse* 1960a: 4) or "When the Allies opened the gates"[123] (*Le Républicain* 1965: 18) now no longer commemorate single events, but rather present an analytical treatment of war events. In addition, through continuous coverage, the newspapers *La Meuse* and *Le Républicain* aimed to publish their articles in a format that allowed the reader to collect them, so that in the end they could be used as a book (see *La Meuse* 1960b: 5). The daily routine of reading is here expanded by the opportunity to archive material. The articles in the *Luxemburger Wort* also increased in length, while common journalistic practice used the date of invasion as serving for the entire period of occupation. The 1960s, however, saw a decline in this detailed and partly documentary-analytical form of remembering; with the exception of major anniversaries, we see an increasing reduction of the obligatory text in favour of a photographic documentation of functions such as wreath-laying ceremonies.

The events of the Second World War are also increasingly interwoven with each other in the papers examined. This is explicitly evident in the connection of two dates, namely, 10 May 1940 and 8 May 1945. The articles concerned covering victory celebrations or reunions of associations suggest that the events of 10 May have begun to lessen in importance in the light of Germany's defeat in 1945. Moreover, by the 1970s, with the commemoration of the Schuman plan announced on 9 May 1950, the unifying European perspective had gained greater relevance. Leading up to the 1980s, we can note a distinct decrease in the quantity of articles about the *Fall Gelb*. In the 1990s, by contrast, there is again an increase that can be explained by the so-called 'history boom' (see Macdonald 2013: 3f.; Assmann 2008: 61ff.), particularly on the 50th anniversary, on 10 May 1990.

---

121 | The predominance of the emotional transmission over a cognitive one is emphasized by Harald Welzer et al. (2002: 200f.) who studied family memories.

122 | Personal translation of: "Histoire de la Guerre 1939-1945 – Il y a aujourd'hui 20 ans."

123 | Personal translation of: "Quand les Alliés ouvrirent les portes."

The analysis of the articles relating to 10 May 1940 shows two major tendencies that apply to the entire survey area: firstly, by the 1960s, the invasion is no longer commemorated every year. Around this time, it is only at important anniversaries that papers run articles on the topic. Their spatial position within the paper also changes and disappears almost completely from the front pages by the 1970s. Secondly, the articles published on the occasion of anniversaries are more differentiated and analytical and show a larger contextualization of the topic of the *Fall Gelb*. From the 1960s onwards, newspaper readers in the border region are thus provided with historical and factual knowledge in journalistic packaging, while the emotional link has all but disappeared. Nevertheless, the trend of a decreasing number of articles about 10 May 1940 does not go unnoticed by Luxembourg's population: recently, readers have voiced their concern that history may be in danger of being forgotten.[124]

5.7.2 'Border Violators' and 'Violated': The Representation of Perpetrators and Victims in the Print Media

A comparison of the newspaper articles reveals certain recurring topoi. In the first three decades after the Second World War, the *Trierischer Volksfreund* simply ignores the subject of the invasion of Luxembourg and Germany's other western neighbours and instead frequently emphasizes the suffering of the German population during the bombing of Trier in the winter of 1944. The border violation is – at best – mentioned in passing in general articles about the Second World War and German readers are addressed using an imagery of victimhood that centre-stages Germany's own suffering.

During the first two decades of the post-war period, the analysis of the newspapers of the western part of the examined border regions displays a distinct contrast between images of perpetrator and victim. This is reflected particularly in the description of the behaviour of German soldiers: "The people of Luxembourg looked on with apprehension as the first unaccustomed grey motor cyclists with the cruel faces and the repulsive helmets clattered past their houses"[125] (*Luxemburger Wort* 1950: 1).[126] The border violation is not only condemned as a breach of international law, but described as an invasion of destitute starvelings

---

[124] | This is for instance mentioned in the *Tageblatt* which does not belong to the source corpus but nevertheless represents an important medium in the border region (see *Tageblatt* 2006: 58).

[125] | Personal translation of: "Das luxemburgische Volk zitterte und sah mit schüchternen Blicken die ersten ungewohnten grauen Motorradler mit den grausamen Gesichtern unter den abstoßenden Helmen an ihren Häusern vorüberrattern."

[126] | There is perhaps one other group, referred to with the abstract and not further explained term of 'the traitor' (*Luxemburger Wort* 1950: 1), which was identified within Luxembourg's population, otherwise marked by a ubiquitous expression of cohesion.

in a prosperous country: a "march of the hungry into paradise, an exodus of the unbeckoned 'have-nots' into the realms of wealth and plenty"[127] (ibid.). Pillage at the cost of the civilian population is therefore, besides the loss of a free and sovereign native country, a further aspect of the topicalized image of victimhood. Finally, however, the accounts of the fatalities among the civilian population of 10 May and the fate of the deportees from the Minette region carry considerably more weight. Only from the 1960s onwards are the latter two aspects addressed more frequently, probably provoked by the interest of the public and the increasing depth and length of the articles. By contrast, the fate of Luxembourg's Jewish population remains almost unmentioned until the 1980s. In the 1950s and 1960s, a very clear differentiation between victims and perpetrators can be observed: values such as humanity and freedom are advocated to the readers – particularly by emphasizing a contrast to the inhuman and despotic Nazi Germany – while at the same time projecting an image of the country's own image of victimhood.

In subsequent decades, this more or less clearly structured binary code of victims and perpetrators became more differentiated: as the Second World War grew more distant in time, we can not only observe a more specific identification of different kinds of victim groups (e.g. 'forced recruits'), concurrently, the perpetrator attributions became more diverse. The generalization and part-demonization of the German military as soldiers that bring only suffering and death began to disintegrate and was contrasted in particular in personal narratives with more positive accounts. One of the individual reports that it was "thanks to the sympathy of some *Wehrmacht* officers"[128] [...] (*Luxemburger Wort* 1965: 20) that the evacuation could be brought to a good conclusion. Moreover, there was a clear departure from the notion, prevalent in the 1950s and 60s, that the entire population of Luxembourg had experienced the invasion as terrifying. The articles of subsequent years focus in detail on the personal experiences of Luxembourgish nationals and their different attitudes towards the German occupiers. In recent years, the distinction between perpetrator and victim attributions is thus no longer exclusively established in accordance with nationality.

Nevertheless, the memory of the Second World War in all the newspapers remains predominantly national. In their regional editions for Luxembourg, the papers *La Meuse* and *Le Républicain* address connecting, binational topics such as the friendship established between Luxembourg and France, a factor that was reinforced, among other things, by France taking in evacuees from the Minette region. But in comparison with the front-page coverage of the celebrations of 8 May in Paris, these articles prove only marginally significant. As to the German

---

127 | Personal translation of: "[...] Marsch der Hungrigen ins Schlaraffenland, ein Auszug der ungerufenen 'Habenichtse' in die Regionen des Wohlstandes und des Überflusses."
128 | Personal translation of: "[...] dem Verständnis einzelner Wehrmachtsoffiziere" [zu verdanken].

coverage, it was only after the 1980s that a more compelling mention of the fate of the population on the other side of the Our, Sauer and Mosel can be observed. Before that time, there is little evidence of identification with the role of the perpetrator regarding 10 May 1940, since the articles reported only in a very implicit manner on the *Fall Gelb*. The newspaper articles published outside Germany generally convey a perception of the border that emphasizes the notion of transgression and – particularly in the first years after the war – affirms the border as a (moral) dissociation from Germany.

5.7.3 Remembering the Second World War Today

If one subscribes to the view adopted by some scholars that the differentiation "between victor and vanquished, on the one hand, and perpetrators and victims, on the other, [constitutes] an essential basis for the comparison of nations and their problems in dealing with their past"[129] (Assmann 2006: 70), then this differentiation proves helpful for the survey area under review here as well: in the examined border regions, the course of the Second Wold War created the situation of positioning the victims of the invasion as victors. The side of the perpetrator on the other hand, Nazi Germany, was seen as coinciding with the vanquished. Particularly from the 1950s until the 1970s, this reversal of power received a great deal of attention in the newspapers: it is to a large extent within this framework of remembering, influenced by the variable binary code of 'victim/perpetrator', that people position themselves towards attributions. In what follows, we will examine which forms of subjectivity manifest themselves in current remembering within the border regions of Luxembourg, France, Belgium and Germany. Here the representative survey serves to shed light on two fundamental questions of current remembering: In the lives of which people currently living in the examined border regions do the memories of the Second World War play a role and what are their sociodemographic features? And what stance do they take with regard to established attributions? The aim here is to reveal identity constructions articulated in the practices of remembering.

Who remembers which contents? The answer to this question gives an indication about which memories the Second World War still plays a role in. Here we can observe a number of common denominators across the political and territorial borders of the survey area: mostly people in the age group of 65 and older display an interest in active memorializing, they most frequently show an interest in memorial events of the neighbouring regions[130] and are furthermore

---

129 | Personal translation of: "Zwischen Siegern und Besiegten einerseits und Tätern und Opfern andererseits [...][besteht] eine unentbehrliche Grundlage für den Vergleich von Nationen und ihren Problemen im Umgang mit ihrer Vergangenheit."
130 | A surprising exception is Rhineland-Palatinate, where the 16 to 24 year-olds show most interest.

the most numerous in stressing the importance of remembering the time of Nazism (see University of Luxembourg, IDENT2 2012/2013 – quantitative survey). These findings clearly show the connection between remembering and personal experience: personal experiences of the war or growing up in a postwar period are shaped by the coming to terms with the aftermath of the war and provide an access to remembering differing from that of following generations, because here it is not only transmission, for instance via print media, that informs the construction of remembering, but primarily personal experience.

Moreover, one can observe a gender-specific manner of remembering, with men more frequently than women showing an interest in active ways of remembering in the form of memorial events of the neighbouring regions. In addition – looking at the survey area in its entirety – it is especially university graduates who confirm that it is necessary to remember the period of Nazism. This might be explained by the fact that this section of the population has acquired a particularly wide interpretational knowledge through continuous access to educational material about history in general and Nazism in particular.

Regarding the content of remembering, we can formulate two theses: they refer primarily to the victim side of the aforementioned binary code, and – considering the survey results of the entire survey area – the border indicated in and by the newspaper articles is ever-present. Within the German border regions, the memories of the aftermath of the war occupy a special place. In the Saarland, family memories of flight[131] are particularly vivid. Also the loss of relatives is most frequently remembered in the Saarland and in Rhineland-Palatinate. A glance at the historical background here shows that memory constructions trace an image of historically proven reality: the population of the German border region was greatly affected by war events, particularly towards the end of the Second World War, because "cities close to the border such as Aachen, Trier and Saarbrücken as well as their environs turned into direct military combat zones"[132] (Düwell 1997: 97).

Memories of Nazi persecution[133] dominate on the other side of the German border: almost a fifth of the respondents from Luxembourg and the border regions of France and Belgium state that family members were interned in a concentration camp (in the Saarland, by contrast, these are 3 % and in Rhineland-Palatinate 6 %). Also experiences of emigration and exile are most frequently remembered in Luxembourg and in the border regions of France and Belgium. What is surprising is that the

---

131 | Deportations were included in the question: "During the Second World War, members of my family were affected by deportation or flight." (University of Luxembourg, IDENT2 2012/2013 – quantitative survey).

132 | Personal translation of: [denn] "grenznahe Städte wie Aachen, Trier und Saarbrücken sowie ihr Umland [wurden] direkt zum militärischen Kampfgebiet."

133 | Respondents were asked about internment in a concentration camp, about emigration and exile.

survey results for Luxembourg reflect no particular memory of the evacuations in the Minette region that were featured in the newspaper articles.

The results show that the partition of the survey area by the border between the German and the neighbouring regions to the west, as indicated in the first step of this case study, remains prevalent. The memory contents do not, however, completely match the contents of the newspaper articles.[134] We can therefore identify a process of remembering that runs contrary to the print media: the border residents thus do not adopt the newspapers' ready-made explanations and identitary attributions, it is rather subjectivations that comprise a substantial part of the constitution of the subject. Here the border drawn by the survey results separates the differently experienced war years.

So far, we have shown that personal memories frequently contradict the discourses in the print media, particularly with respect to victims' memories. Patterns of desirability are a common feature in the newspaper articles: the victim as a moral victor is a desirable transmission that is both ever-present and implied. The more powerful party in this constellation has *per se* a stronger interest in visualizing the past than the perpetrator whose ideas and actions were discredited. For this reason, one can assume that the practices of remembering draw on the implicit values and patterns of interpretation of the victims' memory, while memories of perpetratorship are not included. But which subjectivations emerge in the respondents' response behaviour?

The interest of the respondents from the Saarland and Rhineland-Palatinate in participating in memorial events of neighbouring regions is only marginally smaller than in the border regions of Belgium, France and Luxembourg. The relevance of the subject 'Nazism' for the present, however, is assessed very differently: in Belgium, 84 % of the respondents believe that it is necessary to remember the time of Nazism, in Luxembourg and France it is 83 % – in Rhineland-Palatinate, by contrast, only 68 % and in the Saarland 65 % of respondents gave an affirmative response to this question. Here, the affirmation follows the border indicated in the newspapers, which stresses the fact that the population in the survey area absorbed the experiences of the war period in diverse ways. Queried directly about the relevance of remembering, they chose very different responses among the range of options presented in the questionnaires.

It was possible to clarify the reasons for these differences by putting the very direct question to the respondents whether they had any memory of perpetratorship in their own family: an equally small number of people in the examined border regions remember that family members were involved in

---

134 | One should note the problem inherent in the content-related comparison between transmission and survey results; newspaper articles about 10 May 1940 contain hardly any information about Nazi persecution. Here a thematic expansion of the source corpus of the newspapers would suggest itself, as well as evaluating the survey using additional socio-demographic criteria.

executions. The vehemence with which this memory was expressed and thus the form of subjectivation[135] of the respondents is, however, articulated differently: while 74 to 78 % of the respondents from the border regions of France, Belgium and Luxembourg assertively answered with "no" (no family members were involved in executions) and 15 to 18 % stated "I don't know", 29 % in Saarland and 23 % in Rhineland-Palatinate admitted that they had no knowledge with regard to this question. Concerning the memory of perpetratorship in their own family, the respondents of the German border regions are thus more guarded in their statements. This guardedness can be seen as related to a feeling of shame and repression, but can also be tied to ignorance, because the issue does not feature in the relevant family accounts. Yet both explanations point to different ways of processing these memories in border regions: the observation that on the German side, memories of victimhood are clearly expressed while at the same time, memories of perpetratorship tend to be more vague could suggest that here various codes overlap. Thus, many Germans refused to adopt the attribution of perpetrator made in the border-region newspapers of Belgium, France and Luxembourg. On the contrary, in the Federal Republic of Germany after the Second World War, there prevailed "over many years an attitude of repression which can be described as 'self-victimization' and which makes the own perpetratorship recede behind the self-perception as a victim of Nazi seduction, Anglo-American air raids and the arbitrariness of the Soviet victors"[136] (Sabrow 2006: 134). Thus, in the German case, there was a difference between the forms of subjectivation and the way in which "individuals are addressed as subjects by discourses"[137] (Bührmann/Schneider 2007). In Luxembourg, by contrast, the media addressed subjectifications that – in their attributions of victimhood – were easier to integrate into subjectivations. Hence, on both sides of the indicated border, we see different interpretations of the position of the victims, as on the German side they were influenced more strongly by ambiguities in people's own (family) biographies. These ambiguities are evident today in the respondents' response behaviour.

The fact that memories are relevant for an understanding of history is confirmed by a connection in the memory of the respondents: cross tabellations

---

135 | 'Form of subjectivation' here means the "[...] self-interpretation, the self-experience and the self-perception of individuals and thus their self-understanding in the sense of an 'own identity'" (Bührmann/Schneider 2007). (Personal translation of: "Selbstdeutung, das Selbsterleben und die Selbstwahrnehmung der Individuen und damit ihr Selbstverständnis im Sinne der 'eigenen Identität'").

136 | Personal translation of: [herrschte in der Bundesrepublik vielmehr] "[...] über viele Jahre eine Verdrängungshaltung vor, die sich als 'Selbstviktimisierung' bezeichnen lässt und die die eigene Täterschaft hinter der Selbstwahrnehmung als Opfer brauner Verführung, angloamerikanischer Bombardierung und sowjetischer Siegerwillkür zurücktreten ließ."

137 | Personal translation of: "[...] wie Individuen von Diskursen als 'Subjekte' adressiert werden."

have shown that people with memories of victimhood are particularly frequently of the opinion that the Greater Region has a common history. This connection is not evident with people who have memories of perpetratorship in their family.[138] We can therefore observe a connection between remembering and current positioning in reference to the survey area.

5.7.4 Conclusion

We have shown that practices of remembering in the border regions of Luxembourg, France, Belgium and Germany take on different forms. The presented source corpus allowed us to make a range of further differentiations. This is particularly advantageous in view of the *en bloc* treatment of Luxembourg, France and Belgium conducted here. The approach chosen in this case study represents one of many possibilities of defining identities in border regions in relation to memory.

The evaluation of newspaper articles has shown the distinctiveness of the war experience separating the Rhineland-Palatinate and the Saarland from the survey regions further to the west. In Luxembourg, the border violation of 10 May 1940 is permanently inscribed in the collective memory, while in the French and Belgian border regions, it is addressed in a less intensive but similar way. The survey was also instrumental in making the border visible by how past events are remembered today in various forms of subjectivation; it thus not only divides the memory, transported via the media, of differently experienced war years, but also reacts to the alignment with different "subject models"[139] (Reckwitz 2008a: 139): while the respondents of all regions covered by the survey can identify with the remembered representation of victimhood, the constitution of the subject remains vague when the delicate issue of remembering perpetratorship in the family is addressed. These observations are particularly evident on the German side of the border; the emotional dissonance mentioned earlier, as well as moral dilemmas of the next generation (see Assmann 2006: 159) feature prominently here.

It was also illustrated how the memory of victimhood is dominant within the binary code 'victim/perpetrator', as the former comes to define a culturally desirable subject model. This means that in the examined articles it is primarily values connected with the victims' side that are emphasized: freedom, independence and humanity are implicitly conveyed as features of the victims (and thus ultimately of the victors). The processing of these attributions, as informed and impacted by, amongst others, constantly changing public interpretations of the past, group memories and forms of subjectivation continuously takes on new forms.

---

138 | The empirical data base is very small, due to the few recorded memories of perpetrators: only 67 of the 2,279 respondents state that members of their family had been involved in executions and 102 respondents remember that family members had been involved in lootings.
139 | Personal translation of: "Subjektmodelle."

This case study has shown that the border location is actually the special feature of the survey area: in daily life, it is not necessarily solely people's own memory that is relevant, but also the manner in which they view the neighbouring regions and how they are viewed by their neighbours. It was only possible to bring to light the different forms of subjectivation in contrasting the different border regions. The newspaper articles in particular have helped to show to which degree the view of the 'other' and of one's own role can be subject to change – a result that once again points to the instability of identity models in general.

Sources

La Meuse (1952), VELA: "10 Mai. Mir Letzeburger önner ons", edition of 10.5.1952, 2.
La Meuse (1960a), n. p.: "Histoire de la guerre 1939-1945. 10 mai 1940", edition of 10.5.1960, 4.
La Meuse (1960b), n. p.: "Histoire de la guerre 1939-1945", edition of 11.5.1960, 5.
Le Républicain Lorrain (1965), n. p.: "Quand les Alliés ouvrirent les portes", edition of 2.5.1965, 18.
Luxemburger Wort (1950), n.p.: "Erinnerung", edition of 10.5.1950, 1.
Luxemburger Wort (1965), Jacoby, Al: "Das Generalkommissariat für Evakuierte", edition of 8.5.1965, 20.
Tageblatt (2006), Faber, M.: "Ne pas oublier le 10 mai 1940", edition of 30.5.2006, 58.

5.8 Beyond Luxembourg. Space and Identity Constructions in the Context of Cross-border Residential Migration

Christian Wille, Gregor Schnuer, Elisabeth Boesen

This case study examines the relationship between constructions of space and identity in Luxembourg and the surrounding border regions. A particular focus are cross-border residential migrants, that is, people who have moved from Luxembourg into the neighbouring border regions. This group is compared with other groups in Luxembourg and in the border region with respect to their space- and group-related attitudes and practices. In addition, it serves as a reference category in the sense that the attitudes of the interviewees towards the phenomenon of residential migration provide insights about their self-positionings and group-related identity constructions.

The flow of residential migrants from Luxembourg has been continuous for the last decade and has entailed some considerable structural changes for the communities near the border.[140] This development is primarily due to the low land and real-estate prices in the German, French and Belgian border regions compared to those in Luxembourg. Statistical information about the group of residential migrants is sporadic and incomplete at best[141], so that only limited statements can be made about their prevalence in the survey area. Nonetheless, the findings show that since the beginning of the 2000s, there has been a marked increase of residential migrants and that the two German federal states of Saarland and Rhineland-Palatinate have meanwhile become the preferred target regions. In addition, the overwhelming majority of residential migrants are people employed in Luxembourg, who have, by moving, become cross-border commuters. A third feature of the group that differentiates it from residential migrants of other European border regions is their enormous heterogeneity with regards to national and socio-cultural affiliation.[142]

Besides this relatively recent form of border crossing, the commuter flows into Luxembourg have been playing an increasingly larger role in the border regions ever since the 1980s, so that their other residential population is also highly mobile. Currently around 155,000 people commute daily from the neighbouring regions to their workplace in Luxembourg (see IBA 2013: 81ff.). Among them there are increasingly more 'atypical border commuters', i.e. residential migrants who, after moving away from Luxembourg, continue to work there. The existing evaluations of statistical data on atypical border commuters covering the period from 2001 to 2007 (see Brosius/Carpentier 2010) and the year 2011 (see IBA 2013: 120ff.) not only show that the number of atypical border commuters has increased significantly, but also provide a first indication about the composition of the group of residential migrants. The majority (57 %) is comprised of French, Belgian and, to a lesser degree, German nationals, i.e. persons for whom moving away from Luxembourg meant returning to their country of origin. A further group (10 %) consists of persons of Portuguese nationality, and finally around a quarter of the atypical border commuters are of Luxembourgish nationality (in the year 2011 exactly 3,446 persons).

---

140 | The municipality of Wincheringen in Rhineland-Palatinate can serve as a case in point here: currently the percentage of foreigners living here is as high as 23 % (in 2000, it was 4 %), comprising 33 nationalities (see Schnuer/Boesen/Wille 2013). We can observe a similar development in the Saarland municipality of Perl where the number of residents coming from Luxembourg increased between 1990 and 2010 from 55 to 1,272 (see Nienaber/Kriszan 2013: 5).

141 | The official statistics – where available – do not give a completely truthful picture of the actual development, since a large number of people that move across the border retain their original domicile in Luxembourg.

142 | For instance, persons of Luxembourgish origin, members of different groups of classic work migrants (in particular families of Portuguese origin) as well as members of the highly mobile international elites (finance, European institutions).

Besides the residence and work related mobility, the region under consideration also exhibits a high cross-border mobility in other areas of daily life as shown, among others, by the findings of our survey (University of Luxembourg, IDENT2 2012/2013 – quantitative survey). Thus 76 % of respondents in the entire survey area state that they more or less regularly cross over to a neighbouring country for at least one everyday activity (besides work).

Against the background of these developments and in view of the described heterogeneity, the examined border region constitutes a suitable case for the study of constructions of space and identity on the subject level. Our basic assumption is that concepts of space and identity built on national boundaries or clear-cut categories of 'we' and 'the other' fall short here. The understanding of identity and difference on which the majority of empirical studies in the context of the border are based presumes a binary structure of identity constructions (see Bürkner 2011). This perspective is, however, only insufficiently suited for mapping the everyday realities in the examined border region. We argue that what we are dealing with here is, in more ways than one, a progressive dissolution of clear-cut group structures, and the group of residential migrants is the one that challenges these binary notions of identity particularly strongly. This implies the question in how far the geopolitical structures that are constitutive for the study context of 'border region' are still relevant as categories of perception and identification. What needs to be examined is which constructions of space and identity emerge in the social processes marked by residential migration and other phenomena of mobility and in how far they can serve to overcome concepts based on national borders and binary notions.

The case study attempts to do justice to the particular complexity of the border region by not relying on the given national categories, but considering different everyday-cultural dimensions of differentiation. On the one hand, we differentiate between residential migrants from Luxembourg and the local population in the border region and in Luxembourg, with the group of locals subdivided in autochthonous residents and arrivals from other parts of the country and abroad. On the other hand, cross-border commuters are considered as a distinct social group. Furthermore, we seek to understand the territorial and social dimension of spaces as linked and examine their interaction in processes of identity construction. In line with the praxeological perspective adopted in this chapter, we understand identity constructions as subject constitutions that occur in the interplay of subjectifications and subjectivations. On the basis of empirical data we in particular address the question whether the mentioned mobile practices influence modes of subjectivation.

5.8.1 Space-related Identities

Space-related identities are examined via two complementary approaches (see Sonntag 2013: 46ff. as well as section 2.3 in this volume). One consists in investigating how individuals of the different groups of people described above identify *with* spaces; this primarily concerns a sense of belonging to a cross-border region. With the other approach, we aim to map identifications *of* spaces by revealing space-related representations of a cross-border region. Both approaches provide insights about interpretations and attributions of meaning and deal with different aspects of social practices. On the one hand, we examine the relation between social practices and a sense of belonging to a border region, and on the other, which space-generating discourses and experiences are reflected in space-related representations.

In a first step, the inhabitants of the survey area were asked in how far they have a sense of belonging with respect to different spatial entities. These entities also include the cross-border level of the Greater Region SaarLorLux (see Wille 2012: 106ff.). The results of the quantitative survey show that the majority of all respondents experience a sense of belonging to their respective country of residence and origin (85 % and 81 %), with the inhabitants of Luxembourg in particular (where 43 % of all residents are foreigners) differentiating between country of residence and of origin (93 % and 82 %). By contrast, only a little over a third (35 %) of the respondents identifies with the Greater Region, and this affiliation is more often linked with a sense of belonging to the country of residence than the other way round. This suggests that the identifications with the cross-border level should not be seen as an expression of a general cosmopolitan attitude, but rather as a correlate of other, partly local ties and corresponding spatial appropriation processes. In comparing the national and regional groups, further marked differences emerge with respect to the identification with the cross-border level. Respondents from the Saarland displayed a remarkably high percentage of identification with the Greater Region (63 %); the Luxembourg residential population is still above the average with 44 %, whereas among the inhabitants of Lorraine, only 33 % state having a sense of belonging, followed by 27 % in Rhineland-Palatinate and finally 14 % in Wallonia.

A closer look at the different subpopulations in the border region shows that the identification with the Greater Region is particularly strong with the questioned cross-border commuters (47 %). The residential migrants from Luxembourg, as well as the autochthonous residents, also identify to a relatively high degree with the cross-border level (41 % and 35 %), while the sense of belonging to the Greater Region of those residential migrants not coming from Luxembourg is remarkably low (from the same country: 25 %, from abroad: 26 %). This confirms that the cross-border level is relevant for identity particularly for people with marked local ties and for those who are mobile in the border area. This link between a sense of belonging on the level of the Greater Region, on a local level and the everyday experience of crossing the border is even stronger if further features of the respondents are included. The statistical evaluation of the quantitative data shows that there is a clear link for the entire survey area between the degree of identification with the Greater Region, the cross-border performance of everyday practices, cross-border information behaviour (keeping abreast of current affairs) as well the existence of relations with friends and work colleagues in neighbouring regions.

The most frequent cross-border practices performed "more or less regularly" comprise doing the groceries for daily needs and going shopping (see Fig. 1), trips to the countryside as well as visiting cultural events and friends. In addition, more than half of all respondents (53 %) state that they regularly keep informed about current affairs in the neighbouring country. This cross-border information behaviour is particularly pronounced with the inhabitants of Luxembourg (61 %) and the inhabitants of the francophone regions (Lorraine: 51 %, Wallonia: 59 %) as well as the residential migrants from Luxembourg (70 %).

The connections between spatial identifications and other features discussed so far provide insights about identifications *with* spaces. In a further step, identities *of* spaces, more exactly, of the political-administrative spatial construction 'Greater Region' will be examined in order to understand how the latter is represented. In interviews, it was established whether the term 'Greater Region' was known to the interviewees and if so, what they associate with it. Almost all of them stated being familiar with the term (see in more detail Wille 2009) and addressed the following dimensions of experience.

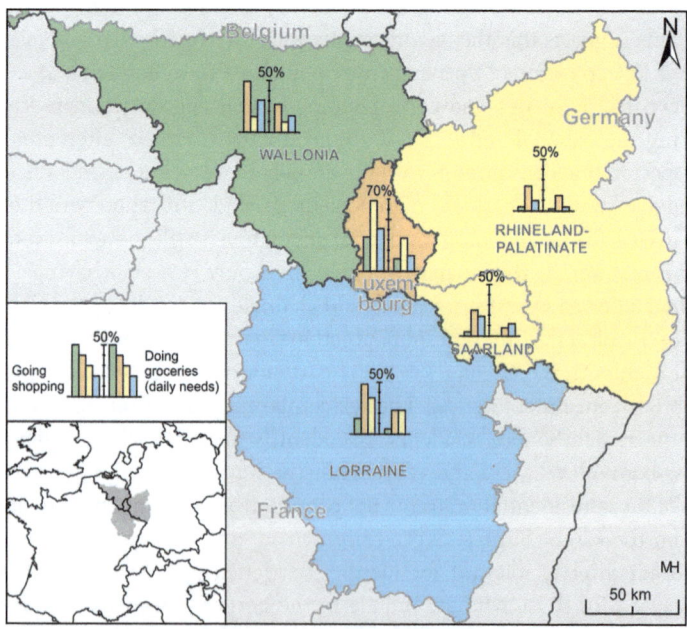

Figure 1: Cross-border everyday practices: shopping and groceries
(University of Luxembourg, IDENT2 2012/2013 – quantitative survey)
(design: Christian Wille, realization: Malte Helfer)
Legend: 69 % of the respondents in Luxembourg shop in neighbouring Germany on a more or less regular basis

A majority of the interviewees first attempts to define the *geographical dimension* of the Greater Region. In doing so, the concept is connected with different levels of scale (national, regional, municipal), with the countries Luxembourg, France and Germany, the regions Province of Luxembourg, Saarland, Rhineland-Palatinate, and the cities Trier, Saarbrücken and Arlon being named most often. The term 'SaarLorLux' is also addressed, the original term for the cross-border cooperation area, pointing to the border region's industrial past and the expanded geopolitical configuration (see Wille 2012: 120ff.). Here, the interviewees make much less specific statements when they describe the Greater Region as consisting of the "cities around Luxembourg", "everything in a radius of 100 km of Luxembourg" or "a bit of Germany, a bit of France and a bit of Belgium." What we can safely say is that the interviewees assume a spatial entity whose representations, however, do not correspond to the shape of the political cooperation area, but rather seem to demarcate a core space within the Greater Region that is probably more relevant for the interviewees' cross-border everyday experiences.

In addition, some of the interviewees in Luxembourg are familiar with the term 'Greater Region' via the *media*. For instance, a radio station is mentioned that emphasizes the fact that it is broadcasting for the Greater Region. They also point to the free papers that are available in the Grand Duchy and in the directly neighbouring towns and in which "you regularly come across the term of Greater Region"[143] (also see section 4.2). Finally, the term is associated with a cross-border cultural project; in 2007 Luxembourg and the Greater Region were the location of the cultural capital of Europe, which is also reflected in the name of the mega event: *Luxembourg and Greater Region – European Capital of Culture 2007*. In terms of marketing, it was at the time important to "highlight Luxembourg in the context of the Greater Region in the sense of an attribution process" and give the region "a (greater-)regional identity" (Reddeker 2011: 196f.).

Some interviewees connect 'Greater Region' *with European and/or regional-political collaboration*, without specifically mentioning any institutions of the political cooperation (see Wille 2012: 119ff.) by name, but rather referring to concrete changes – the abolition of identity checks at borders, the free movement of persons and goods. People emphasized particularly that "much has become simpler" as well as the "ease"[144] with which borders can be overcome nowadays. In this context, 'Greater Region' is also associated with the reconciliation process after the Second World War. What the interviewees thus understand under 'Greater Region' are primarily the results of the institutional cross-border cooperation that are palpable in everyday life.

A further frequently addressed set of subjects with respect to the 'Greater Region' is the *employment of border commuters in Luxembourg*. Thus the interviewees

---

143 | Personal translation of: "[...] man immer wieder von Großregion liest."
144 | Personal translation of: "[...] dass Vieles einfacher geworden ist"; [sowie die] "die Leichtigkeit."

in Luxembourg emphasize that the Grand Duchy relies on the Greater Region "because of the border commuters."[145] And *vice versa*, Luxembourg is described by the inhabitants of the surrounding border regions as the number one employer or as an economic driving force whose effect reaches far into the neighbouring regions. The border commuters among the interviewees connect 'Greater Region' in particular with cross-border commuting, with the geographical distribution of their circle of colleagues and with the advantages of border-commuter employment.

Finally, many interviewees connect 'Greater Region' with the possibility "to be quickly in another country."[146] Here they mention *cross-border daily practices*, primarily involving selective buying of particularly cheap products (petrol, tobacco, coffee, spirits) in Luxembourg and, with a view to the border region, doing general cross-border groceries or shopping, as well as residential migration and visiting friends and acquaintances.

We can safely say that in the identification *of* the 'Greater Region', a variety of everyday-cultural dimensions interact. On the one hand, attempts to depict the Greater Region through geopolitical categories produce the diffuse image of a cross-border region; 'Greater Region' is identified as a variable spatial entity of cities, regions and countries. These demarcations seem partly shaped by media-driven representations and political-administrative discourses. On the other hand, it becomes clear that the representation of 'Greater Region' is primarily connected with the interviewees' cross-border mobile practices and in that sense also with the results of the political-institutional cooperation.

All in all, we were able to establish that the interviewees' identification *with* the cross-border level was relatively weak, but that the identification *of* the Greater Region reflects a strong representation of the cross-border spatial entity that orients itself only to a very small degree along geopolitical categories and even less along the actual territory that is the purview of the bodies of cooperation in the Greater Region. For the interviewees, the experience of crossing the border in the course of everyday practices seemed to be far more relevant. We can assume from this result that the majority of interviewees is engaged in a "*Doing Grande Région*" (Wille 2010), but has little use for the political-administrative concept of 'Greater Region'.

With respect to the spatial aspects of subjectivation processes, there can be little doubt that space in both respects – identification *of* and *with* – proves to be primarily a category of everyday-cultural (and localized) experience. The identification with the Greater Region correlates, as we have seen, with the connectedness to the place of residence, on the one hand, and with cross-border everyday practices (consumption, information, social contacts), on the other. The representations of the Greater Region are also formed by taking recourse to these concrete mobile practices. While we can observe differences between the

---

145 | Personal translation of: "[...] wegen der Grenzgänger."
146 | Personal translation of: "[...] schnell in einem anderen Land zu sein."

examined groups and – partly considerable – differences between the compared regional entities, this in no way changes the basic findings.

5.8.2 Group-related Identities

The results so far suggest that there is a general tendency of an identification *of* and *with* the Greater Region and that this increases with the intensification of cross-border practices and experiences. In a further step, we aim to shed light on the relation between constructions of space and identity from another angle by turning our attention, as mentioned above, to the group of residential migrants and thus to a third form of identification; after having discussed identifications *with* and *of*, what interests us with respect to this group is the 'being identified' (Graumann 1983). We argue that the phenomenon of cross-border residential migration promises to provide particular insights when we try to clarify space-related identity constructions. Living somewhere differs from other cross-border practices (e.g. working, consuming, maintaining contacts etc.), in the sense that settling down in a place initiates a process which usually leads to an identification of a more comprehensive nature than the practices mentioned above. The place becomes a part of one's own identity (see Weichhart 1990). But at the same time, the place is in turn identified with its residents, i.e. the influx of new residents can change the 'character' of a place, a neighbourhood or an entire village. This therefore raises the question whether or in which degree these identification processes take effect in the case of cross-border residential migrants. As mentioned in the beginning, we consider the group of residential migrants in the context discussed here as a reference category. What interests us is how the residential migrants and in particular their relationship to their new place of residence are perceived, in as far as these perceptions reveal something about identification processes in the border regions and in the Greater Region as a whole.

The border area residents that moved from Luxembourg, who meanwhile comprise more than 20 % of the population in some municipalities, represent a very heterogeneous group, and this not only in terms of nationality and socio-economic profiles, but also concerning family structures, even though one can here observe a clear preponderance of young couples who are first property buyers (Brosius/Carpentier 2010: 26). Also because of this diversity, it is difficult to establish a 'common denominator' for the group of residential migrants and the perceptions and identification processes can be assumed to be correspondingly complex.

In order to establish a synopsis of opinions about residential migrants, we formulated twelve statements about "persons who move from Luxembourg into the neighbouring region" (see Table 1) which the respondents could answer using a 4-point scale. In the statistical analysis, we concentrated on those persons of the sample for whom we could assume a daily connection to the phenomenon of residential migration, i.e. on persons who do not live further away than 40 km from the Luxembourg border (n= 1,319). Persons who did not wish to or could not make a statement about the phenomenon of residential migration were left out of consideration.

As Table 1 shows, there is a difference between residents of the examined partial areas in terms of how residential migration is perceived. In order to test this difference for significance and for influences from other relevant variables, logistic regressions were conducted that consider various possible predictor variables. These variables refer to the demographic and socio-economic features as well as to the sense of belonging and to cross-border agency.[147] This procedure enables us to check whether or which predictor variables show a significant difference in response behaviour. Corresponding significances are displayed via probability ratios with respect to the response behaviour.[148] We limit ourselves to showing the regressions with respect to the aspects of 'finances' and 'integration', since they produce the clearest results and offer good possibilities for comparison.

---

147 | Variables considered in the analysis: country of residence (Luxembourg/border region); autochthonous/new arrival; national/non-national; age (ordinal scale); income; household with/without children; urban/suburban/rural life style; cross-border/non cross-border information behaviour; relatives/no relatives, friends/no friends and work colleagues/no work colleagues in the neighbouring regions; criteria for current place of residence as dichotomous; yes/no variables (price, relatives and friends, infrastructure, local public transport connection, connection to the road network); sense of belonging to Greater Region/country of residence/country of origin/region of residence/place of residence (ordinal scales); cross-border/no cross-border practices (shopping, sports, cultural events etc.).

148 | Example: nationals are more likely to agree with the statement "Residential migrants will never become real locals" than non-nationals.

Areas of opinion	Statements The people who move ...	Luxembourg residential population (agreement in %)	Border area residents (agreement in %)
finances	... can't afford to live in Luxembourg.	89	73
	... are primarily concerned about money.	95	82
	... should better invest their money in Luxembourg.	64	39
	... are pushing up the prices.	63	59
quality of life	... enjoy on the whole a higher quality of life.	39	63
	... have their family's best interest at heart.	78	83
national affiliation	... don't feel at home anymore in Luxembourg.	33	35
	... aren't real Luxembourgers.	27	32
integration	... only come home to sleep.	59	51
	... will never become true locals.	60	43
	... keep to themselves.	52	46
	... enjoy participating in village life at their new place of residence.	46	60

Table 1: Statements and opinions about residential migrants (University of Luxembourg, IDENT2 2012/2013 – quantitative survey)

The analysis first shows a significance of the variable 'country of residence', i.e. a difference between the residents of Luxembourg and the surrounding border area with respect to their attitude towards the two discussed aspects of residential migration: it is more likely that those living in Luxembourg believe that the residential migrants would move for financial reasons and would not integrate well in their new place of residence than that the residents of the border region would adopt this view. If, in a second step, the Luxembourg residential population is considered separately, it is only for a small minority of opinions that the regressions point to significant connections. With respect to the view that financial reasons were responsible for the residential migration, the lack of significance can be explained by the fact that the rate of agreement is very high (89 % and 95 %), which suggests that this view in Luxembourg is unquestioned collective knowledge that remains uninfluenced by the variables in question. By contrast, the fact whether in daily life cross-border practices are carried out or not is a significant variable with respect to the opinions about residential migration. Thus people living in Luxembourg who do sports, go out, participate in associations and have friends across the border rate the integration of residential migrants in their new place of residence more favourably than persons not engaging in such cross-border practices. Also, the variable national/non-national proves significant in the analysis of the Luxembourg residential population; people with a migration background rate the participation of the residential migrants in village life and their potential for "becoming real locals" more favourably than Luxembourg nationals.

In the case of the residents of the neighbouring regions, the regressions for the individual subgroups show that certain predictor variables correlate significantly with differences in the opinions of the residents of the respective subregions. In addition, this analysis permits a more extended comparison between Luxembourg and the surrounding border region, i.e. it makes clear that there are not only differing opinions about residential migration, but that opinions in the subregions are in each case influenced by different variables. For the statement "... should better invest their money in Luxembourg" for instance, none of the mentioned variables had a significant influence on the response behaviour of the interviewed border region residents, while in Luxembourg age and cross-border practices play a role.

In the regressions to the other finance-related statements, the variable cross-border migrants/non-cross-border migrants stands out; the cross-border migrants tend to agree more with this statements than the rest of the border region population. A further significant variable is cross-border groceries. This practice correlates positively with the mentioned statements, whereas other cross-border activities turn out to be non-significant variables.

With respect to the integration statements "... like to participate in village life" and "come only home to sleep", the variable national/non-national proves significant in the border region; nationals are clearly more likely to rate the integration of residential migrants at their new place of residence negatively. The cross-border migrant status is here no longer significant. With regard to the statement "... will never become real locals", the variable autochthonous/arrivals from outside is significant.

The regressions on the entire survey area confirm a significant difference between the residents of the border region and those of Luxembourg in their opinions about residential migrants. One should, however, emphasize here that the variables 'national sense of belonging' and nationality have proven to be not significant. In addition, the logistic regressions within both subgroups 'Luxembourgers' and 'border region residents' show not only that the response behaviour and thus the opinions are different, but also that the response behaviour in the two subregions is influenced by different factors. In conclusion, we can make the following observations:

(1) We can identify a general difference between the opinions in Luxembourg and in the border area. This consists chiefly in the fact that, from the perspective of the Luxembourg respondents, moving into the border region is understood more as a choice motivated by the difference in rent and property prices than a choice based on other pragmatic or socio-cultural reasons. For the border region, by contrast, we can observe that the integration of residential migrants is rated more favourably than in Luxembourg.

(2) It has also become clear that certain everyday practices have an influence on how residential migration is assessed, so that the picture indicating a general difference between Luxembourg and the border area in this regard turns out to be an inaccurate one. More detailed analysis, however, shows that this effect does not apply to the opinions as a whole, but only with regard to certain aspects. Thus cross-border social contacts and cultural practices influence the Luxembourg residential population's opinions about integration, while they have no influence on their opinions about the financial aspect of residential migration.

On the whole, the findings support the assessment that the various aspects of residential migration have a more marked influence on opinions where they play a more significant role in everyday life – issues of integration for border region residents and the evaluation of financial advantages and disadvantages for residents of Luxembourg. This observation also offers an explanation for the significance of the variables regarding cross-border practices and relations. In opinions about aspects that play a bigger role in everyday life 'beyond the border', cross-border practices and relations prove to be significant variables. Thus residents living in the border area and engaging in cross-border activities perceive financial advantages and disadvantages in a similar way to Luxembourg residents, and Luxembourg residents engaging in cross-border activities rate integration in a similar way to border region residents. Opinions that play a less important role 'beyond the border' do not seem to be influenced by cross-border practices and relationships. Thus opinions of border region residents regarding integration remain uninfluenced by social contacts in Luxembourg.

5.8.3 Conclusion

In this case study we have concerned ourselves with geographical and political-administrative borders, that is, with the borders between Luxembourg and its neighbouring countries. The object of our research were the different forms in which these borders are crossed and the question how the intensification and diversification of these crossings influence (spatial) identity constructions. In the first step of analysis, we evaluated the quantitative data and the interview material with regard to forms of space-related identification and observed that the cross-border space of all examined groups is appropriated as a space of concrete everyday practices. In addition, we were able to verify that there is a correlation between cross-border practices and spatial identification. In a second step, we attempted to further clarify these cross-border processes by taking a closer look at the group of residential migrants representing this identity construction in a special way. With the aid of logistical regressions, we were able to show in how far the opinions about this group correlate with other features and observe that the response behaviour of the different groups in part differ significantly with respect to these correlations. The statistical results suggest for instance that cross-border practices influence the attitudes of the Luxembourg residential population about residential migration in some aspects more strongly than is the case with border area residents.

In conclusion, we can say that our findings show in particular how difficult it is to make general statements regarding the developments of cross-border spatial identities. Or, returning to our set of theoretical-conceptual tools, that – despite the connection between spatial practices and identifications that can be observed in all groups – it would be mistaken to assume that space-related subjectivation processes and identity constructions would evolve in the same way for all residents of the survey area. Opinions about the group of residential migrants coincide in some aspects, but the statistical analysis of the correlation of voiced opinions, group affiliation and everyday practices allows the guarded conclusion that cross-border practices have up to now not had the general effect of producing a homogenous perception of cross-border residential migration. The group-specific attitudes to residential migrants do not seem to dissolve, but rather become more differentiated.

5.9 Linguistic Identifications in the Luxembourg-German Border Region

Heinz Sieburg and Britta Weimann

The present case study examines internal and external ascriptions of residents in Luxembourg and the surrounding border areas with regard to language, which is seen as an important element of identities (see Bucholtz/Hall 2005: 370). This close connection of language and identity results in particular from the social-symbolic function of language (see Hess-Lüttich 2004) which it has besides its communicative function (see Edwards 2009: 4f.), i.e. language is not only a medium of communication; it also says something about the speakers and their affiliation to a group. The same dichotomy in communicative and symbolic functions can be observed in the assessment of individual languages

5. Space and Identity Constructions through Everyday-Cultural Practices 339

and varieties[149] by their speakers. The communicative value a language has for its speakers does not necessarily need to coincide with its symbolic value (see Edwards 2009: 55f.). Thus the speakers of a language that does not yet or no longer meet communicative requirements – for instance because it has been displaced by another language or variety – may still ascribe high symbolic value to it. Such ambivalent value attributions play a major part in the process of appropriating linguistic identities.

The study focusses on the comparison between Luxembourg and the neighbouring German regions that share a historically evolved dialect continuum and the use of the German standard language.[150] Dialect continua are marked by increasing linguistic differences in their spatial extension with mutual comprehension of neighbouring dialects (see Chambers/Trudgill 2002: 5f.). In this sense, they can be regarded as threshold areas or extended border zones (see section 2.1). If they are intersected by political borders, often two differing areas of language use are created as in the case of Germany and Austria or German-speaking Switzerland, where in each case specific national varieties of German are used and where situations in which the dialect may be used differ (see Riehl 1999: 45 and 48f.). Luxembourg also has its national variety of German (see Sieburg 2013: 100f.). Luxembourgish, by contrast, an 'Ausbau' language with an increasing degree of standardization, has developed from the Moselle-Franconian dialects (see Gilles 1999 and 2009: 186f.), which in the 19th and early 20th century played an important part in shaping a Luxembourgish national identity (see Weimann 2013: 254). Together with French, as the third official language, Luxembourg now has a triglossia situation that has evolved from a purely medium-based one to one that is predominantly concept-driven. The use of the three official languages no longer depends on the medium (written/oral), but increasingly on factors such as proximity/distance and formality/informality (concept). Luxembourgish was for a long time limited to communicative situations that were oral in terms of medium and informal in terms of concept (e.g. everyday conversations), while the two major written languages, French and German, covered the formal (such as parliamentary speeches, sermons) and all written communicative situations. Today, Luxembourgish can be used in all oral and also in written communicative situations of a more informal nature such as chats, SMS, private letters (see section 4.6; see Gilles 2011: 63). The very distinct linguistic constellations in Luxembourg and in the German border regions also came about through the interplay of top-

---

149 | Varieties are various forms of a language such as dialects, regiolects (regional vernaculars), sociolects (group-specific varieties) or standard varieties (standard languages).

150 | The Mosel-Franconian from which Luxembourgish evolved is found on both sides of the Luxembourg-German border; German is also an official language in Luxembourg. Luxembourg shares the use of French with Lorraine and Wallonia. The continuum of West Middle German dialects reaches into both regions.

down implementations (e.g. through the languages act in Luxembourg) and bottom-up realizations (by individual speakers). Thus Luxembourg's languages act determines French as the language of legislation. At school, the alphabetization language is German, while Luxembourgish plays only a minor role in the curricula. These language-related standardizations and practices create a highly variable multilingual space. Since both the German language and the Moselle-Franconian variety cross the national border, but the repertoire of languages and varieties as well as the rules for their use differ in Luxembourg and the German border regions, one can expect ambivalent assessments, affiliations and demarcations.

Our study draws on empirical data from a survey using questionnaires, but also includes statements about language from an interview series (University of Luxembourg, IDENT2 2012/2013 – quantitative and qualitative surveys). Our questions seek to reveal, firstly, what language choices inhabitants of the German border region make in conversational situations for which – thus our assumption – there is no shared cultural code (see Reckwitz 2008: 135f.) in the sense of a transmitted standardization of linguistic behaviour[151] ("How do you answer if addressed in Luxembourgish, or has this never happened to you?"), and secondly, how the choice of one particular variety is assessed and deemed appropriate by Luxembourg's residential population ("What is your opinion when Germans address you in German/their own German local dialect/a mixture of their local dialect and Luxembourgish?"). Finally, a survey of semantic differentials and the question whether Luxembourgish is a dialect of German or a language in its own right, aim at gaining insights about the speakers' emotional connection to their own language and their evaluation of the 'language of the others' and hence about processes of appropriation and attribution.

5.9.1 Language Practices

Different, both active and passive, language competences play a role in everyday life when speakers encounter each other who possess different linguistic repertoires. Even when they share a variety or understand and speak similar varieties, the cultural codes and the choice of the appropriate variety are not necessarily compatible, which often generates misunderstandings.

In the quantitative survey (University of Luxembourg, IDENT2 2012/2013), three quarters of the interviewed residents in Rhineland-Palatinate and Saarland state that they have no competences in speaking Luxembourgish; around 15 % give themselves a low competence; medium and good competences are under 10 %. The question "How do you answer if addressed in Luxembourgish?" aims at revealing the answer strategies employed by the residents of the German border

---

151 | In this case, the code that specifies the choice of a particular variety cannot be identical as the inhabitants of the German border region don't as a rule speak Luxembourgish.

area, the majority of whom do not have the matching variety at their disposal. The languages given by the questionnaire as preset answer options were, in addition to "Luxembourgish" and "German", also "own dialect", "a mixture of my own dialect and Luxembourgish" as well as "other".

Fig. 1 shows the relationships for the entire German residential population. Between Rhineland-Palatinate and the Saarland there are only minor differences. A little over 60 % answer always or often in German, a further 11 % sometimes or rarely. Often the own dialect is also used (always or often: 21,5 %; sometimes or rarely: 21,1 %), which is probably considered adequate due to its similarity to Luxembourgish. Among those who answer with a mixture of their own dialect and Luxembourgish, for which at least rudimentary knowledge of Luxembourgish is required, almost 10 % answer always or often, almost 20 % answer sometimes or rarely. Only a minority of 9 % answer always or often in Luxembourgish. Among the few respondents with an intermediate or full competence in Luxembourgish, just under 50 % answer in this language. A further 7 % always or often use another language.

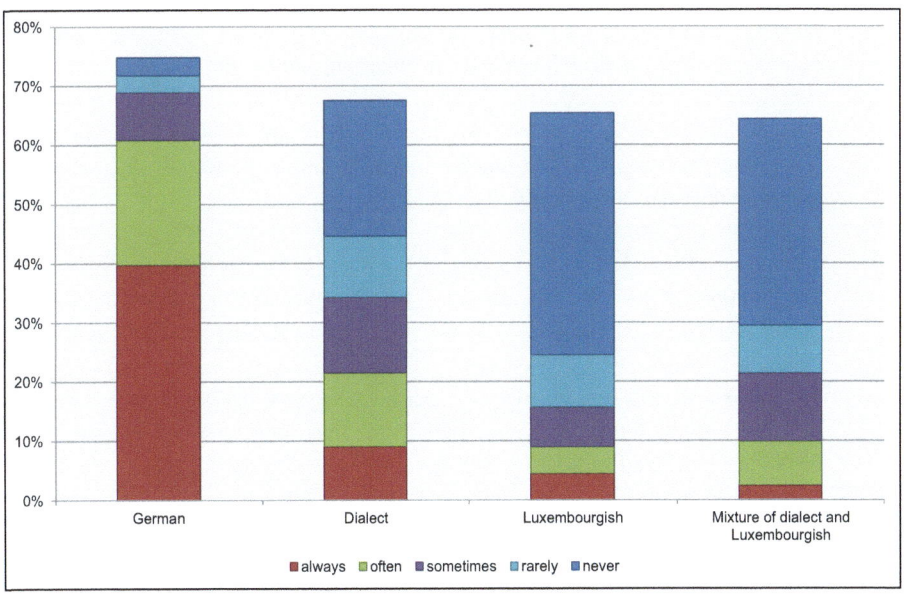

Figure 1: How do you answer if addressed in Luxembourgish? (The answer options "This situation has never happened to me" and "not specified" account for the gaps between percentages and 100) (University of Luxembourg, IDENT2 2012/2013 – quantitative survey)

The similarity between Luxembourgish and the Moselle-Franconian dialects of the German border areas is emphasized in some interviews:

"If we speak our vernacular here, that's maybe a bit faster what the Luxembourgers speak there, but we understand each other. Even though we don't have certain expressions, we don't have the *Chalumeau* (drinking straw) or *Kaweechelchen* (squirrel), but it's almost the same"[152] (male, 45, German, Rhineland-Palatinate).

Also when asked about the Greater Region (1) or cross-border practices (2), linguistic similarity plays a role. Two interviewees mention here the old borders of the Duchy of Luxembourg before the cession of eastern and western territories to Prussia and Belgium in the framework of the Congress of Vienna in 1815 and the Treaty of London of 1839:

(1) "Because already the language. You go to Sankt Vith over there, you go to the Eifel, you also go to... , but that's more or less still the same, I would say. Arlon, the whole area, you can't say that's typical Belgian. You know, maybe reviving the old borders [...]"[153] (female, 39, Luxembourger, Luxembourg).

(2) "I play golf in Klerf and I also play a lot here in Bitburg. There's no difference. There they all talk like us. [...] That side used to be Luxembourg, that's why they all speak vernacular there like we do. As far as Bitburg, you can speak normal. Luxembourgish. That's why there's no problem. Yeah"[154] (male, 62, Luxembourger, Luxembourg).

Despite all linguistic similarity, the interviewee from (2) is sure that he would recognize residents of the German border region (e.g. on holiday) by their language and not take them for Luxembourgers:

"They speak vernacular, a bit like us, but with a German accent, you notice that immediately. And they would also notice immediately that I'm a Luxembourger. If you meet someone like that on your holiday, then you know it immediately"[155] (male, 62, Luxembourger, Luxembourg).

---

152 | Personal translation of: "Wenn wir unser Platt hier sprechen, das ist ja jetzt vielleicht ein bisschen schneller wie das, was Luxemburger da sprechen, aber wir verstehen uns ja. Wir haben zwar bestimmte Ausdrücke nicht, den *Chalumeau* [Strohhalm], oder *Kaweechelchen* [Eichhörnchen] haben wir nicht, aber es ist fast dasselbe."

153 | Personal translation of: "Well schonn alleng mat der Sprooch; Dir gitt op St. Vith dohinner, Dir gitt an d'Äifel, Dir gitt och dann, dat ass dann awer nach relativ d'selwecht, soen ech elo mol sou. Arel de ganze Streech, ne, et kann ee jo elo net soen, dass dat typesch belsch oder sou ass. Sou vun, bëssen déi vläit déi al Grenzen [...] opliewe loossen."

154 | Personal translation of: "Ech spillen zu Klierf Golf, ech spillen awer och vill hei zu Bitburg. Et ass keen Ënnerscheed. Déi schwätze jo och all wéi mir do [...]. Déi Säit war jo fréier Lëtzebuerg, dofir, déi schwätzen all Platt wéi mir. Bis op Bitburg kennt dir normal schwätzen. Lëtzebuergesch. Dofir ass kee Problem do. Jo."

155 | Personal translation of: "Déi schwätze Platt, bësse wéi mir, awer en däitschen Akzent, dat mierkt een direkt. An déi géingen och direkt mierken, dass ech e Lëtzebuerger sinn. Dat ass sou. Wann ee sou ee begéint an der Vakanz, dat dat dat weess een direkt."

5.9.2 Assessment of Language Practices

The Luxembourg residential population was asked a question about the assessment of language choice in the border region: "What is your opinion of Germans talking to you in Luxembourg... in German/their own local German dialect/a mixture of their own local German dialect and Luxembourgish/Luxembourgish?" It aims at evaluating the perceived appropriateness of the particular choice of language. Are the Moselle-Franconian dialects of the border region considered appropriate due to their linguistic proximity to Luxembourgish or not, possibly due to their lower status in comparison to the national language Luxembourgish?

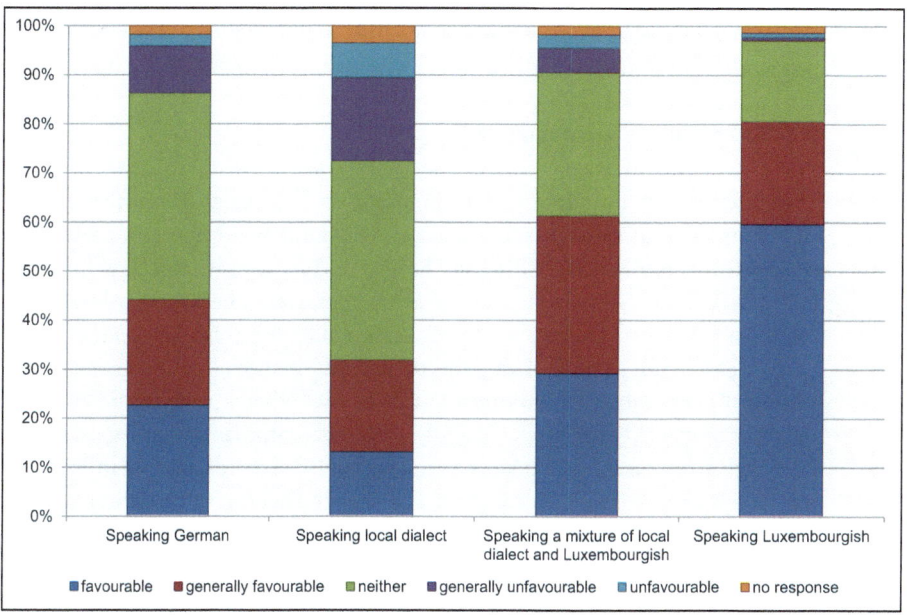

Figure 2: What is your opinion of Germans talking to you in Luxembourg ...?
(University of Luxembourg, IDENT2 2012/2013 – quantitative survey)

The choice for Luxembourgish gets the most favourable evaluation (80 % agreement), the choice of local dialect the most unfavourable, with 24 % rejection. Almost a third, however, has a favourable view of the use of the local dialect. A mixture of dialect and Luxembourgish gets a distinctly better rating with around 60 %. Here the rejection is also, with almost 8 %, clearly lower than in the case of the use of pure dialect. Thus the mixture of dialect and Luxembourgish is seen in a more positive light than the use of German (44 % positive, 12 % negative). If one compares the variants dialect *versus* mixture, dialect *versus* standard German and standard German *versus* mixture, almost half of all respondents give identical ratings in each case. There is therefore nothing to support the view that speaking German or a mixture of dialect and Luxembourgish is generally accorded a better rating. With the other half of the respondents who rate one variety at least one level higher than another, we can see a relatively clear hierarchy: the mixture of dialect and Luxembourgish is rated more frequently (45 %) favourably than the pure dialect (7 %); its preference to standard German is less marked (34 % against 18 %); standard German in turn gets more favourable ratings than the local German dialect (36 % against 12 %).

The findings seem to indicate that Luxembourgers appreciate the effort to learn the national language when Germans use a mixture of their own dialect and Luxembourgish. On the other hand, the switch to standard German, without any accomodation to Luxembourgish, seems to be considered by some speakers more appropriate than the use of a German dialect. Another possible explanation why the use of a German dialect encounters stronger rejection than other answer options could be that respondents assume they would understand the pure dialect less easily than a mixture of dialect and Luxembourgish or than standard German.

5.9.3 Language Assessment

Four different semantic differentials constitute another observation unit within the case study. The aim here was to establish, via a number of important parameters, the proximity or distance of different language communities to Luxembourgish, German and the German dialects of the border area. The necessary limitation to only a few question items led to the selection of semantic differentials which in two cases aim at measuring the degree of emotional connection ("ugly – beautiful", "uncultured – cultured"), and in two other cases, the proximity in terms of practicality ("useless – useful", "foreign – familiar") with regard to each language. In all cases, respondents were asked to fill in corresponding information on a seven-level scale, which comprised besides the neutral value 0 three negative values (-1, -2, -3) and three positive values (+1, +2, +3).

The analysis generally showed that all mentioned languages were rated favourably by all speakers, with the rating of the dialects being lower than for the two standard languages. The following detailed evaluation accordingly focusses on the positive attributions by presenting and describing the data with the help of various bar graphs. This includes a generalization in the sense that favourable ratings of various degrees have been subsumed under one general value. More detailed gradings are only indicated in a few distinctive individual cases. This also applies to other internal differentiations.

'Familiar – Foreign'

Statements under this heading indicate, in general terms, how close respondents feel to a particular language. We can assume here that the response data reflect parameters such as language competence, language contact, but possibly also more affective attitudes.

With respect to Luxembourgish, Fig. 3 shows, as expected, the highest percentage for Luxembourg nationals. A total of 73 % state that they are familiar with Luxembourgish. Only 11 % show ratings in the box 'foreign', 17 % give the indifference value 0.[156] An internal differentiation here shows that the familiarity ratings for respondents of Luxembourgish nationality are even significantly higher with 85 %, with the overwhelming majority (75 %) even giving the highest possible rating (+3). Familiarity with Luxembourgish is, by contrast, considerably lower in other language communities, with a marked gradation between German speaking and French speaking border regions. The ratings for inhabitants of Saarland (40 %) and Rhineland-Palatinate (37 %) here contrast with the percentages of 26 % for inhabitants of Lorraine and 24 % for Wallonians. This corresponds with the figures for the box 'foreign', since here the respondents from Wallonia register the highest rating of 32 %, followed by inhabitants of Lorraine (26 %), of Rhineland-Palatinate (19 %) and Saarland (17 %).

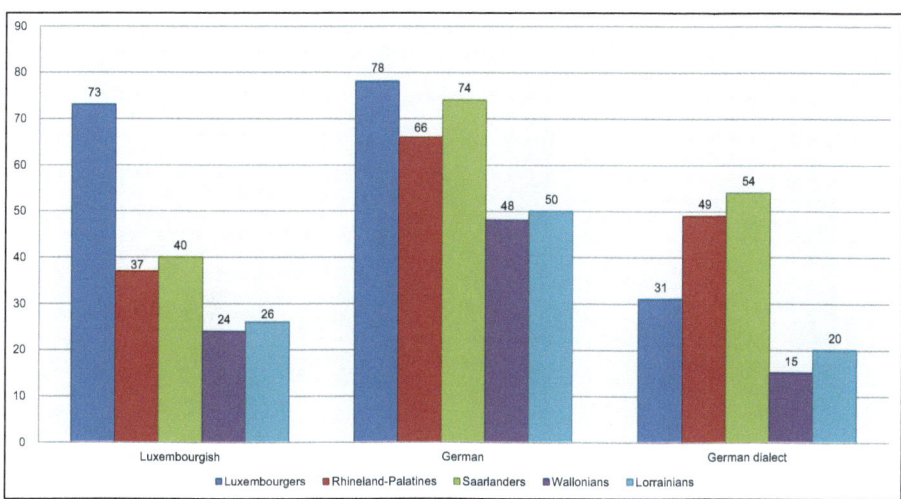

Figure 3: 'Familiar' (in percent) (University of Luxembourg, IDENT2 2012/2013 – quantitative survey)

German scores maximum familiarity values in all language communities. What is remarkable here is that the corresponding statements of the residents of the Saarland (74 %) and of the Rhineland-Palatinate (66 %) are actually lower than those in Luxembourg (78 %). But extreme values (+3) are more frequent in the German speaking regions. On the other hand, (around) half of the respondents from the French border regions state that they are familiar with German. By contrast, merely small minorities rate German as unfamiliar; it is only in Wallonia that we find a double-digit figure (14 %).

---

156 | The fact that the sum of percentages here total 101 is due to the rounding of figures to whole numbers.

Regarding the German dialects, the survey shows familiarity ratings of around 50 % only for the inhabitants of the German border regions. The German dialects are familiar to one third (31 %) of the Luxembourgers according to their own statements, while the corresponding percentages with respect to the francophone border region are significantly lower (20 % and 15 %), whereas the scale values in the box "foreign" with 30 % (inhabitants from Lorraine) and 35 % (Wallonians) are clearly higher. Correspondingly, the neutral value 0 is chosen by (around) half of these respondents.

'Useful – Useless'

The contrasting pair 'useful – useless' measures the practical value of a language, depending on individual communication needs. It cannot be excluded that here also a component reflecting subjective attitudes comes to bear.

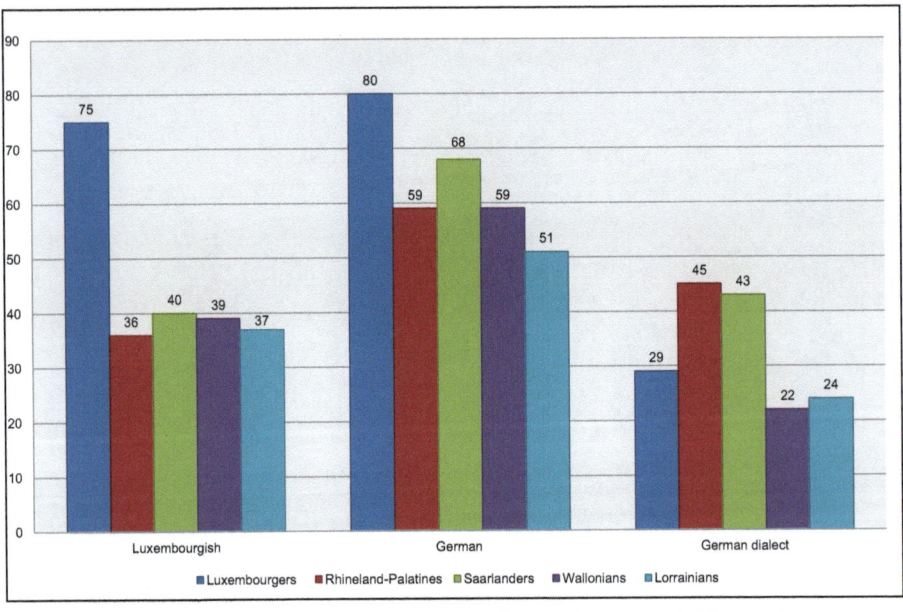

Figure 4: 'Useful' (in percent) (University of Luxembourg, IDENT2 2012/2013 – quantitative survey)

With respect to the usefulness values of Luxembourgish, Fig. 4 shows a clear gradation between Luxembourgers – 75 % (three quarters) of whom made corresponding statements (79 % for respondents of Luxembourgish nationality) – and the inhabitants of the surrounding border area where the corresponding percentages are significantly lower, ranging between 36 % and 40 %. The respective (relative and absolute) majorities make no judgement, choosing the indifference value 0. Only small minorities describe Luxembourgish as fairly useless.

Similar to the familiarity values, the statements on usefulness also show highest values with respect to German, with the percentage of Luxembourgers (80 %) again (significantly) higher than that of the inhabitants of Saarland (68 %) and Rhineland-Palatinate (59 %). Why as much as 6 % of the respondents of these border regions even rate German as fairly useless cannot be wholly explained on the basis of the available language data. But since in both Saarland and Rhineland-Palatinate, rootedness in regional dialects and the dialectically coloured vernaculars is still relatively strong, there is a certain plausibility for the assumption that for some respondents the practical use of standard German tends to be regarded as low.

This assumption is at least in part confirmed by the statements about the usefulness of the German dialects, as these are relatively high for the inhabitants of Rhineland-Palatinate with 45 % and of the Saarland with 43 %. The values of the other language communities, by contrast, are significantly lower, even though as much as 29 % of the Luxembourgers also consider the German dialects useful.

'Beautiful – Ugly'

The differential 'beautiful – ugly' primarily measures attitude values that comprise components of emotional closeness or rejection. One can assume that values such as euphonics, which are however difficult to objectivate, also play a role.

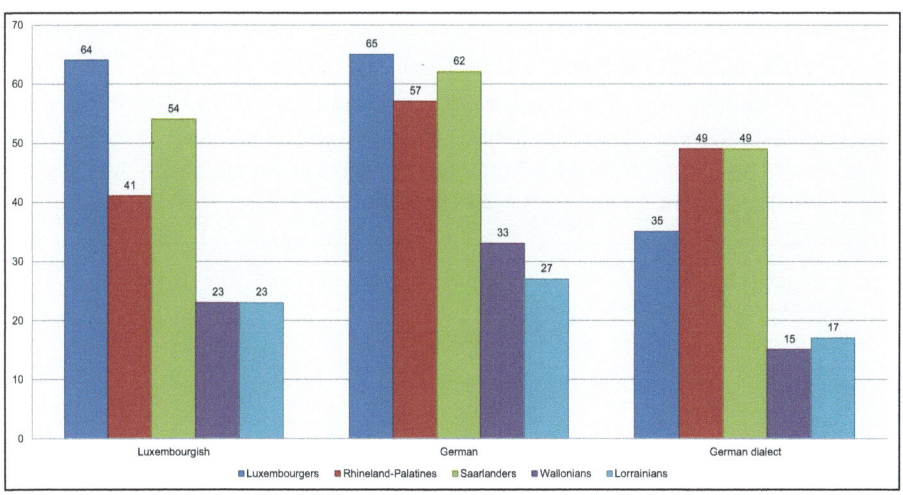

Figure 5: 'Beautiful' (in percent) (University of Luxembourg, IDENT2 2012/2013 – quantitative survey)

A glance at the diagram in Fig. 5 shows that both Luxembourgish and (even more so) German is rated favourably, even though the corresponding attributions of the respondents from Lorraine and Wallonia are significantly lower. For Luxembourgish, we have highest values of positive attribution coming from the Luxembourgers themselves (64 %). For the respondents with Luxembourg nationality, the percentage even increases to 75 % (with a clear preponderance in the extreme values). But also 54 % of the respondents in Saarland state that for them Luxembourgish is fairly beautiful. With the inhabitants of Rhineland-Palatinate there is still a relative majority of 41 %, while 51 % of this group give the mean value 0. The favourable attribution is significantly lower with the inhabitants of the francophone border areas, even though here too the majorities do not regard Luxembourgish as ugly, but make neutral (0) statements.

German here again scores the highest values of favourable attributions. 65 % of Luxembourgers state they find German beautiful, but also 57 % of the respondents in Rhineland-Palatinate and 62 % of those in Saarland make corresponding statements. Here too, the respective values for the inhabitants of Wallonia and Lorraine are considerably lower. As with Luxembourgish, the (relative) majorities refrain from giving ratings.

With respect to the German dialects, favourable attributions are relatively low. Still, a little less than half (49 %) of the German border region inhabitants give favourable ratings. Also around a third (35 %) of the Luxembourgers state they find German dialects fairly beautiful, while only 17 % of the inhabitants of Lorraine and 15 % of Wallonians make the same statements. Even though somewhat more than half of the respondents choose the neutral value, almost a third (each 31 %) describes the German dialects as quite ugly.

'Cultured – Uncultured'

Statements referring to this contrasting pair measure affective, prestige-related attitudes, where we have to assume that also parameters such as the extent to which a variety can produce literature, the degree of its elaboration (including its lexis) and its age as well as its (written) tradition influence the evaluation.

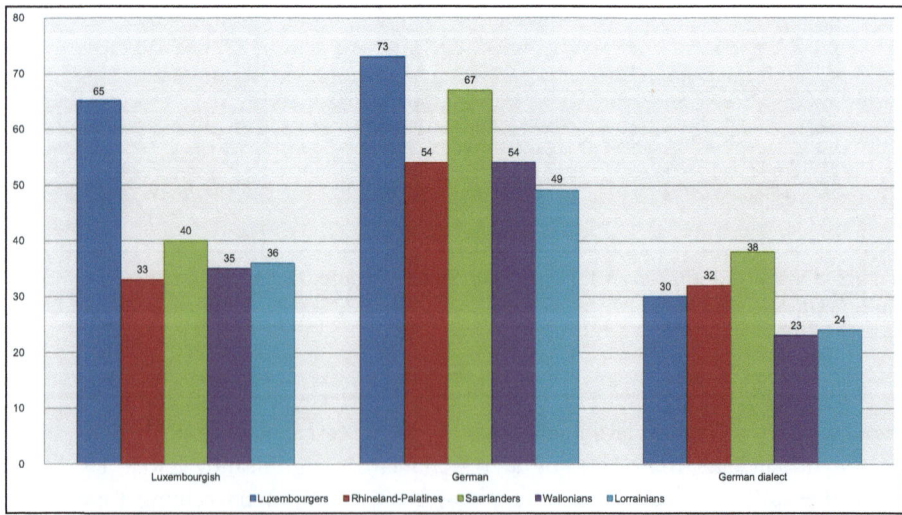

Figure 6: 'Cultured' (in percent) (University of Luxembourg, IDENT2 2012/2013 – quantitative survey)

At first sight, Fig. 6 also shows the already familiar picture. The German language has the highest values of favourable attributions, followed by Luxembourgish. The latter is described by a clear majority of Luxembourgers (65) % as fairly cultured. For respondents of Luxembourgish nationality the corresponding value even increases to 75 %. By contrast, the favourable attributions made by the four other language communities are significantly lower, in a range between 33 % and 40 %. But what these four groups also have in common is that segments of 50 % and more make neutral statements, while the attribution 'fairly uncultured' is made only by 9 to 11 % of the respondents of the border area. The rating 'fairly cultured' is accorded to German by majorities of over 50 % in all language communities, apart from respondents from Lorraine. However, also in this group, the 49 % of favourable attributions reflect the opinion of the relative majority. Luxembourgers regard German as particularly cultured (73 %), followed by Saarland residents (67 %). The favourable ratings by the inhabitants of Rhineland-Palatinate and the Wallonians are equal with 54 %. An unfavourable rating as fairly uncultured is only registered in exceptional cases, in a range between 4 % and 7 %.

Culturedness is not a value that the majority of respondents accords to the German dialects. Less than a third of all language communities accords this predicate, again with one exception: respondents from Saarland state with a substantial 38 % that they regard the dialects as fairly cultured. The respective majorities of respondents choose in this context the indifference value 0. Negative ratings are given by a fifth to a fourth of the respondents.

In conclusion, we can say that the respective groups of speakers show a spatial connectedness which also correlates with the assessment of the languages. This becomes clear in the partly significantly different attributions of value made by respondents from the German-speaking and the francophone border regions. This link is also evident with respect to the assessment of Luxembourgish by Luxembourgers, while we can observe here that comparably high favourable attributions are made with respect to the German language. In general, German scores top ratings for all examined items and in all groups of speakers. Luxembourgish is valued (very) highly in particular by the Luxembourgers themselves. By contrast, the assessments of the German dialects of the border regions are overall significantly lower.

5.9.4 The Status of Luxembourgish

An issue which was for a long time in the forefront in the study of Luxembourgish and still plays a role in 'lay' discussions is the one about the status of Luxembourgish, i.e. whether it is to be considered a dialect of German or a separate language.[157]

---

157 | For instance Peter Gilles (2000: 202): "In the 19th century and well into the 20th century, the discussion around the development trends in Luxembourgish have primarily centered around the question whether Luxembourgish is a dialect of German or a language

Besides members of the Luxembourg residential population expressing their views on both statements, "Luxembourgish is a German dialect" and "Luxembourgish is a separate language", respondents from the Belgian, French and German border regions also comment on "the language of the others."

The rejection of the statement that Luxembourgish is a German dialect is, as can be expected, highest with the Luxembourg residential population with a total of 59 % for "disagree" and "mostly disagree." The inhabitants of the border area show themselves in general more frequently undecided in this question or do not comment ("not specified"). Wallonians and people from Lorraine mostly agree somewhat more frequently than the Luxembourgers or agree entirely. The degrees of agreement in Rhineland-Palatinate and Saarland, by contrast, are hardly any different to those of the Luxembourgers; they are even slightly lower.

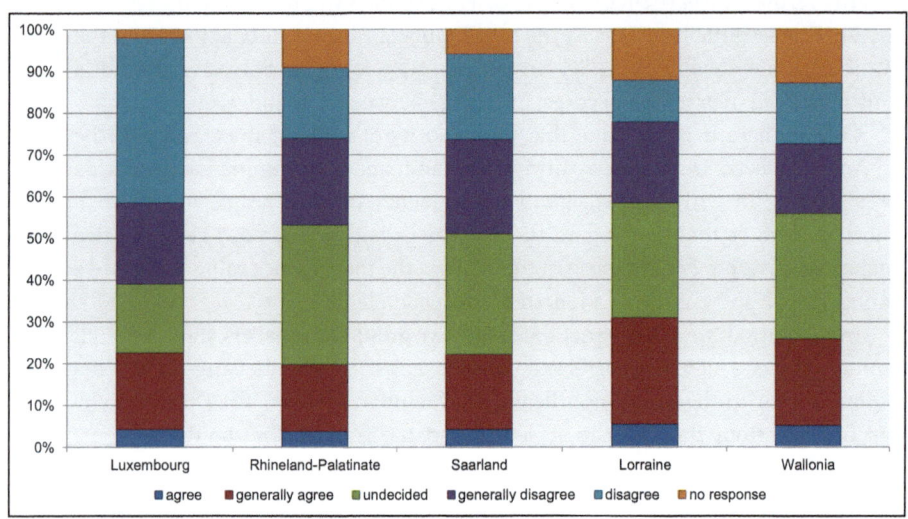

Figure 7: Luxembourgish is a German dialect (Agreement in percent) (University of Luxembourg, IDENT2 2012/2013 – quantitative survey)

The statement that Luxembourgish is a separate language, again, receives the highest approval rate from the Luxembourg residential population, with a total of 83 %. It increases to almost 90 % when only respondents with Luxembourg nationality are considered, an effect that was not observable with the rejection of the dialect status of Luxembourgish. The border area inhabitants exhibit greater undecidedness, as already with the statement about the dialect status.

---

in its own right." (translation of: "Die Diskussion um die Entwicklungstendenzen im Lëtzebuergeschen dreht sich im 19. Jahrhundert und weit ins 20. Jahrhundert hinein primär um die Frage, ob es sich beim Lëtzebuergeschen um einen Dialekt des Deutschen oder um eine selbständige Sprache handelt.") Meanwhile, the language's status has been by and large recognized and the focus is now on other issues.

All in all, they agree less frequently than the Luxembourg residential population with the statement about the language status. The rejection rates of respondents from Rhineland-Palatinate and Saarland are, again, hardly different from those of the Luxembourgers, while Wallonians and respondents from Lorraine, being in their majority francophone, disagree somewhat more frequently than the Luxembourgers with the statement that Luxembourgish is a separate language.

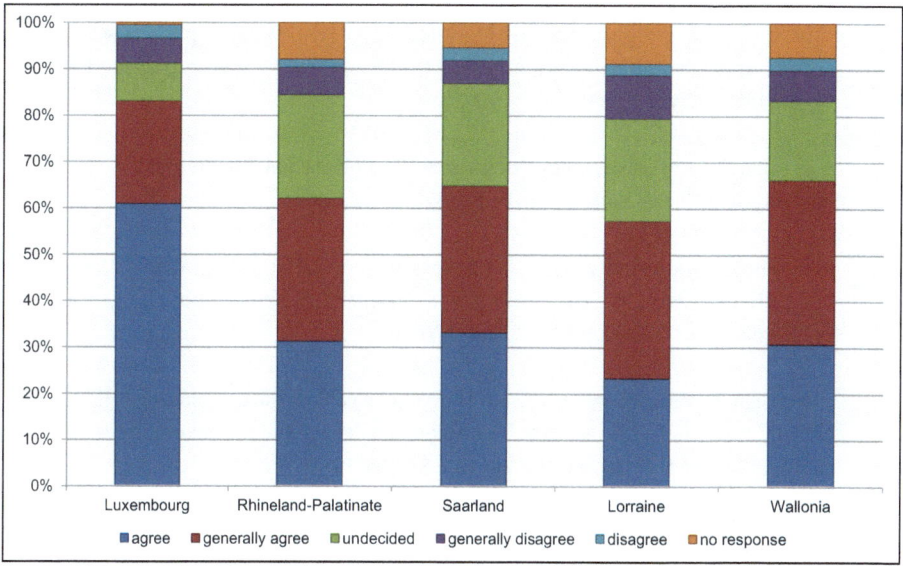

Figure 8: Luxembourgish is a separate language (Agreement in percent) (University of Luxembourg, IDENT2 2012/2013 – quantitative survey)

The criteria for defining the status of Luxembourgish as a separate language are, from a sociolinguistic perspective, primarily the degree of elaboration and standardization, which distances Luxembougish increasingly from the Moselle-Franconian dialects in Germany (see Gilles 2009: 186), as well as the use as offical language. The status as official language and the existence of a grammar is also mentioned by an interviewee who has problems with the ascription of a friend who says Luxembourgish is a German dialect:

"Well, I've only recently found out that Luxembourgish is actually a dialect, actually via a friend of mine who told me she had done it in a [university] course. And there they apparently said it was just another German dialect [...] But for me this is very difficult, I mean to see it that way, because I've already had the idea for so long that Luxembourgish is a separate language. And it's also our official language next to German. It's not an official dialect, after all. That's why it's still a bit difficult for me. After all, we also had Luxembourgish at school, with its own grammar. I don't know, do most dialects have their own grammar?"[158] (female, 24, Luxembourger, Luxembourg).

The attribution of the dialect status instead of the since long internalized language status seems to have shaken the interviewee's linguistic identity. It becomes clear here how the constitution of the subject is destabilized by addressing the mother tongue as a dialect, which collides with the high symbolic value of Luxembourgish, and has to be renegotiated. The big role that Luxembourgish plays as a language in the speaker's subjectivation is also evident in the following passage from the same interview:

"As I said, for me this was quite a shock when she told me that. 'How is that possible, this is my language!'"[159] (female, 24, Luxembourger, Luxembourg).

In appropriation and attribution processes, spatial and linguistic criteria often merge. It is interesting that interviewees frequently also talk about language when discussing affiliation and the Greater Region:

"And then the third [daughter], I'd say she's already a Saarlander. Also language-wise. You mostly define it via the language, the dialect, don't you. And the youngest was born, as I said, in Saarland"[160] (female, 48, German, Saarland).

"Of course, you identify a lot with your country and it's just your language and of course the whole cultural thing"[161] (female, 24, Luxembourger, Luxembourg).

---

158 | Personal translation of: "Also ech hu réischt viru kuerzem erausfonnt, dass Lëtzebuergesch u sech en Dialekt ass, duerch eng Frëndin u sech, wat mer gesot huet, et hätt dat an engem Cours gehat. Et wieren eben däitsch Dialekte gewiescht. [...] Mee fir mech ass dat jo immens schwéier, fir sou, jo einfach sou anzeuerdnen, well ech jo awer lo scho sou laang mat deem Gedanken am Kapp liewen 'Lëtzebuergesch ass eng eege Sprooch'. An 't ass jo awer och eis Amtsprooch niewent dem Däitschen. Et ass jo net en Amtsdialekt. Vun dohier fält mer dat na heiansdo awer bësse schwéier. Mir hate jo och Lëtzebuergesch an der Schoul mat eegener Grammatik. Ech weess net, hunn déi meescht Dialekter eng eege Grammatik?"
159 | Personal translation of: "Wéi gesot fir mech war dat éischter sou e Schock, wéi et mer dat u sech sot. 'Wéi, dat ass dach meng Sprooch!'"
160 | Personal translation of: "Und dann die dritte [Tochter], die würde ich schon zu den Saarländern zählen. Auch so von der Sprache her. Man definiert es ja meistens über die Sprache, den Dialekt. Und die Jüngste, die ist wie gesagt im Saarland geboren."
161 | Personal translation of: "Mä kloer, 't identifizéiert een sech jo vill mat sengem Land an 't ass eben deng Sprooch an natierlech och dat ganzt Kulturellt och einfach."

5.9.5 Conclusion

The evaluation of the questionnaire survey and the interviews has revealed many links of language and identity in linguistic practices and in the assessment of linguistic practices and languages (and their varieties). The point of departure is a twofold construction of linguistic space: on the one hand, a space is constructed via the observed linguistic similarities which transcends the current territorial borders and follows the old Moselle-Franconian dialect continuum; on the other hand, the territorial borders are reflected in a multilingual Luxembourgish language area which is clearly distinct from the neighbouring German language area. The special status of Luxembourgish for the identities of its speakers shows itself in favourable assessments in the semantic differentials and in high approval rates for the statement that Luxembourgish is a language in its own right. One can add to this also the generally more negative assessment of the use of dialects by German speakers in Luxembourg which in comparison to the use of standard German or Luxembourgish is significantly lower. Luxembourgish distinguishes itself from the Moselle-Franconian dialects of the German border area by its language status, its usefulness in communication as well as by the special role it has played in the construction of a national identity (see Fehlen 2011: 571f.) and in the subject constitutions of its speakers. For its speakers, it holds a high communicative and symbolic value, which has the effect that speaking a German dialect in Luxembourg is not regarded as appropriate by all speakers, due to its smaller communicative range and lower status.

5.10 CONCLUSIONS

Following the frequently voiced *desiderat*, the case studies of this chapter sought to present empirical research that links current approaches of spatial and identity studies with those of today's subject analysis. The investigation centred on spatial and identity constructions in border regions and the different ways they articulate themselves in subject constitutions. Building on chapter 3, the present chapter focussed on subjectivations, i.e. the question of how norms and significations are actually lived in everyday-cultural practices. Of particular interest here was, on the one hand, the relationship of subjectifications and subjectivations – or the shifts and creative forms of appropriation they reveal – and the relationship of spaces and identities in cross-border contexts, on the other.

Against this background, a number of case studies elaborated and linked processes of subjectification and subjectivation in the framework of specific contexts. For instance, the everyday dietary practices: these were related to social, cultural and institutional aspects and examined for the subjectivations they express regarding sustainability or 'responsible way of eating'. The findings reflect a largely hedonistic subject constitution of the interviewees that is primarily marked by self-related or health-related subjectivations as well as economic factors rather than general ethical-political subjectivations. The case study has shown that food-related subject constitutions are at the interface of competing subjectification techniques that are appropriated pragmatically and contingently in everyday-cultural practices.

Another case study reconstructed family identities and spatial constructions expressed in practices of commemoration of the dead. The tombstones with their pictorial formulas examined for this purpose represented a visual discourse and the subject constitutions embedded therein. The comparison of Roman pictorial motifs with their local forms of appropriation indicated subjectivations which, while taking up the Roman visual repertoire, negotiate it via differentiated variations and express local identities. Investigation showed, however, that this creative treatment of subjectivations varied in the examined localities, suggesting a social-spatial differentiation of subject constitutions as well as of territorial spaces.

Workers' estates were the subject matter of a study that examined them as a nexus of everyday-cultural practices with a particular interest for material aspects. The subject constitutions revealed here are situated at the interface of entrepreneurial regulation and control and their acceptance or avoidance, with a tendency for a pragmatic adoption of subjectifications. The materialities connected to the location of the workers' estate were not only related to its constitutive practices, but they also possess a strong symbolic relevance for subjectivation processes.

Subject constitutions were also revealed using practices of remembering. This involved making a connection between subjectifications embedded in the commentary on the Second World War in various national newspapers with subjectivations that can be identified from interpretations of meaning and categorizations of individual remembering. The comparison shows an appropriation of the past that frequently runs contrary to that of the print media, even though the coding of victim/perpetrator which they offer is often adopted. The exception here are subject constitutions in the examined German border regions, which are characterized by a diffuse relationship of the perpetrator/victim categories and mark a general faultline in the survey region, dividing past-related attributions and appropriations on either side of the German state border.

The amalgamation of subjectification and subjectivation processes carried out in the case studies has revealed subject constitutions – and thus empirical moments of identity work – that are largely characterized by ambivalent and unpredictable logics of combination. This confirms the creative-processual character of social practices as well as the identity constructions they contain and points to articulations of the 'in-between' which characterize both territorial and categorial border areas. Such border areas and their mechanisms of construction were examined in more detail in further case studies, for instance using subjectivations in connection with gender and space: here the focus was on practical knowledge from which one can deduce space-related identities and the spatial situatedness of social practices whose interpretations in turn have a genderizing effect. The study examined places of restoration, places of corporality and outdoor places that show that the binary coding of public spaces as female/male has partly dissolved. The identified subjectivations seem to overcome the classical spatializing gender discourse, but in qualitative respects, the emerging 'heterosocial border region' remains wedded to traditional subjectifications.

A further case study reconstructed subjectivations with respect to sub- and periurban spaces. The manner in which these were referred to by the inhabitants shows terminological deviations from the subjectivating discourse of space-related planning and highlights the general problem of characterizing 'the space' between city and country or border areas in clear and non-contradictory terms. Instead, it was possible to identify diffuse – but consistently positively connoted – space-related identities that materialize in everyday-cultural practices of appropriation.

Appropriation processes were examined in a further case study with respect to space-and group-related identity constructions, using subjectivations regarding the 'Greater Region', a spatial entity that extends across a number of borders, and the group of cross-border residential migrants. What became clear here was that there is a significant crossing of borders in the course of everyday-cultural practices, even though this variable does not necessarily lead to homogenous space- and group-related identifications in border regions. The relationship between an empirical 'experience of space' and identification processes is also the topic of the study about subjectivations with regard to language. Using linguistic practices and language-related interpretations, this study reconstructs the interplay of space- and language related criteria, pointing to a connection between the interviewees' region of residence and the languages spoken there. The established subjectivations moreover reflect appropriated 'language areas', which cut across borders but also reinforce them.

The research context of the 'border region' investigated in all of these studies not only acts as a scientific experimental field for 'postmodern questions' but is itself a tool of discipline. For, as explained in chapter 2, investigations in 'cross-border contexts' exclude the supposition of fixed spatial entities, preset identities and subjects that derive their agency from social structures. Instead, the authors saw themselves (time and again) obliged to take a genuinely constructivist-relational perspective on their objects of research which in this chapter manifested itself primarily as a decentration of the subject. Here, the empirical subject is effectively replaced by the concept of the subject as socially constituted and as constituting the social, in brief: the subject as an empiricial project. This research perspective – translated to the analytical categories of subjectivation and subjectification – does not only tie in with the approaches of current cultural studies but is a precondition for adequately accessing subjects in the context of the border.

5.11 References

Althusser, Louis (1971 [1970]): "Ideology and Ideological State Apparatuses", in: Lenin and Philosophy and Other Essays (trans. Ben Brewster), Monthly Review Press, 121-176.
Andrikopoulou-Strack, Jeanne-Nora (1986): Grabbauten des 1. Jahrhunderts n. Chr. im Rheingebiet, Köln: Rheinland-Verlag.
Assmann, Aleida (2006): Der lange Schatten der Vergangenheit. Erinnerungskultur und Geschichtspolitik, München: C.H. Beck.
Assmann, Aleida (2008): "Transformations between History and Memory", in: Social Research 75, 49-72.
Baltes-Löhr, Christel (2000): "Migration als Subversion des Raumes", in: Renate von Bardeleben (ed.), Frauen in Kultur und Gesellschaft. Ausgewählte Beiträge der 2. Fachtagung Frauen-/Gender-Forschung in Rheinland-Pfalz, Tübingen: Stauffenburg Verlag, 513-524.
Baltes-Löhr, Christel (2003): "Grenzverschiebungen. Theoriekonzepte zum Begriff 'Grenze'", in: Thomas Geisen/Allen Karchen (eds.), Grenze: Sozial – Politisch – Kulturell. Ambivalenzen in den Prozessen der Entstehung und Veränderung von Grenzen, Frankfurt a.M./London: IKO-Verlag für Interkulturelle Kommunikation, 82-98.
Baltes-Löhr, Christel (2006): Migration und Identität. Portugiesische Frauen in Luxemburg, Frankfurt a.M./London: IKO-Verlag für Interkulturelle Kommunikation.
Baltes-Löhr, Christel (2014): "Geschlechterpluralitäten", in: Heinz Sieburg (ed.), Geschlecht in Literatur und Geschichte. Bilder – Identitäten – Konstruktionen, Bielefeld: transcript.
Bauman, Zygmunt (2000): Liquid Modernity, Cambridge: Polity Press.
Becker, Tom/Hesse, Markus (2010): "Internationalisierung und Steuerung internationaler Wohnungsmärkte – das Beispiel Luxemburg", in: Informationen zur Raumentwicklung 5/6, 403-415.
Becker, Ruth (2008): "Angsträume oder Frauenräume? Gedanken über den Zugang von Frauen zum öffentlichen Raum", in: Feministisches Kollektiv (ed.), Street Harassment. Machtprozesse und Raumproduktion, Wien: Mandelbaum Verlag, 56-74.
Beckmann, Klaus/Hesse, Markus/Holz-Rau, Christian/Hunecke, Marcel (eds.) (2006): Stadtleben. Wohnen, Mobilität und Lebensstil, Wiesbaden: Verlag für Sozialwissenschaften.
Benedikter, Roland (2011): "Subjekt", in: Helmut Reinalter/Peter J. Brenner (eds.), Lexikon der Geisteswissenschaften, Wien/Köln/Weimar: Böhlau Verlag.
Benjamin, Walter (1968 [1955]) "The Work of Art in the Age of Mechanical Reproduction" (trans. Harry Zohn), in: Hannah Arendt (ed.), Illuminations, New York: Harcourt, Brace & World.

Berger, Maxi (2013): "Autonome Subjekte und der Vorrang des Objekts. Überlegungen zu einer Implikation von Praxistheorien", in: Thomas Alkemeyer/Gunilla Budde/Dagmar Freist (eds.), Selbstbildungen. Soziale und kulturelle Praktiken der Subjektivierung, Bielefeld: transcript, 313-328.

Bourdieu, Pierre (1986): "The forms of capital", in: J. Richardson (ed.) Handbook of Theory and Research for the Sociology of Education, New York: Greenwood, 241-258.

Brosius, Jacques/Carpentier, Samuel (2010): "Grenzüberschreitende Wohnmobilität von in Luxemburg ansässigen Erwerbstätigen: Quantifizierung und Charakterisierung des Phänomens", in: Samuel Carpentier (ed.), Die grenzüberschreitende Wohnmobilität zwischen Luxemburg und seinen Nachbarregionen, Luxemburg: Editions Saint-Paul, 15-36.

Brunner, Karl-Michael (2003): "Konsumprozesse im Ernährungsfeld: Chancen für Nachhaltigkeit?", in: Internationaler Arbeitskreis für Kulturforschung des Essens, Mitteilungen 10, 22-29.

Brunner, Karl-Michael (2007): "Ernährungspraktiken und nachhaltige Entwicklung – eine Einführung", in: Karl-Michael Brunner/Sonja Geyer/Marie Jelenko/Walpurga Weiss/Florentina Astleithner (eds.), Ernährungsalltag im Wandel. Chancen für Nachhaltigkeit, Wien/New York: Springer, 1-38.

Bucholtz, Mary/Hall, Kira (2005): "Language and Identity", in: Alessandro Duranti (ed.): A Companion to Linguistic Anthropology. Reprint (= Blackwell Companions to Anthropology, vol. 1), Malden: Blackwell, 369-394.

Bührmann, Andrea/Schneider, Werner (2007): "Mehr als nur diskursive Praxis? – Konzeptionelle Grundlagen und methodische Aspekte der Dispositivanalyse", in: Forum Qualitative Sozialforschung/Forum Qualitative Social Research 8, Art. 28, http://www.qualitative-research.net/index.php/fqs/article/view/237/525, accessed 23.12.2013.

Bührmann, Andrea/Schneider, Werner (2008): Vom Diskurs zum Dispositiv. Eine Einführung in die Dispositivanalyse, Bielefeld: transcript, 176.

Bürkner, Hans-Joachim (2011): "Zwischen Naturalisierung, Identitätspolitik und Bordering – Theoretische Ansatzpunkte für die Analyse von Identitäten in Grenzräumen", in: Wilfried Heller (ed.), Identitäten und Imaginationen der Bevölkerung in Grenzräumen, Berlin: Lit Verlag, 17-56.

Buschmann, Nikolaus (2013): "Persönlichkeit und geschichtliche Welt. Zur praxeologischen Konzeptualisierung des Subjekts in der Geschichtswissenschaft", in: Thomas Alkemeyer/Gunilla Budde/Dagmar Freist (eds.), Selbstbindungen. Soziale und kulturelle Praktiken der Subjektivierung, Bielefeld: transcript, 125-149.

Butler, Judith (1997): The Psychic Life of Power: Theories in Subjection, Stanford CA: Stanford University Press.

Caregari, Laure/Leboutte, René/Sauer, Arnaud/ Scuto, Denis (2012): "Histoire industrielle – Bilan & Perspectives", in: Hémecht 64/4: Actes des 4e Assises de l'historiographie luxembourgeoise.

Caregari, Laure/Lorang, Antoinette (2013): "Werkswohnungsbau in der Großregion. Eine Forschungsbilanz", in: Mutations. Mémoires et perspectives du Bassin Minier 6, 47-60.

Carlsson-Kanyama, Annika (1998): Climate Change and Dietary Choices. How Can Emissions of Greenhouse Gases from Food Consumption be Reduced?, in: Food Policy 23/3-4, 277-293.

Chambers, J. K./Trudgill, Peter (2002): Dialectology, 2nd edition, Cambridge: University Press.

Champion, Anthony Gerard (1989): Counterurbanization: The Changing Pace and Nature of Population Deconcentration, London: Arnold.

Cloke, Paul (2011): "Urban-rural", in: John Agnew/David Livingstone (eds.), The Sage Handbook of Geographical Knowledge, London/Thousand Oaks/New Delhi: Sage, 563-570.

Commaille, Laurent (2004): "Ein neues Bild der Arbeitersiedlungen in Lothringen", in: Hans-Walter Herrmann/Rainer Hudemann/Eva Kell (eds.), Forschungsaufgabe Industriekultur. Die Saarregion im Vergleich, Saarbrücken: Merziger Druckerei und Verlag, 361-374.

Crenshaw, Kimberlé (1991): "Mapping the Margins: Intersectionality, Identity Politics and Violence Against Women of Color", in: Stanford Law Review 43/6, 1241-1299.

Dasen, Véronique/Späth, Thomas (2010): Children, Memory & Family Identity in Roman Culture, Oxford: Oxford University Press.

Degele, Nina (2010): Andere Räume. Soziale Praktiken der Raumproduktion von Drag Kings und Transgender, Bielefeld: transcript.

Deppmeyer, Korana (2005): "Das Akkulturationsmodell", in: Günther Schörner (ed.), Romanisierung – Romanisation. Theoretische Modelle und praktische Fallbeispiele, Oxford: Archaeopress, 57-63.

Dirksmeier, Peter (2009): Urbanität als Habitus. Zur Sozialgeographie städtischen Lebens auf dem Land, Bielefeld: transcript.

Dörhöfer, Kerstin (2000): "'Halböffentlicher Raum' – eine Metapher zur Auflösung (nicht nur) räumlicher Polarität", in: Monika Imboden/Franziska Meister/Daniel Kurz (eds.), Stadt – Geschlecht – Raum. Beiträge zur Erforschung urbaner Lebensräume im 19. und 20. Jahrhundert, Zürich: Chronos, 101-118.

Düwell, Kurt (1997): "Trier und sein Umland in der Schlußphase des Zweiten Weltkriegs", in: Kurt Düwell/Michael Matheus (eds.), Kriegsende und Neubeginn. Westdeutschland und Luxemburg zwischen 1944 und 1947 (= Geschichtliche Landeskunde: Veröffentlichungen des Instituts für Geschichtliche Landeskunde an der Universität Mainz, vol. 46), Stuttgart: Franz Steiner Verlag, 97-106.

Eberle, Ulrike/Hayn, Doris/Rehaag, Regina/Simshäuser, Ulla (2006): Ernährungswende: Eine Herausforderung für Politik, Unternehmen und Gesellschaft, München: Oekom.

Edwards, John (2009): Language and Identity. An Introduction, Cambridge: University Press.
European Environment Agency (EEA) (2005): Household Consumption and the Environment, EEA Report 11/2005, Kopenhagen/Luxemburg: Office for Official Publications of the European Communities.
European Environment Agency (EEA) (2012): Consumption and the Environment: 2012 Update. The European Environment State and Outlook 2010, Kopenhagen: EEA.
European Commission (2010): Violence against Women and the Role of Gender Equality, Social Inclusion and Health Strategies, Luxemburg: Publications Office of the European Union.
ESPON/University of Luxembourg (2010): Metroborder. Cross-border Polycentric Metropolitan Regions. Final Report, n. p.
Fasold, Peter (1998): Bestattungssitte und kulturelle Identität. Grabanlagen und Grabbeigaben der frühen römischen Kaiserzeit in Italien und den Nordwest-Provinzen, Köln: Rheinland-Verlag.
Featherstone, Mike (1995): Undoing Culture: Globalization, Postmodernism and Identity, London: Sage.
Fehlen, Fernand (2011): "'Letzebourger Deutsch'. Aus der Vorgeschichte der Luxemburger Sprache (1815-1830)", in: Association luxembourgeoise des enseignants de l'histoire (ed.), Du Luxembourg à l'Europe. Hommages à Gilbert Trausch à l'occasion de son 80ᵉ anniversaire. Luxemburg: Editions Saint-Paul, 571-591.
Fleischhauer, Rob (2013): Lasauvage. Le fer des nobles, Differdange: Amis de l'Histoire.
Foucault, Michel (2000): "The Subject and Power", in: Michel Foucault, Power, James D. Faubion (ed.), Essential Works of Foucault 1954-1984, vol. 3 (trans. Robert Hurley), New York: The New York Press, 326-348.
Foucault, Michel (2002 [1969]): The Archeology of Knowledge (trans. A. M. Sheridan Smith), London and New York: Routledge.
Freigang, Yasmine (1997): "Die Grabmäler der gallo-römischen Kultur im Moselland. Studien zur Selbstdarstellung einer Gesellschaft", in: Jahrbuch des Römisch-Germanischen Zentralmuseums Mainz 44, 277-440.
Friedrich, Malte (2010): Urbane Klänge: Popmusik und Imagination der Stadt, Bielefeld: transcript.
Füller, Henning/Marquardt, Nadine (2009): "Gouvernementalität in der humangeographischen Diskursforschung", in: Georg Glaszke/Annika Mattissek (eds.), Handbuch Diskurs und Raum. Theorien und Methoden für die Humangeographie sowie die sozial- und kulturwissenschaftliche Raumforschung, Bielefeld: transcript, 83-106.
George, Michele (ed.) (2005a): The Roman Family in the Empire. Rome, Italy and Beyond, Oxford: Oxford University Press.

George, Michele (2005b): Family Imagery and Family Values in Roman Italy, in: Michele George (ed.), The Roman Family in the Empire, Oxford: Oxford University Press, 37-66.

Gergen, Kenneth (1991): The Saturated Self: Dilemmas of Identity in Contemporary Life, New York: Basic Books.

Gertenbach, Lars (2012): "Governmentality Studies. Die Regierung der Gesellschaft im Spannungsfeld von Ökonomie, Staat und Subjekt", in: Stephan Moebius (ed.), Kultur. Von den Cultural Studies bis zu den Visual Studies. Eine Einführung, Bielefeld: transcript, 109-127.

Gilles, Peter (1999): Dialektausgleich im Lëtzebuergeschen. Zur phonetisch-phonologischen Fokussierung einer Nationalsprache (= Phonai, vol. 44), Tübingen: Niemeyer.

Gilles, Peter (2000): "Die Konstruktion einer Standardsprache. Zur Koinédebatte in der luxemburgischen Linguistik", in: Dieter Stellmacher (ed.), Dialektologie zwischen Tradition und Neuansätzen. Beiträge der Internationalen Dialektologentagung. Göttingen, 19.-21. Oktober 1998 (= Zeitschrift für Dialektologie und Linguistik, supplement 109), Stuttgart: Franz Steiner Verlag, 200-212.

Gilles, Peter (2009): "Luxemburgisch in der Mehrsprachigkeit – Soziolinguistik und Sprachkontakt", in: Michael Elmentaler (ed.), Deutsch und seine Nachbarn, Frankfurt a.M.: Peter Lang, 185-200.

Gilles, Peter (2010): "Sprache im Minette", in: Mutations. Mémoires et perspectives du Bassin Minier 1, 111-123.

Gilles, Peter (2011): "Mündlichkeit und Schriftlichkeit in der luxemburgischen Sprachgemeinschaft", in: Georg Mein/Heinz Sieburg (eds.), Medien des Wissens. Interdisziplinäre Aspekte von Medialität (= Literalität und Liminalität, vol. 4), Bielefeld: transcript, 43-64.

Goethert-Polaschek, Karin (1980): Römische Gläser im Rheinischen Landesmuseum Trier, Trier: Selbstverlag des Rheinischen Landesmuseums.

Graumann, Carl Friedrich (1983): "On Multiple Identities", in: International Social Science Journal 35, 309-321.

Habermas, Jürgen (1990[1988]): The Philosophical Discourse of Modernity (trans. Frederick G. Lawrence), Cambridge: Polity Press.

Haffner, Alfred/von Schnurbein, Siegmar (2000): Kelten, Germanen, Römer im Mittelgebirgsraum zwischen Luxemburg und Thüringen. Akten des Internationalen Kolloquiums zum DFG-Schwerpunktprogramm "Romanisierung" in Trier vom 28. bis 30. September 1998, Bonn: Dr. Rudolf Habelt.

Harris, Richard/Larkham, Peter (eds.) (1999): Changing Suburbs: Foundation, Form and Function, London: Spon.

Harris, Richard (2006): Creeping Conformity. How Canada Became Suburban 1900-1960, Toronto: University of Toronto Press.

Harris, Richard (2010): "Meaningful Types in a World of Suburbs", in: Research in Urban Sociology 10 (Suburbanization in Global Society), 15-47.

Heinzelmann, Michael/Ortalli, Jacopo/Fasold, Peter/Witteyer, Marion (2001): Römischer Bestattungsbrauch und Beigabensitten in Rom, Norditalien und den Nordwestprovinzen von der späten Republik bis in die Kaiserzeit. International Colloquium, Rome 1-3 April 1998, Wiesbaden: Dr. Ludwig Reichert.

Herde, Adina (2005): Kriterien für eine nachhaltige Ernährung auf Konsumentenebene, Discussion Paper 20/05, October 2005, Berlin: Technische Universität Berlin, Zentrum Technik und Gesellschaft.

von Hesberg, Henner (2008): "The Image of the Family on Sepulchral Monuments in the Northwest Provinces", in: Sinclair Bell/Inge Lyse Hansen (eds.), Role Models in the Roman World. Identity and Assimilation, Ann Arbor: The University of Michigan Press, 257-269.

Hesse, Markus (2010): "Suburbs: The next Slum? Explorations into the Contested Terrain of Social Construction and Political Discourse", in: Articulo – Journal of Urban Research 3, http://articulo.revues.org/1552, accessed 20.02.2014.

Hess-Lüttich, Ernest W. B. (2004): "Die sozialsymbolische Funktion der Sprache. The Social Symbolic Function of Language", in: Ulrich Ammon/Norbert Dittmar/Klaus J. Mattheier/Peter Trudgill (eds.), Sociolinguistics. Soziolinguistik. An International Handbook of the Science of Language and Society. 2nd completely revised and extended edition. Volume 1 (= Handbücher zur Sprach- und Kommunikationswissenschaft, vol. 3.1), Berlin/New York: de Gruyter, 491-502.

Hingley, Richard (2010): "Cultural Diversity and Unity: Empire and Rome", in: Shelley Hales/Tamar Hodos (eds.), Material Culture and Social Identities in the Ancient World, Cambridge: University Press, 54-75.

Hodos, Tamar (2010): "Local and Global Perspectives in the Study of Social and Cultural Identities", in: Shelley Hales/Tamar Hodos (eds.), Material Culture and Social Identities in the Ancient World, Cambridge: University Press, 3-31.

Hudemann, Rainer/Wittenbrock, Rolf (eds.) (1991): Stadtentwicklung im deutsch-französisch-luxemburgischen Grenzraum (19. u. 20. Jh.) (= Veröffentlichungen der Kommission für Saarländische Landesgeschichte und Volksforschung, vol. 21), Saarbrücken: SDV.

Huebner, Sabine (2011): "Household Composition in the Ancient Mediterranean – What do we really know?", in: Beryl Rawson (ed.), A Companion to Families in the Greek and Roman Worlds, Malden/Oxford: Blackwell, 73-91.

Huskinson, Janet (2011): "Picturing the Roman Family", in: Beryl Rawson (ed.), A Companion to Families in the Greek and Roman Worlds, Malden/Oxford: Blackwell, 521-541.

Interregionale Arbeitsmarktbeobachtungsstelle (IBA) (ed.) (2013): Die Arbeitsmarktsituation in der Großregion. 8. Bericht an den Gipfel der Großregion, Saarbrücken.

Jaksche, Jutta (2005): "Ernährungspolitik – Zum Wohle des Verbrauchers" in: Karl-Michael Brunner/Gesa Schönberger (eds.), Nachhaltigkeit und Ernährung. Produktion – Handel – Konsum, New York/Frankfurt a.M.: Campus, 263-276.

Jameson, Fredric (1991): Postmodernism or the Cultural Logic of Late Capitalism, Durham: Duke University Press.

Kant, Immanuel (1786): Grundlegung zur Metaphysik der Sitten, Riga: Johann Friedrich Hartknoch.

Kant, Immanuel (1999): Critique of Pure Reason (trans. and eds. Paul Guyer and Allen W. Wood) (The Cambridge Edition of the Works of Immanuel Kant), Cambridge: Cambridge University Press.

Keupp, Heiner/Ahbe, Thomas/Gmür, Wolfgang/Höfer, Renate/Mitzscherlich, Beate/Kraus, Wolfgang/Straus, Florian (2006): Identitätskonstruktionen. Das Patchwork der Identitäten in der Spätmoderne, Reinbek bei Hamburg: Rowohlt.

Kieffer, Marcel (2006): "Kind der Kolonien", in: Ville d'Esch-sur-Alzette (ed.), 100 Joer Esch. 1906-2006, Luxembourg: Editions Guy Binsfeld, 306-311.

Kirby, Andrew/Modarres, Ali (2010): "The Suburban Question: An Introduction", in: Cities 27/2, 65-67.

Kloosterman, Robert/Musterd, Sako (2001): "The Poycentric Urban Region: Towards a Research Agenda", in: Urban Studies 38/4, 623-633.

Knebeler, Christophe/Scuto, Denis (2010): Belval. Passé, présent et avenir d'un site luxembourgeois exceptionnel (1911-2011), Esch-sur-Alzette: Editions Le Phare.

Kockel, Valentin (1993): Porträtreliefs stadtrömischer Grabbauten. Ein Beitrag zur Geschichte und zum Verständnis des spätrepublikanisch-frühkaiserzeitlichen Privatporträts, Mainz: Verlag Philipp von Zabern.

Krause, Jens-Uwe (2003): "Antike", in: Andreas Gestrich/Jens-Uwe Krause/Michael Mitterauer (eds.), Geschichte der Familie, Stuttgart: Alfred Kröner Verlag.

Kudera, Werner/Voß, Günter (2000): Lebensführung und Gesellschaft. Beiträge zu Konzept und Empirie alltäglicher Lebensführung, Wiesbaden: Verlag für Sozialwissenschaften.

Latour, Bruno (1993): We Have Never Been Modern (trans. Catherine Porter), Cambridge Massachusetts: Harvard University Press.

Lefèbvre, Louis (1975): "Les sculptures gallo-romaines du musée d'Arlon", in: Bulletin trimestriel de l'Institut archéologique du Luxembourg, Arlon 7, 1-91.

Lemke, Thomas (2008): "Gouvernementalität", in: Clemens Kammler (ed.), Foucault-Handbuch. Leben – Wirkung – Werk, Stuttgart/Weimar: Metzler, 260-263.

Lorang, Antoinette (1994): Luxemburgs Arbeiterkolonien und billige Wohnungen: 1860 - 1940. "...wo der Arbeiter sich daheimfühlt und die Schnapskneipe meiden lernt", Luxembourg: Ministère du Logement.

Macdonald, Sharon (2013): Memorylands. Heritage and Identity in Europe Today, London: Routledge.

Mariën, Marcel Edouard (1945): Les monuments funéraires de l'Arlon romain (= Annales de l'Institut Archéologique du Luxembourg, vol. 76), Arlon: Institut Archéologique du Luxembourg.

Marx, Karl/Engels, Friedrich (1970): The German Ideology (trans. W. Lough, C. Dutt and C. P. Magill), London: Lawrence & Wishart Ltd.
McCarthy, James (2008): "Rural geography: Globalizing the countryside", in: Progress in Human Geography 32/1, 129-137.
Michel, Joël (1989): "Die industriellen Beziehungen im französischen Bergbau vom Ende des 19. bis in die 70er Jahre des 20. Jahrhunderts", in: Gerald D. Feldman/Klaus Tenfelde (eds.), Arbeiter, Unternehmer und Staat im Bergbau. Industrielle Beziehungen im internationalen Vergleich, München: Beck, 220-225.
Mitchell, Clare J. (2004): "Making Sense of Counterurbanization", in: Journal of Rural Studies 20/1, 15-34.
Moebius, Stephan (2008): "Handlung und Praxis. Konturen einer poststrukturalistischen Praxistheorie", in: Stephan Moebius/Andreas Reckwitz (eds.), Poststrukturalistische Sozialwissenschaften, Frankfurt a.M.: Suhrkamp, 2008, 58-74.
Nicolaides, Becky (2006): "How Hell Moved from the City to the Suburbs", in: Kevin Kruse/Thomas Sugrue (eds.), The New Suburban History, Chicago/London: University of Chicago Press, 80-98.
Nienaber, Birte/Kriszan, Agnes (2013): "Entgrenzte Lebenswelten: Wohn- und Arbeitsmigration als Ausdruck transnationaler Lebensentwürfe im deutsch-luxemburgischen und deutsch-polnischen Grenzraum", in: Raumforschung und Raumordnung 71/3, 221-232, http://link.springer.com/article/10.1007%2Fs13147-013-0230-2, accessed 20.02.2014.
Nietzsche, Friedrich (2009 [1885]): Digitale Kritische Gesamtausgabe (eKGWB), www.nietzschesource.org/#eKGWB/NF-1885,38, accessed 20.02.2014.
Paasi, Anssi (2002): "Bounded Spaces in the Mobile World. Deconstructing 'Regional Identity'", in: Tijdschrift voor economische en sociale Geografie 93/2, 137-148.
Paasi, Anssi (2003): "Region and Place: Regional Identity in Question", in: Progress in Human Geography 27/4, 475-485.
Pagliarini, Luciano/Heng, Clemens (2009): L'autre mine. La mine dite "Bei de Collaren" à Esch-sur-Alzette. Période de 1726 à 1912, Esch-sur-Alzette: Editons Schortgen.
Paluch, Didier (1997): Périurbanisation: une croissance continue. Nord-Pas-de-Calais Profils, Lille: INSEE Nord-Pas-de-Calais.
Parr John B. (2004): "The polycentric urban region: a closer inspection", in: Regional Studies 38/3, 231-240.
Pflug, Hermann (1989): Römische Porträtstelen in Oberitalien. Untersuchungen zur Chronologie, Typologie und Ikonographie, Mainz: Verlag Philipp von Zabern.
Piorr, Annette/Ravetz, Joe/Tosics, Ivan (2011): Peri-urbanisation in Europe. Towards European Policies to Sustain Urban-Rural Futures. Synthesis Report, Frederiksberg: University of Copenhagen/Forest & Landscape.

Pirling, Renate (1986): Römer und Franken am Niederrhein, Mainz: Verlag Philipp von Zabern.
Pratt, Geraldine (1994): "Suburbs", in: Ron Johnston/Derek Gregory/David Smith (eds.), Dictionary of Human Geography, 3rd edition, Cambridge: Blackwell, 606-607.
Prykhodko, Olena (2008): "Are Mini Skirts Guilty? The Discourse on Sexual Harassment as Cultural Phenomenon in Public Spaces", in: Feministisches Kollektiv (ed.), Street Harassment. Machtprozesse und Raumproduktion, Wien: Mandelbaum Verlag, 37-54.
Quasten, Heinz (1970): Die Wirtschaftsformation der Schwerindustrie im Luxemburger Minett, Saarbrücken: Universität des Saarlandes.
Raco, Mike (2006): "Building New Subjectivities: Devolution, Regional Identities and the Re-scaling of Politics", in: Mark Tewdwr-Jones/Phil Allmendinger (eds.), Territory, Identity and Spatial Planning, London: Routledge, 320-334.
Reckinger, Rachel (2007a): "Le vin", in: Sonja Kmec/Benoît Majerus/Michel Margue/Pit Péporté (eds.), Lieux de mémoire au Luxembourg, vol. 1: Usages du passé et construction nationale, Luxembourg: Editions Saint-Paul, 305-310.
Reckinger, Rachel (2007b): "La bière", in: Sonja Kmec/Benoît Majerus/Michel Margue/Pit Péporté (eds.) Lieux de mémoire au Luxembourg, vol. 1: Usages du passé et construction nationale, Luxembourg: Editions Saint-Paul, 311-317.
Reckinger, Rachel/Baltes-Löhr, Christel/Prüm, Agnès/Wille, Christian (2011): "Everyday Cultures and Identities", in: IPSE (ed.), Doing Identity in Luxembourg. Subjective Appropriations – Institutional Attributions – Socio-Cultural Milieus, Bielefeld: transcript, 233-290.
Reckinger, Rachel/Schulz, Christian/Wille, Christian (2011): „Identity Constructions in Luxembourg", in: IPSE (ed.), Doing Identity in Luxembourg. Subjective Appropriations – Institutional Attributions – Socio-Cultural Milieus, Bielefeld: transcript, 291-294.
Reckinger, Rachel (2011): "De la terre natale symbolique au terroir sensoriel. Usage politique et normativité didactique du discours sur l'origine des vins", in: Serge Wolikow/Olivier Jacquet/Christophe Lucand (eds.), De Jules Guyot à Robert Parker: 150 ans de construction des territoires du vin, Dijon: Editions Universitaires de Dijon, 259-268.
Reckinger, Rachel (2012a): Parler vin. Entre normes et appropriations, Tours/Rennes: Presses Universitaires François Rabelais/Presses Universitaires de Rennes.
Reckinger, Rachel (2012b): "Produits culinaires régionaux", in: Sonja Kmec/Pit Péporté (eds.): Lieux de mémoire au Luxembourg, vol. 2: Jeux d'échelles, Luxembourg: Editions Saint-Paul, 181-186.
Reckinger, Rachel (2013): Der Gouvernementalitätsbegriff. Eine Perspektive zur Untersuchung von Raum- und Identitätskonstruktionen (= IDENT2-Working Papers 4), Luxemburg, http://wwwen.uni.lu/content/download/62474/745288/file/IDENT2_Working-Paper_04-2013.pdf, accessed 23.12.2013.

Reckwitz, Andreas (2003): "Grundelemente einer Theorie sozialer Praktiken. Eine sozialtheoretische Perspektive", in: Zeitschrift für Soziologie 32/4, 282-301.

Reckwitz, Andreas (2004): "Die Entwicklung des Vokabulars der Handlungstheorien: Von den zweck- und normorientierten Modellen zu den Kultur- und Praxistheorien", in: Manfred Gabriel (ed.), Paradigmen der akteurszentrierten Soziologie, Wiesbaden: Verlag für Sozialwissenschaften, 303-328.

Reckwitz, Andreas (2006): Das hybride Subjekt. Eine Theorie der Subjektkulturen von der bürgerlichen Moderne zur Postmoderne, Weilerswist: Velbrück Wissenschaft.

Reckwitz, Andreas (2008a): Subjekt, Bielefeld: transcript.

Reckwitz, Andreas (2008b): "Subjekt/Identität", in: Stephan Moebius/Andreas Reckwitz (ed.), Poststrukturalistische Sozialwissenschaften, Frankfurt a.M.: Suhrkamp, 75-92.

Reckwitz, Andreas (2009): "Praktiken der Reflexivität: Eine kulturtheoretische Perspektive auf hochmodernes Handeln", in: Fritz Böhle/Margit Weihrich (eds.), Handeln unter Unsicherheit, Wiesbaden: Verlag für Sozialwissenschaften, 169-182.

Reckwitz, Andreas (2010): "Auf dem Weg zu einer kultursoziologischen Analytik zwischen Praxeologie und Poststrukturalismus", in: Monika Wohlrab-Sahr (ed.), Kultursoziologie. Paradigmen – Methoden – Fragestellungen, Wiesbaden: Verlag für Sozialwissenschaften, 179-205.

Reddeker, Sebastian (2011): "Collective Symbols and (New) Identity Options in Luxembourg's Advertising", in: IPSE (ed.), Doing Identity in Luxembourg. Subjective Appropriations – Institutional Attributions – Socio-Cultural Milieus, Bielefeld: transcript, 190-202.

Reuter, Julia (2008): "Globalisierung: Phänomen – Debatte – Rhetorik", in: Stephan Moebius/Andreas Reckwitz (eds.): Poststrukturalistische Sozialwissenschaften, Frankfurt a.M.: Suhrkamp, 263-276.

Riehl, Claudia Maria (1999): "Grenzen und Sprachgrenzen", in: Monika Fludernik/Hans-Joachim Gehrke (eds.), Grenzgänger zwischen Kulturen (= Identitäten und Alteritäten, vol. 1), Würzburg: Ergon, 41-56.

Rose, Hannelore (2007): "Privatheit als öffentlicher Wert – Zur Bedeutung der Familie auf Grabmonumenten der Gallia Belgica", in: Elisabeth Walde/Barbara Kainrath (eds.), Die Selbstdarstellung der römischen Gesellschaft in den Provinzen im Spiegel der Steindenkmäler, Innsbruck: Innsbruck University Press, 207-224.

Rothe, Ursula (2009): Dress and Cultural Identity in the Rhine-Moselle Region of the Roman Empire, Oxford: Archaeopress.

Ruhne, Renate (2011): Raum Macht Geschlecht. Zur Soziologie eines Wirkungsgefüges am Beispiel von (Un)Sicherheiten im öffentlichen Raum, Wiesbaden: Verlag für Sozialwissenschaften.

Sabrow, Martin (2006): "Die NS-Vergangenheit in der geteilten deutschen Geschichtskultur", in: Christoph Kleßmann/Peter Lautzas (eds.): Teilung und Integration. Die doppelte deutsche Nachkriegsgeschichte als wissenschaftliches und didaktisches Problem (= Reihe Politik und Bildung, vol. 41), Schwalbach/Ts.: Wochenschau, 132-151.

Schmid, Christian/Brenner, Neil (2011): "Planetary Urbanisation", in: Matthew Gandy (ed.), Urban Constellations, Berlin: Jovis, 10-13.

Schmidt, Robert (2012): Soziologie der Praktiken. Konzeptionelle Studien und empirische Analysen, Frankfurt a.M.: Suhrkamp.

Schmitz, Walter (2007): "Die europäische Stadt: Teil unseres kulturellen Erbes", in: Erich Greipl/Stefan Müller (eds.), Zukunft der Innenstadt. Herausforderungen für ein erfolgreiches Stadtmarketing, Wiesbaden: Gabler Verlag, 33-45.

Schnuer, Gregor/Boesen, Elisabeth/Wille, Christian (2013): "We, You, the Others. Constructions of Difference and Identity in the Greater Region", lecture at the 12th International Conference "European Culture", Universitat Internacional de Catalunya, Barcelona.

Scholz, Markus (2012): Grabbauten des 1.-3. Jahrhunderts in den nördlichen Grenzprovinzen des Römischen Reiches, vol. 1, Mainz: Verlag des Römisch-Germanischen Zentralmuseums.

Schörner, Günther (2005): "Einführung", in: Günther Schörner (ed.), Romanisierung – Romanisation. Theoretische Modelle und praktische Fallbeispiele, Oxford: Archaeopress, V-XVI.

Schrott, Karin (2005): Das normative Korsett. Reglementierungen für Frauen in Gesellschaft und Öffentlichkeit in der deutschsprachigen Anstands- und Benimmliteratur zwischen 1871 und 1914, Würzburg: Königshausen & Neumann.

Sedlacko, Michal/Reisch, Lucia/Scholl, Gerd (2013): "Sustainable Food Consumption. When Evidence-Based Policy-Making Meets Policy-Minded Research. Introduction to the Special Issue", in: Sustainability: Science, Practice & Policy 9/2, 1-6, http://sspp.proquest.com, accessed 20.02.2014.

Setzwein, Monika (2006): "Frauenessen – Männeressen? Doing Gender und Essverhalten", in: Petra Kolip/Thomas Altegeld (eds.), Geschlechtergerechte Gesundheitsförderung und Prävention. Theoretische Grundlagen und Modelle guter Praxis, Weinheim/München: Juventa Verlag, 41-60.

Sieburg, Heinz (2013): "Die Stellung der deutschen Sprache in Luxemburg. Geschichte und Gegenwart", in: Heinz Sieburg (ed.), Vielfalt der Sprachen – Varianz der Perspektiven. Zur Geschichte und Gegenwart der Luxemburger Mehrsprachigkeit (= Interkulturalität. Studien zu Sprache, Literatur und Gesellschaft, vol. 3), Bielefeld: transcript, 81-106.

Sonntag, Monika (2013): Grenzen überwinden durch Kultur? Identitätskonstruktionen von Kulturakteuren in europäischen Grenzregionen (= Luxemburg-Studien/Etudes luxembourgeoises, vol. 3), Frankfurt a.M.: Peter Lang.

STATEC (Statistics Portal Grand-Duchy of Luxembourg) (2012): Luxemburg in Zahlen, Luxemburg: STATEC.
STATEC (Statistics Portal Grand-Duchy of Luxembourg) (2013): Luxemburg in Zahlen. Edition 2013, Luxemburg: STATEC.
Strüver, Anke (2010): "KörperMachtRaum und RaumMachtKörper: Bedeutungsverflechtungen von Körpern und Räumen", in: Sybille Bauriedl/Michaela Schier/Anke Strüver (eds.), Geschlechterverhältnisse, Raumstrukturen, Ortsbeziehungen. Erkundung von Vielfalt und Differenz im spatial turn, Münster: Westfälisches Dampfboot, 217-237.
Sustainable Development Commission (SDC) (2009): Setting the Table: Advice to Government on Priority Elements of Sustainable Diets, London: Sustainable Development Commission.
Tenfelde, Klaus (1991): "Ende der Arbeiterkultur: Das Echo auf eine These", in: Wolfgang Kabuschka/Gottfried Korff/Bernd Jürgen Warneken (eds.), Arbeiterkultur seit 1945. Ende oder Veränderung?, Tübingen: Tübinger Vereinigung für Volkskunde, 19-30.
Trausch, Gilbert (2000): L'ARBED dans la société luxembourgeoise, Luxemburg: V. Bruck.
Vaughan, Laura/Griffiths, Sam/Haklay, Muki/Jones, Catherine Emma (2009): "Do the Suburbs Exist? Discovering Complexity and Specificity in Suburban Built Form", in: Transactions of the Institute of British Geographers 34, 475-488.
Vicenzotti, Vera (2011): Der "Zwischenstadt"-Diskurs. Eine Analyse zwischen Wildnis, Kulturlandschaft und Stadt, Bielefeld: transcript.
Walde, Elisabeth/Kainrath, Barbara (eds.) (2007): Die Selbstdarstellung der römischen Gesellschaft in den Provinzen im Spiegel der Steindenkmäler. IX. internationales Kolloquium über Probleme des provinzialrömischen Kunstschaffens, Innsbruck: Innsbruck University Press.
Wastl-Walter, Doris (2010): Gender Geographien. Geschlecht und Raum als soziale Konstruktionen, Stuttgart: Franz Steiner Verlag.
Weichhart, Peter (1990): Raumbezogene Identität. Bausteine zu einer Theorie räumlich-sozialer Kognition und Identifikation, Stuttgart: Franz Steiner Verlag.
Weimann, Britta (2013): "Überlegungen zur Entwicklung der Mündlichkeit und Schriftlichkeit in Luxemburg", in: Heinz Sieburg (ed.), Vielfalt der Sprachen – Varianz der Perspektiven. Zur Geschichte und Gegenwart der Luxemburger Mehrsprachigkeit (= Interkulturalität. Studien zu Sprache, Literatur und Gesellschaft, vol. 3), Bielefeld: transcript, 251-262.
Welzer, Harald/Moller, Sabine/Tschuggnall, Karoline (2002): "Opa war kein Nazi." Nationalsozialismus und Holocaust im Familiengedächtnis (= Die Zeit des Nationalsozialismus, vol. 15515), Frankfurt a.M.: Fischer.
West, Candace/Zimmerman, Don H. (1987): "Doing Gender", in: Gender & Society. Official Publication of Sociologists for Women in Society 1, 125-151.

von Massow, Wilhelm (1940): "Bronzestatuette einer Göttin aus Belginum", in: Trierer Zeitschrift 15, 28-34.
Wille, Christian (2009): "Eine namenlose Region", in: Forum 288, 30-31.
Wille, Christian (2010): "'Doing Grande Région.' Espace entre transgression et construction à l'exemple du frontalier", in: Gaëlle Crenn/Jean-Luc Deshayes (eds.), La construction des territoires en Europe. Luxembourg et Grande Région: Avis de recherches, Nancy: Presses universitaires de Nancy, 81-93.
Wille, Christian (2012): Grenzgänger und Räume der Grenze. Raumkonstruktionen in der Großregion SaarLorLux (= Luxemburg-Studien/Etudes luxembourgeoises, vol. 1), Frankfurt a.M.: Peter Lang.
Wineburg, Sam (2001): "Sinn machen: Wie Erinnerung zwischen den Generationen gebildet wird", in: Harald Welzer (ed.), Das soziale Gedächtnis. Geschichte, Erinnerung, Tradierung, Hamburg: Hamburger Edition, 179-204.
Woods, Michael (2007): "Engaging the Global Countryside: Globalization, Hybridity and the Reconstitution of Rural Place", in: Progress in Human Geography 31/4, 485-507.
Wucherpfennig, Claudia (2010): "Geschlechterkonstruktionen und öffentlicher Raum", in: Sybille Bauriedl/Michaela Schier/Anke Strüver (eds.), Geschlechterverhältnisse, Raumstrukturen, Ortsbeziehungen. Erkundung von Vielfalt und Differenz im spatial turn, Münster: Westfälisches Dampfboot, 48-74.
Würzbach, Natascha (2014): "Raumdarstellung", in: Vera Nünning/Ansgar Nünning (eds.): Erzähltextanalyse und Gender studies, Stuttgart: JM Metzler, 49-71.
Young, Doug/Wood, Patricia/Keil, Roger (2011): In-Between Infrastructure: Urban Connectivity in an Age of Vulnerability, Toronto: Praxis (e)Press.
Zanker, Paul (1975): "Grabreliefs römischer Freigelassener", in: Jahrbuch des Deutschen Archäologischen Instituts 90, 267-315.

6. "Luxembourg is the Singapore of the West" – Looking Ahead

Markus Hesse

"'Luxembourg is the Singapore of the West', he says, meaning it as the greatest compliment. With rule of law and little corruption, the country is at the same time multicultural and very international. Other positive aspects are the strategic thinking and the easy access to the political establishment and authorities"[1] (*Luxemburger Wort* 2014: 59).

The following contribution aims to cast a final glance across the borders of the subjects and approaches discussed in this book. Here too, the term of border is a polysemous one. On the one hand, our endeavour is about the spatial borders of Luxembourg and the Greater Region that form the territorial frame or the respective backdrop for the considerations presented in this volume.[2] Border crossings here means directing the focus to the region's international and global dimension and at the same time challenging conventional notions of space and region. On the other hand, this contribution addresses a central defining factor in the constitution of space: mobility. The circulation of people and commodities, of information and currencies across the borders of space and time is not only of central importance in the case of the region(s) analysed here. Mobility is in that sense the opposite or the counterpart of place. Both condition each other, both are elementary parts of the development of regions. On the basis of these border

---

1 | Personal translation of: "'Luxemburg ist das Singapur des Westens', sagt er und meint das als höchstes Kompliment. Rechtsstaatlich mit geringer Korruption, sei das Land gleichzeitig multikulturell und sehr international. Weitere positive Aspekte seien das strategische Denken und der einfache Zugang zur Politik und den Behörden."
2 | Here we refer primarily to the Grand Duchy of Luxembourg, in particular its capital, not to the Greater Region as a whole. In this outlook, 'Luxembourg' stands, both metaphorically and ideal-typically, for tendencies discussed beyond the frame of research presented in this volume. The basic pattern of the phenomena and processes relevant here is, however, not conceivable without the entanglement of the country and its capital with the bordering areas.

crossings, this contribution aims to explore the terrain for further questions that have emerged after completing this book and the work it is based on. Inevitably, categories such as identity and space play an important role here.

The quote at the beginning is from the new director and Chief Country Officer of a German bank in Luxembourg, who was interviewed by the country's largest paper after assuming his position in early 2014. Before coming to Luxembourg, he had worked in the bank's offices in North America, Hongkong and Singapore. There is much here that reminds him of the Asian city state. The similarities between the two locations are obviously great: niches of sovereignty have contributed a great deal to the economic success of the city state there and the mini-state here; the same applies for the transparency of political conditions. A sense of tradition and understatement, on the one hand, a commitment to change and the very determined integration into larger spatial contexts, on the other, make both cases both unusual and also attractive for analysis.

Today, both locations probably represent a new type of city or space: they are "relational" (Sigler 2013). This means that they have derived their significance from a specific positioning with respect to other urban locations. Neither local location factors nor their size are relevant here, but rather the specialization of their function in the web of larger spatial relationships and flows. It is no coincidence that both places are important hubs of the global financial industry (see QFC/TZG 2014). Behind this economic niche lie complex socio-cultural preconditions: historically, both societies have internationalized themselves in a very brief period of time, both cases are marked by very specific – and clearly less internationalized – practices of political regulation. National actors and institutions here play a key role, which also disproves the downfall of the national state sometimes predicted in the globalization debate. Sidaway (2007) sees in this context even the emergence of a new "metageography of development", which has developed from niche strategies and owes its current importance to the specific interplay of spaces, flows and politics.

The Luxembourg as we know it and the "Singapore of the West" can also be seen as complementary images or identities of one and the same space. The analogies or overlaps between both images are at any rate evident: the small country and its capital, which only recently acquired the status of a 'major city' (*Großstadt*)[3], have a functional significance, which, measured against criteria such as surface area or population, is developed far above average. This holds true, for instance, for the already mentioned feature as a global financial centre, but also for aspects such as international connectivity or political importance. In addition, the corresponding changes have occurred in historically short periods of time. From this, one can conclude that in these cases a favourable structure was turned to account or exploited by the determined action of subjects, which is to mean

---

3 | Since autumn 2012, the city of Luxembourg has more than 100,000 inhabitants and has in purely statistical terms acquired the status of a metropolis (*Großstadt*).

that this development was in itself not an inevitable outcome. This dimension of change also provides a number of links to the subjects, approaches and empirical case studies of this volume. Luxembourg and Singapore are not spaces pre-existing *per se* that could be described via classical categories such as spatial location, accessibility or resources. Rather, these spaces were 'made': in one way or another, they have been 'produced' and are thus the result of social practices. They are constituted via specific establishments and removals of borders and via specific identity constructions.

It is against this background that two questions present themselves that can be read as logical extensions of our research into spaces, identities and borders in the context of Luxembourg and its border areas as well as a perspective towards future work: (1) What consequences does a wider perspective have that goes beyond the survey area in this volume, all the way to the global level? (2) Which epistemically significant role does the term mobility play in this context, i.e. the mobility of persons, commodities, ideas, information and also economic values? In what way do these flows contribute to the constitution of spaces?

(1) The various contributions of this book have approached their subject with a constructivist, relational understanding. We understand spaces and regions – in much the same way as borders and identities – as an expression of social practices, not as already fixed analytical categories merely applied to the respective subject of research. Terminologies such as 'doing space', 'doing identity' or 'practices of the border' point to the relationship of space or identity and society (in the broadest sense). This relationship was reversed in contrast to traditional analyses: it is not 'space' or 'identity' that play a determining role for social developments, rather, it requires social practices to bring forth different spatial contexts and identities. Our research questions were elaborated with different empirical foci that are reflected in three methodological perspectives: politics and institutions (see chapter 3); media and representations (see chapter 4); and subjectifications and subjectivations (see chapter 5). The considerations that guided research precede the empirical case studies of these three chapters.

What connects these different viewpoints particularly in the space-related perspective is the examination of space and region in their contingency and their character as something produced. This foil of inquiry consists of the Grand Duchy of Luxembourg and the surrounding border areas, which are marked by a closely knit web of socio-economic relationships: migration, commuting, residential mobility or political cooperations are only a few examples. This relational scenario is in its essence organized horizontally, and is most visibly exhibited in cartographic works, i.e. in topographical representations. The geography illustrated or produced in them reflects very diverse processes that can be observed on a two-dimensional surface of the survey area. This in turn has good reasons connected to epistemically significant points of focus and limitations in terms of practical research. Yet the image of space this conveys tends to be incomplete: it focusses on processes in the two-dimensionally and horizontally conceived space, compared to which vertical interdependencies remain subordinate. It is these latter that will be the subject of further observations: practices and correlations established via these between the survey area examined in this volume, on the one hand, and the policies, representations, subjectivations/subjectifications and identifications situated externally, on the other.

The vertical level has been for a considerable time the point of departure of far-reaching dynamics in the socio-economic development that have had a particular impact in scholarly discussion. This refers in particular to processes of transnationalization and globalization. They have moved a key category of recent spatial research into the centre of discussion: the concept of scale. This category addresses the over time increasing interlinkage of processes at different locations on Earth and the specific interplay of the respective levels of scale between local, regional, international and global levels (see Massey 2005; Cox 2010). An example for this is the emergence of world trade or global tourism, but also changes in the system of political control, for instance through federalism or decentralization. In this context, it seems generally agreed that a purely territorial, two-dimensional view of regions is no longer suited to appropriately reproduce the complex interplay of the respective factors and contexts. At the same time, however, the linkage thus taken into account of horizontal and vertical scales, of internal and external, the blending of discourse and materiality, the development of different notions of space (lived space, space of representations) has led to much confusion and insecurity regarding the assumed 'correct' approach to this category. This also applies to the space of politics: it not only comprises the territorially defined, clearly demarcated political-administrative space, which constitutes the arena for the interaction of very diverse regional actors, but also the space of representation – i.e. the space of political instrumentation and symbolic representation, which is definable via images and terms, attributions of meaning and identifications.

A variety of scientific concepts and terms, some of them very abstract, have emerged to do justice to these complex constellations of space and region. These include for instance "soft spaces" (see Allmendinger/Haughton 2009 and section 2.1 in this volume), "variable" or "flexible geometries" (see Dahl/Tufty 1973) or "assemblage" (Anderson/McFarlane 2011). All of them seek to relate to each other objects of very diverse nature which only remain loosely and precisely *not* causally connected. These approaches no doubt have their justification, since they may convey an analytically more appropriate, more timely image of their subject. But they have also been criticized as being too random or too apolitical (see Cox 2013). The great challenge for research here is certainly not to every time draw the most recent picture of spatial conditions with the maximum attention-grabbing effects within academia. Rather, it makes more sense to firmly address on a very robust epistemic foundation the overlap of scientific interpretations and representations on the one hand, and the ways of (practically) dealing with material realities on the other.

A constructivist approach to space and focussing on social practices have direct effects on research practice: if the continuously increasing complexity of the material space no longer permits us to clothe regions in a fixed territorial passepartout, then the consequence can only be to examine spatial (see section 2.3) or social (see section 2.1 and 2.3) processes of differentiation along different levels of scale, and no longer (primarily) territorial spaces and political borders.

(2) Mobility and movement are constitutive for today's appearance of the Grand Duchy and the neighbouring areas. The rise of Luxembourg to one of the seats of the European Union, to a financial hub and a magnet of an international labour market would have been unthinkable without the cross-border mobility of people, goods, ideas, information as well as financial values (commodities). This dynamic is not so much linked to the endogenic developmental path of the country which has in the past always reinvented itself successfully. It is primarily due to Luxembourg's ongoing internationalization. Luxembourg and its neighbouring regions are in this sense a model for active spatial construction which only became possible through the attraction and organization of flows. This modernizing power of mobility is a fundamental one; or in other words: mobility and movement are immanent to a general logic of development (or of progression) of modern societies (see Münch 1998: 225). In anglophone countries this view has informed studies on cultural and sociological theory already since the 1990s: "Modern society is a society on the move. Central to the idea of modernity is that of movement, that modern societies have brought about some striking changes in the nature and experience of motion or travel" (Lash/Urry 1994: 225). In the economic and social fragmentation processes that have been observable for some time now spatial-temporal disembedding and dissolution of borders seem to be playing a crucial role. Social differentiations, temporal compression and spatial expansion enter a specific association here which to a large degree relies on circulation, mobility and traffic.

The relationship between space and movement has traditionally played an important role in geography, for instance in the work of Edward Ullman, who has analysed the concrete *site* in its character as conditioned through the interaction with other sites (*situation*) (see Ullman 1954). The part of this relationship concerned with movement has, however, been long neglected in social sciences and humanities. Basically, it was only the paradigm of the *new mobilities* emerging in the late 1990s that has contributed in making this dimension more visible and in examining its special significance more thoroughly. Authors such as John Urry or Tim Cresswell have advanced these issues in the field of social and cultural theory. For a long time, a dichotomous, polarizing notion of spatial interaction – i.e. of social practices and relationships in partial areas or between these – had been at the centre of attention. According to Cresswell (2006: 126), this is the metaphysics of sedentarism and nomadism, the antagonistic relationship of fixity and flows. Mobility is in this way confronted and challenged by space; the same applies in the reverse direction.

If one follows the view of the more recent mobilities studies, i.e. the studies on mobility in the social context inspired by social and cultural theory, the development of space, on the one hand, and movement or flexibility, on the other, are closely and systematically intertwined – even in a hitherto unknown way. Luxembourg is prototypical in this regard: here, mobility is everyday-cultural practice of many people working there, who are either circularly mobile as cross-border commuters (see Wille 2012) or work and live there temporarily as employees of the financial site or as experts of European institutions. Households that move across the border to buy property retain their workplace in Luxembourg for the time being, as well as their social networks (see section 5.8). However, they need to synchronize their everyday activities more and more in terms of space and time, develop complex routines or develop new relationships. Or, as also discussed in this volume: petrol stations that used to serve a clear purpose suddenly acquire a particular socio-economic but also socio-cultural role under the influence of Luxembourg's strategy of creating niches of sovereignty: through the generation of 'accises' they contribute considerably to the national income, provide young people with meeting places and they are a nucleus for cross-border socialization processes (see section 4.7).

Finally, there is an increasing mixing of different spatial levels of scale: local, regional and superordinate functional systems increasingly overlap, they cover different catchment areas and are each specifically localized (see Affolderbach/Carr 2014). The classical image of the spatial organization on the basis of centrality has here lost much of its interpretative power. In this context, Manuel Castells (1985) has spoken, in a very abstract way, of a "space of flows" with which he later also conceptualized his theorem of "network societies" (Castells 1996). According to this concept, the space constituted through material and information flows enters into a specific connection with the physical space, impacting social practices and spatial concepts. The blending of different levels of scale is visible in many ways in quasi-metropolitan Luxembourg, as well as in other places of the country: for instance, in the mobile functional elites that are very present in the public space, in the mega projects of the built city, in the overloading of infrastructures. In its sum, this complexity of levels of scale compounds the orientation in the social and particularly political space. And this challenges political-administrative functional systems all the more. The geographer Kevin R. Cox has described this problem as the relationship between the area of a region and the difficult to define "out there" (2010: 216). This relationship not only makes political decision-making processes very complex, but also disrupts transmitted notions of the order of space and the world.

In this sense, mobilities contribute to the liquidation of spatial conditions and they have considerable repercussions on the spatial objects on all levels of scale. At the same time, they mobilize our notions, images and discourses with respect to these objects. It is not least this fact that makes the categories and research subjects examined here – space, border, identity – an extremely interesting object of analysis and scientific discussion that raises a host of further questions. It should be clear from the observations made in this chapter, as well as the findings presented in this book as a whole, that social sciences, cultural studies and the humanities are making relevant and original contributions to this research.

REFERENCES

Affolderbach, Julia/Carr, Constance (forthcoming): "Blending Scales of Governance: Land Use Policy and Practices in a Small State", in: Regional Studies.
Allen, John/Cochrane, Allan (2007): "Beyond the Territorial Fix: Regional Assemblages, Politics and Power", in: Regional Studies 41/9, 1161-1175.
Allmendinger, Phil/Haughton, Graham (2009): "Soft Spaces, Fuzzy Boundaries, and Metagovernance: the New Spatial Planning in the 'Thames Gateway'", in: Environment and Planning A 41/3, 617-633.
Anderson, Ben/McFarlane, Colin (2011): "Assemblage and geography", in: Area 43/2, 124-127.
Castells, Manuel (1985): "High Technology, Urban Restructuring and the Urban-Regional Process in the United States", in: Manuel Castells (ed.), High Technology, Space and Society (= Urban Affairs Annual Reviews 28), Newbury Park: Sage, 33-40.
Castells, Manuel (1996): The Rise of the Network Society. The Information Age: Economy, Society, and Culture, vol. 1, Malden/Oxford: Blackwell.
Cox, Kevin R. (2010): "The Problem of Metropolitan Governance and the Politics of Scale", in: Regional Studies 44/2, 215-222.
Cox, Kevin R. (2013): "Territory, Scale, and Why Capitalism Matters", in: Territory, Politics, Governance 1/1, 46-61.
Cresswell, Tim (2006): On the Move. Mobility in the Western World, London/New York: Routledge.
Dahl, Robert Alan/Tufte, Edward R. (1973): Size and Democracy, Stanford: Stanford University Press.
Harvey, David (1989): The Condition of Postmodernity. An Enquiry into the Origins of Cultural Change, Malden/Oxford: Blackwell.
Lash, Scott/Urry, John (1994): Economies of Signs and Space, London et al.: Sage.
Luxemburger Wort (2014), Adam, Andreas: „Klares Bekenntnis zum Standort", edition of 28.02.2014, 59.
Massey, Doreen (2005): For Space, Thousand Oaks: Sage.
Münch, Richard (1998): Globale Dynamik, lokale Lebenswelten. Der schwierige Weg in die Weltgesellschaft, Frankfurt a.M.: Suhrkamp.
Qatar Financial Centre and the Z/Y Group (2014): The Global Financial Centres Index 15, London.
Sidaway, James (2007): "Enclave Space: A New Metageography of Development?", in: Area 39/3, 331-339.

Sigler, Thomas J. (2013): "Relational Cities: Doha, Panama City, and Dubai as 21st Century Entrepôts", in: Urban Geography 34/5, 612-333.

Ullman, Edward L. (1980 [1954]): Geography as spatial interaction, Seattle: University of Washington.

Wille, Christian (2012): Grenzgänger und Räume der Grenze. Raumkonstruktionen in der Großregion SaarLorLux (= Luxemburg-Studien/Etudes luxembourgeoises, vol. 1), Frankfurt a.M.: Peter Lang.

7. Interview Guidelines

1. LIVING IN THE GREATER REGION

For those who regularly undertake activities in a neighbouring country:

1.1 Why do you travel from your local area to neighbouring countries on a more or less regular basis for [3 activities stated in the questionnaire]?

For those who never undertake activities in a neighbouring country:

1.2 Many people go shopping in neighbouring countries. Why don't you travel to a neighbouring country to shop?

1.3 Recently there has been much talk of the Greater Region; do you know what this is about?

- What does the Greater Region mean to you?
- Do you feel (no) sense of belonging to the Greater Region?

1.4 How would you react if you were outside the Greater Region and you met someone from Luxembourg (or someone from another neighbouring region)?

- Why (not)?
- Differences/commonalities
- And how would you react if you met someone from one of the other three Greater Region areas?

1.5 Recently, an increasing number of people have been moving to neighbouring regions:

- (Also you). What kind of people in general do you think these are?
- Why did they move to the border area?
- How do you think they are getting on there?
- What is your personal opinion of this development?

1.6 In your experience: what do you think is the opinion of people who have lived here for a long time of the fact that many people from Luxembourg have moved here?

1.7 In your experience: what is the general opinion in Luxembourg of your decision to move?

- Do people in Luxembourg also ask how the experience is like for you?

1.8 Did your circle of friends and acquaintances before you moved include people who had also moved into the border area?

- Did you get any tips from them? What were they?
- Did you have information what this experience was going to be about? Did you have any idea how this experience was going to be like?

1.9 Why do you (not) undertake these activities [from question 1.1] in your place of residence?

1.10 When you meet people who don't know the area here, how do you describe where you live?

1.11 When you meet acquaintances who know the area very well, how do you describe where you live?

1.12 You indicated in the quantatitve questionnaire that your place of residence is [urban/suburban/rural]. Why do you describe/qualify it in this way?

1.13 You were asked in the questionnaire whether you feel a sense of belonging to your place of residence.

- Could you elaborate on this?
- Why is this?

2. EATING AND DRINKING

2.1 What do you consider to be a 'good' diet/way of eating for our society? Why?

2.2 You said in the quantitative questionnaire that you shop in the shopping venues [mention names here]:

- Why is this?
- How did this come about? Has it always been the case?
- If you had the choice, would you shop elsewhere?
- Are there shopping venues which you would never visit? Which ones? Why?

2.3   What do you consider important when choosing your food?

2.4   Do you consider the area from which your food comes to be important?

- [Yes] Why do you buy food from this area? What does this mean to you?
- [No] What is important to you instead? Why are the criteria [from question 2.3] more important to you?

2.5   Are there any foodstuffs which you buy/have bought directly from the producers?

2.6   Do you know any associations relating to food and drink, such as a consumer association or something similar?

- Are you a member of any? Why?
- Why not?

3. LEISURE

3.1   Which petrol station do you drive to most often?

3.2   What things would you never buy or do at a petrol station?

3.3   What do you associate with petrol stations in general?

3.4   Has anything unusual ever happened to you at a petrol station? Have you ever noticed anything unusual at a petrol station?

3.5   What have you seen at the theatre during the past year? Do you remember the titles of the shows?

3.6   In your opinion, what sets the quality of Luxembourg's theatre landscape?

3.7   What would have to be different for you to visit the theatre (more often)?

4. MEN AND WOMEN

4.1 In your opinion, are there places/areas where men feel particularly threatened?

4.2 In your opinion, are there places/areas where women feel particularly threatened?

4.3 Do you know any places where men or women have been threatened?

4.4 In your opinion, at what moments during the course of the day do places/areas give an impression of being threatening (or not)?

- Is it affected by levels of light or dark?
- Why do you think this is so?

4.5 Is there a place where you have ever been threatened?

- [Yes] Where did this threat take place?

4.6 What would you recommend that young people or young adults do when they spend time in public, in order to prevent such situations from ever arising?

8. Authors

Christel Baltes-Löhr (Assoc. Prof. Dr.) is the University of Luxembourg's gender representative and works in the fields of migration and gender. She represents Luxembourg at the European Commission as a gender expert in the EU Helsinki Group *Women and Science* and she is a member of the *European Migration Network – National Contact Point – Luxembourg*.

Luc Belling (Dr.) is a sociolinguist in the field of media linguistics at the University of Luxembourg. His PhD thesis discusses communicative and linguistic varieties of Luxembourgish on wall posts as well as social network analyses.

Andrea Binsfeld (Assoc. Prof. Dr.) teaches ancient history at the University of Luxembourg. Her research and interests focus on history and archeology of Roman Gaul and ancient social history.

Elisabeth Boesen (Dr.) is a cultural anthropologist and conducts research at the University of Luxembourg on the topics of mobility and socio-cultural change, including in rural areas of the Greater Region SaarLorLux.

Julia de Bres (Assoc. Prof. Dr.) is a sociolinguist at the University of Luxembourg. Her research interests are multilingualism, minority languages and language ideologies.

Laure Caregari (M.A.) is a historian and art historian. She is engaged in research for the oral history project *Terres Rouges – Histoire de la sidérurgie luxembourgeoise* and conducts interviews with former mine and steel workers.

Till Dembeck (Dr.) is a research scientist for modern German literature at the University of Luxembourg. His current research interests are literary multilingualism and poetry.

Martin Doll (Jun. Prof. Dr.) holds a degree in media and cultural studies and teaches media studies at the Heinrich Heine University Düsseldorf. His research focus includes politics and media, mediality of architecture, utopian architecture and media utopias of the 19th century as well as forgery and hoax.

Fabian Faller (Dr.) works as postdoctoral researcher at the University of Kiel, Institute of Geography. His research focus lies on 'green' regional transitions. His present contribution emerged from his PhD thesis at the Universities of Luxembourg and the Saarland where he examined the energy transition from the perspective of environmental economic geography.

Paul di Felice (Dr.) teaches history of modern and contemporary photography and art didactics at the University of Luxebourg. He is coordinator of *Mois européen de la photographie* and founding member of the art journals *Café Crème art magazine* and *lacritique.org*.

Johanna M. Gelberg (M.A.) holds a degree in literary studies. She is currently engaged as a doctoral candidate in the ATTRACT-project *Ästhetische Figurationen des Politischen* (Aesthetic figurations of the political) funded by the *Fonds National de la Recherche* at the University of Luxembourg. Her research focus includes border research, literature of the German division and political aesthetics.

Markus Hesse (Prof. Dr.) is a geographer and spatial planner, working as professor of urban studies at the University of Luxembourg. His research focuses on theoretical and practical issues of metropolitan development as well as spatial governance.

Eva Maria Klos is a doctoral candidate at the University of Luxembourg. In her PhD project funded by the *Fonds National de la Recherche*, she examines memory cultures in Luxembourg, France and Belgium.

Sonja Kmec (Assoc. Prof. Dr.) teaches history and cultural studies at the University of Luxembourg. Her research focus lies on European history (16th-21st century), memory culture and identity constructions.

Bernhard Kreutz (Dr.) is a historian and conducts research on the history of the Rhine-Moselle region and the history of nobility and castles in the Middle Ages.

Elena Kreutzer (Dr.) has a degree in social sciences and cultural studies. She graduated at the University of Luxembourg and the University of the Saarland under a *cotutelle* agreement (joint degree). Her research focus is the comparative content- and discourse-analytical investigation of migrants in the media of the SaarLorLux region.

Heike Mauer (Dr.) holds a degree in political sciences and social studies. She obtained on her PhD at the University of Luxembourg with a thesis analyzing the historical problematization of prostitution in Luxembourg from an intersectional and governmental perspective.

Agnès Prüm is senior lecturer in English and American studies at the University of Luxembourg. Her research interests include gender and writing, sustainability and speculative fiction as well as spatial and identity constructions in (fictional) narratives.

Rachel Reckinger (Dr.) is a cultural anthropologist and a sociologist, working as scientific project coordinator at the University of Luxembourg. Her research focus includes food-related reflexivity, transitions to sustainable food practices and governmentality.

Céline Schall (Dr.) holds a doctorate in communication studies (Avignon, France) and one in museology (UQAM, Canada). She is currently conducting research on Luxembourg museums at the Institute for Romance, Media and Art Studies of the University of Luxembourg.

Gregor Schnuer (Dr.) is a sociologist and works as research associate on the project *Cross border residence. Identity experience and integration processes in the Greater Region (CB-RES)* at the University of Luxembourg.

Benno Sönke Schulz is a student at the University of Trier. Since 2010 he has been working there in the Research Cluster. In 2012, he was an assistant in the *PARTIZIP2* project of the University of Luxembourg.

Heinz Sieburg (Assoc. Prof. Dr.) teaches German linguistics and medieval studies and is the head of the Institute of German Language, Literature and Intercultural Studies at the University of Luxembourg.

Britta Weimann (Dr.) graduated in linguistics and is currently working as a scientific assistant in the project *Die Wortbildung des Luxemburgischen. Historische Voraussetzungen und kontrastive Analyse* (WBLUX2) (Word formation in Luxembourgish. Historical preconditions and contrastive analysis) at the University of Luxembourg.

Christian Wille (Dr.) graduated in social sciences and cultural studies and is currently coordinator of the UniGR-Center for Border Studies and the Key Area Multilingualism and Intercultural Studies at the University of Luxembourg. His research focuses on border studies and spatial research from a cultural studies perspective.

Julia Maria Zimmermann (M.A.) is writing her PhD thesis on gender constructions in debates of the European Parliament at the University of Luxembourg. She also examines masculinities and identity constructions in postmodern societies.